THE FORMATION AND PERCEPTION
OF THE MODERN ARAB WORLD

STUDIES BY MARWAN R. BUHEIRY

MARWAN R. BUHEIRY

THE FORMATION
AND
PERCEPTION
OF THE
MODERN ARAB WORLD

STUDIES BY MARWAN R. BUHEIRY

Lawrence I. Conrad, Editor

The Darwin Press, Inc.
Princeton, New Jersey

Library of Congress Cataloging in Publication Data

Buheiry, Marwan R., 1934–
    The formation and perception of the modern Arab world.

    Includes index.
    1. Middle East—Foreign relations—United States.
2. United States—Foreign relations—Middle East.
3. Middle East—Relations—Europe. 4. Europe—
Relations—Middle East. 5. Lebanon—History—
1516–1918. 6. Israel-Arab conflicts. I. Conrad,
Lawrence I., 1949–   .   II. Title.
DS63.2.U5B82   1989   327.56073   89–11608
ISBN 0–87850–064–2

Second printing, 1990

Printed in the United States of America

CONTENTS

The Plate section follows page 599

PREFACE

This volume comprises a selection of 28 studies by Marwan R. Buheiry, who died suddenly in London on 17 February 1986. The loss of this eminent Lebanese historian deprived scholarship on the modern Arab world of one of its most original and stimulating representatives, and in the months following his death the idea of collecting and republishing his most important work was one that naturally arose among his friends and colleagues.

Such a volume also seemed valuable for other reasons. Firstly, Buheiry had been an active participant in the lively interchange of ideas that was so characteristic of the Beirut intellectual scene, and some of his studies thus appeared in French or Arabic in publications rarely encountered outside the Arab world and not found in the collections of even major centers of Arabic and Middle Eastern studies in the West. A volume drawing together these essays thus presented an opportunity to make the author's scholarship available to a much wider audience. Secondly, although fluent in both French and Arabic, Buheiry regarded English as his primary vehicle for scholarly expression and always wrote in that language: studies published in French and Arabic were invariably translated by others from texts prepared by the author in English. In some cases the original texts were abridged in accordance with the limitations or needs of the journal or volume concerned. In others the problems inherent in translation arose. And in the unstable conditions prevailing in Beirut and Lebanon through much of his career, it was often impossible for the author to check the translated versions or to correct proofs, and some of these therefore contain misprintings and infelicities not found in the English text. A meticulous scholar who set high standards for his own work, Buheiry also tended to revise and expand on already published work, with the result that several articles published in French or Arabic now stand superseded by fuller but hitherto unpublished English texts.

For these reasons, it was decided that the studies included in this volume should be published in their original English form. Although the original handwritten or typed manuscripts fortunately have in all cases survived among the author's papers, certain difficulties did arise in editing them for publication. In some cases, lost pages or quotations cited in Arabic (with Arabic publication in mind) had to be retranslated back into English from the published versions; and in others, collation indicated places where Buheiry had made revisions or additions to the translated texts. Where this material seemed clearly to be the work of the author himself, the English has been revised accordingly. In the case of quotations from English language sources or diplomatic material for which an official English version exists (e.g., Foreign Office documents, joint communiqués), that version has been used. Spelling and other similar conventions have been standardized, and all Arabic terms and titles and all but the most generally known names (e.g., Faysal, Nasser, Sadat) have been transliterated according to a uniform system. In cases where it has been necessary to furnish notes or add to existing ones, the additional material has been set off in square brackets.

A meeting between the editor, Professor Tarif Khalidi, Dr. Basim F. Musallam, and Mrs. Leila Ghantous Buheiry in Oxford in September 1986 resulted in agreement on the selection and arrangement of the material to be published. Although factors of distance and the pressure of other commitments did not allow for the joint editing enterprise originally envisaged, I am grateful to both Professor Khalidi and Dr. Musallam for their suggestions and assistance in planning this work, to Professor Khalidi for his contribution to the Introduction, and to Dr. Musallam for dealing with one of the passages requiring retranslation from Arabic into English.

It is also my pleasant task to acknowledge the valuable assistance contributed by others. This volume could not have appeared without the enthusiastic support, encouragement, and assistance of Mrs. Leila Ghantous Buheiry, who placed all the necessary materials at the editor's disposal, provided photographs from her late husband's valuable collection, fielded many queries, and contributed to the reading of all of the proofs. I am also grateful to Mr. Nadim Shehadi, director of the Centre for Lebanese Studies, Oxford, for the Centre's financing and supervision of the preparation of the index, and to Professors A.A. Duri, Albert Hourani, and Samir Seikaly for assistance with several bibliographical questions. The book has benefitted much from the fine work of Marika Antoniw, who computer typeset the text at the Wellcome Institute in London, from the advice of my colleagues Dr. Dominik Wujastyk and Helen Gibson on matters regarding the computer formatting, and from the keen editorial eye of Albert McGrigor at the Darwin Press. My thanks also to Edward Breisacher, managing director of the Darwin Press, for his cooperation in coordinating a project proceeding on two continents at once, and to all of the publishers—indicated at the beginning of the studies concerned—who generously gave their permission for the use of essays that had originally appeared in their publications.

Lawrence I. Conrad

17 February 1989

INTRODUCTION

Marwan Buheiry was born in Beirut on 3 December 1934, the son of Ra'fat Buheiry and Anne Sarrafian. His father was a pioneer commercial designer and printer, descended from a family of Tripoli *'ulamā'*. His mother was the daughter of a family of Lebanese Armenian intellectuals, artists, and pioneer photographers. Buheiry was heir to a rich cultural and linguistic heritage, and his professional interests as a historian were later to reflect that variegated background. Most of his published work was to deal, in one way or another, with those areas of history where one culture or system perceives or affects another.

At the American University of Beirut, where he first developed his serious interests in history, a group of Arab historians—trained mostly at Princeton, Chicago, or London—had created a *turāth*, or heritage, originating in the 1930s and composed of the critical reexamination of medieval and modern Arabic history and of assessing the relevance of that history to the contemporary problems of Lebanon and the Arab East. The encounter with the West loomed large among these problems. Beirut itself, prismlike, refracted the intellectual pursuits of those scholars and of their foreign colleagues. Outside the walls of the University, a vivid consciousness of history being made and unmade, coupled with an intense commentary and debate about events conducted in three languages, gave the student of history at that particular juncture of Beirut's fortunes ample scope to reflect upon the judgment that "all history is contemporary history."

The most outstanding quality about Buheiry as a historian was his·constant mining of the present for clues to help him understand the past. He was an avid student of political power, economics, and the arts. He was keenly aware of the finer nuances of the language and processes of power and diplomacy, had a marvellous grasp of the theory and practice of economics, and was endlessly fascinated by the possibilities inherent in the history of art. The present supplied him with the imagination needed to investigate the past. This imagination was put to use in his striving to expand the spectrum of his interests and to offer—from each of his specialized topics—some view, gracefully expressed, which formulated the relevance of his own research to scholars in adjacent fields. With what he knew he was immensely generous. For knowledge imparted, he was immensely grateful. About what he really knew, he was often unduly modest.

A scholar of uncompromising integrity and a tireless advocate for a critical and comprehensive approach to historical problems, Buheiry was keenly

committed to the enhancement of the intellectual and pedagogical infrastructure essential to the promotion of sound historical scholarship. At the
American University of Beirut he served on numerous Faculty and Administration committees and bodies and was an enthusiastic teacher and a dedicated advisor to his students. He was a vocal supporter of interdisciplinary
studies generally, and of the University's interdisciplinary Cultural Studies
Program in particular, and lectured extensively in the Beirut community at
large. His last year, spent in Britain, was in large part dedicated to efforts
to establish the Centre for Lebanese Studies (Oxford), of which he was the
first director.

The essays and articles reprinted in this volume fall under four main
themes: European perceptions of the Orient, the superpowers and the Arab
world, the economic history of the Middle East, and intellectual and artistic
history. In all these themes Buheiry was concerned with the unravelling of
illusions. Himself unsaddled by any attachment to ideology or creed, he was
sensitive, nonetheless, to the impact that such attachment could have on
the lives of men. The reader, we think, will note that the author's presence
is strongly in evidence in his writings. He enjoyed not only what he had
unravelled, but also how a historian unravels history. In conversation with
him, one sometimes felt that he could *see* the past moving before his eyes like
a film. His concern for art sharpened his perception of the interplay between
appearance and reality. Thus, he was one of the earliest investigators of the
phenomenon of Orientalism, but he was also among the first historians to be
concerned with the genesis and development of Lebanon's modern economic
history, as actuality and as thought.

There is a certain poignancy in the premature death of a historian. It
is as if the discipline itself has rudely reached out to reclaim one of its
own, before he has completed his exploration of the Other Great Unknown.
For Buheiry, the past was not so much a "foreign country" as much as
an impressionist painting whose subtle and devious relationship to reality
was always a pleasure for him to examine. If there is one single reason for
believing that these essays will live and inspire, it is the sense of freshness,
wonder, and committed humane purpose that their author brought to any
history he studied, leaving a field better comprehended or more fertile where
he had sown.

Part I

European Perceptions of the Orient

1

Changes in French Colonial Perceptions 1789–1830: From the New World to Egypt and Algeria*

IN THIS STUDY the aim has been to chart the significant changes in French colonial perceptions—and to a lesser extent in policy—from the old colonial empire of India and the New World constructed by the Ancien Régime, to the French Revolution, to the perspectives opened by Napoleon's colonial interlude in Egypt, and finally to the renewed colonial vision and activities during the ensuing Bourbon Restoration, particularly the motivation for the conquest of Algeria. In this respect the study will stress the importance of economic interpretations of the changes in perceptions as well as of the decision to lay the foundation of a new empire closer to France in the Mediterranean, specifically in Algeria.

The French Colonial Empire After 1789

With only a few minor outposts sprinkled here and there, France could hardly be called a leading colonial power in 1789.[1] The old empire con-

---

*From *Al-Abhath*, 28 (1980), pp. 49–67. © 1980 by the American University of Beirut. Reprinted courtesy of the Center for Arab and Middle East Studies, American University of Beirut.

[1]The literature of France's colonial empire is indeed vast. General works include the following: Gabriel Hanotaux and Alfred Martineau, eds., *Histoire des colonies françaises et de l'expansion de la France dans le monde* (Paris: Plon, 1929), in 6 volumes; Henri Blet, *Histoire de la colonisation française* (Paris: Arthaud, 1946), in 3 volumes; Alfred Rambaud, *La France coloniale* (Paris: A. Colin, 1895); J. L. de Lanessan, *L'Expansion coloniale de la France* (Paris: F. Alcan, 1886); M. Raboisson, *Étude sur les colonies et la*

structed by Richelieu and Colbert was lost in a series of disastrous wars: Canadian and French claims in India were surrendered to the victor, England. Further losses were incurred during the Revolutionary and Napoleonic era. The pearl of the sugar isles, Santo Domingo, revolted against the mother country and became the independent Republic of Haiti; the vast region of Louisiana was purchased by the United States in 1803.

The tattered remnants of a once prosperous empire languished for a variety of reasons. The abolition of the slave trade, one of the principal pillars of the old colonial system, reduced the importance of outposts in the Senegal region and cast a shadow on the future of slave-based plantations. The settlement of Guyana suffered for lack of funds and colonizing skill. Most serious of all, the rapid growth of sugar beet agriculture within France brought home the fact that colonial sugar was not an indispensable item. Yet, in theory at least, the whole purpose of a colony in the dominant mercantilist dogma was to provide the tropical products that could not be grown in the mother country and, in general, to remain totally subservient to her interest. In the words of one analyst, the mercantilist *empire exotique* was a ripe lemon to be squeezed "until the pips screamed;"[2] and the euphemism for this kind of exploitation was called the *pacte colonial*.[3] By the end of the eighteenth cen-

colonisation (Paris: Challamel, 1877); Henri Brunschwig, *La Colonisation française; du pacte colonial à l'union française* (Paris: Calmann-Lévy, 1949); Léon Deschamps, *Histoire de la question coloniale en France* (Paris: Plon, 1891); Hubert Deschamps, *Les Méthodes et les doctrines coloniales de la France* (Paris: A. Colin, 1953); Victor Piquet, *Histoire des colonies françaises* (Paris: Payot, 1931); J. B. Piolet, *La France hors de France* (Paris: Falcan, 1900); Georges Hardy, *Histoire sociale de la colonisation française* (Paris: Larose, 1953); Paul Gaffarel, *Les Colonies françaises* (Paris: F. Alcan, 1899); Albert Duchêne, *La Politique coloniale de la France* (Paris: Payot, 1928); Maurice Besson, *Histoire des colonies françaises* (Paris: Boivin, 1931); Herbert Ingram Priestley, *France Overseas: A Study of Modern Imperialism* (New York: D. Appleton-Century, 1938); Louis Vignon, *L'Expansion de la France* (Paris: Hachette, 1892); Jacques Stern, *Les Colonies françaises* (New York: Brentano, 1943). Works specializing in the period before 1815 include Herbert Ingram Priestley, *France Overseas Through the Old Régime* (New York: D. Appleton-Century, 1939); Louis Pauliat, *La Politique coloniale sous l'ancien régime* (Paris: Calmann-Lévy, 1887); J. Saintoyant, *La Colonisation française sous l'ancien régime* (Paris: La Renaissance du livre, 1929), in 2 volumes; J. Saintoyant, *La Colonisation française pendant la période napoléonienne* (Paris: La Renaissance du livre, 1931); Carl L. Lokke, *France and the Colonial Question* (New York: Columbia University Press, 1932); Vincent Confer, "French Colonial Ideas Before 1789," *French Historical Studies*, 3.3 (Spring 1964), pp. 338–59.

[2] H. Oppenheimer, *Le Libéralisme français au début du XIXe siècle* (Paris: Sirey, 1930), p. 16.

[3] The term *pacte* suggests some sort of mutual agreement. In fact, it was a unilateral imposition. See Lokke, *France and the Colonial Question*, p. 27.

tury, the *pacte*—also referred to as the *exclusif*—showed signs of increasing anachronism which did not escape the attention of many critical observers.

In actual fact, the critique of the *pacte colonial* had started half a century earlier. In practical terms, the *exclusif*—a monopoly of trade, slave trade, and shipping—mainly served the cause of seaports like Bordeaux and Nantes, bringing to them an unprecedented era of prosperity during the eighteenth century. However, the French colons residing in the isles found the system unduly restrictive because they were not allowed to engage directly in international trade or to develop their own industries.

The influential physiocratic doctrine of political economy represented by Quesnay, Mirabeau, and Turgot was also disenchanted with the colonial system of relations. Believing as it did in a natural order of things and in agriculture as the true producer of wealth, it tended to view trade, especially colonial trade—as sterile, costly, and artificially sustained. Quesnay denounced the system of colonial mercantilism: it enriched, on one hand, only a restricted elite of *négociants* and, on the other, it diverted enormous wealth from investment at home in agriculture.[4] Mirabeau stressed its undesirable monopolistic features and drain in human resources, while Turgot compared colonies to "fruits which detached themselves from the tree when ripe."[5] The American example was indeed a vivid one.

Mention should also be made of the sociological and humanitarian consequences of the *pacte*. After 1750, the widely read works of travellers (Bernardin de Saint-Pierre), publicists (Abbé Raynal), and *philosophes* of the Enlightenment (Voltaire) devoted some attention to the brutality and corruption of slave-based systems.[6] More concrete results were expected when Condorcet, Siéyès, and Brissot founded in 1787 the Société des amis des noirs, which actively campaigned for slave abolition and colonial reform.[7]

Another line of critique suggested that the French lacked genius in the colonial field, that the national character was ill-suited to the heavy demands of colonization. The repeated failure of projects in the Guyana region, including those involving convicts and "dangerous classes," was a constant

---

[4] *François Quesnay et la physiocratie* (Paris: Institut National d'Études Démographiques, 1958), II, 656, 663.

[5] Lucien Brocard, *Les Doctrines économiques et sociales du Marquis de Mirabeau* (New York: Franklin, 1970), p. 215; Deschamps, *Les Méthodes et les doctrines*, p. 81.

[6] Bernardin de Saint-Pierre, *Voyage à l'Ile de France* (Amsterdam: Merlin, 1773); Abbé Raynal, *Histoire philosophique et politique des établissements et du commerce des européens dans les deux Indes* (Geneva: J.-L. Pellet, 1780); Voltaire, *Candide* (London: Penguin, 1970).

[7] Lokke, *France and the Colonial Question*, p. 90.

reminder.[8] And in the final analysis, whereas France accomplished great
things in Europe, she seemed unable to hold on to her colonies in times of
war. Her vocation was clearly continental rather than *outre-mer*, in spite
of the romance of the Crusades and of the short Indian and North American interlude. There also appeared around 1800 De Pradt's prophetic vision
of decolonization. Referring in his *Les Trois âges des colonies* to Europe,
he remarked: "Ses colonies sont à la veille de lui échapper."[9] As things
stood they were inevitably set on the road to independence, whether through
forcible means or by mutual arrangement.[10] But De Pradt also suggested
that the mother country could become stronger by relinquishing colonial
territory, and he cited the example of the Turkish empire: giving up the
Asian provinces of Syria and "turbulent Egypt" would constitute, in fact, a
gain.[11] The idea of strength through separation was, of course, not entirely
novel. Adam Smith and especially Josiah Tucker maintained that the separation of the American colonies was not a loss to England. In 1781, Tucker
published under the title *Cui Bono* a series of letters to Neckar forcefully
advocating this interpretation of colonial contraction.[12] A few years later,
in 1793, Jeremy Bentham addressed his famous call to the French National
Convention, *Emancipate Your Colonies*, demonstrating the debilitating effect of colonies:

> Your predecessors made me a French citizen: hear me speak like
> one. War thickens round you: I will shew you a vast resource—
> Emancipate Your Colonies!...[13]

There was also the faint stirrings of opposition to the *pacte* from the rising
school of free traders and economic liberals. However, in France this critique
reached fruition after 1815. With the progress of the industrial revolution,
the mercantilist system of colonial protection and preferences appeared increasingly anachronistic; to the physiocratic critique was now added that of

---

[8]De Pradt, *Les Trois âges des colonies* (Paris: Giguet, 1801), I, 150; Maurice Allard,
Considérations sur la difficulté de coloniser la Régence d'Alger (Paris: Selligue, 1830), pp.
26–27. Allard compared the hundred years of stagnation in Louisiana under the French
with the tremendous growth achieved in 25 years by the Americans.

[9]De Pradt, *Les Trois âges*, I, 1.

[10]*Ibid.*, II, 278, 361.

[11]*Ibid.*, II, 510–11.

[12]Carl Bodelsen, *Studies in Mid-Victorian Imperialism* (Copenhagen: Glydendalske,
1924), p. 14.

[13]Jeremy Bentham, *Emancipate Your Colonies* (London: Heward, 1830), p. 1.

the rising economic liberalism closely associated with the person of Jean-Baptiste Say.[14] This important exponent of free-trade ideas distinguished three varieties of colonies: trading posts, plantation-type settlements utilizing slave labor, and European settlements in relatively unpopulated regions such as in Pennsylvania—his ideal model. While bitterly opposed to the first two varieties, Say saw great possibilities in the third. Trading posts and sugar isles brought about war, the commercial wars of the seventeenth century.[15] Moreover, he went on to criticize such outposts on social and economic grounds. The prevailing social system was the master-slave relationship with its indolence and human debasement: "intelligence usurped by violence and brutality."[16] Another consequence was the creation of a peculiar colonial class of administrators with a vested interest in perpetuating the absolutist link between the home country and colonies which alone guaranteed job security. There was obviously a proliferation of posts providing an ideal opportunity for the interplay of favor and patronage at home.[17] In social terms, the colonial system was guilty beyond redemption, in economic terms it spelled disaster through the imposition of monopoly and protection: the *exclusif*.[18] Colonial products were priced far above their natural price, thus inhibiting consumption and the possibility of normal exchange.[19] In

---

[14] Jean-Baptiste Say (1767–1832), son of a Protestant merchant, studied commerce in England together with his brother Horace Say, and was deeply influenced by Adam Smith: "I revere Adam Smith," he wrote to Malthus in 1821, "he is my master." See J.-B. Say, *Letters to Malthus* (London: George Harding, 1936), p. 20. His brother Horace, who became a *polytechnicien* and a member of the Institut d'Égypte, died during Napoleon's abortive siege of Acre, Palestine. J.B. Say's career combined journalism, public administration, industrial enterprise, and education. From 1794 to 1799, he wrote for the *Décade philosophique* on economic questions, then was appointed to the government's Finance Committee. In 1803, he achieved fame as an original economic theoretician with the publication of his *Traité d'économie politique* (five editions in 25 years). He was reasonably successful as a cotton industrialist in Pas-de-Calais. The Restoration sent him on a fact-finding mission to Great Britain in 1815, where he was offered Adam Smith's chair at Glasgow University. In the same year, he initiated a course in economics at the Athéné in Paris and published several editions of his popular *Catéchisme d'économie politique*. His career as Professor of Political Economy included positions at the Conservatoire des Arts et Métiers and at the Collège de France. His most important contribution, *Cours complet d'économie politique*, was published in 1828. See Charles Coquelin, *Dictionnaire de l'économie politique* (Paris: Guillaumin, 1852–53), II, 591–95.

[15] J.-B. Say, *Cours complet d'économie politique* (Paris: Guillaumin, 1840), I, 20.

[16] J.-B. Say, *Traité d'économie politique* (Paris: Crapelet, 1803), I, 215–16.

[17] Say, *Cours complet*, I, 632.

[18] *Ibid.*, I, 633.

[19] *Ibid.*, I, 634.

short, Say concluded that "colonies were enormous economic burdens that ought to be gotten rid of...; far from contributing to the prosperity of the mother country, they acted as obstacles."[20]

Why then could such an anomalous reality persist? First, there was the colon, and Say presented an interesting insight into the colon's unnatural attachment to his mother country: "The white population of the sugar isles could not possibly keep a black population fifteen or twenty times its own size in total servitude without the help of the armed forces provided by the mother country; the colon hated the yoke of the mother country, yet he would not want independence."[21] The other reason was the vested interest of the colonial administration fighting to keep the status quo.[22]

With respect to the third variety of colonial establishment, that of excess population from the Old World seeking to colonize unpopulated areas beyond Europe, Say warmly approved this option. In fact, he wrote:

> [Les Européens], en raison du génie entreprenant qui les distingue, et par suite des étonnants progrès qu'ils ont faits dans toutes les branches des connaissances humaines, sont destinés sans doute à subjuguer le monde, comme ils ont déjà subjugué les deux Amériques.[23]

Say went on to add that the task would not require military action and preponderance since this factor, he thought, was becoming increasingly incidental in European life. Rather, the task would be done through "enlightenment and institutions."[24] And contrary to what has often been repeated by many scholars of French imperialism, Say was even in favor of conquest and colonization close to the southern shores of Europe;[25] in this particular expansionist venture, however, he seemed to have had second thoughts about his earlier anti-militarist position: "If the European powers were really conscious of their best interests, the immense armies, wealth, and tactics that

---

[20] *Ibid.*, I, 636.

[21] *Ibid.*, I, 640.

[22] Oppenheimer, *Le Libéralisme français*, p. 53.

[23] Say, *Cours complet*, I, 666.

[24] *Ibid.*

[25] In the literature of French colonialism there is a general feeling that all liberal economists (except for Sismondi) were opposed to colonies. Ch. An. Julien maintained this position in 1922 and 1964: "L'Avenir d'Alger et l'opposition des libéraux et des économistes en 1830," *Bulletin de la Société de Géographie d'Oran*, 42 (1922), p. 19; and *Histoire de l'Algérie contemporaine*, I, 45; also René Vâlet, *L'Afrique du Nord devant le Parlement* (Algiers: Imprimerie La Typo-litho, 1924), p. 29; and P. Leroy-Beaulieu, *L'Algérie et la Tunisie* (Paris: Guillaumin, 1897), p. 4.

they use to hurt each other could be employed, instead, to introduce European civilization into North Africa; the powers would form colonies, soon to become independent—as all colonies should—and to supply precious foodstuffs in return for European manufactured products."[26] He saw colonization as a middle-class enterprise, not as a panacea for the poor: "C'est des classes moyennes que sortent les fondateurs d'une colonie."[27] Furthermore, new colonial establishments, if founded in deserted regions or underpopulated areas, would advance the cause of human progress.[28]

At this point, one may wonder at the apparent confusion in J.-B. Say's thought; in actual fact, there was none. To many liberals—and Say was regarded as one of the movement's leading lights—the old colonialism, involving slavery and protectionism, was morally bankrupt and economically disastrous; but they did see interesting possibilities in a neo-colonialism geared to liberal *laissez-faire* ideas in politics and economics. In short, Say was moving in the direction of an imperialism of free trade.

Nonetheless, throughout the period under consideration, the term colony remained primarily associated with mercantilism: hence the powerful economic overtones evoked by the term. Montesquieu in *L'Esprit des lois* and Diderot's *Encyclopédie* ascribed to it essentially this meaning. But it found ideal expression in the instructions of Choiseul to the governor of Martinique in 1765:

> The colonies of Europe were established only in order to be useful to the mother countries...they are to be regarded exclusively as commercial establishments....The more a colony differed from the mother country in the products yielded, the more perfect it was; this difference determined its aptitude and final purpose...colonies must be placed under the severest *prohibition* in favor of the mother country.[29]

To use Henri Brunschwig's characterization, colonies under this strict form of colonial mercantilism were seen in the final analysis as "an accounting problem, the interest was in things more than in people."[30] To most Frenchmen, the archetypal colony was the plantation-based sugar isle in the

[26] Say, *Cours complet*, II, 191.
[27] *Ibid.*, II, 192.
[28] *Ibid.*
[29] Brunschwig, *La Colonisation française*, pp. 11-12.
[30] *Ibid.*

Antilles, in the New World, requiring the importation of slave labor from Africa.

Talleyrand, Napoleon, and the Importance of Egypt

However, at the close of the eighteenth century, a new perspective on the colonial question began to emerge: a gravitation of interest from the New World to the Old World. Moreover, while the economic concern was maintained, political and strategic considerations intruded more forcefully. And with Napoleon, a distinct note of militarism was injected into the colonial equation.[31] Several interrelated factors provoked the reorientation: the debate concerning the abolition of the slave trade and of slavery; the scientific and especially the geographical discovery of the African continent;[32] perhaps the awareness of a Malthusian situation developing in France; and in the case of Talleyrand and Bonaparte, a new geopolitical perception of French power.

With the loss of the American domain, the constant threat of further dispossession in the Carribean, and the awareness of an impending slave emancipation, voices were heard advocating colonial experiments in Africa with free labor. The idea was appealing: instead of transporting black slaves all the way to America to plant sugar cane, cotton, and tobacco, why not try the cultivation of tropical crops on African ground with free or freed native labor. This was the substance of Dupont de Nemours' proposal made in the year 1796.[33]

In the rich annals of colonialism, whether Napoleon's initiative with regard to the conquest and planned colonization of Egypt represented a new departure is likely to remain a moot point. However, his bold move in the land of the Nile revealed original features. To begin with, the project involved the mobilization of a wide range of the nation's resources—muscle power as well as brain power—whereas colonialism under the *pacte*'s spirit had always been a constricted enterprise involving a minority of settlers, traders, and colonial administrators. This is not to suggest that the idea of a colonial venture in Egypt was totally new: Leibnitz had proposed it to King Louis XIV—an opportunity for the Sun King to acquire a place in the sun. Similar projects were also formulated in the following period. Upon his

---

[31] Duchêne, *La Politique coloniale*, p. 144.

[32] Hubert Deschamps, *L'Europe découvre l'Afrique* (Paris: Berger-Levrault, 1967), pp. 23–24.

[33] Carl Lokke, "French Dreams of Colonial Empire Under Directory and Consulate," *Journal of Modern History*, 2 (1930), p. 238.

return from America the sagacious Talleyrand made his often-cited plea for an active colonial expansion.[34] In his inaugural address as member of the Institut de France in 1797, he read a paper entitled, *Essai sur les avantages à retirer des colonies nouvelles dans les circonstances présentes*, arguing that France ought to turn away from the New World—seen as the upcoming sphere of influence of the United States—and to concentrate instead on the Old World. The Mediterranean appeared a more suitable terrain on which to challenge her mortal enemy, Albion. Talleyrand selected Egypt as the new focal point: properly colonized it would replace all of France's lost possessions and present the added strategic advantage of threatening England's position in India.[35] The importance of Talleyrand's initiative cannot be overstressed.

In the same year, Napoleon declared that Egypt had to be conquered in order to ruin English power. The whole operation would be conducted along rational and scientific lines to suit the new spirit of the age. With the active assistance of the Institut d'Égypte, founded in 1798, the Egyptian population would be introduced to modern Western civilization and persuaded to adopt the revolutionary dynamism of the French. Thus the GNP of Egypt would be dramatically increased under French supervision. The archeological and scientific expertise—including some of the more esoteric branches such as aerostatics—would constitute, as it were, the fringe benefits of what was to remain, in effect, a carefully planned system of colonization under the direction of Menou.[36]

From the standpoint of Bonaparte, military audacity and bold experimentation were the order of the day. Other features of the conquest and colonization of Egypt were equally significant. The military campaign was given an enormous amount of publicity: in other words, the public relations aspect of militarism in the colonial field was not neglected. This included a carefully prepared proclamation to the Egyptians explaining France's purpose and plans. Napoleon and Menou tried very hard to project an Islamic image. There was some attention paid to a *politique indigène*—perhaps a new departure in the story of French colonialism.[37] In any case, a certain amount of self-interested consideration was shown to the native culture and mores. Not surprisingly, the Egyptian people were not impressed.

---

[34] Lokke, *France and the Colonial Question*, p. 166.

[35] *Ibid.*, p. 174.

[36] *Ibid.*, p. 213.

[37] Blet, *Histoire de la colonisation*, II, 31.

The expedition to Egypt carried out with such unconventional flourish ended in disaster, but it did strike deeply into the imagination of the French people: they had tasted the romantic trappings of empire and identified closely with the popular hero who believed he was the embodiment of the principles of 1789. In many ways the abortive campaign served as a dress rehearsal for the Algerian project. Bourmont's proclamation to the Algerians is reminiscent of Bonaparte's to the Egyptians. The whole story of the conquest and colonization of Algeria is replete with allusions to the Egyptian model.[38] Public opinion saw this French enterprise through the hazy vision of Imperial Grandeur, and the press certainly contributed to preserve the aesthetic image.

Thereafter, colonialism could no longer remain the exclusive domain of mercantilism. To a great extent, it became associated with the pageant of militarism: the transition from the *pacte colonial* to colonialism as a national undertaking was being effected.[39]

Although the powers had left France with only the shreds of an empire at the Congress of Vienna in 1815, the popular phantasm of a French expansion overseas remained virtually intact. There may even have been a psychological imperative: it was, after all, part of the Napoleonic legend.

The Colonial Policy of the Restoration

The Bourbon Monarchy's first task after Napoleon's demise was to assert its presence once more at the head of the French state. Priority was given both to internal reconstruction along the principles of the Charter and to the strengthening of the Restoration's rural constituency. The nation was gingerly trying a novel experiment, constitutional monarchy. Considerable attention was also devoted to the country's continental position and to foreign affairs. On the other hand, the colonial question was regarded as relatively unimportant in the face of such pressing matters at home and in Europe.

From 1815 to 1821, the Restoration's colonial policy was directed by a capable Bordelese *négociant*, Baron Portal, who may be described as somewhat of an innovator in colonial matters. The opposite trend—resistance to colonial reform—was represented by the Villèle ministry which came to power in 1821, causing considerable dismay to the trading and shipping circles of Bordeaux.

---

[38] J. J. Baude, *L'Algérie* (Paris: A. Bertrand, 1841), I, 32.

[39] Hardy, *Histoire sociale*, p. 138.

Portal appreciated, perhaps more consciously than most of his political contemporaries, the devolution of the old colonial system. In his view, it was neither possible nor desirable for France to reconstruct an empire based on a narrow adherence to the *pacte colonial.*[40] Influenced no doubt by a certain trend in Bordelese *négociant* opinion, he sought to enlarge the scope of export activity, particularly to the newly freed Latin American republics and to Southeast Asia. There is some evidence that he toyed with the idea of informal empire—juxtaposed to the remnants of the formal empire—which would not require direct control.[41] And he wanted to move in the direction of limited free trade, or at least the easing of protective tariffs. But in all these areas he came into headlong clash with a colonial lobby jealously guarding their monopoly of sugar cane exports to France from encroachment by cheaper Cuban and Indochinese sugar.[42]

From 1822 to 1828, the colonial lobby's powerful representation in Paris, supported by many ultra-Legitimists, was able to influence colonial legislation, acting as it did as an advisory council to the Minister of Colonies. The lobby fought successfully to maintain high protective tariffs on foreign sugar and to retard slave emancipation, using the pretext that blacks first had to be "prepared" for freedom.[43]

The field of action of the post-1815 colonialism was also enlarged to include a lively policy of colonization to be effected by white settlers, free or freed labor, and imported coolies. Portal had in mind three distinct areas: Senegal, Guyana, and Madagascar. High expectations were placed on an intensive cultivation of cotton and indigo in Senegal: in the Cap-Vert region a Société coloniale philanthropique made various attempts which all ended in failure. A member of this society, L.B. Hautefeuille, continued to press for colonization in spite of the lack of success, proposing a colonial establishment of a new type: "a feudal regime with severe laws."[44] In addition to poor climatic conditions, the local population showed very little sympathy to the colonization projects being carried out by the energetic Governor

---

[40] Duchêne, *La Politique coloniale*, p. 166.

[41] *Ibid.*, p. 175.

[42] *Ibid.*, p. 173.

[43] *Ibid.*

[44] L. B. Hautefeuille, *Plan de colonisation des possesions françaises dans l'Afrique occidentale au moyen de la civilisation des nègres indigènes* (Paris: Levasseur, 1830), p. 8. Many distinguished names were associated with various projects in Senegal: Hogendorp, Schmaltz, and Baron Roger. However, the results with cotton were very mediocre. Senegal continued to depend on her traditional export of gum. See Blet, *Histoire de la colonisation*, II, 71.

Schmaltz: in fact, traditional rivals got together to offer armed resistance against what undoubtedly was felt to be a direct intrusion into their socio-economic structure. Schmaltz, to be sure, found it expedient to blame it all on British machination.[45]

In Guyana the problem was a little different. The native inhabitants were not "hostile," but they were not deemed capable of working the land. Colonization had to depend therefore on white colons, who usually tried to avoid the colony except when deported there, or else on imported slaves.[46] However, with the abolition of the slave trade other sources of labor had to be located. Captain Philibert thought of a scheme to organize Chinese coolies, and was in fact entrusted with a recruiting mission which took him to Southeast Asia. He finally did manage to find 27 Chinese and five Malays who accompanied him to Guyana, where nine of them died. The rest were repatriated, but one of them made it to Paris and received a pension from the King.[47]

Various plans utilizing deported criminals and political prisoners were tried during the Ancien Régime and the Revolution; Napoleon also favored them on the ground that they provided a golden opportunity "to purge the Old World and people the New."[48] During the first half of the nineteenth century, some of France's acute social problems included widespread poverty, illegitimate children, foundlings, and orphans. Middle-class opinion was prone to view such groups as dangerous to the political and social order of society, a phenomenon which has received the careful attention of Louis Chevalier in his work *Laboring Classes and Dangerous Classes*; the fear of criminality—and of those responsible for it—permeated the atmosphere of daily life during this period.[49] This question may have played a more important role than is normally suggested in determining official as well as popular

---

[45] Georges Hardy, *Histoire de la colonisation française* (Paris: Larose, 1928), p. 153.

[46] André Vigé, *La Colonisation pénale* (Toulouse: Imprimerie du Sud-Ouest, 1911), pp. 15–16. Guyana's experience with penal colonization and settlements is a rich one. In 1763 there was the notorious failure of the Kourou River settlement, which cost the lives of over 1000 beggar-settlers and engulfed 25 million francs. The Convention also made use of the colony as a place of deportation for criminals and political prisoners. Finally a proper penal establishment was organized in 1854.

[47] Hardy, *Histoire de la colonisation*, p. 154.

[48] Vigé, *La Colonisation*, pp. 15–16.

[49] Louis Chevalier, *Laboring Classes and Dangerous Classes in Paris During the First Half of the Nineteenth Century*, translated by Frank Jellinek (New York: Fertig, 1973), p. 3.

attitudes towards colonialism. And it needs further exploring in connection with the problem of Algerian colonization.

In 1822, a pilot project was tried in Guyana, initiated more out of domestic than colonial imperatives.[50] Fifty orphans of both sexes and a handful of retired military personnel were settled in the Mana region at a cost of over one million francs. Again the scheme ended in total failure, with only three families installed in this "Nouvelle Angoûleme," as it was called. Still another attempt was made by Madame Jahouvey of the Sisters of Saint Joseph in 1828: her 40 farmers returned to France at the end of their three-year term.[51] Clearly, then, French colons did not seem willing to work under tropical conditions and at such great distances from home, thus confirming the thesis of the agrarians and physiocrats concerning the national character of the French people.

The third area envisaged by Portal, Madagascar, differed from Senegal and Guyana in that it required a military takeover from the ruling Hovas. In 1818, an expedition was sent out to the east coast; the island of Sainte-Marie, together with some territory along the Bay of Tintingue, was secured. The plan included the setting up of a fortified military position on the bay and the colonization of Sainte-Marie with the help of Malgache labor purchased locally as slaves, who were to be liberated and then signed on for 14-year terms of work on plantations.[52] Again, high hopes were entertained: the venture was in the charge of an experienced colonial hand, Sylvain Roux; moreover the Malgache population—or the Hovas, as they were called— had achieved a measure of progress by Western standards under Radama, their modernizing king.[53] However, the Hovas were determined to offer resistance: by 1824, they had ousted the French from all points except Sainte-Marie. Another campaign was mounted during the last two years of the Restoration; the navy bombarded the ports of Tintingue and Tamatave, but the expeditionary force could not maintain a permanent foothold on the coast.[54] A period of stalemate ensued which was finally broken by the July Monarchy's decision to abandon the conquest: General Sebastiani, the new

---

[50] Hardy, *Histoire de la colonisation*, p. 159; Blet, *Histoire de la colonisation*, II, 77.

[51] Priestley, *France Overseas*, p. 10.

[52] Blet, *Histoire de la colonisation*, II, 76.

[53] Gabriel Gravier, *Madagascar* (Paris: Delagrave, 1904), p. 478; Antony de Fontmichel, "Considérations inédites sur Madagascar et sur les résultats de la nouvelle colonisation française de cette île," *Revue des deux mondes*, Second Series, 2 (May-June 1830), p. 336.

[54] Gravier, *Madagascar*, pp. 483–84.

Minister of Marine, known for his scepticism regarding colonial expansion, gave the order soon after the July Monarchy was installed in 1830.[55]

Thus, all of Portal's endeavors to extend French colonization in Senegal, Guyana, and Madagascar met with unmitigated failure. And it is surprising that the Bourbon ruling elite could initiate such costly involvement given the fact that France had an army tied down in Spain, another being prepared for intervention in the Greek War of Independence, and a potentially dangerous situation on the Rhine frontier. With relatively few resources available for far-ranging colonial operations, it would seem that the aims of the Restoration's colonial policy bordered on the quixotic. Moreover, French colonial planners seemed to possess an extraordinary capacity for misjudging their countrymen's predispositions: Frenchmen, unlike Englishmen, did not wish to emigrate, particularly as colons to distant tropical regions. But despite the failure of systematic colonization, the policymakers had provided an opportunity for an improvement of technical skills in the colonial field, the rising middle classes were constantly reminded of the lure of riches and glory in far-off places, and, in general, the ground was being prepared for future expansion.

More fruitful was the Restoration's record with other aspects of colonialism, such as exploration, publicity, and the revival of religious missionary activity. In West Africa, Gaspard Mollien explored the sources of the River Senegal in 1818; a few years later René Caillié, dressed as an Arab, undertook his famous 4000-mile voyage to Timbuktu. His success was all the more exciting because it was contested by the British. Predictably, the Société de géographie (founded in 1821) awarded him its valuable prize for the Timbuktu trip.[56] In the Pacific region Freycinet (Australia), Duperrey (New Guinea), and Bougainville (Southeast Asia) carried out their exploration and hydrographic surveys, which attracted attention, helping to focus interest a little more on that portion of the globe.[57]

The Catholic religious revival in France contributed to a renewed interest in foreign missions. The government was willing to cooperate with the Church on the question of support for missionary activity—the aim be-

---

[55] *Ibid.* It is interesting to note that Fontmichel, in his article "Considérations inédites," p. 357, called upon his fellow citizens to emulate the British: "Je termine cet article en faisant appel aux armateurs, aux grands capitalistes, aux hommes et industrieux; je les invite à montrer un peu plus d'ardeur pour les expéditions maritimes."

[56] Hubert Deschamps, *L'Europe découvre l'Afrique*, pp. 66, 103.

[57] J. Tramond and André Reussner, *Eléments d'histoire maritime et coloniale* (Paris: Challamel, 1924), pp. 5, 22.

ing to counter British Protestant expansion, especially in Oceania; Polignac pursued this policy zealously. As to the navy, on whose effectiveness depended the maintenance and further growth of France's maritime empire, the Restoration sought to increase its strength in spite of the lukewarm feeling in the House regarding expenditure.[58] Finally, the Bourbon Monarchy became engrossed in the Algerian affair, and, in so doing, helped to set in place what eventually became the cornerstone of France's new colonial empire.

The Conquest of Algeria: An Economic Interpretation

The domestic crisis faced by the Bourbon Restoration in its closing days under Polignac contributes much by way of explaining the decision to go ahead with the Algerian expedition, but it was far from being the sole motivation. The relationship between political decisions and commercial interests has always been difficult to document; however, in the case of the Algerian affair, there is evidence pointing to its presence as an important factor. Historically, the south of France had a Mediterranean mystique which may be described as a mixture of religious zeal for the land of Saint Augustine, the scene of King Saint Louis' crusade in Tunis, and specific economic interests. The whole basin was the traditional domain of a group of business firms located in Marseilles: the Maghrib, in particular, was virtually their monopoly.[59] The North African coast was viewed as a kind of cornucopia; during the Revolutionary Wars it had supplied a starving Midi with vast quantities of grain. As early as 1776, the Marseilles Chamber of Commerce had minted a commemorative medal picturing North Africa holding a cornucopia overflowing with grain.[60]

However, in the first quarter of the nineteenth century trade with the Levant was on the decline, relentlessly taken over by the products of British manufacturing. The emergence of an independent Greek nation threatened Marseilles' weak position further; for the Greeks represented skilled competitors, well-acquainted with the nature of the Levant trade. Vigorous action on the North African coast was a most popular idea in the city and found

---

[58] *Ibid.* The Ministry of Marine budgets for 1819, 1822, and 1823 gave rise to acrimonious debates in the House. For Portal's defense of his Marine and Colonies budget, see *Archives parlementaires*, XXIV, 4 June 1819, p. 751.

[59] Lucette Valensi, *Le Maghreb avant la prise d'Alger, 1790-1830* (Paris: Flammarion, 1969), pp. 70-74. The *grand négoce* of Marseilles was characterized as Europe's Trojan horse in the region (*ibid*).

[60] Ferhat Abbas, *La Nuit coloniale* (Paris: Julliard, 1962), p. 49.

echoes in the lone intervention in the House by the deputy of Marseilles, Pierre Honoré Roux, in May 1828. His speech was noteworthy on more than one count: he reminded the Bourbon regime that the port was interested in going beyond the mere destruction of piracy, that France ought to conquer several points on the Algerian coastline, that "the region which is almost within sight of Marseilles was extremely fertile," and that "civilization would turn the bedouin nomads into agriculturists."[61] Significantly, Roux was much more sceptical, in the same speech, of Greece, and felt that France ought to pay closer attention to the lucrative exchange with Turkey.[62] The Chamber of Commerce and the local press also reminded the nation of the attractive possibilities present in Algeria.[63] That this opinion was noted by the principal military figures of the campaign is not at all surprising; the commander-in-chief of the expedition, Bourmont, addressed the Chamber of Commerce on the eve of the sailing date and announced France's colonial projects in Algiers.[64] Obviously, it was the kind of policy that was expected; the *grand négoce* of Marseilles was less impressed by the avenging-of-the-king rhetoric than by the prospect of a rich colonial settlement within a stone's throw from its shores.

Religious fervor and economic expansion went hand in hand for two of the most articulate champions of colonization in the first half of the nineteenth century: Lyon and Marseilles. Pauline Jaricot, daughter of a Lyon silk magnate, provided the impulse for the work of the Propagation de la foi and the Société des missions étrangères.[65] Nor was the patriotic connection with this evangelism absent: the Minister of the Navy, referring to the work of the congregation of Picpus in the Pacific, commended the missionaries for displaying "evangelical zeal as well as the purest patriotic sentiment."[66]

In actual fact, the idea of overseas expansion and colonization—whether in North Africa or elsewhere—was in vogue not only in the Midi but also

---

[61] *Archives parlementaires*, LIV, 13 May 1828, pp. 31–32.

[62] *Ibid.*

[63] Pierre Guiral, "L'Opinion marseillaise et les débuts de l'entreprise algérienne," *Revue historique*, 213 (June 1955), p. 10.

[64] Julien, "L'Avenir d'Alger, p. 4; Claude Ambroise Fernel, *Campagne d'Afrique en 1830* (Paris: Barrois, 1831), p. 1; François Alexandre Desprez, *Journal d'un officier de l'armée d'Afrique* (Paris: Anselin, 1831), p. 7.

[65] John Laffey, "Roots of French Imperialism in the Nineteenth Century: The Case of Lyon," *French Historical Studies*, 6 (1969), p. 78.

[66] *Revue de l'Orient*, 1 (1843), p. 393.

in the numerous studies commissioned by different ministries.[67] Prior to the conquest, the *Revue des deux mondes* published an unsigned article advocating the establishment of a substantial French colony of two million European immigrants in Algeria.[68] Reference has already been made to J.-B. Say's vision of an expanding European order incorporating vast regions of the globe; Charles Ganilh, a popular economic publicist, also shared this vision, as did Sismondi with specific reference to Algeria.[69]

If the year 1829 was bad for the Bourbons, it was disastrous for Marseilles; the regime knew it and had ample opportunity of being acquainted with the city's wishes regarding conquest and colonization. Thus, underlying the rhetoric of vengeance and the suppression of piracy was a calculated move to counter opposition at home and—of equal importance—to implement the Mediterranean outlook of the Midi.

In conclusion, of the many explanations for Algeria's conquest and colonization, two expressed on the eve of the expedition are particularly valuable: Alexandre Colombel and J.C.L. Simonde de Sismondi, enthusiastic supporters of colonial expansion and of the Algerian project.

What differentiated Colombel from the vast majority of his contemporary commentators was the socio-economic orientation of his reasoning.[70] The conclusions he derived from an appraisal of the internal condition of France led him to campaign for a crash program in empire building. "Ever since the French Revolution," he wrote, "the country has experienced an overabundance of population."[71] And in addition to this demographic increase, there were grave social problems threatening society: "The painful contrast of opulent wealth and misery was generalized and conspicuous..., cries of distress reverberated; an active industry was exhausting itself in superfluous efforts; production seemed to have exceeded everywhere the limits of con-

---

[67]F. Charles-Roux, *France et Afrique du Nord avant 1830* (Paris: Alcan, 1932), pp. 661–65.

[68]"Du territoire et de la ville d'Alger," *Revue des deux mondes*, Second Series, 1 (Jan. 1830), pp. 160–61.

[69]Charles Ganilh, *Dictionnaire analytique d'économie politique* (Paris: Ladvocat, 1826), p. 121; J.C.L. de Sismondi, "De l'expédition contre Alger," *Revue encyclopédique*, 46 (May 1830), pp. 277–83.

[70]Alexandre Colombel, a little-known publicist—his name does not figure in any of the five standard biographies of the period—is the author of *De la guerre d'Orient, ou des plans d'invasion de la Russie* (Paris: Dupont, 1828); *De la chambre des députés, de la chambre des pairs* (Paris: Delaunay, 1839); and *Du parti qu'on pourrait tirer d'une expédition d'Alger* (Paris: Delaunay, 1830).

[71]Colombel, *Du parti*, p. 10.

sumption and was on the verge of devouring itself unless new opportunities were made available."[72] The ideal solution was colonial expansion: "France must fix the roots of a colonial domain...she needs colonies urgently."[73]

Colombel had the vision of a mixed formal and informal empire founded in the Mediterranean basin with Algeria forming "the nucleus of a vast colonial establishment and the advance sentinel of Europe on the African coast."[74] The colony would serve as a base for the future conquest of Tunisia as well as the key to trade with the African interior. In addition to Tunis, France could also gain direct control of Tripoli, the Sudan, and Morocco, and could act as protector over Cyprus. This was the broad outline of his *nouveau système colonial* in the Mediterranean.[75]

As to Algeria itself, in addition to the advantages already mentioned, Colombel proposed that it serve as France's Botany Bay to take care of criminals and convicts. He liked to argue that "a crook married to a prostitute could produce an honest child in such places."[76] Finally, he did advocate as a motive to the conquest "the reintegration of the Barbary coast to civilization."[77]

J.C.L. Simonde de Sismondi (1773–1842) was a Genevan economist who rejected the anti-colonial arguments of the political opposition in France; the article he published in the *Revue encyclopédique* in May 1830 was a deliberate rebuttal to their sharp barbs. The motive for the conquest was not, in his view, the cultivation of popularity at home; rather, it was a response to "a higher, more general" imperative.[78] Algeria was useful to France for basic socio-economic reasons; and, besides, "there was glory in reintroducing civilization to the home of Saint Augustine."[79] Its crucial importance, in his view, was clear: Algeria ought not to be regarded as a mere object of conquest but as "a colony, a new land ready to soak up the surplus population and excessive economic energies present in French society." [80]

---

[72] *Ibid.,* p. 11. Colombel was familiar with British economic literature and quoted Adam Smith and Malthus (*ibid.,* p. 9).

[73] *Ibid.,* p. 9.

[74] *Ibid.,* p. 35.

[75] *Ibid.,* pp. 42, 48, 59, 60.

[76] *Ibid.,* p. 74.

[77] *Ibid.,* pp. 23–24.

[78] "De l'expédition contre Alger," pp. 276–77.

[79] *Ibid.,* p. 283.

[80] *Ibid.,* pp. 284–85.

To Sismondi, a rich and vast nation like France could undoubtedly absorb "twice the population and present level of investment, but that in the prevailing social order, property was, so to speak, chained."[81] France was progressing gradually—at a rate he deemed proper and which he did not want to see accelerated for fear of falling into the pattern of social perturbations experienced by England—but in the meantime, openings had to be secured for the excess material and human energy present in the nation:[82]

> C'est encore un fait que les manufactures, l'agriculture et le commerce ne récompensent qu'imparfaitement l'activité qu'on y emploie; que la vente de tous les produits ou bruts ou ouvrés est difficile, que les marchandises, en prenant ce mot dans l'acceptation la plus large, dépassent les besoins du marché, ou la capacité des acheteurs; qu'enfin, les capitaux surabondent....Toute cette masse de talens, de connaissances, d'activité et de capitaux que produit la France avec surabondance, demande impérieusement de l'emploi; elle le demande pour le repos de la France; car tant d'activité non employée est une cause permanente de troubles... Chacun des grands Etats de l'Europe, la France seule exceptée, a un débouché....La France seule se sent à l'étroit, resserrée dans des frontières qui ne peuvent s'étendre. Faut-il donc qu'elle soit laissée en arrière par toutes ses rivales!....Que l'Afrique lui soit ouverte...."[83]

Because of its close proximity to French shores—"one day's span by steamship navigation from Toulon"—Algeria was seen as representing a crucial strategic advantage to a continental power such as France.[84] In this respect it differed from the distant and vulnerable colonial outposts; it was not at the mercy of the foremost maritime power: a value that the Genevan economist did not fail to stress.[85]

In many ways Colombel and Sismondi foreshadowed the Hobson-Lenin explanation of colonial expansion. The elements were there: overproduction, underconsumption, maldistribution of wealth, and social unrest, leading to a search for outlets. However, Colombel and to a lesser extent Sismondi did

---

[81] *Ibid.*
[82] *Ibid.*
[83] *Ibid.*, pp. 285–87.
[84] *Ibid.*, p. 284.
[85] *Ibid.*, p. 291.

not emphasize the determining role of finance capital—indeed, it would have been strange for the period if they had.

To be sure, unlike Hobson, whose answer to the socio-economic imbalance lay in a more equitable distribution of wealth, thus neutralizing the need for imperialist expansion, Sismondi, a political conservative who basically accepted the existing system of relations, preferred the short-term palliative: the creation of external outlets through colonial conquest.

In explaining the causes of the Algerian conquest, seen as a deliberate neo-colonial move, one ought to stress the alliance of three principal factors: first, the internal socio-economic condition of France and the anxieties it generated, as suggested by Sismondi; secondly, the personality of Polignac—"a mystic of another age,"[86] his Mediterranean vision, and the high expectations that were placed in him to save a tottering regime; and thirdly, the specific commercial and trading interests in the port of Marseilles and, to a lesser extent, elsewhere in the Midi, who made their voices heard in the right places.[87] In this complex alliance of factors and subfactors, the third factor may very well have outweighed the others.

[86]Hubert Deschamps, *Méthodes*, p. 99.

[87]Yves Lacoste *et al., L'Algérie: passé et présent* (Paris: Éditions sociales, 1960), pp. 239–40.

2

The Conquest of Algeria and the Apocalyptic Vision of La Gervaisais*

IN THE ANNALS of the French opposition to the conquest and colonization of Algeria during the period of the Bourbon Restoration and the July
Monarchy of Louis Philippe, the figure of the Marquis de la Gervaisais is
largely ignored. Yet he is the author of about 200 widely circulated pamphlets and booklets predicting, among other things, an era of violent revolts,
the falls of the Bourbon Restoration and the July Monarchy, the return of
a Republican order to France, and the coming of a new Napoleon. Many of
his works included sharp attacks on the social and economic systems, the
new industrial middle class, and French militarism in Algeria.

The personal history of this unusual and little-studied publicist (a brief
biography published in 1850 appears to be one of the few exceptions) was
marked by tragedy and bitter disappointment, which might explain his characteristic compulsion for apocalyptic writing. He was eager to have his works
brought to the attention of political circles and was requested, on one occasion, to stop using the secretariat of the two Chambers of Representatives
for purposes of disseminating his polemical literature.[1]

Born in 1765 near Saint-Malo in Brittany, the Marquis embarked on what
was to become a conventional military career. While visiting one of France's
more prestigious watering places, he fell in love with a Princess Bourbon

*From *Al-Abhath*, 27 (1978–79), pp. 39–47. © 1979 by the American University of
Beirut. Reprinted courtesy of the Center for Arab and Middle East Studies, American
University of Beirut.

[1](A. de Laborde and La Gervaisais), *Correspondance inédite, à la fois instructive et
amusante, entre un des questeurs de la Chambre et un des docteurs de la presse* (Paris:
Pihan, n.d.).

de Condé who apparently returned his love, but their marriage was not deemed possible because of important differences in their respective family stations. Thereupon, the officer, wounded in his heart and pride, resigned his commission and went on a self-imposed exile to Switzerland to get over his unlucky fate. The Princess retired eventually to a nunnery.[2]

Meanwhile, in his home country a new page in world history was being written. In 1789 the Parisians stormed the Bastille, placing France in a momentous revolutionary situation. La Gervaisais returned home only to be repelled by the spectacle of devastation and the radical dismantling of a cherished Ancien Régime. Deeply shaken, he went again into exile in Wales in 1791, but was forced to return after two years to save a family estate that was being decimated by the anti-noble legislation enacted by the French Revolution. Not unexpectedly, his writings are characterized by a bitter oppositon to all revolutions and revolutionary situations.[3]

It is not entirely clear how he fared under Napoleon, whom he regarded as a reckless adventurer. However, the Restoration of the Bourbons in 1815 enabled the Marquis to rebuild, to some extent, his former position. But he did not get along too well with the returning Bourbons and, in fact, opposed the Villèle ministry on the ground that it was spelling the ruin of the monarchical system by permitting the erosion of the King's prerogatives.[4] After the downfall of Charles X, he took his distance from the Bourbon Legitimist camp without declaring a definite support for the new liberal bourgeois order represented by the July Monarchy. To be sure, like most aristocrats of the Ancien Régime he thoroughly detested the liberal bourgeoisie's accession to power and privilege: "It is *avide*," he wrote, "like all dominant classes, and blind like all *parvenus*."[5] He also gave vent to his feelings on its role as follows:

> There is talk about freedom only in order to better construct authority which is then used to formulate laws. In turn, legislation serves to rivet the chains. Industry on a grand scale serves to concentrate wealth and aggravate poverty. Thus, increasingly, vested interest takes over from real need. Nine-tenths of France

---

[2] Damas Hinard, *Un Prophète inconnu* (Paris: Ledoyen, 1850), pp. 15, 79.

[3] La Gervaisais, *La Catastrophe* (Paris: Pihan, 1835), p. 11. He described the scene in France as follows: "Nous sommmes en France, en 1789. Dans cette nation rien n'annonce une chose publique. Il ne s'y rencontre que des castes, des classes, chacune concentrée en elle-même, toutes isolées, oposées entre elles" (*ibid.*).

[4] *Ibid.*, p. 20.

[5] La Gervaisais, *La Raison des temps* (Paris: Pihan, 1836), p. 27.

suffers while barely a tenth is satisfied, and we return to a barbarism under the sign of liberalism.[6]

Having noted that the interest of the vast majority was being sacrificed for the sake of a new plutocracy eager to maintain a predominance in politics and economics, he therefore exhorted Louis Philippe to move closer to the real France, to become the King of the poor and the dispossessed. One of his pamphlets—*À Philippe*—advising the monarch to wake up before he suffered the fate of his Bourbon predecessor was seized and further publication was prohibited.[7]

La Gervaisais' shrewd observation of his contemporary society undergoing industrial as well as political revolution—both of which he vehemently denounced—provides an insight into his pessimistic personality. Before attempting to examine his appraisal of French colonialism, which he linked, albeit vaguely, to financial interests residing in the capital, it would be useful to outline his more general views on the political economy of a changing France.[8] These will include: the deep split between state and country, the pernicious influence of the bourgeoisie, the extreme polarization of society between a handful of haves and a great mass of have-nots, and the permanent state of internal war leading inevitably to bloody revolution.

The state was seen as a fictitious abstraction in sharp contrast with the real and positive *Pays*, which alone encompassed the nation's living forces. In characteristic fashion, he exclaimed: "The state is taken for the *Pays,* or rather the state is taken for everything, the *Pays* for nothing."[9] Moreover, France was nine-tenths agricultural while Paris, the remaining tenth, was capitalist. Yet the tenth prevailed over all others: "La ville est tout, le pays n'est rien."[10] As to the locus of political power, he concluded that it resided in the one million political militants split into Constitutionalists, Legitimists, and Republicans tearing each other apart, whereas the remaining 31 million acted as "passive spectators always prepared to surrender their children and gold to any government."[11]

It is clear, then, that the neo-physiocratic tendencies, to which must be added the nostalgia for the decentralized political life that had once pre-

[6] La Gervaisais, *Exposé de la ligne politique* (Paris: Pihan, 1835), pp. 120–21.

[7] La Gervaisais, *À Philippe* (Paris: Pihan, 1835). See also his work, *Mise à l'index* (Paris: Pihan, 1835).

[8] La Gervaisais, *De la loi économique* (Paris: Pihan, 1830), pp. 26–27.

[9] La Gervaisais, *L'État et le pays* (Paris: Pihan, 1835), p. 7.

[10] La Gervaisais, *De la loi économique*, p. 26.

[11] La Gervaisais, *La Raison du temps*, p. 29.

vailed in the province of Brittany, turned the Marquis against an emerging industrial urban civilization, which he saw as the creation and centralized domain of a new plutocratic bourgeoisie characterized as "the true barbarians threatening society."[12] But he did recognize their revolutionary role in politics as well as in economics: "La révolution fut faite par la classe moyenne, contre la classe alors supérieure; et la révolution serait faite par la classe infime, contre la classe maintenant éminente."[13]

A clear notion of class struggle leading to revolution was ever-present in his writings; for instance, a recurring theme was "la guerre sociale est en permanence."[14] In fact, as early as 1830, he had noted a connection between the industrial revolution and the political revolution rocking France. In a work entitled *Les Périls du temps*, he had described, in vivid images, "the wild expansion of industry creating, on one hand, a concentration of factories owned by the few, and, on the other, a whole population of dispossessed and impoverished serfs ready to revolt against its masters."[15]

Thus, a full decade before Karl Marx, the Marquis de la Gervaisais described the bourgeois class as selfishly forging society in its own image: "It is as though society were identified by, incarnated in, a certain class that looked upon itself as the society and egotistically promoted its own exclusive interest."[16] Why is it, he asked, that equitable distribution of such an unprecedented quantity of wealth was not forthcoming? He blamed it on the "abstract principles of economists: *laissez-faire, laissez-passer*;" and he added ironically: "It does not really matter if a person has no arm—*qu'on le laisse faire*, and he who has no legs—*qu'on le laisse passer*."[17] In his own peculiar way, he called the nineteenth century the "Age of Lead, an age totally incapable of love and appreciation."[18]

The power and influence generated by an expanding credit, manipulated in the interests of the middle class, retained his critical attention. To begin with, it was of no benefit to the vast majority of Frenchmen; in fact, La Gervaisais suggested that it was intimately linked to war, although the connection was not made very clear. "By a strange paradox," he wrote, "war commanded credit and vice-versa; war increased the load of taxation,

---

[12]La Gervaisais, *Les Vrais barbares* (Paris: Pihan, 1834), p. 3.

[13]La Gervaisais, *La Raison du temps*, p. 26.

[14]La Gervaisais, *L'État de guerre dans la société* (Paris: Pihan, 1833), p. 22.

[15]La Gervaisais, *Les Périls du temps* (Paris: Pihan, 1830), p. 3.

[16]La Gervaisais, *L'État de guerre dans la société*, p. 17.

[17]La Gervaisais, *Exposé de la ligne politique*, p. 109.

[18]La Gervaisais, *Premières ombres de la barbarie* (Paris: Pihan, 1836), p. 14.

which combined with the heavy demand for recruits to place a crushing burden exclusively on the people. Thus, the people always paid both for the war, which stimulated credit expansion, and for the credit expansion, which brought about war."[19]

Continuing his account of the pernicious influence of the July Monarchy's bourgeoisie, the Marquis stressed the fact that it had secured an exclusive monopoly over privilege, wealth, and lucrative positions in the administration. Moreover, the industrial revolution, having destroyed the old cottage industry of the country, completed thereby the polarization of society.[20] No intermediaries were left in the fabric of society to soften the *choc* of explosion.[21] Such observations undoubtedly influenced his formulation of apocalyptic visions of fire and destruction reminiscent of Biblical thunderings, ending in the victory of the *prolétaires* and *semi-prolétaires*:[22]

> Face à face, se rencontreraient les deux bandes, l'une rare en
> nombre, timide de coeur, glacée d'épouvante, et l'autre énorme
> de masse, bouillante de furie, enivrée de confiance. Combat à
> outrance, victoire à coup sûr, défaite à plate couture, ruine à ras-
> terre, et subversion des choses, dévoration des êtres, conflagration
> du sol: ainsi, cela se passerait.[23]

The grave industrial insurrections of Lyons served to confirm his belief in the existence of a permanent "struggle between the possessing and non-possessing classes" caused by an unrestrained expansion of industry.[24] Turning to the industrial elite of Lyons, he compared its relationship with the proletariat as one of colonizer to colonized: "The industrialist resided in the midst of his slaves like a colon, and the revolt in Lyons was akin to a Santo Domingo colonial revolt."[25]

La Gervaisais was as bitter an opponent of the old colonial empire of France as he was of his nation's expansion into new overseas territories, Algeria being the case in point. His critique was both economic and political:

---

[19] La Gervaisais, *Cinq chapitres du resumé des vues économiques* (Paris: Pihan, 1832), p. 3.

[20] La Gervaisais, *Exposé de la ligne politique*, pp. 108–109.

[21] La Gervaisais, *La Raison des temps*, p. 26.

[22] *Ibid.*, pp. 26–27; *Exposé de la ligne politique*, p. 110, for his usage of the terms *prolétaires* and *semi-prolétaires*.

[23] La Gervaisais, *La Raison du temps*, pp. 26–27.

[24] La Gervaisais, *Les Vrais barbares*, pp. 1–3.

[25] *Ibid.*

the cost was too high for such insignificant returns, and political emancipation of the colonies was anyway overdue. The reason, he maintained, for the continued imposition of a useless colonial burden was the vested interest of an elite who knew both how to exert political pressure in Paris and how to make themselves heard to the public through the press. Without making the link explicit, he suggested that the colonial system followed from the fact that a capitalist Paris predominated over an agrarian France: "As to the sugar islands," he wrote, "the powerful colons resided and dominated in Paris."[26] The well-articulated but narrow interests of a tiny minority required the imposition of prohibitive tariffs and taxation in order to subsidize the colonies.[27] The other economic disadvantages included a military expenditure of 40 million francs a year to safeguard the colons and their obsolete system of plantations.[28] These factors were responsible for the increase in the general level of prices in France.[29]

To be sure, emancipating the colonial empire was an economic imperative, but it was also an urgent political task. He saw the role of the colon as nearing the end, and the colonial system had to be artificially sustained by national charity.[30] There were also signs that a kind of decolonization process was taking place. The colonial revolt of Santo Domingo was very much on La Gervaisais' mind, and he tended to generalize from that single but important example. Furthermore, if the natural and inevitable process of emancipation was delayed, the colonies of the old empire would surely succumb to social disorders and even to massacres.[31] "For it is impossible," he wrote, "for two enemy races to keep the peace when serious perturbations were taking place in the mother country."[32]

Again, one is reminded of the specter of new Santo Domingo revolts, caused by the internal situation at home in France, threatening the tattered remnants of a once-extensive colonial system. He was obviously thinking of the parallel between the revolutionary situation of 1789 and 1830.

So much for the old colonial empire. But when the Marquis turned his attention to France's military action in North Africa, he appeared to have lost control of his pen. Frequently, his outbursts became so emotional as

---

[26] La Gervaisais, *De la loi économique*, pp. 26–27.
[27] *Ibid.*
[28] *Ibid.*, pp. 30–32.
[29] *Ibid.*
[30] La Gervaisais, *Alger* (Paris: Pihan, 1834), p. 6.
[31] La Gervaisais, *De la loi économique*, pp. 30–31.
[32] *Ibid.*

to lose coherence. He lashed out at the motive of the Bourbons in calling for the expedition in the first place, at the reasons why the enterprise was being continued and expanded under the July Monarchy, at the methods used to dupe the public, and finally, at the brutal impact, both on France and on Algeria itself, of a new colonialism, masquerading under the civilizing mission of colonization.

On the causes of the Bourbon decision to invade the Algerian Regency, La Gervaisais offered the familiar explanation of a political move dictated solely by domestic considerations, a move designed to check the growing influence of the Liberal opposition which was causing discomfort, even fear, to the regime.[33] He did not indicate the precise location of the decision-making process, although he did suggest that it was inspired by "royal anger, which propelled the enterprise forward, hoping thereby to raise the regime to new heights of popularity and power, whereas the opposite, in fact, happened and the throne collapsed."[34] The ministers welcomed the plan because "they felt the ground no longer secure under their feet and were therefore grabbing support from any quarter."[35] In short, the men in power hoped to neutralize the domestic opposition and to consolidate the throne by a brilliant victory achieved against an unpopular enemy, the Dey of Algiers.

It is clear that the Marquis' analysis was restricted to political and domestic factors with no suggestion of other hidden or conscious motives for the conquest. The commercial interests of southern France, the shipping interests of Marseilles and Toulon, the attempt to compensate for the loss of the old empire and more importantly for territory on the Rhine borderland, and the desire to emulate Napoleonic victories, were not mentioned.

The official account of the famed "fly-whisk" stroke which served as a pretext for the war against Algiers did not impress him. It was his view that "Algiers was taken supposedly to avenge an insult to France's national honor whereas, in fact, it was the French consul who had provoked the Dey by insulting him in the first place."[36] And as to the destruction of an alleged pirates' lair, what France had really initiated was a "vast campaign of ravage and massacre."[37]

To La Gervaisais, if the decision of the Bourbons to capture Algiers was dishonest and wrong, the policy of the July Monarchy, which aimed at the

---

[33] La Gervaisais, *Alger*, p. 28.

[34] *Ibid.*

[35] *Ibid.*, p. 1.

[36] *Ibid.*, p. 28.

[37] *Ibid.*

conservation and extension of the conquest, was even more disastrous. It was, in addition, an incredible anachronism:

> The conservation of Algiers with expansion in the interior was the stupidest of ideas....Not even permissible during the dark ages of barbarism, it was now being unashamedly applauded in a century of enlightenment, priding itself on having reached the peak of civilization.[38]

As to the establishment of a formal colonial empire in the Regency, he sarcastically saw it as a "glorious thought of gigantic proportion, almost equal to the spirit of Attila the Hun."[39] In fact, he pointed out, the pretended glory of it was subordinate to the lure of riches: "à peine entrent en compte les fleurs de gloire, vis-à-vis les fruits du lucre...; accourez, indigos, sucres, cafés, cotons!"[40] The reasons advanced for the retention of Algiers were always numerous: glory, a misplaced national honor, the pretense of a civilizing mission for France in Africa, and above all, the thought of a new Eldorado within easy reach of the shores of southern France. However, the sceptical Marquis stressed the profit motive: Algeria was being kept because people believed it to be a Garden of Eden, and, "as in the case of the Terrestrial Paradise, they expected that a plentiful supply of sugar, coffee, indigo, cochineal, pepper, and ginger would be had for the asking."[41]

The methods utilized by the vested interests in sustaining their projects of conquest and colonization were varied. Above all, the growing power of the press was harnessed to their cause—a power which La Gervaisais denounced as immoral, omnipotent, and a danger to the nation because it inhibited the free and rational discussion of important issues. The exercise of statesmanship became virtually impossible. The government feared the press to such an extent that it found itself paralyzed and could therefore do nothing to check military expenditure and colonizing schemes.[42] Even the royalist press unexpectedly pressured the regime to hold on at all costs to "cette plaie dévorante en existences, en fortunes, en moeurs, cet ulcère d'Alger."[43] Therefore, the ministers, always cautious and on the defensive,

---

[38] La Gervaisais, *L'État et le pays*, p. 7.
[39] La Gervaisais, *De la capitation saline* (Paris: Pihan, 1834), pp. 35–36.
[40] *Ibid.*
[41] La Gervaisais, *Alger* (Paris: Pihan, 1835), p. 28.
[42] *Ibid.*, p. 26.
[43] *Ibid.*, p. 32.

found it expedient to treat the Algerian expansion as a question of national honor and ride on the crest of the popular wave.[44]

To La Gervaisais, it was neither the vested interests nor the ruling elite that paid the 40 million francs wasted year after year on a futile venture. It was the people, through what he described as the "suction pump of taxation, which, added to the high rate of French casualties, combined to place severe hardships on the nation."[45] Perhaps not unexpectedly, he singled out the salt tax which, in his view, sustained a reckless and immoral war.[46] Regarding his general attitude toward taxation, his publications persistently called for the abolition of property and personal taxes. On the other hand, he felt that industrial machinery ought to be heavily taxed in order to protect small-scale artisanal industry—a typical agrarian and neo-physiocratic response.[47]

But interested as he was in the analysis of the motives and methods for sustaining the Algerian venture, it was the actual consequences of the war of conquest and the policy of expanded colonization that retained his full attention. He was moved to depict scenes of fire, social dislocation, and massacre on the colonial front, which paralleled his apocalyptic visions of class warfare and destruction on the domestic scene. In pamphlet after pamphlet bearing such grim titles as *Premières ombres de la barbarie* (1836), *Les Vrais barbares* (1834), *Le Dix-neuvième siècle à l'oeuvre* (1836), *Alger* (1834 and 1835), *La Catastrophe* (1835), *Le Siècle de l'absurde* (1832), he painted the tragic consequences of war and colonization on France as well as on the new colony. He saw very clearly that the logical outcome of agricultural colonization was inevitably the expulsion and extermination of the indigenous populations: "Au développement de la colonisation agricole, s'attacherait une fatale et détestable nécessité, celle d'expulser et d'exterminer les indigènes."[48]

Algeria, he noted, offered a spectacle of devastation more despicable than the worst era of barbarism.[49] The razing of the city of Mascara was one such incident which he regarded as a preview to the "war of total destruction aimed against the Arab populations."[50] The unrestrained shedding of blood led him to write: "Moloch sourit à ce que tes contrées soient encore fertilisées

---

[44] La Gervaisais, *Alger* (1834), p. 5.

[45] *Ibid.*, p. 4.

[46] La Gervaisais, *De la capitation saline*, p. 22.

[47] La Gervaisais, *La Catastrophe.*

[48] La Gervaisais, *Alger* (1834), p. 1.

[49] *Ibid.*

[50] La Gervaisais, *Le Dix-neuvième siècle à l'oeuvre* (Paris: Pihan, 1836), p. 2.

par le sang."[51] And he dwelt at length on the horrors of an interminable war of conquest: peaceful herdsmen slain in their tents, women and children uprooted, countryside ravaged, and crops burnt. One idea haunted him all the time: his nation was responsible for the systematic extermination of a people.

As to the impact of the war on the domestic front in France, he felt that an entire army was being decimated in the Algerian deserts for no good reason. French blood, he thought, ought to be shed only in defense of the nation. In addition, the remnants of this tattered army, if they ever were fortunate enough to return home, would never be the same human beings again; they would be disillusioned and ill-disposed toward society.[52]

One direct outcome of this militarism was reflected in a general decline of the sense of justice, a weakening of what constituted a moral action. La Gervaisais frequently denounced his countrymen's "cynical disregard for the shedding of blood,"[53] their tacit acceptance of violence and extermination as normal behavior worthy of the nineteenth century. "Will no one condemn this devastation," he exclaimed, "before Muslim blood pouring in the Mediterranean washes on the coast of France."[54]

Not content with criticizing France, he turned his full blast on Europe at large and on its so-called civilization of the nineteenth century: "Europe! l'histoire t'atteigne au front, te marque en traits indélibles, de ces deux stygmates sanglants, Pologne, Afrique; l'une vouée aux tortures, et l'autre au ravages."[55]

But Algeria augured even more sinister consequences for contemporary European civilization than did Poland:

> Alger, hélas! signe funèbre, présage sinistre... Certes, Varsovie, Pologne, détachent ce honteux et hideux siècle de la civilisation; et le rejettent au plus loin, sous la date des temps de barbarie. Mais Alger, mais Afrique, tranchent plus fortement encore: n'annonçant point de terme, point de fin, et de plus, advenant sans aucune raison, sans motif quelconque.[56]

---

[51] La Gervaisais, *Alger* (1835), p. 29.

[52] La Gervaisais, *Alger* (1834), p. 3.

[53] *Ibid.*, p. 4. He also wrote elsewhere: "Certes, cela coute à l'esprit juste du siècle, que de cette façon, on vienne sanctifier, canoniser en Afrique les horreurs sans terme commises en Pologne." See La Gervaisais, *Alger* (1835), p. 29.

[54] La Gervaisais, *Alger* (1834), p. 6.

[55] La Gervaisais, *Le Dix-neuvième siècle à l'oeuvre*, p. 9.

[56] *Ibid.*, pp. 7–8.

As one might expect, there were very few Frenchmen who were prepared to recognize the analogy between Russia's action in Poland and their nation's action in Algeria. But the Marquis de la Gervaisais did and it is to his credit. He even went further, believing that France's action was aiding and abetting the Tsar: "The Russian was heartened by what was taking place in Algeria, it gave him the incentive to persevere even more in his sinister task of repression in Poland."[57] If it did occur to La Gervaisais that the Tsar did not need the example of Algiers, he did not say it.

The question of the civilizing mission, which was being discussed with great pride by the advocates of European expansion, was also touched upon by La Gervaisais. However, he did not follow the trend of self-congratulation and ego gratification. On the contrary, he was indignant. "So it is clear!," he wrote, "France is so oversaturated with civilization that she feels compelled to get rid of the surplus, to export it overseas, so to speak."[58] To him, the much-vaunted civilizing mission was in fact a barbarizing mission of wanton destruction. And he again summoned apocalyptic visions on colonization in his century:

> Et mosquées, sépulcres violés; et propriétés spoliées, indigènes expulsés; et bestiaux enlevés, campemens incendiés; et pays à feu et à sang; mode nouveau de civilisation! mode très ancien de colonisation.[59]

---

[57]La Gervaisais, *Alger* (1835), p. 29.

[58]*Ibid.*, p. 30.

[59]La Gervaisais, *Le Dix-neuvième siècle à l'oeuvre*, p. 2. For a more comprehensive discussion of anti-colonialism in the period 1830–48, see Marwan Buheiry, "Anti-Colonial Sentiment in France During the July Monarchy: The Algerian Case," Ph. D. Dissertation: Princeton University, 1973, from which this study is taken.

3

Planat de la Faye: A Critic of France's Algerian Mission in the 1840s*

THE EXPERIENCE OF COLONIALISM is a familiar one. The colonized is usually either destroyed, assimilated, or segregated, while the colonizer, self-confident in this assertion of power, may yet feel urged to seek justification for his action. Hence, the so-called civilizing mission of imperialism. In actual fact, far from being a "cause" for the phenomenon of imperialist expansion, the mission is merely a moral sanction— or a rationale—for a process already in motion. Horace and Virgil, poets who sang the glory of *imperium*, discovered a divinely ordained mission for Rome—to unite and bring peace by force to the world—only after her legions had substantially accomplished the task.

This is also true of the modern era. Once colonialism gathered momentum, the *mission civilisatrice* was conjured up. In time, it became the brighter side of an image growing increasingly dismal; other poets, the Kiplings, depicted it as a burden carried by the white man to the "half-devil, half-child" wearer of darker skins.[1] Thus the colonizer could be made proud of a dubious achievement. As he saw it, a once-barbarous world had been reclaimed by the self-appointed watchdogs of civilization.

Cultural imperialism has been defined as "the process that describes the permeation and pervasion of one culture by the thought, habit, and purpose of another....Civilization can be defined as the machinery of culture,

---

*From *Al-Abhath*, 26 (1973–77), pp. 19–25. © 1977 by the American University of Beirut. Reprinted courtesy of the Center for Arab and Middle East Studies, American University of Beirut.
[1]From Rudyard Kipling's poem "The White Man's Burden" (1899).

as the aspect a culture takes on when it wants to accomplish something."[2] During the period of the Bourbon Restoration and of its successor the July Monarchy (1815–48), Frenchmen invoked a glorious mission for Europe, and particularly for their own fatherland, to civilize the Afro-Asians. They insisted for the most part on motives that were not materialistic, stressing instead honor, duty, and uplift as reasons for imperialist expansion. Of course, one may ask: Is it possible for a culture to judge other cultures as candidates for civilization without developing at the same time a contempt for them? Most likely not. At the very least, the Asians and Africans were regarded as "control groups against which Europeans could measure their own achievements."[3]

Even more presumptuous was the fact that academic, intellectual, and religious groups debated, in all seriousness and with considerable energy, whether the non-European, especially the African, was civilizable in the first place. And science, the newly installed god, was summoned to give its learned opinion.[4]

In the first half of the nineteenth century, the civilizing mission of Europe was still largely dominated by overt religious considerations: the spread of Christianity, the thrusting back of Islam, and the rivalry between Latin Catholics and Anglo-Saxon Protestants. In certain cases, however, the mission took on a more secular aspect, as for instance with the Saint-Simoniens, although it may be argued that the followers of Saint-Simon had erected a new religion. At any rate, both trends—the religious and the quasi-secular— will be considered.

In 1830, Clermont-Tonnere, Minister of War of Charles X, described the Algerian conquest to his monarch as "a glorious act reserved to France by Providence to civilize the Arabs and make them Christians."[5] Likewise, in a pamphlet published in 1846 and entitled *À MM. Thiers et Barrot: L'Algérie, son influence sur les destinées de la France et de l'Europe,* H. Lamarche remarked: "Our aim in the conquest—an aim that need not be hidden from Europe or the Arabs—is the propagation of Christian civilization in Africa."[6]

---

[2] A. P. Thornton, *Doctrines of Imperialism* (New York: J. Wiley, 1965), p. 187.

[3] Philip D. Curtin, *The Image of Africa* (Madison: University of Wisconsin Press, 1964), p. 245.

[4] Scientists like Blumenbach, Laurence, Lamarck, and especially George Cuvier contributed to these debates (*ibid.*, pp. 230–31).

[5] J. B. Piolet, *Les Missions catholiques françaises au XIXe siècle* (Paris: Armand Colin, 1902), V, 11.

[6] H. Lamarche, *À M M. Thiers et Barrot...* (Paris: Paulin, 1846), p. 38.

And, in much the same vein, M. Roy saw the colonization of Algeria as the "imposition of law and of the benefits of civilization on savage inhabitants, the most rational manner being through Christian colonization and religious civilization (*celui d'une colonisation chrétienne et de la civilisation par la religion*)."[7] There was a tendency shared by the publicists and doctrinaires of the *mission* to use the terms civilization and colonization interchangeably, to define the one by the other.[8]

To be sure, there were also those who saw the civilizing mission in more secular terms, the imposition of French law, institutions, language, technical skills, and capital investments—in short, of modernization. This was particularly true of the Saint-Simoniens and other early modernizers: their Algerian vision was the object of Planat de la Faye's bitter sarcasm.[9] Not surprisingly, even the popular attitude toward Algeria—although eclectic—reflected an element of mission: a fair example of it may be found in the lengthy title of A. Fromental's pamphlet, *Essai sur la pacification, la colonisation, la civilisation, la sécurité, la prospérité, la force et la gloire de l'Algérie* (Nancy: Hinzelin, 1837). As to the term *mission civilisatrice* it was in use during the period of the July Monarchy by pro-colonialists as well as by the rare anti-colonialists.[10] And it is possible to find an early version of the White Man's Burden theme in Rozet's *Voyage dans la Régence d'Alger*, a call to Europe and America to participate in a glorious humanitarian undertaking in Africa: "Generous men, filled with a love for humanity, have sacrificed their existence in order to instruct the savage nations and extend the boundaries of civilization."[11]

But bringing civilization to a region did not always imply that the native would become the beneficiary. In fact, at times, he was considered as some kind of physical obstacle; those who clamored for his disappearance

---

[7] M. Roy, *Illustrations de l'histoire d'Algérie* (Paris: M. Ardant, 1844), pp. 237–38.

[8] *Le Globe*, 10 November 1831, "Alger politique générale;" J. B. Flandin, *Régence d'Alger, peut-on la coloniser?* (Paris: Feret, 1833), p. 12.

[9] Leo Lamarque, *Colonisation, chemins de fer et canaux en Algérie* (Algiers: Besancenez, 1841), iv–v.

[10] Armand Carrel, *Oeuvres politiques et littéraires d'Armand Carrel*, edited by M. Littré (Paris: Chamerot, 1857), IV, 401. Carrel was an ardent pro-colonial publicist. For anti-colonialist expression, see A. de Gasparin, *La France doit-elle conserver Alger?* (Paris: Béthune et Plon, 1835), p. 37. In addition to the term *mission civilisatrice*, variations such as *oeuvre civilisatrice* or *conquête civilisatrice* were widely used: see G.R. de Flassan, *Solution de la question d'Orient* (Paris: Dentu, 1840), p. 32.

[11] Claude Antoine Rozet, *Voyage dans la Régence d'Alger* (Paris: Bertrand, 1833), III, 412.

as a prerequisite to civilized life in Algeria were more than an isolated few. An article in 1846 published in a Bordeaux newspaper expressed this belief without regrets, without any sign of a pricking of conscience: "To justify our conquests we need only to say that we are the instruments of civilization."[12] The author then went on to clarify what he had in mind for the native inhabitant of Algeria: "The bedouins are the Red Indians of Africa; in the process of the French colonization of Algeria the same fate will be reserved for him as it was for the Red Indian during the Pioneers' colonization of America; he will disappear from the surface of the earth."[13]

* * * *

Planat de la Faye, an aide-de-camp to Napoleon Bonaparte, was a determined opponent of French colonial expansion. After the debacle of the Hundred Days, he accompanied Napoleon to Plymouth on board the *H.M.S. Bellerophon* and was chosen to share his exile in Saint Helena. However, he lost this privilege at the last moment when England decided to reduce the number of Napoleon's companions in exile; instead, he found himself interned in Malta for a year and got his name crossed off the officer list by the Bourbon Restoration.[14] Attempts at rehabilitating his position proved fruitless even under the July Monarchy: he had presented an eloquent petition to Louis Philippe in 1839.[15] This luckless officer remained convinced that he had been the victim of unjust treatment, and he did not hide his disillusion with the Bourbons and the July Monarchy.

Planat de la Faye's personal life presents interesting facets. He and his wife, a Bavarian, were probably the first Unitarian Protestants in France.[16] He admired Garibaldi considerably and corresponded with him regularly.

[12] André Jean Tudesq, *Les Grands notables en France, 1840–1849: étude historique d'une psychologie sociale* (Paris: Presses Universitaires de France 1964), II, 827, quoting *Courrier de la Gironde*, 6 June 1846.

[13] *Ibid.* Similar views were expressed by Eugène Bodichon, "Disparition des Musulmans," *Revue de l'Orient, de l'Algérie, et des Colonies*, 10 (1851), pp. 39–40; also *L'Echo d'Oran*, 2 May 1846, proposing that the extinction of the Arab race in Algeria and Morocco was a positive act, that real philanthropy consisted in destroying the races that stood in the face of progress; also V. A. Hain, *À la nation, sur Alger* (Paris: Lachevardière, 1832), p. 108.

[14] *Vie de Planat de la Faye: souvenirs, lettres et dictées* (Paris: Ollendorf, 1895), vii, edited by his wife.

[15] Planat de la Faye, *Mémoire présenté au Roi* (Paris: Delanchy, 1839), p. 10. He wanted confirmation of the rank received at Waterloo.

[16] *Vie de Planat de la Faye*, vii.

Furthermore, he was a free trader who devoted much attention to economic questions: developments of railways,[17] colonization, reduction of tariffs, and publication of free trade doctrines. In this respect, he was a disciple of F. Bastiat, one of France's foremost liberal economists, who was also opposed to colonialism in Algeria.[18] France's war of conquest and expansion in North Africa received Planat's critical attention, and he addressed two studies to both Chambers of France in 1836: *De la nécessité d'abandonner Alger* and *Supplément aux motifs pour l'abandon d'Alger: ce que c'est que la colonisation.* They reflect a profound knowledge of the Algerian problem and a skill at polemical writing, although Planat de la Faye claimed that he belonged to no party or côterie, adding that his pleas were objective because he was not interested in advancing his fortune or career.[19]

The Algerian question was in his view "nothing more than misplaced national pride promoted in the first place by extremist sections of the opposition, then by political dreamers, and finally by certain vested interests."[20] As a possession, it brought no wealth to the country, having practically no commercial or agricultural value; the war was ruinous and constituted a dangerous military liability for the home front in the event of a European crisis.[21]

He attempted to understand the underlying motives for the peculiar behavior of the Chambers and of the press regarding this "all-important veiled question:"[22] a behavior characterized by extreme caution and deliberate vagueness. Why is it, he asked, that the government could not bring itself to abandon such a ruinous venture?[23] The most serious reason, he thought, lay in the newly acquired commercial interests of Marseilles: Algeria had turned into a convenient and highly profitable marketplace for Marseilles and its immediate hinterland, although he felt that the importance of the

---

[17] Planat de la Faye, *Des encouragements à donner par l'État aux entreprises de chemins de fer* (Paris: Delanchy, 1840), p. 9. He wanted the state to promote railways by granting a subsidy per constructed kilometer.

[18] *Vie de Planat de la Faye*, p. 563. Planat de la Faye claims (*ibid.*) that he was a close friend of the liberal economist F. Bastiat, and that he formed an association in Paris to spread Bastiat's ideas through popular editions of his works. Other interested members of the association included Michel Chevalier, Horace Say, and the Duke d'Harcourt, a militant free trader from Bordeaux.

[19] Planat de la Faye, *De la nécessité d'abandonner Alger* (Paris: Dezauche, 1836), p. 4.

[20] Planat de la Faye, *Supplément aux motifs pour l'abandon d'Alger: ce que c'est que la colonisation* (Paris: Dezauche, 1836), p. 3.

[21] *Nécessité*, pp. 6, 13.

[22] *Ibid.*, p. 5.

[23] *Ibid.*, p. 7.

trade to France as a whole was vastly exaggerated. It was restricted almost exclusively to the consumer demands of the French occupying forces and did not involve the Algerian Arabs.[24]

Another explanation was "the private interests of well-placed individuals who speculated on extensive property newly acquired in the colony under the guise of colonization schemes."[25] A third reason given was the government's fear of Bourbon Legitimist intriguers who would seize the abandonment of Algeria as a golden opportunity to play on the nationalistic sentiments of the French population, thus causing a popular reaction against the regime of the July Monarchy.[26] The region of Marseilles was one of the Bourbon opposition's principal strongholds, hence the object of constant preoccupation of Louis Philippe's government.

To be sure, the regime had also to take into account the popularity of the Algerian campaign in professional military circles: "The occupation of Algeria led to extraordinary promotions, to a stream of decorations, and mentions in dispatches."[27] Planat de la Faye pointed out that "from Marshals down to Second Lieutenants all were ardent partisans of the Algerian venture and of further military expansion."[28] He could have added that the campaigns brought national celebrity to politically ambitious generals such as Clauzel and Bugeaud.[29]

However, the most original reason provided by the former aide-de-camp of Napoleon was the *exutoire* argument: Algeria as a safety valve for discontent at home, a field for the more violent to work out his passion. It was touched upon briefly in his first work, *De la nécessité,* and taken up in expanded form in the second of his works, *Supplément aux motifs pour l'abandon d'Alger.* Thus, he wrote:

> The revolution of July was effected by the people and awoke in them many ambitions. . . . The government found it convenient to offer Algeria as a field for new opportunities. Africa then became *une sorte d'exutoire qui débarrassait la France d'une partie de ses humeurs viciées.* At the same time, the warlike tendencies in French society were aroused after fifteen years of slumber and threatened to push the country into a European war

---

[24] *Ibid.,* p. 9.

[25] *Ibid.,* p. 8.

[26] *Ibid.,* p. 9.

[27] *Ibid.,* p. 10.

[28] *Ibid.*

[29] Paul Azan, *L'Armée d'Afrique de 1830 à 1852* (Paris: Plon, 1936), p. 17.

that it wanted to avoid at all costs. For this reason, the government was very happy to redirect these martial instincts by
offering, to the most ardent, *un simulacre de guerre*, and, to the
most avid, chances for employment, decoration, and promotion.
I don't think that the cabinet ever recognized other advantages
in the Algerian possession....[30]

Turning to internal conditions in France, he dwelt on the many opportunities present for the poor and the unemployed for developing the vast land
resources that the country blindly neglected. He even suggested a possible
link between social unrest, unemployed resources, and wastage in colonialism. Serious riots, he maintained, would have occurred less frequently if the
180 million francs already wasted in Algeria had been used instead to finance
large agricultural and public works enterprises utilizing unemployed labor in
France.[31]

The arguments put forth by the military and their defenders for the
retention of Algeria were also criticized by Planat de la Faye. It was often
repeated that the new acquisition "provided a school of warfare for the army
as well as an opportunity of fostering the martial spirit (*l'esprit militaire*)."[32]
On the contrary, he saw this spirit undermined by injustices committed in
the form of unusually rapid promotions for some and by the immorality of
officers getting wealthy on fraud and on land speculation. Besides, the cost
of maintaining a special school of combat and of sustaining a rather doubtful
stimulus for the martial spirit was not one that the nation could afford.[33]
Nor did the military conception of colonization appeal to him, for he could
not see the value of a "colony bristling with bayonets, where the colon held
the saber in one hand, the plow in the other."[34]

What annoyed him particularly—quite understandably in view of his long
association with Napoleon—was the behavior of young officers comparing
their small engagements in Algeria to Napoleon's great campaigns: "They
think they are really engaged in warfare whereas, in fact, they are chasing
a few white *bournouses* across the desert."[35] He deplored the pompous

---

[30] *Supplément*, p. 16.

[31] *Ibid.*, p. 17.

[32] *Ibid.* The military journal *L'Armée*, no. 2 (2 July 1837), characterized the new colony
as "a practical school of warfare, a testing ground for a young army."

[33] *Supplément*, pp. 10–11.

[34] *Ibid.*, p. 15.

[35] *Ibid.*, p. 12. The *bournouses* refer to the white dress worn by the Algerians.

bulletins full of fiction announcing, in glowing terms, yet another victory which the press obligingly published:[36]

> Mais il est douloureux pour les vieux soldats de Napoléon de voir...user (l')ardeur guerrière contre des Bédouins, en de sottes escarmouches, dont les pompeux récits nous rendent la risée de l'Europe militaire.[37]

Finally, the strategic implications of a massive military involvement in continuous warfare in Algeria did not escape his notice. In the event of a war in Europe, the possession would present a serious handicap, necessitating the rapid evacuation of the colony or else the possibility of having the expeditionary forces subjected to certain destruction: France, lacking the naval strength to sustain her forces in North Africa, would also feel the need of such troops in the defense of the homeland.[38]

Without elaborating the theme deeply or dwelling on its implications, Planat de la Faye pointed out the paradox of progressive idealists faced with the problem of colonial expansion. "How is it," he asked, "that the defenders of the principles of liberty, equality, and the independence of nations can advocate, at the same time, the founding of a colony that could only be accomplished through violence."[39] At the same time, he stressed the rejection of French civilization by the Algerians: "The indigenous inhabitants do not need our civilization, which is rejected *avec mépris par principe religieux et politique*; they know very well that their hard life, soberness, and even their privations, are the finest guarantee of independence."[40] In this respect, he was vindicated: 130 years of French imposition did not significantly erode the native culture.

However, Planat de la Faye was not merely content with providing answers for the peculiar behavior of the government and with exposing the special interest groups who found a lucrative field in the new colony for their activities. He also criticized the self-confident arguments of publicists and theoreticians who rationalized the retention and, indeed, the further expansion in North Africa in the name of the *mission civilisatrice* of France.

The Saint-Simoniens—Michel Chevalier and Enfantin—as well as the followers of Fourier, were ardent advocates of colonization linked with social

---

[36] *Ibid.*, pp. 10–11.
[37] *Nécessité*, pp. 12–13.
[38] *Ibid.*, pp. 13–14.
[39] *Supplément*, p. 10.
[40] *Nécessité*, p. 9.

experiments on new ground, believing as they did in a universal global civilization to be achieved through their missionary activities.[41] Their journal *Le Globe* characterized colonization as "l'intervention de la civilisation chez les peuples barbares."[42] Planat de la Faye heaped sarcasm on some of their cherished ideas: the sublime fusion of Orient and Occident and the civilizing mission.[43] France had no reason to "pay the wedding costs" of a union that he regarded as mystical and that apparently was to be consummated, of all places, in Algiers.[44] Although willing to recognize the humanitarianism of such progressive circles and their endeavor to bring civilization and instruction to Africans, he nevertheless felt that France lacked the material and perhaps even the spiritual conditions for such a grandiose undertaking. "Before we think of civilizing, of colonizing Africa," he wrote, "let us begin by civilizing France—she needs it far more than is generally thought of; let us start by cultivating the vast expanse of unreclaimed lands that are a disgrace to the [nineteenth] century and that, to the surprise of our neighbors, still form one eighth of total French ground."[45] Countering the argument that France was wealthy enough to afford any cost for the sake of glory, he exclaimed: "This France, so rich and powerful, cannot even afford to keep up her communications network."[46]

Moreover, he believed that French culture and civilization were restricted to a tiny minority, "the great mass of the people being sunk in ignorance and

---

[41] *Le National*, 25 August 1833. Another example of the modernizing vision of this railway magnate was his criticism of the commission of scholars sent by the French government to study Algeria. Instead, he proposed young engineers and technicians. *Ibid.*; Marcel Blanchard, "Lettres d'Enfantin sur l'Algérie," *Revue historique*, 182 (1938), p. 340. The considerable and direct influence of the Saint-Simoniens in the conquest and colonization of Algeria has been demonstrated by Marcel Emerit in *Les Saint-Simoniens en Algérie* (Paris: Société d'édition "Les Belles Lettres," 1944). Enfantin's own "scientific" system of colonization was described in his *Colonisation de l'Algérie* (Paris: Bertrand, 1843). He also founded a short-lived newspaper in 1844, *L'Algérie*, to expound his Algerian and colonial vision; see Blanchard, "Lettres d'Enfantin," pp. 346–47. The Saint-Simoniens were by no means the only entrepreneurs and futurists concerned with grandiose schemes of expansion and development. They were followed by the Fourierists, the "Master" having envisaged as early as 1821 the colonization of North Africa, the reclaiming of the Sahara Desert, and the settlement in the highlands of the Atlas of four million Europeans. See Marcel Emerit, "L'Idée de colonisation dans les socialismes français," *L'Age nouveau*, 24 (1947), p. 104.

[42] *Le Globe*, 18 November 1831, article entitled "Alger: politique générale."

[43] *Supplément*, p. 6.

[44] *Ibid.*, p. 8.

[45] *Nécessité*, p. 15.

[46] *Supplément*, p. 7.

unenlightenment."[47] He then referred to the disgraceful excesses committed by Frenchmen in the Tlemcen area of Algeria and wondered "on which side was civilization and who were the barbarians."[48] Clearly, then, not every Frenchman was the spiritual son of a Montaigne, Voltaire, or Rousseau—particularly in the colonial field. Yet when faced with the culture of others, many Frenchmen succumbed to the temptation of seeing themselves as special wardens of civilization.

Although Planat de la Faye's anti-colonial ideas and his criticism of France's colonial venture in Algeria had a negligible—if any—impact on public opinion or the centers of power, he must nevertheless be granted recognition as a courageous publicist who saw in the *mission* a shameful imposture unworthy of his country and of his age. Far from being carried away by the so-called humanitarian component of the colonial enterprise, he saw it for what it truly was: violence in the natural state. In this respect he is an early precursor—albeit timid—of Frantz Fanon, author of the *Wretched of the Earth* and one of the most perceptive analysts of colonialism in our time.[49]

---

[47] *Nécessité*, p. 15.

[48] *Ibid.*

[49] For a comprehensive discussion of anti-colonialism in the period 1830–48, see Marwan Buheiry, "Anti-Colonial Sentiment in France During the July Monarchy: The Algerian Case," Ph.D. Dissertation: Princeton University, 1973.

4

Tocqueville on Islam[*]

THAT ALEXIS DE TOCQUEVILLE (1805–59) was an original thinker who carefully observed his contemporary scene is not in doubt. His interest ranged far and wide in politics, history, public administration, ethics, sociology, and religion, but the two principal works on which his reputation as a genial scholar is founded are *De la démocratie en Amérique* and *L'Ancien régime et la révolution.* He was less successful in the field of active politics. In spite of a long and intensive participation in French politics, he failed to emerge as a public figure, which has led to a questioning of his talent as an actor in the political arena. According to Gustave de Beaumont, his life-long friend and biographer, Tocqueville was "too good a writer to have made a good orator in Parliament."[1] Be that as it may, he could not be accused of ivory-tower intellectualism.

Born into an aristocratic Catholic family, Tocqueville was both profoundly interested in religion and sensitive to its importance as a factor in the social and political life of a people. The place of religion in his thought has been widely studied;[2] but his preoccupation with Islam is generally ig-

[*]From *Al-Abhath,* 24 (1971), pp. 103–109. © 1971 by the American University of Beirut. Reprinted courtesy of the Center for Arab and Middle East Studies, American University of Beirut.

[1]Oeuvres et correspondance inédites d'Alexis de Tocqueville, edited by Gustave de Beaumont (Paris: Lévy, 1861), I, 63. According to Beaumont (*loc. cit.*), Tocqueville did not shine in the House: his style was cold, analytical, and lacked passion.

[2]The literature includes Joachim Wach, "The Role of Religion in the Social Philosophy of Alexis de Tocqueville," *Journal of the History of Ideas,* 7 (1946), pp. 74–90; Jack Lively, *The Social and Political Thought of Alexis de Tocqueville* (Oxford: Clarendon Press, 1962); Antoine Redier, *Comme disait M. de Tocqueville* (Paris: Perrin et Cie, 1925); J. P. Mayer, *Alexis de Tocqueville* (New York: Harper, 1960); Doris Goldstein, "The Religious Beliefs of Alexis de Tocqueville," *French Historical Studies,* 1 (1958–60), pp. 379–93; *Alexis*

nored, and the main concern of this essay will be to examine his assessment of Islam at a time when Europe was posing a grim military and cultural challenge to Muslim societies in North Africa, the Near East, and India. This will include primarily his view of the Qur'ān, the Prophet, the absence of a Muslim priesthood, the consequences of the blending of temporal and spiritual powers, and the so-called decadence of Muslim society. The place of Christianity in his thought will be touched upon briefly and only by way of background to his treatment of Islam.

Disagreement persists regarding Tocqueville's personal commitment to Catholicism and attitude to the Church. In his youth, he came under the powerful influence of the family tutor, a devoted Catholic churchman of the traditional school. He then appeared to move toward a thoroughgoing scepticism, only to return, late in life, to the Church. Finally, he ended his days as a believer, but without completely conforming to Catholic orthodoxy. His unbelief, however, was not a source of pride; at the height of his doubting period, he ardently defended the spiritual grandeur of Christianity, attaching great importance to its values of freedom and tolerance as well as to its goals, which he considered superior to those of other faiths. In a letter written in 1843 to Arthur de Gobineau, author of the *Essay on the Inequality of Races,* he revealed: "I am not a believer (which is far from a boast), yet I cannot help being overcome by the deepest emotion when reading the Gospels...I cannot understand how, when you read them, your soul does not soar with that higher sense of inner freedom that their pure and stately morality evokes in my own."[3] Furthermore, he viewed religion as a moral regulator, hence indispensable to the body politic, and Christianity, in particular, as a revolutionary force that had created a new order. Writing to a somewhat sceptical Gobineau, Tocqueville outlined the far-reaching changes effected by Christianity:

> It seems to me that Christianity accomplished a revolution—you may prefer the term considerable change—in all the ideas connected with rights and duties: ideas that, after all, are the basic matter of all sound morality....The magnificent achievement of

---

de Tocqueville, Livre du centenaire 1859-1959 (Paris: Centre national de la recherche scientifique, 1960); for a brief critique of Goldstein's article see John Lukacs in *French Historical Studies,* 2 (1961–62), pp. 123–25.

    [3] Alexis de Tocqueville, *Oeuvres complètes,* edited by J. P. Mayer (Paris: Gallimard, 1961–[77]), IX, 57. The parentheses are Tocqueville's own; all translations from Tocqueville's works are my own.

Christianity is to have constructed a human community beyond all national societies.[4]

Nevertheless, the organizational aspects of his contemporary Church and the emphasis it placed on external observances deeply troubled Tocqueville. He also disapproved of excessive religious zeal, mysticism, and stress on other-world salvation, and he criticized the clergy for encouraging such trends. At the same time, feeling as he did that the growing gap between liberalism and the Church was too dangerous to be left unchecked, he sought to diminish the existing tension and to bring about an "alliance between the liberal and religious elements" in France.[5]

Tocqueville's motivation for the study of Islam arose more from political needs than from romantic curiosity or scholarly interest.[6] After 1830, his country was engaged in a bitter and costly conquest of Algeria, the herald of a new colonial empire. French arms, administration, norms, and laws were involved in a headlong clash with an Islamic society whose resistance to alien intrusion was maintained with fierce determination. To Tocqueville, the outcome was of crucial importance; he regarded Algeria as "la plus grande affaire de la France" and one of the most neglected,[7] a theme he often repeated in his interventions in Parliament. That his country's new involvement led him to a study of Islam was made clear in a letter addressed to Arthur de Gobineau: "I have studied the Qur'ān deeply because of our position vis-à-vis the Muslim populations of Algeria and of the Orient."[8] During his tour of Algeria in 1841, he had discussed the Qur'ān with a French Orientalist, a student of De Sacy, most probably Louis-Jacques Bresnier, who had impressed him with the need for a proper translation of the Qur'ān together with the five or six indispensable explanatory commentaries. In that connection, Tocqueville was to note:

---

[4] *Ibid.*, IX, 45–46.

[5] Lively, *The Social and Political Thought of Alexis de Tocqueville*, p. 184.

[6] The principal sources of Tocqueville's remarks on Islam include his two letters on Algeria written in 1837, his notes on the Qur'ān taken in 1838, the notes he prepared for his Algerian trip, the notes taken in Algeria in 1841, and the correspondence with A. de Gobineau and to a lesser extent with Kergolay. For a treatment of Tocqueville's interest in the Algerian question, see André Jardin, "Tocqueville et l'Algérie," *Revue des travaux de l'Académie des sciences morales et politiques et comptes rendus de ses séances*, 4th Series, 115.1 (1962), pp. 61–74.

[7] *Oeuvres* (Mayer), III, 300.

[8] *Oeuvres* (Mayer), IX, 69.

> The Qur'ān is the source of laws, ideas, customs of all this
> Muslim population with whom we have to deal. The first task
> of the government ought to be the translation of the text and
> commentaries—a better task than the spending of 500,000 francs
> on the relatively useless Scientific Mission in Algeria.[9]

It is perhaps not surprising that Tocqueville approached Islam as would
an aristocratic European Christian intellectual of the early nineteenth century convinced of the superiority of Western civilization over all others.
Thus, he showed little sympathy or understanding for the Islamic ethos, and
was generally critical of its creed. In fact, on many occasions, he was presumptuous enough to remark to such friends as Gobineau and Kergolay that
Islam and the Prophet caused more calamity than good and were to blame
for the decadence of the Muslim world.[10] But his definition of decadence, as
will be shown later, remained ambiguous, and like many nineteenth-century
European intellectuals who looked at Islam, he preferred to pass judgment:
Islam was false; the Prophet, at best, was a clever manipulator; the Qur'ān
was little more than a copy of earlier sources. Tocqueville, therefore, joined
the long-standing tradition of Western Christian estimates regarding Islam
and the Prophet. As Albert Hourani had remarked in his treatment of "Islam
and the Philosophers of History:"

> In this thousand-year-long process of thought, there is one fac-
> tor which is almost constant. The attitude of Western Europe
> towards Islam is one of judgement. Islam is being weighed in
> the balance against something other than itself, being assigned
> a place in a scale.[11]

---

[9] *Oeuvres* (Mayer), V.2, 206–207.

[10] *Oeuvres* (Mayer) IX, 69; *Oeuvres* (Beaumont), I, 355, 356. In 1838 he had written to
Louis de Kergolay, who incidentally was the first officer ashore at Sidi Ferrush (Algeria)
during the 1830 invasion: "La doctrine de Mahomet a exercé sur l'espèce humaine une
immense puissance que je crois, à tout prendre, avoir été plus nuisible que salutaire." See
Oeuvres (Beaumont), I, 356.

[11] Albert Hourani, "Islam and the Philosophers of History," *Middle East Studies*, 3 (1966–
67), p. 219. Other works on the subject include J.W. Fück, "Islam as an Historical
Problem in European Historiography since 1800," *Historians of the Middle East*, edited
by Bernard Lewis and P. M. Holt (London: Oxford University Press, 1962), pp. 304–14;
Norman Daniel, *Islam and the West: The Making of an Image* (Edinburgh: University of
Edinburgh Press, 1960); J.J. Waardenburg, *L'Islam dans le miroir de l'Occident* (Paris:
Mouton, 1962).

A major source for Tocqueville's views on Islam is contained in notes he left on the Qur'ān: in 1838, he took up the study using Savary's translation.[12] The notes he left behind appear mostly as direct quotes from verses he considered important, with personal comments added occasionally. Apparently, his work did not go beyond the first eighteen *sūras*. It is clear that the links with earlier religions received his careful attention, noting very early in his study that the Qur'ān was "closely allied to, and a continuation of, the Old Testament, with a conscious effort to take Islam back to the origins of creation."[13] This feature, the link with creation, he characterized as a "first need of every religion."[14] He claimed Judaism as the root of Islam: "racine de l'islamisme dans le judaisme."[15] Moreover, he felt that Muḥammad had managed very dexterously to connect Abraham with Islam, the Arabs, and the construction of the first Temple of Mecca.[16]

In regard to the Prophet, Tocqueville remained sceptical of the authenticity of his mission; his notes on Sūra IV reveal Muḥammad as "careful to present Qur'ānic prescriptions as emanating from God and to promise paradise to obedient followers."[17] In addition, Tocqueville also remarked: "As almost everywhere else in the Qur'ān, Muḥammad is preoccupied much more with inducing people to believe him than he is with prescribing moral laws; terror is his favorite tool."[18]

The skill of the Prophet in dealing with sensitive issues was a constant theme in the notes. In his analysis of Sūra XI, which contains the answer to be given to disbelievers who question the divine origins of the Qur'ān and who treat it as Muḥammad's own handicraft ("let them produce ten chapters similar to the ones contained therein") Tocqueville observed: "Mahomet tire là très habilement d'affaire le prophète en tirant parti du grand écrivain."[19]

---

[12] C. E. Savary, *Le Coran, traduit de l'arabe, accompagné de notes et précédé d'un abrégé de la vie de Mahomet* (Paris: Knapen et Onfroy, 1783), in two volumes. Alexis de Tocqueville may have been influenced by Savary's estimates of the Qur'ān, the Prophet, and Islam in general. Savary, a humanist and somewhat of a sympathizer, tended to present the Prophet as a wise though subtle politician who adapted preexisting doctrines and moral precepts to suit the requirements of desert society. Tocqueville appears to have adhered to this estimate, albeit with less enthusiasm for the value of the Qur'ān and the personal qualities of the Prophet.

[13] *Oeuvres* (Mayer), III, 154.

[14] *Ibid.*

[15] *Ibid.*, III, 155.

[16] *Ibid.*, III, 156.

[17] *Ibid.*

[18] *Ibid.*, III, 160.

[19] *Ibid.*, III, 159.

Similarly, on the question of miracles demanded as proof of the genuineness of the prophetic mission, he believed that the Prophet ingeniously attempted to deal with this predicament by asserting that God could have undoubtedly granted him the power of miracle-making, but that the unbelievers would have still remained as obdurate as ever.[20]

Throughout the notes, there is little evidence of real concern with the spiritual message of the Qur'ān. In characteristic fashion, Sūra XII, containing the dramatic story of Joseph, was dismissed in one sentence: "Nothing else than the story of Joseph, son of Jacob, with unimportant variations;" as was Sūra XIV: "Nothing new, always the same pictures of the punishment awaiting those who refuse to believe in prophets;" and again, as was Sūra XV: "Grandeur of God depicted, warning against unbelievers, *rien de particulier ni de pratique.*"[21] With such simplifications, important differences between Qur'ānic and Biblical narratives were missed. For in the Qur'ān, Jacob refused to accept the account of Joseph's death as reported by his brothers and patiently awaited God's unveiling of the mystery in His own good time—a kind of Jobian Jacob.

Furthermore, in interpreting the Qur'ān, Tocqueville concluded that "everything pertaining to war is clearly spelled out, whereas the moral content is general and confused, with the exception of the precepts governing almsgiving."[22] But, he did not even want to speculate on the reasons for the attention to almsgiving in Islam, which he recognized, on more than one occasion, as being more spelled out than in the Bible.[23] This is all the more surprising in the light of his keen interest in sociological explanations of religious behavior.

Another and perhaps more significant preoccupation with Islam was evident in a question Tocqueville formulated and then attempted to answer: "Why is it that one does not come across an organized priestly function, a *sacerdoce* in Islam?"[24] He began his investigation by assuming a simple cult, Muḥammad having had to preach his message to a primitive population of nomads and warriors. According to Tocqueville, the basic aim of the new religion was to wage wars of conquest and expansion, hence a simple cult with a few practical precepts was all that was called for. He argued that complicated cults with elaborate ritual practices would normally require temple

---

[20] *Ibid.*, III, 160.
[21] *Ibid.*, III, 161.
[22] *Ibid.*, III, 159.
[23] *Ibid.*, III, 160.
[24] *Ibid.*, III, 173.

construction, a sedentary population, and the habits of peace.[25] There was, therefore, no objective need for the development of a priestly function—an unusual feature with far-reaching consequences; for, as he put it, "all religions, especially the ones exerting powerful influences on the human imagination, have had to rely on an effective *corps sacerdotal*, separated from the rest of the nation, with an elaborate organization of its own."[26] And this brings to light what Tocqueville thought was a more important explanation for the absence of a priestly structure and function:

> In Islam, more than in any other religion, the spiritual and temporal powers were blended together so that the high priest is necessarily the prince, and the prince the high priest; virtually the entire civil and political life was regulated by religious law. This being the case, the development of a *corps*, separated from the civil and political society and whose function was to direct the religious society, such as one finds in Catholicism, was impossible for Islam.[27]

To an anti-clerical Tocqueville, the absence of a clerical organization in Islam was an original and positive contribution. Believing, as he did, that a *corps sacerdotal* led to grave social ills, he praised Islam for having escaped the fate of other religions. However, he pointed out what in his view was a double-edged nature of this mixed blessing: "If on the one hand," he wrote, "the fusion of the spiritual and the temporal powers effected by Muḥammad is distinctively good, on the other hand, the fusion is also the principal cause of the despotism and social immobility prevalent in Muslim nations, which makes them succumb before the nations who adopted the separation of the two powers."[28]

Two explanations, thus, were offered for the absence of a priestly structure in Islam: the primitive, nomadic character of the setting, and the successful efforts of the Prophet to fuse the spiritual and temporal powers. Tocqueville, of course, took for granted the nomadic nature of the Arabian setting, disregarding the existence of highly urbanized centers such as Mecca and Medina—cities that depended principally on trade. He also failed to take account of the elaborate rituals connected with pre-Islamic cults in Mecca,

---

[25] *Ibid.*, III, 174.
[26] *Ibid.*
[27] *Ibid.*
[28] *Ibid.*

although his notes on the Qur'ān did mention the existence of temple religion in the Arabian peninsula. In other words, he did not choose to question
the presuppositions of European scholarship regarding Islam, presuppositions that stressed the primitive quality of a religion specifically tailored for
a nomadic-warrior society.

To Alexis de Tocqueville, the blending of the spiritual and temporal
powers led to a number of calamities: despotism, social immobility, and the
inability to resist the encroachments of Western Europe. It explained, in
short, the so-called decadence of Islam, which, in actual fact, he simply took
for granted. The voluminous correspondence he maintained with Arthur de
Gobineau sheds further light on this all-important question. Gobineau, to
be sure, was something of a romantic in his admiration for the Orient: one
of his lady friends described him as a dreamer, swearing by the Prophet, and
forcing his guests to sit "à la façon orientale."[29] But his defence of Islam
and, incidentally, of Buddhism, was more than mere eccentricity. He felt
that they contained sound moral principles, that they desired the perfection
of man through his own effort and through a sense of duty, and that they had
contributed immensely to civilization.[30] As one might well imagine, these
affirmations were not to Tocqueville's liking, and he retorted in a letter in
which he derided his friend for entertaining such positive views on the Islamic
religion and culture.[31]

Twelve years later, in 1855, Tocqueville again referred to the theme of
decadence in his correspondence with Gobineau, France's chargé d'affaires
in Tehran:

> You are in the heart of the Asian and Muslim world; I am very
> eager to know to what you attribute the swift and apparently
> inevitable decadence of the races you have encountered, a deca-
> dence that has already placed some and may in fact place all
> under the supremacy of our little Europe whereas in the past it
> often trembled before them. Where is the worm that is eating
> into this vast body?[32]

Gobineau did contribute a partial answer to the question. To start with,
he concurred that Europe's domination of Asia was a foregone conclusion:
"The expansion of European power to this tattered empire was as certain

---

[29] *Ibid.*, IX, 22.
[30] *Ibid.*, IX, 65.
[31] *Ibid.*, IX, 69.
[32] *Ibid.*, IX, 242.

as a law of physics."[33] The Asians would accept this domination. As to the cause of this inevitable occurrence, he explained: "We will dominate because we are more disciplined and more energetic in our thinking."[34] And he pointed to the sorry state of moral as well as scientific education in the Asian continent. However, Gobineau fell short of attributing it all to religion.

To conclude, Alexis de Tocqueville judged Islam and found it wanting. He claimed, rather gratuitously, that its principal aim was war. He characterized it as fossilized and especially as decadent without really defining what he meant, although he did seem to find the sign in the fact that the Islamic world was unable to resist European domination. The penetrating insights he had revealed in his studies of European and North American societies were significantly absent in his consideration of Islam. He never asked how Islamic civilization with its literature, law, and social organization, not only survived the relative collapse in politics, but managed somehow to spread into regions far beyond its epicenter. In short, he failed to appreciate its staying power and spiritual content.[35]

Perhaps the explanation for this lack of empathy is not all that hard to detect. Europe seems to have developed a marked interest in Islam concurrently with its preparation for hegemony over Asia and Africa. And in this respect, Tocqueville's interest after 1830 was undoubtedly symptomatic. The connection between European scholarship on Islam and the requirements of European colonial policy remains to be further explored. Tocqueville was a representative of the 1830s while C. Snouck Hurgronje—the "savant-politicien," to use J.J. Waardenburg's characterization[36]—was an example of

---

[33] *Ibid.*, IX, 246.

[34] *Ibid.*, IX, 254.

[35] Letter to Kergolay in *Oeuvres* (Beaumont), I, 355.

[36] Waardenburg, *L'Islam dans le miroir de l'Occident*, p. 21. C. Snouck Hurgronje (1856–1936), son of a Dutch Reform Church minister, wanted originally to follow in his father's footsteps. In 1878 he changed his mind about the priesthood and studied Islam: his doctoral thesis was on the Meccan pilgrimage. In 1881 he joined the faculty of a Dutch institute specialized in the training of colonial administrators. In 1885 he visited Mecca under the assumed name of 'Abd al-Ghaffār and made contact with Muslim Indonesians residing in the holy city. From 1887 to 1889 he taught Islamics at the University of Leiden, then joined the Dutch Colonial Department in Indonesia in 1889. Thereafter, and until 1906, he led a distinguished career as a principal adviser on Muslim affairs in the Dutch colonial empire, and his role in the suppression of the Atjeh uprisings in Sumatra was particularly important. After 1906 he returned to his teaching duties in Leiden while remaining a counsellor to his government on Islamic affairs. His colonial policy—which he characterized as "realist"—aimed at preserving the Indonesians from unscrupulous exploitation. *Ibid.*, pp. 18–22. [Cf. also p. 116 below.]

the 1890s. Tocqueville wanted to understand the Muslim Algerian in order to better implant a European settler community in North Africa. Snouck Hurgronje, a distinguished Islamicist, was also an important advisor on colonial affairs and an expert on conflict management in the Dutch colonial empire of Muslim Indonesia. The imperatives of the colonizer and the requirements of scholarship make strange bedfellows; they are basically incompatible.

5

Islam and the Foreign Office: An Investigation of Religious and Political Revival in 1873*

ON 22 AUGUST 1873, a brief circular of instructions was dispatched by Foreign Minister Granville to Her Majesty's consuls in a vast area designated as the East and China:

> The proceedings of Mussulmans in Eastern countries, partaking in some degree of the character of a religious and political revival, have lately attracted considerable attention; and I should be glad to receive from you a Report in regard to any circumstances which may come under your observation, calculated to show the existence and objects of any movement of the kind among the Mussulman population of the country in which you reside. [signed] Granville.[1]

The responses received and incorporated in a special "Confidential Print" report were 29: ten from Anatolia and the European provinces of Turkey; eight from Syria, Lebanon, Palestine, Iraq, and Egypt; two from North Africa

---

*From *Studia Arabica et Islamica: Festschrift for Iḥsān 'Abbās on His Sixtieth Birthday*, edited by Wadād al-Qāḍī (Beirut: American University of Beirut, 1981), pp. 47–59. © 1981 by the American University of Beirut. Reprinted courtesy of the American University of Beirut.

[1] Great Britain, Foreign Office, Confidential Print no. 2621, *Correspondence Respecting the Religious and Political Revival Among Mussulmans 1873–1874* (London, July 1875) [abbreviated hereafter as FOCP, 2621, *Correspondence*], item 4, "Circular Addressed to H. M. Consuls in the East and also to Mr. Wade and to Consuls and Vice-Consuls in China," Granville, 22 August 1873.

(Libya and Tunisia); one consolidated memorandum on India from the India Office; and eight from China.

The principal objective of this study will be to examine the motivation of the Foreign Office investigation, the consuls' interpretations of the terms Muslim "political and religious revival," their analysis of the presence or absence of such phenomena in their respective areas of assignment, the value of the observations contained in the reports, and the extent to which they shed light on the question of Arab separatist or proto-nationalist sentiment. Attention will be focused on the European and Anatolian provinces of Turkey and on the Arab world; China and India will be excluded.

* * * *

One of the first questions that comes to mind is what could have triggered such an investigation of political and religious revival in Muslim societies stretching from Bosnia to Formosa. Three factors—more properly documents—are explicitly cited in the Confidential Print; they serve as background or introduction to Granville's circular: a Dutch memorandum expressing concern over Atjeh (Sumatra); from the India Office, a request for information on Najd, Lahj (Yemen), Kashgaria (Chinese Central Asia), and Yunnan (China); and a somewhat puzzling report from Aleppo regarding problems with law courts.[2]

A month before Granville's circular of instructions, a memorandum was communicated to the Foreign Office (19 July 1873) by Count Bylandt, Holland's ambassador in London, deploring a new current, which he felt was present, "to bring Muslim populations everywhere towards unity."[3] The Sultanate of Atjeh in northern Sumatra, or Atchin as he called it, was using religion in a bitter struggle against the Dutch colonial power. Its special envoy in Istanbul had visited Mecca and contacted Muslim pilgrims from Java and Sumatra and was in fact seeking "l'intervention du Calife et insistant spécialement sur le côté religieux de sa mission."[4] Bylandt claimed that the Turkish press was supporting the Atjian struggle; he further insisted to Granville that this Muslim revival would have serious consequences on the "Christian 'powers'...qui ont des intérèts majeurs à sauvegarder dans ces parages, en premier lieu pour les Pays-Bas et la Grande Bretagne."[5]

---

[2] *Ibid.*, item 1; item 2, "Memorandum communicated to Earl Granville by Count Bylandt, 19 July 1873;" item 3, Grant Duff, India Office, 9 August 1873.

[3] *Ibid.*, item 2, Bylandt to Granville.

[4] *Ibid.*

[5] *Ibid.*

It is interesting to note that in a reference to the role of the Reuter telegraphic agency as a disseminator of news all over the globe, Bylandt implied that it was causing a disservice to the colonial enterprise; and he went on to stress the crucial role of Mecca and of the *hajj* in "calling attention to symptoms of a Muslim revival."[6] To Bylandt, therefore, the revival was linked with the resistance of the Atjians against forcible incorporation into the Dutch colonial empire of the East Indies. Clearly, the importance of the document lies in its synthetic view of the Ottoman capital, Mecca, the pilgrimage, the new role of the press and of the telegraphic agencies, and the problems caused to the colonial powers.

In the stormy history of the Archipelago, the struggle of the West for the control of Atjeh's pepper trade was prominent. In 1824 the Dutch had pledged to Britain not to extend their colonial holdings into the Sultanate of Atjeh, the only remaining independent state in Sumatra.[7] In 1850 the Sultanate appears to have renewed its ancient relations with the Ottoman Empire and had "sought aid from the Sublime Porte (and other powers) in the 1860's against Dutch interference in its affairs."[8]

A new treaty with Britain in 1871 gave Holland a free hand in Atjeh and opened the way to a costly colonial war of conquest which began in 1873 and lasted until 1910 under the last two Sultans, Maḥmūd Shāh (1870–74) and Muḥammad Da'ūd Shāh (1874-1903). According to the historian William Roff, the resistance to the Dutch invaders "assumed the character of a *jihād*" and was led by *'ulamā'* who traditionally "were either Arabs or, more specifically, of Ḥaḍramī sayyid descent," and who made use of "political pan-Islamic ideas."[9] In Atjeh the powerful Ḥaḍramī *sayyid* Ḥabīb 'Abd al-Raḥmān al-Ẓāhir had organized the campaign to win Ottoman and other Muslim support through a network of emissaries. An appeal was made to Istanbul in 1868 and was renewed actively in 1873, representing, almost certainly, the initiative referred to in Bylandt's memorandum to Granville. Both appeals apparently failed. Nonetheless, "belief that help would be forthcoming from the Ottomans gained ground in Atjeh itself, in the Straits Settlements (British Empire), and throughout the Archipelago."[10] The *hajj*

---

[6] *Ibid.*

[7] A. J. Piekaar, "Atjeh," EI², I, 744; *The Cambridge History of Islam*, edited by P.M. Holt, Ann K.S. Lambton, and Bernard Lewis (Cambridge: Cambridge University Press, 1970), II, 179. The relevant chapter is by William Roff.

[8] *Cambridge History of Islam*, II, 179.

[9] *Ibid.*, II, 178, 179.

[10] *Ibid.*, II, 179, 180.

was widely seen as a spiritually and politically energizing force—one that may have promoted the spread of the *tarīqas*, particularly the Naqshbandīya and Qādirīya, into rural areas.[11]   The driving force of resistance against Dutch colonialism by the Atjians was Islam. Thus both Holland and Britain feared that colonial resistance in Atjeh would have serious repercussions on their empires in Southeast Asia and the Archipelago. In fact, in the words of William Roff, "millenarian expectations that a union of the Islamic people would shortly arise and defeat the West" remained in force for a considerable time after 1873.[12]

Another factor for the investigation originated from the India Office on 9 August 1873, and took the form of a call for a report on Muslim actions in the East, a watch on Turkish actions in Najd and Lahj and Muslim insurrections in Kashgaria and Yunnan, plus a request to Granville for "any information which may tend to throw light upon this important subject."[13]

The interest in Najd is not surprising. The heartland of Wahhābism had been under careful observation by the British in India for two principal reasons: the security of the Gulf coastline and waters, and the effects of the Wahhābī *da'wa* on Indian and Central Asian Muslims. Lewis Pelly, the Political Resident in the Gulf from 1862 to 1873, had paid an important visit to the legendary Fayṣal ibn Sa'ūd in Riyadh in 1865. The death of this effective ruler, followed by the internecine quarrels of his sons, 'Abdallāh and Sa'ūd, had provided an ideal opportunity for a Turkish invasion of Najd aimed at the destruction of the Wahhābī state. Prepared by Midḥat Pāshā, then *vālī* of Baghdad, a Turkish military expedition brought Najd under Ottoman authority after 1871.

The British colonial authorities in India were opposed to this Turkish initiative. In this respect the testimony of Midḥat's son and biographer, 'Alī Ḥaydar Midḥat, sheds light on an important aspect of Britain's concern:

> Midhat was aware that certain delicate international questions
> might arise in the course of the expedition. The policy of Eng-

---

[11] *Ibid.* The Beirut journal *Al-Jinān*, edited by Salīm al-Bustānī, devoted in 1873 several articles to the question of Western expansion in Central Asia, Sumatra, and Africa— articles that often paraphrased the London or St. Petersburg press. The war in Atjeh was covered in "Al-Ḥarb fī Sūmaṭra," no. 10 (15 May 1873), p. 329, and in "Atchīn wa-Hūlanda," no. 13 (1 July 1873), in which *Al-Jinān* alluded to sovereignty links with the Ottoman Empire.

[12] *Ibid.*

[13] FOCP, 2621, *Correspondence*, item 3, Grant Duff, India Office, 9 August 1873. The Beirut journal *Al-Jinān* referred to Muslim insurrections in China in "Al-Islām fī l-Ṣīn," no. 3 (1 February 1873), pp. 78–79.

land, as represented by its Indian government, had always been to favour rather than to discourage the desire of independence on the part of the Arab chiefs in this part of the world. A serious and systematic attempt, therefore, to suppress their independence and to attach these distant members permanently to the body of the Ottoman Empire might seem to run counter to the policy of the Indian government on the shores of the neighbouring Persian Gulf. Midhat had always been a stout and consistent supporter of the English Alliance, but he was by no means inclined for that reason to sacrifice to that alliance the essential interest of the Ottoman Empire; and he did not hesitate, in spite of a certain amount of sympathy manifested by England towards Saood, to proceed with the expedition he had resolved upon.[14]

As to the references in the India Office memorandum to Lahj, Kashgaria, and Yunnan, with the opening of the Suez Canal in 1869 the Ottomans found it much easier to expand their control of the Yemen. By 1872 Aḥmad Mukhtār Pāshā was exercising direct Ottoman rule from Sanaa itself and laying claims to Lahj and to other territories under the nominal control of Aden.[15] In 1873 the Turks went as far as to occupy the Sultan's palace at Lahj, a move that aroused the British in Aden sufficiently to mount a military expedition against the Turks. Therefore, in the Najd, as in the Yemen-Aden border region, the Ottomans made advances perceived by the British as being detrimental to their imperial interests in the strategic Red Sea and Gulf zones along the routes to India.

In the Chinese provinces of Kashgar (Chinese Central Asia) and Yunnan, periodic outbreaks of Muslim insurrection in the nineteenth century caused considerable concern to the Manchu dynasty. However, these references in the Foreign Office investigation will not be dealt with as they are outside the scope of this study.[16]

---

[14] Ali Haydar Midhat, *The Life of Midhat Pasha* (London: John Murray, 1903), pp. 56–57.

[15] Fārūq Abāẓa, *Al-Ḥukm al-'uthmānī fī l-Yaman, 1872–1918* (Cairo: Al-Hay'a al-miṣrīya al-'āmma li-l-kitāb, 1975), p. 90; Harold Ingrams, *The Yemen* (London: John Murray, 1963), p. 57. An editorial in *Al-Jinān* deplored the war on the Yemen-Aden border: no. 23 (1 December 1873), p. 793.

[16] FOCP, 2621, *Correspondence*, item 24, Albaster to Granville, 7 October 1873; item 26, Parker to Granville, 1 November 1873; item 27, Robertson (Canton) to Hammond, 11 November 1873; item 28, Harvey to Granville, 21 October 1873; item 29, Hughes' report from Hankow, 7 November 1873; and especially item 33, Wade's comprehensive survey to Granville from Peking, 10 February 1874.

The third factor or document, which, it is presumed, prompted the investigation, was a report by the British consul in Aleppo claiming that the courts were not exercising sufficient impartiality in local disputes. Such observations have to be seen in the context of the traditional hostility displayed by consular authorities towards the *'ulamā'*—a phenomenon that A.L. Tibawi has pointed to in his valuable *Modern History of Syria*:

> Apparently commercial tribunals did not give full satisfaction to demanding foreigners. Take for example the tribunal in Aleppo which in 1871 had four Muslim members including the chairman, four native Christians and four Europeans. The British consul complained of its inefficiency, and, despite a clear Christian majority, complained that Islamic law was a great hindrance to its operation. The truth is that, from the Crimean era onwards, British consuls in Syria began to show a prejudice against the ulema as a class. They favoured their replacement on provincial and district councils and commercial tribunals by business men who, it was assumed, would be more pliable.[17]

In this respect, an economic explanation for the actions of the consuls and the *'ulamā'* is called for. The *'ulamā'* were expressing the feelings of the Aleppo artisans and local traders, who were finding it increasingly hard to compete with the intrusion of Europe's industrial order. In short, theirs was an early form of "economic nationalism" seeking to protect the domestic economy from foreign hegemony. On the other hand, the task of the consul was to ensure his country's economic supremacy under the guise of free-trade ideas and with suitable institutional reforms, including European-style commercial courts.

* * * *

These, then, were the three factors (documents) included in the "Confidential Print" as introduction or background for the circular of instructions launching the investigation of "religious and political revival [which] have lately attracted considerable attention...."[18]

There may have been other factors prompting the investigation. In Istanbul, for example, Nāmiq Kemāl had taken over the newspaper *'Ibret* in

---

[17] A. L. Tibawi, *A Modern History of Syria, Including Lebanon and Palestine* (London: Macmillan, 1969), p. 140.

[18] FOCP, 2621, *Correspondence*, item 4.

June 1872, and was talking and writing about *ittiḥād-i Islām* and *iḥyā-i Islām* (unity of Islam and regeneration of Islam).[19] Moreover, on 1 April 1873, Nāmiq Kemāl's play *Vaṭan Yākhūd Silistre* (Fatherland or Silistria), dealing with the theme of patriotism, was first performed "amid scenes of wild enthusiasm; the next day and following days letters of rapturous praise and support were published in *Ibret*."[20] According to Bernard Lewis:

> All this was not viewed with favour by the authority...any man-
> ifestation of popular enthusiasm was suspect, all the more so
> when it was associated with the alien and subversive idea that
> the people owed loyalty not to the Sultan and his ministers, not
> to the Islamic community and its authorized exponents, but to
> an abstract and unfamiliar entity called the Fatherland.[21]

A few days later the newspaper was suspended on the grounds of irresponsible behavior; Nāmiq Kemāl was deported under close arrest to Famagusta, Cyprus, and placed, for some time, in solitary confinement. This imprisonment and exile lasted until the deposition of Sultan 'Abd al-'Azīz in 1876.[22]

This was also the period when the *nahḍa* in Syria, Lebanon and Palestine—but more particularly in Beirut—acquired increased impetus in its literary, educational, scientific, newspaper publishing, and perhaps even political manifestations. Likewise, reform movements were under way in Egypt and Tunisia, led by such outstanding figures as al-Afghānī and Khayr al-Dīn.

* * * *

As to the consular responses, they were transmitted with haste in most cases, particularly from locations in the European and Arab provinces of the Ottoman Empire. Within a fortnight, the consuls in Roumania had telegraphed that there were no Muslims in residence in their areas and therefore nothing to report bearing on Granville's instructions. From Albania, Consul Reade reported that he had heard "some months ago of the alleged existence of such a movement elsewhere in Turkey, the object of which was said to be

---

[19] Niyazi Berkes, *The Development of Secularism in Turkey* (Montreal: McGill University Press, 1964), pp. 267–68, quoting M. N. Ozön, *Namik Kemal ve Ibret Gazetesi* (Istanbul, 1938), pp. 74–78.

[20] Bernard Lewis, *The Emergence of Modern Turkey*, 2nd edition (Oxford: Oxford University Press, 1968), p. 158.

[21] *Ibid.*

[22] *Ibid.*, p. 159. Bernard Lewis has perhaps overstressed the "unfamiliarity" of Muslim society with the "abstract...entity called the Fatherland."

the unity of Islamism...." But he went on to add that there was no trace of that in his own district.[23] The use by Reade of the term "Islamism" is noteworthy.

From Bosnia, Consul William Holmes composed a racist report. To begin with, he interpreted "revival" as meaning the "rise of intolerance...[and] the revival of fanaticism."[24] He then went on to add: "The character of the Bosniacs, both Mussulman and Christian, is intensively bigoted and fanatical; they are all equally ignorant, given to boasting and bullying, and in general are essentially cowards."[25] Nor was his colleague in Belgrade, Consul-General Longworth, any less prejudiced.[26] In stating what he believed to be "the inherent characteristics of Islamism" (again the use of the term "Islamism" is to be noted), Longworth made frequent use of pejorative terminology: "deficient in vitality," "aggressive," and "carrying in its bosom the seeds of decay," etc.[27] And to round off his report he enclosed the 69th Report of the British and Foreign Bible Society, the section marked Turkey.[28]

So much for the consuls residing in the European provinces of the Ottoman Empire, who either had no relevant material or, as in the case of Holmes and Longworth, reported fanaticism and intolerance—basically their own prejudices. More interesting was the assessment of Acting-Consul Hillebrandt in Crete. Answering the circular on 4 October 1873, he spoke of "the existence of two so-called religious associations both composed entirely of Mussulmans...: one is called the Bektashy, which was organized since the last Cretan insurrection; the second is named the Mevlévis, whose organization in Crete dates from December 1872...."[29] Hillebrandt did not provide any assessment as to whether these constituted a revival in religious terms; he did, however, believe that the associations exercised a growing control over the political and administrative life of the island.[30]

---

[23] FCOP, 2621, *Correspondence*, item 7, Reade (Scutari) to Granville, 9 September 1873.

[24] *Ibid.*, item 9, Holmes (Bosna Serai) to Granville, 12 September 1873.

[25] *Ibid.*

[26] *Ibid.*, item 22, Longworth (Belgrade) to Granville, 8 September 1873.

[27] *Ibid.*

[28] For the highly colored reporting of consuls Holmes and Longworth on other matters, see Gordon Iseminger, "The Old Turkish Hands: The British Levantine Consuls, 1856–1876," *Middle East Journal*, 22 (1968), pp. 300–301, 312–13.

[29] FOCP, 2621, *Correspondence*, item 18, Hillebrandt (Crete) to Granville, 4 October 1873.

[30] *Ibid.*

From Anatolia, one of the earliest and longest reports was from Consul Cumberbatch, located in the bustling seaport of Smyrna. Writing within twenty days of the date of the circular, the consul outlined his views of the effects of Western education and provided a brief sketch of economic integration in the Smyrnan society, together with the impact of such integration on social harmony.

Answering the circular directly, Cumberbatch did not believe a religious revival was under way. "Far from any religious revival amongst the Mussulmans of this district," he wrote, "I can assure your Lordship that quite the opposite has taken place."[31] He could speak with this degree of certainty because of the excellent connections he claimed to have had with the Muslim population of the Smyrna district—and hence, he insists, he would have easily detected a revival if there was one. As to the question of education, many Smyrnan Muslims, having studied abroad, "have in most instances returned discontented with their own country's institutions and have abandoned their religion without adopting another and I might almost say have become the followers of Voltaire, and other sceptic leaders."[32] On the subject of harmony between the various components of Smyrnan society, Cumberbatch affirmed: "One thing mainly contributes in this district to the harmony with the Christian population, and that is the intimate relations which have existed for the last two centuries in commercial affairs, there are few speculations in which both Christians and Mussulmans are not interested."[33]

From the Black Sea port of Trebizond, Vice-Consul Alfred Biliotti reported very briefly that he had not observed any political or religious revival in his consular district.[34] In contrast, Consul J. Taylor, writing from Erzerum on 23 November, attempted to interpret the terms used in the circular of instructions, and in so doing he echoed the intolerance and inclinations of his colleagues Holmes and Longworth:

> If under the denomination "religious revival," anything like spiritual impulse, the consequence of missionary zeal and preaching is presupposed, real or pretended, or even the ordinary devotional features attending Christian demonstrations of the like nature, it is as well to discard the supposition....[35]

---

[31] *Ibid.*, item 8, Cumberbatch (Smyrna) to Granville, 11 September 1873.

[32] *Ibid.*

[33] *Ibid.*

[34] *Ibid.*, item 21, Biliotti (Trebizond) to Granville, 25 September 1873.

[35] *Ibid.*, item 30, Taylor (Erzerum) to Granville, 23 November 1873.

Taylor attributed it all to the "very lax religious spirit" prevalent in the region. In fact, he went on to add, an examination of the state of public morals would lead to the opposite conclusion of revival. "The use of spirits," he wrote, "is largely on the increase....Other detestable Eastern vices, that can hardly find name here, continue to be practised as heretofore unblushingly and openly."[36] He also claimed bribery and corruption were on the rise, and strongly implied that the population was incapable of true religious and moral life.[37] Needless to say, such high-handed attitudes and stereotyping were especially common in the second half of the nineteenth century. Of the three facets of Orientalism as analyzed by Edward Said (an academic discipline, a style of thought, and a discourse in the Foucault sense aimed at "dominating, restructuring, and having authority over the Orient"), the last two were in evidence in Holmes, Longworth, and Taylor, who thus shared in the vast and integrated enterprise to *create* the Orient, the Oriental, and his world."[38]

* * * *

Reports were also sent in from Egypt, North Africa, and the Mashriq. From the increasingly important port of Suez, Consul West sent an early answer to the circular. No signs of religious or political revival came to his notice; but he did take the opportunity to transmit a few observations. "The native population," he explained, "on the borders of the Red Sea, those of Suez included, would prefer being considered Hegazi to being Egyptians, as they look toward their Holy Cities, and not toward Cairo or Constantinople, for persons as well as things that ought to be revered."[39] Consul West also referred to one profound negative impact caused by the opening of the Suez Canal; many conveyors of pilgrims to the Holy Cities—traditionally an important resource to the town—lost their means of livelihood, having been replaced by "the [Egyptian] Viceroy's steamers navigating the Red Sea."[40] Moreover, he detected dissatisfaction with the increase in taxation, which the inhabitants of Suez "look upon as a European innovation."[41]

---

[36] *Ibid.*

[37] *Ibid.*

[38] Edward Said, *Orientalism* (New York: Vintage Books, 1978), pp. 2–3, 40.

[39] FOCP, 2621, *Correspondence*, item 10, West (Suez) to Granville, September 1873. Is it possible that Consul West was hinting at the possibility of the Sharīf of Mecca as an alternative to Sultan or Khedive?

[40] *Ibid.*

[41] *Ibid.*

His colleague Consul Stanley in Alexandria, in contrast, affirmed that a revival was under way: "There is in Egypt," he said, "as in other parts where the Mahommedan religion prevails, a revival of Mahommedan religious feeling... [which] has not yet taken the form of fanaticism."[42] This did not mean, however, that its manifestations were "evident to a casual observer." There was also some ambiguity in the revival because of the presence of many signs of "laxity" such as drinking, "ladies going to French plays, driving about with the thinnest of veils, and returning the salutes of gentlemen...."[43] As to the positive indicators of a revival in Egypt, Stanley observed: "One of the chief instruments is the press, and it may be taken for granted that the literature of a country is a good index of the religious feelings of the people. This shows that there is among the people a new interest in matters of religious faith."[44] He also noted the ferment in publishing, and the role played by al-Azhar in generating and disseminating religious books, including commentaries on the Qur'ān. Furthermore, he had gained the impression of a rise in mosque attendance; and in concluding the section of the report dealing with the religious aspect of the revival, he wrote: "To sum up, the signs that I see of a revival of Mahommedan religious feeling are, (1) the changed literature of the country, (2) greater attention to prayer, (3) greater deference by the government to the religious feeling of the people."[45]

Significantly, Stanley made a connection between religious and political revival. "With regard to the political aspect of this revival," he observed, "the whole civil life of the Mahommedans is so bound up with their religious life, that any religious revival, if successfully persevered in, must necessarily have more or less remote political consequences."[46] In closing, Stanley wrote to Granville: "I am aware that this is but an imperfect sketch on a difficult subject." Yet it is clear that in comparison with most of his colleagues who replied to the circular, he need not have been so modest. While it is true that his report was somewhat marred by the confusion between "revival" and "fanaticism," his observations were nevertheless balanced; and he did acknowledge that he consulted widely in preparing his report.

From Cairo, Consul Rogers mentioned that he had not observed "any manifestation of fanatical feeling... nor been able to gather that any religious

---

[42] *Ibid.*, item 13, Stanley (Alexandria) to Granville, 29 September 1873.
[43] *Ibid.*
[44] *Ibid.*
[45] *Ibid.*
[46] *Ibid.*

or political revival exists."[47] He seemed to ignore the stirrings of reform in the capital of Egypt. Instead, he went into a colorful account of visits to *dhikr* ceremonies and to "the Sheikh Al-Bakir" which he described as "chief of all the sects of Derviches in Egypt."[48] He appeared to be impressed by the argument that the mere presence of non-Muslims and foreigners at such popular ceremonies was an indication of the absence of fanaticism, and did not consider the touristic factor, the appeal of the ceremonies in vogue at the time. It is also remarkable that there was no mention of al-Afghānī's activities, nor of the attempts to modernize al-Azhar and the ensuing ferment among the *'ulamā'* opposed to such innovation.[49]

From Tripoli, Libya, Consul-General Drummond Hay reported "no mouvements among the Mussulman population of this country in any way partaking of the character of a religious and political revival."[50] His fellow-consul in Tunis, Richard Wood, like many others, read the circular in terms of "fanaticism."[51] He did, however, report signs of more zeal among the religious orders, which were quoted as "the Bektashy, Abdul Kader el Bagdady, the Khowan (Fraternity), Issawiyé, and Darkawy," and whose mission had a "politico-religious character."[52] Wood also emphasized their wide diffusion throughout the world of Islam, and their methods of communication. "The emissaries of these societies," he wrote, "meet annually at Mecca during the season of the pilgrimage to give and receive information, to exchange ideas, and to concert fresh measures for the future."[53] Nor did the consul neglect the factor of improved steam navigation in the Mediterranean, Red Sea, Indian Ocean, Gulf, and beyond: "With the present regular and rapid communication between the principal centres of Mahommedanism, the societies are placed in a more favourable position to combine their measures and to simultaneously carry them out; they require therefore, to be watched with

---

[47] *Ibid.*, item 16, no. 2, Rogers (Cairo) to Granville, 24 September 1873.

[48] *Ibid.*

[49] Albert Hourani, *Arabic Thought in the Liberal Age, 1798–1939* (Oxford: Oxford University Press, 1962), p. 109; Afaf Lutfi al-Sayyid Marsot, "The Beginnings of Modernization Among the Rectors of Al-Azhar, 1798–1879," in *The Beginnings of Modernization in the Middle East: the Nineteenth Century*, edited by William R. Polk and R.L. Chambers (Chicago: University of Chicago Press, 1968), pp. 278–80.

[50] FCOP, 2621, *Correspondence*, item 14, Drummond Hay (Tripoli) to Granville, 17 September 1873.

[51] *Ibid.*, item 17, Richard Wood (Tunis) to Granville, 4 October 1873.

[52] *Ibid.*

[53] *Ibid.*

greater vigilance....."[54] It is interesting to note that Wood did not report on Khayr al-Dīn's political initiatives aimed at "confirming the position of Tunis as an autonomous part of the Ottoman Empire."[55]

Turning to the Mashriq—to Syria, Lebanon, Palestine, and Iraq—the first answer to the Foreign Office circular came from Damascus, actually from the summer residence of Blūdān. Consul Green confirmed that he had sent dispatches on this very subject in May and July in which he "made direct allusion to the existence of a feeling among the Mahommedans of Syria of the approaching opportuneness of reasserting Moslem ascendancy."[56] He went on to describe public feeling in the country regarding the outcome of the Franco-Prussian War: "In Syria the disasters of France have been diligently held up as a providential interference."[57] This is not surprising. The memory of the aftermath of the 1860 communal upheaval, the threat of French intervention, and the nature of Turkish justice must have been very much present. Fu'ād Pāshā had dealt with the outbreaks of 1860 with speed and blind severity. As soon as the news of the French expedition to Syria broke out, and in an obvious move to placate the French, the Ottoman authorities executed a number of Damascene notables (with hardly a trial), exiled and imprisoned several hundred more, and, "as a final blow that part of the male population of Damascus [which was] eligible for conscription was forcibly recruited into the Ottoman army."[58] A great deal of scapegoatism had undoubtedly taken place, with many innocents having suffered, while an even greater number of culprits escaped punishment.

Consul Green also noted public resentment against Russian expansion in Muslim Central Asia, specifically the military expedition sent to the khānate of Khīva. Having conquered the khānates of Kokand and Bukhārā, the Russian Empire had turned its attention to the remaining khānate of Central

---

[54] *Ibid.*

[55] Hourani, *Arabic Thought in the Liberal Age*, p. 85.

[56] FCOP, 2621, *Correspondence*, item 12, W. K. Green (Blūdān, Damascus) to Granville, 17 September 1873.

[57] *Ibid.*

[58] Kamal Salibi, *The Modern History of Lebanon* (London: Weidenfeld and Nicolson, 1965), p. 108. In a book published in 1879, the Damscene Nu'mān Qasātilī wrote that seventy people were hanged, one hundred eleven were executed by firing squads, some *'ulamā'* and notables were exiled, and "about four thousand youths from the populace were drafted into the army...;" Nu'mān Qasātilī, *Kitāb al-rawḍa al-ghannā' fī Dimashq al-fayḥā'* (Beirut: Maṭba'at al-amrīkān, 1879), p. 92. See also Kamal Salibi, "The 1860 Upheaval in Damascus as Seen by al-Sayyid Muhammad abu'l-Su'ud al-Hasibi," in *The Beginnings of Modernization*, pp. 201–202.

Asia, Khīva. In 1873, four Russian columns were engaged in crossing the Khīvian deserts in which two previous expeditions had foundered.[59] Their progress was receiving the attention of the press: throughout 1873, Salīm al-Bustānī's *Al-Jinān* (Beirut) published articles on the Tsarist advances.[60] Green was sensitive to the new role of the press in molding public opinion: "The Constantinople and local native papers, keep on the alert the belief of Moslems that the supremacy of the Caliphate" was forthcoming.[61] He did not name the newspapers, but it is surmised that he was probably referring to the semi-official *Ḥadīqat al-akhbār* (Beirut), founded in 1858 by Khalīl al-Khūrī, to *Al-Janna* and *Al-Junayna* of Beirut, founded in 1870 and 1871 by Salīm al-Bustānī, to the fortnightly *Al-Jinān,* to the only Damascene paper published at the time, the official gazette *Sūrīya,* founded in 1865 and printed in both Arabic and Turkish, and finally to Aleppo's official gazette, *Al-Furāt,* founded in 1867 and also printed in both Arabic and Turkish.[62] In the early 1870s the real breakthrough of the Arabic press in terms of independently owned newspapers had not yet occurred. A growing public of readers had to content themselves with official and semi-official papers. Nevertheless, there was enough political coverage in the sheets to generate ferment—a striking fact noted with increased frequency in Western diplomatic and consular reports. The following assessment of the influence of Istanbul's newspapers made in 1882 is indicative and applies to other cities in the Empire:

> It is hardly possible to exaggerate the evil influence of the Turkish newspapers. The old "story-teller" of the bazaars and cafés has given place to the newspaper reader; and the arrival of the mail is eagerly watched for, and the reader at the café is surrounded by listeners who carry away to their villages such version of politics as is contained in the articles. . . . [63]

---

[59] Geoffrey Wheeler, *The Modern History of Soviet Central Asia* (London: Weidenfeld and Nicolson, 1964), p. 86.

[60] *Al-Jinān,* "Rūsīyā wa-Khīwa," no. 2 (15 January 1873), p. 39–40; also no. 8 (15 April 1873), p. 259, and no. 13 (1 July 1873), p. 437; and especially "Ḥamlat Khīwa," no. 15 (1 August 1873), p. 514.

[61] FOCP, 2621, *Correspondence,* item 12.

[62] Philippe de Ṭarrāzī, *Kurrās al-nasharāt al-dawrīya al-'arabīya* [(Arabic Periodicals Fascicle), in *A Post-War Bibliography of the Near Eastern Mandates,* edited by Stuart C. Dodd (Beirut: American Press, 1933) = De Ṭarrāzī's *Ta'rīkh al-saḥāfa al-'arabīya,* IV] (Beirut: Al-Maṭba'a al-amīrkīya, 1933), pp. 4, 42, 53, 107.

[63] Great Britain, Confidential Print, *Affairs of Turkey,* FO 424–126, Sir C. Wilson to the Earl of Dufferin, Constantinople, 25 August 1882.

To Green, in short, there was political agitation in Damascus connected, to some extent, with the expansion of European powers in Muslim lands. He did not think, however, that it was rooted in the general population: "The danger of a Mahommedan outbreak," he wrote, "does not arise from a *bona fide* religious revival, but from exaggerated assumption of religious sentiments by those in authority...."[64] One is tempted to speculate on how Richard Burton, who was the British consul in Damascus from 1869 to 1871, would have answered the circular.

From Beirut, or rather here again from the summer resort of Aley, Consul-General Eldridge provided a somewhat different kind of response, expressing open disagreement with his subordinate in Damascus. "From what I can observe," Eldridge wrote, "there does not appear to me to exist any organized mouvement in the direction indicated."[65] There were isolated manifestations of unrest but nothing unusual. "I should be inclined to say," he continued, "that on the whole the fanatical spirit of the Mussulmans is rather diminishing than increasing, which is, no doubt, to be attributed to the spread of education in the country."[66] And on the subject of the Syrians' falling in line with a Turkish initiative of any kind, he remained sceptical because of the presence of a fundamental conflict of interest: "I cannot refrain from expressing," he clarified, "that the Mussulmans of Syria, who are Arabs, are not very likely to find favour in any mouvement to revive the political importance of the Turks whatever they may be inclined to do towards a religious revival in which I do not believe."[67]

Eldridge's perceptive remarks have to be considered within the context of a trend which began early in the 1860s, and which drew some Muslims and Christians to work in common for decentralization in government and the renaissance of Arab culture and language. A.L. Tibawi has cogently argued that one such manifestation, *Al-Jam'īya al-sūrīya al-'ilmīya* (founded in Beirut in 1857 and reconstituted in 1868), cut across sectarian lines. Presided over by the Druze intellectual Amīr Muḥammad Arslān, its 150 members included influential Christians and Muslims such as Salīm al-Bustānī and Ḥusayn Bayhum.[68] Tibawi has also concluded that Ottoman

---

[64] FOCP, 2621, *Correspondence*, item 12.

[65] *Ibid.*, item 20, Eldridge (Aley) to Granville, 2 October 1873.

[66] *Ibid.*

[67] *Ibid.*

[68] Tibawi, *Modern History of Syria*, pp. 158–61; 'Ādil al-Ṣulḥ, *Suṭūr min al-risāla* (Beirut: 'Ādil al-Ṣulḥ, 1966), pp. 36–37. The following example of social harmony is indicative. At the height of the civil strife in Mount Lebanon between Druzes and Ma-

reforms in the mid-nineteenth century caused discontent among Arab Muslims, which "developed into a separatist tendency with the aim of creating an Arab Islamic state...."[69] Such aspirations for a revived Islam under an Arab Caliphate drew the attention of consular authorities. And in this connection Tibawi has referred to an important observation by Consul Skene in Aleppo in 1858. After underlining the "hatred felt by the Arab population of this part of Syria for the Turkish troops and officials," the consul went on to add: "The Mussulman population of northern Syria hope for a separation from the Ottoman Empire and the formation of a new Arabian state under the sovereignty of the Sharif of Mecca...."[70]

Yet fifteen years later, Consul Skene was certain there was no religious or political revival under way in Aleppo. He also expressed his satisfaction that the local authorities were showing impartiality in legal disputes and with matters pertaining to the courts—an obvious allusion to his earlier report indicating problems in this area. His colleague in Baghdad, Consul-General Herbert, also reported the absence of revivalist movements in his consular district of central Iraq.[71] Likewise, Consul Moore in Jerusalem sent the following assessment on 26 September 1873:

> I do not observe amongst the Mussulmans of this city any sign
> of the mouvement referred to in that dispatch. These, indeed,
> would, I think, be amongst the last to join in any such mou-
> vement, by reason of the spirit of comparative liberalism which
> their long and constant contact with Christians, their pilgrims
> and travellers, establishments and institutions, has engendered
> in them. In the other inland towns of Palestine, namely Nablous

ronites, Consul-General Moore reported to the Foreign Office from Beirut (9 June 1860) on the state of security and on the Christian refugees streaming from the mountains into the city: "It affords me much pleasure to report to your Excellency [Sir H. Bulwer] that many of the Mahometan inhabitants of Beyrout, both of the superior and lower classes, have behaved with great humanity to the poor fugitive Christians now at Beyrout. They have opened a subscription in their favour to supply them with food and other necessaries, and afforded them shelter...;" F.O., Accounts and Papers, 69 (1860), *Despatches from her Majesty's Consuls in the Levant Respecting Past or Apprehended Disturbances in Syria 1858–1860*, Consul-General Moore to Sir H. Bulwer, Beirut, June 1860, p. 571.

[69] Tibawi, *Modern History of Syria*, p. 161.

[70] *Ibid.*, p. 159, quoting dispatch from Skene to Alison (31 July 1858), FO 78–1389.

[71] FOCP, 2621, *Correspondence*, item 19, Skene (Aleppo) to Granville, 30 September 1873; item 23, Herbert (Baghdad) to Hammond, October 7, 1873: "Nothing in the proceedings of the Mussulmans of this country indicates the character of a religious and political revival, neither is there any evidence of the existence or object of any mouvement of the kind."

and Hebron, and the unfrequented port of Gaza, the old Mohammedan spirit is much stronger....[72]

* * * *

To conclude, a number of observations are in order. In the first place, the circular of instructions was insufficiently clear as to what was wanted by way of information. Nor were the terms "political and religious revival" defined by the Foreign Office; hence the variety of responses.

Secondly, the consuls—largely "old Turkish hands" with many years' service in the Ottoman Empire—remained the prisoners of Victorian colonial attitudes and conventions.[73] According to one of them, Robert Stuart, the Ottoman Empire required the special skills of experienced staff: "The Consul is always regarded as a political and representative officer, and as a repository of the views of his government on questions of state policy."[74] On the thorny question of qualifications, Stuart was equally emphatic. A consul had to see things "through the English medium," because:

> If his notions and sympathies are local, they influence his judgement, his mode of reasoning, and habit of thought. They colour his despatches, so that, writing according to his own appreciations, he might, in all good faith, represent a state of things very different to what it would appear to English eyes. Now, it is the English, not the Eastern, view of things that is required by our Government....Our Government as well as our capitalists and merchants, are directly interested in knowing the real state of things in Turkey. And for such knowledge they are almost, if not altogether, dependent on Consular Reports.[75]

With this observation in mind, how useful is the data contained in this wide-ranging investigation? On balance, more is revealed about the official thinking and concern of the Foreign Office and its consuls on such matters as the impact of the press and the telegraph on Muslim opinion than is revealed about the nature of Muslim religious revival, whether in potential or actual terms. Similarly, a central paradox is illuminated—the fact that Western technological breakthroughs in communication (steam navigation, Suez

---

[72] *Ibid.*, item 15, Moore (Jerusalam) to Granville, 26 September 1873.
[73] I owe this formulation to Gordon Iseminger, "The Old Turkish Hands," pp. 297–316.
[74] *Ibid.*, p. 306.
[75] *Ibid.*, p. 307.

Canal, telegraph, and the press), while greatly facilitating the dominance of Europe over the world, also served to create a common consciousness in opposition to such enterprise. The inherence of decolonization in the colonial process was thus intensified.

Thirdly, most consuls equated revival with fanaticism. Yet few saw a link between religious and political revival. Those who did focused attention on the role of the *ṭarīqa*s and the growing importance of the pilgrimage in Muslim life.

Finally, at least one report revealed a fundamental conflict of interest between the Arab population and the Turkish authorities, with significant political undertones and overtones that sounded clearer in the course of the next decade.

6

Theodor Herzl and the Armenian Question*

HISTORIOGRAPHICAL—including hagiographic—contributions to the Zionist movement and its leading figures are plentiful. This is especially true of the founding father, Theodor Herzl, who continues to enjoy pride of place in the literature: there is hardly a facet of his life, personality, and endeavor that has not received at least some attention.[1] One topic, however, has been relatively neglected: Herzl's initiatives regarding the Armenian question, more specifically his parallel attempts at the instigation of the Sublime Porte, first, to persuade Armenian revolutionary committees in Europe to submit to Sultan 'Abd al-Ḥamīd, and second, to influence the European press to give less prominence to Armenian affairs and to reduce its generally pro-Armenian position.

Significantly, these represent some of Herzl's earliest political acts on behalf of the nascent Zionist movement, occurring as they did a year before the convening of the First Zionist Congress at Basle in 1897. Equally important is the fact that his intervention took place at a particularly critical juncture in the development of the Armenian question, which was a national and revolutionary question to most Armenians.

---

*From the *Journal of Palestine Studies*, 7.1 (Autumn 1977), pp. 75–97. © 1977 by the *Journal of Palestine Studies*. Reprinted courtesy of the Institute for Palestine Studies.

[1]Two more biographies of Herzl have recently appeared: Desmond Stewart, *Theodor Herzl* (New York: Doubleday, 1974); Amos Elon, *Herzl* (New York: Holt, Rinehart, Winston, 1975). Stewart devotes some attention to Herzl and the Armenian question; Elon does not.

The Armenian Question to 1896

Strategically located between the Black Sea, the Caucasus Mountains, the Caspian Sea, and the Taurus range, Armenia (Hayastan, as it is known to Armenians) has borne the brunt of countless invasions, coming under the sway, *inter alia*, of Hellenes, Parthians, Romans, Byzantines, Seljuks, Tartars, Mamlūks, Safavids, Russians, and Ottomans. According to statistics established by their Patriarchate in 1882, the total number of Armenians in the Ottoman Empire was close to 2.7 million and was concentrated in six Anatolian *vilāyets*—usually referred to as the six Armenian *vilāyets*—and in the cities of Constantinople and Smyrna.[2] There were also large concentrations in the two Russian Armenian provinces of Erivan and Nakhitchevan and to a lesser extent in Persia.

Properly speaking, the Armenian question became a hotly disputed international issue with the accession of Sultan 'Abd al-Ḥamīd in 1876. Like other national groups contained within such decaying multi-ethnic empires as those of the Russian Tsar, Austrian Hapsburgs, and Ottoman Sultan, the Armenians went through several stages of development during the course of the nineteenth century: from educational enlightenment, to cultural romanticism, to political nationalism bent on achieving autonomy as a minimum and independence as a long-term ideal. Restricted at first to a minority of intelligentsia, "nationalism became a profession of faith for the mass of the people" by the mid-1880s.[3] Leadership was provided traditionally by the Church, but also increasingly by cultural clubs, patriotic organizations, secret societies, and eventually by full-fledged political parties: 1) the Armenakan, founded in 1885 in the Vān region under the ideological guidance of M. Portugalian; 2) the Henshag, founded in Geneva in 1887 as a socialist revolutionary party led by Avetis Nazarbekian (also known as Nazarbek) and Mariam Vardanian, who were the target of Theodor Herzl's diplomatic attention in 1896; and 3) the Tashnag, also known as the Armenian Revolutionary Federation, founded in Tiflīs (Transcaucasia) in 1890 by C. Michaelian, R. Zorian, and S. Zavarian, and influenced by Russian populism.

---

[2] Marcel Léart, *La Question arménienne à la lumière des documents* (Paris: Challamel, 1913), p. 59. The specifically Armenian character of the six *vilāyets*—Erzarūm, Bitlis, Vān, Diyārbekr, Ma'mūrat al-'Azīz (Kharpūt), and Sīvās—was rejected by both Ottomans and modern Turks.

[3] A.O. Sarkissian, *History of the Armenian Question to 1885* (Urbana: University of Illinois Press, 1938), p. 136.

Some of the revolutionary activity in the six *vilāyets* and urban centers of Turkey was coordinated by special committees in exile that sought to win support for their cause from Western intellectuals, politicians, clergymen, and radical organizations. They also conducted propaganda campaigns in the world press against the despotism of Sultan 'Abd al-Ḥamīd and his repressive regime. Other opposition groups in exile, particularly the Young Turks and the Macedonian committees, cooperated with the Armenians on many issues.

In short, one aspect of the Armenian question—a question which increasingly caught the attention of Europeans after the 1870s—was the struggle for democratic reforms, autonomy, or in rarer cases, for total independence, waged by the Armenian national and revolutionary movement in Turkey, Russia, and in western and central European capitals. A second aspect was the perennial problem of protection from nomadic tribes which were at times beyond the reach of the central authority. But while the frequent raids by Kurdish and Circassian tribesmen on the Armenian peasantry may be seen as a grim reminder of Ibn Khaldūn's law of conflict between settler and nomad, there was the additional factor of religious and ethnic manipulation. As one analyst put it:

> At home Abdul Hamid's exploitation of religion as an adjunct of despotism indirectly led to the most hideous episode of his reign—the Armenian massacres. To punish the Armenians for the nationalist agitation that had developed among some of the Armenian communities in the wild mountainous region near the Caucasian border, the Sultan in 1891 authorized the use of Kurdish tribesmen as auxiliary police to put down the unrest....To send them into the Armenian areas to track down suspected nationalist revolutionaries was a sure recipe for religious and race war.[4]

The third aspect of the Armenian question was the diplomacy of the Great Powers regarding the Ottoman Empire: their constant pressure on the Sultan to reform his autocratic system, and their traditional self-imposed role as protectors of the Christian minorities, which was seldom motivated by genuine humanitarian concerns.

The acknowledged watershed in the Armenian question is the Berlin Congress of 1878. A delegation presided by Archbishop Khrimian attended

---

[4]Edmond Taylor, *The Fossil Monarchies* (London: Penguin Books, 1967), p. 156.

the conference and formally requested administrative autonomy—along the lines of the *Mutaṣarrifīya* of Mount Lebanon—for an extensive region mapped out as Turkish Armenia, backed by a gendarmerie and a militia which excluded non-Armenians. The request was not taken into consideration; instead, a watered-down provision—Article LXI—was incorporated into the final draft of the Treaty of Berlin, engaging the Sublime Porte to effect reforms "in the provinces inhabited by Armenians, to guarantee their security against the Kurds and Circassians, and to report periodically to the Powers on the measures taken in this respect, while the Powers would supervise their application."[5] Very little was done in spite of strong representations and of the "Collective Note of 1880" presented by six European powers. "The so-called Armenian reforms," wrote Bismarck in 1883, "are ideal and theoretical aspirations, which were given an appropriate place in the ornamental part of the transactions of the Congress, so that they could be used for parliamentary purposes. Their practical significance, whatever the final outcome, is very doubtful and cuts both ways so far as the Armenians are concerned."[6]

The question of whether it was a major diplomatic blunder by the Great Powers, or a deliberate expression of bad faith by a wily 'Abd al-Ḥamīd eager to find issues that would later enable him to divide the Europeans, is interesting but academic. To the bulk of Ottoman opinion at the turn of the century, the Sultan's refusal to grant reforms under pressure was interpreted as a defense of the empire's sovereignty and integrity. To European public opinion, the Sultan's behavior was further corroboration of the widely circulated epithet "Abdul the Damned." To the Armenians, this was both a reason for further alienation from a regime that showed little interest in their protection and a call for militant action. To a modern Turkish scholar, the Sultan with all his despotism and cruelty was basically right to reject the diplomatic initiatives of the Powers in 1880 and 1895 with respect to reforms: "Why should the Armenians be specifically singled out?"[7]

---

[5] Léart, *La Question arménienne*, p. 31.

[6] William Langer, *The Diplomacy of Imperialism* (New York: A Knopf, 1960), p. 153, quoting *Die grosse Politik*, IX, no. 2183, footnote.

[7] I. C. Ozkaya, *Le Peuple arménien et les tentatives de réduire le peuple turc en servitude* (Istanbul: I.C. Ozkaya, 1971), pp. 164, 167. "Abd-ul-Hamid était despote, tyran, cruel, rapace, pusillanime et tout ce que l'on voudra, mais Abd-ul-Hamid eut parfaitement raison de laisser sans réponse la note collective que les gouvernements des grandes puissances de l'époque lui remirent en 1880 pour demander des réformes pour les provinces habitées par les Arméniens." *Ibid.*, p. 164.

In the brief period between 1890 and 1896, Armenian demonstrations in the cities and uprisings in the rural areas, as well as Turkish repression, reached crisis proportions and reverberated across the diplomatic corridors and press offices of Europe. To some observers the cycle of uprising and bloody repression was made worse by British intervention. "The Turk begins to repress because we sympathize," wrote David Hogarth in his *A Wandering Scholar in the Levant*, "and we sympathize the more because he represses...."[8]

In the year 1890 the Henshag party organized a protest march from the Armenian quarter of Qum-Qapi in the capital to Yildiz Palace in support of reforms—it ended in bloody riots. In the same year, Russian Armenian militants of the Tashnag party staged the Gugunian raid by penetrating into the Turkish eastern border provinces to spark off an uprising. The raid ended in failure, principally because of the collusion between Turkish and Russian authorities, both eager to dismantle the Armenian national and revolutionary movement.[9] This cooperation between two habitual enemies was thereafter intensified.

Three years later, the Henshag organized a carefully coordinated campaign involving the massive distribution of revolutionary pamphlets, throughout the southern provinces, calling on the Turks to overthrow the Ḥamīdian regime. More serious was the rebellion of the mountaineers in the district of Sāsūn in the autumn of 1894. Led by experienced Henshag activists, the Armenians conducted a fierce guerrilla campaign in their mountain strongholds, provoking a large-scale mobilization of Ottoman forces. The rebellion was finally repressed with considerable bloodshed and devastation of villages, prompting in turn the intervention of the Powers; an international Commission of Inquiry was formed with instructions to investigate the entire question of uprisings and reforms. Of course, the Sultan was quick to recognize this as a golden opportunity for vacillation and delaying tactics.[10] The following year, a similar rebellion broke out in the Zaytūn highlands; it was contained with great difficulty and was finally ended through a compromise formula negotiated by European consuls, pleasing neither the Sublime Porte nor the Armenians. In the meantime, ominous clouds were gathering in Constantinople, where Nazarbek had prepared the ground for a demonstration

---

[8] Langer, *The Diplomacy of Imperialism*, p. 159.

[9] *Ibid.*

[10] H. Pasdermadjian, *Histoire de l'Arménie* (Paris: Librairie Orientale, 1964), pp. 346, 347; Louise Nalbandian, *The Armenian Revolutionary Movement* (Berkeley: University of California Press, 1963), p. 122.

at Bāb 'Alī coupled with the circulation of a manifesto to all the foreign embassies stressing its peaceful character and aim: to press for reforms in the Armenian provinces and for civil rights for all Ottoman citizens. In the wake of the bloody reaction which followed, the revolutionaries realized their primary objective, which was to force the attention—perhaps even the intervention—of England and other sympathetic nations.

At this point the Armenian question was taken up in earnest by the chancelleries of Europe. Salisbury, taking over from the retiring Gladstone, was in favor of concerted action to force the hand of the Sublime Porte. Moreover, he felt the time was ripe for negotiations on a partition of the Ottoman Empire, proposing that the Russians "occupy the Armenian provinces of Turkey in return for recognition of Britain's special position in Egypt and perhaps with some compensation for France in Syria."[11] This ambitious scheme did not, however, materialize due to the basic cleavages in the European alliance system. In addition, Tsar and Sultan shared a common interest in thwarting the Armenian national movement: the Russian foreign minister opposed the use of coercion as proposed by Britain, and urged the Sublime Porte not to yield to any European pressure for reforms. The shrewd political sense of 'Abd al-Ḥamīd appeared vindicated; sooner or later the Powers would quarrel over the Armenian question. Besides, even Salisbury had remarked in public: "No fleet in the world can get over the mountains of Taurus to protect the Armenians."[12]

To bring this brief examination of the Armenian question to a close, one must recall the dramatic events of 1896. In the eastern borderland region of Vān, a rare case of cooperation between the three Armenian revolutionary parties took place in the defense of the city of Vān and the neighboring towns against the combined assaults of Turks and Kurds. These bloody events occurred during the month of June, acting as backdrop to Theodor Herzl's first visit to Constantinople in connection with the "charter" for Syria-Palestine and the assistance his movement could offer the Sultan in his campaign against the Armenian committees in Europe.

In August, Tashnag revolutionaries mounted a daring attack on the Imperial Ottoman Bank in Constantinople. Attempts to dislodge them by force failed, and the militants threatened to blow up the premises with everyone in them unless a list of demands was met within 48 hours. With the approval of the Sublime Porte, the foreign ambassadors acted as negotiators, agreed

---

[11] Langer, *The Diplomacy of Imperialism*, p. 197.
[12] A.L. Kennedy, *Salisbury, 1830–1903* (London: John Murray, 1953), p. 273.

to comply with the demands, and arranged a safe conduct out of the country for the militants. Rioting broke out in the capital and the Armenian quarter was sacked with substantial loss of life.

For the Henshag party, 1896 was a painful year. The personal and ideological quarrels between pro-Nazarbek and anti-Nazarbek factions reached breaking point. The former tended toward extreme social-democratic positions, whereas the latter wanted the party to move in the direction of integral nationalism. A splinter group led by A. Arpirian and L. Pachalian founded a new party: the Henshag Veragazmial. Not only the Henshag but the whole Armenian revolutionary movement found it virtually impossible to maintain a lasting cohesion or common front: the committees in exile, plagued by internal rifts and disappointed at the failure of the Powers to coerce the Sublime Porte into granting the promised reforms, were assessing the results of their revolutionary offensive. One of their objectives, the rousing of European public opinion and conscience, had been largely achieved: a flood of books and pamphlets denouncing the Turks appeared, especially in England, between 1894 and 1897.[13] Nonetheless, the cost in lives of Armenian artisans and peasants had to be weighed in the balance. The committees did not have the means adequately to arm and protect their people in the cities, highlands, and valleys of Anatolia.

It was at this point that Theodor Herzl, who had recently embarked on his Zionist venture, was persuaded by Newlinsky, a special agent of the Sultan, to work for the capitulation of the Armenian revolutionary committees in return for advantages that might later accrue to Zionist diplomacy in Constantinople, particularly in connection with the colonization "charter" which he then sought for Syria-Palestine.

Herzl, Newlinsky, and the Sultan's Armenian Mission

Before 1895 there was little indication that Theodor Herzl, a Viennese Jewish journalist, would ever devote serious attention to the politics of his community, or that he would propose the creation of an exclusive Jewish state as a modern solution to the problem of Jews living in an age of increasing nationalism and anti-Semitism in Europe. On the contrary, he had always regarded assimilation into the world at large as both desirable and ineluctable.[14] But

[13] Sir Edwin Pears, *Life of Abdul Hamid* (London: Constable, 1917), p. 240; Nalbandian, *The Armenian Revolutionary Movement*, p. 125.

[14] Alex Bein, *Theodor Herzl: A Biography* (Philadelphia: Jewish Publication Society of America, 1941), pp. 94–95, 100–101. In his capacity as literary critic, he had once

at the age of 35 he made the transition from the world of journalism and letters to that of politics and diplomacy, and also the more radical transition from assimilation to Zionism. Such drastic changes of mind and heart are not easily explained, and his conversion remains somewhat of a mystery.[15] To be sure, his personal experiences of the Dreyfus Affair in Paris, the unexpected manifestation of a virulent anti-Semitism, and the ensuing sense of injured pride, were contributing factors. This is the stock explanation. But there are others as well. Peter Loewenburg, in his controversial psychoanalytical study of Herzl, maintains:

> Zionist hagiography would have it that Herzl came to his Jewish nationalism by firsthand observation of the Dreyfus case as a correspondent in Paris. I suggest that Herzl's Zionist calling was determined by a personal need to be a messiah-saviour-political leader.[16]

And in a recent biography Desmond Stewart added an additional factor to the stock explanation. The death of a wealthy father-in-law gave Herzl, who had failed to make a mark in the literary field, an option in politics: the possibility of using his wife's fortune to advance a new career.[17] Herzl, in a revealing entry in his *Diaries* dated 20 October 1895, had asserted: "I shall be the Parnell of the Jews."[18] In that year, a turning point in his life, as well as in the contemporary history of the Jews, he embarked on the eventful road that took him to the centers of power in Europe in search of an internationally sanctioned "charter" of immigration and colonization, which he felt was an indispensable condition for the founding of a Jewish national home.

Throughout the month of June 1895, Herzl exerted himself in vain to win the support of the Jewish philanthropist Baron Maurice de Hirsch for

---

made fun of the proto-Zionist ideas contained in Alexandre Dumas' play *La Femme de Claude*; moreover, Herzl had even gone so far as to propose the mass conversion of Jews to Christianity as the correct solution to the Jewish question. *Ibid.*

[15] In this connection Herzl himself stressed "the realm of the Unconscious" in his diaries, *The Complete Diaries of Theodor Herzl*, edited by R. Patai (New York: Herzl Press, 1960), I, 13.

[16] Peter Loewenberg, "Theodor Herzl: A Psychoanalytical Study in Charismatic Political Leadership," in B.B. Wolman, *The Psychoanalytical Interpretation of History* (New York: Basic Books, 1971), p. 151.

[17] Stewart, *Theodor Herzl*, p. 168.

[18] *Diaries*, I, 248. Charles S. Parnell (1846–91) was a prominent Irish political leader who fought for Irish independence.

his political solution. He also wrote to Bismarck, the retired Iron Chancellor, whom he admired so much, in an attempt to find out whether his plan was "a truly saving idea or an ingenious fantasy."[19] The letter remained unanswered. In the meantime, he had composed a long study entitled "Address to the Rothschilds," which in effect served as an outline for the major political writing of his career—*Der Judenstaat.*

A visit to Paris in November 1895 aimed at winning French Jewish religious and political leaders to his project also proved quite fruitless. However, he probably gained his first convert there: Max Nordau, who recommended England, and in particular the prestigious Jewish Maccabean Club of London, as a more fruitful scene for his endeavors. Nordau outlined the advantages of direct contact with leading Jewish figures and especially with the influential Jewish press; Herzl duly recorded in his *Diaries* (19 November): "The campaign's center of gravity is shifted to London."[20]

The reception in London turned out to be warmer than it had been in Paris. Israel Zangwill, a widely acclaimed man of letters, sponsored his introduction to the world of British Jewry. Sir Samuel Montagu MP informed him that he would very much like to settle in Palestine; Herzl noted: "He has in mind a Greater Palestine rather than the old one."[21] His lecture to the Maccabeans was well received, and he was unanimously elected as an honorary member. Furthermore, the London *Jewish Chronicle* published his article, "The Solution of the Jewish Question," which attracted some international attention. All in all, the British trip was successful; the contacts he established would later prove valuable in connection with the Armenian mission.

Shortly thereafter, in mid-February 1896, *Der Judenstaat* was released in Vienna, and events began to move rapidly. A week after the book was on sale Herzl noted in the *Diaries* the name of Newlinsky:

> Dr. Landau (a journalist) proposed to me the founding of a weekly paper for the movement. That suits me, and I shall look into it. This weekly will become my organ. Landau had another good idea. Newlinsky, the publisher of the *Correspondance de l'Est,* is a friend of the Sultan's. He might be able to procure for us a status of sovereignty—for baksheesh (a gratuity).[22]

---

[19] *Diaries,* I, 120, letter to Bismarck, 19 June 1895.

[20] *Ibid.,* I, 272, 276.

[21] *Ibid.,* I, 280.

[22] *Ibid.,* I, 305. Philip Michael de Newlinsky (1841–99) was a "multiple-agent" (for numerous European states, the Ottoman Sultan, and Theodor Herzl), a Polish nobleman,

Additional offers of help materialized. The Reverend William H. Hechler, chaplain of the British Embassy in Vienna and a dabbler in prophecy, visited Herzl, "waxed enthusiastic over [his] solution," and offered to act as a propagandist for *Der Judenstaat* with a number of German princes and to arrange an audience with one of the most powerful rulers of Europe—Kaiser Wilhelm II.[23] At the audience, Herzl was to ask the Kaiser to convince the Sultan to grant the Zionists a charter on the Rhodesian model which would enable Jewish economic activities and settlement in Palestine.

The center of gravity was gradually shifting eastward in the direction of Constantinople. On 3 May 1896, Dionys Rosenfeld, editor of the Constantinople *Osmanische Post*, visited Herzl in Budapest and proposed his services as intermediary to the Sultan. He was confident that the time was ripe for the Zionist project because of Turkey's financial plight, and he promised to arrange an audience at the Yildiz Palace for the end of May.[24]

The next visitor on the list appeared four days later, Philip Michael de Newlinsky, a Polish political adventurer, who in describing himself had once said: "Since I cannot shape the politics of my nation, I don't care a rap for anything. I go on artists' tours in politics, like a piano virtuoso—that is all."[25] Herzl's lengthy diary entry describing their first encounter is characteristic, comprehensive, and requires no additional commentary:

> May 7, evening
>
> Newlinsky came to see me after I had telephoned him. In a few words I brought him *au courant*. He told me he had read my pamphlet before his last trip to Constantinople and discussed it with the Sultan. The latter had declared that he could never part with Jerusalem. The Mosque of Omar must always remain in the possession of Islam.
>
> "We could get around that difficulty," I said. "We shall extraterritorialize Jerusalem, which will then belong to nobody and yet to everybody—the holy place which will become the joint pos-

---

an international diplomatic adventurer, and a journalist whom Herzl described as "the most interesting figure I have had to deal with since I carried on the Jewish cause" (*Diaries*, I, 390). His contribution to the early diplomacy of Zionism has been studied by N.M. Gelber, "Philip Michael de Newlinsky: Herzl's Diplomatic Agent," in *Herzl Yearbook: Essays in Zionist History and Thought*, edited by R. Patai, 2 (1959), pp. 113–52.

[23] *Diaries*, I, 310.

[24] *Ibid.*, I, 345.

[25] *Ibid.*, I, 390.

session of all believers. The great condominium of culture and morality."

Newlinsky thought that the Sultan would sooner give us Anatolia. Money was no consideration to him; he had absolutely no understanding of its value—something that may frequently be observed among rulers. But there was another way of winning the Sultan over: through supporting him in the Armenian situation.

Newlinsky is even now on a confidential mission on behalf of the Sultan to the Armenian Committees in Brussels, Paris and London. He is to induce them to submit to the Sultan, whereupon the latter will "voluntarily" grant them the reforms which he refuses to accord under pressure of the Great Powers. Newlinsky now asked me to procure for him the support of the Jews in the Armenian situation; in return he would tell the Sultan that Jewish influence had rendered him this service. The Sultan would show his appreciation of this. This idea immediately struck me as excellent, but I told him that we shall not give our aid away free, i.e., give it only in return for positive counter-services to the Jewish cause.

At this, Newlinsky proposed that no more than an armistice be obtained from the Armenians. The Armenian Committees were preparing to strike some time in July. They ought to be persuaded to wait for a month. We would use that period for negotiations with the Sultan. Since Newlinsky himself is becoming an interested party to the Jewish cause, he wants to drag out the Armenian matter profitably, so that one cause may promote the other.

I said: "The Jewish cause will bring you greater returns than the Armenian. I have nothing to do with money matters, to be sure, but I shall give you a recommendation to our wealthy men...."[26]

Waxing enthusiastic over Newlinsky's imaginative if circuitous approach to the politics of Yildiz Palace, Herzl wasted little time in mobilizing his press and political connections to induce the Armenian revolutionary committees to meet the Sultan's terms. He tried to draw Max Nordau into the project,

---

[26] *Ibid.*, I, 345–46.

but the reply was cabled back in a single emphatic "No!"[27] He discussed the mission of the Sultan's confidential agent with Reverend Hechler, suggesting that he inform his friend, Ambassador Sir Edmund Manson. The latter would then bring the matter to Lord Salisbury's attention, placing him in a position to achieve "a great and effortless diplomatic success"[28] by bringing about a reconciliation between the Sublime Porte and the Armenians. Herzl then decided to send Newlinsky to London while he remained in Vienna to direct the operation.

Combined Explorations from London and Vienna: May 1896

Feverishly pursuing his efforts at mediation, Herzl enlisted the help of the Russian translator of *Der Judenstaat*, S. Klatschko, a Jewish journalist and former nihilist, who was acquainted with Alawerdov (Alawerdian), the leader of the Tiflīs Committee and one who could make contact with Armenian revolutionaries in London. Klatschko was asked to write to them stressing that Herzl considered the Sultan's offer to be genuine and that his personal envoy could be trusted.[29]

From Vienna, Herzl wrote to Newlinsky in London on 15 May to inform him that the ground had been prepared with Lord Salisbury and that friends were contacting Armenian leaders in London and Tiflīs. He also offered this advice: "You will have to overcome the mistrust of the Armenians. Their leaders will believe that we want to compromise them by a fruitless submission which will cripple the entire movement. Actually, on the basis of information which I received last night, we could get them to conclude an armistice without any detrimental effects."[30]

It is difficult to establish from the *Diaries* alone the extent of Herzl's and Newlinsky's expertise regarding the state of the Armenian revolutionary movement in 1896, or to reconstruct all the specific details of their interventions. Nor is N. M. Gelber's study "Philip Michael de Newlinsky" very helpful in this connection, although it makes use of Herzl's unpublished papers.[31] In fact, Gelber devotes relatively little attention to the important Armenian dimension of the Herzl-Newlinsky association; when he does, he generally relies on the *Diaries* rather than on unpublished archival material.

---

[27] *Ibid.*, I, 349.

[28] *Ibid.*, I, 348.

[29] *Ibid.*, I, 349–50.

[30] *Ibid.*, I, 351.

[31] See n. 22 above.

However, he refers to three items which may help to shed some light: Newl-insky, according to Gelber, briefed Herzl on "the situation of the Armenian organizations in London and Paris." The references cited are two letters dated 8 and 9 May 1896, from the Zionist Central Archives, Jerusalem.[32] Gelber also writes: "Newlinsky vainly tried with the help of Sidney Whitman to win over Mayer who was Rothschild's *alter ego*. Mayer told him frankly he considered the Armenian affair as hopeless."[33] The Mayer in question is most probably Sir Carl Meyer, a leading Jewish financial expert and head of the Rothschild office. It would be interesting to know whether Meyer gave Newlinsky the reasons for his estimate of the Armenian affair, and whether the Polish adventurer in turn relayed this information to Herzl.

On the other hand, Joseph Fraenkel's study *Lucien Wolf and Theodor Herzl* quotes from documents in the Herzl archives directly related to the Armenian mission: the full text of a letter dated 27 May from Newlinsky to Lucien Wolf, and substantial excerpts from a revealing letter from Herzl to Solomon J. Solomon, President of the London Maccabeans, dated 22 May.[34]

With the help of the *Diaries* and archival material contained in Gelber and Fraenkel, the firm outlines of the picture emerge, though many crucial questions remain unanswered.

To return to the initiatives in London, urgent messages indicated that in spite of Herzl's efforts, progress was very slow for the Sultan's confidential agent: he wanted in particular to be received by Lord Salisbury and to win an entrée into the influential circles of the British press, traditionally hostile to 'Abd al-Ḥamīd. Newlinsky wired Herzl for "an introduction to Sir Edward Lawson, the son of Joseph Moses Levy of the *Daily Telegraph*."[35] He also tried to lobby with Branting, the editor of the influential *Contemporary Review*.[36] In answer, Herzl telegraphed a letter of introduction to Lucien Wolf, a leading British journalist, requesting help with the British press. He could not have found a better-placed person.[37]

Although opposed to Zionism—in fact, he published an article entitled "The Zionist Danger"—Lucien Wolf was drawn to Herzl and rendered as-

---

[32] Gelber, "Philip Michael de Newlinsky," p. 125, quoting *Gebeimarchiv Herzl fasz*. H. 613a.

[33] *Ibid.*, p. 126.

[34] Joseph Fraenkel, *Lucien Wolf and Theodor Herzl* (London: Jewish Historical Society, 1960), pp. 9–10.

[35] *Ibid.*, p. 9.

[36] Gelber, "Philip Michael de Newlinsky," p. 126.

[37] *Diaries*, I, 355; Fraenkel, *Lucien Wolf*, p. 9.

sistance to him and to Newlinsky in connection with the Armenian mission and negotiations with the Sultan. This is how Newlinsky described his confidential mission in a letter to Lucien Wolf:

> The object is to persuade the Armenian Committees to approach the Sultan, who is guided by the best intentions, direct. A sincere and complete reconciliation could be brought about. The Armenians will of course also have to consider the very difficult situation in which the Sultan finds himself. This would enable him to grant them more than any naval demonstration could ever achieve. The main thing, as you know, is to establish an understanding with the Sultan personally without the intervention of his ministers or foreign diplomats which has spoilt everything in the past....[38]

And Newlinsky went on to request an introduction to Mr. Lawson of the *Daily Telegraph*, "whose important position is well known to us and whose goodwill and support would be of great importance for us."[39]

But a letter from the Zionist leader to Solomon J. Solomon dated 22 May 1896 is even more revealing with respect to: a) the importance of winning the support of the British press for the Sultan's Armenian initiative (one might add, parenthetically, with the help of influential Jewish journalists); and b) the highly controversial nature—bordering on the devious—of Herzl's overtures to the Armenian leaders. The letter has been quoted only partially by Fraenkel, and the omissions may be quite significant:

> I would request you to speak to Mr. Lucien Wolf and ask him what our friends could do in this matter. The Armenians should not know that our participation is based on our own national interests. Should it not be possible to intervene directly, could not a climate of opinion in favour of the Armenian submission be created in the British press?... Lucien Wolf will have no difficulty in realizing the significance of this action, and I hope that he will help as much as possible. Our aim is to induce the Armenian Committees, which intend to renew the struggle in July, to conclude an armistice until August. I say armistice, and not peace, since in the meantime we may be able to deal with the Sultan and obtain some concessions for ourselves. Is it understood that

---

[38] Fraenkel, *Lucien Wolf*, p. 9.
[39] *Ibid.*

I may count on you, Mr. Wolf and our friends in London? We must act without delay![40]

In one respect at least, the Newlinsky-Herzl mission was successful; there was some coverage in the British press concerning the Sultan's offer of reforms in return for submission. An article entitled "The Sultan and the Armenians: The Truth About the Secret Mission" was published in the *Observer* (7 June 1896). The Armenian leaders were warned not to allow themselves "to be enticed into a false position by lending a too willing ear to the interested counsels of the Young Turkish Party."[41] Lucien Wolf himself contributed an unsigned article which drew the response of James Aratoon Malcolm, a British Armenian—former archivist of the Armenian Patriotic Association—who does not appear to have had intimate connections with the revolutionary circles of such militants as Nazarbekian. In actual fact, his reply is the more illuminating in view of his pro-Zionist tendencies and of the useful service he later rendered to Weizmann in connection with the negotiations over the Balfour Declaration.[42]

In the letter he published in July 1896, Malcolm discerned the important bearing that a proposed Jewish state would have on the future of Armenia. He also assessed the reasons for the non-implementation of the Armenian reforms clause in the Treaty of Berlin, suggesting that the Sultan had tricked Disraeli by dangling an attractive bait:

> Among those who have for years worked for Armenia and have had opportunities of learning what was going on behind the scenes it is well known what the real reason of the non-fulfilment of the now notorious Article 61 of the Berlin Treaty was. At the same time that this international contract was signed there is no doubt [England]...intended that the promised reforms should at least be introduced into the government of the Armenian provinces....But the Turk, wily as ever, though crippled and back-broken, threw out a hint to Lord Beaconsfield [Disraeli] that an autonomous Palestine might also be arranged if only the Sultan were given time for spontaneous action. And who, indeed, similarly placed would not have been tempted with such a bait?

[40] *Ibid.*

[41] *Ibid.*, p. 10.

[42] Leonard Stein, *The Balfour Declaration* (London: Valentine, Mitchell, 1961), pp. 354–55, 362–66. Malcolm was a businessman and his family was of Persian-Armenian origin.

> The introduction of the reforms in Armenia were consequently put off *sine die.* . . .[43]

Malcolm went on to claim that having been successful once with the policy of gaining time, the Sublime Porte was "again trying on the same game." He then added by way of conclusion: "The probabilities are at the present juncture, at the sacrifice of another 30,000 or 40,000 Armenians, the Jews may get the grant of some lands in Syria for their settlements, but if they wish for the realization of their legitimate ambition—a proper Jewish state, an autonomous Palestine—nothing, in my opinion, would hasten it more than an autonomous Armenia."[44]

Though the campaign to win the British press was yielding some fruit, the equally crucial political campaign to secure Lord Salisbury's mediation in the Armenian mission was getting nowhere. On 26 May, when Newlinsky telegraphed that Salisbury refused to see him, Herzl advised an early return to Vienna and a postponement of the initiative with the British statesman until the planned visit by the leader of the Zionist movement to London in late June. Instead, he proposed an immediate trip to Constantinople where Newlinsky would introduce him to 'Abd al-Ḥamīd. "Let the Sultan give us that piece of land," he said, "and in return we shall set his house in order, straighten out his finances, and influence public opinion all over the world in his favour."[45]

The Klatschko-Alawerdian probe with the Armenian committees in London had also failed to yield any concrete result. Nazarbekian in response stressed his distrust of the Ottoman Sultan but thanked "the leader of the Jewish movement for his kind sentiments."[46] To remain in the picture, the train ride to Constantinople with Newlinsky and an audience with the Sultan appeared all the more urgent.

The Constantinople Visit: June 1896

As the Orient Express left Vienna for Constantinople on 15 June it had on board Theodor Herzl. At Budapest Newlinsky got on and introduced him to three Turkish dignitaries travelling to the capital of their empire. Herzl

---

[43] Fraenkel, *Lucien Wolf*, p. 11, quoting Malcolm's letter published in the *Observer*, 6 July 1896.

[44] *Ibid.*

[45] *Diaries*, I, 356, 363.

[46] *Ibid.*, I, 359.

brought along with him his master plan for the purchase of Palestine; at Newlinsky's suggestion, he also carried a basket containing "strawberries, peaches, grapes, asparagus—all imported from France."[47] The fruit was destined for the Turkish court. The master plan he reserved for 'Abd al-Ḥamīd, and hoped that it would meet the Sultan's approval.

In the dining car Herzl discussed the plan with the Sultan's confidential agent, who had also become perhaps the first agent of the Zionist movement: "20 million pounds—of which two millions would be earmarked as an immediate advance for the cession of Palestine, and 18 million for the freeing of the Turkish government from the (Debt) Control Commission." Newlinsky objected vehemently and suggested instead a counterplan divided into three parts: "One third we pay cash. For the second third we take the responsibility (or rather, if we become a vassal state, this third is credited against our tribute). On the remaining third we pay interest from the revenues taken away from the present (Control) Commission and assigned to us." And he added : "We could perhaps stipulate several additional concessions and thus facilitate our payments—e.g., an electric power monopoly for all of Turkey, etc." Herzl's reaction as recorded in the *Diaries* was: "I have slept on this and think that Newlinsky is right."[48]

Disappointment awaited him. Once in Constantinople, Newlinsky reported that 'Izzet Bey, the Sultan's First Secretary, was hostile to the project—"Too many commissions are being promised in this matter! he said."[49] More ominously, 'Abd al-Ḥamīd was reportedly ill and did not receive Newlinsky. Herzl wondered whether his expected audience was in jeopardy. Nevertheless, after dinner, he accompanied Newlinksy to an Italian light opera performance where he met Jawād Bey, the son of the Grand Vizier. Herzl's diary entry is revealing:

> We sat on a garden bench, the operetta tunes sounded distantly from the arena stage as I acquainted the still youthful State Councillor with the project. His objections were: the status of the Holy Places. Jerusalem, he said, must definitely remain under Turkish administration. It would run counter to the most sacred feelings of the people if Jerusalem were ceded. I promised

---

[47] *Ibid.*, I, 366.
[48] *Ibid.*, I, 369.
[49] *Ibid.*, I, 370–71.

a far-reaching extra-territoriality. The Holy Places of the civilized world must belong to no one, but to everyone.[50]

The next day, he outlined the plan to the Grand Vizier himself. "Palestine is large," replied the Vizier, "what part of it do you have in mind?" Herzl answered: "That will have to be weighed against the benefits we offer. For more land we shall make greater sacrifices."[51] And as the Ottoman official inquired about the terms, Herzl explained carefully that these were only for the Sultan's ears; and if accepted in principle, Sir Samuel Montagu would then submit the financial program of the Zionist movement. In the evening, Newlinsky returned to the hotel again with bad news and ordered "only half a bottle of champagne *en signe de deuil*."[52] Pādishāh 'Abd al-Ḥamīd had rejected the plan totally:

> If Mr. Herzl is as much your friend as you are mine, then advise him not to take another step in this matter. I cannot sell even a foot of land, for it does not belong to me, but to my people. My people have won this empire by fighting for it with their blood and have fertilized it with their blood. We will again cover it with our blood, before we allow it to be wrested away from us. The men from two of my regiments from Syria and Palestine let themselves be killed one by one at Plevna. Not one of them yielded; they all gave their lives on that battlefield. The Turkish empire belongs not to me, but to the Turkish people. I cannot give away any part of it. Let the Jews save their billions. When my empire is partitioned, they may get Palestine for nothing. But only our corpse will be divided. I will not agree to vivisection.[53]

Herzl, however, did not lose hope. He wanted Newlinsky to renew his efforts to obtain an audience.

On 21 June Newlinsky came out with the reason for the Sultan's refusal to receive the author of *Der Judenstaat*. His Majesty was annoyed with the Viennese newspaper for which Herzl worked. But there was hope. This is how Herzl recorded the episode in the *Diaries*:

> ['Abd al-Ḥamīd] could not and would not receive me as a journalist after the experience he had had with Bacher and the *Neue*

---

[50] *Ibid.*, I, 371–72.
[51] *Ibid.*, I, 375–76.
[52] *Ibid.*, I, 378.
[53] *Ibid.*

Freie Presse. A few months after Bacher's audience our paper had published the most malicious attack on his person that had ever appeared in the press—including the English and Armenian papers....On the other hand, he could and would receive me as a friend—after I had rendered him a service. The service he asks of me is this: For one thing, I am to influence the European press (in London, Paris, Berlin, and Vienna) to handle the Armenian question in a spirit more friendly to the Turks; for another, I am to induce the Armenian leaders directly to submit to him, whereupon he will make all sorts of concessions to them....I immediately told Newlinsky that I was ready *à me mettre en campagne.* Let them give me a pragmatic presentation of the Armenian situation: which persons in London are to be brought round, what newspapers to be won over, etc. Of course, my efforts would be greatly facilitated if the Sultan were to receive me. Newlinsky said: "He will receive you afterwards and confer a high decoration on you." I answered: "I don't need a decoration. All I want now is an audience with him...."[54]

This was 21 June. A week later he had second thoughts. He told Newlinsky "with reluctance and secret shame:"

If the Sultan won't receive me, he should at least give me a visible token that, after listening to my proposal and rejecting it, he still wants to remain *en coquetterie* with me. A high decoration would be suitable for that. But I implore you not to take me for a decoration hunter. I have never given a hoot for decorations, and I don't give a hoot now. But for my people in London I badly need a sign of favour from the Sultan.[55]

If the confidential agent could not secure for him an audience he could manage a decoration. On the eve of their departure from the Ottoman capital, and as he got back to the Hotel Royal to collect his luggage, "Newlinsky, who was writing letters in his underwear...handed [Herzl] a box containing the Commander's Cross of the Mejidiye Order."[56] And as the Orient Express sped along to Sofia, the double agent confided: "The Sultan now expects you to help him in the Armenian matter. Moreover he wishes you to

---

[54] *Ibid.*, I, 386–87.
[55] *Ibid.*, I, 397–98.
[56] *Ibid.*, I, 400.

procure for him a loan based on a lien on the revenue from the lighthouses. For that purpose he is sending you the contract with Collas. The revenue is 45,000 Turkish pounds annually. The loan is supposed to amount to two million pounds."[57]

The bemedalled Herzl was now ready to confront his London friends.

London, July 1896: Herzl meets with Nazarbekian

The next phase of Zionist diplomacy in the Armenian mission required careful planning. The stakes, according to Newlinsky, were high and success assured if three conditions were fulfilled: "Si vous arrivez à pacifier les Arméniens, si vous faites l'emprunt de deux millions de livres sur les phares (lighthouses), et si nous avons la lettre de Bismark—nous enlevons la chose en huit jours."[58] The outlook seemed bright.

At first sight, finding the two millions in the City of London—the world's financial center—appeared easy. According to Sir Samuel Montagu, the Hirsch Foundation alone had at its disposal ten million sterling.[59] British Jewry was wealthy and—Herzl thought—immediately interested in his Palestine project. Besides, he was offering the prospect of lucrative investments; this loan—and others like it—would be tied to concessions on public utilities: the European scramble for such concessions was at its height, as he had learned on his recent visit to Constantinople. London was also the base for many Armenian revolutionary committees—particularly for Nazarbekian and the Henshag. As to the Bismarck angle, Newlinsky said he would arrange an introduction with the Iron Chancellor through a common friend, Sidney Whitman, a journalist in the service of the Ottoman Pādishāh.

To prepare some of the ground Herzl met in Vienna (2 July) with the Armenian leader Alawerdian—with Klatschko serving as interpreter—and offered his services as a conciliator between the Sultan and the Armenians. Alawerdian was not particularly forthcoming. Herzl noted: "He didn't seem to trust me. We finally agreed that he will announce me in London as a friend of the Armenians and act as a pacifier in his circle."[60]

With this hesitant endorsement, the leader of the Zionist movement boarded the train which took him to Brussels and Ostend, and ran into "some ugly waves" as he crossed the Channel to Dover. On 4 July he was

---

[57] *Ibid.*, I, 401.
[58] *Ibid.*, I, 403–404.
[59] Stewart, *Theodor Herzl*, p. 246.
[60] *Diaries*, I, 404.

in London where he hoped, among other things, to lay the foundation of the
"Society of Jews"—the political arm of the Zionist movement. For all these
efforts he needed the help of the Maccabeans, of his friends in the press, and
of English Jews in politics and finance. Having been interviewed by Lucien
Wolf and Israel Zangwill he was able to record: "During the past few days all
the local papers have started to make a noise."[61] He also got the Armenian
mission started by asking Lucien Wolf "to initiate a little press campaign for
the cooling of tempers in the Armenian Question." To Newlinsky he wired:
"Lighthouse and Armenian affairs effectively launched."[62] But he was having trouble with the financial sector: "If I cannot have the *superos* [top men]
of Jewish finance for the lighthouse loan which the Sultan desires, I shall
move Acheron (the Underworld of Greek mythology)." He then thought of
trying to float the loan "through bankers of the second rank, through the
Africanders like Barnato."[63] The doors of Mammon would not easily open.

Herzl's overtures to the politicians appeared more promising. Sir Samuel
Montagu received him in the House of Commons and showed interest in
his account of the Constantinople trip. Herzl also asked Alfred Cohen to
get him an introduction to Salisbury through Rothschild, claiming that he
"wanted to do Lord Salisbury's policy the favour of settling the Armenian
question and thus restoring the lost English influence in Constantinople."
Cohen promised "to discuss it with Rothschild while riding horseback."[64]
On 10 July he asked Colonel Goldsmid of the British Hovevei Zion to obtain
for him an introduction to the Duke of Argyll—"who is important on the
Armenian Committee"—through Arthur Cohen, the Queen's Counsel.[65] He
also wanted an introduction to the Russian Tsar through the Prince of Wales.

The Zionist leader's next moves were aimed at direct contact with Armenian revolutionaries in London. On 11 July, he was interviewed by Rapoport,
a journalist well-acquainted with Armenian circles, particularly with the
Henshag leader Nazarbekian. Herzl's record of the encounter is revealing:

> Rapoport indicated to me that he suspected the Armenian rev-
> olutionaries were being supported with money by the English
> government. I asked him to put me in touch with Nazarbek. I
> want to make it clear to this revolutionary that the Armenians

---

[61] *Ibid.*, I, 407. The interviews were for the *Sunday Times* and the *Daily Graphic.*
[62] *Ibid.*, I, 410–11.
[63] *Ibid.*, I, 407–12.
[64] *Ibid.*, I, 413.
[65] *Ibid.*, I, 414.

should now make their peace with the Sultan, without prejudice to their later claims when Turkey is partitioned.[66]

Two days later, Theodor Herzl took the underground to Shepherd's Bush for the long-awaited meeting with Nazarbekian—one of the principal reasons for his London trip. This is how he recorded the scene.

> The house is noisy, second-rate, middle-class elegance, and from time to time wild Armenian faces appear in the crack of the door. They are refugees who find shelter here.
>
> The Russian Rapoport had introduced me. Together with him and Mme. Nazarbek I waited in the living-room for the man of the house. I said that I had not had my lunch yet, whereupon the woman with an unfriendly expression had a piece of meat brought out to me.
>
> Nazarbek came home. The head of a genius, the way they are fixed up in the Quartier Latin. Black, tangled serpentine locks, black beard, pale face.
>
> He mistrusts the Sultan and would like to have guarantees before he submits. His political ideas are confused, his acquaintance with the European situation downright childish. He said: Austria is building fortifications on the Black Sea!
>
> And as it seems, his word is obeyed by the poor people in Armenia who are being massacred. He lives in London, not uncomfortably.
>
> I asked whether he knew who was finally benefitting from all this unrest, Russia or England?
>
> He replied that he did not care; he was revolting only against the Turks.
>
> The woman kept interrupting us, speaking in Armenian and evidently against me. She has a wicked look; and who knows how much she is to blame for the bloodshed. Or is it the evil look of the frightened, the persecuted?
>
> I promised I would try to get the Sultan to stop the massacres and new arrests, as a token of his good will. But he would hardly release the prisoners in advance, as Nazarbek desired. I explained to him in vain that, after all, the revolutionaries could watch the

---

[66] *Ibid.*, I, 414–15.

course of the peace negotiations without disarming, with their guns at their feet.[67]

Before leaving London, Herzl met Montagu again in connection with political support for his Armenian mission. In particular, he sought the good offices of Francis S. Stevenson MP, Vice-President of the Anglo-Armenian Committees.[68] "I am satisfied with the result of my trip to London," he jotted down in his *Diaries,* adding: "The conditional promise of Montagu and Goldsmid to join us if Edmond Rothschild and the Hirsch Fund participate and the Sultan enters into positive negotiations, suffices me for the present."[69] As it turned out later, he lost the support of Montagu (and the *superos* of British Jewry) because, according to Fraenkel, of a "postcard which he sent [Montagu] on a Sabbath."[70]

Conclusion

In the ensuing months the Armenian question lost its urgency and news-making power in the chancelleries and press offices of Europe. The storm center shifted to the Balkans where a Greco-Turkish war broke out in April 1897. Herzl immediately responded with a pro-Turkish stand, raising funds for the Turkish war efforts, arranging for volunteers, including doctors, to participate on the Turkish side. Predictably, he wrote a secret message to the Turkish ambassador in Vienna stressing that the Jews were eager to use this opportunity to show their devotion to Turkey.[71] The Armenian question receded to the background, and with it one of the first diplomatic initiatives of the emerging Zionist movement.

Prodded on by the Ottoman Pādishāh, who dangled the prospect of a charter, Theodor Herzl in 1896 had spent three intense months in trying to achieve a breakthrough with the Armenian revolutionary committees in Europe. In this respect he could not report much progress. Nonetheless, the whole episode demonstrated his capable handling of the press, his recognition of its power, rapidly expanding role, and its vulnerability to influence, and his ability to persuade well-placed journalists to come to his aid. At the same time it highlighted the Zionist leader's propensity for involvement

---

[67] *Ibid.,* I, 417–18.
[68] *Ibid.,* I, 422.
[69] *Ibid.*
[70] Fraenkel, *Lucien Wolf,* p. 15.
[71] *Diaries,* II, 541–42.

with the political and diplomatic *demi-monde* of Europe peopled by shady adventurers and eccentrics gravitating around thrones in decline.

That Herzl manipulated the Armenian question to further his own ends is clear, although the details and consequences of the manipulation would have to await the opening of additional archival material, in particular the Herzl *Geheimarchiv* referred to in Gelber's study.[72] To the President of the Maccabeans, Solomon J. Solomon, Herzl had written: "The Armenians should not know that our participation is based on our own national interests."[73] This and similar references point to the perception of the Armenian national movement as a possible rival. The attitude of early Zionism to the various nationalisms present in the Ottoman Empire has been insufficiently studied. Nevertheless, Gelber's reference to Newlinsky's reports and Herzl's request for a briefing in Constantinople would indicate at least an interest in keeping a sharp lookout on the activities and development of a rival national movement capable of drawing popular sympathy and political support in Europe. This also raises the question of the extent of early Zionist monitoring of other nationalisms, such as the nascent Arab nationalist movement. A 5 March 1904 entry in Herzl's *Diaries* reads: "There is an Arab movement which intends to make a descendant of Muhammad Caliph."[74] Three years later, another Zionist leader, Chaim Weizmann, on his first visit to Palestine reported he "first heard something of the nascent Arab national movement" from Victor Jacobson, branch director of the Anglo-Palestine Bank.[75]

Some of Herzl's colleagues had doubts about the morality of Herzl's stand on the Armenian question. Bernard Lazare, one of Theodor Herzl's earliest supporters, resigned from the Zionist movement's directing Actions Committee in protest over his leader's links with 'Abd al-Ḥamīd.[76] In 1902 he published a scathing attack on Zionism in the French-Armenian journal *Pro-Armenia*. Herzl's reaction in the *Diaries* was characteristic: "Bernard Lazare published in the propaganda sheet *Pro-Armenia*, a vulgar nasty article against me apropos of the exchange of greetings between the Zionist Congress and the Sultan. Apart from a handsome gesture what interest could he have in defending the Armenians?"[77] Nor was Herzl alone in his

[72] Gelber, "Philip Michael de Newlinsky," p. 125, note 19.
[73] Fraenkel, *Lucien Wolf*, p. 9.
[74] *Diaries*, IV, 1616.
[75] Chaim Weizmann, *Trial and Error* (New York: Schocken Books, 1966), p. 125.
[76] Lazare Prajs, *Peguy et Israël* (Paris: Nizet, 1970), pp. 64–65, 70.
[77] Nelly Jussem-Wilson, "Bernard Lazare's Jewish Journey," *Jewish Social Studies*, 26 (July 1964), p. 165.

views. His great successor, Chaim Weizmann, writing to his future wife in 1902, reported: "I had a long talk with [Edward] Bernstein and his daughter in Berlin. I took him to task for taking up the cause of the Armenians and not taking up the Jewish cause."[78]

---

[78] *The Letters and Papers of Chaim Weizmann*, edited by Leonard Stein (London: Oxford University Press, 1968), Series A, I, 389.

7

Colonial Scholarship and Muslim Revivalism in 1900*

IN THE SUMMER OF 1897 a pageant to end all pageants was staged in London in celebration of Queen Victoria's diamond jubilee and of Britain's paramount position in the hierarchy of imperial powers. This is how Carlton Hayes described the occasion in his stimulating study, *A Generation of Materialism 1871–1900*:

> A procession, such as the world had not previously beheld, passed from Buckingham Palace up Constitution Hill, through Picadilly, Trafalgar Square, the Strand and Fleet Street, to [a] solemn service of Thanksgiving in St. Paul's. First went detachments of armed forces from beyond the seas: Dyak police from North Borneo, Maoris from New Zealand, Hausas from West Africa, twenty-six cavalrymen from Cape Colony, forty-two helmeted soldiers from Hong-kong, black fighters in the employ of the Royal Niger Company, mounted Zaptiehs from Cyprus, a contingent of Rhodesian horsemen, men of Australia clad in brown, and Canadians in variant uniforms of thirty military organisations. Followed Dominion premiers in sober black and scores of colonial governors with swords and gold lace; next, representatives of all ranks of the royal navy; then, for the army of the United Kingdom, scarlet coats, Highland kilts, Coldstream Guards, Dragoons, generals and field marshals. After which

*From *Arab Studies Quarterly*, 4 (1982), pp. 1–16. © 1982 by the Association of Arab-American University Graduates and the Institute of Arab Studies. Reprinted courtesy of the Institute of Arab Studies.

went carriages with ministers and ambassadors accredited to
the Court of St. James's, foreign princes, kings, and emperors,
and the Queen's family—she had nine children, forty grandchil-
dren, and thirty great-grandchildren. Finally, passed Victoria,
Queen and Empress, in coach of gold and crimson drawn by
eight cream-coloured horses and surrounded by a bodyguard of
Indian soldiery.[1]

In many respects, 1897 was indeed the apotheosis of the British Empire,
the living example of social Darwinism on a global scale. Perhaps even the
order of the procession—beginning with the Dyaks of North Borneo and
ending with the Queen's own Royal Guards—was an unconscious reflection
of the social Darwinian ladder as perceived by the intellectual and political
elites and the public.

France's Third Republic was not far behind Victorian England in both
theory and practice. One of its most influential theorists of colonialism, Jules
Harmand, provided the current justification of imperial expansion, along social Darwinian lines, as the prerogative and mission of superior civilizations:

We must therefore accept as our basic principle the fact that a
hierarchy of races and civilizations exists, and that we belong to
the highest race, the highest civilization. But we must realize,
too, that our superiority imposes important duties on us, as well
as giving us certain rights. For we are superior not only in the
economic and military, but especially in the moral, sense. That
fact constitutes our main justification for the conquest of native
peoples.[2]

Inaugurated by France's conquest of Tunisia in 1881 and Britain's conquest of Egypt in 1882, the modern scramble for colonies—generally referred
to as the "new imperialism"—brought the two powers into intense competition. That they did not go to war was probably due to the fact that the
colonial cake was immense: everyone could pretend to possess the lion's
share.

While Britain dreamt and planned an African empire with a north-south
axis of unbroken territory stretching from the Cape to Cairo, France pushed

---

[1] Carlton Hayes, *A Generation of Materialism 1871–1900* (New York: Harper, 1963),
p. 315.

[2] Jules Harmand, *Domination et colonisation* (Paris: Flammarion, 1910), p. 156, quoted
in Harvey Goldberg, *French Colonialism* (New York: Rinehart, 1959), p. 4.

hard on a west-east axis from Senegal on the Atlantic to Somalia on the Red
Sea. The strategic point of intersection, as yet unconquered by the colonial powers, was the upper Nile basin of the Sudan. A preemptive French
expedition would obstruct British hopes for a continuous north-south axis
and vice versa. It is in this sense that Foreign Minister Hanotaux told the
leader of the French expedition, Captain Marchand, that "France was going
to fire her pistol," which she almost did when Marchand's column arrived at
Fashoda in southern Sudan in 1898. Meanwhile, Kitchener advanced from
Cairo, defeated the Khalīfa—successor of the Mahdī—at Atbara and Om-
durman, and confronted Marchand at Fashoda. For a while, there was talk
of war between the two colonial powers. Then France reluctantly withdrew
from Fashoda, but had her claim to Wadai (east of Lake Chad) recognized
by Britain in return for recognition of Britain's claim in the Sudan.[3]

In colonial terms there were only a few more "gaps" to fill before the
whole continent would be painted in the respective colors of the colonial
powers. One such "gap" was represented by Morocco, which France eagerly
sought and was soon to appropriate with British help. Along the whole of
the French and in substantial portions of the British axis, colonialism had
met fierce Muslim resistance to conquest and colonization. In this uneven encounter, old ruling elites were destroyed while the intrusion of new economic
forces brought changes in social relations. The colonial victim was subjected
to either destruction, assimilation, association, or segregation, while the colonizer in this self-confident assertion of his power, justified his actions in the
name of the civilizing mission.[4]

With a vast colonial domain in Africa, and with wide-ranging ambitions
in the Ottoman Empire, France's *politique musulmane* held the intense concern of cabinet ministers, the colonial army and administration, and the
growing establishment of scholars specialized in Oriental studies. Their
combined effort aimed—in the words of Edward Said—at "dominating, restructuring, and having authority over the Orient."[5] Would Islam, both as
religion and social organization, retain its traditional opposition to Western
hegemony and colonization? Would it continue to do so if it were suitably
"Europeanized"? With the destruction of the old indigenous elites, who
would fill the vacuum and what type of educational formation was needed
for the new elites? How was France to face the paradoxical fact that West-

---

[3]Hayes, *A Generation of Materialism*, pp. 318–19.

[4]Marwan Buheiry, "Planat de La Faye: A Critic of France's Algerian Mission in the
1840s," *Al-Abhath*, 26 (1973–77), p. 19 [= p. 45 above].

[5]Edward Said, *Orientalism* (New York: Vintage Books, 1978), pp. 2–3.

ern technological breakthroughs in communications (the press, railways and steamship navigation, the Suez Canal, and the telegraph), while facilitating colonial dominance, also served to tie Muslim societies from the Atlantic seaboard to the confines of the Far East? What was the reason for and significance of the Islamic revival in the nineteenth century? These, among others, were important stock questions that the entire colonial establishment sought answers to.[6]

Whither Islam in 1900: The Perception of Orientalistes and Arabisants

In 1901 one of the prestigious organs of the colonial press, the fortnightly *Questions diplomatiques et coloniales* conducted a comprehensive investigation of the prospects for Islam in the twentieth century. At this point in time, a newly founded Colonial party (1894) was served in Paris by 45 newspapers and periodicals eagerly diffusing expansionist and jingoist themes. An examination of the list of patrons and of members attending the special "colonial banquets" organized by the journal *Questions diplomatiques et coloniales* lends support to the theses of Henri Brunschwig and Charles-Robert Ageron that the Parti colonial was essentially a loose grouping of notables, associations, and committees.[7]

The motive for the *Questions diplomatiques et coloniales* investigation was clearly stated: "France is—and will naturally become more and more—a great Muslim power. Therefore the evolution and probable destiny of Islam in the twentieth century ought to become the passionate concern of every French patriot."[8] The editor in charge of this special *enquête*, Edmond Fazy, prefaced the investigation with the statement that Islam was in a state of revival, as indicated by its resolute expansion in the African continent.

The results of the investigation were published over several months. They consisted mainly of careful responses by at least eighteen prominent contrib-

---

[6] For a British investigation of Muslim political and religious revival in the mid-seventies, see Marwan Buheiry, "Islam and the Foreign Office: An Investigation of Religious and Political Revival in 1873," in *Studia Arabica et Islamica: Festschrift for Iḥsān ʿAbbās on His Sixtieth Birthday*, edited by Wadād al-Qāḍī (Beirut: American University of Beirut, 1981), pp. 47–59 [= pp. 65–82 above].

[7] Henri Brunschwig, *Mythes et réalités de l'imperialisme colonial français* (Paris: Colin, 1960), pp. 113–15; Charles-Robert Ageron, *France coloniale ou parti colonial?* (Paris: Presses universitaires de France, 1978), p. 131.

[8] *Questions diplomatiques et coloniales*, 15 May 1901, p. 579.

utors from all over the world, with short commentaries by the editor. The contributors were:

> French (six): Bernard Carra de Vaux, Clément Huart,
>   René Basset, Edmond Doutté, William Marçais, and Henry
>   de Castries.
> British (three): Edward G. Browne, Malcolm MacColl,
>   and F.G. Aflalo.
> Dutch (two): L.W.C. Van den Berg and C. Snouck Hurgronje.
> Hungarians (two): Ignaz Goldziher and Arminius Vámbéry.
> German (one): Martin Hartmann.
> Russian (one): Eugene de Roberty.
> Turko-Greek (one): Musurus-Ghikis Bey.
> Persian (one): Muḥammad Ḥasan Sirjānī.
> Algerian (one): Muḥammad Ben Raḥḥāl.

The substance of their observations and assessments may be grouped into the following five areas of concern: 1) the prospect for Muslim revival in the twentieth century and Europe's task; 2) the Caliphate and pan-Islam; 3) Islam south of the Sahara; 4) the Arabisants school and the problem of old and new elites; and 5) in defense of Islam.

The Prospect for Muslim Revival

Leading the *enquête*, and portrayed by the editor as a keynote address, was the answer of Baron Carra de Vaux of the Catholic Institute, a specialist on Ibn Sīnā (Avicenna) who left no doubt as to where he stood on the subject. "To begin with," wrote Carra de Vaux, "Islam is an institution possessing a character of exceptional fixity...which places its adherents in an uncritical frame of mind opposed to progress."[9] He believed that with the exception of Persia, which he saw in terms of the "Aryan spirit reacting against the Semitic," Islam would remain in the twentieth century what it was in the nineteenth, and that change could only be brought about through external forces.[10] These were the Christian powers who exercised hegemony over major portions of the Muslim world. "Islam is today vanquished," affirmed Carra de Vaux, "its political decadence was inevitable...and in regard to its temporal destiny, *l'Islamisme est une religion finie*."[11]

---

[9] *Ibid.*, p. 580.
[10] *Ibid.*, pp. 581–82.
[11] *Ibid.*

Yet all was not well. Colonization, he recognized, was a slow process and the native reaction remained unpredictable. "The great and general danger menacing the Christian powers in their relations with the Muslim world was pan-Islam; a simultaneous uprising from the Maghrib to the Far East, although improbable, was still possible at any time and without any clear pretext."[12] Europe was not fully capable of understanding the "mysterious and secret" currents that produced the Mahdī phenomenon with its "system of occult propaganda" and which was most likely to find fruition in Morocco and Tripolitania.[13]

If the stereotyping conformed to the standard colonial and Victorian norms of Orientalism (fixity, decadence, mystery, irrationality, and menacing peril) what then was the possible answer? Carra de Vaux's magic formula was the policy of segmenting the unity of Islam:

> I believe that we should endeavor to split the Muslim world, to break its moral unity, using to this effect the ethnic and political divisions....Let us therefore accentuate these differences, in order to increase on the one hand national sentiment (*sentiment de nationalité*) and to decrease on the other that of religious community (*communauté religieuse*) among the various Muslim races. Let us take advantage of political conditions. Egypt, for example, governed today by British power, must form a moral entity clearly distinct from French Sudan or from Arabia, which remains free. Let us make of Egypt a barrier between African Islam and Asian Islam. In one word, let us *segment Islam*, and make use, moreover, of Muslim heresies and the Sufi orders.[14]

The task, in his view, was "to weaken Islam...to render it forever incapable of great awakenings."[15]

Different and more complex was Eugene de Roberty's assessment, although he did offer similar advice in the end. This Russian freethinker and sociologist, author of *La Sociologie* (1880) and *Frederic Nietzsche* (1902), did not attach any importance to religious belief, which, in his view, played a passive, symptomatic role only. Modernization, to him, was a universal model and in this respect he wanted Europe "to work on the Muslim elite...by sending Western scholars, artists, engineers, and workers, while

---

[12] *Ibid.*, p. 587.

[13] *Ibid.*

[14] *Ibid.*, p. 588.

[15] *Ibid.*

keeping strictly at home in Europe the Catholic, Protestant, and Orthodox priests and missionaries." The real task was to build railways in the world of Islam and to proceed with a secular colonization of land and industry. Moreover, Roberty clearly favored the segmenting of the principal Muslim power, the Ottoman Empire, into multiple political centers including: "an independent and free Armenia..., a Jewish republic along the equitable Zionist plan, an Egypt delivered from Britain's selfish and useless tutelage, a federation of small Arab principalities, and so on."[16]

Another opinion regarding Islam's prospects was expressed by Musurus-Ghikis Bey, a Turko-Greek political figure in exile in Europe, who argued that while he "could not envisage the Arab tribes of Najd, Hijaz, and Yemen displaying a warm desire by the year 2000 for taxation, military service, tribunals, schools, etc., and for debates in Parliament relating to budgets and expenditures," he could nevertheless picture their coreligionists in Bosnia accepting Western civilization. He also felt that the Turks were "perfectly prepared to receive most, if not all, the institutions of the West...and to become with the Greeks the agents of progress in the Orient, sharing with them the honor of being the guardians of the European and Asian littoral of the Aegean Sea, for the greater good and security of the principal Mediterranean powers." In short, Musurus-Ghikis Bey appeared as an enthusiastic precursor of some of NATO's arguments.[17]

Martin Hartmann, one of Germany's eminent scholars, also contributed his views, concentrating with some ambivalence on the much-debated phenomenon of Muslim revivalism in his time. "There is no Islamic peril," he wrote, "but certain precautions are indicated; the growing ferment in the Muslim world needed careful watching so that it did not become a danger."[18] "In 1800," he argued, "Islam as a political power appeared dead, whereas today it was on the eve of a new evolution" with two dimensions: 1) an inner renewal calling for a strict adherence to religious practice and belief and leading to the birth of a multitude of Ṣūfī orders (*confréries*); and 2) Western borrowings in the military field, and more particularly in education, the press, and female progress.

On the level of global politics, Hartmann felt that Islam was resigned to the loss of Africa, and to the sharing of Iran and Central Asia between Britain and Russia. Only Turkey was left to assume the mantle of Muslim

---

[16] *Ibid.*, pp. 591–92.

[17] *Ibid.*, pp. 595–96.

[18] *Questions diplomatiques et coloniales*, 15 July 1901, p. 84.

leadership, and in this respect he affirmed that "in the twentieth century a new Turkey would occupy the center of the political stage at the head of a powerful ascending Islam." He ended on a characteristic social-Darwinist note: "Conflict equals progress."[19] Hartmann's stress of Ottoman leadership echoed the *Weltpolitik* of Kaiser William II, and the strategic importance of the alliance with Turkey.

The Caliphate and Pan-Islam

That the *enquête* should devote some attention to the Ottoman Empire is not surprising. In this respect the views of Snouck Hurgronje from Sumatra were given prominence: his essay "Islam and the Phonograph" was described by the editor of the investigation as "classique dans le monde des Orientalistes."[20]

Snouck Hurgronje prefaced his report to *Questions diplomatiques et coloniales* by stressing the growing political and administrative roles and travels he had to undertake in Indonesia, complaining that he was no longer able to keep abreast of the state of research in Europe. As to the question of the Caliphate on which he concentrated attention, he felt there was a great deal of confusion in the minds of Western political decision-makers, and far too much fuss made over the subject. The issue ought to be played down. He pointed to the danger of admitting "Muslim political and religious beliefs into the arena of international relations" and the colonial venture. If the colonial powers accepted the principle and implications of the Caliphate, their Muslim subjects would then be placed in the position of having to accept their present rulers "as an anomaly."[21]

To be sure, Sultan ʿAbd al-Ḥamīd was delighted to be addressed as Caliph by European officials and press; this gave him the opportunity to enlarge his field of action and to legitimize the policy and ideology of pan-Islam. But Snouck Hurgronje insisted that in reality "the Caliphate was over because the political unity of Muslims had ended forever, and the religious unity was held not by the Caliph but by the *ʿulamāʾ*."[22]

Moving next to the loudly voiced question of reforms in the Ottoman Empire, Reverend Malcolm MacColl proclaimed that equal justice to all the subjects of the Sultan was impossible in Turkey, that Islam excluded "any

---

[19] *Ibid.*, pp. 85–88.
[20] *Ibid.*, p. 73. [On Snouck Hurgronje, cf. p. 63, note 36, above.]
[21] *Ibid.*, p. 81.
[22] *Ibid.*, p. 82.

development or progress beyond the contents of the Qur'ān,"[23] and that for Muslims "patriotism was a question of religion rather than of country (*pays*)." How then should Europe proceed with reforms in Turkey? His advice, a mixture of paternalism and *Realpolitik*, was very much in line with the conventional wisdom of Western chancelleries:

> Coercion exercised by a superior force was the only argument capable of persuading the Sultan to grant a reform violating articles of the sacred law. How is it that during these last years the Christian powers have overlooked this basic truth in their negotiations with the Sublime Porte? Let them offer the Sultan a reform project accompanied by an ultimatum demanding a full compliance under penalty of war at a given date, and the Sultan would undoubtedly have to yield, on the advice of the Shaykh al-Islam, whom he must consult.[24]

In this wide-ranging investigation another issue received the attention of many contributors. "My fifty years of Muslim ethnographic studies," observed Arminius Vámbéry, "causes me to answer a host of such questions as: does pan-Islam really exist; is it likely to pose, in Asia, for example, a danger to the political and civilizational enterprise of the West?"[25] Vámbéry had the reputation of being a confidant of the Sultan and the answers he sent in to *Questions diplomatiques et coloniales* included the origins of the pan-Islam movement which, in his view, first grew in "India during the Crimean War when modest attempts were made in India and Java to provide assistance to the Turkish army in the form of funds and rice." However, it was in recent times, as he put it, that the "victories of Christian armies in the Caucasus, Algeria, and the Indies had awakened the Believers to their own dangerous predicament and material decline, causing them to seek closer fraternal bonds with each other." From Constantinople, the center of pan-Islam, "the cunning Sultan personally manipulated the strings of the great intrigue."[26] But Vámbéry believed neither in the present nor future effectiveness of the movement: in the absence of concerted effort and proper social organization, "Pan-Islam would never possess sufficient power to score

---

[23] *Questions diplomatiques et coloniales*, 1 August 1901, p. 152.
[24] *Ibid.*, p. 155.
[25] *Ibid.*, p. 147.
[26] *Ibid.*, p. 148.

a specific success, and with the possible exception of Africa, it could not halt the victorious forward march of the Occidental world."[27]

In somewhat similar terms, yet signalling a lurking danger (possibly with German implications), Musurus-Ghikis Bey outlined his impressions of pan-Islam:

> Pan-Islam, which appears to trouble the sleep of publicists in London and Paris and which miracle workers preach in the antichambers of Yildiz Palace, is of theoretical importance only, because it lacks sufficient material resources. It would pose a danger to the tranquility of British and French colonies only if, in response to motives that the supporters of changes in the present status quo will easily guess, the Sultan will place himself under the exclusive sway of a leading military monarchy whose ambitious political project he will serve.[28]

Islam South of the Sahara

The impact of European colonial expansion on Muslim societies and institutions was the subject of universal attention. In this respect, French contributors to the *enquête* revealed significant perceptions regarding the nature and prospects of Islam in Black Africa.

In his *L'Islam: impressions et études* (first published in 1896 and running into its seventh edition by 1928), Count Henry de Castries observed that "Islam was being studied by two categories of individuals: erudite Orientalists, and those who for lack of a better title could be called *les arabisants d'Algérie*."[29] Castries placed himself with the latter group, admitting that the Orientalists produced "infinitely superior scientific contributions compared to the *arabisants*, but that the latter nevertheless possessed a rightful claim to Islamic studies by virtue of their intensive daily contact with Muslims."[30]

For the *Questions diplomatiques et coloniales enquête* of 1901, Castries sent in a general response on the hotly debated topic of the diffusion of Islam in Black Africa and its alleged retreat before Christian missionary activity. Castries recognized that Islam had made powerful inroads in the

[27] *Ibid.*, p. 149.
[28] *Ibid.*
[29] Henry de Castries, *L'Islam: impressions et études* (Paris: Armand Colin, 1928), p. 7.
[30] *Ibid.*

interior of the continent, attributing its success to what he termed "its simple dogma...and complacent morality."[31]   Castries' observations find echoes in William Roome's articles, written from the vantage point of Protestant missions and published in the *Moslem World.*[32]

Of special significance was an additional dimension to Islam which Count Castries claimed was little-known as yet: the absence of racial prejudice. In contrast, this prejudice "was an enduring feature of the Christian missionary even when he gave the Black his most tender compassion and even when he proclaimed him to be his brother."[33]

Castries was then moved to consider what he felt was an important consequence of the European colonial expansion: "If Europe's domination had not expanded as rapidly in Africa as it had done in the last thirty years, profoundly modifying the situation of Muslims, it is almost certain that the whole continent would have turned Muslim, despite the efforts of Christian missionaries." He thought that, in the long run, the African convert to Christianity would rise above the African Muslim in the hierarchy of civilization and draw closer to the European, whereas Islam had the effect of distancing the African from the West. In conclusion he painted a most somber picture of the future of Islam in Africa: "Its faith will not be refined, its morality will not progress...and even after several centuries, its population will continue to live as dispersed tribes, incapable of both social and individual activity."[34]   Like many of his contemporaries, the Count was an articulate exponent of France's *mission civilisatrice.*

In a similar vein, René Basset, a leading expert in Berber and Ethiopian studies and a scholar-troubleshooter for his government in Africa, pondered over France's policy toward Islam. As director of the École superieure des lettres d'Alger and the successor of Masqueray, he appeared to be particularly concerned "to bring order and prosperity to a land dominated over the centuries by anarchy."[35]   Basset started by making a fundamental distinction between North Africa and the Sudan-Senegal region. In the former, France was faced with a *fait accompli*: the population was Muslim, "and voluntary conversions could not be counted upon...the time for inquisitions and *drag-*

---

[31] *Questions diplomatiques et coloniales*, 1 November 1901, p. 533.

[32] William Roome, "The Dead Weight of Islam in the Western and Eastern Sudan," and "The Dead Weight of Islam in Equatorial and Southern Africa," *The Moslem World*, 4 (1914), pp. 120–36, 273–90.

[33] *Questions diplomatiques et coloniales*, 1 November 1901, p. 533.

[34] *Ibid.*

[35] *Questions diplomatiques et coloniales*, 1 October 1901, p. 386.

onnades was past."[36] The *confréries* needed to be placed under surveillance, but they were not as dangerous as was generally believed. Instead, far more attention—in his opinion—ought to be devoted to the Ottoman press and its pan-Islamic message and to the pilgrimage scene in Mecca. The immediate task for France in North Africa was to "win over the masses through material prosperity and to work slowly on *l'esprit des classes élevés.*" Reforms should proceed gradually and Frenchmen should not be impatient about progress. However, in the Sudan-Senegal colonial domain, Basset proposed a determined effort "to stop the growth of Islam by supporting the action of Christian missionaries, particularly French ones; it was still possible," he argued, "to check Islam's progress, but in half a century it would be too late."[37]

The *Enquête sur l'avenir de l'Islam* also printed the testimony of Clément Huart, introduced to the readers as diplomat, Orientalist, man of letters, professor of Persian at the École des langues orientales and a leading authority on Bābism. Islam, as he saw it, was in a state of rapid expansion in China and Africa, where its prestige rested on the individual exertions of powerfully motivated believers.[38] In this respect he felt that the Sunnī branch was leading the movement of expansion and winning new adherents to the faith; in addition, the twentieth century would be marked by the triumph of Sunnī "orthodoxy over heterodoxy." As to the spread of Islam in England (Liverpool) and France (Pontarlier), he did not attach too much importance to the phenomenon, which he dismissed as *fantaisies individuelles.*[39]

The Arabisants School and the Problem of Old and New Elites

The French conquest and colonization of Algeria had profoundly altered the political organization, economic structure, and demographic balance of the country. Moreover, the Algerians had offered continuous and effective resistance, punctuated by armed rebellion, against the colonial intrusion. Uppermost in the official mind of the European administration (both military and civil) was therefore the identification of actual and potential "hostile" as opposed to "accommodationist" social groups in the Algerian colonial crucible, and by extension in Tunisia and eventually in Morocco. This was a

---

[36] *Ibid.*, p. 388.
[37] *Ibid.*, pp. 388–89.
[38] *Questions diplomatiques et coloniales*, 1 August 1901, p. 156.
[39] *Ibid.*, p. 157.

core item in the formulation of France's *politique musulmane* in North Africa, in which the Arabisants school participated fully. In fact, as pointed out by Jacques Berque, many soldiers and administrators adhered to the school.[40] A contemporary example of the literature is A. Le Chatelier's comprehensive study, "Politique musulmane."[41]

It is not surprising, therefore, to find in the *enquête* two young *arabisants* of the Algerian school, Edmond Doutté and William Marçais, taking positions on the perennial debate regarding the impact of French colonialism on traditional elites and the emergence of new and more acquiescent social groups. Writing from Fez, and displaying incredibly poor taste in the process by referring to this masterpiece of architecture as a "sad and gloomy town with its labyrinth of narrow and dark streets," Doutté formulated the following question: "What was the future of North African Islam in the presence of modifications caused by European civilization on the social state of Muslims."[42] His answer was perceptive. "Europe provoked the rapid diffusion of a relatively pure Muslim orthodoxy; people who were lax in their religious practices now observed stricter principles under our domination." This, he remarked, was due to two causes: "First, communications have generally improved and religious instruction has spread; second, it is a natural phenomenon that Islam when in contact with Christianity is accentuated and exalted."[43]

To Edmond Doutté old elites could not be trusted: "The educated Muslim has moved farthest away from us, whereas it was the native worker who fraternized with French colons." The task was to "favor the birth of a new Islam more inclined toward compromise and tolerance of Europe; to encourage the young '*ulamā*' inclined in this direction; to increase the number of mosques, *madrasas*, and Muslim universities and to staff them with adherents of the new theories."[44]

Doutté also addressed another dimension in France's *politique musulmane*: the possibility of creating a rival to the Ottoman Sultan under French sponsorship. On the eve of the formal takeover of Morocco, Doutte wrote:

---

[40] Jacques Berque, "Cent vingt-cinq ans de sociologie maghrebine," *Annales: économies, sociétés, civilisations*, 2 (1956), p. 302.

[41] A. Le Chatelier, "Politique musulmane," *Revue du monde musulman*, 12 (1910), pp. 1–165.

[42] *Questions diplomatiques et coloniales*, 1 October 1901, pp. 390–91.

[43] *Ibid.*, pp. 395–96.

[44] *Ibid.*

It is in Fez that the destiny of Algero-Moroccan Islam should be centered, for there, in fact, resides the Imam, the Sharif....The elaboration of a *politique musulmane* from Fez would imply the question of appropriate balance between the two great sovereigns of Islam, the Mongol of Istanbul, and the Arab of Marrakesh and Fez. It is known that the latter does not recognize the former's right of being the Imam of the Believers. The Imam, in actual fact, must be of Arab descent, and as Sharif, at least from the tribe of Quraysh. However, the Sultan of Istanbul is only a Turk, a Grand Turk it is true, but still a Turk. No one should therefore be surprised that we aspire to this policy; the task we are pursuing in Algeria and Tunisia gives us every right to do so.[45]

A decade before the *enquête*, A. Le Chatelier argued that in the urban regions of Algeria the task was "to create a new society that would no longer be Muslim and yet, without becoming French, would remain Algerian (la création d'une société nouvelle qui ne serait plus musulmane et, sans devenir française, resterait algérienne.)"[46]

This was also, in effect, the substance of the Morley-Minto reforms in India based on the existence of "a class of persons, Indian in blood and colour, but English in taste, in opinion, in morals, and intellect."[47] Clearly, in both cases new elites regarded as *évolués* and grouped in a nascent native bourgeoisie—the product of the colonial encounter—were counted upon to ease the task of the European intrusion. An influential newspaper, writing in 1908, argued that "the bourgeoisie in the process of formation in Algeria will usefully support French influence."[48] However, this entailed the isolation of Islam; contact through the press or pilgrimage was perceived as dangerous.

Oriented toward sociological analysis and leaning in the direction of secular solutions like Roberty, whom he cites, William Marçais saw France's hope residing in *"l'Islamisme nouveau"* or *"l'Islam moderne"* (Marçais used both terms)—essentially a French colonial creation in the Maghrib. It is important to note that this scholar of Algerian epigraphy was director of the *madrasa* of Tlemcen, founded by the colonial authorities to form Al-

---

[45] *Ibid.*, p. 398.

[46] Statement by A. Le Chatelier in 1888, quoted in Charles-Robert Ageron, *Les Algériens et la France 1871–1919* (Paris: Presses universitaires de France, 1968), II, 823–24.

[47] Quoted in Geoffrey Barraclough, *An Introduction to Contemporary History* (London: Penguin Books, 1967), p. 167.

[48] Ageron, *Les Algériens*, II, 824.

gerian *qāḍīs* along French "rationalist" lines.[49] Marçais' starting point, as he put it, was that "in the past 70 years, a new element has entered the economy of Islam in the Maghrib; a European power has established itself in the land."[50] The implications were not without significance. The ideas and habits of Western civilization exercised their most profound influence on urban elites in closest contact with "the daily life of the colonial victors." It was in those elites, particularly among the newly trained in French schools, that his hope for an appropriate transformation of Islamic society resided. Its adherents, in his view, were eager to harmonize the Qur'ān with modern science, and to espouse rationalism, a certain degree of relativism, and Mu'tazilite doctrines.

Marçais, however, did note the artificial nature of this new creation: "This elite. . . was not a natural and necessary growth from population strata which Roberty has spoken of. Rather, it saw the light under a foreign influence; there was not germination from within, but penetration from without. It must therefore be considered as an artificial entity, certainly not a spontaneous creation."[51] The scope and pace of its influence was therefore severely limited, and he did not think that anyone could in 1901 hazard a guess as to the balance sheet of modifications in the year 2000.

What is striking is that none of the Orientalists or Arabisants in the *enquête* raised the possibility that such elites might lead the process of decolonization.

In Defense of Islam

Among the eighteen printed responses, three were in defense of Islam: Muḥammad Ḥasan Sirjānī, Muḥammad Ben Raḥḥāl, and Edward Browne. Muḥammad Ḥasan Sirjānī, founder of several schools in Tehran specializing in the teaching of the French language, directed the Persian section of the Paris *Exposition.* He was granted the title of "Cheikh el-Molk" by the Shah. Described by the *Questions diplomatiques et coloniales* as a friend of France, Sirjānī sent in his observations which included a defense of Islam against "widespread European charges that it was opposed to science," and a statement to the effect that the differences between the Sunnīs and the Shī'a were

---

[49] William Marçais, *Musée de Tlemcen* (Paris: Leroux, 1906); *idem,* "Un Siècle de recherches sur le passé de l'Algérie musulmane," *Histoire et historiens de l'Algérie* (Paris: Librairie Félix Alcan, 1931), pp. 139–75.

[50] *Questions diplomatiques et coloniales*, 1 October 1901, p. 400.

[51] *Ibid.*, p. 403.

only minor. Moreover, "as brothers in Islam, they would succor each other when menaced by great dangers."[52] It may be interesting to note that in Paris Sirjānī contributed frequently to the Persian section of Ya'qūb Sānū's journal *Al-Tawaddud.*

Muḥammad Ben Raḥḥāl, an Algerian *caïd* of the Oran province, a member of the Société asiatique, and a participant in the Congrès des orientalistes, presented to the readers of the *Questions diplomatiques et coloniales* an impassioned defense not so much of Islam as his own existential situation. He dwelt on the qualities of justice, mercy, and tolerance in Islam, and on the strong bonds present in the Muslim family. He also underlined the absence of class struggle in Muslim society, the cooperation between capital and labor, and the social and economic harmony realized by the prohibition of interest. He felt that there was a revival in the world of Islam provoked to some extent by a common experience of reverses, a revival which Europe in its blindness sought to check by superior military might.[53] The Muslim possessed qualities of infinite resistance and patience. Muslim states were now divided but would rise once more with the help of education; the hostile behavior of Christendom would serve to unite them.[54]

In fact, wrote Ben Raḥḥāl, "hostility is the dominant note in Europe's sentiment toward Islam;. . .if the Muslim defends his home, religion, or nation, he is not seen as a patriot but as a savage; if he displays courage or heroism, he is called a fanatic; if after defeat he shows resignation, he is called a fatalist." In short, Islam is "ostracized, systematically denigrated, and ridiculed without ever being known."[55]

Ben Raḥḥāl thought that the resolution of this deeply ingrained hostility in the twentieth century would take the form of "either a catastrophe or peace." His final indictment of the colonial venture was noted, and disclaimed, by *Questions diplomatiques et coloniales*: "Dreaming to annex half a continent and to reduce the native—even by legal means—to misery is no policy, charging him with all kinds of crimes is no justification and no solution."[56]

Edward Browne, a leading authority in Persian studies, made a careful and critical survey which earned him the title of "islamophile" by *Questions diplomatiques et coloniales*. He reminded his readers of the Prophet's grand

---

[52] *Questions diplomatiques et coloniales*, 1 August 1901, pp. 157–59.

[53] *Questions diplomatiques et coloniales*, 1 November 1901, pp. 545–46.

[54] *Ibid.*, p. 547.

[55] *Ibid.*

[56] *Ibid.*, p. 550.

vision and work: "Muḥammad achieved the unification of the Arab tribes, he awakened in his people the spirit of patriotism...[and] conceived the grand idea of the solidarity and fraternity of all Believers."[57] Browne also defended Islam against the usual stereotypes prevailing in the West: intolerance and fatalism.

Going against the current trend of his contemporaries, Browne was critical of Europe's imperialism and jingoism (he used both terms). He was much more worried about his own society at the dawn of the twentieth century than he was about the future of Islam or of the Orient:

> To my mind, Asia is right to be wary of Western civilization, of the rapacity and materialism which are direct and necessary consequences of the blind attachment to the natural sciences....It is more the future of Europe than that of Asia which preoccupies me, which provokes my anxiety. How can one construct a pure and disinterested ethic on the basis of a theory which clearly declares that it is the strongest and the most rapacious that have the right to survive; a theory that lacks compassion for the weak. Such a theory can only lead to unending war between nations.[58]

Conclusion

Writing to his friend Gobineau in the decade following France's invasion of Algeria, Tocqueville confided that he had taken up the study of Islam because of his country's newly acquired colonial status.[59] Thereafter, Europe developed a marked interest in Islam concurrently with colonial expansion: the link between scholarly and political research on Islam and the imperatives of colonial policy remained strong. From Tocqueville to C. Snouck Hurgronje, to the *arabisants* of the Algerian school, manipulation was more important than scholarly detachment. Furthermore, and recalling Muḥammad Ben Raḥḥāl's sensitive cry, manipulation went hand in hand with hostility. Signs of resurgence or revival were therefore interpreted as dangerous, characterized as fanatical, and generally opposed by every means. This, in short, was one of the fundamental lines of continuity in the Western encounter with Islam in the nineteenth century. The world of Islam, like the rest of the Afro-Asian world, was not only the object of conquest, but of denigration.

---

[57] *Questions diplomatiques et coloniales*, 15 May 1901, p. 592.

[58] *Ibid.*, p. 594.

[59] Marwan Buheiry, "Tocqueville on Islam," *Al-Abhath*, 24 (1971), p. 104 [= p. 57 above].

Islam was perceived as a threat, and Carra de Vaux's dictum of "segmenting the Muslim world" was a reflection of the conventional wisdom of European policymakers. Yet, at the same time, the leading colonial powers made use of Islam in their rivalries and struggles, just as today superpowers attempt to mobilize Muslim sentiment against each other's interventions. This is often done in the name of the defense of Islam, as during the recent intervention in Afghanistan. However, one must note that when Israel conquered Jerusalem, one of Islam's holiest cities, the West did not object.

Part II

The Superpowers and the Arab World

8

External Interventions and Internal Wars in Lebanon: 1770-1982[*]

IT IS A FACT that in modern times Lebanon has experienced several instances of external interventions and internal wars which have helped to shape the course of its troubled history. This is as true of the post-1943 independence period as it was of the pre-independence period, perceived at the time by European interests and diplomacy in the context of the Eastern Question—i.e. the fate of a declining Ottoman Empire, its partition, and the eventual restructuring of strategic portions of it as mandates under the League of Nations after 1919.

It is also clear that this striking phenomenon, common to both periods in modern Lebanese history, has attracted attention but relatively little study. Today, of course, the interest is greater and more absorbing than ever before in the past because of the unprecedented scale of human losses, political fragmentation, and material destruction that threatens the foundations of the state and the very existence of the nation as a unified whole. Never has the Lebanese arena of conflict received so much attention from within and from without: from pen, gun, explosives, money, diplomacy, and TV camera.

The main objective of this study is to examine the historical record by isolating the many instances of external intervention and internal war, and to determine broad trends as well as the possible interplay between the external and internal dimensions. The period under consideration is roughly

[*]From *Lo Spettatore internazionale*, 19 (1984), pp. 56–60. © 1984 by the Istituto di affari internazionali. Reprinted courtesy of the Istituto di affari internazionali. An Arabic version of the study was also published as "Al-Tadākhulāt wa-l-ḥurūb al-ahlīya fī ta'rīkh Lubnān al-ḥadīth," *Al-Wāqi'*, 2.6–7 (1983), pp. 23–30.

1770 to the present. External intervention is defined here as overt military action by an external force involving one or more of the following: sustained naval and/or aerial bombardment, amphibious landing in battalion strength or more, and the crossing of borders in battalion strength or more. In this definition, covert operations as well as political, economic, or cultural interventions on their own (i.e., without overt military action) are excluded. This survey is intended as an interpretative essay of an exploratory nature rather than as a systematic study of the origins and consequences of such conflicts in the country's modern history.

Between 1770 and 1982 there have been eight instances of internal war and/or external intervention:

1. 1770–74: the Russo-Turkish War and the siege of Beirut.

2. 1831–41: the intervention of Muḥammad ʿAlī of Egypt and the counter-intervention of Britain and Austria.

3. 1858–61: the internal wars in Mount Lebanon and the French intervention.

4. 1912: the Italian bombardment of Beirut.

5. 1914–18: the First World War and the Allied intervention.

6. 1939–45: the Second World War and the Allied intervention.

7. 1958: the internal war in Lebanon and the American intervention under the Eisenhower Doctrine.

8. 1975 to the present: everything—a long list of local and foreign contenders, Lebanese, Palestinians, Syrians, and Israelis attracting the attention of the Arab Deterrent Force (ADF), numerous United Nations contingents (UNIFIL), and the Multinational Force (MNF); the countryside and the cities transformed into a shifting arena for internal, proxy, regional, and perhaps even global conflicts.

The first instance occurred in the context of the Russo-Turkish War of 1768–74 and the decisions of Ḍāhir al-ʿUmar of Palestine and the Mamlūk ʿAlī Bey of Egypt to seize the occasion to seek independence from the Sublime Porte with the help of the Russian fleet.[1] What is of direct concern

---

[1] Kamal Salibi, *The Modern History of Lebanon* (London: Weidenfeld and Nicolson, 1965), p. 15.

to us here is the Russian intervention along the Lebanese coast, which took the form of periodic bombardments of Beirut by the Eastern Mediterranean Squadron of the Tsarina Catherine II, culminating in the siege by land and sea of Beirut from 8 July 1773 until its final surrender on 10 October.[2] This intervention neither preceded nor followed an internal war. However, it did have an impact on the local scene, particularly in the struggle for power between the Amīr of Lebanon, Yūsuf Shihāb, and Aḥmad al-Jazzār, who was at the start of a tumultuous career that would lead him several years later into a successful defense of the city of Acre against Napoleon Bonaparte. There is evidence that Amīr Yūsuf persuaded the Russian squadron to eliminate al-Jazzār's fortified positions in Beirut.[3]

There is no need to dwell, in this article, on this curious episode. It was, to be sure, a novel incursion by the Russians into the eastern Mediterranean— a first in the annals of the Eastern Question, aimed at diverting attention from the principal military front in Europe by creating pressures on Turkey's exposed southern flank in the Middle East. And one might add on a light note that the occasion provided an entertaining exchange of correspondence between Catherine and Voltaire, with the French philosopher advising the Russian empress to include in her Eastern policy: 1) the restoration of Jews to Palestine ("rebâtir le Temple de Jérusalem et y rappeler tous les juifs"); 2) the extension of her dominion into Egypt, retaining the Mamlūk 'Alī Bey as her viceroy, and sending her Academy of Sciences of St. Petersburg there to study the archeological wealth of ancient Egypt; and 3) Voltaire deplored the fact that Lebanon's cedar trees were becoming extinct, implying a reforestation program.[4] Thus, Voltaire may be said to be a precursor of the Zionist project in Palestine, a precursor of Napoleon's scientific expedition to Egypt, and a precursor of the Plan Vert, a comprehensive plan for Lebanon's rural development, including reforestation, elaborated in the late 1950s.

The second instance, that of the intervention of Muḥammad 'Alī of Egypt into Lebanon and the region had, to be sure, a far greater and lasting impact. To begin with, it placed an intolerable pressure on the Amīr Bashīr II, caught between two irreconcilable opponents: on the one hand, Muḥammad 'Alī of

---

[2] R.C. Anderson, *Naval Wars in the Levant 1559–1853* (Liverpool: University Press, 1952), pp. 298, 302.

[3] Ḥaydar Aḥmad al-Shihābī, *Lubnān fī 'ahd al-umarā' al-shihābīyīn* (Beirut: Université libanaise, 1956), I, 95–101; Henri Lammens, *La Syrie* (Beirut: Imprimerie catholique, 1921), II, 110–14.

[4] *Documents of Catherine the Great*, edited by W.F. Reddaway (Cambridge: Cambridge University Press, 1931), pp. 59ff.

Egypt, an ally of France, and, on the other, the Ottoman sultan aided by a powerful Anglo-Austrian coalition. Britain perceived Muḥammad ʿAlī as an economic threat to its industrial and market interests and as a strategic threat both to the then-important Euphrates route to India and to the Red Sea route, while Austria saw him as a destroyer of the balance of power and as a revolutionary adventurer. Amīr Bashīr could not maintain his precarious balance on the tightrope indefinitely, and his amīrate did not survive the upheavals of one of the country's most decisive decades.

The intervention of Muḥammad ʿAlī also provoked serious communal cleavages and conflicts of interest, a major cause for the bitter internal wars of 1841 and 1844. In addition, it had led to a counter-intervention by British and Austrian naval and infantry units accompanied by a massive distribution of arms, especially at Jounieh, to foster a Lebanese popular insurrection against the Egyptians. One official British report of the period indicated the landing of 23,500 muskets in 1840, and it is known that Abū Samra Ghānīm, one of the principal popular leaders of the Maronite peasantry, received 4000 muskets for his men.[5] The traditional feudal leaders probably received even larger shares.[6]

This, very briefly, is the picture; and there are at least four lasting conclusions that may be drawn from the 1831 to 1841 experience of intervention and intercommunal conflict. The first is the internationally recognized importance of Lebanon in the regional balance—an importance which will be commented on later in the concluding remarks. And it is indeed relevant, in this connection, that a Prince Metternich stressed this dimension when referring to "ce petit pays qui est si important" in the 1840s.[7] Likewise, shortly thereafter, Friedrich Engels, in an article for the *New York Daily Tribune* written at the request of Karl Marx on the subject of Turkey and the Great Powers, declared that whenever the Eastern Question was raised, "the only portions taken into consideration were Palestine and the Christian valleys of the Lebanon."[8] When such symbols of the conservative and radical spirits of the mid-nineteenth century are in rare accord, it is significant.

---

[5]R. Byham's report of 22 March 1841 in Great Britain, Foreign Office, *Accounts and Papers*, XLV, 595; Toufic Touma, *Paysans et institutions féodales chez les druses et les maronites du Liban* (Beirut: Université libanaise, 1971), I, 188.

[6][The arming of the Lebanese peasantry was discussed in greater detail by Buheiry in a later study. See below, pp. 499–512.]

[7]Salibi, *Modern History of Lebanon*, p. 1.

[8]Article by Friedrich Engels in *New York Daily Tribune*, 7 April 1853, in S. Avineri, *Karl Marx on Colonialism and Modernization* (New York: Doubleday, 1968), p. 48.

A second consideration is related to the question of external intervention, which in this case, and this case alone, preceded the outbreak of internal war. The point here is the paradoxical nature of intervention: the paradox of a European power, Great Britain, the traditional protector of the Druzes, actually arming the Maronites against the Egyptians, who were being assisted by France, the traditional protector of the Maronites ever since the Crusades.[9] There are also paradoxes with reference to the Egyptian intervention, which experienced a reversal of alliances with the Maronites and the Druzes.

A third consideration is that intervention, in this particular instance, did provoke internal conflicts in Mount Lebanon and that the two phenomena are therefore linked, although a great deal of research has yet to be done to clarify the nature and dynamics of this linkage.

A fourth consideration is that intervention brought the various religious communities of Lebanon together, despite obvious conflicts of interest and deep-seated rivalries. In May 1840, Druze and Christian representatives from the districts of the Shūf and the Matn met in a Druze *khalwa* (a place of religious assembly and sanctuary) in Dayr al-Qamar to lay the foundations of a council of mutual defense.[10] About a week later, Christians, Druzes, and Muslims assembled at the Maronite Church of St. Elie in Antīlyās, near Beirut, and agreed to make plans for a common resistance against the Egyptians: they swore solemnly "not to betray each other and not to serve as accomplices for some against others."[11] Clearly these two events constitute crucial landmarks on the road to the National Pact of 1943, which in turn is the cornerstone in Lebanon's consensus edifice and one of the preconditions for any peaceful integration of this pluralist society.

The third instance of intervention, that of France under Napoleon III, is also linked—as in the second—to internal war, but the order is reversed. The French expeditionary force arrived in late 1860, at the end of a particularly bloody intercommunal war characterized by the worst excesses and by massacres on Mount Lebanon and in Damascus. Undoubtedly, this traumatic experience has left deep scars that are far from being healed; if anything, they have been rendered more virulent by the recent experiences of 1958 and more particularly of 1975 and after.

---

[9] Daad Bou Malhab Atallah, *Le Liban: guerre civile ou conflit international* (Beirut, 1980), p. 152.

[10] Asad Rustum, *Bashīr bayna l-sulṭān wa-l-ʿazīz* (Beirut: Université libanaise, 1957–66), I, 174.

[11] Touma, *Paysans et institutions féodales*, I, 170, 179.

Perhaps the paradox of the French intervention of 1860 is that its deep-seated causes are to be found as much in the economic situation in France at the time as in what was happening on Mount Lebanon and in Damascus. As demonstrated by Marcel Emerit, the silk industry in France was going through a severe supply crisis between 1853 and 1860 (especially in 1857), caused by a silkworm disease that devastated French production in the Rhone Valley and Languedoc and paralyzed the weavers.[12] This would perhaps explain why the French expeditionary force in Lebanon was so eager to engage in reconstruction work, with particular attention to the restoration of Lebanon's raw silk sector, which was controlled to an appreciable extent by French investments. The principal market for this valuable raw material was the Lyon region. Emerit described the reconstruction work as follows:

> The first priority of General Hautpoul was to put the Lebanese back to work. A committee of assistance was established, presided over by Fu'ād Pāshā. French officers were given the task of reconstructing houses, opening workshops, repairing looms, installing dye-houses, and hiring the necessary workers....France advanced the salaries. Reconstruction gave entire satisfaction to the French industrialists.[13]

Thus, reconstruction served the interests of both France and Lebanon.

The intervention hastened the process of political reorganization. Mount Lebanon emerged as an autonomous Ottoman province under the guarantee of the European signatory powers, a far-reaching step in the evolution of the country toward independence. One could also argue that despite the internal war of 1860, the principle of consensus politics did not disappear and was relocated in the elected Conseil administratif, representing the different religious communities. Thus, the pluralist model in Lebanon's development was enhanced and the country was better placed to take advantage of the expansion of trade, services, and communications effected by Europe's industrial revolution. The rapid growth of the city of Beirut as the leading center of political, economic, and intellectual activity dates from this period.[14]

The fourth, fifth, and sixth instances of intervention (1912, the First World War, and the Second World War) will be mentioned only in passing. None were linked with internal wars, and, in the case of the 1912 Italian

---

[12] Marcel Emerit, "La Crise syrienne et l'expansion économique française en 1860," *Revue historique*, 207 (1952), pp. 224–25.

[13] *Ibid.*, p. 226.

[14] [On the rise of Beirut, see below, pp. 535–57, 536–38.]

intervention, it took the form of a naval bombardment of Beirut without, however, any troop landings. As to the two world wars, Lebanon was simply caught up in cosmic events totally beyond its control.

The last two remaining examples of internal war and external intervention (that is, the seventh and eighth) occurred in the period of independence. The seventh instance, that of the American intervention during the Lebanese internal war of 1958 and following the military coup d'état which ended the monarchy of Iraq, provides a good study of the paradoxes of intervention. The stress in this article will not be on the Lebanese component of the story, but rather on the political behavior of the United States in its use of military power as a political instrument.

Why did the Americans intervene? Or, what was the primary motivation for the intervention? There are various explanations. For example, Malcolm Kerr has argued that the primary reason was to prevent a chain reaction that could have led to another Arab-Israeli war, whereas William Quandt, in contrast, has argued in Blechman and Kaplan's *Force Without War* that it was because President Eisenhower and Secretary of State Dulles wanted to deter Soviet expansion in the Middle East and to check the growing influence of Nasser in the Arab countries: in other words, that intervention was aimed primarily against communism and Nasserism.[15] A third explanation, that the Americans came in to save the presidency of Camille Chamoun is, of course, much less plausible. According to the then American ambassador in Lebanon, Robert McClintock,[16] who incidentally was opposed to intervention, the US made it clear as early as 9 May 1958 that troops would not be sent in to keep the President in office after the expiry of his term. And President Chamoun, in his book *Crise au Moyen-Orient*, did observe with some bitterness that "the friends of yesterday had become burdens to be gotten rid of."[17]

The explanations of Quandt and Kerr are in fact complementary. In the cold-war atmosphere of the fifties, the Atlantic Alliance was in constant fear of losing influence in this strategically and economically vital region. Hence the plans for the Middle East Command of British inspiration, the

---

[15] Malcolm Kerr, "The Lebanese Civil War," in *The International Regulation of Civil Wars*, edited by Evan Luard (London: Thames and Hudson, 1972), pp. 79–80; William Quandt, "Lebanon 1958 and Jordan 1970," in *Force Without War: The US Armed Forces as a Political Instrument*, edited by B. Blechman and S. Kaplan (Washington: Brookings Institution, 1979), p. 230.

[16] Quandt, "Lebanon 1958 and Jordan 1970," p. 229.

[17] Camille Chamoun, *Crise au Moyen Orient* (Paris: Gallimard, 1963), p. 11.

Baghdad Pact, and the Eisenhower Doctrine, which of all the Arab states only Lebanon had accepted. Another significant initiative included Anglo-American contingency planning in 1957 "for military intervention in Lebanon and Jordan in the event of an actual or imminent coup d'état in either country."[18] And there was always a role earmarked for Israel.

As it turned out, the American intervention did not take place in early May, when the Lebanese internal war erupted, but in mid-July, following the Iraqi revolution and in combination with a British intervention in Jordan. There were other paradoxes too. If the original motive was to stop Nasser, America's special envoy, Robert Murphy, in the wake of the intervention soon managed to strike a deal with Nasser. Whereas President Eisenhower in his 15 July address to the American nation implied that communism lay behind the internal war in Lebanon, his envoy on the spot quickly concluded that "communism had nothing to do with the crisis in Lebanon."[19] Whereas the US intervention was a concrete example of the application of the Eisenhower Doctrine, what happened in fact was that the United States proceeded to scrap the Doctrine after the intervention. Likewise, while Britain's intervention was intended not only to protect King Hussein, but also to serve as a nucleus for a push into Iraq if conditions permitted, the Americans on the other hand "had no intention of helping to restore British primacy in Iraq."[20]

For Lebanon, also, the intervention was not inconsequential, although in a different sense. It provided the impetus for a political resolution to the internal war. Further fighting seemed pointless, and attention was turned to the important task of finding a strong, unifying presidential candidate capable of attracting broad support. The principle of consensus politics was restored, perhaps even invigorated, by the promise of social reform, and the transition to the presidency of Fu'ād Shihāb was accomplished smoothly and constitutionally.

As to the eighth and hopefully last instance of internal war and intervention, one obvious observation is in order. None of the participants could predict that it would last so long, take the course that it did, cost so much in human and material terms, and lead to such unexpected results.

---

[18] Quandt, "Lebanon 1958 and Jordan 1970," p. 228.
[19] *Ibid.*, p. 236.
[20] William B. Quandt, "The Western Alliance in the Middle East: Problems for US Foreign Policy," in *The Middle East and the Western Alliance*, edited by Steven L. Spiegal (London: Allen and Unwin, 1982), p. 10.

The Lebanese were not fully conscious of the fragility of their political system at a crucial conjuncture during which social change provoked by rapid modernization and asymmetrical development became intertwined with other factors, such as the armed presence of the Palestinian revolution and the demographic explosion of the urban underprivileged.

The Palestinians never expected that they would be so inextricably caught in the contradictions of a Lebanese reality they scarcely understood. They did not imagine they would be pushed beyond the Litani by an Israeli invasion in 1978, and by a repeat invasion in 1982 that pushed them to Khaldeh and then out of Beirut.

The Arab League, the much-heralded guardian of the pan-Arab ideal and of collective security, never thought how paralyzed and ineffective it could become on an issue of such crucial importance.

The Syrians never imagined the complexity of their role, the ambiguities involved, the reversal of alliances, the difficulty of constructing a policy in an ever-shifting context of conflicting and converging interests, nor the level of internal resistance they eventually encountered, particularly from the Lebanese Forces.

The Israelis could hardly have envisaged the extent of damage caused to their own internal order by their massive intervention in Lebanon—that is, the damage to self-image and reputation in the wake of their destruction of Beirut and of the massacres of Ṣabra and Shaṭīla.[21] The fabric of Israeli society and the precarious harmony between Ashkenazim and Sephardim were severely strained. Nor did they ever dream that the protest movement would involve the highest ranks of their professional military elites as well as their reservists. Nor could they have foreseen how questionable was the myth of their being a strategic ally or asset to the United States in the Middle East.

Concluding Remarks

1. Taking the eight cases of internal war and/or external intervention, whereas there have been cases of external intervention without internal wars (Russia in 1770, Italy in 1912, the Allies in the First World War and the Second World War), there is no instance of internal war without external intervention. In all four cases (1840, 1860, 1958, 1975) the two phenomena are closely linked, constituting perhaps a "law" of Lebanese history. A fur-

---

[21] Jacobo Timerman, *The Longest War* (New York: Vintage Books, 1982), p. 138.

ther observation is also clear: it is not possible to estimate the length and intensity of the crisis, who will intervene, and how the resolution will take place. The parallel with the Spanish Civil War is striking.

2. The importance of Lebanon may be summed up as follows: in strategic terms, as a crossroads and bridge (an accident of immutable geography); in political terms, because of the age-old links with Christian Rome and Paris, on the one hand, and with the Arab and Muslim interior, on the other; also, since independence, because of its membership in the Arab League, its position in the regional balance and, potentially at least, the weight of its emigrants. Socially, and as a product of human will, Lebanon is important because it has chosen to develop as a refuge for various communities and to engage in a social experiment of pluralism that might yet merit the attention of the world, while culturally it remains deeply rooted in the regional environment and is not an external implant or artificial creation.

But this pluralistic composition, however exciting and original it may be, has also provided a fertile ground for the patron-client game in international relations, with all the major components of the Lebanese body politic possessing or believing that they possessed one or more traditional sponsors, giving rise therefore to a sense of pride and fulfillment matched by a real sense of inadequacy in those without equivalent sponsorship. This pluralism explains, in part, the relative ease and frequency of internal wars, external interventions, and the interplay between the two. In other words, what is being stressed is again a paradox: the importance of Lebanon in the great game of nations is due, in part, to its vulnerability as a pluralism where the forces of coalescence are in precarious balance with the forces of dispersion and disintegration, vertically and horizontally, intra- and intercommunally.

3. On balance, it is clear that the pull of cohesion has been stronger than the push of dislocation, but it is also clear that the testing of this principle in 1958 and again in 1975—that is, twice in the short 35-year span of independence—is an unnecessary exercise.

4. One lesson from this experience of internal wars is that no community should be faced with the choice between total mobilization for war and total surrender. For example, the choice that lay before the Maronites in February and March of 1976 and before the Druzes in 1982 must not be repeated for any community. There is no room for zero-sum situations in the politics of pluralism.

The territorial imperative is profoundly ingrained in the consciousness of the various Lebanese religious communities. Finding ways of reducing the negative effects of this atavism—an indispensable measure in the promotion of integration—has not been seriously undertaken to date, neither by the state nor by any of the traditional institutions of the various communities, and there are, of course, no easy answers.

5. Despite the eight-year nightmare of internal wars and external interventions, there is scope for a guarded optimism. And there are one or two bright spots even. One is the extraordinary economic resilience of the Lebanese and their resolve not to sink into moral or political despair. More profound perhaps (and constituting the greatest potential gain and qualitative difference in behavior) is the heightening of consciousness that the old attitudes of indifference or complacency toward the state and the army are suicidal, and that there is no substitute for a strong and just state in the task of constructing a modern integrated nation capable of meeting the arduous challenges of the years ahead: a state that would also have to be sensitive to the issues of economic deprivation and of political freedom in an atmosphere of internal conflict and foreign occupation.

Finally, the Western community of nations, after an irresponsible and damaging eclipse, had shown a rare resolve to help Lebanon's internal and external security and economic recovery—a return to the spirit of the Tripartite Declaration of 1950. The multinational force (MNF) comprising elite contingents from the USA, Italy, France, and the United Kingdom was an effective symbol of such resolve and was a positive contribution to the complex art of peacekeeping combined with the protection and advancement of strategic interests. It was also an expression of Italy's enhanced role in the eastern Mediterranean.

The MNF in the Sinai and then in Lebanon also serve as a "workshop" for a more coherent cooperation of Americans and West Europeans in the crucible of Middle Eastern realities. The danger is that they may be drawn into confrontationist postures with the Soviet Union.[22]

---

[22]Marwan Buheiry, "The Atlantic Alliance and the Middle East in the Early 1950s and Today: Retrospect and Prospect," in *Palestine and the Gulf*, edited by Rashid Khalidi and Camille Mansour (Beirut: Institute for Palestine Studies, 1982), p. 158 [= p. 245 below.].

9

The Israel-South Africa Alliance and the Third World*

IN SEPTEMBER 1976, the United Nations Special Committee Against Apartheid published its *Report on the Relations Between Israel and South Africa*, which helped to focus more world attention on a unique and long-standing relationship with grave implications to the well-being of Third World nations. At the same time, the character of this link and the parallelism between the two states raised important moral questions that trouble many sympathizers of Israel and South Africa in the Western world.

The intimate connection betwen Zionism, Israel, South Africa, and imperialism is indeed a long one; in broad terms it has gone through three phases. Beginning with the late 1890s it involved Theodor Herzl, Cecil Rhodes, and Joseph Chamberlain, Britain's Colonial Secretary, and the quest for vast colonization schemes of Jewish settlement in the Arab world and Africa. The second phase (1917 to 1948), dominated by such figures as Chaim Weizmann, General Ian Smuts, Lord Balfour, and Lloyd George, was principally concerned with extracting a British promise for a Jewish national home in Palestine, consolidating Zionist presence during the Mandate period, and paving the way for recognition of a Zionist state. Following the establishment of Israel in 1948 the connection entered a third phase, characterized by

*From the original English text translated and published as "L'Alliance Israël-Afrique du Sud et le Tiers-Monde," *Revue d'études palestiniennes*, 13 (Autumn 1984), pp. 59–70. Parts of earlier versions of the text were translated and published as "Maʿānī l-taḥāluf bayna Junūb Ifrīqiya wa-Isrā'īl," *Qaḍāyā ʿarabīya*, 6.7 (November 1979), pp. 229–36; and "Al-ʿAlāqāt bayna Junūb Ifrīqiya wa-Isrā'īl," *Qaḍāyā ʿarabīya*, 8.3 (March 1981), pp. 43–49.

increased interdependence in the military, economic, geopolitical, psychological, and particularly in the nuclear and advanced technological fields.

Whereas the first two phases of the connection involved a triangular relationship combining the interests of the World Zionist Organization (WZO),
South Africa, and imperial Britain, the third phase has taken the direction
of a bilateral symbiosis between South Africa and Israel. Nevertheless, the
third component of the triangle has not altogether disappeared; in fact, it
has been diversified and strengthened by additions from the European community of nations and the United States, which has aimed, since Vietnam,
at "the formation of special relationships with regional sub-imperial powers
so that military intervention could be delegated to junior partners."[1]

It is clear that this close association of interests, which today has grown
into an interdependence of the two colonial outposts (or regional sub-imperial
powers), presents a grave challenge to the Arab world and more generally
the Third World, as the following analysis will show. Soon after the UN
Security Council imposed an arms embargo on South Africa in November
1977, the Israeli ambassador to Johannesburg proclaimed that it was more
important than ever for Israel and South Africa to stick together in order to
confront the alliance of Africa and the Arab world.[2]

Herzl, Rhodes, and Chamberlain

Large-scale colonization projects in progress in South Africa during the last
decade of the nineteenth century involving mechanized mining, advanced
technology, and substantial investments fascinated Theodor Herzl. From
the evidence of his principal treatise, *Der Judenstaat*, written in 1895, and
of his utopian novel, *Altneuland*, it is clear that the South African experience

---

[1] Richard Falk, "Exporting Counter Revolution," *The Nation*, 9 June 1979, p. 659. See
also James H. Mittelman, "America's Investment in Apartheid," *The Nation*, 9 June 1979,
pp. 684–89.

[2] Perceptive critiques of the Israel-South Africa experience include George Jabbour,
Settler Colonialism in Southern Africa and the Middle East (Beirut: Palestine Liberation
Organization Research Center, 1970); George J. Tohmeh, *The Unholy Alliance: Israel and
South Africa* (New York: New World Press, 1973); Abdelkader Benabdallah, *L'Alliance
raciste israelo-sud-africaine* (Montreal: Éditions Canada, 1979); *Settler Regimes in Africa
and the Arab World: The Illusion of Endurance*, edited by Ibrahim Abu-Lughud and
Baha Abu-Laban (Wilmette: Medina University Press, 1974); *Israel and South Africa:
The Progression of a Relationship*, edited by Richard Stevens and Abdelwahab Elmessiri
(New York: New World Press, 1976); Kunirum Osia, *Israel, South Africa, and Black
Africa: A Study of the Primacy of the Politics of Expediency* (Washington: University
Press of America, 1981).

served as inspiration, model, and source of funds, the South African wing of the Zionist movement being, in relative terms, one of the wealthiest.

Following his official appointment as head of the Zionist movement at the Basle Congress of 1897, Herzl sought to link Zionism to the rising fortunes of Great Britain using the argument of Jewish colonization at strategic locations in the Near East and Africa in close support of Britain's imperial aims. England was to him the "Archimedean point" for the Zionist enterprise, and in this respect he suggested to Lord Rothschild the sponsorship of an extensive colonization blueprint in Sinai, Palestine, and Cyprus: "You may claim high credit from your government," he wrote in 1902 to the acknowledged leader of Britain's Jews, "if you strengthen British influence in the Near East by a substantial colonization of our people at the strategic point where Egyptian and Indo-Persian interests converge."[3]

In much the same vein Herzl also unfolded to the British Colonial Secretary, Joseph Chamberlain, a comprehensive Zionist colonization project backed by "a Jewish Eastern Company with £5 million sterling capital" for settlements in Cyprus and the Sinai (al-'Arīsh).[4] It is interesting to note in passing that one of the Zionist movement's foremost colonial experts was a South African Jewish engineer, Leopold Kessler, who was sent on a mission to the Sinai in 1903 to assess the al-'Arīsh project. Joseph Chamberlain was somewhat hesitant about Cyprus, more enthusiastic about al-'Arīsh, and finally offered his own "Uganda project" to Herzl, involving a Jewish colonial settlement in a prime agricultural region of the East African—actually Kenyan—colonial domain. The motivation for the offer was largely a consequence of events in South Africa. In the aftermath of a ruinous Boer War, which ended with the victory of the British over the Boers of South Africa, he wanted to attract additional Jewish investments to Africa, particularly in such sectors as mining, industry, real estate, and general postwar reconstruction. The Rand Territory in South Africa, famed for its fabulous wealth and investment opportunities, attracted many Jewish entrepreneurs who also served as principal figures of the rising South African Zionist movement. The Colonial Secretary felt that the Ugandan project would further consolidate Jewish presence in the African continent within, of course, a British imperialist framework; it is therefore not surprising that South African Zion-

---

[3] Richard P. Stevens, *Weizmann and Smuts: A Study in Zionist-South African Cooperation* (Beirut: Institute for Palestine Studies, 1975), p. 16.
[4] *Ibid.*, p. 17.

ists enthusiastically endorsed what Israel Zangwill called a "British-Jewish Crown Colony" in reference to the Ugandan project.[5]

Yet another noteworthy example of the "triangular" relationship is Theodor Herzl's admiration of Cecil Rhodes, the archetypal model of the successful colonizer whom he sought to emulate, especially in connection with the British South African Company. Despite strenuous efforts, a meeting with Rhodes could not be arranged, but Herzl's *Diaries* contain the text of a revealing memorandum addressed to Rhodes on 11 January 1902: "How do I happen to turn to you, seeing this is a matter so remote to you? How? Because it is colonial, and because it presupposes an understanding of a development that requires twenty to thirty years."[6] To the founding father of the movement, Zionism was indeed a colonial movement requiring the sponsorship of British imperialism. And as George Jabbour has shown in his study *Settler Colonialism in Southern Africa and the Middle East*, from the very beginning the Zionist project was perceived and executed in terms of settler colonialism.[7]

Weizmann and Smuts

The long personal friendship between General Ian Christian Smuts, principal architect of the South African state, and Chaim Weizmann, a leading Zionist figure and Israel's first president, was an important contributing factor in the gains achieved by the Zionist movement since the outbreak of the First World War. But this relation is also significant in other aspects. For, as Richard Stevens in his study *Weizmann and Smuts: A Study in Zionist-South African Cooperation* has cogently argued:

> It helps to put in perspective the contradictions of Western liberalism and the psychological climate which rationalized the dominant position of a white minority in South Africa and of a new European settlement in Palestine. It also underscores the crucial relationship between Zionism and South Africa, a relationship drawing its strength first from the Zionist character of the South African Jewish community with its privileged economic position;

[5]Israel Zangwill, *The Voice of Jerusalem* (New York: Macmillan, 1921), p. 254.

[6]Theodor Herzl, *The Complete Diaries of Theodor Herzl*, edited by Raphael Patai (New York: Herzl Press, 1960), III, 1193–94. The Memorandum of January 1902 was not sent. Cecil Rhodes died shortly thereafter in March 1902.

[7]Jabbour, *Settler Colonialism in Southern Africa and the Middle East*, pp. 28–29.

secondly, from the very nature of the South African economic-political system; and thirdly, from the imperial factor as it affected South Africa's domestic and international situation.[8]

It is remarkable that the same handful of leading politicians decided the political future of both South Africa and Palestine: Lord Milner, Lord Selbourne, Lord Balfour, Joseph Chamberlain, and General Smuts contributed to the birth of the South African Union of 1910 and to the Balfour Declaration of 1917. In both cases the idea was to place power in the hands of those who, to use the words of Balfour, "think like us."[9] An African majority was thus placed under a minority of white masters and an Arab majority was left to the tender mercies of an East European minority of settler-colons, the Zionist Organization, in Palestine. The rationale, a legitimizing of inequality, as spelled out by Balfour, was: "You cannot give the natives in South Africa equal rights with the whites without threatening the whole fabric of white civilization."[10] Or as Lord Curzon remarked to Balfour shortly after the publication of the Balfour Declaration in reference to the real aims of the Zionist Executive in Palestine: "He [Weizmann] contemplates a Jewish state, a Jewish nation, a subordinate population of Arabs ruled by Jews; the Jews in possession of the fat of the land and directing the administration."[11]

To be sure, General Smuts realized that Zionism was part and parcel of the imperial scheme, particularly in that crucial strategic area, the Palestine-Suez Canal axis, at the very crossroads of Africa and Asia. Furthermore, he appreciated, as Chamberlain had done, the vital economic role of Jews in South Africa and their strong commitment to Zionism and to the imperial ideal. Similarly, Chaim Weizmann, who had become a British subject in 1910, believed that the success of his movement depended on the link with British imperialism and, in return, viewed a Zionist Palestine as "a very great asset to the British Empire."[12] In this respect he adhered closely to Herzl's political vision. Writing to Balfour from Palestine in 1918, he drew attention to the intimate nature of this relationship: "I see that the welfare of Zionism is intimately linked up with the strength of British policy in the East, and I feel that London, Cairo, Jerusalem, and Delhi, are very

---

[8]Stevens, *Weizmann and Smuts*, ix.

[9]*Ibid.*, xi.

[10]*Ibid.*

[11]Quoted in Christopher Mayhew and Michael Adams, *Publish It Not: The Middle East Cover-Up* (London: Longman, 1975), pp. 144–45.

[12]Leonard Stein, *Weizmann and England* (London: W.H. Allen, 1964), p. 15.

intimately connected, and the weakness of a link in this important chain may have serious consequences."[13]

The outbreak of the First World War and the fateful participation of the Ottoman Empire on the German side provided Weizmann with the opportunity to lead the Zionist movement along Herzlian paths. In 1914 he suggested to a friend:

> We can reasonably say that should Palestine fall within the British sphere of influence and should Britain encourage a Jewish settlement there, as a British dependency, we could have in twenty to thirty years a million Jews out there, perhaps more. They would develop the country, bring back civilization to it and form a very effective guard for the Suez Canal.[14]

The simplistic arrogance of the civilization mission that rationalized all European expansion is also revealed elsewhere in his writings: in a paper entitled "The Position in Palestine" (1929), he viewed the Zionist enterprise as the fight between "progress and stagnation," between "civilization and the desert."[15]

Chaim Weizmann contributed to the wartime effort by placing his scientific skill at the disposal of the Ministry of Munitions; his discoveries in the production of acetone for high explosives were recognized as valuable. He was therefore well placed to build upon the contacts of his predecessor Herzl with the British ruling circles. Lord Balfour, Winston Churchill, Lord Selbourne, Lord Milner, General Smuts, and Lloyd George became the target of his interested friendship. And these, to be sure, played a prominent role in the formulation of the Balfour Declaration and the implementation of postwar imperial policy in the Near East.

Having secured a major political gain in the form of a Declaration, which, for all its ambiguity, recognized Zionist aspirations, Weizmann's next task was to extract the maximum advantage from its promises. This clearly meant, in practice, that the rights of the Palestinian Arabs would be trampled upon without any hesitation.

The first years of Zionist consolidation in Palestine with the active help of an imposed Mandate system coincided with the period of General Smuts'

---

[13] *Ibid.*, pp. 15–16.

[14] Chaim Weizmann, *Trial and Error: The Autobiography of Chaim Weizmann* (London: Hamilton, 1949), p. 191.

[15] Chaim Weizmann, "The Position in Palestine," *Palestine Papers*, no. 2 (London: Jewish Agency for Palestine, 1929-30), pp. 24–25.

first ministry, 1919–24. In South Africa the General pursued anti-African policies, which culminated in the Port Elizabeth and Bulhock massacres (1921) and the Native Affairs Act excluding Africans from Parliamentary life. At the same time, he sought the help of the powerful South African Jewish community while extending considerable support to the World Zionist Organization. Speaking in Johannesburg in November 1919, Smuts spelled out his view of the common bond between Boer culture in South Africa and Jewish tradition as he interpreted it. "I need not remind you," he said in his address to the South African Jewish Board of Deputies and the Zionist Federation, "that the white people of South Africa, and especially the older Dutch population, has been brought up almost entirely on Jewish traditions." And he added: "We are standing together on a common platform, the greatest spiritual platform the world has ever seen. On that platform I want us to build the future of South Africa."[16]

Thus for more than three decades (1917–50), whether in office or out, General Smuts supported the Zionist cause, using his considerable influence in the British corridors of power to further its fortune; and Weizmann could always count on a swift and effective response to urgent calls for help. This included, first and foremost, the Balfour Declaration, and was followed in 1920 by a joint Weizmann-Smuts attempt to extend the northern and eastern borders of the Palestine mandate in order to expand the potential for Jewish colonization to the Litani River in southern Lebanon, and beyond the River Jordan.[17] The South African Prime Minister actively defended the Zionist policy of large-scale immigration, which was being accomplished in total disregard of Arab views and apprehensions and of the country's absorption capacity; and he also sponsored fund-raising campaigns in South Africa with frequent personal appearances on platforms.

Smuts' political support was especially crucial in the wake of such revolutionary Palestinian reactions to the growing threat of the Zionist presence as the Jaffa Rebellion in 1921, the concerted actions on Zionist colonial settlements in 1929, and notably during the Palestinian National Revolt of 1936. Smuts' frequent high-level interventions to undermine the Palestinian Arab case and his successful attempts to thwart the initiation and implementation of an evenhanded Mandate policy were decisive in preserving Zionist gains, particularly in the sphere of immigration and land acquisi-

---

[16] Stevens, *Weizmann and Smuts*, p. 33.

[17] *Ibid.*, p. 34.

The Formation and Perception of the Modern Arab World

tions. Smuts worked closely with Weizmann to present Arab nationalism as a threat to Britain's imperial geopolitical position, and Zionism as a valuable prop.

During the Second World War and its immediate aftermath, a period with fateful consequences to Palestine, the South African leader assisted Zionist diplomacy to counter Arab influence in America, particularly during the San Francisco Conference, and to oppose some of the recommendations of the Anglo-American Committee of Inquiry on Palestine. He also placed the resources of the South African delegation to the United Nations at its disposal. Finally, he completed the work started with the Balfour Declaration by extending *de facto* recognition to the state of Israel on 24 May 1948, *de jure* recognition following two days later.

One of the most interesting manifestations of the triangular connection, Zionism-Britain-South Africa, is Weizmann's "Memorandum on Africa" addressed to Smuts in 1943: a remarkable postwar plan of development for the African continent that aimed, in effect, at reinforcing British and South African imperialism by economic means. In short, he was advocating a brand of neo-colonialism aimed at safeguarding their plunder of strategic raw materials. Weizmann's scheme, "based on the assumption," as he put it, "that Africa will probably become the backbone of the British Colonial Empire after this war," involved extensive utilization of carbohydrates for a new chemical industry to replace petroleum and coal. And, of course, a special place in the project was reserved for the Jewish National Home: it would serve as "the laboratory or the pilot-plant for the big factory into which the African Continent under this scheme might eventually develop."[18]

One must also recall the fact that many prominent South African Jewish figures, including Abba Eban, Arthur Lourie, and Major Comay, joined the ranks of Israel's ruling elite: all three assumed prominent positions in the diplomatic infrastructure of the newly founded Jewish state. South Africans played a prominent role in the formation of Israel's Air Force. It is also interesting to note that the El Al airline grew out of Universal Airways, a company started by the South African Zionist Federation.[19]

---

[18] *Ibid.*, pp. 124, 126–27.

[19] *Encyclopedia of Zionism and Israel*, edited by Raphael Patai (New York: Herzl Press, 1971), II, 1063; Antoine Bullier, "Les Relations entre l'Afrique du sud et Israel," *Revue française d'études politiques africaines*, November 1975, p. 60.

After 1948

The death of General Ian Smuts in 1950 brought to a close one of the many chapters of the South Africa-Israel connection. Nonetheless, the cooperation is more intense today than it ever was. Their everyday perceptions of each other, as reflected in the press and the media, their strong collaboration in the political, military, and economic fields, their updated versions of the "Weizmann Memorandum" (Israel as a "pilot-plant for the big factory" of South Africa), and frequent visits such as the April 1976 visit by South Africa's Prime Minister Vorster to Israel, are all eloquent reminders, as are their repeated violations of human rights. The Sharpville and Soweto repression, as well as the treatment accorded by the apartheid regime to such Black leaders as Steve Biko, find parallels in the equally brutal routine of Israeli repression in the West Bank and in Lebanon. The practice of torture is widespread, and political detainees are known to have died under both systems of detention. According to Alfred Moleah's "Violations of Palestinian Human Rights: South African Parallels:"

> Between August 1976 and September 1977, twenty political detainees are known to have died in security police custody; but this figure is probably low since some people known to have been detained have simply disappeared. In September 1977, the whole world was shocked by the death of the Black Consciousness leader Steve Biko, while in police custody. However, he was just one of many Black Consciousness leaders to meet such a cruel fate. And, while police brutality is particularly directed at political prisoners, it is also routinely applied to the Black population as a whole....[In the West Bank] Mr. Taysir al-Aruri, a physicist and member of the mathematics faculty at Bir Zeit University, was held in administrative detention from April 1974 to January 1978 without charges being filed against him. His detention was routinely renewed every six months....There are many reports of Israeli torture of Palestinian detainees and prisoners. The National Lawyers Guild delegation made a careful and detailed investigation of the charge and concluded that it was true....Other organizations, such as the highly regarded London *Sunday Times* Insight Team, the International Committee of the

Red Cross, Amnesty International and others, have also come to similar conclusions.[20]

This commonality of experience and perception is reflected in other dimensions. The organ of the National Party of South Africa, *Die Burgher*, put it succinctly on 29 May 1968:

> Israel and South Africa have a common lot. Both are engaged in a struggle for existence, and both are in constant clash with the decisive majorities in the United Nations;...it is in South Africa's interest that Israel is successful in containing her enemies, who are among South Africa's own enemies.[21]

While on a visit to South Africa, Amnon Kapeliouk, one of Israel's leading journalists, also noted the peculiar symmetry:

> Un Israélien en visite en Afrique du Sud est accueilli par des manifestations d'estime et d'admiration; les Afrikaaners (les Boers) voient en lui le symbole d'une minorité qui a toujours raison, ainsi qu'un allié dans la lutte contre les "rouges". Ici, on ne lui pose pas de questions embarrassantes sur les Palestiniens ou sur les territoires occupés. On s'intéresse plutôt à des problèmes "opérationnels". "Comment arrivez-vous à maintenir calmes plus d'un million de personnes?," demandait-on, paradoxalement, le jour même où l'agitation en Cisjordanie était à son comble. "Comment organisez-vous votre défense civile?"[22]

With such symmetry in experience and perception, it is therefore neither surprising to find the two isolated states actively in concert against national liberation movements, nor to note the magnitude of the association in the armaments industry and the nuclear field, which is far above what is officially revealed or recognized. This is of particular importance in the combat aircraft and naval industries: the Kfir fighter, the Reshef and Ramta ships, and the advanced Gabriel guided missile are the most recent vivid examples. But the cooperation extends to other weapons systems. South Africa and Israel

---

[20] Alfred T. Moleah, "Violations of Palestinian Human Rights: South African Parallels," *Journal of Palestine Studies*, 10.2 (Winter 1981), pp. 34–35.

[21] *Israel-South Africa: Cooperation of Imperialistic Outposts*, edited by *Dritte Welt Magazin* (Bonn: Progress Dritte Welt Verlag, 1976), p. 18.

[22] Amnon Kapeliouk's article in *Le Monde*, 25–26 April 1977.

have supplied tanks to each other at various times, and Israel regularly exports to the apartheid state light weapons, sophisticated electronic systems, and anti-guerrilla equipment, specifically designed to fight African liberation movements. Defense Minister Ariel Sharon visited in secret South African military bases along the Angolan-Namibian border in December 1981.[23]

In November 1977 *The Economist* (London) revealed that Kissinger in early 1975 had secretly asked the Israeli government to send troops to Angola to support the South African army in fighting the Popular Movement for the Liberation of Angola:

> The Israelis...sent South Africa some military instructors specializing in anti-guerilla warfare plus equipment designed for the same purpose. In return, the Israelis took Mr. Kissinger's request as the green light for an Israeli-South African partnership. In May 1976, South Africa's prime minister, John Vorster, arrived in Israel for an offical visit. He signed a row of economic and military collaboration agreements that centred on South Africa's willingness to finance some of Israel's costlier military projects. Israel was to reciprocate by supplying weapons systems and training.

The Economist then went on to analyze additional areas of close collaboration in advanced warships and tanks:

> South Africa, for its part, put up the money for the next generation of Israeli warships. Now under construction is a new version of the Reshef, larger than the current one, more like a miniature aircraft-carrier able to carry a helicopter....The highly advanced weapons aboard the boat will again include the Israeli Gabriel surface-to-surface missile. The new Reshef's range will be 6,000 to 7,000 sea miles, and it will have a crew of sixty....As a return on its investment, South Africa will cream off the first four or five new boats as they are produced in 1979–80.
>
> The two countries are also collaborating in armour development. In earlier years Israel had ransacked world markets in vain for the rare type of steel it wanted to sheath its Chariot [Merkeva] tank. Then, in 1976, along came Mr. Vorster and offered Israel

---

[23] Penny Johnson, "Israel and South Africa: The Nuclear Axis," in Israel Shahak, *Israel's Global Role: Weapons for Repression* (Belmont, Mass.: Association of Arab-American University Graduates, 1982), p. 50.

not only the steel it wanted, but also the most advanced technology in steel manufacture to enable Israel to renovate its old-fashioned steel industry. Israel in return undertook to modernize 150 South African Centurion tanks.[24]

Equally extensive is the scope and volume of economic cooperation and exchange: trade in diamonds, raw materials, and finished products, joint projects in energy and in the steel industry, the exchange of production techniques, investment and financing, and the mutual circumvention of embargoes and boycotts. This web of relations was neatly characterized by Itzhak Unna, Israeli ambassador to Pretoria in 1974: "With South Africa's abundance of raw materials and Israel's know-how, we can really go places."[25]

Yet another example of interdependance, one with sinister overtones and implications for the not-too-distant future, is in the nuclear field. South Africa is one of the world's principal producers of uranium and is known to possess an impressive nuclear weapons capability. Israel, for its part, contributes advanced laser technology and its application to the nuclear field (the work of physicists Isaiah Nebenzahl and Menahem Levin), a long experience in the chemical reprocessing of nuclear material as well as in the clandestine testing of nuclear devices and delivery systems. Many analysts believe that the September 1979 nuclear test in the southern Atlantic was a joint Israeli-South African undertaking (as revealed, for instance, by an Israeli radio correspondent, Dan Raviv, and by two journalists from *Haaretz*, Eli Teicher and Ami Dor-On).[26] Significantly, both states have refused to sign the nuclear non-proliferation treaty.

As to the close identity of their ideological perceptions and emotional ties, examples abound. Within the vast community of nations only two countries saw fit to celebrate Transkei's "independence": South Africa and Israel. On the evening of 28 October 1976, Israeli television viewers watched a special program on the new Transkei prepared by South African television, and many undoubtedly dreamt of "Transkeis" in the West Bank. In addition, news events in Africa are routinely described in Israeli mass media from the perspective of minority settler-colonial regimes. The Soweto protests were

---

[24] *The Economist*, 5 November 1977, p. 90.

[25] *Financial Mail*, June 1974, quoted in *Israel-South Africa: Cooperation of Imperialistic Outposts*, p. 49.

[26] Robert Pranger and Dale Tahtinen, *Nuclear Threat in the Middle East* (Washington: American Enterprise Institute, 1975), p. 13; Penny Johnson, "Israel and South Africa," pp. 49–50.

portrayed in the Vorster government's version as "criminal violence created by communist elements and outside agitators."[27]

The solution envisaged for Africans and Palestinians alike is permeated by what one might call "Bantustanism." To recall once more the testimony of Amnon Kapeliouk:

> Quand on demande à un Blanc comment organiser les relations avec la majorité, la réponse est simple: les Bantoustans. Les Noirs voteront pour le Parlement de ces États et continueront de travailler dans la République Sud-Africaine. L'Israélien de passage songe aussitôt au plan qu'élaborèrent naguère le général Dayan et M. Pérès. Les habitants arabes de la Cisjordanie devaient voter pour le Parlement jordanien tout en restant sous occupation israélienne.[28]

Samih Farsoun has argued that "the pivotal attribute of settler colonial regimes is their relationship to the indigenous population."[29] They are prone to establish what Van den Berghe has called a "*Herrenvolk* democracy:" a strict dualism where the colonizers rule themselves in accordance with normal democratic forms while denying them to the original inhabitant, the native. Political and economic exploitation is thus facilitated and often legalized.[30]

To conclude, in recalling the long-standing connection from Herzl and Rhodes, to Weizmann and Smuts, to Rabin and Vorster, and most importantly today, one ought not to lose sight of the basic impulses that have served to reinforce their community of interests in the political, military, economic, and colonial spheres. In the words of one analyst:

> Each took for granted the moral legitimacy of the other's position. Thus, not a word is to be found in Weizmann's correspondence or writings questioning either the racial basis of the South African state on which Zionism was so dependent or Smuts' role in upholding its racist system: the subordinate position of the African majority in South Africa posed no moral difficulty [for

---

[27] Benjamin Beit-Hallahmi, "South Africa and Israel's Strategy of Survival," *New Outlook*, April-May 1977, pp. 56–57.

[28] Amnon Kapeliouk in *Le Monde*, 25–26 April 1977.

[29] Samir Farsoun, "Settler Colonialism and Herrenvolk Democracy," in *Israel and South Africa*, p. 14.

[30] *Ibid.*

Weizmann]....Similarly, Smuts assumed without question "the right" of Jewish settlers to occupy Palestine without regard to the rights of the indigenous Palestinian Arabs. In both cases, Smuts and Weizmann epitomized the capacity of Western civilization to rationalize domination and exploitation, conquest and control....[31]

And it is abundantly clear that the increased isolation of the two states has reinforced such characteristics: to use the explosive statement of former South African Prime Minister Dr. Verwoerd, whose authority on the nature and function of apartheid is clearly manifest: "The Jews took Israel from the Arabs after the Arabs had lived there a thousand years. In that I agree with them; Israel, like South Africa is an apartheid state."[32] It is interesting to note that Verwoerd was eulogized by the Chief Rabbi of South Africa as "the first man to give apartheid a moral basis."[33]

Throughout the three phases, the implication to the Third World of this cooperation and interdependence has been particularly grave. In the broadest terms, one would begin with the general phenomenon of imperialism of the post-1880 era: a seamless web encompassing the globe with strategic constructs such as the Route to India and the Cape to Cairo Route. Today the emphasis is also on the direct policing of the Red Sea and the Indian Ocean. In addition, there was, and there still is, the economic plunder of the Third World and the enforced colonization of the land. Kessler of South Africa was Theodor Herzl's expert on colonization, with a specific mission to examine the Zionist al-'Arīsh project in Sinai in 1903. General Ian Smuts, the principal architect of the South African state, closely identified with Chaim Weizmann and the project to construct a Zionist state during the Mandate period. He exerted considerable influence in London to advance the cause of Zionist immigration and territorial gains and to neutralize the struggle of the Palestinian Arabs for independence and nationhood. Smuts also lent valuable support to Weizmann during the Second World War and at the San Francisco Conference. In more recent times one would also recall

---

[31] Stevens, *Weizmann and Smuts*, x.

[32] *Rand Daily Mail*, 23 November 1961; quoted in *Israel-South Africa: Cooperation of Imperialistic Outposts*, p. 12.

[33] Robert G. Weisbord, "The Dilemma of South African Jewry," *Journal of Modern African Studies*, 5 (1967), pp. 233–41; also *South Africa and Israel*, 2nd edition (Madison: Madison Area Committee on Southern Africa, 1971), p. 1.

the sponsorship by South Africans of *moshav* colonization projects such as the Neot Hakikar settlement.[34]

Today the interdependence has reached new heights both in conventional armaments and in the nuclear field. The implications are obvious and the challenge to the Arab and African worlds is clear. "Denying the humanity of the natives is the *sine qua non* of settler colonialism," wrote Alfred Moleah.[35] And the Bantustan syndrome dominates both apartheid and Zionism.

---

[34] *Jerusalem Post*, 18 December 1974, p. 3.
[35] Moleah, "Violations of Palestinian Human Rights," p. 15.

10

Alfred T. Mahan: Reflections on Sea Power and on the Middle East as a Strategic Concept*

IN A RECENTLY PUBLISHED ARTICLE entitled "Naval Competition and Security in East Asia," Admiral Kazutomi Uchida of the Japanese Navy paid tribute to the continuing importance of Alfred T. Mahan. "It is difficult," said Uchida, "to write on the subject of sea power without acknowledging the debt that we owe to such men as Alfred Thayer Mahan, who was the first to theorize about sea power, and Halford Mackinder, who reminded people of the importance of sea power by formulating his theory of power on land."[1] Such tributes abound in the literature on sea power, a phrase that Mahan is believed to have invented. Forty years ago, one of the leading American scholars on Mahan, Professor M.T. Sprout, wrote:

> No other single person has so directly and profoundly influenced the theory of sea power and naval strategy as Alfred Thayer Mahan. He precipitated and guided a long-pending revolution in American naval policy, provided a theoretical foundation for Britain's determination to remain the dominant sea power, and gave impetus to German naval development under Wilhelm II and Admiral Tirpitz. In one way or another his writings affected the

---

*From the original English text translated and published as "Alfred T. Mahan: afkār wa-ārā' ḥawla al-qūwa al-baḥrīya wa-l-Sharq al-Awsaṭ ka-mafhūm istrātījī," *Al-Fikr al-istrātījī al-'arabī*, 5 (October 1982), pp. 183–95.

[1] Admiral Kazutomi Uchida, "Naval Competition and Security in East Asia," in *Sea Power and Influence: Old Issues and New Challenges*, edited by Jonathan Alford (London: International Institute of Strategic Studies, 1980), p. 104.

character of naval thought in France, Italy, Russia, Japan, and lesser powers. He was a historian of distinction and, at the same time, a propagandist for the late nineteenth century revival of imperialism. By direct influence and through the political power of his friends, Theodore Roosevelt and Henry Cabot Lodge, he played a leading role in persuading the United States to pursue a larger destiny overseas during the opening years of the twentieth century.[2]

In considering the theory and practice of sea power, there are remarkable elements of continuity as well as change. This study of A.T. Mahan will seek to survey the following areas: the relation between sea power and national greatness, naval warfare and strategy, the contribution of Mahan to the "creation" of the Middle East as a strategic concept, and finally, the influence that Mahan exerted on the naval thinking of Germany, Britain, and France.

Mahan's theories and observations are not arranged systematically in one work, but are scattered throughout a dozen books and several dozen essays. And this presents a serious problem to the analyst. In addition, his work is both prescriptive (saying what nations and navies *should* do) and descriptive (examining, for instance, the pros and cons of a "lesser" use of the sea, such as in the case of *guerre de course* or commerce raiding, where the object is not to engage and destroy the opponent's main battle strength). It is also important to note that Mahan made a careful distinction between naval strategy, based on broad foundations and remaining to some extent immutable, and naval tactics, i.e., combat operations and the science of using weapons, which, because they have been manufactured by man, may change: for instance, with the development of new weaponry.[3] The solid reputation of Mahan is to a large extent founded upon the clear distinction he made between naval strategy and naval tactics.

Mahan's Life and Works

Admiral Alfred Thayer Mahan (1840–1914) was born at West Point, New York, into a military family; his father was a professor of military engineering at the United States Military Academy. Mahan chose a career in the Navy

---

[2] M.T. Sprout, "Mahan: Evangelist of Sea Power," in *Makers of Modern Strategy*, edited by E.M. Earle (Princeton: Princeton University Press, 1971), p. 415.

[3] Alfred T. Mahan, *The Influence of Sea Power Upon History, 1660–1783* (London: Sampson Low, 1890), pp. 8–10.

and eventually took up the position of lecturer in naval history and strategy at the Naval War College, becoming its president in 1885. The work for which he has become famous, *The Influence of Sea Power Upon History, 1660–1783* (published in 1890), was composed out of a conviction that sea power exerted a powerful influence on the destiny of nations, and that its historic significance, especially in terms of control of the sea, had generally been neglected by statesmen, academic historians, and military strategists. This first book in a trilogy was followed by two others: *The Influence of Sea Power Upon the French Revolution and Empire* (1892), and *The Life of Nelson* (1897), in which he examined the career of one of Britain's principal commanders. Other important writings include *Naval Administration and Warfare: Some General Principles* (1918), *Lessons of the War with Spain* (1918), and especially *The Interest of America in Sea Power: Present and Future* (1898). He also contributed dozens of articles in various journals and periodicals in which he constantly repeated his principal theses of naval history and strategy, and there is no doubt that his doctrines stimulated the interest in and growth of navies in the two decades preceding the First World War, particularly in Europe and America.

Mahan's importance is in the dimension of strategy rather than in tactics, in the perceptive analysis of the elements of sea power rather than in the details of sea battle. There is also an interesting paradox in this man of the sea. As one of his biographers, Robert Seager, put it:

> Mahan remains one of the few military figures in American history whose brain power was his main shield and buckler....He was an intellectual in uniform, and his busy pen was mightier than his sheathed sword. As a seagoing naval officer....Mahan was a disaster. He was an indifferent seaman. Indeed, he feared and hated the sea, its storms, its moods, its loneliness. But as a propagandist for sea power, especially as it was represented by the Navy in the years 1890 to 1914, he was a genius.[4]

Mahan epitomized the battleship and offensive naval concentration in an age of pre-1914 imperialism, made possible by the industrial revolution and the scramble for colonies. Through his writings and personal friendship with prominent decision-makers, "he helped to crystallize influential opinion favoring the outward thrust of American policy based on sea power, resting

---

[4] Quoted in Thomas Etzold, "Is Mahan Still Valid?," *Proceedings of the US Naval Institute*, August 1980, p. 43.

on coastal and island bases."[5] In one of his most influential articles, entitled "The United States Looking Outward," he developed economic and strategic arguments for American expansion in the world in protection of vital national interests and as a matter of necessity.[6]

The Middle East as a Strategic Concept

Before 1900, the terms "Orient" or "East" were generally used by the West to denote the vast expanse of territories in the Ottoman Empire, Persia, India, and beyond. However, in the 1890s, a certain differentiation began to appear in geographical and geopolitical usage both in the press and in official Western circles. The term Near East or Nearer East had crept into fairly common usage, and was given a degree of diffusion in the influential work of geography *The Nearer East*, published in 1902 by the English archeologist D.G. Hogarth. It is significant to note that Hogarth stressed the fact that "the Nearer East was a term of current fashion for a region which formerly was simply called the East." In this novel usage, Hogarth proceeded to include within its boundaries Albania, Montenegro, southern Serbia and Bulgaria, Greece, Egypt, the Arab provinces of the Ottoman Empire together with Anatolia, the entire Arabian peninsula, and the whole region between the Caspian Sea and the Indian Ocean.[7]

Likewise, it is of particular interest that in the same year in which Hogarth's definition appeared, a new term, soon to become associated much more with strategic and geopolitical dimensions, was also born. In fact, this new term, the Middle East, was an invention of Alfred Thayer Mahan, who first used it in an article he wrote in 1902 for the prestigious London periodical, the *National Review*. The article was entitled "The Persian Gulf and International Relations," and in it Mahan examined the traditional Anglo-Russian rivalry in Persia and Central Asia near the borders of India in the light of a new element to which he accorded much importance: the projected *Baghdadbahn*, the German Berlin-to-Baghdad railway with its terminus in the Kuwait region of the Gulf. What is noteworthy is that Mahan urged Anglo-German cooperation to check the Russian advance in this general

---

[5] *Selected Readings in American History*, edited by John A. De Novo (New York: Scribner, 1969), II, 179.

[6] Alfred T. Mahan, *The Interest of America in Sea Power: Present and Future* (London: Sampson Low, 1898), pp. 3–27.

[7] R. Davison "Where is the Middle East?," in *The Modern Middle East*, edited by R. Nolte (New York: Atherton, 1963), p. 16.

area, and he urged Britain to improve its strategic naval position by acquiring additional bases in the Gulf. It is in this context that he invented the term Middle East:

> The Middle East, if I may adopt a term which I have not seen, will some day need its Malta, as well as its Gibraltar....The British Navy should have the facility to concentrate in force, if the occasion arises, around Aden, India, and the Gulf.[8]

Mahan did not have in mind a definite geographical boundary for his term. He saw it much more as a shifting strategic concept than as immutable geography. For him, the Middle East "was an indeterminate area guarding a part of the sea route from Suez to Singapore" and a reference area where the major imperialist powers of Europe converged for global supremacy; in short, what the distinguished geopolitician Halford Mackinder referred to as the struggle between "rimland and heartland."[9] Mahan was in fact drawing attention to the Middle East and the Gulf as a permanent arena of strategic confrontation between rival powers as early as 1902.

But if Mahan was the inventor of the term and concept, the real propagator and propagandists were the London *Times*, which immediately appropriated Mahan's terminology and published a series of articles by its Foreign Editor, Valentine Chirol, on this all-important subject, with minor modification and emphasis. While acknowledging that Alfred Mahan invented the term Middle East as a strategic concept, Chirol defined it as encompassing "those regions in Asia which extend to the borders of India or command the approaches to India, and which are consequently bound up with the problems of Indian political as well as military defense."[10] Chirol also perceived the Middle Eastern question as the "outcome of that constant projection of European forces—moral, commercial, and military—into Asia which is slowly but steadily transforming all the conditions that enabled (Britain) to achieve...a position of unparallelled ascendency in the Asiatic continent."[11] The central problem as he saw it at the turn of the century was how to preserve this position of unrivalled hegemony acquired in the past through the Royal Navy's control of the seas, under new conditions in which land power, exemplified by Tsarist Russia's thrust in Central Asia, was growing at an

---

[8] *Ibid.*, p. 17.

[9] *Ibid.*

[10] Valentine Chirol, *The Middle Eastern Question or Some Political Problems of Indian Defence* (London: John Murray, 1903), p. 5.

[11] *Ibid.*

alarming rate.[12] In the succeeding decades, the Mahan-Chirol definition and strategic elaboration conditioned the thought and perhaps the planning of Anglo-American policy-makers and military commanders.

Sea Power and National Greatness

The first chapter of Mahan's *The Influence of Sea Power Upon History* is devoted to a discussion of the elements of sea power, which he sees as composed of six fundamental factors: "1) geographical position; 2) physical conformation; 3) extent of territory; 4) number of population; 5) national character; and 6) character and policy of governments."[13]

In his view the first factor could be seen best in the example of Britain with her insular position as compared with her traditional rivals, Holland and France: close enough to Europe yet far enough to be relatively safe from invasion. England could operate from a centrally located home base, concentrating her forces for any blockading or other duties, whereas France was forced by geography to divide her naval forces between the Atlantic and the Mediterranean.[14]

The second factor, physical conformation (or configuration) dealt with the nature of the national domain, which had an important determining influence on a people's inclination towards the sea. For instance, the great extent and fertility of French soil did not really force the French to look to the sea. On the other hand, the character of the English coastline made the people of that island drift naturally into dependence on the sea. In a profound sense a coastline is like a frontier (i.e., a nation can choose to defend it, or else it can serve as a starting point for further extension).[15]

The third factor, extent of territory, is closely linked to the fourth, number of population. And in this regard, a large territory may be a weakness rather than a strength, if it lacks a sufficiently numerous population and other resources. Mahan gave the example of the southern United States during the American Civil War of 1861–65 as an instance of an area with too much land and coastline in relation to its population. The same, for instance, would be applicable to most of the Arab world, which possesses extensive land areas and one of the lengthiest coastlines in the world with-

---

[12] *Ibid.*, p. 394.
[13] Mahan, *Influence of Sea Power*, 2–58.
[14] *Ibid.*, pp. 29–31.
[15] *Ibid.*, pp. 35–37.

out, however, the necessary backing (from the standpoint of sea power) of a large population.

The fifth factor, national character, is also an important dimension. It is a fact that some nations are trade-oriented and are drawn to the establishment of trading outposts and colonies. This means that in peacetime such a population builds and maintains a seagoing tradition: sailors, navigators, ships, and supplies. All this can be easily transformed to sea power in times of crisis or war. Added to this are the specialized technical skills that a sea-oriented people possess and nurture, which can be easily actualized into the many complicated tasks that warfare upon the sea demands. In short, Mahan argued that "the tendency to trade, involving of necessity the production of something to trade with, is the essential chacteristic most important to the development of sea power."[16] And closely associated with trade, in Mahan's view, was the planting of colonies, a field in which England excelled and which he hoped his own country would imitate.

The sixth and last factor, the character of government, was also of vital importance in any growth of sea power. In this respect, Mahan singled out the persistent effort of Britain's government to foster the national interest in seagoing matters, including the assertion of commercial, colonial, and naval supremacy. Strangely enough, in the case of England, Mahan attributed this determination to a single class—the landed aristocracy—whereas it is perhaps more correct to attribute it to the powerful middle class in England, which always showed a marked interest in trade and colonies. Mahan also believed that it was the duty of governments to persuade the population to turn their eyes to the sea, in peacetime as well as in times of war and crisis.[17]

Mahan and Naval Strategy

We have seen what in Mahan's view are the influential elements of sea power. Indeed, the proper utilization and actualization of sea power, he felt, influenced the destiny of nations. We now turn to another area of Mahan's concern: his study of naval warfare in order to derive some fundamental principles of naval strategy. In this regard, it is said that he was influenced by the thought of Antoine Henri Jomini, a Swiss military expert who rose to the rank of general in the French army and whose writings on warfare were appreciated by Napoleon Bonaparte.[18]

---

[16] *Ibid.*, pp. 53.
[17] *Ibid.*, p. 87.
[18] Sprout, "Mahan: Evangelist of Sea Power," p. 430.

To Mahan, position, lines, communications, and especially concentration were the components of successful strategy. A central position offered tremendous advantages in that it gave "interior lines, shorter lines, by which to attack." On the question of communications, he was certain that they represented "the most important single element in strategy, political or military."[19] Sea power depended on control over them. Equally fundamental was the *concentration of force*, which is facilitated by the availability of central positions.

Mahan's principal prescription was concentration and engagement. This to him was the central purpose of naval warfare: "the power of offensive action" aimed at preponderance over the adversary's naval forces, and the control of the sea. The power of offensive action was the only way to "break up the enemy's power on the sea, cutting off his communications with the rest of his possessions, drying up the sources of his wealth in his commerce, and making possible a closure of his ports...."[20] Such an objective could not be accomplished without concentration and power. This meant that the heavy "ships-of-the-line" in the days of sailing or the large battleships in his own days were the backbone of fleet strength and the indispensable instrument for the mastery of the sea.

Such mastery of the sea (through battleships) would ensure the proper use of sea lanes for moving men, materials, and weapons to the places where they are needed. The opponent, on the other hand, would be relegated to a "lesser use" of the sea, for instance, the *guerre de course* or commerce raiding that Mahan associated with French naval strategy and that he felt could not lead to decisive long-term results.

The German Navy

Mahan's writings had a powerful influence on decision-makers in Germany. With the fall of Bismarck and the end, so to speak, of Germany's exclusive focus on European affairs, Kaiser Wilhelm II's proclaimed goal of *Weltpolitik* could be realized. This involved turning Germany into a paramount *world* empire combining political, economic, and cultural interests backed by a powerful oceangoing navy: a dream shared by the Kaiser, his minister for foreign affairs Bülow, and above all by Admiral Alfred Tirpitz, whose task was to translate this dream into efficient reality.

---

[19] Alfred T. Mahan, *Naval Strategy Compared and Contrasted with the Principle and Practice of Military Operations on Land* (London: Sampson Low, 1911), pp. 31ff.

[20] Mahan, *Influence of Sea Power*, p. 288.

Tirpitz's plan in 1898 involved getting the Reichstag to vote the necessary funds for a long-term construction program instead of the usual annual credit appropriation. In this respect the naval program began to resemble, in its long-term commitment, the provisions of the army program. Another aspect of Tirpitz's program—one which echoed Mahan's own grand design— was the construction of a "battle fleet" composed of two squadrons of eight modern ships each designed for size, fire power, and for duty on the high seas. As Oron Hale described this initiative, "thus the decision in the German navy fell in favor of Admiral Mahan's theory of a large striking force that would bid for control of the seas rather than a navy concentrating on cruiser warfare, commerce destruction, and coastal defense."[21] Tirpitz's view was that this "battle fleet," without matching Britain's in terms of size, would nevertheless act as an effective deterrent, particularly because Britain's navy would normally be dispersed over the four corners of the globe. In short, with a battle fleet of two squadrons Germany could pick a suitable location where it could challenge Britain's control of the seas. This capability was further enhanced two years later, in 1900, when the projected size of the battle fleet was doubled to reach the figure of four squadrons of eight ships each. Britain's security in the Atlantic and in the North Sea was clearly in jeopardy.[22]

In addition to his theory of sea power (battleships to control the sea rather than cruisers to disrupt the enemy's commerce), Mahan was very influential as a propagandist. Wilhelm and Tirpitz had to sell the concept of sea power to the German people, who did not really possess a naval history or tradition. The Navy League (*Flotteverein*) waged a determined campaign to win hundreds of thousands of Germans into its association and to popularize the concept of naval power. Mahan's numerous writings were translated and disseminated: Ernst von Halle, one of the influential figures of the movement to popularize naval might, contributed a study entitled *Die Seemacht in der deutschen Geschichte* (1907), in which he applied Mahan's doctrines to the events of German history.[23] Of course the ideas of Mahan combining external trade, colonial possessions, bases, technology, and sea power found fertile ground in Germany. The Kaiser himself wrote to a friend in 1894: "I am just now not reading but devouring Captain Mahan's book, and am trying to learn it by heart. It is a first-class work and classical in

---

[21] Oron Hale, *The Great Illusion 1900–1914* (New York: Harper, 1971), p. 232.

[22] *Ibid.*, p. 234.

[23] Sprout, "Mahan: Evangelist of Sea Power," p. 442.

all points. It is on board all my ships and constantly quoted by my captains and officers."[24]

Britain's Naval Expansion Plan

From Mahan's exploration of the factors conditioning sea power, it is clear that Britain's supremacy was the product not only of material strength combined with the superior tactical knowledge of her Navy, but also of what Mahan saw as "the control of the narrow seas". Areas such as the English Channel, the Straits of Gibraltar, Bab al-Mandab in the Red Sea, or the Straits of Hormuz were characterized as outposts of naval power capable of controlling larger bodies of water, and were therefore seen as a precondition to the worldwide command of the oceans. During centuries of struggle Britain had specialized in this aspect of geopolitics, and enjoyed an important headstart over other seafaring nations.

Mahan also argued persuasively—and in an age when such arguments were likely to be endorsed by a Europe that had become the center of the world—that to maintain her dominant position as the principal sea power, Britain needed three factors: 1) a large volume of trade, 2) modern industry, 3) an extensive colonial domain spanning the entire globe. In short, Britain's success was explained by the fact that she had transformed "the principal sea routes of the world [into] the internal communications network of the British Empire."[25] Sea lanes were British highways. And it is therefore not surprising that Mahan's *The Influence of Sea Power Upon History*, as well as his other writings, were received with great enthusiasm in England. In other words, in the late eighties when imperialist rivalry was at its height among European nations competing for overseas markets, raw materials, and especially opportunities for capital investments, Mahan's book appeared at exactly the right time to explain, justify, and propagandize the complete dependence of Britain upon supreme command of the oceans, not only for her present condition of greatness, but also for her very survival.

In 1889, the British Parliament was presented with an ambitious naval expansion program based on the so-called two-power standard: i.e., a navy equal to any two other European nations. This was the occasion of lively debates. The British Army, for instance, tended to argue that Britain's protection could be better secured by fortifications along the entire coastline

---

[24] *Ibid.*
[25] *Ibid.*, p. 440.

of the British Isles. Mahan's book, with its timely appearance, provided ideal ammunition for the naval lobby and the general public, swinging this crucial debate to their side. Characterizing Mahan as "the single most important factor in making the whole British nation navy-minded," Professor M. Sprout has written:

> It is not difficult to understand the appeal of Mahan's ideas to the British people. He had perceived beneath the maze of events in English naval and political history the basic principles which had made Britain mistress of the seas, and he stated these principles in a form even laymen could understand. With an ancient tradition of sea power behind them, with a naval race already in progress, and a new era of imperialism in the making, it is no wonder that Englishmen at once eulogized his work.[26]

The influence of Mahan's ideas on England can also be seen in the fact that he was awarded honorary degrees by Oxford and Cambridge, and received as a guest of honor by the very exclusive Royal Navy Club—the first foreigner to be so. The London *Times*, usually very sober with its prose, said that he had done "for naval history what Copernicus had done for astronomy."[27] A British naval expert said that for the first time Britain "had a philosophy of sea power built upon history."[28]

Finally, it must be mentioned that Admiral Alfred Mahan personally contributed to the creation of what might be called the "Atlantic Feeling": the feeling that there is a common heritage between the British and the Americans that is not only linguistic, cultural, and political. To Mahan, Anglo-American cooperation was also dictated by the logic of geopolitics and strategy. In this respect Mahan is acknowledged as one of the precursors of the Atlantic Alliance, with particular reference to its Anglo-American core.[29]

The French Debate on the Guerre de Course

In addition to the influence he exerted on German and British naval developments, Mahan also was widely used in the heated debates of French

---

[26] *Ibid.*, p. 441.

[27] *Ibid.*

[28] *Ibid.*

[29] A.T. Mahan, "Possibilities of an Anglo-American Reunion," in Mahan, *The Interest of America in Sea Power*, p. 128. In this respect Mahan joined Andrew Carnegie and Sir George Clarke in advocating either a federative union or a naval alliance (p. 107).

naval strategists before the First World War. In the early 1880s an impressive school of naval thought, led by Admiral Théophile Aube, developed the strategy of *guerre de course* based to some extent on the experience of the French Navy in the wars of the eighteenth century, but which also took account of technological progress in naval weaponry and shipbuilding, specifically the torpedo and the high-speed torpedo boat, the forerunner of the modern destroyer.[30] This school, known as the Jeune école, argued from the premise that France could not afford to match the British Navy in terms of size and tonnage, and that any future war of revenge against Germany would be primarily a land affair. Hopes of an effective blockade of Germany were regarded as slim, nor was it realistic to plan landing operations in the face of a well-trained and numerous German army backed by excellent internal communications and Europe's finest railway system.[31]

From their basic premise that France was largely self-sufficient whereas England was not, the Jeune école's principal strategy rested on the disruption of the adversaries' shipping and lines of communication, causing panic and severe economic disruption. This involved a strategy of effective coastal defense combined with a modern version of the traditional *guerre de course* (commerce raiding) using technological advances in naval craft and armaments, such as the fast patrol boat, submarine, and the torpedo.

Of course, not all French strategists shared the *guerre de course* concept, and in their debates they made use of Mahan. In this respect, Theodore Ropp, who has studied French doctrines of sea power, has concluded:

> Mahan's insistence on battle and the importance of the organized force was a necessary corrective to the Jeune école's extravagant enthusiasm for the latest technical wrinkles and their hopes of gaining a cheap victory by attacking only non-military objectives....[32]

The big question is whether Mahan, the great proponent of sea power based on the battleship, is still relevant today in the age of air power, submarines, and nuclear missiles. The answer is, of course, complex. The sinking of the *Eilat* by a small Egyptian naval craft armed with ship-to-ship missiles is a good example of the vulnerability of big craft to small units. In

---

[30] Admiral Théophile Aube's most important work is his *A terre et à bord, notes d'un marin* (Paris: Berger-Levrault et Cie, 1884).

[31] T. Ropp, "Continental Doctrines of Sea Power," in *Makers of Modern Strategy*, pp. 447–49.

[32] *Ibid.*, p. 450.

the days of Mahan, only a battleship could sink another battleship. Today, it is possible for smaller countries to impose high costs in conflict with much larger states through the rational use of naval technology. However, it is also a fact that the six principles outlined by Mahan have a somewhat immutable quality to them.

11

Anthony Eden and the Arabs: The Failure of a Policy*

ANTHONY EDEN, Earl of Avon (1897–1977), was born into an ancient landowning aristocratic family in the year of Queen Victoria's diamond jubilee, the climax of Britain's imperial era. When he died 81 years later, Britain had not only lost her empire, but also her ranking as a superpower in a troubled world. In fact, Eden's political life spanned the years of his nation's precipitous decline from imperial apogee to post-Suez nadir. Not that Eden could be held personally responsible for all of it. Suez was surely a symptom rather than a cause for the end of the *Pax Britannica*.

Nonetheless, Anthony Eden was largely responsible for the construction of an Arab policy during the years of the Second World War that could be described as promising in some of its features. But it did founder on two basic crises: Palestine, for which he was only indirectly responsible because a Labor government was then in power; and Suez, for which there is no escape, because he was personally involved as Prime Minister.

In this study, the main emphasis will be on the examination of Eden's policy and personality. We will begin by presenting, in outline form, the major policy decisions of Eden regarding the Arab world during the Second World War, with special emphasis on the pan-Arab dimension and the Alexandria Protocol. We will then move to consider the complex problem of Eden's personality, relying in this respect on the recent studies of David Carlton, Donald Neff, and Chester Cooper. And we will end by examining Eden's political behavior during the Suez crisis.

---

*From the original English text translated and published in Arabic as "Anthony Eden wa-l-'arab," *Al-Mustaqbal al-'arabī*, 57 (November 1983), pp. 35–47.

Anthony Eden, Arab Unity, and the Elements of a Policy

On the eve of the Second World War, there was a consensus among the active and conscious Arab political class that the Mandate system of Britain and France should be ended by force if necessary, that various Arab states should become sovereign and independent members of the world community of nations, and that despite regional and personal rivalries, the powerful current toward unity should be reinforced. At the same time, there appeared to be a growing willingness to develop the mechanisms of common action in the pursuit of these objectives. The two pan-Arab conferences of 1937 and 1938, and the London Round Table Conference of 1939, were examples of this Arab collective phenomenon.

But Britain and France were not prepared to give up their privileged positions in these strategic zones, at the very intersection of their empires. And they entered the Second World War with an attitude of complacency toward the aspirations of the Arab people. Despite some warnings by such experts as Lord Lloyd, Winston Churchill preferred to overestimate Turkey's potential as an active ally and to favor the Zionists of Palestine over the Arabs, viewed either singly or as a collective.[1] Thus, the pro-Turkish bias appeared in a surprising suggestion by Britain to the French authorities in Syria in 1940 that some territories and airfields in northern Syria should be handed over to Turkey, a suggestion which Puaux, the French High Commissioner in Lebanon and Syria, rejected.[2]

It is of course clear that such attitudes and policies could not escape Arab notice for long, and they helped to provide Germany with the opportunity to score some successes in an Arab world that was somewhat clouded by the dangers and flux of the early years of the Second World War. In this respect, the German Declaration of October 1940 favoring the Arab struggle for independence, the activities of Otto von Hentig, which sought to establish contact with Arab nationalists, and, more importantly, the April 1941 coup of Rashīd ʿAlī al-Kaylānī in Iraq, were developments that threatened Britain's position and traditional interests in the Middle East. And the British counteroffensive came in the form of Anthony Eden's Mansion House declaration of 29 May 1941—a policy statement widely regarded as being of some importance:

---

[1]George Kirk, *The Middle East in the War* (Oxford: Oxford University Press, 1952), pp. 237–38.

[2]Stephen Longrigg, *Syria and Lebanon Under the French Mandate* (Oxford: Oxford University Press, 1958), p. 296.

This country has a long tradition of friendship with the Arabs, a friendship that has been proved by deeds, not words alone. We have countless well-wishers among them, as they have many friends here. Some days ago I said in the House of Commons that His Majesty's Government had great sympathy with Syrian aspirations for independence. I should like to repeat that now. But I would go further. The Arab world has made great strides since the settlement reached at the end of the last War, and many Arab thinkers desire for the Arab peoples a greater degree of unity than they now enjoy. In reaching out towards this unity they hope for our support. No such appeal from our friends should go unanswered. It seems to me both natural and right that the cultural and economic ties between the Arab countries, and the political ties too, should be strengthened. His Majesty's Government for their part will give their full support to any scheme that commands general approval.[3]

This statement of policy was greeted with satisfaction all over the Arab world, although, in the words of Elizabeth Monroe, "it was calculated more with reference to Iraq, where Nuri Pasha and others had long cherished a scheme for union with immediate neighbours, than to Egypt."[4] Nonetheless, the esteem for Britain was widespread. In November 1941, the newspaper *Filasṭīn* wrote: "Britain's stock now stood higher than ever before. She had given evidence of her good intentions to the Arab peoples."[5] Similar views were echoed by Fikrī Abāza in the newspaper *Al-Muṣawwar* (6 June 1941).[6] Equally, the impetus for Arab unity grew considerably, as evidenced, for instance, by Prime Minister Naḥḥās in his 13 November 1942 address to the Wafd Party on the subject of the bonds that bind the Egyptians to the Arab people. One ought to mention also the publication in 1941 in Beirut of 'Abdallāh al-'Alāylī's *Dustūr al-'arab al-qawmī*, which gave solid expression to the scope and dynamics of Arab unity,[7] and the publication in Baghdad in 1943 of Nuri al-Said's *Arab Independence and Unity*.[8] Shaykh

---

[3] Kirk, *The Middle East in the War*, p. 332.

[4] Elizabeth Monroe, *Britain's Moment in the Middle East* (London: Chatto and Windus, 1981), p. 92.

[5] Great Britain, Foreign Office, FO 371/45241, Research Department, 28 March 1947.

[6] 'Alī Muḥāfaẓa, "Al-Nash'a al-ta'rīkhīya li-l-Jāmi'a al-'Arabīya," in *Jāmi'at al-Duwal al-'Arabīya: al-wāqi' wa-l-ṭumūḥ* (Beirut: Center for Arab Unity Studies, 1983), p. 40.

[7] 'Abdallāh al-'Alāylī, *Dustūr al-'arab al-qawmī* (Beirut: Maktabat al-'irfān, 1941).

[8] Nuri al-Said, *Arab Independence and Unity* (Baghdad: Government Press, 1943).

Ḥāfiẓ Wahba, Saudi Arabia's representative in England, went as far as to urge Anthony Eden to plan an Arab federation in consultation with Arab governments as early as August 1941.[9] The stage was being set for more formal consultations between Arab states on the question of Arab unity, culminating in the Alexandria Protocol of 1944 and the founding of the Arab League, particularly after "Eden made his second public statement of support for Arab unity (February 1943) stressing, however, that the initiative must come from the Arabs themselves."[10]

A study of the foundation of the Arab League in 1944–45 and of the various Arab unity projects advanced at the time in Cairo, Baghdad, Damascus, and Amman is beyond the scope of this survey. Recent studies by Ahmad Gomaa and 'Alī Muḥāfaẓa have shed much light on the above.[11] We will concentrate, rather, on presenting four British official estimates made in late 1944 on the prospects for the Arab League in the wake of the Alexandria Protocol and the significance it might have for British interests and policies.

Writing to Anthony Eden in October 1944, Terence Shone, Britain's Minister in Cairo, was impressed by the fact that the Arabs, despite "divisions, jealousies, as well as the instability of the Arab states (which) may militate against effective implementation of the resolutions" of the League, had nevertheless created a suitable machinery to give "permanence and method" to Arab political, social, and economic cooperation. Shone felt relieved that the Arab states had avoided "impracticable ideas such as those of immediate administrative unions or federations."[12] And as regards the impact on Britain, he commented:

> The conference constitutes a step forward towards the political solidarity of the Egypto-Arab world against European encroachment. This political development will not only affect our position in the Arab countries proper but also in Egypt, which is on the verge of putting forward its claims for treaty revision, complete independence, etc. The terms of these resolutions accentuate the unity of attitude to be adopted by the States of the Egypto-Arab world towards States outside it, of which we are the principal one. We are regarded as having promoted this Arab unity movement,

---

[9]Ahmad Gomaa, *The Foundation of the League of Arab States* (London: Longman, 1977), p. 107.

[10]*Ibid.*, pp. 154–55.

[11]See notes 6 and 9 above.

[12]FO 371/39991, E6477/41/65, Shone to Eden, Cairo, 10 October 1944.

and the general feeling still is that we will welcome its fruition. It is not impossible that this solidarity of the Egypto-Arab world may be conciliated with our essential interests of communications and oil supplies, provided we are able to adapt ourselves to the new conditions quickly enough.[13]

Also writing to Eden, Britain's Resident Minister in the Middle East, Lord Moyne, who was generally regarded as being pro-Arab (he was assassinated by Zionist terrorists a month later), agreed with Shone that the setting up of "machinery to give the League concrete expression" was an important outcome. But he was also more eager to underline the positive aspects that he felt would favor Britain. The Arabs are "willing, and indeed anxious, to co-operate with Great Britain on a basis of independence and free association; they believe that this will be to the mutual advantage of both, since it gives the best guarantee on the one side of the security of the Arab countries, and on the other side of the maintenance of British imperial communications."[14] He warned of the growing prestige of the Soviet Union in the Middle East and of the "risk of the whole orientation of the Arab bloc of countries being changed to some other direction." In addition, he noted the orientation toward the future and the substantial contribution made by the League toward the international order:

The conference marks a considerable advance in constructive political thinking on the part of the Middle East States. The protocol looks to the future, not the past. The era of recriminations over such matters as the MacMahon Correspondence seems at last to be over. The delegates have shown in conversations that they are aware of having made a fresh start and that they look for a response in kind from His Majesty's Government. The general spirit in which the conference appears to have been conducted, and the lines of the protocol itself, show, moreover, that the States of the Middle East have not been slow to learn the new technique of international co-operation developed in war-time United Nations conferences such as those at Bretton Woods and Dumbarton Oaks. "Regionalism" is in the air, and it is noteworthy that it should be the newly-developed States of

---

[13] *Ibid.*

[14] FO 371/39991, E6697/41/65, Moyne to Eden, 19 October 1944.

the Middle East who have taken the lead in attempting to work
out a practical scheme of regional co-operation.[15]

A similar assessment was presented by the Political Intelligence Centre, Middle East (PIC). In a comprehensive report entitled "Notes on the
Meeting of the Preparatory Committee of the Arab Unity Conference in
Alexandria, 25 September–6 October 1944," PIC remarked: "On the whole
the Conference has been a success...a document drafted with considerable
skill and statesmanship has been produced," adding that, in the words of
a delegate, "while the rest of the world has been talking for a number of
years of regional councils and federation, the Arabs have been the first to
get down to work and produce a concrete plan."[16] On the thorny question
of Palestine, the report felt that the British government would not "object to the Palestine resolution, which in fact, though not explicitly, is a declaration in favour of the White Paper: the first time that the Arabs have ever
openly accepted a declared policy of HMG (His Majesty's Government) on
the subject of Palestine."[17] The conference was seen as a "notable triumph
for moderate Arab Nationalism" and as providing a distinct advantage for
Britain in the Middle East over other powers:

> If one reads the Protocol carefully, and if at the same time one
> takes into account the views and the outlook of the men who
> made it, it will be seen that the Protocol envisages that the
> Arab world should have one, and only one, orientation to the
> outside world: there is no room for two orientations, taking dif-
> ferent parts of the Arab world in different directions. Now in the
> existing circumstances this can only mean one thing: that the
> direction envisaged is one of co-operation with Great Britain to
> the exclusion of other Powers. Thus although the question of the
> French in the Levant is not mentioned, it is quite clear what the
> Protocol means; and no doubt the French will take this as one
> more piece of evidence of the British-inspired character of Arab
> nationalism.[18]

This brings us to our last example of British official reactions to the
Alexandria Protocol. Reporting to Anthony Eden from Baghdad, Sir Ki-
nahan Cornwallis provided a thought-provoking evaluation of the risks and

---

[15] *Ibid.*
[16] FO 371/39991, PIC/71.
[17] *Ibid.*
[18] *Ibid.*

opportunities offered by the newly established Arab League, especially over such questions as Palestine and the future prospects for Britain's strategic interests in the Middle East. To Cornwallis, the inclusion of a reference to the White Paper was motivated by a feeling that Britain stood by the side of the Arabs. As to the actual phrasing used, it was the result of a desire to find a formula that would be acceptable "to Jamal Husseini, who had actually, despite Amin Husseini's threats, initialled the White Paper (with trifling reservations), together with Musa al-Alami in Nuri Pasha's house in May 1940; it was therefore felt appropriate to make a reference to it (the White Paper)."[19]

Cornwallis did not minimize the significance of the acceptance of the White Paper by the Palestinians and of its endorsement by the Alexandria Protocol. It meant on the one hand that Britain had the "general support of the Arab world for the policy enshrined (in the Paper); but, that on the other hand, it meant equally that any serious divergence from that policy would confront HMG (His Majesty's Government) not only with the hostility of the Palestine Arabs, but with that of all the signatories to the Alexandria Protocol."[20] This issue, together with the British "guarantee of Syria and Lebanon" formed an "integral part of their (the Arabs') scheme for Arab Unity, a movement which (Britain) had undertaken to support." Thus any serious opposition by Britain would "lose the confidence and...friendship which has proved such an asset." And Cornwallis, after stressing that "Arab Unity must be considered first and foremost from the point of view of British interests," ended his evaluation to Eden by indicating the choice before Britain with respect to Arab unity in the aftermath of this momentous preparatory conference. "If we are ready," he wrote, "to support the plan fully and openly, and to respond to the invitation which has been given to us to act as the guide and mentor of the Arab world, then I see every reason to hope that Imperial interests in the Middle East will be maintained and safeguarded more surely than ever before, and that a period of stability and prosperity lies before us." But he also warned: "If, on the other hand, we are not able or willing to do so...we shall suffer in this part of the world a blow which will not only involve us and the Middle East in unrest, violence and confusion, but in the eyes of its inhabitants will abase our honour and prestige irreparably."[21]

---

[19] FO 371/39991, E7213/41, Cornwallis to Eden, Baghdad, 25 November 1944.
[20] *Ibid.*
[21] *Ibid.*

It is clear that the makers of Britain's Middle East policy appreciated the opportunities and risks presented by the Alexandria Protocol, a landmark on the road to Arab unity for which Britain was largely responsible. Yet as soon as the League of Arab States showed signs of independent behavior and the defense of Arab interests, Britain adopted an attitude of self-righteous indignation toward it and exacerbated the natural divisions contained within this body. In the long run, Britain's failure to build on the opportunities offered by the Arab League led to the catastrophe that Cornwallis had warned against, and to the loss of Britain's privileged position in the Middle East.

The Problem of Anthony Eden's Personality

It is a fact that before the Suez crisis the factor of Eden's complex personality was rarely invoked as a problem in the analysis of his political behavior. For example, Dennis Bardens, in a biography he published in 1955 before the Suez crisis, attempted to deal with "Eden the Man" in the final chapter. Bardens concluded that Eden was "one of the best-known yet least understood men in the world," that his "psychic make-up was so elusive," and that he was "given to flashes of temper, although overwork or emotional strain could have accounted for much of that."[22] In the aftermath of Suez, the personality problem of Eden became a favorite puzzle that delighted both biographers and the reading public. Speculation, some of it wild and based on very slim evidence, was of course stimulated by the tragic turn of events ending with Eden's defeat. There are four areas of attention: 1) the influence of Eden's parents; 2) his complex relation with Winston Churchill, a much resented father figure and capricious political patron; 3) the apparent antiappeasement stand of Eden and the determination to transfer this anti-Munich complex to the post-Second World War imperial scene in the Middle East; and 4) the factor of Eden's prolonged and painful illness and the drastic medication that may have impaired his judgment at crucial moments. These are seen by such analysts as David Carlton, Donald Neff, Kennett Love, Anthony Nutting, Mohamed Hassanein Heikal, and Chester Cooper as having influenced in various ways Eden's clashes with Acheson, Dulles, and Nasser.

In writing his recent biographical study of Anthony Eden, David Carlton made judicious use of the official papers of Eden covered by the Thirty-Year Rule of government archives (i.e., up to 1949 or 1950). But Eden's

---

[22]Dennis Bardens, *Portrait of a Statesman* (London: Muller, 1955), pp. 312–14.

private papers, presumably reserved for the authorized biography that is yet to be commissioned by the family, were not available to him. Other papers, including those of Chamberlain, Truman, Acheson, and Dulles were utilized, as was the important and revealing diary of Sir Evelyn Schuckburg, Eden's Principal Private Secretary in the early fifties, the period still blocked by the Thirty-Year Rule. However, Carlton does not appear to have had access to the private papers of Winston Churchill, presumably because they are being used by Churchill's biographer, Martin Gilbert; but Carlton is planning to publish an updated and expanded edition in 1987, when the Suez episode, as well as the crisis with Musaddeq, could be written from the opened British government archives. In the meantime, he recognizes that parts of the present biography "should therefore be seen as an interim verdict."[23]

From the standpoint of our study of Eden and the Arabs, the most relevant sections of Carlton's book include the complex relations with Winston Churchill (in many ways a resented father figure to Eden), the very difficult relations with Acheson and Dulles against a background of serious Anglo-American divergences over Iran and the Arab states, and, of course, the analysis of the Suez crisis, which contains new information gathered from American sources.

Carlton cautiously suggests that there is a flaw in Eden's personality that is perhaps traceable to his early childhood experience, although this is not fully explored. His father was an eccentric verging on the insane who was known for his violent temper and biting ridicule and who terrified his children and spared no one else. His mother, less eccentric but somewhat distant, does not appear to have given much protection to her children. In fact, Patrick Cosgrave, in a recent study of R.A. Butler, one of Eden's principal Conservative Party rivals for high office, records Butler as saying acidly: "Anthony's father was a mad baronet and his mother was a very beautiful woman. That is what Anthony is, half a mad baronet himself and half a beautiful woman."[24]

There were many personal tragedies in his life that affected him profoundly. He lost two brothers in the First World War and a beloved eldest son during the Second World War. Moreover, his first marriage ended in separation and divorce, and he was plagued by a long series of severe health

---

[23] David Carlton, *Anthony Eden: A Biography* (London: Allen Lane, 1981), p. 10. [Dr. Carlton (personal communication, 15 January 1988) advises the editor that this second edition of the book is now in course of preparation].

[24] John Rodgers, "Top Failure," *London Review of Books*, 3.17 (September 1981), p. 7.

problems necessitating powerful medication while in office and in retirement. This factor will be examined later and in relation to the Suez crisis.

Yet in another sense, Anthony Eden was the very image of success, moving effortlessly through Eton and Christ Church (Oxford University), where he studied for a degree in Oriental languages, Arabic and Turkish. He entered politics, winning a seat to Parliament in 1923, at the age of 26. He became a junior Minister in the Foreign Office at age 34, then a Foreign Secretary, a position that he was to hold on three occasions, first at the age of 40. Finally, in 1955, he realized his political dream of leading his nation as Prime Minister, succeeding Winston Churchill after long delays, and an incredible story of broken promises made by Churchill to step down in favor of his protégé, Eden. Another mark of his success was his composed, suave, and elegant manner: the very model of the "perfect diplomat" and the epitome of the carefully nurtured ruling Establishment, with all its mannerisms, tribal loyalties, and sense of mission.[25] He was also a man of courage, resigning from Chamberlain's cabinet in 1938 over the appeasement of Mussolini, although in this respect Carlton shows that Eden was not the consistent antiappeaser that was generally recognized, and he appears to have had a rather positive view of Hitler when he first met him. On the other hand, Carlton gives Eden credit for his role as peacemaker over Vietnam in the face of much American resentment. While still on the subject of appeasement and Munich, it is interesting to note that Carlton also casts doubt on Winston Churchill's much-advertised antiappeasement stand. It is by no means clear how far Churchill was willing to go in making concessions as a peace offer to Hitler, through the mediation of Mussolini, which possibly included the giving up of certain colonies and the recognition of Hitler's overlordship of Europe. In the event, Mussolini, who was about to enter the war, was not interested in mediation. But the episode does raise many questions. Would Hitler have accepted an offer that would have given him the opportunity to invade the Soviet Union? Perhaps Martin Gilbert will help to shed light on this matter, which may alter the traditional view of Winston Churchill as a determined opponent of all appeasement policies.

Until then, and as David Carlton suggests: "The role of both Eden and Churchill in connection with pre-war 'appeasement' will be increasingly critically scrutinized. For evidence is gradually emerging which modifies the simplistic picture of the two men as models of heroic consistency: distinctions

---

[25] Chester Cooper, *The Lion's Last Roar: Suez 1956* (New York: Harper and Row, 1978), p. 79.

between 'appeasers' and 'anti-appeasers' in the Conservative Party were less sharp than has been popularly supposed."[26]

Eden, the Americans, and the Road to Suez

With the Conservative victory of 1951, Eden was given the post of Foreign Secretary for the third time. As regards his stormy relations with the Americans, it is interesting to note that he had a showdown with Acheson over Iran as a sort of prelude to his graver showdown with Dulles and Eisenhower over the Suez fiasco. There were serious divergences with Acheson over Egypt even before the Free Officers' Revolution. Acheson's view was that Britain should accept Egypt's repudiation of the 1936 treaty; furthermore, the American Secretary of State "rejected the idea of a token American presence at Suez and regarded the Middle East Command (MEC) idea as a forlorn hope unless the British first restored full Egyptian sovereignty."[27] There was also opposition to Britain's repressive measures in the Canal Zone (particularly in Ismailia, where 43 Egyptians had been killed by British troops), culminating in the "Black Saturday" demonstrations in Cairo in 1952. On this occasion, Acheson told the British Ambassador: "The splutter of musketry apparently does not stop things as we had been told from time to time that it would."

As to the showdown over Iran, the full extent of Acheson's bitterness is revealed in the following excerpt from recollections taped in 1954:

> The Foreign Office view—that is, Eden's personal view—of things was that he, Anthony Eden, understood and knew the Persians ...he had gone to Persia as a private citizen and on a visit. And like so many people who have been briefly in a part of the world, his whole knowledge was colossal as a result of that one visit. He knew the Persians; he had been there, and in his view they were rug dealers and that's all they were. You should never give in; they would always come around and make a deal with you if you just stayed firm. As far as there being any danger that the Persian economy would go to pieces, it was always in pieces, and it couldn't be much worse than it was and it didn't make any difference. It was a matter of unimportance to anybody.

[26] Carlton, *Anthony Eden*, p. 481.
[27] *Ibid.*

Carlton's verdict is that "Eden's showdown with Washington might thus easily have come over Iran rather than Egypt." If so, he adds, "perhaps Acheson rather than Dulles would have been the villain of Eden's memoirs."[28]

As one might easily suspect, the Anglo-American rivalry over Iran had a strong smell of oil about it, with Acheson, at one stage, proposing financial aid coupled with an invitation to Musaddeq to visit Washington—an initiative bitterly opposed by Eden. In general, the American view was that the incompetence of the Anglo-Iranian Oil Company (AIOC) was matched by the political incompetence of the Foreign Office on Iranian Affairs, and that both factors acting in concert were driving the Iranians into the Soviet camp.

With the coming to power of Nasser, the stage was being set for Eden's final act in politics. Yet relations with Egypt were fairly cordial at first. And at one stage Churchill even raged against Eden, accusing him of appeasement toward Nasser by saying: "He (Churchill) never knew before that Munich was situated on the Nile," a remark that must have struck a sensitive chord. It is significant that Eden took a pro-Egyptian stance on the question of the Aswan Dam. In fact, according to American sources, Eden went as far as to threaten that if America did not join Britain in building the Aswan Dam, the British "would no longer restrict their trade" with the Soviet Union. Furthermore, in his famous Guildhall speech, Carlton believes that:

> Eden went much further than Dulles in urging Israel to disgorge territory. He favored a compromise between the armistice frontiers of 1949, which Israel desired, and the UN-recommended borders of 1947, which were more favorable to the Arabs. This plainly implied a larger loss of territory by the Israelis than the triangles in the southern Negev suggested by Dulles. Even Nasser praised Eden's initiative though he did not commit himself to accepting any particular solution. The Israelis, by contrast, were outraged and felt confirmed in their view that Eden was an extreme Arabist.[29]

If relations with Acheson were bad, those with Dulles were much worse. As Herman Finer pointed out in his study *Dulles Over Suez*, there was profound mutual aversion between the two leaders: "(Dulles) detested Eden and Eden detested Dulles."[30] Although ten years younger than Dulles, Eden

---

[28] *Ibid.*, pp. 316–17.

[29] *Ibid.*, p. 390.

[30] Herman Finer, *Dulles Over Suez* (London: Heineman, 1964), p. 83.

had "some historic successes to his credit, including his participation in the decisive policies made during World War II when Dulles was only a distant off-stage theorist." The American saw his British counterpart in the 1950s as a "world rival running the foreign policy of a country that was on the downgrade in world power."[31] It was now America's turn, and the English would have to know it. Besides, Eden had personally appealed to Eisenhower not to appoint Dulles as Secretary of State, an incredible initiative.

How does one fully explain the *volte-face* at Suez when a supposedly anti-Zionist Eden joined Israel and France in a concerted invasion of Egypt, the very country it was supposed to protect by treaty? We cannot be reasonably sure until the full record and the various private papers are open to investigation. However, and in the meantime, we would have to rely on the significant pieces of information that are revealed from time to time. For instance, both David Carlton and Donald Neff have made good use of newly available American sources. Carlton pointed to the serious breakdown in personal communications between Eden and Eisenhower, with the American President proceeding at the height of the Suez crisis to deal with three of Eden's Cabinet ministers without the knowledge of either Eden or the Foreign Office, an astonishing departure from accepted diplomatic practice. In this context, it is also interesting to note that the French government was much more eager to cooperate with Washington during the Suez fiasco than was America's traditional partner in the Atlantic Alliance, Britain.

But to return to the Suez crisis, which, in the words of Albert Hourani, "certainly made a deeper impact on the political consciousness of England than any event since the Second World War ended," there is general agreement that the British Cabinet's position was widely supported by the nation. In fact, to quote Hourani once more, "it is doubtful whether an attack on any other people in the world would have aroused so much enthusiasm in England as an attack on the Egyptians."[32] But in addition to this factor of popular appeal over a confrontation at Suez and the generation of jingoist sentiment, there was the powerful personality clash between Eden and Nasser against a backdrop of irreconcilable worldviews and conflicting strategic interests.

The two had met only once, and inauspiciously, in February 1955 at a dinner in the British Embassy in Cairo, which was, in the words of Mohamed Hassanein Heikal, "the symbol of colonial domination; the fate of Egypt was

---

[31] *Ibid.*

[32] Albert Hourani, "The Middle East and the Crisis of 1956," *St. Antony's Papers*, 4: Middle East Affairs, no. 1 (London: Chatto and Windus, 1958), pp. 9–10.

always made there and Nasser felt the humiliation of Egypt's subservience when he walked through its gates."[33] The meeting did not go well; Eden was annoyed at Nasser's persistent opposition to the Baghdad Pact and adopted, according to Heikal's account of the meeting, a haughty attitude with Nasser, giving him the deliberate impression that he was treating him as an inferior. A different account is given by Selwyn Lloyd, Eden's Foreign Secretary. "Eden told me," wrote Selwyn Lloyd, "that the (meeting) had been quite friendly but Nasser had annoyed him by suddenly holding hands as the photographer was about to photograph them."[34]

Eden mentioned this episode in his memoirs, *Full Circle*. The two paragraphs on the Cairo visit stressed Nasser's agreement with Britain's overall strategic appraisal, but also the Egyptian leader's determination to oppose the Baghdad Pact. There is also a reference to Eden's official report to London on the reasons for Nasser's opposition. "No doubt jealousy plays a part in this and a frustrated desire to lead the Arab World," is all that Eden seemed to offer by way of explanation.[35] Curiously, Eden ended his two paragraphs on the Cairo visit with the photograph episode: "As the flashlights went off, he (Nasser) seized my hand and held it."[36] What is the significance of this inclusion, without comment, in the memoirs? The matter is open to speculation.

In a classic statement on the inextricable confusion of personal and impersonal forces in moments of negotiations and crises, Harold Nicolson observed:

> Yet it must be realised that the texture of any international negotiation is formed of diverse strands, some stretching back into the remoter recesses of national tradition, some being derived from previous commitment, and some owing their presence within the fabric to personal antipathies, chance misunderstandings, and sudden improvisations. The structure of any international crisis is organic rather than artificial; it is the result of gradual growth; and however much one may seek to detach and mount the specimens for purposes of exposition, it must never be forgotten that at the time they were part of the thought, feeling, and action

[33] Mohamed Hassanein Heikal, *Nasser: The Cairo Documents* (London: Mentor Books, 1973), p. 73.

[34] Selwyn Lloyd, *Suez 1956* (London: Jonathan Cape, 1978), p. 27.

[35] Anthony Eden, *Full Circle* (London: Cassell, 1960), p. 221.

[36] *Ibid.*

of sentient beings, exposed to all the impulses and fallibility of human nature.[37]

How very true is this of Eden, Dulles-Eisenhower, and Nasser with respect to the Suez crisis.

On the question of tradition and the conventional wisdom of the British Establishment, Anthony Eden's stand in 1956 finds an important echo a decade earlier. During a House of Commons debate in May 1946, occasioned by the question of renegotiating the Anglo-Egyptian treaty of 1936, Eden revealed a toughness of attitude on treaty rights and strategic interests. He argued that on the question of Britain's strategic imperative in the Suez Canal, the treaty must be maintained, not altered. He compared Britain's position with that of Soviet rights to bases in Finland and to America's position over the Panama Canal. Eden was giving notice that on such questions as treaty rights and vital strategic interests, his country had equal status with the United States and the Soviet Union in the postwar world of Yalta.[38] Nor is the Munich dimension of lesser importance. Its frequent and intense intrusion in the memoirs is obsessive—or is it the justification for the Suez aggression? An interview conducted in 1970 by Jean Lacouture with Guy Mollet, the French Prime Minister who played such a crucial role in the Tripartite invasion of Egypt, underlines the importance of the Munich-transposed-on-the-Nile factor in Eden's life. Mollet told Lacouture:

> And make no mistake: this is the key to Eden's attitude, so inexplicable to many. Without this key, it is impossible to understand my colleague's decision. He had been courageously anti-Munich and wished to remain loyal to his past.[39]

The defiant decision of Nasser to exercise the sovereign rights of Egypt over its Canal, added to his firm opposition to the Baghdad Pact, were judged by Eden as being intolerable, and irritated the Prime Minister personally and profoundly.

The "personal" factor was aggravated by the failure of the Templar mission and the dismissal of Glubb in March 1956. Kennett Love's study places great emphasis on this incident, which "unhinged Eden's judgement: he jumped to the emotional and inaccurate conclusion that Nasser was behind

---

[37] Quoted in Finer, *Dulles Over Suez*, p. 87.

[38] House of Commons, *Debates*, 423, cols. 701–708, 24 May 1946.

[39] Jean Lacouture, *Nasser: A Biography*, translated by Daniel Hofstadter (New York: A. Knopff, 1973), p. 175.

all his troubles in the Middle East; he made a fateful decision that Nasser must be destroyed in order to restore Britain's international prestige and his own political leadership."[40] Anthony Nutting, at the time Minister of State for Foreign Affairs (and very close to Anthony Eden) is equally emphatic:

> As one who spent the evening and half the night after Glubb's dismissal arguing with Eden, I can testify that, at the time, he put all the blame on Nasser...and on that fatal day he decided that the world was not big enough to hold both him and Nasser....From now on Eden completely lost his touch.[41]

Furthermore, when Nutting tried to reason with Eden he was told: "I want [Nasser] destroyed, can't you understand? I want him removed, and if you and the Foreign Office don't agree, then you'd better come to the Cabinet and explain why." And when Nutting suggested the implications of such an action in the absence of a viable alternative to the Egyptian leader, Eden shouted back: "But I don't want an alternative; and I don't give a damn if there's anarchy and chaos in Egypt."[42]

Finally, the controversial question of Prime Minister Anthony Eden's physical illness, the consequence of an unsuccessful gallstone operation in 1953, must be raised. Anthony Nutting describes an episode, at the height of the Suez crisis, when Eden lost his temper and adds: "What I did not know was how much of this metamorphosis was due to sickness and to the poison from a damaged bile-duct, which was eating away at his whole system." Donald Neff, in a recent study of the Suez crisis, based largely on the Eisenhower papers, offers an even more damaging analysis of the impact of Eden's illness and drug intake:

> To control an incurable infection in the damaged duct, Eden thereafter had to take antibiotics. Stress and fatigue aggravated the duct, suddenly sending his temperature soaring and further debilitating his strength and mental faculties. He bolstered his waning energies by taking amphetamines, which in those days were not widely understood by physicians to have such potent psychedelic effects.[43]

---

[40] Kennett Love, *Suez: The Twice-Fought War* (London: Longman, 1970), p. 207.
[41] *Ibid.*, p. 213.
[42] *Ibid.*, p. 215.
[43] Donald Neff, *Warriors at Suez* (New York: Linden Press, 1981), p. 182.

The Suez crisis is most frequently portrayed as a classic Greek tragedy. What is equally tragic is the fact that in the Mansion House statement of 1941, in the support for the Alexandria Protocol of 1944, and in the Guildhall speech of 1955, Eden had shown that British policy could be in substantial harmony with at least some of the Arab world's aspirations. Yet all this was put in serious jeopardy by a combination of personality flaws aggravated by illness and the imperial mind-set—the inheritance of a whole generation of British ruling Establishment—with its traditional blind spots regarding the Arab world.

12

From Truman to Kissinger: American Policy-Making and the Middle East*

UNTIL THE SECOND WORLD WAR, American interest in the Middle East in general and the Arab world in particular was restricted to commercial exchanges and missionary activities in which education figured prominently. The strategic importance of the region, however, did not escape American notice. In 1902 a distinguished US naval strategist, Admiral Alfred Mahan, argued that the Middle East—both as strategic concept and reality on the southern periphery of the Mediterranean and of Asia—was necessarily the scene of strategic confrontation between rival powers.[1] In those days the rivalry was between Tsarist Russia and imperial Britain; today it is between the United States and the Soviet Union. Following the Balfour Declaration, which the United States supported, an additional factor of interest developed: the growth of the Zionist movement in Palestine, its national-political future, and the repercussions on the American domestic scene. Another interest which ran concurrently and with growing strategic importance was the oil dimension: the massive entrance of American oil companies into the Arab world, which gave them the opportunity "to eventually dispose of more than two thirds of the Arab oil entering world markets."[2]

---

*From the complete English text of the study abridged and translated into Arabic as "Min Truman ilā Kissinger" and published in *Al-Mustaqbal al-'arabī*, 29 (July 1981), pp. 73–85. The printed Arabic version does not contain the final section on Arab linkage strategy.

[1] Alfred T. Mahan, "The Persian Gulf in International Relations," *National Review* (London), 40 (September 1902–February 1903), pp. 27–45.

[2] Robert Stookey, *America and the Arab States: An Uneasy Encounter* (New York: J. Wiley, 1975), p. 76.

During the Second World War the strategic function of the Middle East assumed much greater importance in American eyes. The region proved to be a major center of land, sea, and air communications; moreover, its rich petroleum resources helped the Allies to carry on the war. After 1945, and as the Cold War and the "containment" of the Soviet Union became the dominant concern of US government and diplomacy, the strategic relevance of the Middle East climbed to new heights. Henceforth American strategists argued that Soviet presence or penetration in the region would outflank NATO and "bring a decisive shift in the world balance."[3] A second argument was that "Soviet control of Middle Eastern oil would disrupt the economy of the free world."[4] A third argument, heard less often than the former two, was that "the triumph of communism in the heart of the Islamic world could be the prelude to its triumph throughout Asia, Africa, and Europe."[5]

In this brief and necessarily selective survey of American policy-makers and policy-making as they relate to the Middle East, concentration is placed on the American perception of its overriding interest—security in the broadest sense. In dynamic terms, this involves denying as many strategic advantages as possible to rivals; but it also involves politico-economic expansion into new areas in the name of security (or in the name of the more dramatic and emotive term that is often used, survival). Thus security becomes a cover for the preservation of a superpower's political hegemony, and of its high-growth economic system based on utilization and control of ever-increasing quantities of raw material, energy resources, and markets.

The emphasis in this survey is not on the comprehensive picture, but rather on doctrines, pacts, and policy behavior under crisis conditions. Particular attention is devoted to Kissinger's policy vis-à-vis Arab linkage strategy and the oil embargo.

Policy-Making in Perspective

There are various ways of explaining decision-making in American foreign policy. One leading analyst, William Quandt, sees it in terms of "four distinctive, though often complementary, approaches:"[6]

---

[3] John Campbell, *Defense of the Middle East: Problems of American Policy* (New York: Harper, 1960), p. 4.

[4] *Ibid.*, p. 5.

[5] *Ibid.*

[6] William Quandt, *Decade of Decisions* (Berkeley: University of California Press, 1977), p. 3.

1. *The strategic or national-interest perspective*, which is probably the most commonly employed and stresses the global view.
2. *The domestic politics perspective*, which stresses the role of lobbies, Congress, and public opinion in formulating policies.
3. *The bureaucratic politics perspective*, which emphasizes the role of the Executive branch and the professionals in shaping and implementing policies.
4. *The Presidential leadership perspective*, which emphasizes the view that it is the President and his closest advisers who make high-level policy. This perspective tends to assume that foreign policy is the product not of abstract forces but of individuals.[7]

Thus the first perspective is really stressing that foreign policy is the "rational adaptation of means (resources) to ends (national interests)," the use of economic and military power to attain desirable goals. In this respect the Arab world is seen in terms of a global strategy dominated by superpower rivalry. Typically, American strategic analysis will emphasize the pattern of alliances, the nuclear balance, and control of vital resources. The Arab world and the Middle East in general are viewed as part of the American and West European global defense system against the Soviet Union. The doctrine of "containment" of the Soviet Union is held sacrosanct; détente tends to remain a tactical tool, despite the rhetoric.

The second perspective tends to look into the domestic realities of the United States: the lobbies' activities, Congressional behavior, election issues, and the mood of the public. As far as the Middle East is concerned, the activities of the various pro-Israel lobbies (particularly the American Israel Public Affairs Committee—AIPAC), the oil lobby, and the defense lobby have helped to shape policy at certain crucial moments. The pro-Israel lobbies, because of the "law of anticipated reaction," act as powerful constrainers on policy-makers. In other words, they do not always need to mobilize support in a confrontation with the White House: their mere presence and the nuisance value of their "anticipated reaction" is often as effective in the formulation and implementation of policy.[8]

The third perspective emphasizes the importance of the rivalries among the various bureaucracies controlling the vast field of foreign affairs: rivalries between the Department of State, the Pentagon, the CIA, and the National Security Council (NSC), with the White House often making political capital

---

[7] *Ibid.*, p. 4.
[8] *Ibid.*, p. 20.

out of these divergences. Classical examples of bureaucratic rivalries have been those between the State Department and the White House during, for instance, Truman's policy of recognition and support of Israel in 1948, and between the State Department and the NSC (more specially between William Rogers and Henry Kissinger) during the whole episode of the ill-fated Rogers Plan, as well as between Cyrus Vance and Zbigniew Brzezinski in the Carter years.

In this connection the crucial role of the NSC deserves careful study. During the short period that General George Marshall held the office of Secretary of State (1947–49) in the Truman administration, far-reaching changes occurred in the formulation and implementation of American foreign policy. As one analyst put it:

> Marshall himself played a major role in the development of new administrative devices to meet the challenge of the Cold War. In July 1947, the National Security Act became law, creating a new agency, the National Security Council, to coordinate military and foreign policy in the interest of national defense and security. Although that agency recognized the supremacy of the civilian authorities in the determination of foreign policy, it gave new importance to military factors. The Secretary of State was a member of the Council, but he was seemingly outflanked by the military departments, for the Secretaries of Defense, the Army, the Navy, and the Air Force were also members. Since Marshall himself was a soldier and since other soldiers held important diplomatic posts, it appeared to critics that the military had indeed captured control of foreign policy.[9]

Although the military content of the NSC eventually became less conspicuous, and despite the fact that the fortunes of the NSC have varied—with each President using it in different ways—in time it helped to displace the State Department as the fulcrum of decision-making. And while it is true that in the Johnson years the NSC lost some of its decisive attributes, with the Nixon-Kissinger tandem in the White House it not only regained its losses, but moved ahead to become the effective rival of the State Department. Today, the fundamental rivalry between the various bureaucracies concerned with foreign policy matters is as sharp as ever. Whether General Alexander Haig, who is in some ways reminiscent of General George

---

[9] Norman Graebner, *An Uncertain Tradition: American Secretaries of State in the Twentieth Century* (New York: McGraw-Hill, 1961), p. 160.

Marshall (with an additional faint touch of Kissinger) will be able to defend his perimeter against such consummate bureaucratic experts as Casper Weinberger and George Bush remains to be seen.

A major assumption is that the President plays a pivotal role in foreign policy matters, although there are sharp differences of opinion as to the definition of this role. But the question of the psychology of decision-making and the personality of the President remains central. This is how one analyst sees the problem:

> It is less the personality of the President that must be understood than the way he and his advisers view the world and how they reason. Policy-making is an intellectual process embedded in a social context. It is not merely an acting out of one's deepest fears, anxieties, and aspirations. Two points can be made to clarify the ambiguous link between personality and policymaking. First, individuals with remarkably different personal backgrounds are typically found supporting similar policies. In fact, it is rare that serious arguments over policy take place at high levels in government. The tendency is toward consensus and toward reinforcement of prevailing views....Second, the same individual, with no noteworthy alteration in his personality or his psychodynamics, may very well change position on given policy issues....The question to be asked is not whether policy decisions are rational or irrational, but rather what kind of calculation goes into them....On most issues of importance, policy-makers operate in an environment in which uncertainty and complexity are the dominant realities....The result is often a cautious style of decision-making that strives merely to make incremental changes in existing policies.[10]

In short, policy-making appears here as rational calculations by Presidents and their closest advisers acting in a given social context with well-established guidelines: a reinforcement of continuity and consensus. How then can change take place? And what is the importance of Presidential leadership in this connection? The key lies in the frequency and magnitude of crisis situations, for it is in such moments that a President becomes personally involved in management. Large crises often cause surprises, bring a sense of urgency into decision-making, expose the defects in older guidelines

---

[10]Quandt, *Decade of Decisions*, pp. 29–31.

and assumptions, and can, on occasion, produce change in both perspective and policy.

Because the Middle East is the region of the world where crises occur very frequently (usually provoked by superpower interplay and Israel), one would expect to read a story of *change* rather than of *continuity* in American policies. Yet, it is the latter trend that tends to dominate the dismal story. The question is why? The answer is because as soon as the crisis is managed or resolved, the old stable *conventional wisdom* reasserts itself, the new nuances perceived in the heat of the crisis regress, and the Administration tends to slide back into the traditional modes and premises, with minor cosmetic changes here and there when necessary.

Of course, the policy-making elite in the United States is far from being a monolithic block; any discussion of the conjunctures that lead to continuity or change must take account of the important dichotomy between the "Cold Warriors" school and the "Regionalists" school. As outlined by Malcolm Kerr in his recent study, *America's Middle East Policy: Kissinger, Carter and the Future:*

> The Cold Warriors school of thought is based on the idea of the balance of power, a conception with strong roots in the European diplomatic tradition from Machiavelli to Talleyrand to Bismarck to Churchill....Since 1945 in America it has focused on the Soviet Union as a strategic rival, and on the post-colonial Third World as a soft area of "power vacuums" that one of the two superpowers must inevitably fill, before the other one does, by cultivating local clients if not by inserting its own direct control....The opposing school of thought, which we shall term the Regionalist, does not deny the importance of the American-Soviet global rivalry, but denies that local issues around the world should be primarily approached in those terms; instead, the Regionalists insist, it should always be recognized that local problems have their own substance to be dealt with in their own terms, if the US is to hope for positive relationships with the local societies and their governments. Nor are these societies inevitably the exclusive clients of any great power: their outside attachments, including their orientation to Cold War issues between the superpowers, will depend significantly on who assist them in solving problems that they cannot solve alone.[11]

Leading Cold Warriors include Hans Morgenthau, Dean Acheson, John Foster Dulles, Henry Kissinger, John Connolly, Henry Jackson, Ronald Reagan, and Alexander Haig. The smaller, and far less influential, Regionalist school has included Dean Rusk, Adlai Stevenson, George Ball, J. William Fulbright, William Rogers, Cyrus Vance, and Jimmy Carter (at least at the outset of his administration).[12]

Some attention must also be paid to the "Arabist" presence in the State Department, which has been under constant attack by the powerful pro-Israel lobbies. "Arabists" tend to include career diplomats with long service in the Arab countries who believe that it is in the US national interest to improve relations with the Arab world by developing "even-handed" policies and correcting the persistent pro-Israel tilt. However, they are not a cohesive group and their ability to influence policy has not always been decisive, particularly when Israel is involved.[13]

The Truman Years and the Politics of the Cold War

It is after 1945 that the main lines of America's policy in the Near East were established by the administration of President Truman in the confrontationist Cold War atmosphere of the post-Second World War years. To a large extent they were inherited from imperial England or developed in response to domestic pressures—particularly in the case of Palestine. In addition, a cornerstone was the determination to "contain" the Soviet Union, which meant in effect a policy to keep it out of the Middle East and the Arab world. However, the main lines hardly took account of the hopes and fears of the Arabs—an observation that is corroborated by American analysts.[14]

In March 1947, Truman announced his Doctrine, which applied primarily for the defense of Greece and Turkey, but which soon expanded to cover

---

[11]Malcolm Kerr, *America's Middle East Policy: Kissinger, Carter and the Future* (Beirut: Institute for Palestine Studies, 1980), pp. 10–11.

[12]*Ibid.*

[13]Quandt, *Decade of Decisions*, pp. 25–26. Arabists, for instance, were strongly divided over the proper policy toward Nasser's Egypt. The Rogers Plan represents perhaps the apogee of their influence. Moreover, because of the dynamics of crisis situations, analyzed above, the chances of having their policy recommendations adopted tend to recede.

[14]See William Polk, *The United States and the Arab World*, 3rd edition (Cambridge, Mass.: Harvard University Press, 1975), p. 363.

other zones as well. It also signified the extension of the Marshall Plan to cover the Middle East. The implications of the Doctrine were clear: America would henceforth assume direct involvement not only in Western Europe, but also in the eastern Mediterranean and the Near East, aimed at providing military and economic assistance to nations and governments opposed to Soviet ideology and policies.[15]

The Truman Doctrine meant, in effect, the setting in place of joint defense pacts in the region. In many Arab states—Iraq, Jordan, and Egypt—Britain maintained a powerful influence bolstered by an extensive network of land, sea, and air bases centered on the Suez Canal base complex. It is out of considerations such as the Truman Doctrine and the continuing British presence that the concept of the Middle East Command (MEC) was born. The United States and Britain asked France and Turkey to join them as sponsors of the proposal, to which Egypt held the key by virtue of the Suez Canal position and its leadership of the Arab League. The idea was that if Egypt accepted the MEC, other Arab states would follow suit.[16] It is significant that the MEC proposals were presented to Egypt by the governments of the United States, Britain, France, and Turkey on 13 October 1951 (and rejected by Egypt two days later), while the principles underlying this controversial defense pact were published by NATO a month later.[17] At the same time, invitations to participate in the MEC were addressed to Australia, New Zealand, and South Africa. The principal points in the proposal required Egypt to furnish the MEC with "such strategic defence and other facilities on her soil as are indispensable for the organisation in peacetime of the defence of the Middle East...[and] undertake to grant forces of the Allied Middle East Command all necessary facilities and assistance in the event of war, imminent menace of war, or apprehended international emergency, including the use of Egyptian ports, airfields, and means of communications."[18] In return, Britain would abrogate the Anglo-Egyptian Treaty of 1936 and withdraw military forces not earmarked for the MEC.

It was clear to Arab opinion that the MEC was merely a device to perpetuate a somewhat disguised imperial domination of the region. The government of Naḥḥās Pāshā replied by abrogating, unilaterally, the Anglo-Egyptian Defence Treaty of 1936 and the Anglo-Egyptian Condominium of

---

[15] Arthur Link, *American Epoch* (New York: A. Knopf, 1965), p. 708.

[16] Campbell, *Defense of the Middle East*, p. 42.

[17] Stookey, *America and the Arab States*, p. 133.

[18] Text in *Documents on the Middle East*, edited by Ralph Magnus (Washington: Enterprise Institute, 1969), p. 76.

1899 over the Sudan. The evacuation of the Canal Zone was also demanded. Yet there was no let-up in US pressure, perhaps reflecting the principle of bureaucratic inertia. As William Polk put it: "Despite the Egyptian rejection and Soviet protests that the United States was trying to draw the Middle East into the 'aggressive Atlantic bloc,' the government tried to keep the project alive until the May 1953 visit of Secretary Dulles to the Middle East."[19]

President Truman made two other important initiatives—in addition to the Truman Doctrine and the particularly abortive proposal for the MEC—that related directly to the Middle East and had important consequences for the sovereignty and well-being of Arab countries: 1) support for the partition of Palestine and the establishment of the Zionist state; and 2) the Tripartite Declaration of May 1950.

Harry Truman's policy of supporting the Zionist program and his unconscionable neglect of Palestinian interests, and Arab interests generally, remains a classic example of how domestic political pressures, under certain circumstances, can directly influence the decision-making of a head of state. Hence, Truman played the leading role in the passage of the partition resolution by the General Assembly of the United Nations on 29 November 1947, and later recognized the Zionist state within ten minutes of its declaration.[20]

In explaining Truman's policy decisions, which conflicted sharply with the views of such senior members of his administration as Secretary of State George Marshall and Secretary of Defense James Forrestal, it is important to recall that 1948 was a presidential election year. Truman's chances appeared slim and his Republican opponent, Governor Thomas Dewey of New York, was making a determined effort to capture the Jewish vote concentrated in a few but vitally important urban areas, particularly in the State of New York. Despite urgent pleas by leading officials of his administration to keep controversial foreign policy issues out of narrow domestic and electioneering politics, Harry Truman, to win as many Jewish votes from his opponent as possible, took the advice of Clark Clifford and David Niles—his advisers on election strategy—and committed the United States to virtually unqualified support of Zionist consolidation and expansion: a position that was subse-

[19] Polk, *The United States and the Arab World*, p. 373.
[20] [Two pages containing the four preceding paragraphs were missing from the author's English text, and have been restored by retranslation from the published Arabic text and collation with a similar passage below (pp. 231–32).]

quently adhered to by succeeding Presidents, with the notable exception of President Dwight Eisenhower.[21]

As to the Tripartite Declaration on arms shipments to the region, which also affirmed "unalterable opposition to the use of force or threat of force between any of the states in that area," the three governments of the United States, Britain, and France aimed at preserving frontier and armistice lines drawn in Mandate times and redrawn in the aftermath of the first Arab-Zionist war. The principal beneficiary was, of course, Israel. Moreover, the Arabs correctly read the Tripartite Declaration as an infringement of their independence and sovereignty. The Arab League regarded it as a usurpation of its regional security function and as a device to maintain the old colonial dominance in new forms. Asserting that a rational policy of arms acquisition was a vital necessity for "the legitimate defense of their *neutrality*," the Arab League also rejected the paternalistic "right" of the three powers to decide the appropriate scale of armament of Arab states.[22] The irony of the Tripartite Declaration is that within six years, two of the guarantors of the sovereignty of Middle Eastern states (i.e., Britain and France) joined Israel in a tripartite aggression against Egypt.

The Eisenhower-Dulles Era: The Quest for Pacts

It is perhaps significant that the Middle East was not mentioned in President Eisenhower's inaugural speech in January 1953; the United States was concerned more about events in the Far East and, of course, in Europe. The new Secretary of State, John Foster Dulles, was "terrified of the spectre of international communism and it was that spectre which shaped most of his thought on the world situation."[23] His views on the Middle East were dominated by the Soviet threat, and he expressed both shock and dismay "to find that the responsible leaders in the Middle East did not see the world in his terms."[24]

Following Dulles' first tour of the Middle East in May 1953, it is possible to discern the following broad conclusions. Of all the states in the region, it was what he called the "Northern Tier" (Greece, Turkey, Iraq, and Pakistan) that shared his views about the Soviet menace and hence were qualified to be

---

[21] Stookey, *America and the Arab States*, p. 115.

[22] *Ibid.*, p. 133.

[23] William Polk, *The Elusive Peace: the Middle East in the Twentieth Century* (London: Croom Helm, 1979), p. 116.

[24] *Ibid.*

associated with the network of treaties established in Europe and Southeast Asia. Secondly, he concluded that most Arab leaders did not share his views regarding regional security. To them the real threats came from Israel and from Western imperialism. "Many Arab League countries," reported Dulles to the American public, "are so engrossed with their quarrels with Israel or with Great Britain or France that they pay little heed to the menace of Soviet communism."[25] It was obvious that they did not want to be linked with Western defensive arrangements, and that there was little point in pressuring or persuading them to do so. Instead, the concentration of effort ought to be in the direction of strengthening the "Northern Tier;" problems like Suez or Palestine would be given a low order of priority.[26] Creating an exact parallel to NATO in the Middle East was not feasible for the moment, but the United States could lay the foundation for extending the "Northern Tier" concept into the Baghdad Pact, thus completing the belt of defensive treaties—what Halford Hoskins would call "situations of strength"—from Europe to the Far East. The Soviet Union would be more firmly contained than ever.[27]

Originating as a Pact of Mutual Cooperation between Iraq and Turkey (signed in Baghdad on 24 February 1955) and subsequently acceded to by Britain, Pakistan, and Iran, the Baghdad Pact did not include the United States as a formal member. In practice, however, the United States was a full participant in the alliance: the communiqué issued at Bermuda by President Eisenhower and British Prime Minister Macmillan on 24 March 1957 affirmed the "willingness of the United States...to participate actively in the work of the Military Committee of the Baghdad Pact."[28] In this case the communiqué merely gave public recognition to a long-existing state of affairs: America's military and economic commitment to the pact was there from the very start.

As to Britain's leading position, it was best expressed by Anthony Eden's Foreign Secretary, Harold Macmillan, at the Conservative Party Conference in October 1955:

> In the Middle East, we have an area of vital importance to Great Britain. It is vital strategically because it is no good producing

---

[25] Text in *Department of State Bulletin*, XXVIII, 729 (15 June 1953), pp. 831–35.

[26] Campbell, *Defense of the Middle East*, pp. 49–50.

[27] See Halford Hoskins, *The Middle East: Problem Area in World Politics* (New York: Macmillan, 1954), particularly Chapter 14, "The Search for Situations of Strength."

[28] US Department of State, *United States Policy in the Middle East, September 1956– June 1957: Documents*: (Washington: Government Printing Office, 1957), p. 421.

stability in the wings if the centre gives. It is vital from an economic point of view because in an age when coal is getting harder and more expensive to win, and when atomic power cannot be developed on a great scale for many a long year, oil is a vital fuel and a vital means of power production for the world. We have in the Baghdad Pact perhaps the most important, anyway in embryo the most important, organisation other than NATO which we are now trying to build up. There lies the strength and protection of the other world. Already Turkey, Iraq, Pakistan and Britain are members of the Pact. We hope for other partners in due course....[29]

Iran adhered to the pact a month later. However, no Arab state decided to take advantage of the clause in the Turkish-Iraqi pact "inviting the accession of any member of the Arab League or any other state effectively interested in the peace and security of this region."[30]

In fact, the Western powers and Turkey had either totally misread Arab opinion or else were willing to proceed against it. The ill-fated decision of Nūrī al-Saʿīd's government to join the Baghdad Pact was an open challenge to the Arab League Collective Security Pact, and was countered by the determination to build an Arab alliance that excluded Iraq. Thus, Egypt, Syria, Saudi Arabia, and the Yemen joined in an effective alliance, while Lebanon declared it would follow a neutral course (and worked for the ending of Iraq's isolation). In the meantime, Britain's efforts at pressuring Jordan into adherence to the Baghdad Pact backfired: Prime Minister Samīr al-Rifāʿī's government declared Jordan's refusal to join the Pact on 8 January 1956, and King Hussein proceeded to purge Jordan's army of British officers, led by General John Glubb. The net result of the disastrous policy of Western-sponsored pact-making was the creation of a conflict of interest between the so-called Northern Tier states (including Iraq) and the bulk of the Arab states (or the southern tier of nations, as perceived by US strategic mappers). It also sharpened anti-Western feeling in the Arab world. Finally, it provided an opportunity for the Soviet Union to improve its position in parts of the Arab world. Thus, a policy that was designed to keep the Soviets out had the opposite effect.[31]

---

[29] Guy Hadley, *CENTO-The Forgotten Alliance* (Brighton: Institute for the Study of International Organisation, University of Sussex, 1971), p. 3.

[30] Campbell, *Defense of the Middle East*, p. 55.

[31] The intention is not to minimize the importance of the propensity in Arab decision-makers of the period and the rivalries that led to a bitter Arab cold war. However, one

A great deal has been written regarding the troubled relations between President Nasser and the Eisenhower administration following the arms deal with the Soviet Union, the American fiasco in the Aswan Dam affair, and the nationalization of the Suez Canal. Secretary of State Dulles never understood Arab nationalism, and viewed with profound hostility Arab determination to participate responsibly in the politics of positive neutralism and nonalignment aimed at opposing foreign domination and the pursuit by the superpowers of "spheres of influence" diplomacy.[32] Nonetheless, the positive stand adopted by the Eisenhower administration following the Tripartite aggression on Egypt in 1956 was a unique moment of wisdom and global statesmanship in the long and dreary annals of American policy decisions regarding the Arab-Israeli conflict.

On the other hand, the Eisenhower administration formulated the Eisenhower Doctrine, the striking feature of which, as one analyst has put it, "was that America's own national interest was deemed to justify American armed intervention in the Middle East at America's exclusive discretion."[33] In one important aspect, it was undoubtedly an attempt to bolster America's regional security and oil interests in the Middle East in the wake of the dismal failure of the Baghdad Pact and the Allied political debacle in the Suez War. The fact that this short-sighted doctrine of intervention received such little support in the Arab world was noted by none other than John Kennedy: "The Aswan Dam refusal, the concept of the Baghdad Pact, and the Eisenhower Doctrine, which is being rejected really in every country—all these, I would think, are unhappy monuments to Mr. Dulles in the Middle East."[34]

Johnson and the June 1967 War

There has of course been a veritable deluge of books, articles, and press reports on the subject of the June 1967 war. And it will be some time before access to the American archives is possible for analysts: around the year 1997. Some facets of the two crucial weeks preceding 5 June will probably remain obscure for a considerable time, if not forever. Nevertheless, it is

---

ought not to neglect the combined Anglo-American interest in provoking splits, or at the very least in exacerbating the propensities. Archival material to be released in the forthcoming years will undoubtedly help to throw light on this relatively neglected area of perceptions and policy-making.

[32] For a particularly good treatment of this subject, see Fayez Sayegh, *The Dynamics of Neutralism in the Arab World: A Symposium* (San Fransisco: Chandler, 1964).

[33] Herman Finer, *Dulles Over Suez* (London: Heineman, 1964), pp. 499–500.

[34] John Kennedy, *The Strategy of Peace* (New York: Popular Library, 1961), p. 261.

possible on the basis of a careful reading of Heikal, Quandt, Aronson, and Eveland to fit some pieces of the story together. What concerns us here is the controversy surrounding the issue of the American "green light." Did Johnson give the Israelis a "green light" to go ahead with their preemptive aggression? If it was not a "green light," was it a broad hint? And were such signals further intensified by initiatives from the Pentagon and the CIA?

Heikal's analysis stresses the difference between the Arab-USSR relationship and the Israel-US relationship in 1967. Whereas Moscow fed Cairo with alarmist news regarding the crisis, in the case of Washington and Tel-Aviv the roles appeared to be reversed: "It was Israel which fed Washington with alarmist stories as part of the process of keeping the Americans involved in its fate. America's relations with Israel were, so to speak, conducted from the inside, whereas Russia's relations with the Arabs were conducted from the outside. The Arabs were always insisting to the Soviet Union on their independence, while the Israelis preferred to emphasize to the Americans their close mutual dependence. This difference was to have important consequences both during and after the 1967 war."[35]

In his insightful chapter entitled "The Trap," Heikal argues that the newly installed Soviet leadership was hesitant and lacking an overall strategy for the Arab world. It "was advocating caution and preservation of the status quo," whereas President Johnson "was stirring up violent change." In May 1967, the Soviets were behaving in a confused manner, "speaking two languages at the same time, the language of alarm and the language of restraint."[36]

Thus, according to Heikal, during the crucial final week of May 1967, Kosygin on the one hand advised Shams al-Dīn Badrān (Egypt's Defense Minister) "to cool things down and not give Israel or the imperial forces any cause for triggering off an armed conflict," while Marshal Gretchko, on the other hand, was urging him to "stand firm," adding: "Whatever you have to face, you will find us with you; don't let yourselves be blackmailed by the Americans or anyone else."[37] The impression given by Heikal is that the Soviet leadership was outmaneuvered by the Israelis and Americans, especially on the question of the preemptive strike option, the determining factor in modern war. The Soviet ambassador in Tel Aviv "emphasized Israel's wish to avoid a conflict." In addition, there was that frantic message from Kosy-

---

[35] Mohamed Hassanein Heikal, *Sphinx and Commissar: the Rise and Fall of Soviet Influence in the Middle East* (London: Collins, 1978), p. 171.

[36] *Ibid.*, p. 175.

[37] *Ibid.*, p. 179.

gin to President Nasser to the effect "that the Americans had contacted the Russians with the report of an impending Egyptian attack" and in a sense getting President Nasser to declare that "Egypt had no such plan."[38] Heikal hints strongly that the Soviets' concern with détente influenced their actions. Meanwhile, the Israelis had all the time in the world to prepare a devastating preemptive strike, in the full knowledge that everyone was urging Egypt to restraint while Israel was receiving the green light from the US President to go ahead. Moreover, once the war started the Soviet response to urgent requests of assistance, including an airlift, was seen by Heikal to be dilatory and hesitant.

If the Soviets emerge in negative terms in Heikal's account, so does the role of UN Secretary General U Thant, particularly in connection with the crucial 30 May message cabled to Nasser, with American and Russian agreement, which stated that Israel would not be taking any offensive action before 14 June and which urged "special restraint and the foregoing of belligerence."[39]

Quandt's analysis is more cautious. But he does raise the question of the green light. On 26 May Abba Eban had gone to the Pentagon, where he was told by the military chiefs and by CIA Director Richard Helms that the Israelis would easily win.[40] There was also that cryptic phrase, repeated on so many occasions during those crucial crisis days before 5 June, "Israel will only be alone if it decides to go alone"—which Quandt argues was read in Israel as containing a "hint of a green light to Israel."[41] Perhaps even more important was the secret visit to Washington on 30 May by Meir Amit, Israel's chief of intelligence, who got the impression from Robert McNamara (Pentagon) and Helms (CIA) that "if Israel were to act on her own, and win decisively, no one in Washington would be upset."[42]

This is also confirmed by Shlomo Aronson, who cites Meir Amit's clearance in Washington as the second of three crucial factors that decided Israel to launch its preemptive aggression against the Arab states: "Meir Amit reported from Washington that the US administration...would not oppose Israel if it decided to take unilateral action."[43]

---

[38] *Ibid.*

[39] *Ibid.*

[40] Quandt, *Decade of Decisions*, p. 50.

[41] *Ibid.*, p. 56.

[42] *Ibid.*, p. 57.

[43] Shlomo Aronson, *Conflict and Bargaining in the Middle East* (Baltimore: Johns Hopkins University Press, 1978), p. 74.

As to Wilbur Eveland's account in his *Ropes of Sand: America's Failure in the Middle East*, this former adviser to the CIA and former member of the policy-planning staffs of the White House and Pentagon is of the opinion that there was very close coordination between Minister Counsellor Ephraim Ebron of the Israeli Embassy in Washington and James Angleton of the CIA. A channel had been established between the two that permitted the by-passing of regular diplomatic channels. The "feasibility of an attack on Egypt with the objective of toppling Nasser" had been discussed.[44] Eveland states that "President Johnson authorized Angleton to inform Evron that the US would prefer Israeli efforts to lessen the tension but would not intervene to stop an attack on Egypt. The American position stipulated that there must be no Israeli military action against Jordan, Syria, or Lebanon."[45]

What adds plausibility to the "green light" thesis is President Johnson's behavior following the June 1967 war. In sharp contrast with President Eisenhower's position in 1956, Johnson's declaration of 19 June 1967 in effect maintained that Israel was not obligated to return conquered Arab territory. Moreover, in private, "Americans stated the strategic and political conditions under which this declaration held: Israel's ability to hold on to its conquests by itself without impairing US vital interests."[46] Within three months Johnson reportedly assured Levi Eshkol that substantial quantitites of the high-performance F-4 Phantom fighter-bomber would be supplied to Israel.

America had greeted Israel's victory with unconcealed satisfaction and public jubilation at the highest official levels. It was assumed that the post-war balance of power had shifted appreciably in favor of the US. But not all American analysts saw the outcome of the June 1967 as being favorable to American interests in the Near East. Robert Stookey, in particular, saw it in terms of "the failure of American policy" and drew the following seven-point negative balance sheet of the state of American interests in the wake of the war:

> 1. The United States had sought in the interest of its own security...the maintenance of stability in the Middle East and the settlement of disputes by peaceful means. Instead, the region was rocked by a war from which America's moral authority,

---

[44] Wilbur Eveland, *Ropes of Sand: America's Failure in the Middle East* (New York: Norton, 1980), pp. 323–24.

[45] *Ibid.*

[46] Aronson, *Conflict and Bargaining*, p. 86.

compromised by its own warlike actions in Southeast Asia, was helpless to deter even Israel.

2. Whereas free communications across the area were acknowledged to be a major American interest, the principal surface artery, the Suez Canal, was closed at the onset of war by the sinking of block-ships held in readiness for the purpose; thenceforth shipping between Atlantic and Mediterranean waters to the Indian Ocean and adjacent seas was forced to circumnavigate the African continent.

3. Access to Middle Eastern oil, recognized as a vital interest, was denied entirely by the Arabs for a time to the United States and its major ally. Added impetus was given to the movement to alter, to Western disadvantage, the terms of its availability.

4. The territorial integrity of all countries in the area, for which the United States had consistently proclaimed support, was sharply impaired by Israeli occupation of significant portions of Syria, Jordan, and Egypt.

5. Whereas the United States had sought to contain the expansion of Soviet influence in the Middle East, the Arab defeat forced Syria, Egypt, and Iraq into sole and urgent reliance on the Soviet Union for their national security and the rehabilitation of their armed forces; in exchange, the Russians acquired the use of important naval and aviation facilities as well as an enhancement of their political position. In countries such as Yemen and the Sudan, American aid was no longer an alternative to dependence on Soviet, Chinese, and East European assistance for purposes of economic development.

6. The United States had failed to win practical support from either its allies or the communist countries for its long-standing policy of limiting the Middle East arms race, unsettling both to inter-Arab and Arab-Israel relations, or even to abide by it itself.

7. The United States had sought friendly relations with all Arab states regardless of ideological orientation; it now had no official contact with half the Arab countries, representing a substantial majority of the Arab peoples.[47]

---

[47] Robert Stookey, *America and the Arab States*, pp. 208–209.

Kissinger vs. Arab Linkage Strategy and the Oil Embargo

Shortly after taking office, President Nixon began the search for a broad framework that would set the tone and direction for his foreign policy, what later came to be known as the Nixon Doctrine. With Vietnam at the top of the list of his administration's priorities, it was inevitable that the Doctrine would reflect on the one hand the need to reassure a disenchanted public opinion at home that the Vietnam involvement would be gradually ended, and on the other hand the need to secure from America's allies a greater burden in defense expenditure without making them feel insecure as to the ability of the United States to conduct an effective foreign policy globally. Outlined in a press conference at Guam in July 1969, this new doctrine for Asia, with applications elsewhere, was ambiguous and open to a wide variety of interpretations. In the words of Henry Brandon: "To some, the Nixon Doctrine was a rationale for the retreat of American power; for others, it was an exercise in rhetoric to justify the continuing US involvement in the world."[48]

But on one issue the Doctrine was clear: friends and allies would be given massive aid and armaments as an invitation to participate more fully in regional security tasks deemed necessary by the United States. In this respect the direct outcome for the Middle East was the enhancement of the Shah of Iran's role as regional policeman in the traditional perimeter of the Arab-Israeli conflict.[49]

The extent to which the Rogers initiative harmonized or was at variance with the Nixon Doctrine is open to a great deal of debate. But in any case, the whole episode is a clear manifestation of Henry Kissinger's ability to undercut William Rogers' plan on the grounds, as he tells us, that "it made no strategic sense." Besides, Kissinger tells us that he "was always opposed to comprehensive solutions."[50]

---

[48] Henry Brandon, *The Retreat of American Power* (New York: Delta Books, 1974), p. 80.

[49] By the time Nixon visited Tehran in May 1972, the extent of the massive American commitment to supply modern arms to the Shah had become clear. See Robert Pranger and Dale Tahtinen, "American Policy Options in Iran and the Persian Gulf," *AEI Foreign Policy and Defense Review*, I.2 (1979), pp. 3–4. As to the Israeli supply, despite the fact that Egypt and Jordan had accepted the Jarring mission, whereas Israel had rejected it, the year 1971 "was the highwater mark of American military aid to Israel, $600 million worth, or seven times as much as ever given by the Johnson administration." See Polk, *The United States and the Arab World*, p. 398 n.

[50] Henry Kissinger, *White House Years* (Boston: Little, Brown, Little, 1979), p. 1279.

Within the Nixon administration two opposed teams struggled for control of America's foreign policy. For the Middle East the NSC team led by Henry Kissinger included Alexander Haig, Peter Rodman, and Winston Lord, as well as specialists Harold Saunders and his deputy William Quandt. The Department of State's team included William Rogers, Joseph Sisco, Alfred Atherton, and three of the leading "Arabists" in the Department: Richard Parker, in charge of Egyptian affairs; Talcott Seelye, covering Jordan, Lebanon, Syria, and Iraq; and Deputy Assistant Secretary Roger Davies.[51]

Soon, however, Kissinger took over Rogers' post at the State Department while retaining his own position at the head of the NSC. With this powerful combination, he became the undisputed Caesar of US foreign policy, particularly as the shadow of Watergate hung over the White House. What is of special concern to us here is that Kissinger was determined to break the ranks of Arab unity in the aftermath of the Ramadan War and the imposition of the Arab oil embargo. This fact he personally revealed to a group of leading American Jews in 1975.[52]

A week after the outbreak of the Ramadan War, Secretary of State Henry Kissinger declared at a press conference: the "Middle East may become in time what the Balkans were in Europe before 1914, that is to say, an area where local rivalries... have their own momentum that will draw in the great nuclear powers into a confrontation." He then went on to warn the Arab world of a massive airlift of American military hardware to Israel.[53] Three days later President Nixon raised the specter of intervention by characterizing current US policy as being "like the policy followed in 1958 when Lebanon was involved."[54] According to William Quandt, these comments caused consternation in Arab diplomatic circles.[55]

As the massive airlift surged forward and saved the Israeli army from a dire predicament, the Organization of Arab Petroleum Exporting Countries (OAPEC), meeting in Kuwait on 17 October, responded with a scheduled five percent cutback in oil production each month until Israel withdrew from all occupied Arab territory. Two days later, President Nixon asked Congress for $2.2 billion in military assistance to Israel. On 19 October, King Fayṣal,

---

[51] Quandt, *Decade of Decisions*, pp. 74–75 n.

[52] For a transcript of these revealing conversations, see *Journal of Palestine Studies*, 10.3 (Spring 1981), pp. 186–95.

[53] *Department of State Bulletin*, LXIX, 1792 (29 October 1973), pp. 534–39.

[54] Quandt, *Decade of Decisions*, p. 187.

[55] *Ibid.*

who had called for a ten percent cut in production, imposed an oil embargo on the United States and Holland; Kissinger received the news during his flight to Moscow. One of the major assumptions of American policy, namely that the Arabs would not use the oil weapon, went up in smoke together with other assumptions concerning the determination and ability of Arab nations to wage a war against Israel, a state enjoying "special relationship" status with the United States.

In actual fact, there were indices to suggest that the oil weapon was being prepared by the Arabs. At the Khartoum Summit of 1967, King Fayṣal had led Arab oil states in setting up a regular contribution to help the confrontation states that had suffered in the 1967 war. Nonetheless, as late as July 1973 he appeared to oppose the utilization of the oil weapon. But a month later, according to Heikal's account, the Saudi monarch told President Sadat: "Give us time. We don't want to use our oil weapon in a battle which only goes on for two or three days and then stops. We want to see a battle which goes on for long enough for world public opinion to be mobilized." Yet Heikal is of the opinion that there was no "precise plan for the use of the oil weapon" on the eve of the Ramadan War.[56]

An examination of the nuclear confrontation between the two superpowers with vital interests in the outcome and aftermath of the war is not within the scope of this survey article. Concentration instead will be placed on the US response to Arab linkage strategy: the linking of the lifting of the embargo to withdrawal from occupied territories. In the American response, the threat of military intervention was repeatedly used as an instrument of policy.[57] Significantly, President Nixon revealed in his memoirs: "From the moment the Arab oil embargo began [his administration] worked unceasingly to end it."[58]

On 21 November Kissinger spoke in sharp terms about "Arab pressure" and "Arab shutdown of oil," affirming that the US would not be influenced in changing its policy because of the oil embargo, and warning of the possibility of "countermeasures" against oil producers.[59] The following day Shaykh Aḥmad Zakī Yamānī warned that Arab states "could cut production by 80

---

[56]Mohamed Hassanein Heikal, *The Road to Ramadan* (London: Fontana, 1976), pp. 266–67.

[57]For a detailed analysis of this policy, see Marwan Buheiry, *US Threats of Intervention Against Arab Oil, 1973–1979* (Beirut: Institute for Palestine Studies, 1980) [= pp. 249–310 below].

[58]R. Nixon, *Memoirs of Richard Nixon* (London: Arrow Books, 1979), p. 986.

[59]*International Herald Tribune*, 22 November 1973, p. 1.

percent" if the United States, Japan, or the EEC took punitive counter-measures. Moreover, he said that his country might blow up some of its oil fields and installations in the event of an American military intervention, and invited the Western Alliance to carefully consider the potency of the Arab oil weapon. He also linked the resumption of oil supplies to Israeli withdrawal from the occupied territories.[60]

A week later it was James Schlesinger's turn to announce his country's intention to maintain an important naval presence in the Indian Ocean aimed at protecting US interests in the Gulf in the wake of the Ramadan War and the oil embargo.[61] This initiative was most probably a reaction to Arab solidarity and to the resolution to maintain the oil weapon adopted at the Sixth Arab Summit Conference of 26 November, specifically the item regarding the "continuation of the embargo in relation to countries supporting Israel."[62]

The intervention threat also retained the attention of President Boumedienne of Algeria, who warned on 4 December that Arab oil workers would react swiftly to military intervention: "...if the West tries to act with arrogance or to use force, it would suffer a catastrophe. All the wells will be set on fire, all the pipelines will be destroyed, and the West will pay the price."[63]

The year 1973 ended on a grave keynote of warning and counterwarning, including hints of American military intervention in the Gulf and the increase of the aircraft carrier task force deployed in the Indian Ocean.[64] Then came Schlesinger's thinly veiled threat of 7 January, warning the Arabs that force may be used against them if the oil weapon was carried too far. And once again the riposte was abundantly clear to everyone. Saudi Arabia and Kuwait announced their determination to blow up the oil fields and installations in the event of a military intervention. Kuwait's foreign minister was quoted as stating that the oil fields were surrounded by an explosive belt, explodable the moment actual American military intervention was sensed. Authoritative statements were made regarding the placing of explosive charges in the Saudi Arabian oil fields. Arab commentators, particularly in Damascus and Algiers, also made statements to the same

---

[60] *International Herald Tribune*, 23 November 1973, p. 1.

[61] *New York Times*, 1 December 1973.

[62] *International Documents on Palestine, 1973*, edited by Jorgen S. Nielsen (Beirut: Institute of Palestine Studies, 1976), p. 524, doc. 331.

[63] *International Herald Tribune*, 5 December 1973, p. 2.

[64] Edward Sheehan, "Step by Step in the Middle East," *Journal of Palestine Studies*, 5.3–4 (Spring-Summer 1976), p. 27.

effect.[65] There is conclusive evidence that American officials took the Arab riposte seriously and appreciated the full extent of both the devastation and the oil shutdown that would be triggered by armed intervention.[66]

In the meantime, Dr. Kissinger had left Washington to embark on his shuttle diplomacy in earnest, with the agitation over military intervention as his supporting background. Ending the embargo, getting a disengagement agreement signed, and countering Arab linkage strategy were his highest priorities. In this respect, there is a strong suggestion in Nixon's *Memoirs* that the Americans were able to count on President Sadat's early cooperation. In December Kissinger had told Nixon in a memo: "Sadat promised me he would get the oil embargo lifted during the first half of January and said that he would call for its lifting in a statement which praised your personal role in bringing the parties to the negotiating table and making progress thereafter."[67] Nixon followed up on 28 December 1973 with a letter to Sadat: "I must tell you in complete candor," he wrote, "that it is essential that the oil embargo and oil production restrictions against the United States be ended at once. It cannot await the outcome of the current talks on disengagement."[68] Nixon also relates that Sadat sent him a message through the US delegate to the United Nations, Shirley Temple Black, who had seen the Egyptian president privately: "I will lift the embargo," he told her; "I will lift it for President Nixon."[69]

For the Nixon administration, ending the Arab oil embargo was dictated by several crucial factors: 1) on the domestic scene the need to neutralize the effects of the Watergate scandal through dramatized "successes" in foreign policy; 2) the need to restore a badly shaken Western Alliance and a Trilateral world facing the prospect of deep economic recession; 3) the national interest of the US in the context of Big Power rivalry; 4) the energy requirements of the US and the prospect of a depletion in its strategic reserves; 5) the need to prevent the EEC and Japan from moving in the direction of the Arab states in terms of arms sales, technological transfers, renegotiated oil supplies, the direct access to energy, and quasi-independent diplomatic initiatives. And the closer Dr. Kissinger got to an agreement on

---

[65] William Coughlin, "Fears of Invasion by US Rise in Mideast: Oil Fields Mined," *International Herald Tribune*, 12–13 January 1974, p. 2.

[66] *Ibid.* See also D. Middleton, "Intervention in the Middle East," *International Herald Tribune*, 14 January 1974, p. 2.

[67] Nixon, *Memoirs*, p. 986.

[68] *Ibid.*, p. 987.

[69] *Ibid.*

the disengagement of forces in the Suez Canal area, the more King Faysal was pressed to persuade OAPEC to lift the embargo in recognition of the American effort.

The Saudi monarch made it clear that he was interested in seeing progress toward disengagement equally on other fronts.[70] What would happen if, with the embargo lifted, Kissinger's ardor sagged and Israel's obdurate posture increased? Syria, fighting a heroic and single-handed war of attrition in the Golan, would then be left out in the cold, as would Jordan and the Palestine Liberation Organization. The unity of the Arabs would have eroded, especially as it was becoming more obvious that step-by-step was designed by Kissinger to mean little-by-little and the breaking of Arab ranks. Once lifted, the reimposition of the embargo would be a risky undertaking. Nevertheless, the Arab position was sufficiently flexible to accommodate the possibility of easing or lifting the embargo at the forthcoming February meeting of OAPEC. The Arab oil states were quick to realize that an escalation in cutbacks could push the industrialized world "to the brink of ruin long before any significant progress was achieved towards the fulfilment of [Arab] objectives."[71] The moderate course of action of OAPEC, with its carefully balanced but potent mix of sanctions and incentives, was therefore clear to everyone. Yet Nixon and Kissinger chose the path of confrontation, characterizing the projected OAPEC meeting as yielding to the logic of American pressure diplomacy and warning that failure to put an early end to the embargo would be read as a form of "blackmail." In reaction, OAPEC postponed its February meeting.[72] In this vitally important and highly complex web of diplomacy, an additional Arab initiative requires stressing: President Asad's trip in early February to Saudi Arabia and Kuwait, where he is believed to have received firm pledges linking the lifting of the embargo with successful disengagement in the Golan and assurances of support regarding Palestinian rights.[73]

Perhaps for the first time in the annals of the Arab-Israeli conflict, Arab diplomacy was trying out a sophisticated form of linkage strategy—and with some measure of success. Of course, the conjuncture of events was of great

---

[70] *The Economist*, 26 January–1 February 1974, p. 36.

[71] Fuad Itayim "Strengths and Weaknesses of the Oil Weapon," in *The Middle East and the International System* (London: International Institute for Strategic Studies, 1975; *Adelphi Papers*, no. 115), p. 3.

[72] Joe Stork, *Middle East Oil and the Energy Crisis* (New York: Monthly Review Press, 1975), pp. 240–41.

[73] *Ibid.*; *Arab Report and Record*, 1–14 February 1974, pp. 51, 53.

help. The impressive performance of the Syrian and Egyptian forces, the world energy crisis, the relative success of the Arab embargo (unlike its ill-fated counterpart imposed in 1967), and the organized drive by a united front of oil producers to keep the price of crude from falling, impacted directly on the US scene and even more dramatically on that of its allies. Undoubtedly, the US displayed annoyance at the use of its favorite strategy by others; superpowers have a tendency to regard linkage strategy as their own very private possession. Hence, the strenuous attempts by the Nixon administration to deny the existence of linkage between oil and disengagement diplomacy. Yet, as pointed out by Edward Sheehan, although Dr. Kissinger denied linkage, "his Syrian shuttle was the price he paid to end the embargo."[74] On 6 March, President Nixon acknowledged that "progress on the diplomatic front, while it is not linked to lifting the embargo, inevitably has an effect on it."[75] And in sharp contrast to the tough language he had earlier used to indicate that American pressure would force the lifting of the embargo, he now thought it more advisable "to leave that decision to the Arabs."[76]

By mid-March, the fact that some progress had been made with respect to military disengagement in the Golan, combined with nervousness on the part of OPEC, seemed to warrant a reconsideration of this embargo. Thus in the Vienna meeting of 18 March, the oil ministers of OAPEC outlined the linkage between oil measures, the drawing of world attention to the Arab cause, and encouragment to be granted to "countries which showed readiness and willingness to work for a just remedy to the cause which would lead to the complete termination of the Israeli occupation and to the restoration of the legitimate rights of the Palestinian people."[77] The meeting also expressed, perhaps too hastily, recognition of the emergence of a new American policy more compatible with justice toward Arab and Palestinian rights: an "adjustment" which has not materialized to date. Furthermore, two crucial decisions were taken: to treat Italy and the West German Republic as friendly states and to meet their petroleum needs,[78] and second, to lift the embargo on oil supplies to the US. The decision on the embargo was subject to review at the next OAPEC meeting in June 1974, with Egypt and Saudi Arabia providing assurances against its reimposition—a point duly noted by

[74]Sheehan, "Step by Step in the Middle East," p. 27.
[75]*Department of State Bulletin*, LXX, 1813 (25 March 1974), pp. 294–95.
[76]*Ibid.*
[77]*Middle East Economic Digest*, 22 March 1974, pp. 324–42.
[78]*Ibid.*

the American Secretary of State.[79] On the other hand, the embargo on Holland, Portugal, South Africa, and Rhodesia was maintained. The question whether OAPEC sheathed the oil weapon too soon remains the subject of controversy, as does the role of the Egyptian president.

Arab linkage strategy had made a convincing debut. The careful planning and military successes, the avoidance of some pitfalls strewn along its paths, the tough stand adopted in the face of the thinly veiled threats of intervention, and the selection of the appropriate forums did not fail to impress international opinion. Not that the Arab states were enduringly united. In measuring the effectiveness of the oil weapon one has to admit that the embargo did not work properly.[80] Nonetheless, despite President Sadat's propensity to strike out on his own, sufficient consensus was maintained to ensure the credibility of the strategy and to soften the impact of the threats of intervention.

US policy-makers were annoyed and preoccupied by Arab linkage strategy. President Nixon went so far as to assert on 15 March in Chicago that oil pressure would have "a countereffect on [the US] effort to go forward on the peace front, on the negotiation front, because it would simply slow down...[US] efforts to get the disengagement on the Syrian front and also to move towards a permanent settlement."[81] Yet the recognition that it was a new and important factor, that there was no longer room for the old complacency, may be gauged by the following Presidential assessment made just after the lifting of the oil embargo: "It is in the interest of those countries that imposed it as well as the United States that it be lifted. The two should be parallel. Inevitably, what happens in one area affects the other."[82]

In short, the Arabs had left it to the Americans to choose between having the embargo as a semipermanent imposition or living with it as an Arab tactical weapon. The first alternative was particularly intolerable. Predictably, the US chose the second, especially as it presented certain advantages stemming from the limitations of the embargo as a tactical weapon in the absence of a state of war, and with the element of surprise no longer obtaining.

The oil embargo was lifted five months after it was imposed, not as fast as the Nixon administration would have liked, despite the harsh campaign of threats and the war of nerves, but faster than the Arab interest would

[79] Stork, *Middle East Oil and the Energy Crisis*, p. 242.

[80] Hanns Maull, *Oil and Influence: The Oil Weapon Examined* (London: International Institute for Strategic Studies, 1975; *Adelphi Papers*, no. 117), p. 6.

[81] *New York Times*, 16 March 1974, p. 12; Nixon, *Memoirs*, p. 987.

[82] *New York Times*, 20 March 1974, p. 28.

have otherwise dictated. Yet one thing was made clear: the consequences of that display of combined military and economic power were likely to be long-lasting in terms of political and economic dividends for the Arab nation as a whole, provided Arab solidarity was maintained.

There were other gains. On the eve of the October War of 1973, the United States still regarded the region of the Arab Gulf and the heartland of the Arab-Israeli conflict (Syria, Jordan, Palestine, Egypt, and Lebanon) as two separate and distinct areas or arenas. The October War, the coordinated Arab moves, the determination and sacrifice of Arab armies in the battlefields, and the skillful use of the oil factor shattered this old US illusion born of misplaced self-interest, the exertions of the pro-Israel lobby, and the deep aversion for Arab nationalism in general. Arab linkage strategy tended to dispel them. A new strategic reality was born, despite the joint American-Israeli effort to minimize its importance.

13

The Atlantic Alliance and the Middle East in the Early 1950s and Today: Retrospect and Prospect*

IN SHARP CONTRAST to the political and colonial interests of Britain, France, Tsarist Russia, or Italy, the interest of America in the Middle East before the First World War focused in the main on commercial and missionary activity, including education. However, this picture was to change gradually. Following the Balfour Declaration and the mandate system, which the United States supported, an additional factor developed: the growth of political Zionism in Palestine and its repercussions on the American domestic scene. Furthermore, in the late thirties the Middle Eastern oil dimension and the entrance of American oil companies into the Arab world assumed strategic importance and inextricable linkage with politics and defense.[1]

During the Second World War the strategic importance of the Middle East was fully recognized by policy-makers and public opinion in America. The region at large was shown to be a crucial center of land, sea, and air communications, as well as an indispensable reservoir of petroleum that helped the Allies' war effort. It is also significant that despite their wartime alliance against the Axis powers, the United States and the Soviet Union

---

*From *Palestine and the Gulf*, edited by Rashid Khalidi and Camille Mansour (Beirut: Institute for Palestine Studies, 1981), pp. 120–60. © 1981 by the Institute for Palestine Studies. Reprinted courtesy of the Institute for Palestine Studies. A French version of this study, "L'Alliance atlantique et le Proche-Orient, au début des années cinquante et aujourd'hui," appeared in *Revue d'études palestiniennes*, 7 (Spring 1983), pp. 53–81.

[1] Marwan Buheiry, "Min Truman ilā Kissinger," *Al-Mustaqbal al-'arabī*, 29 (July 1981), p. 73 [= p. 189 above].

clashed on the question of Iran even while the war was in progress: the Soviets supported separatist movements among the Kurds and Adharbayjānīs,
and, in 1944, "even attacked the presence in Iran of the American troops
who were bringing lend-lease supplies to Russia."[2] This episode confirms
the perception of Admiral A.T. Mahan, who drew attention to the Middle
East and the Gulf as a permanent arena of strategic confrontation between
rival powers as early as 1902.[3] Whatever the definition, the Middle East was
and remains above all a strategic, rather than a geographic, concept.

After 1945, as the Cold War and the containment of the Soviet Union
became the dominant concern of the Western allies, the strategic importance
of the Middle East reached new heights. Henceforth it was argued that Soviet
penetration of the region would outflank the Atlantic Alliance, causing a
decisive rupture in the world balance. A second perception was that Soviet
control over Middle East oil resources would dislocate the economy of the
Western world.[4]

In the late forties and early fifties, during the process of formalizing
the Atlantic Alliance as NATO, questions of linkage with the Middle East
and the enlargement of the NATO area of responsibility were raised and
several options debated. Thereafter, interest in this thorny matter fluctuated
according to the level of tension in the world. Today, it is evident that the
expansion of the Alliance's zone of operation is once more the subject of
intense deliberation and concern: the logic of a new Cold War is being
imposed on the Middle East, while NATO appears intent on bringing the
area into association with it by extending the perimeter of action beyond the
Tropic of Cancer (the traditional limit of NATO deployment as specified in

[2] George Lenczowski, *United States Interests in the Middle East* (Washington: American
Enterprise Institute, 1968), p. 13.

[3] Alfred T. Mahan, "The Persian Gulf and International Relations," *National Review*
(London), 40 (September 1902–February 1903), pp. 27–45.

[4] John Campbell, *Defense of the Middle East: Problems of American Policy* (New York:
Harper, 1960), pp. 4–5. A third argument heard perhaps less often than the other two was
(*ibid.*) that "the triumph of Communism in the heart of the Islamic world could be the
prelude to its triumph throughout Asia, Africa and Europe." An influential example of a
"grand design" policy paper is the NSC–68, the product of Dean Acheson in 1950, which in
his words stated the conflicting aims and purposes of the two superpowers: "The priority
given by the Soviet rulers to the Kremlin design, world domination, contrasted with the
American aim, an environment in which free societies could exist and flourish." This major
policy paper recommended "specific measures for a large and immediate improvement of
military forces and weapons, and the economic and morale factors which underlay our
own and our allies' ability to influence the conduct of other societies." See Dean Acheson,
Present at the Creation (New York: Norton, 1969), pp. 375–76.

the Organization's charter) and by formal and informal arrangements with some of the region's states.

The purpose of this study is to examine the dynamics and implications of this fateful trend, both in its first manifestations in the early 1950s and today, with major emphasis placed on the United States and Britain.

The Alliance and the Middle East in the Early 1950s

In the confrontationist atmosphere of the Cold War, the administration of President Truman established the main lines of America's Middle East policy. To some extent these were inherited from imperial Britain or developed in response to domestic pressures, particularly in the case of Palestine. Another influence flowed from the nature and scope of America's wartime strategy, exemplified by the sharing with Britain of the Persian Gulf Command, the supply channel to the Soviet Union through Iran, and the construction of an air base at Dhahran during the final year of the war. There was also the factor of oil.[5]

A cornerstone of America's policy was the global containment of the Soviet Union, which in effect meant keeping it out of the Middle East and the Arab world, as well as other regions. Dominated as it was by Cold War and Globalist outlooks, the main lines of US policy hardly took account of Arab hopes and fears: Arab nationalism and the drive for Arab unity, decolonization, full sovereignty, and non-alignment were generally seen in terms of conflict with or obstruction of American and Allied global aims and objectives. All this was reinforced by the traditional penchant in favor of Israel.

When Britain gave notice in early 1947 that it was no longer able to fulfill its economic and military commitments to Greece and Turkey, the Truman administration (particularly Averell Harriman, Dean Acheson, George Marshall, James Forrestal, and, of course, the President himself) stepped in with the Truman Doctrine: perhaps the first evidence of the application of

---

[5]On the complicated question of America's wartime oil policy, there was a great deal of concern on the part of the Office of Mobilization about the depletion of America's domestic oil reserves caused by the requirements of war. An abortive plan for the government to nationalize American foreign oil holdings in support of the war effort was even considered. The thorny questions of the competition between foreign and domestic oil and of the public versus private ownership of the oil industry tended to be adjudicated by considerations of national security. One ought not to forget also the crucial importance of Middle Eastern oil in the European recovery program. See Robert Stookey, *America and the Arab States* (New York: J. Wiley, 1975), pp. 69–70.

containment in the Middle East, with clear implications for its extension anywhere in the world. Furthermore, the doctrine opened the way to other major moves on the bipolar and Cold War checkerboard: the Marshall Plan of 1947, the North Atlantic Treaty of April 1948, and the North Atlantic Treaty Organization of August 1949 (although the last two also evolved from the 1947 Anglo-French Treaty of Dunkirk and the Brussels Pact of 1948). Yet another step was the Point Four proposal of 1949, which extended the principle of economic development and recovery to the less-developed areas of the world.

NATO's original membership of 12 included the United States, Canada, Great Britain, Iceland, Norway, Denmark, France, Belgium, Luxembourg, Holland, Portugal, and Italy. Sweden was pressured to join but refused to do so. Later on, Greece, Turkey, and West Germany were brought into the alliance, raising the membership to 15. From the very start there were reservations about the Treaty both in America and in Europe. Voices were heard in Congress against stationing American forces in Europe. The mutuality of obligations set out in the key operative Articles III and V were judged to be too precise and restrictive. Also, in the words of a group of Brookings Institution analysts writing in the mid-fifties: "Public feeling became restive at the implication that United States policy was abandoning the United Nations, was organizing a military coalition against the Soviet Union, and was moving toward developing military means to achieve its objectives."[6]

In Europe too, the northern states were not altogether happy about the widening scope of commitments. To cite one example, reflecting on the problem of additional membership in NATO, Dean Acheson remarked:

> A press leak in May (1951) that Britain, France and the United States were consulting together about invitations to Greece and Turkey alarmed and annoyed the other allies. The "North Atlantic" had been stretched in 1949 to include Italy; now we were trying to take in the Eastern Mediterranean, a snake pit of troubles. How could Northern European statesmen convince their people that attacks in the Levant should be regarded as attacks on Scandinavia or the Low Countries? In carrying the debate for the invitations, I pointed out the absence of any feasible alternative. A year before, recognizing the importance of Greece and Turkey as an eastern flank of European defense, the Nato Coun-

---

[6]William Reitzel, Morton Kaplan, and Constance Coblenz, *United States Foreign Policy 1945-1955* (Washington: The Brookings Institution, 1956), p. 127.

cil had decided to associate the two countries through a defense agency, but it had not worked. They wanted full membership, which from our point of view had the advantage of mutuality of obligations.[7]

As to the Middle East, the leading partners in the Alliance (America, Britain, and France) perceived the region as one of vital strategic importance in relation to the Soviet Union, and, on occasion, in relation to each other. France and Britain were colonial powers with special interests in the eastern Mediterranean and a long tradition of rivalry. In this respect, Britain's perception of French rivalry and fears may be gauged by a Permanent Under-Secretary's Committee paper on the Middle East (30 April 1949). The French attitude toward the region was seen as "a combination of fear that the area may be given undue attention to the detriment of security arrangements in Western Europe; of desire to retain or partially recover France's interests (largely cultural) and prestige, especially in the Levant States; and of concern for continued or increased supplies of Middle East oil." The Committee's paper acknowledged French interest in Palestine's Holy Places, "largely in response to Catholic opinion."[8] As to the recent origin and consequences of this rivalry, the paper perceived it in familiar terms:

> The French blame British policy in 1942 and after for the loss of their position in the Levant States, and they regard with the highest suspicion any positive move by the United Kingdom to co-operate with Syria or the Lebanon for security purposes. They are inclined to attribute to His Majesty's Government Machiavellian schemes to counter French influence and to absorb the Levant States into a British-controlled Greater Syria. In order to combat these imaginary schemes, they are all too ready to intrigue against us and we must accept that France's policy is likely to be one of mistrust and covert opposition to us. There have been recent instances of this on the occasion of M. Bidault's visit to the Levant States, and over Persian oil.[9]

While recognizing that such feelings of mistrust were present to a greater extent in Frenchmen in the Middle East than in the government in Paris,

---

[7] Acheson, *Present at the Creation*, p. 570.
[8] *Foreign Office* (FO) 371/75067, PUSC (19) on Middle East, 30 April 1949.
[9] *Ibid.*

the Committee also felt that France was "preoccupied with the risk of the growth of Arab nationalism in North Africa, and consequently opposed to manifestations of Arab national unity in the Middle East, and in particular a revival of the Arab League or the realization of plans for Greater Syria or the Union of the Fertile Crescent."[10]

However, Anglo-French relations did improve with the joint US-British-French statement on the Middle East of 25 May 1950 (the Tripartite Declaration). Yet here again, the Foreign Office appeared less than enthusiastic about France's association, preferring to bring France in at the last moment (in fact, almost as a *fait accompli*).[11] And there was some opposition by British diplomats in the Middle East. Sir Ronald Campbell's opinion from Cairo, as late as 30 April 1950, was that the declaration would "be stronger if confined to the United Kingdom and the United States since France is unfortunately regarded here as weak and also self-seeking."[12]

In addition to the Anglo-French rivalry, account had to be taken of the fact that not everyone in the world was willing to abide by the bipolar logic: a third bloc, voicing the politics of neutralism and non-alignment, was manifesting its presence at the United Nations. Nonetheless, the mood in the United States suggested a different order of priorities. A year before announcing his doctrine, Truman had stated:

> The Near and Middle East comprise an area which presents grave problems. This area contains vast natural resources of enormous value. It lies across the most convenient routes of land, air, and water communication between the west and east. It is consequently an area of great strategic importance. In this area there are a number of friendly sovereign states, members of the United Nations. They are not strong enough individually or collectively to withstand armed aggression on the part of any great power. It is easy to see, therefore, how the Near and Middle East might become an arena of intense rivalry between outside powers, and how such rivalry might suddenly erupt in armed conflict.[13]

---

[10] *Ibid.*

[11] FO 371/81910; E 1023/91; 8 May 1950: "Possibility of Statement by Americans and Ourselves and Perhaps the French About the Middle East."

[12] FO 371/81907; E 1023/15: Campbell to FO.

[13] Reitzel, *et al.*, *United States Foreign Policy 1945–55*, p. 210.

Viewed in the context of global containment and NATO, there is a strong implication that commitments could be extended beyond the core area of the North Atlantic and the western hemisphere in general.

American and British Perceptions of NATO's Extension: 1949–50

In March 1949 Secretary of State Dean Acheson set the general tone for the debate. "During the drafting of the North Atlantic Pact," he declared at a press conference, "we were aware of the possibility that our formal expression of serious interest in the security of countries in the North Atlantic area might be misinterpreted as implying a lessening of our interest in the security of countries in other areas, particularly the Near and Middle East." After stressing the special importance of Turkey, Greece, and Iran, he went on to say: "In the compact world of today, the security of the United States cannot be defined in terms of boundaries and frontiers."[14] At this point, it may be of interest to recall that the National Security Council considered that the United States had "greater long-range strategic interests in the military establishments of Turkey than in those of Greece."[15]

On the question of extension, a long memorandum prepared by Gordon P. Merriam of the State Department's Policy Planning Staff (dated 13 June 1949 and marked "Top Secret") is a reflection of the official position at the time. It began with a statement of "The Problem: To determine whether the North Atlantic Treaty should be extended to include Middle Eastern countries, and the possibility of creating one or more additional Article 51 treaties embracing the Middle East... considered for the purposes of this discussion [as] Greece, Turkey, Syria, Lebanon, Israel, Jordan, Egypt, the Sudan, Eritrea, Ethiopia, Saudi Arabia, Iraq, Iran, Afghanistan, Pakistan and India."[16] The memo acknowledged that American security requirements were "closely interwoven with those of Great Britain."[17]

Merriam concurred that it would be unwise, because of the limitations of US resources and the potential provocation to the Soviet Union, "a) To send US Forces to Greece, even as token forces; b) To construct medium bomber and fighter fields in Turkey with a view to use by US Forces; c) To stock existing Turkish airfields with aviation gasoline to be held for use by

---

[14] Quoted in *Foreign Relations of the United States*, 1949, VI, 44.

[15] *Foreign Relations of the United States*, 1949, VI, 40 (NSC report 42/1 of 22 March 1949 to President Truman).

[16] *Foreign Relations of the United States*, 1949, VI, 31.

[17] *Ibid.*, p. 32.

US Forces." On the other hand, it was considered desirable "to construct a suitable air-field in the Suez area which could be used by US bombers."[18]

Turning to the Arab countries, Merriam observed that all had "indicated at one time or another a desire to enter into a military alliance or other military arrangements with the US or with both the US and the UK...[yet] with the exception of Saudi Arabia, none of the Arab governments could enter into an alliance with the US at this time due to the deterioration of relations resulting from the Palestine question."[19] The early reference to the impact of the Palestinian question is to be noted. As will be shown below, this factor figured prominently in the calculations of such American and British foreign affairs policy-makers as Ernest Bevin, George McGhee, and Loy Henderson.

As to the steps open to the United States, Merriam listed six that could be taken singly or simultaneously (and as options they appear to retain relevance for policy even today):

> a) Continuing along present lines, i.e. by unilateral diplomatic, economic, and military support as determined by us on the basis of *ad hoc* need and availabilities, but refraining from any mutual commitment except as provided by the UN Charter, with such assistance and cooperation as other like-minded nations, particularly the UK, can and will provide.
>
> b) Extension of the North Atlantic Treaty to include certain selected countries in the area.
>
> c) Creation of a regional pact, pure and simple.
>
> d) Creation of a regional pact linked to the strongest members of the North Atlantic Treaty system.
>
> e) Creation of a regional pact having some kind of association, or possibility of association, with the North Atlantic Treaty.
>
> f) Creation of a new UN procedure.[20]

The first step offered the "advantage of simplicity," but also the disadvantages inherent in an *"ad hoc,* country by country basis," which would undermine what Merriam called the "area approach"—the preferred course given the circumstances. But the prerequisite for the "area approach," which he saw as being the "friendship, trust and cooperation" of the Arab countries, was lacking. Hence he felt that the "acquisition or construction of

---

[18] *Ibid.*

[19] *Ibid.*, p. 133.

[20] *Ibid.*, pp. 33, 34.

adequate facilities" in Arab countries would be "extremely difficult if not impossible so long as the US maintained a policy of favoritism in regard to Israel."[21] Merriam argued that a relationship of friendship and trust with the Arabs had once existed, but that it had "suffered severe though not irreparable damage." As to the implications:

> Until the damage has been repaired, [the US] task of supporting the integrity of the three northern countries of Greece, Turkey and Iran will be that of holding up an arch which lacks foundations. Furthermore, the relations between the various countries of the area must be on a sound basis. The Palestine question has caused the contrary effect.[22]

The second option, extension of NATO to include selected countries (primarily Greece and Turkey), was rejected as an immediate possibility for two reasons. Firstly, with the inclusion of Norway and Italy, the area of commitment had grown considerably. Secondly, the inclusion of Greece would "throw the question of aid to Greek guerrillas into the NAP framework and risk magnifying the question into a crude and primary power issue."[23] Besides, the extension in the direction of the Middle East would be vulnerable if Germany became a security risk.

The third option (creation of a regional pact, pure and simple) offered no solution, again because of regional discord created by the Palestine question, and also because "the area lacked a power center on the basis of which a pact could be built."[24] The fourth option, linking a regional pact with strong NAP (North Atlantic Pact) members such as the US and the UK, placed too heavy a burden on the two Atlantic allies. Besides, as Merriam put it, "the Arab countries, while having a pervading fear of the USSR, have a closer and more immediate problem in Israel."[25] Finally, there was a basic difference between the US and the UK:

> The US has supported and favored Israel, and endeavored at the same time to remain on friendly terms with the Arab states. The UK, on the contrary, places Arab relations ahead of relations

---

[21] *Ibid.*

[22] *Ibid.*

[23] *Ibid.*

[24] *Ibid.*, p. 35.

[25] *Ibid.*

with Israel, and has temporarily departed from this policy only when necessary in the interest of Anglo-American relations.[26]

For much the same reasons, the fifth option—a regional pact linked in some form with the NAP—was not immediately viable, although it did offer positive prospects "if the Middle East [could] be sufficiently pulled together."[27] It could help to resolve some of the area's chronic tensions and possessed more flexibility in its linkage structure than other options. In addition, individual requests might be formulated with more moderation because of group consideration.

The last option was developing existing UN machinery not subject to veto "to contribute to general international security including the security of the Middle East."[28] The idea here proposed was to give more muscle to the General Assembly so that there would "be a judgment of the international community on the facts of any situation in which armed attack is alleged and the Security Council fails to take adequate measures."[29] Merriam felt that the proposal was immediately practicable and could make "a significant political contribution to security as a deterrent, particularly in regions outside the Western Hemisphere and the North Atlantic area."[30]

This in short was Merriam's argument and list of options. How representative his views and options were of the conventional wisdom in Washington and London is not easily answered. But they do offer a useful framework for the subject under study. How true was Merriam's contention that American security requirements were "closely interwoven" with those of Britain? Was Britain's definition of the Middle East substantially similar? Was Merriam's hesitancy regarding further extensions and entanglements shared by American representatives on the spot in the Middle East? One might also ask the question as to whether Merriam's view of the centrality of the Palestine question was shared by others.

The Centrality of the Palestine Question

Following high-level talks in 1947 that drew the principal guidelines for Anglo-American policy toward the Middle East, the two Atlantic partners continued to hold their periodic and closely coordinated reviews of questions

[26] *Ibid.*, p. 36.
[27] *Ibid.*, p. 37.
[28] *Ibid.*
[29] *Ibid.*, p. 38.
[30] *Ibid.*, p. 39.

related to defense of the region, arms transfers, economic aid, oil policy, the desirability of regional security pacts, base facilities, and the Palestine question. Differences of perception and policy were never absent. For instance, at the 1947 talks the Palestine question was deliberately kept out of the discussions in order to facilitate progress on other issues.[31] Later, during the George McGhee-Michael Wright negotiations of November 1949, the British record reveals vigorous discussions on the Palestine issue, with American opposition to the British plan to incorporate Arab Palestine into Jordan shifting from a question of principle to one of timing.[32] Britain and the United States were drawing closer, but differences remained. In an important paper dated April 1949 the Permanent Under-Secretary's Committee (PUSC) in the Foreign Office argued:

> We want the whole of the Middle East, including Israel, to be friendly towards us. If, however, we were to secure the friendship of Israel at the expense of the friendship of the Arab countries, we should lose economically and strategically more than we should gain. Our object must be, therefore, to endeavour to promote friendly relations with Israel, but not to the point of losing the friendship of the Arab world. Strategically, facilities in Israel would be no substitute for facilities in Egypt and other Arab countries.[33]

A month later, a document entitled "Policy Towards Israel" bearing Ernest Bevin's signature expressed the same concern and priority: "If for any reason we are faced with the position of having to choose between Israel and the Arabs our overriding interest must be to do our utmost to preserve our position in the Arab countries."[34] The other bone of contention was oil. A Foreign Office minute on "Conversations with the Americans About the Middle East," dated 19 December 1949, recorded: "Issues such as Palestine and Middle East oil [are] capable of leading to such a degree of friction and tension with the United States as to endanger the general policy embodied

---

[31] Paul Jabbet, *Nor By War Alone* (Berkeley: University of California Press, 1981), p. 70.

[32] *FO 371/78056*; E 14770/1026/65. Record of discussion between Mr. Michael Wright and members of the State Department, 14 November 1949 (Discussion on a Palestine Settlement).

[33] FO 371/75067; PUSC (19) on Middle East, 30 April 1949.

[34] FO 371/75054; E 6145/1026/65: "Policy Towards Israel," signed Ernest Bevin, 20 May 1949.

in the Atlantic pact and the European Recovery Programme."[35] The Foreign Office was expressing the hope that by 1951 82 percent of Britain's oil would be drawn from the Middle East.[36] The stakes were enormous.

The Policy Planning Staff of the State Department believed that US support for the partition of Palestine could adversely affect the development of Middle Eastern petroleum, thus presenting "a serious threat to the overall success of the Marshall Plan" for the recovery of Europe.[37] The National Security Council (NSC) was even more emphatic on this point, linking Palestine with US strategic interests and security directly. As A.D. Miller, author of *Search For Security: Saudi Arabian Oil and American Foreign Policy 1939–1949*, put it, the NSC argued "that unrestricted access to Middle Eastern oil was essential to the economy of the United States and to the economic recovery of Europe under the ERP (Economic Recovery Program)."[38] Similar views were also shared by Loy Henderson, head of the State Department's Office of Near Eastern and African Affairs (NEA), and by the Joint Chiefs of Staff (JCS).

Henderson pointed to the American stake in Middle Eastern oil and to the lurking danger in late 1947:

> We shall need Arab friendship if we are to retain our petroleum position in the Arab world. During the next few years we are planning to obtain huge quantities of oil from Iraq, Bahrein, Kuwait, and Saudi Arabia, not only for our use but for the reconstruction of Europe. Furthermore we are intending to transport oil from Persia, Iraq, and Saudi Arabia across a number of Arab countries by pipelines to the Mediterranean ports. Already, partly as a result of our policies regarding Palestine, the attitude of Saudi Arabia towards the United States has changed sharply....[39]

In this respect Tapline and its 300,000 barrels-a-day capacity was seen as an indispensable component of Europe's economic recovery, and therefore of the Alliance's security. As for the military planners, the Joint Chiefs of Staff warned: "The most serious of all possible consequences from a military

---

[35] FO 371/78056: E 15252/1026/65 by Michael Wright, 19 December 1949.

[36] FO 371/78067; PUSC (19), 30 April 1949.

[37] A.D. Miller, *Search for Security: Saudi Arabian Oil and American Foreign Policy 1939–1945* (Chapel Hill: University of North Carolina Press, 1980), p. 192.

[38] *Ibid.*, p. 193.

[39] *Ibid.*, pp. 186–87.

point of view is that implementation of a decision to partition Palestine would gravely prejudice access by the US to [Middle East] oil."[40]

Finally, the centrality of the Palestine question was reflected in an important report to the House Committee on Foreign Affairs by Assistant Secretary of State George McGhee in February 1950:

> Let me speak very frankly on this question. The political loss of this area to the Soviet Union would be a major disaster comparable to its loss during war....The Near East may be critical to our national interests in time of war, but it is vital to us in time of peace.
>
> Against this background, our solicitude for the Palestine refugees, partly based on humanitarian considerations, has additional justification. As long as the refugee problem remains unresolved, the delicate equilibrium affected by the armistices is endangered. As long as this problem remains unresolved, attainment of a political settlement in Palestine is delayed, and a major source of friction between Israel and the Arab states is perpetuated to the detriment of peace in the entire Near East. Finally, as long as this problem remains unresolved, the refugees themselves will continue to serve as a natural focal point for exploitation by Communist and disruptive elements which neither we nor the Near Eastern governments can ignore. In this critical area we can ill afford to stand by in the face of any major security threat. The presence of three quarters of a million idle, destitute people—a number greater than the combined strength of all the standing armies of the Near East—whose discontent increases with the passage of time, is the greatest threat to the security of the area which now exists.[41]

Where is the Middle East: The Inner and Outer Rings

Writing in 1903 (and acknowledging that Alfred Mahan invented the term Middle East as a strategic concept), Valentine Chirol, foreign editor of the *Times*, defined it as encompassing "those regions in Asia which extend to the borders of India or command the approaches to India, and which are

---

[40] *Ibid.*

[41] Quoted in FO 371/81907; E 1023/8-11.

consequently bound up with the problems of Indian political as well military defence."[42] Chirol also perceived the Middle Eastern question as the "outcome of that constant projection of European forces—moral, commercial and military—into Asia which is slowly but steadily transforming all the conditions that enabled [Britain] to achieve. . . a position of unparalleled ascendancy in the Asiatic continent."[43] The central problem as he saw at the turn of the century was how to preserve this position of unrivalled hegemony, acquired in the past through the Royal Navy's control of the seas, under new conditions in which land power, exemplified by Tsarist Russia's thrust in Central Asia, was growing at an alarming rate.[44]

There has never really been a consensus on where the Middle East is, nor an accepted core for it. In the mid-fifties, John Foster Dulles defined it in Congress as the "area lying between and including Libya on the West and Pakistan on the East and Turkey on the North and the Arabian Peninsula to the South," plus the Sudan and Ethiopia.[45] As mentioned earlier in this paper, our contention is that it is better understood as a shifting strategic concept than as "immutable geography."[46]

Nonetheless, the two Atlantic allies did not widely differ on the question of definitions. Ernest Bevin defined it in one document as "the area stretching from Corfu to Kabul which is next in strategic importance after Europe to our interests as a whole."[47] The reference to Afghanistan is of some interest. The document bears the following note: "There are traditional links between Afghanistan, Persia, and Turkey, and from the Soviet point of view if not from ours Afghanistan is strategically important to Middle East defence. Inclusion of Afghanistan in a Middle Eastern Pact would therefore be logical."[48]

But if agreement existed as to definition, there was a fundamental divergence of views regarding the relative importance of the outer and inner rings.

---

[42]Valentine Chirol, *The Middle Eastern Question or Some Political Problems of Indian Defence* (London: John Murray, 1903), p. 5.

[43]*Ibid.*

[44]*Ibid.*

[45]Roderic Davison, "Where is the Middle East?," in *The Modern Middle East*, edited by Richard Nolte (New York: Atherton Press, 1963), p. 14. Davison (p. 18) sees the term as "a projection of European, particularly British, thinking." Equally valuable is Nikkie Keddie, "Is There a Middle East?," *International Journal of Middle East Studies*, 4 (1973), p. 257.

[46][Cf. further pp. 160–62 above.]

[47]FO 371/75079; E 5020/1074/65; Ernest Bevin.

[48]*Ibid.*

And in this respect the assessment of B.A.B. Burrows, a British diplomat reporting from Washington in September 1950, is especially perceptive and deserves lengthy quotation:

> I am assuming that it is still very much our wish to have the Americans strategically committed in the Middle East, even though at the present time there is a higher priority for giving practical effect to the general commitment they are undertaking to put more troops into Europe. I feel that one of the factors which influences the divergent views on Middle East strategical priority held by us and the Americans is that their thoughts always start from the outer ring of Greece, Turkey and Persia, whereas ours start from Cairo and radiate outwards. The Americans think like this partly because Greece, Turkey and Persia border on Russian or satellite territory, and therefore the first attack on the Middle East must come through them, and the first impact of such an attack on American opinion will be related to these countries and not to the Arab world. This way of thinking has become crystallised and confirmed because Greece, Turkey and Persia are treated together in both Congressional and State Department practice for purposes of military assistance, and because the State Department put Greece, Turkey and Persia together in a single office under the Near Eastern, South Asian and African Affairs Bureau. These factors are reinforced by a perhaps sub-conscious reluctance on the part of the State Department to consider commitments in the Arab world, owing to memories of the emotional pressure exercised by Jewish groups here and by more national misgivings about the local and economic conditions in most of the Arab states.[49]

On the question of Merriam's hesitancy regarding extension of the Atlantic Alliance being shared by American representatives in the Middle East, the records of the Istanbul (November 1949) and Cairo (March 1950) Conferences of American diplomats indicate downright opposition to any further commitments. At Istanbul the Conference recommended that the United States "should not attempt to negotiate multilateral or bilateral security pacts with the Near Eastern States, at least until such time as it is prepared to commit military forces required to carry out the guarantees given."[50]

---

[49] FO 371/81967; E 1195/3/G, Burrows to Wright, 14 September 1950.
[50] *Foreign Relations of the United States*, 1949, VI, 169.

The Cairo Conference "confirmed the continued validity of the (Istanbul) position."[51] But despite the very real caution discussed above, and the danger that the Atlantic Alliance might find itself involved in the region's conflicts, including the Arab-Israeli or inter-Arab conflicts, the Cold War perspective of Secretary of State Dean Acheson dominated the scene. In February 1950 he had asserted that "the only way to deal with the Soviet Union...is to create situations of strength."[52] In this respect it was pointed out shortly thereafter that the Middle East was "a region that seemed to call preeminently for creating a 'situation of strength'...[for it] seemed almost to invite a Soviet push that would split the free world along its North-South axis, deny it the abundant oil resources of Iran, Iraq, and the Arabian peninsula, and open a path for the extension of Soviet influence westward across Africa and eastward into Pakistan and India."[53]

In early 1949 Ernest Bevin had remarked: "Once the Atlantic Pact is concluded...we shall then be free to give more attention to the area stretching from Corfu to Kabul."[54] The abortive proposals for the Middle East Command (MEC), the Middle East Defense Organization (MEDO), as well as various blueprints for Mediterranean pacts, the Baghdad Pact, and CENTO, flowed from the logic of both Dean Acheson and Ernest Bevin. In virtually every instance, formal linkage with the North Atlantic Alliance, particularly Merriam's options d) and e), was established, and the spectrum of responsibilities as well as the area of deployment and operations expanded, without much concern for the aspirations of the peoples of the Middle East, especially the Arabs. In this type of grand design, particularly in view of the zero-sum game atmosphere of the Cold War, the regional population tended to recede from the concerns of policy-makers, giving way to the "realism" of eyeball-to-eyeball confrontation between "rimland and heartland."

The Arab Response

It is a fact that the official Arab response to the debate on the extension of NATO and the setting up of Western-sponsored Middle East pacts modelled on the Atlantic Pact was varied. But on the level of public opinion it was one of angry opposition. To cite one or two examples: In April 1950 Maʿrūf

---

[51] *Foreign Relations of the United States*, 1950, V, 3.

[52] Jaber, *Not By War Alone*, p. 3.

[53] *Ibid.*, quoting Richard Stebbins, *et al.*, *The United States in World Affairs, 1950* (New York: Harper, 1951), p. 307.

[54] FO 371/75079; E 5020/1074/65; Ernest Bevin.

Dawālibī denounced the policy of Western pacts and called for a treaty of friendship with Russia, which Soviet diplomat Daniel Solod quickly took up by offering Syria a treaty of friendship and credits for the purchase of Soviet and Czech armaments. There was also the mainstream Arab nationalist answer to all such pacts, as expressed in early 1952 by George Ḥabash, who was then a fifth-year medical student at the American University of Beirut (AUB). In the course of a lecture at West Hall (AUB) sponsored by the influential AUB Arab nationalist student association *Al-'Urwa al-wuthqā*, Ḥabash argued that during the First and Second World Wars the Arabs had adopted a policy of cooperation with the Allies. He asked what this policy brought other than occupation, partition, and disaster upon disaster. Besides, the pacts were clearly designed to perpetuate the condition of semi-sovereignty and to inhibit the Arabs from changing their internal status quo.[55]

The MEC and MEDO proposals provide interesting cases in point. They meant, in effect, the setting in place of joint defense pacts with NATO linkage. In many Arab states—Iraq, Jordan, and Egypt—Britain maintained a powerful influence bolstered by an extensive network of land, sea, and air bases centered on the Suez Canal base complex. It is out of considerations such as the Truman Doctrine of containment and the continuing British military presence that the concept of the Middle East Command (MEC) was born. The United States and Britain asked France and Turkey to join them as sponsors of the proposal. Egypt held the key by virtue of the Suez Canal position and its leadership of the Arab League. The idea was that if Egypt accepted the MEC, other Arab states would follow suit.[56] It is significant that the MEC proposals were presented to Egypt by the governments of the United States, Britain, France, and Turkey on 13 October 1951 (and rejected by Egypt two days later), while the principles underlying this controversial defense pact were published by NATO a month later.[57] At the same time, invitations to participate in the MEC were addressed to Australia, New Zealand, and South Africa. The principal points in the proposal required Egypt to furnish the MEC with "such strategic defence and other facilities on her soil as are indispensable for the organisation in peacetime of the defence of the Middle East. . . [and] undertake to grant forces of the Allied Middle East Command all necessary facilities and assistance in the event of

[55] George Ḥabash, "Al-Difā' al-mushtarak," *Manshūrāt Jam'īyat al-'Urwa al-Wuthqā* (Beirut: American University of Beirut, 1952).
[56] Campbell, *Defense of the Middle East*, p. 42.
[57] Stookey, *America and the Arab States*, p. 133.

war, imminent menace of war, or apprehended international emergency including the use of Egyptian ports, airfields, and means of communication."[58] In return, Britain would abrogate the Anglo-Egyptian Treaty of 1936 and withdraw military forces not earmarked for the MEC.

It was clear to Arab opinion that the MEC was merely a device to perpetuate a somewhat disguised imperial domination of the region. The government of Naḥḥās Pāshā replied by abrogating, unilaterally, the Anglo-Egyptian Defence Treaty of 1936 and the Anglo-Egyptian Condominium of 1899 over the Sudan. The evacuation of the Canal Zone was also demanded. Yet there was no let-up on the part of the senior partners of the Alliance. Analyzing this episode, Halford Hoskins wrote:

> ...in an announcement by the Department of State on October 24, 1951...the United States intended to establish a Middle East defense command despite Egypt's refusal to join. Plans were being worked out for the cooperation in this task of the United States, Britain, France, Turkey, New Zealand, Australia, and the Union of South Africa. Once plans had been completed, invitations to membership might be extended to the Arab states and Israel. Meanwhile, the announcement implied, the Suez Canal would continue to be used as a base of operations.[59]

Again there was no progress, and the MEC project was abandoned in favor of MEDO, sponsored by the same countries, and which Hoskins characterized as "consisting essentially of a committee of generals to plan the defenses of the area, [and to be] concerned also with the issues making for instability:" i.e. the Arab-Israeli conflict, Iran under Mossadeq, and Egypt in revolution.[60]

Labyrinthine and often disingenuous explanations have been provided for the failure of the MEC and MEDO projects. The true explanation is, however, much simpler. For the Arabs, these initiatives generally spelled a return to, or a maintenance of, dependent status; besides, the immediate object of Arab apprehension was Israeli expansionism. One consequence of their failure was that Western interest shifted to the Northern Tier or Outer Ring, where there was a more pronounced willingness to come under the

---

[58] Text in *Documents on the Middle East*, edited by Ralph Magnus (Washington: Enterprise Institute, 1969), p. 76.

[59] Halford Hoskins, *The Middle East: Problem Area in World Politics* (New York: Macmillan, 1954), pp. 282–83.

[60] *Ibid.*, p. 284.

Alliance's umbrella, and where the Central Treaty Organization (CENTO) was ultimately established.

The Atlantic Alliance and the Middle East Today

There is growing evidence today of a renewed interest in extending NATO's perimeter beyond the Tropic of Cancer and in enlarging the scope and membership of the Alliance, especially by informal means. This evidence is to be found in the official pronouncements of many Western political figures, military commanders, and parliamentary bodies, as well as in the position papers of authoritative experts and in the publications of leading Western research institutes. Although such material is fundamentally different in nature from the unpublished primary documents that underpinned the earlier sections, it reveals elements of continuity in several themes from the post-war period until the 1980s.

Views From Britain

Clear signs that a more forceful British strategic posture was in the making began to emerge in the press in 1979. In September of that year the weekly *The Economist* called for a vigorous program of Western "counter-arming" to rectify a vulnerable situation that, it felt, would grow strategically worse in the following two or three years. Three especially grave vulnerabilities were singled out: in the US, in Europe, and in "areas important to the West in other parts of the world."[61]

First, argued *The Economist*, by 1982 Russia's missile force could destroy enough American land-based, submarine, and air-launched missiles in a surprise attack on the United States to make it impossible for the surviving American nuclear arsenal to destroy Russia's still unused warheads. Second, Europe also was placed in an increasingly vulnerable situation because of the massive deployment of Soviet SS-20 missiles and Backfire bombers. Third, areas important to the West in other parts of the world were likewise in an exposed position. Russia's decade of rearmament had equipped it with sufficient aircraft and ships to deploy troops anywhere in the globe. The well-informed weekly observed: "Once the Russians and their allies have established non-nuclear superiority in a given area, they can put it to use

---

[61] *The Economist*, 8 September 1979, pp. 15–17.

under the protection of their new nuclear power. It is they, not the West, who will be holding the nuclear umbrella. ...."[62]

In answer, *The Economist* proposed for the West an ambitious program of counter-arming that would "set out to do four specific things: 1) as soon as possible, to make some of America's land-based missiles invulnerable, by making them mobile; 2) to give America's nuclear force the ability to hit more of Russia's missile silos, so as to reduce the damage Russia can do to America; 3) to restore the balance of shorter-range nuclear weapons in Europe; 4) to strengthen the West's conventional forces, so that they have a better chance of holding off Russia's without resorting to the threat of going nuclear."[63]

This was in September 1979. With the Soviet intervention in Afghanistan in December, British fears, together with Western fears in general, reached a high point. As Gregory Treverton of London's International Institute of Strategic Studies put it: "Most past so-called crises in the Alliance have been pre-eminently about fashioning new Alliance political arrangements to reassure ourselves. In contrast, this crisis is about confronting an adversary, about the stakes, about perceptions and capabilities of Europe and America. It cuts to the bone."[64] There was a growing feeling of insecurity. Whereas in 1977 only 14 percent of Europeans felt they might be involved in a war in the next ten years, a 1980 poll indicated that 35 percent felt this way.[65]

It is perhaps not surprising that Britain developed and released plans to press ahead with the development of intervention units and strike forces, as the next two examples will show. The *International Herald Tribune* in a special report on the new strategy of NATO wrote in July 1980:

> Britain has earmarked Marine Commandos for intervention out-side NATO. Margaret Thatcher's government also favors recreat-ing an assault paratroop battalion trained to jump in enemy-held terrain, and the Royal Air Force has started lengthening the fuse-lages of their C-130 Hercules—the transport used by Israel in the Entebbe raid. Welcoming the new European capability, a US of-ficial said: "There are scenarios France or Britain could handle alone, avoiding any superpower involvement."[66]

---

[62] *Ibid.*

[63] *Ibid.*

[64] Joseph Fitchett, "Nato Seeks New Strategy," *International Herald Tribune*, 18 July 1980, p. 1.

[65] *Ibid.*

[66] *Ibid.*

Britain's 1980 Defence White Paper stated: "The Services should also be able to operate effectively outside the NATO area without diminishing our central commitment to the alliance."[67] Such recent Command Papers as *Defence in the 1980s* and *Statement on the Defence Estimates: 1981* are much more explicit in their emphasis on action over a wider area than the traditional NATO perimeter. This ambition to establish such strike forces capable of intervention—for example in the Gulf and Indian Ocean—has led to a debate as to the nature of the force. One school of thought sees it in terms of a parachute battalion, possessing its own stockpiles of equipment, and requiring the services of RAF Hercules transport aircraft.

This capability is envisaged in modest terms, with tasks ranging from gaining rapid control of an air field, to providing assistance to friendly governments "threatened by rebellion," to acting in support of US operations in the Gulf.[68] But the cost involved could run to tens of millions of pounds, which would have to be reallocated from within the existing defense budget.

On the other hand, another school represented by Field Marshal Lord Carver, a former Chief of Defence Staff, has dismissed such ideas of seeking to reassert Britain's "imperial past on this small scale as military poppycock." He did not think it wise "to extend NATO's area of responsibility east of Suez or south of the Tropic of Cancer."[69] And with respect to unilateral intervention, he noted a growing trend in the Western world "to threaten military force without any credible means of implementation, or conception of the risks and costs involved." The only effective military power Britain could deploy quickly anywhere in the Middle East, in his view, was air power; and in this context, if Britain was really determined to make a contribution, "the best move could be to reactivate the RAF base at Akrotiri, in Cyprus, for strike, reconnaissance and transport operations."[70]

Which school of thought will win in the eighties? Britain will probably resort to the proverbial compromise and end up combining a parachute assault force with the Akrotiri option. The stress in any case will most likely be on the contribution that can be made within a larger American-dominated framework, if some recent official positions are any indication.

In March 1981, Prime Minister Thatcher expressed unrestrained enthusiasm for a joint NATO Rapid Deployment Force, although her Common

---

[67] David Fairhall, "Assault Battalion Idea is Poppycock," *The Guardian Weekly*, 6 July 1980, p. 4.

[68] *Ibid.*

[69] *Ibid.*

[70] *Ibid.*

Market partners appeared far less enthusiastic about such prospects, particularly her pledge to President Reagan that began with the words: "There is an urgent need for a new defence policy beyond the North Atlantic."[71]

In this respect, a close look at *Defence in the 1980s*, prepared by the British Minister of Defence, is instructive, particularly paragraphs 401, 402, 408, and 409, where the following arguments are developed:

> 1. In common with NATO allies, we also have wider interests outside the NATO area....We depend on the developing world for many raw materials. The security of our trade routes is therefore of vital importance to our economy....[72]
>
> 2. The West must make it clear to the Soviet Union and its allies that it is capable of protecting essential interests by military means should the need arise. That task should not be left to the United States alone. Of our European partners, France has major defence commitments in Africa and elsewhere, and retains permanent forces in the Indian and Pacific Oceans. Vessels of the Federal German, Italian and Dutch navies undertake occasional deployments beyond the NATO area. Belgium provides training assistance to Zaire. All such activities help to protect Western interests worldwide.[73]
>
> 3. The government believes that the Services should also be able to operate effectively outside the NATO area....British forces will therefore continue to deploy and exercise outside the NATO area from time to time....From April this year (1980) one parachute battalion will always be available to provide a parachute capability at seven days notice.[74]

This capability was upgraded in John Nott's *Statement on the Defence Estimates: 1981* (Chapter Four: Wider Defence Interests) in terms of dropping "an entire battalion group if necessary within 15 minutes."[75] The *Statement* also spoke of a three-fold task for the Services: "assistance, deployment (including periodic exercises) and intervention;" and referred to a

---

[71] *Guardian*, 3 March 1981.

[72] *Defence in the 1980s* (London: H.M. Stationery Office, April 1980), I, Command Paper 7826-1, p. 39.

[73] *Ibid.*, p. 41.

[74] *Ibid.*

[75] *Statement on the Defence Estimates: 1981* (London: H.M. Stationery Office, April 1981), Command Paper 8212-1, p. 32.

Royal Navy Task Group Deployment (RNTGD) comprising two destroyers, three frigates, and the three Royal Fleet Auxiliaries with which "the United Kingdom was able to respond promptly [with] a naval presence in the Gulf of Oman" at the outset of the Iraq-Iran war of 1980.[76]

Western Security Perceptions by Four Western Institutes

The trend toward greater NATO involvement in the Middle East extends beyond the US and Great Britain. In this context the cooperation of four influential Western institutes in preparing the report *Western Security: What has Changed? What Should Be Done?* was an unprecedented event. The report carried the signatures of Karl Kaiser, Director of the German Foreign Policy Institute, Winston Lord, President of the Council on Foreign Relations (US), Thierry de Montbrial, Director of the Institut français des relations internationales (IFRI), and David Watt, Director of the Royal Institute of International Affairs (London). As the report saw it, Western security can no longer be limited to events and threats occurring in the NATO region alone, because of: a) "increased tensions between East and West and enhanced Soviet military threats both in Europe and in Third World regions;" b) the fact that "the West will also be facing an increasingly unstable and volatile Third World upon which it will depend more and more for its economic survival (this is particularly true of the Persian Gulf region);" and c) the fact that "the period ahead will also be one of prolonged economic crisis worldwide."[77]

Neither was it possible "to isolate European security from crises arising in other regions vital for the West." The report's central theses stated "that the days of the old Atlantic system, based on US predominance and its corollary European reluctance to take wider responsibilities, are over."[78] It added that the Arab-Israel conflict of 1973, oil dependence, and the Soviet intervention in Afghanistan have contributed to produce "a new arena of the East-West conflict outside the traditional NATO area and imposed it on the existing regional conflicts."[79] The report recommended a Western naval task force able to keep open the Straits of Hormuz, and approved of the RDF. It also recognized that the failure to resolve the Palestinian problem is a permanent cause of instability.

---

[76] *Ibid.*, p. 30.

[77] Karl Kaiser *et al.*, *Western Security: What Has Changed? What Should Be Done?* (London: Royal Institute of International Affairs, 1981), p. 7.

[78] *Ibid.*, p. 17.

[79] *Ibid.*, p. 23.

Furthermore, the report injected a note of realism regarding the formal expansion of NATO: "We do not propose," said the directors, "that NATO undertakes major institutional innovations, concerning political and security developments in the Third World. To enlarge formally its geographical responsibility would require fundamental amendment of the Treaty and ratification in fifteen parliaments. Such change would be highly contentious."[80] What they urged instead was a "thicker web of consultations" by adding to the NATO forum the seven-nation summit of leaders of the advanced industrialized countries that began in Rambouillet in 1975. This seven-nation summit should also expand its concerns to political and military issues. In addition, a mechanism called the Principal Nations Approach, with a core group composed of the US, Britain, France, Germany, and Japan, should be established at once to deal with "developments in the Gulf and South West Asia" on a continuing "watch" basis.[81]

Views of NATO Assemblies, Military Commanders, and Lobbies

There is mounting evidence of this trend towards the expansion of Alliance interests southward and eastward in the deliberations of NATO and its associated bodies. At the 26th Annual Session (November 1980) of the North Atlantic Assembly (which provides a forum for 150 Alliance parliamentarians representing the 15 member countries) were four observers from the Spanish Cortes, and, for the first time, eight members of the Japanese Diet. The overriding theme of the session was the situation in the Gulf and its implications for Western security. Despite a critique of the RDF by Colonel Jonathan Alford, Deputy Director of the International Institute of Strategic Studies, characterizing this enterprise as a "King Lear Syndrome" ("I will do such things—what they are yet I know not—but they shall be the terror of the earth."), the Assembly voted a resolution on the Gulf urging member countries "to deal effectively with conflicts in other areas where the NATO Treaty cannot be applied."[82]

Also in the same year, J.M. Luns, Secretary-General of NATO, made a speech at the Royal Institute for International Relations in Brussels entitled "NATO in the Present World Situation" in which he concluded:

> I am not suggesting that any attempt be made to amend the
> North Atlantic Treaty. What I am suggesting is that it will not

---

[80] *Ibid.*, p. 44.
[81] *Ibid.*, p. 46.
[82] *NATO Review*, February 1981, p. 23.

suffice in the future for the Alliance to confine its attentions to the territorial limits embodied in that Treaty if it is to duplicate its past success in protecting the vital interests of its member states.[83]

Similarly, the final communiqués of the NATO Council, meeting in Ministerial Session in Rome in May 1981, devoted considerable attention to the Gulf area and how to cope with emergency situations outside the Alliance's traditional boundaries. In particular, Article 5 of the Defence Planning Committee's final communiqué recognized that "situations outside NATO's boundaries may...threaten the vital interest of the West and therefore have implications for the security of members of the Alliance." It called for consultations when members of the Alliance "are considering out-of-area deployment of forces." The communiqué also recognized that "common objectives identified in such consultations may require members of the Alliance to facilitate out-of-area deployments in support of the vital interests of all."[84]

Writing in the June 1981 issue of the *NATO Review*, General Bernard Rogers, Supreme Allied Commander Europe (SACEUR), argued that the strategic environment of the 1980s contained an "added challenge outside the boundaries of NATO" that had to be met as well. An adequate response, in his view, involved the following steps:

> The first step is to acknowledge that, to meet these challenges, member nations must provide additional forces and resources, not simply redistribute already inadequate ones. The second is to recognize that only a few member nations have the military capability to protect common vital interests in external regions. Thus, these few Allies must rely on the remainder to take up the slack within NATO for any forces committed outside its area. Specifically, our force planning must address candidly the challenges posed by the possible commitment of the US Rapid Deployment Force (RDF) to an outlying area which would reduce the number of US forces and resources available to reinforce Europe.[85]

Such views are shared by Admiral Harry D. Train, Supreme Allied Commander Atlantic, who argued that from the very first days of the Alliance

---

[83] J.M. Luns, "NATO in the Present World Situation," *Studia Diplomatica*, 33.6 (1980) p. 646.

[84] *NATO Review*, June 1981, p. 30.

[85] General Bernard Rogers, "Increasing Threats to NATO's Security Call for Sustained Response," *NATO Review*, June 1981, p. 5.

"an informal agreed interpretation" of consultations as specified in Article 4 of the Treaty applied to threats in any part of the world. "Simply stated," said Train, "there is no NATO border. Time—not distance—must determine NATO's sphere of geopolitical interest."[86] As to the restriction contained in Article 6 defining the Tropic of Cancer as boundary, it applied, in his view, to a *casus belli* and was never meant to "prevent collective planning, maneuvers, or operations south of the Tropic of Cancer."[87]

In a lecture at the Royal Institute of International Relations (November 1980) on the subject of "NATO's Maritime Increased Challenges" (*sic*), Admiral Train stressed the growing power of the Soviet Navy and its projection capabilities, which necessitated that NATO "look beyond national and Atlantic interests and embrace a fundamental philosophy of world-wide maritime commitment."[88] The United States and NATO were commited "to a policy of maritime superiority" to ensure control over vital sea lines of communications and choke points, such as the Straits of Hormuz, "during periods of crisis or general war."[89] He believed "this basic premise of maritime power [to be] one of the most challenging aspects of geopolitics," that a war between NATO and the Warsaw Pact was "more likely to start in a remote region such as the Mideast or Persian Gulf," and that during this decade of the dangerous eighties, "the regional inferiority of NATO must be offset by confronting the Warsaw Pact, and especially the Soviets, with a global strategy."[90]

This major perception of crises originating beyond NATO's traditional sphere of military responsibilities also found expression in an article by Sir John Killick (Britain's Permanent Representative to NATO from 1975 to 1979) entitled "Is NATO Relevant to the 1980's?," and is shared by Air Chief Marshal Sir Alasdair Steedman, a former British Military Representative of NATO. In Killick's view, the chief threats "presented themselves outside the area of the North Atlantic Treaty...[and] the Alliance recognized in the Ottawa Declaration that developments outside the Alliance area could have implications for the interests of the Allies." While acknowledging that

---

[86] Admiral Harry D. Train, "NATO's Maritime Increased Challenges," *Studia Diplomatica*, 33.6 (1980), p. 651.

[87] *Ibid.*

[88] *Ibid.*, p. 654.

[89] *Ibid.*, p. 658–59.

[90] *Ibid.* See also Harry D. Train, "Preserving the Atlantic Alliance," *Proceedings of the US Naval Institute*, January 1981, pp. 24–28.

a "political consensus does not now exist in favor of the expansion of the responsibilities of the Alliance as such," Killick nevertheless urged that:

> ...extra-Alliance situations must therefore remain the responsibility for those member countries, acting individually or in consortium, who are willing and able to take action—political, economic or even military....The Allies concerned will not be acting under a NATO label, but NATO must continue to provide the forum for the monitoring and exchange of information about extra-Alliance developments and their implications....[91]

In a similar vein, Air Chief Marshal Steedman, in arguing that "NATO is much more than a military alliance; it is a political military alliance," has also concluded that the boundaries of NATO and the "inhibitions which this has imposed upon a number of the members who tend to sit upon those boundaries looking inwards at the day to day minutiae of their own country" constitute a very real problem. Drawing support from Lord Hill-Norton's book *No Soft Options*, Marshal Steedman added: "There is no question that there is a real need to look outside because that is now where the biggest threat is."[92]

We bring to an end this review of NATO's renewed interest in expanding its perimeter beyond the Tropic of Cancer by examining the perceptions and recommendations of various NATO "lobbies:" the Atlantic Council of the United States, the Institute for the Study of Conflict (London), and the Foreign Affairs Research Institute (London).

Nearly three years ago, the Atlantic Council of the United States and the Japanese Research Institute for Peace and Security (RIPS) began an unprecedented joint project on common security concerns. The joint working group, under U. Alexis Johnson and George R. Packard (Dean of the John Hopkins School of Advanced International Studies, SAIS), published a summary of their assessment and recommendations in the *NATO Review* (February and May 1981) under the title "The Common Security Interests of Japan, the United States, and its NATO Allies." As it saw it, NATO and Japan's dependence on Middle Eastern oil would remain critical for the foreseeable future. Consequently, a substantial military force should be "positioned in the area before access is denied, either by Soviet military power

---

[91] Sir John Killick, "Is NATO Relevant to the 1980's," *The World Today*, January 1980, p. 7.

[92] Air Chief Marshal Sir Alasdair Steedman, "Problems of Coalition War," *Royal United Services Institute Journal*, 126 (September 1981), pp. 11, 13.

or by local political upheavals."[93] The United States was seen as "the only country capable of taking the lead in this operation." But there were also important roles for other North Atlantic Treaty nations and Japan:

> France, the Federal Republic of Germany, the United Kingdom and Canada should provide appropriate military assets to the Middle East-Persian Gulf area to enhance allied capability and to demonstrate allied solidarity; other NATO Europe nations and Japan should apply their own civil assets, including airlift and sealift, to support this allied presence in the Middle East-Persian Gulf area. Countries with past operational experience in the Middle East region could provide valuable intelligence and training support for forces in, or being deployed to, the area.[94]

Another group of the Atlantic Council, the Special Working Group on the Middle East, published its report *Oil and Turmoil: Western Choices in the Middle East* in September 1979, three months before the Soviet intervention in Afghanistan. In contrast to the above-mentioned working group of the US, Japan, and NATO, and reflecting the atmosphere of détente that prevailed even in late 1979, this special Middle East group's recommendations were much more moderate. Convened in the aftermath of the Iranian revolution and the collapse of the Shah's regime, its membership of 30 experts included many former ambassadors to Arab countries, and their recommendations tended to mirror the State Department's conventional balance of approaches to the region, focusing on five major areas of policy: "availability of oil, Arab-Israeli settlement, strengthening of Turkey, a stronger military posture, and political relations."[95]

While opposing any revival of CENTO, or the building of "a new alliance linking Middle East states with the West," or finding a "new policeman of the Gulf to replace Iran," the report nevertheless urged a "strengthening of the US military posture through the increase of US naval power in the Indian Ocean supplemented by forces of allied navies," in response to what was perceived as a growing Soviet military threat.[96]

---

[93] *NATO Review*, February 1981, p. 12.

[94] *Ibid.*, April 1981, p. 14.

[95] John Campbell, Andrew Goodpaster, and Brent Scowcroft, *Oil and Turmoil: Western Choices in the Middle East* (Boulder, Colorado: Western Press, September 1979), pp. 9–11.

[96] *Ibid.*, pp. 33–35.

On the question of Palestine, acknowledged by the working group as "remain[ing] at the heart of the Arab-Israeli conflict," the report concluded: "We do not see any solution possible unless the negotiators take up the hard questions of Palestinian self-determination together with those relating to borders and security arrangements, aiming at an eventual total package that can reconcile Palestinian rights to self-government with Israel's right to security."[97] However, the report thought that this was not "the moment to bring the PLO into active negotiations," but that this "should not rule out informal contacts between the United States and the PLO with the purpose of ascertaining the latter's views and modifying them."[98] Indeed, elsewhere in the report, the implications to the Western alliance of the failure to resolve the issue of Palestinian self-determination were forcefully stated:

> The question of Palestinian self-determination in the West Bank and the Gaza Strip is crucial to the process of negotiation and to the prospects of a political settlement. Unresolved, it will continue to drive wedges between the US and a number of states in the Middle East whose cooperation it needs, Saudi Arabia in particular. America's European and Japanese allies, for whose vital interest in Middle East oil the cooperation of the producing states is essential, also have strong reasons to see the Palestinian question resolved. Thus, lack of progress on this question threatens not only the Israeli-Egyptian peace treaty but other essential American interests, including the cohesion of the Western Alliance.[99]

Compared to the Institute for the Study of Conflict's special paper written by Admiral of the Fleet (ret.) Lord Hill-Norton (which was also published in September 1979), the Atlantic Council's report is mild. Lord Hill-Norton estimated that Soviet behavior in Angola, Afghanistan, and the region of the Horn of Africa necessitated a vigorous response by NATO and its associates through the immediate establishment of an allied "constabulary force on the seas," the abandoning of the restrictive Tropic of Cancer limit, the enlargement of NATO (because of the demise of SEATO and CENTO) to include Japan, ASEAN, and others, and, on the level of strategic planning, a "shift from the land-air confrontation in Europe to the steadily increasing risks...on and over and under the world's oceans." Waxing nostalgic

---

[97] *Ibid.*, pp. 36–37.
[98] *Ibid.*
[99] *Ibid.*, p. 19.

while contemplating this dramatic swerve "from the narrow confines of the European theatre to the great oceans of the world," the Admiral asked: "Who better to take the lead than the United Kingdom, whose *Pax Britanica* was the longest and greatest maritime success story in the history of the world?"[100]

In the same category, one would also find proposals by the Foreign Affairs Research Institute (London)—a consistent advocate of the unrestrained expansion of NATO. It has promoted the case for expansion in its own conferences—Winchester in 1976, Brighton in 1978, and Leeds Castle, Kent in 1980—with such papers as "Reclaiming the Initiative From the Soviet Heartland, the Case For a Tri-Oceanic Alliance of the Imperiled Rimlands;" "A Strategy For the Coming Resource War;" "Will the United States Formulate and Implement a Grand Strategy For Global Freedom;" "The One Open Highway;" and a call by Dr. Jun Tsunoda, Director of the Japanese Centre for Strategic Studies, for the construction of "a Super-NATO...equipped with a system of regular summit and ministerial conferences with a small but efficient permanent secretariat."[101]

Concluding Remarks

We have now assembled a body of evidence of differing kinds relating to NATO and the Middle East in two distinct periods. The following observations concerning continuity and change can be made in conclusion.

a) With respect to the Middle East, there is a remarkable permanence of certain basic geographic realities and strategic concepts. Ernest Bevin's definition of the Middle East as stretching from Corfu to Kabul holds substantially true today, with perhaps one important difference: the expansion

---

[100] Admiral Lord Hill-Norton, "World Shipping at Risk: The Looming Threat to the Lifelines," *Conflict Studies*, 111 (September 1979), pp. 9, 14. There is a perception in NATO that Soviet naval doctrine has been increasingly emphasizing the interruption of sea lines of communications (SLOC), what Maurizio Cremasco of the Istituto Affari Internazional (Rome) has called a "return to concepts expounded by Marshall Sokolovski in the 1962 edition of his famous book *Military Strategy*." Thus, whereas the mission of "disrupting the enemy's ocean and sea communications" was listed by Admiral Gorshkov in 1971 as the lowest priority of the Soviety Navy, the same task was moved in 1976 from last to third place in his article in the *Soviet Military Encyclopedia* and in his book *The Sea Power of the State*. See Maurizio Cremasco, "The Mediterranean, the Atlantic and the Indian Ocean: A Difficult Strategic Equation," *Lo Spettatore internazionale*, 15.1 (January-March 1980), p. 8.

[101] *Towards a Grand Strategy of Global Freedom* (London: Foreign Affairs Publishing Co., 1981), pp. 9, 34, 51, 58, 106.

southward to include at least half of the Indian Ocean, with anchor points at the French island of Reunion and the Anglo-American base at Diego Garcia.

b) For the years 1948 to 1951, it would appear from the Foreign Office archives that the moving force behind the expansion of commitments into the "inner ring" was Britain, and that the Americans were being persuaded to join in defense arrangements there by the British. In the "outer ring," however, the roles were reversed, and Britain initially opposed the entrance of Turkey into NATO. Today, there appears to be a blurring of the distinction between outer and inner rings, particularly in the views of Secretary of State Alexander Haig. This is to some extent a reflection of renewed Cold War atmosphere. From a report to the US Senate Committee on Foreign Relations, "Perspectives on NATO's Southern Flank," prepared by a fact-finding mission of Senators who visited the region, it would appear that Oman, Turkey, Greece, and Italy are considered to be crucial in any examination of "problems facing American foreign policy on the southern flank of Nato and in the securing of oil flowing to the West from the Persian Gulf."[102]

Also on the question of the inversion of roles, today the pressure for additional involvement of NATO in the Middle Eastern region—such as the calls for the reinforcement of support facilities in Europe, the setting up of joint naval task forces, and the creation of a Multinational Force—is being exerted largely by the United States. In this respect, the Multinational Force, as indeed the Rapid Deployment Force and Allied Deployment Force (suggested by Jonathan Alford, a Director of the International Institute for Strategic Studies, London), may be seen as informal expansions of NATO. The fact that four European members of NATO have concerted to act together in the Middle East outside the framework of the United Nations is a grave precedent in terms of troop commitment and responsibility.[103]

c) On the question of support for Israel, the difference between the British and American positions, which dates from the late forties, remains an element of remarkable continuity. Thus, Gordon Merriam's contention, referred to earlier, still holds true: "The US has supported and favored Israel, and endeavored at the same time to remain on friendly terms with the Arab states [while] the UK, on the contrary, places Arab relations ahead of relations with Israel, and has temporarily departed from this policy only when

[102] US Senate, Committee on Foreign Relations, *Perspectives on NATO's Southern Flank* (Washington: Government Printing Office, 1980), iii.

[103] Jonathan Alford, "Les Occidentaux et la sécurité du Golfe," *Politique étrangère*, 3 (September 1981), p. 681.

necessary in the interest of Anglo-American relations."[104] Another element of continuity is the persistent attempt to bring Arab states to join Israel in a Western-sponsored alliance (or "strategic consensus") against the Soviet Union, undeterred by a long record of failure since the late forties (MEC, MEDO, the Baghdad Pact, and CENTO), and seemingly oblivious of Arab public opinion's profound attachment to non-alignment.

The change from the late forties is that Israel has been promoted to the rank of a "strategic asset" possessing F-15s and F-16s, a nuclear option, and what has been described as the most rapid of all rapid deployment forces. The danger posed to the Arab states, including those of the Arabian peninsula, is obvious.

d) It is a truism that NATO has become the victim of its own relative success in protecting the economic recovery of Europe in the late forties and in providing an adequate defense shield thereafter. There has been, of course, much controversy and friction within the Alliance, while beyond the traditional NATO perimeter, interests and policies have diverged more sharply still. In this respect, the Middle East has been a focal point of major conflicts of interest: Algerian decolonization, the Suez War of 1956, the Arab-Israeli War of 1973, the ensuing energy crisis, and the Venice Declaration. From both sides of the Atlantic, the bulk of writings and analysis speak of an unprecedented disarray of the Alliance. There are sharp divisions over such matters as volatile interest rates, trade wars, grain supplies to the Soviet Union, the Siberian gas pipeline to western Europe, the North-South dialogue, sanctions against the socialist bloc, Cruise missiles, Central America, and Europe's Arab and Palestinian policy. To this must be added America's fears of European "Finlandization" and Europe's corresponding fear of "decoupling."

Security in the West has traditionally been perceived in military terms. Today, however, it is clear that in the West, the concern for economic security is taking precedence. The United States is being perceived more often as a bitter rival than as an ally in this context. In the fifties, the Middle East was an important factor in the economic recovery of Europe. Today, the sheer survival of the European economy is perceived as being at stake and as depending largely on Third World energy resources, raw materials, markets, and investments, all in open competition with the United States. This does not mean that the unravelling of the Alliance is a real danger, particularly its Anglo-American core. The Trident connection is equivalent to the cementing

---

[104] *Foreign Relations of the United States*, 1949, VI, 36.

experience of the Polaris. However, the reluctance of the Allies to follow America's lead and order of priorities, and the ensuing annoyance with what are perceived in Washington as recalcitrant Allies, will continue to trouble the Alliance in this decade. The principal challenge for the Arab states will consist of maintaining non-alignment on the one hand and countering Israel's hegemonic objectives on the other.

As regards the prospect of NATO extension, the significance of the growing strategic weight of Europe (both economic and military) within the Alliance is an open question, as is the impact of this weight on Arab options for the 1980s.

14

U.S. Threats of Intervention Against Arab Oil: 1973–79*

> "It is not possible for us to calculate, like housekeepers, exactly how much empire we want to have. Do not be put off by Nicia's arguments for non-intervention." Alcibiades in Thucydides, *The Peloponnesian War* (Book Six).
>
> "Beneath the nuclear umbrella, the temptation to probe with regional forces or proxy wars increases." Henry Kissinger, 1976 (quoted in P. Mangold, *Superpower Intervention in the Middle East*, p. 9).

EVER SINCE THE OCTOBER WAR of 1973, the administrations of Presidents Nixon, Ford, and Carter have repeatedly relied on a policy of threatening military intervention against oil-producing countries: the peculiar foreign policy vocabulary of power-seeking to impose congenial behavior by others. Normally, this type of projection of power by the powerful is addressed to potential or real adversaries. But in the contemporary world, the superpowers increasingly deter, threaten, and frighten potential or real allies and the non-aligned.

This study has two primary objectives. Firstly, it examines the historical record by identifying the incidence, context, and vocabulary of the threats issued by US officials, the Congress, and related actors in the media and the world of scholarship, as well as the help proposed in this endeavor by interested proxies, particularly Israel. Secondly, it examines the Arab riposte

---

*IPS Papers, No. 4E (Beirut: Institute for Palestine Studies, 1980). © 1980 by the Institute for Palestine Studies. Reprinted courtesy of the Institute for Palestine Studies.

and the doubts voiced in the United States, the Arab world, and elsewhere regarding America's ability to implement such threats. It also assesses the effectiveness (or lack of it) of this US policy.

In broad terms, US government and academic circles reflecting government policy have envisaged intervention in six conditions: in response to 1) Soviet attempts to take over oil fields or to block key oil shipping lanes; 2) oil embargoes by the Organization of Arab Petroleum Exporting Countries (OAPEC); 3) "unacceptable" price increases or production shortfalls by OAPEC or OPEC; 4) the invasion of oil-producing states labelled as "friendly" by regional states perceived as "radicals;" 5) the revolutionary overthrow of friendly regimes in the area which involves a high risk of interference with oil production or shipment; 6) instances of "massive violations of human rights"—the rarely invoked "humanitarian intervention."[1]

There is a seventh circumstance or situation in which such intervention might be envisaged: in the service of a imperial *Pax* (Kissingeriana or à la Camp David). Although it is hotly denied by the Establishment, this view is widely shared by the radical critics of US policy, who often subsume many of the other six under this heading.

The general conclusion drawn is that the policy of threatening intervention is ill-considered, counter-productive, and likely to provoke economic and political disasters of unprecedented magnitude. Or put differently, the policy of threatening intervention against Arab oil-producing countries is likely to trigger the very apocalyptic event that it is supposedly trying to prevent.

The study covers the period from the October War of 1973 to the Soviet intervention in Afghanistan in the closing days of 1979, an intervention that finally consecrated the interdependence of four strategic zones of confrontation: the Horn, the Gulf, the Indian Ocean, and the traditional core of the Arab-Israeli conflict. As the year drew to a close, it became clear that the Palestine question, in both its spatial and temporal dimensions, had expanded immeasurably, with attending risks but also with new opportunities.

Nixon, the Oil Embargo, and Arab Linkage Strategy

US Threats in the Wake of the Oil Embargo

A week after the outbreak of the October War, Secretary of State Henry Kissinger announced at a press conference: the "Middle East may become

---

[1]William V. O'Brien, "US Military Intervention: Law and Morality," *The Washington Papers*, 68 (Beverley Hills: Sage Publications, 1979), p. 82.

in time what the Balkans were in Europe before 1914, that is to say, an area where local rivalries...have their own momentum that will draw in the great nuclear powers into a confrontation." He then went on to warn the Arab world of a massive airlift of American military hardware to Israel: "We have made a very serious effort, in this crisis, to take seriously into account Arab concerns and Arab views. On the other hand, we have to pursue what we consider to be the right course; we will take the consequences in pursuing what we consider to be the right course."[2] Three days later President Nixon raised the specter of intervention by characterizing US policy as being "like the policy we followed in 1958 when Lebanon was involved, it is like the policy we followed in 1970 when Jordan was involved."[3] According to William Quandt, these comments caused consternation in Arab diplomatic circles.[4]

As the massive airlift surged forward, the Organization of Arab Petroleum Exporting Countries, meeting in Kuwait on 17 October, responded with a scheduled five percent cutback in oil production each month to be effective until Israel withdrew from all occupied Arab territory. Two days later, President Nixon asked Congress for $2.2 billion in military assistance to Israel. On 19 October, King Faysal, who had called for a ten percent cut in production, imposed an oil embargo on the United States and Holland; Kissinger received the news during his flight to Moscow. One of the major assumptions of American policy, namely that the Arabs would not use the oil weapon, went up in smoke together with other assumptions concerning the determination and ability of Arab nations to wage war against Israel, a state enjoying "special relationship" status.

In actual fact, there were indices to suggest that the oil weapon was being prepared by the Arabs. At the Khartoum Summit of 1967, King Faysal had led oil states in setting up regular contributions to help the confrontation states which had suffered in the 1967 war. Nonetheless, as late as July 1973 he appeared to oppose the utilization of the oil weapon. But a month later, according to Mohamed Hassanein Heikal's account, the Saudi monarch told President Sadat: "Give us time. We don't want to use our oil as a weapon in a battle which only goes on for two or three days and then stops. We want to see a battle which goes on for long enough for world public opinion

---

[2] *Department of State Bulletin*, 29 October 1973, pp. 534–39.

[3] William B. Quandt, *Decade of Decisions* (Berkeley: University of California Press, 1977), p. 187.

[4] *Ibid.* Nixon placed a force of 20,000 American troops on alert and sent additional naval units into the Mediterranean. See R. Nixon, *Memoirs of Richard Nixon* (London: Arrow Books, 1979), p. 485.

to be mobilized."[5] Heikal is of the opinion that there was no "precise plan for the use of the oil weapon" as the October War was ignited.[6]

However, according to a heavily classified (but nonetheless leaked) report, both the Central Intelligence Agency and the National Security Agency had eavesdropped on meetings between Faysal and Sadat, and had reported that in August 1973, agreement had been reached on war against Israel, economic aid to Egypt of $600 million for the war, and the use of oil as a political weapon.[7]

It is not within the scope of this paper to examine the worldwide alert of 25 October and the nuclear confrontation of the two superpowers.[8] Instead, the threats of American military intervention will be examined both in the context of the Arab oil embargo and Dr. Kissinger's step-by-step diplomacy. In his memoirs President Nixon asserted: "From the moment the Arab oil embargo began we had worked unceasingly to end it."[9]

On 21 November Kissinger spoke in sharp terms about "Arab pressure" and an "Arab shutdown of oil," affirming that the US would not be influenced in changing its policy because of the oil embargo, and warning of the possibility of "countermeasures" against oil-producers.[10] The following day Shaykh Aḥmad Zakī Yamānī, Saudi Arabia's oil minister, responded by warning that Arab states "could cut production by 80 percent" if the United States, Japan, or the EEC took punitive countermeasures. In fact,

---

[5] Mohamed Heikal, *The Road to Ramadan* (London: Fontana, 1976), pp. 266–67.

[6] *Ibid.*

[7] Seymour Hersh, "Senate Report Criticizes US Intelligence on Oil Embargo," *New York Times*, 21 December 1977.

[8] The notable fact is that the United States and the Soviet Union have been in a state of quasi-permanent naval confrontation in the Mediterranean for the past fifteen years. As to the Ramadan War of October 1973, both the Soviets and the Americans carried out a large-scale reinforcement of their naval positions in the Mediterranean. On the eve of the war the Soviets had the normal complement of 56 units deployed, but by 31 October the total strength had risen to an all-time record of 96 ships. The US Sixth Fleet, normally consisting of 45 ships (including two aircraft carriers and one helicopter carrier with an 1800-marine assault contingent), was also reinforced by a third aircraft carrier task force and a second helicopter carrier with an 1800-marine amphibious force. One naval expert, Robert Weinland, believes that the US navy enjoyed a clear advantage in the confrontation by having insured "superior military capability in the critical place and the critical time..., making Soviet intervention in the conflict, at best, potentially very costly, and at worst, militarily infeasible." See Robert Weinland, "Superpower Naval Diplomacy in the October 1973 Arab-Israeli War," *The Washington Papers*, 61, Pt. II (Washington: Center for Strategic and International Studies, 1979), p. 90.

[9] Nixon, *Memoirs*, p. 986.

[10] *International Herald Tribune*, 22 November 1973, p. 1.

he said that his country might blow up some of its oil fields and installations in the event of an American military intervention. While recognizing that the United States and its allies could take some countermeasures, he went on to say: "...if I were an American, or European, or Japanese, for that matter, I would also carefully consider what the Arab states have in their hands. I think what we have as an oil weapon is far greater."[11] During the same televised interview he linked the resumption of oil supplies to Israeli withdrawal from the occupied territories.

A week later it was James Schlesinger's turn to announce his country's intention to maintain an important naval presence in the Indian Ocean aimed at protecting US interests in the Gulf in the wake of the October War and the oil embargo.[12] This initiative was most probably a reaction to the resolution to maintain the oil weapon adopted at the Sixth Arab Summit Conference of 26 November, specifically the item regarding the "continuation of the embargo in relation to countries supporting Israel."[13]

The intervention threat also retained the attention of President Boumedienne of Algeria. Speaking to Lebanese and Egyptian newsmen in Algiers on 4 December, he warned that Arab oil workers would react swiftly to Western military intervention: "...if the West tries to act with arrogance or to use force, it would suffer a catastrophe. All the wells will be set on fire, all the pipelines will be destroyed and the West will pay the price."[14]

As the year 1973 ended on a grave keynote of warning and counter-warning "buttressed by murky hints of American military intervention in the Gulf," it was announced that the nuclear-powered frigate *Bainbridge* would join the carrier task force in the Indian Ocean.[15] Then came Schlesinger's thinly veiled threat of 7 January, warning the Arabs that force might be used against them if the oil weapon were carried too far. And once again the riposte was abundantly clear to everyone: Saudi Arabia and Kuwait announced their determination to blow up the fields and installations in the event of a military intervention. Kuwait's foreign minister was quoted as stating: the "oil fields have been surrounded by an explosive belt, explod-

---

[11] *International Herald Tribune*, 23 November 1973, p. 1.

[12] *New York Times*, 1 December 1973.

[13] *International Documents on Palestine, 1973*, edited by J. Nielsen (Beirut: Institute for Palestine Studies, 1976), p. 524, doc. 331.

[14] *International Herald Tribune*, 5 December 1973, p. 2.

[15] Edward Sheehan, "Step-by-Step in the Middle East," *Journal of Palestine Studies*, 19–20 (Spring-Summer, 1976), p. 27.

able the moment actual American military intervention is sensed."[16]   Authoritative statements were made regarding the placing of explosive charges in the Saudi Arabian Ghawar oil field, the largest known reserve in the world. Arab commentators, particularly in Damascus and Algiers, made statements to the same effect.[17]

There is conclusive evidence that some American officials took the Arab riposte seriously and appreciated the full extent of the devastation and the potential oil shutdown which would be triggered by armed intervention.[18] On the other hand, militant Zionist groups in America, such as the B'nai B'rith, initiated a virulent anti-Arab campaign with the accent on oil. Full-page advertisements poured hate on Arab rulers in tones that some observers described as "verging on the incendiary."[19] The Zionist Organization of America and its monthly journal, *The American Zionist,* were particularly active in this campaign.[20] In the meantime, Dr. Kissinger had left Washington to embark on his shuttle diplomacy in earnest, with the agitation over military intervention as his supporting background. Ending the embargo, getting a disengagement agreement signed, and countering Arab linkage strategy were his highest priorities. In this respect, there is a strong suggestion in Nixon's *Memoirs* that the Americans were able to count on President Sadat's eager cooperation. In December Kissinger had told Nixon in a memo: "Sadat promised me he would get the oil embargo lifted during the first half of January and said that he would call for its lifting in a statement which praised your personal role in bringing the parties to the negotiating table and making progress thereafter."[21] Nixon followed up on 28 December 1973 with a letter to Sadat: "I must tell you in complete candor," he wrote, "that it is essential that the oil embargo and oil production restrictions against the United States be ended at once. It cannot await the outcome of the current talks on disengagement." Nixon also relates that Sadat sent him a message through the US delegate to the United Nations, Shirley Temple Black, who

---

[16]William Coughlin, "Fears of Invasion by US Rise in Mideast: Oil Fields Mined," *International Herald Tribune,* 12–13 January 1974, p. 2.

[17]*Ibid.*

[18]*Ibid.*; see also D. Middleton, "Intervention in the Middle East," *International Herald Tribune,* 14 January 1974, p. 2.

[19]R. Evans and R. Novak, "Tuning Down the Zionists," *International Herald Tribune,* 27 December 1973, p. 4.

[20]"War by Oil," *The American Zionist,* December 1973; Abel Jacob, "Oil Fuel for a New Anti-Semitism," *The American Zionist,* January 1974; and Jacques Medecin, "Europe's Servitude," *The American Zionist,* February 1974.

[21]Nixon, *Memoirs,* p. 986.

had seen the Egyptian President privately: "I will lift the embargo," he told her; "I will lift it for President Nixon."[22]

President Sadat's own memoirs are no less revealing. He recalls that he decided "to lift the oil embargo when we realized it began to affect the interests of the American people;" a few pages later he also wrote: "The moment we felt that the oil embargo had started to hit the American citizen, it was lifted. Our objective was never to penalize the American or Western citizen, but simply to point out that a blind partiality to Israel has a price."[23]

Linkage Strategy

For the Nixon administration, ending the Arab oil embargo was dictated by several crucial factors: 1) on the domestic scene the need to neutralize the effects of the Watergate scandal through dramatized and widely reported grandstand acts of diplomatic skills; 2) the need to restore a badly shaken Western alliance and a Trilateral world facing the prospect of deep economic secession; 3) the national interest of the US in the context of Great Power rivalry; 4) the energy requirements of the US and the prospect of a depletion in its strategic reserves; 5) the need to prevent the EEC and Japan from moving in the direction of the Arab states in terms of arms sales, technological transfers, renegotiated oil supplies, the direct access to energy, and quasi-independent diplomatic initiatives. And the closer Dr. Kissinger got to an agreement on the disengagement of forces in the Suez Canal area, the more King Faysal was pressed to persuade OAPEC to lift the embargo in recognition of the American effort.

The Saudi monarch made it clear that he was interested in seeing progress toward disengagement equally on other fronts.[24] What would happen if, with the embargo lifted, Kissinger's ardor sagged and Israel's obdurate posture increased? Syria, at the time waging a single-handed war of attrition in the Golan, would then be left out in the cold, as would Jordan and the Palestinians.

The unity of the Arab front—a key card—would have eroded, especially as it was becoming somewhat clearer that step-by-step was designed by Kissinger to mean little-by-little, country-by-country, and bilateral. Once

---

[22] *Ibid.*, p. 987.

[23] Anwar al-Sadat, *In Search of Identity* (New York: Harper and Row, 1977), pp. 300, 304.

[24] *The Economist*, 26 January-1 February 1974, p. 36.

lifted, the reimposition of the embargo would be a risky undertaking; the element of surprise would no longer be present. Nevertheless the Arab position was sufficiently flexible and conciliatory to indicate a fair measure of progress toward an easing or lifting of the embargo at the forthcoming February meeting of OAPEC. The Arab oil states were quick to realize that an escalation in cutbacks could push the industrialized world "to the brink of ruin long before any significant progress was achieved towards the fulfilment of [Arab] objectives."[25] According to Fuad Itayim's figures, Arab oil-supply shortfalls against September 1973 production (in million barrels per day) were as follows: November 1973, 4.2; December, 3.9; January 1974, 2.4; February, 2.0; March, 1.5.[26] The moderate stand of OAPEC, with its potent mix of incentives and sanctions, was therefore clear. Yet both President Nixon and Dr. Kissinger inhibited additional progress by characterizing the projected OAPEC meeting as yielding to the logic of American pressure and by suggesting that failure to put a early end to the embargo would be interpreted as a form of blackmail. In reaction, OAPEC postponed its February meeting.[27] In this whole diplomatic episode an additional Arab move requires stressing: President Asad's trip in early February to Saudi Arabia and Kuwait, where he is believed to have received firm pledges linking the lifting of the embargo to successful disengagement in the Golan and assurances regarding Palestinian rights.[28]

Perhaps for the first time in the annals of the Arab-Israeli conflict, Arab diplomacy was trying out a sophisticated form of linkage strategy—and with some measure of success. Of course the conjuncture of events was of great help. The impressive military performance of the Arabs, the world energy crisis, the relative success of the Arab embargo (unlike its ill-fated counterpart imposed in 1967), and the organized drive by a united front of oil producers to keep the price of crude from falling (in fact, OPEC had decided to double oil prices on 23 December) impacted directly on the US scene and even more dramatically on that of its allies. Undoubtedly the US displayed annoyance at the use of its favorite strategy by others—superpowers have a tendency to regard linkage strategy as their own very private possession.

---

[25] Fuad Itayim, "Strengths and Weaknesses of the Oil Weapon" in *The Middle East and the International System*, II: *Security and the Energy Crisis* (London: International Institute for Strategic Studies, 1975; *Adelphi Papers*, no. 115), p. 3.

[26] *Ibid.*

[27] Joe Stork, *Middle East Oil and the Energy Crisis* (New York: Monthly Review Press, 1975), pp. 240–41.

[28] *Ibid.*; *Arab Report and Record* (London), 1–14 February 1974, pp. 51, 53.

Hence the strenuous attempts by the Administration to deny the existence of linkage between oil and disengagement diplomacy. Yet, as pointed out by Edward Sheehan, although Dr. Kissinger denied linkage, "his Syrian shuttle was the price he paid to end the embargo."[29] On 6 March, President Nixon acknowledged that "progress on the diplomatic front, while it is not linked to lifting of the embargo, inevitably has an effect on it."[30] And, in sharp contrast to the tough language he had earlier used to indicate that American pressure would force a lifting of the embargo, he now said that he had decided "to leave that decision to them [the Arabs] because indicating what they will do might lead them to do otherwise."[31]

By mid-March sufficient progress had been made in the Golan disengagement talks to warrant a reconsideration of the embargo. Thus, in the Vienna meeting of 18 March, the oil ministers of OAPEC outlined the linkage between oil measures, the drawing of world attention to the Arab cause, and encouragement to be granted to "countries which showed readiness and willingness to work for a just remedy to the cause which would lead to the complete termination of the Israeli occupation and to the restoration of the legitimate rights of the Palestinian people."[32] The meeting also expressed, perhaps too hastily, recognition of the emergence of a new American policy more compatible with justice toward Arab and Palestinian rights. Furthermore, two crucial decisions were taken: to treat Italy and the West German Republic as friendly states and to meet their petroleum needs,[33] and second, to lift the embargo on oil supplies to the US. The decision on the embargo was subject to review at the next OAPEC meeting in June 1974 with Egypt and Saudi Arabia providing assurances against its reimposition—a point duly noted by the American Secretary of State.[34] On the other hand, the embargo on Holland, Portugal, South Africa, and Rhodesia was maintained. The question of whether OAPEC sheathed the oil weapon too soon remains the subject of controversy, as does the role of the Egyptian President.

Arab linkage strategy had made a convincing debut. The careful planning, the avoidance of the many pitfalls strewn along its paths, the tough stand adopted in the face of thinly veiled threats of intervention, and the selection of the appropriate forums did not fail to impress international opin-

---

[29]Sheehan, "Step by Step," p. 27.

[30]*Department of State Bulletin*, LXX, 1813 (25 March 1974), pp. 294–95.

[31]*Ibid.*

[32]*Middle East Economic Digest*, 22 March 1974, p. 324–42.

[33]*Ibid.*

[34]Stork, *Middle East Oil*, p. 242.

ion. Not that the Arab states were enduringly united. In measuring the effectiveness of the oil weapon one has to admit that the embargo, as Hanns Maull indicated, "did not work properly for two reasons: firstly, some Arab oil evidently 'leaked' to the United States despite the embargo, and secondly, the international oil distribution system was managed by oil companies in such a way as to spread the damage fairly evenly, by diverting Arab oil away from embargoed ports and replacing it with non-Arab oil."[35] Nonetheless, despite President Sadat's propensity to strike out on his own, sufficient consensus was maintained to ensure the credibility of the strategy and to soften the impact of the threats of intervention.

The US repeatedly showed annoyance with Arab linkage strategy. President Nixon went so far as to assert on 15 March in Chicago that oil pressure would have "a countereffect on [US] effort to go forward on the peace front, on the negotiation front, because it would simply slow down...[US] efforts to get the disengagement on the Syrian front and also to move towards a permanent settlement."[36] Yet the recognition that it was an important factor, that there was no longer room for the old complacency, may be gauged by the following Presidential assessment made just after the lifting of the oil embargo:

> It is in the interest of those countries that imposed it as well as the United States that it be lifted. The two should be parallel. Inevitably, what happens in one area affects the other, and I am confident that the progress we are going to continue to make on the peace front in the Mideast will be very helpful in seeing to it that an oil embargo is not reimposed.[37]

In short the Arabs had left it to the Americans to choose between having the embargo as a semi-permanent imposition or living with it as an Arab tactical weapon. The first alternative was intolerable. Predictably the US chose the second, especially as it presented certain advantages stemming from the limitations of the embargo as a tactical weapon in the absence of a state of war and with the element of surprise no longer obtaining.

The oil embargo was lifted five months after it was imposed, not as fast as the Nixon administration would have liked (despite the campaign of threats and the war of nerves), but faster than Arab interests would have otherwise

---

[35] Hanns Maull, *Oil and Influence: the Oil Weapon Examined* (London: International Institute for Strategic Studies, 1975; *Adelphi Papers*, no. 117), p. 6

[36] *New York Times*, 16 March 1974, p. 12; Nixon, *Memoirs*, p. 987.

[37] *New York Times*, 20 March 1974, p. 28.

dictated. Yet one thing was made clear: the consequences of that display of power were likely to be long-lasting in terms of political and economic dividends for the Arab collectivity, provided the precarious balance between *raison de la nation* and *raison d'état* tipped, however slightly, in favor of Arab solidarity.[38]

There were other gains. On the eve of the October War of 1973, the United States still regarded the region of the Arab Gulf and the heartland of the Arab-Israeli conflict (Syria, Jordan, Palestine, Egypt, and Lebanon) as two separate and distinct areas or arenas. However the October War, the coordinated Arab moves, and the skillful use of the oil factor shattered this old illusion born of misplaced self-interest, the exertions of the pro-Israel lobby, and the deep aversion for Arab nationalism in general, and Nasser in particular. If there were any doubts left, Arab linkage strategy tended to dispel them.

Would the United States recognize this revolutionary change in the geopolitical equation for what it really was, namely a positive fact, possessing deep organic roots? Would it then proceed to a radical policy reevaluation in this new light? And would it have the will to resist Israel's attempt to block such reevaluation? In the ensuing months, at any rate, the Kissinger-Sadat tandem on the road to Sinai II, the fascination with *Pax* rather than with peace, and the untimely assasination of King Faysal were factors which worked against the maintenance and promotion of Arab consensus politics. The memory of US threats of intervention may also have been a factor in this process.

The Ford Administration and the Intervention Debates

With the lifting of the oil embargo and the achievement of a separation of forces agreement in the Golan, the pressure on Dr. Kissinger's shuttle diplomacy eased considerably. For months the focus of attention of US diplomacy, and of the Secretary of State himself, were located in the Near East. Then in mid-year, President Nixon, following in Kissinger's footsteps, made his grand tour of the region, which included visits to states never before visited by an American president. The objective, as publicly stated, was to consolidate the change in US policy and the new relationship with the Arab world that his Administration had painstakingly constructed. The

---

[38] Walid Khalidi, "Thinking the Unthinkable: A Sovereign Palestinian State," *Foreign Affairs* (New York), July 1978, pp. 696–713.

other objective was a desperate attempt to elude Watergate and escape impeachment.

Following the lifting of the embargo, the threat of military intervention as an instrument of policy had been quietly shelved—at least for a short while. And Nixon's tour, loudly proclaimed as a statesman's initiative, was the wrong time and place for saber-rattling. Nonetheless, the picture was to change with the denouement of Watergate, and the center of gravity, with respect to the conduct of Near Eastern policy, returned to Washington with the newly installed Ford administration.

As the winter of 1974 approached, the American public was informed of an impending energy crisis and was led to believe that an oil price of nearly $10 a barrel was prohibitively high and would lead to economic disasters of unprecedented magnitude. This concern over oil prices was a thorny domestic issue for President Ford, but it was also magnified and used as a cover for the failure to develop an effective energy policy combining energy conservation, the search for alternative sources, and additional investment. Also missing from US policy were the political incentives necessary to ensure OAPEC's cooperation in terms of supplies and prices and to persuade Arab producers to charge less than the market price for their depletable reserves and to pump more than was in their short-term or long-term interests.

The prophecies of doom spread by the political alarmists did not materialize. There was no chaos in the Trilateral world in the ensuing months. In fact, an even higher level of prices eventually led to an economic recovery helped along by a massive recycling of petrodollars. Yet the US government had adopted a strategy of extreme pressure, including threats against OPEC (and especially against OAPEC) to force down price levels.

A second consideration influencing the strategy of threats was the Rabat Arab Summit of late October 1974, which ran counter to Kissinger's plans and expectations, and apparently caused him "considerable annoyance and dismay."[39] The unanimous Arab consecration of the PLO as the sole le-

[39]Quandt, *Decade of Decisions*, p. 257. In assessing US reactions to the Rabat Summit, Yasir Arafat stressed the recognition by Kissinger that this Arab summit "had upset American plans and calculations." Therefore the Secretary of State moved urgently "first, to strike at the heart of Arab steadfastness, notably the allies of the Ramadan War— Egypt, Syria, and the Palestine revolution; next, to break the oil weapon as an effective factor in the Arab nation's battle." The Palestinian leader went on to say: "We have to concede that Kissinger's counterattack has had considerable success." Consequently, one of the priorities for the Arab nation was to reestablish the oil weapon as a decisive weapon. *Wafa*, 1 January 1977: Message of PLO Chairman Arafat to the Palestinian people on the occasion of the 12th anniversary of the outbreak of the Palestinian revolution.

gitimate representative of the Palestinian people was a blow to the existing American-Israeli consensus on the conduct and substance of negotiations. Moreover, the growing recognition of the PLO by the international community, symbolized by the historic appearance of Yasir Arafat at the United Nations on 13 November (which the United States had opposed), was a further embarrassment. The campaign of threats may be seen as a punitive measure directed particularly against the Arab moderates for failing to toe the Kissinger line.

Bearing also on the evolution of American strategy was the Israeli position, made abundantly clear in Prime Minister Rabin's interview with *Haaretz* (3 December 1974), where the "Seven Lean Years" theory was elaborated. To Rabin the cardinal principle was to gain time: periods of stalemate, he felt, were to Israel's advantage. The implication was that the Zionist state—with its grandiose vision of an expanding settler colonialism as yet unrealized—had to work to that end. How much time? Seven years. "Seven lean years" as Rabin put it—the length of time he hoped was needed for the world to become independent of Arab oil.[40]

In the same interview Rabin also declared that Israel had to pay "a reasonable price, another interim settlement with Egypt," in order to ensure the breakup of the solidarity of the Egypt-Syria front and to keep Egypt away from the Soviet camp.[41] In this respect, differences between Rabin and Kissinger were almost imperceptible, and the road to Sinai II was being paved. For all the above reasons, unleashing a war of nerves against the Arab states in general and their oil weapon in particular, through threats of military intervention, was probably seen as holding some promise.

In this examination of the Ford administration's campaign of military threats against Arab oil, attention has been focused on four areas: 1) the statements of the highest ranking officials; 2) the interventionist scenarios of Tucker and Ignotus; 3) the critics who argued against intervention on moral or practical grounds; 4) the study prepared for the House Committee on International Relations entitled *Oil Fields as Military Objectives: A Feasibility Study*, which has been described as the most serious unclassified study of the topic and which was published in August 1975.[42]

---

[40] *Haaretz* (Tel Aviv), 3 December 1974.

[41] *Ibid.*

[42] John Collins and Clyde Mark, *Oil Fields as Military Objectives: A Feasibility Study* (Washington: Government Printing Office, August 1975), prepared for the Committee on International Relations, US Congress.

Ford, Kissinger and Schlesinger, and the Threats of Military Intervention

In late September 1974, the newly installed Ford administration launched a tough policy on oil prices. Believed to have been orchestrated by Dr. Kissinger himself, with public warnings before the UN and at the Detroit Energy Conference that "what has gone up by political decision can be reduced by political decision,"[43] the campaign aimed at attracting support from hesitant allies for a united front against OPEC. Another motive was to make a dramatic impact on the domestic scene in support of a much-weakened Republican Party on the eve of midterm elections involving 34 out of 100 Senate seats, all of the 435 seats in the House of Representatives, and 35 out of 50 state governorships.

It is in this context that the question of projected military action against Arab oil was repeatedly raised, attracting wide attention. The press, of course, participated fully in the campaign. Early in October, *Newsweek* magazine ran a lengthy article entitled "Thinking the Unthinkable," based on interviews "with a number of government officials, military strategists, and experts on the Mideast."[44] The editor concluded that the three most talked about options were: 1) psychological warfare aimed at "unnerving the enemy;" 2) covert operations aimed at terrorizing Arab shaykhs; and 3) military intervention in the form of American parachute assaults—supported by similar Israeli moves—to quickly seize the major Arab oil fields. According to *Newsweek*, the idea of military intervention was gaining respectability in the Western world.[45] Likewise, *Business Week*, in a controversial interview with Dr. Kissinger, supplied further confirmation: "One thing we also hear from businessmen," volunteered the interviewer, "is that in the long run the only answer to the oil cartel is some sort of military action."[46]

The press campaign against Arab oil interests, including military seizure, continued throughout November and December. The columnist Jack Anderson, who is reputed to have excellent contacts in the corridors of power in Washington, observed in the *Washington Post* (8 November) that a military take-over of Libyan oil fields would not require more than a couple of US Marine divisions.[47] This recipient of many well-timed official leaks also

---

[43] *Newsweek*, 7 October 1974, pp. 15–17.

[44] *Ibid.*

[45] *Ibid.*

[46] *Business Week* (New York), 13 January 1975, p. 69. Kissinger's statements will be discussed in detail below.

[47] *Arab Report and Record*, 1–15 November 1974, p. 486.

claimed for Israel the role of seizing Kuwait's rich oil fields.[48] And Paul
Seabury contributed his "Thinking About an Oil War" to the *New Leader*
of 11 November.[49] In short, seizing Arab oil was being portrayed almost as
a patriotic duty and a necessary action in the defense of the West, as Washington witnessed an atmosphere reminiscent of the jingoism of the 1890s.

Whether the threats were real or illusory is of course a moot point. For
their part, the Arab oil producers stood their ground firmly. "The era of
using military force is gone," retorted Shaykh Aḥmad Zakī Yamānī; the
risk involved could be too great, and "the danger of reducing the oil supply
[was] very clear."[50] American behavior was widely seen by the Arabs as a
new form of economic imperialism.[51] Similarly, George W. Ball, a former US
Under-Secretary of State, criticized the fact that "not only the Secretaries of
State and Treasury but the President himself made harsh, brooding speeches,
overlaid with frustration, anxiety and shadowy threat but empty of content
or any reasoned program."[52] To Ball the option of military seizure was
clearly not viable, and he spoke out sharply against the practice of thinly
veiled threats:

> Such talk is archaic fantasy, for this is no longer the nineteenth
> century. It is a period of nuclear parity and strategic stalemate.
> There is a powerful Soviet fleet in the Mediterranean, Soviet
> missiles are targeted on Western capitals and the USSR clearly
> has a compelling interest in the Middle East. That a military
> move by one superpower in that area would automatically be
> countered by the other was vividly demonstrated last October
> at the time of the American worldwide military alert....We had
> better stop muttering under our breath. Great nations should
> not even hint at threats they have no intention of carrying out.[53]

In actual fact, the campaign of threats appears all the more surprising
in the context of an Arab policy of calculated moderation. Arab oil producers led by Saudi Arabia had worked out the consequences of the dramatic
geopolitical and energy changes in the wake of the 1973 war. Likewise, they

---

[48] *Jerusalem Post,* 10 November 1974, p. 5.
[49] Paul Seabury, "Thinking About an Oil War," *New Leader* (New York), 11 November
1974.
[50] *Newsweek,* 7 October 1974, p. 19.
[51] *Arab Report and Record,* 16–30 September 1974, p. 416.
[52] George W. Ball, "No Time For Threats," *Newsweek,* 7 October 1974, p. 19.
[53] *Ibid.*

had embarked on a giant recycling of petrodollars to prop up the flagging economy of the Western world, and on an ambitious second five-year plan (1975–80) involving the expenditure of $141 billion. In November Saudi Arabia, the United Arab Emirates, and Qatar even lowered oil prices a little, while increasing taxes and royalties paid by the oil companies.[54] The option selected was cooperation between equals with the clear understanding that oil prices and recycling would be linked to political issues such as progress toward Israeli withdrawal from Arab territory, including East Jerusalem, and the recognition of the legitimate rights of the Palestinians as a people. Nevertheless, Arab moderation and cooperation were not recognized by the Western media, which in general persisted in its inflammatory campaign, while responsible officials in Washington provided both direct and indirect help to the provocation campaigns by, for instance, suggesting that Arab petrodollars could be made available in the form of aid to Israel. Gerald L. Parsky, Deputy Secretary of the US Treasury, suggested the possibility of "even providing Israel with Arab oil money under a three-party agreement."[55]

Since the embargo had been lifted back in March 1974, there remained only two issues: the reduction of oil prices, and the question of linkage between the price and availability of supplies and the resolution of the Arab-Israeli conflict. The principal figures at the State Department took pains to make the separation clear. Thus, on the eve of his October departure for yet another round of talks in the Middle East in connection with Sinai II, Dr. Kissinger asserted:

> ...The impact of the high oil prices is not inevitably linked to the Arab-Israeli negotiations. And we are negotiating these two issues separately...we are conducting them in separate forums.[56]

A month later, the Under-Secretary, Joseph Sisco, also reflected the US position on this sensitive question. In response to a statement that affirmed the existence of a link between Kissingerian peace diplomacy and oil sanctions, Sisco said:

> Well, we certainly do not make this link. But as the Secretary has said quite recently in a press conference, obviously oil is a

---

[54] *New York Times*, 12 November 1974, p. 60. For details of the Saudi plan, see Kingdom of Saudi Arabia, *Second Development Plan 1395–1400 A.H.* (Riyad: Planning Ministry, 1975).

[55] *Daily Star* (Beirut), 6 September 1974, p. 6.

[56] *Department of State Bulletin*, LXXI, 1844 (28 December 1974), pp. 565–67.

factor. The threat of embargo is one that we always have to bear in mind and take into account.[57]

Why this ambivalence with regard to the issue of linkage, since no one in the area or in the know was really fooled? Perhaps the best explanation came from Senator Fulbright, who stressed the central fact that "for domestic political reasons the [US] is exceedingly reluctant to acknowledge the close relationship between the Arab-Israeli conflict, and the price and availability of oil."[58]

In the final weeks of the year 1974, the threat of oil seizure—whether real or a mere diplomatic ploy—loomed larger. The carrier *Constellation*, escorted by two guided-missile destroyers, appeared in the waters of the Gulf on what was officially described as a "familiarization" tour, raising speculation of a possible action against certain oil installations. This was clearly an ominous move, both because of the general context of harrassment and because no American aircraft carrier had entered the waters of the Gulf since 1948.[59] At the same time, the US press continued to echo the likelihood of a move against Arab oil producers.[60]

On 13 December, Dr. Kissinger denied reports of US military training for intervention in Arab oil-producing countries: "There is no American army," he said, "that is being trained to take over Arab oil fields."[61] Yet ten days later he did not entirely rule out this possibility in the course of a controversial interview accorded to *Business Week*. In response to a question on military action against oil, the State Secretary remarked:

> A very dangerous course. We should have learned from Vietnam
> that it is easier to get into a war than to get out of it. I am
> not saying that there is no circumstance where we would not use

---

[57] Text of US Under-Secretary of State Joseph Sisco's USIS interview (Washington, 18 November 1974); published by the US embassy, Beirut, 20 November 1974.

[58] Senator Fulbright's Fulton, Missouri speech of 2 November 1974, in *International Documents on Palestine, 1974*, edited by J. Nielsen (Beirut: Institute for Palestine Studies, 1977), p. 346, doc. 168.

[59] Michael Klare, "La Stratégie américaine dans le golfe arabo-persique," *Le Monde diplomatique* (March 1976), p. 6. See also Peter Mangold, *Superpower Intervention in the Middle East* (London: Croom Helm, 1978), p. 74: "In late November 1974 a United States carrier suddenly broke off from a CENTO exercise and entered the Gulf, the first visit by an American carrier for twenty-five years." These naval exercises were the largest in CENTO's history and were held in the Arabian Sea near the mouth of the Gulf.

[60] *Christian Science Monitor* (Boston), 26 November 1974; *US News and World Report* (Washington), 2 December 1974, pp. 18–20.

[61] *Department of State Bulletin*, LXXII, 1854 (6 January 1975), p. 2.

force. But it is one thing to use it in the case of a dispute over price, it's another where there's some actual strangulation of the industrialized world.[62]

During the same interview Kissinger raised the specter of intervention twice when he went on to affirm that "the use of force would be considered only in the gravest emergency." Yet, he also remarked: "I don't anticipate an oil embargo in the absence of war. I am not even sure of an oil embargo in the event of a war. It would now be a much more serious decision than it was the last time."[63] Why then the campaign of warnings and threats? What did "strangulation" and "gravest emergency" mean? And whose policy was really doing the strangling?

Following the release of the "strangulation" remarks by Kissinger, President Ford, questioned on the prospect of America using force in the Middle East, replied:

> I stand by the view that Henry Kissinger expressed in the *Business Week* [interview]. Now, the word strangulation is the key word. If you read his answer to a very hypothetical question, he didn't say that force would be used to bring a price change. His language said he wouldn't rule force out if the free world or the industrialized world would be strangled. I would affirm my support of that position as he answered that hypothetical question.[64]

In the same interview the President regarded the prospects of renewed fighting between the Arabs and Israelis as being very serious.

Such tactics of intimidation elicited sharp reactions from Arab leaders, including President Boumedienne of Algeria, PLO Chairman Yasir Arafat, and Libyan Premier Jallūd. The Palestinian press warned its readers of the existence of coordinated invasion plans by Israel, the United States, and the Shah of Iran.[65]

On the other hand, William Quandt did not appear to take military intervention too seriously. In a lecture delivered at the Lebanese University in Beirut in January 1975, he downplayed the whole issue:

---

[62] *Business Week*, 13 January 1975, p. 69.

[63] *Ibid.*

[64] *Time*, 20 January 1975, pp. 27–28.

[65] *Filasṭīn al-thawra* (Beirut), 3 November 1974; 22 December; and especially "Al-Tahdīd al-amīrikī," 12 January 1975; and 2 February 1975.

I think that there is a small element of psychological warfare involved in statements of this sort. I personally don't think they are to be taken very seriously. If the US had in mind the resort to force, it certainly would not be advertising it. Therefore I think it is either simply an irrelevant statement of an empirical reality—namely, that conditions could become so bad that irrational action might be considered—or a gambit in a bit of psychological warfare which probably is ill-considered.[66]

This was hardly the end of the "strangulation" affair. In a Washington press conference on 21 January, the President, far from ducking questions concerning the prospect of intervention, took his time to field them.[67] Such a desire on the part of the Administration to encourage questions and speculation on the subject of military force was noted by observers. Again on 23 January the President in a televised interview was asked: "The other day at your press conference, you were asked about Dr. Kissinger's quote and the possibility of military intervention and something surprised me, Sir. You have been in politics for a long time and you are as expert a question-ducker as anybody in that trade. Why didn't you duck that question. Why didn't you just say that's hypothetical? You did go into some detail on it."[68] And the President's answer is revealing: "I wanted it made as clear as I possibly could that this country, in case of economic strangulation—and the key word is 'strangulation'—we had to be prepared, without specifying what we might do, to take the necessary action for our self-preservation."[69]

The President was also asked whether, even under such circumstances, it was moral to take another nation's natural resources. While recognizing that the question was troublesome and while hoping military intervention would not be necessary, he nevertheless remarked: "It may not be right, but I think if you go back over the history of mankind, wars have been fought over natural resources from time immemorial...; history, in the years before us, indicates quite clearly that was one of the reasons why nations fought one another."[70] This "saber-rattling" has to be seen in the context of a leak—confirmed by the Pentagon—that three American divisions were being prepared for the Middle East: one airborne, one armored, and one air

---

[66] *Monday Morning* (Beirut), 13–19 January 1975, p. 34.
[67] *Department of State Bulletin*, LXXII, 1859 (10 February 1975), p. 179.
[68] *Department of State Bulletin*, LXXII, 1860 (17 February 1975), p. 220.
[69] *Ibid.*
[70] *Ibid.*, p. 222.

mobile.[71] In addition, there was a great deal of muttering concerning the need to upgrade the Diego Garcia base in the Indian Ocean; Britain and Oman were also asked for the use of the Masirah Island air base, which is within 400 miles of the entrance of the Gulf.

Just as ominous were Defense Secretary Schlesinger's remarks. On 14 January 1975, he indicated that the US would have to have recourse to force in the gravest emergency, and that from a military point of view intervention both in the Middle East and the Gulf was a realistic option: "It is indeed feasible to conduct military operations if necessity should arise."[72] To him, gravest emergency meant "the likelihood of the strangulation of the industrial economies of the West."[73] In the same interview he said that there was nothing unusual about American amphibious exercises in the Mediterranean, and he refused to comment on whether the US carrier *Enterprise,* which was in the Indian Ocean, was heading for the Gulf. And yet in almost the same breath he insisted that the United States aimed at maintaining "friendly relations with the nations of the area." However, this discrepancy in Schlesinger's statement did not escape unnoticed. One of the reporters present remarked:

> Mr. Secretary, I must say, Sir, you sound rather Delphic this morning. As far as I am concerned, I am trying to sort out some of the enigmas you pose. On one hand you say we desire friendly relations with all the nations of the Middle East, but you are not hesitant, nor was Secretary Kissinger, nor was the President, about tossing about the necessity to take military actions should the gravest of circumstances arise. I have trouble putting together these two, if I may use the term, "saber-rattling" expressions.[74]

Such examples of statements made by some of the highest ranking figures of the United States Government, including Kissinger, Ford, and Schlesinger, comprised only part of the campaign. Equally important were the contributions by various individuals and pressure groups which added fuel to the near-hysteria surrounding the topic of oil crisis and military intervention.

---

[71] *Ibid.*, p. 220. See also *New York Times*, 22 January 1975, for reports regarding the use of bases in the Arabian Sea and Oman.

[72] Transcript of US Secretary of Defense Schlesinger's press conference at the Pentagon, 14 January 1975.

[73] *Ibid.*

[74] *Ibid.*

In this case, however, the campaign reached new heights, with scholars, think-tank analysts, armchair strategists, and the media joining the Ford administration on the "seize Arab oil" bandwagon.

In contrast, and throughout the campaign, the Arab states, while demonstrating their firm resolve to counter any military intervention by blowing up the oil fields and installations, were also prepared to show responsible restraint, especially as the specter of "strangulation" was clearly a Kissingerian red herring. "Since oil constitutes a part of the national sovereignty of each oil-producing country," observed President Boumedienne, "any attempt by a foreign state to impose certain conditions on its exploitation must be regarded as violation of national sovereignty."[75] And the Algerian leader went on to characterize the threats as being "out of place, to say the least," particularly because no one had "threatened the US with strangulation, and it was impossible for any country to do so."[76]

In making threats against Arab oil states, the United States faced the prospect of wider reaction than from the organization of Arab producers (OAPEC) and the risk of an even tighter embargo. In April 1975, the Conference of Sovereigns and Heads of State of OPEC went on record with a solemn declaration confirming their readiness to "counteract...threats with a unified response whenever the need arises, notably in the case of aggression."[77] The solidarity of OPEC held firm in the face of the Ford administration's offensive.

Intervention Scenarios

In the January 1975 issue of *Commentary*, an influential journal published by the American Jewish Committee and regarded as one of the principal forums of the American Jewish intellectual establishment, Professor Robert Tucker took up the technical feasibility of seizing Arab fields by means of military intervention. He began by emphasizing that the oil crisis was one of the turning points of history and that until recently it would never have occurred "because of the prevailing expectation that it would have led to armed intervention."[78] He argued firmly that without intervention there was a distinct possibility of an economic and political disaster

---

[75] *Arab Report and Record*, 1–14 February 1975, quoting an interview with the Iranian news agency PARS.

[76] *Ibid.*

[77] Collins and Mark, *Oil Fields as Military Objectives*, p. 10.

[78] Robert Tucker, "Oil: the Issue of American Intervention," *Commentary*, 59 (January 1975), p. 22.

"bearing more than a superficial resemblance to the disaster of the 1930s."[79] Therefore, to Tucker, this led to the question of "employing extraordinary means" to deal with the oil crisis. "Is military intervention technically feasible?," he asked. His answer was yes, and it depended on "geography" in the first place: "Since it is impossible to intervene everywhere, the feasibility of intervention depends upon whether there is a relatively restricted area which, if effectively controlled, contains a sufficient portion of present world oil production and proven reserves to provide reasonable assurance that its control may be used to break the present price structure by breaking the core of the cartel politically and economically...."[80] Such a convenient area, in his view, existed—and it happened to be the Arab shoreline of the Gulf; a new Eldorado waiting for Tucker's conquistadores:

> The one area that would appear to satisfy these requirements extends from Kuwait down along the coastal region to Qatar. It is this mostly shallow coastal strip less than 400 miles length that provides 40 percent of present OPEC production and has by far the world's largest proven reserves (over 50 percent of total OPEC reserves and 40 percent of world reserves). Since it has no substantial centers of population and is without trees, its effective control does not bear even remote comparison with the experience of Vietnam.[81]

He was prepared to dismiss the possibility of Russian counter-intervention, principally because the Soviets did not possess the necessary naval capabilities for such action in the Gulf, and even if they did "the balance of perceived interest" was against them: they simply did not have, in his view, the overriding interests that the Americans had in the area.[82] He recognized that intervention would have to be undertaken by the United States unilaterally, and "initially at least in the face of condemnation by most of the world." This did not seem to worry him. What mattered was Western Europe and Japan; and these, later on, would be won over to the American action—because there would be something in it for them too: namely oil, allocated "evenhandedly."[83] Significantly, he also argued that American seizure of Arab oil fields would "markedly improve Israel's position," adding:

---

[79] *Ibid.*

[80] *Ibid.*, p. 25.

[81] *Ibid.*

[82] *Ibid.*, p. 26.

[83] *Ibid.*, p. 28.

"It would be both useless and insincere to deny the benefits accruing to Israel from intervention, just as it is both useless and insincere to deny the present linkage between the oil crisis and the steady erosion of Israel's position."[84] As to the reaction of American public opinion, he felt that "if intervention were to promise success at relatively modest cost, opinion might well move in the direction of support."[85] One might mention in passing that in the November 1975 issue of *Commentary* he urged Israel to adopt a defense policy "based on a known nuclear deterrent."[86]

The remarks of Kissinger backed by Ford and Schlesinger, together with Professor Tucker's controversial and much-advertised article, stimulated military discussion. The consensus among senior naval and military officers, as reported by the *New York Times,* was that the operation would be "militarily feasible but politically disastrous."[87] In addition to the very serious problems of the maintenance and consolidation of US forces in the oil fields in the post-intervention period, almost all the senior American and European military men consulted emphasized the domestic and international implications: "It could create the damnedest row in years," said one general, "and who would be blamed: us, not the Government." And he added: "The United States Army didn't order itself into Vietnam, the Administration did; but when things went sour, we got the blame." Another general felt that the American people would oppose the move: "the 'no more Vietnams' trauma was still very powerful."[88] There was disagreement as to the preferred target. Tucker's choice, as was mentioned earlier, was for the 400-mile stretch from Kuwait down the Saudi Arabian coast to Qatar. This terrain, containing no large population and "no trees," appeared to some to have significant advantages from the point of view of seizure and control.

Other military strategists preferred the Libyan target, arguing that the factor of surprise would be difficult to achieve in the Gulf area, where airborne troops would have to be flown in either from Mediterranean bases or from a naval task force in the Indian Ocean. Detection would be inevitable and the element of surprise gone. On the other hand, surprise, it was argued, would be more easily achieved in Libya through a combined air and sea

---

[84] *Ibid.,* p. 29.

[85] *Ibid.*

[86] *Time,* 17 November 1975, p. 23.

[87] Drew Middleton, "Military Men Challenge Mideast Force Strategy," *New York Times,* 10 January 1975, p. 3.

[88] *Ibid.*

strike.[89] However, operations in this part of the Mediterranean were also very risky. Admiral Thomas H. Moorer, former Chairman of the Joint Chiefs of Staff, and former Chief of Naval Operations Admiral Elmo Zumwalt, Jr., had both warned that "it is dangerous for the United States now to deploy, in a bilateral confrontation with the Soviet Union in the Eastern Mediterranean, its fleet because the odds are that the fleet would be defeated in a conventional war."[90]

Blueprints for such take-overs remained the subject of open discussion. In an article entitled "Kissinger Views Make Serious Speculation of Idle Talks," Clifton Daniel of the *New York Times* affirmed: "Military action to solve the oil problem, once a matter for cocktail-party conversation in Washington, has become the subject of serious speculation."[91] And Senator J.W. Fulbright, who had just retired as chairman of the Senate Foreign Relations Committee, said he had "heard intervention discussed at dinner tables and in Capitol cloakrooms."[92] The pro-Israel lobby also joined in the game and geared it to the campaign against arms supplies to Saudi Arabia. Thus the *Near East Report* remarked in mid-January: "Didn't Kissinger warn that we might have to take over oil-producing countries to avert 'strangulation'? Then why arm them against us?"[93]

Along the lines of Tucker's article, Miles Ignotus (presumably the pseudonym of Edward Luttwak, according to William Quandt) published his article "Seizing Arab Oil" in the March issue of *Harper's*.[94] Ignotus, identified as a Pentagon consultant "with intimate links to high-level U.S. policy-makers," developed a rapid deployment and strike scenario.[95] The 82nd Airborne Division, strengthened by two "air-cavalry" battalions, would embark on giant C-5 and C-141 jet transports, refuel at Israeli bases, and proceed to drop paratroopers at key Saudi oil fields, installations, and airports. Escort would be provided by Phantom fighters "based on Israeli fields or aboard carriers in the Arabian Sea."[96] The airborne division would pave the way

---

[89] *Ibid.* In the Gulf "the Arabs would have adequate warning of the force's approach... and would have enough time to destroy oil-field installations before the intervention force could arrive" (*ibid*).

[90] Collins and Mark, *Oil Fields as Military Objectives*, p. 25.

[91] *New York Times*, 7 January 1975, p. 2.

[92] *Ibid.*

[93] *Near East Report*, XIX.3, 15 January 1975, p. 9.

[94] Quandt, *Decade of Decisions*, p. 260, note.

[95] Miles Ignotus, "Seizing Arab Oil," *Harper's*, March 1975, pp. 45ff.

[96] *Ibid.* (*miles ignotus* is the Latin for "unknown soldier").

for the large Marine contingents who would arrive on the scene 72 hours later.

So much for logistics. As for some of the tactical problems—like the very real chance of fire in the oil fields—Ignotus was not unduly alarmed: "The world's supply of oil field firefighter talent is to be found in Texas."[97] He minimized the possibility or effectiveness of Saudi armed opposition to intervention. As for the strategic problems, he felt that the balance of risks was to the Soviet Union's disadvantage: "To seize the oil, the United States must seize some tracts of desert. To deny the oil, the Russians must kill American troops."[98] Besides, the rewards of inaction were high for the Soviets: "Even if the Russians do nothing at all, their prestige and influence would immediately increase all over the Middle East, and beyond. Let the Russians have the influence, and let us [the US] have the oil."[99] To Ignotus, "direct Russian counter-intervention need barely be considered."[100] Finally, there was a role for the Shah to play. He would be asked "discreetly...to 'protect' Kuwait—and, incidentally, appropriate their oil."[101]

In his comprehensive strike scenario, Ignotus—like Tucker before him—was mesmerized by the factor of trees: "If Vietnam was full of trees and brave men, and the national interest was almost invisible, here there are no trees, very few men, and a clear objective. There could be serious risks in the operation, but at least there would be no sense of futility with 200 million barrels of oil underfoot."[102]

A similar scenario was reported in the *Sunday Times* on 9 February and was quoted in the *Arab Report and Record* as follows:

The US National Security Council had completed a detailed review of a top-secret Department of Defense plan to invade Saudi Arabian oil fields in the event of another Middle East war resulting in a further Arab oil embargo, the London *Sunday Times* reported on February 9. The paper said that the plan, code-named Dhahran Option Four, had been drawn up by the Pentagon and provided for a US attack on the oil field of Ghawar, which contains 40 percent of the world's known oil reserves. The

[97] *Ibid.*
[98] *Ibid.*
[99] *Ibid.*
[100] *Ibid.*
[101] *Ibid.*
[102] *Ibid.*

attack would be led by nine airborne infantry battalions based in North Carolina, which would be flown under escort to Dhahran in the Gulf by way of the Israeli air base at Hatserim. The infantry battalions would seize the oil field at Dhahran, evacuate US personnel, and move inland to Ghawar after capturing landing jetties and storage tanks at Ras Tanura. They would be joined three days later by a Marine division of some 14,000 men who would be sent to the Gulf by sea.[103]

Another contribution to this literature came from the pen of Walter Goodman. In a article entitled "Fair Game," published in the *New Leader,* Goodman argued: "Should [military intervention in the Gulf] be successful, should the troops move in, quickly take over the fields and get the oil flowing again without much delay or opposition, my guess is that the polls would show overwhelming support for the action." And he added: "We should see a flowering of friendship for the Israelis, who would then, willy nilly, be our main allies in the area. At home, American Legionnaires and Zionists would be trading plaques at patriotic banquets."[104] On the other hand, if this scenario did not work and the military situation became messy, "it could be bad for Jews here at home."[105]

The close connection between pro-Israeli stands and American intervention to seize Arab oil, which found expression in the Zionist press, was denounced by I.F. Stone, a prominent Jewish intellectual critical of Israel. He warned American Jews against proposing solutions through war or stimulating "hate the Arabs" campaigns. He was troubled by Tucker's article: "*Commentary* is published by the American Jewish Committee. Nothing could be more dangerous for American unity, for the future of the American Jewish Committee, and for Israel itself than to have it look as if Jewish influence were trying to get the US into war with the Arabs, and take their richest resource from them."[106] Significantly, I.F. Stone's article was criticized in turn by Walter Goodman.[107]

---

[103] *Arab Report and Record,* 1–14 February 1975, p. 116.

[104] Walter Goodman, "Fair Game," *New Leader,* 17 March 1975, p. 15.

[105] *Ibid.*

[106] *Ibid.*

[107] See *Jerusalem Post Weekly* (overseas edition), 28 January 1975, 4 and 25 February 1975. Throughout this period, the Israeli press devoted some attention to oil exploration in the Ramallah area of the occupied West Bank, and a "Public Committee for Abu Rudais" was formed in Israel to campaign against the return of the Sinai oil fields to Egypt.

Moral and Practical Criticism of Intervention

There were some articulate voices in the United States who expressed reservations about intervention either on moral grounds or because of the serious risks involved. Arnaud de Borchgrave's article "Intervention Wouldn't Work" was one such contribution. After a visit to the scene of the proposed intervention he concluded: "The notion is considered too absurd to contemplate; intervention would precipitate the very event it is supposed to prevent: the economic strangulation of Western industrialized society."[108] The opinion of Frank Jungers, chairman of the Saudi-owned Arabian American Oil Co. (Aramco), as reported by De Borchgrave, was equally emphatic: "If anyone were mad enough to commit such an act of folly, Aramco's production, a quarter of the world's oil exports, requiring the service of one-third of the world's tanker fleet—would be out of commission for at least two years."[109] Much of Saudi Arabia's oil equipment was unique and gigantic (one-of-a-kind items) and virtually irreplaceable. Besides, De Borchgrave was informed by Saudi experts on the spot that the whole oil operation could be swiftly knocked out of action without even having to blow up wells and cause widespread damage. This was a technical problem involving the destabilization of water or gas injection plants, to cite one example.

On the floor of the American Senate there was some criticism in January 1975 of the Ford administration's repeated statements regarding military intervention. A few Senators denounced the fact that oil seizure was being presented to the nation as a viable policy option. In this respect, Oregon Senator Mark Hatfield's reaction to the Secretary of State's threat of intervention was particularly sharp. On 21 January in the Senate, he decried the mounting campaign of reports concerning direct military intervention against oil producers and deplored the threat to world peace caused by such unwarranted tactics. Hatfield remarked:

> I will not stand before you today and pretend to understand the nuances and subtleties of Dr. Kissinger's moral juxtaposition, or what possible purpose he hopes to achieve by threatening overtly the countries of the Middle East and the fragile peace of a troubled world. For I can sense little reason for hope in the Secretary's remarks. Let me speak plainly. As every American realizes, Dr. Kissinger is not talking in the abstract about

[108] Arnaud de Borchgrave, "Intervention Wouldn't Work," *Newsweek*, 31 March 1975, p. 27.
[109] *Ibid.*

imaginary crises, or hypothetical situations. He is talking and
threatening military action.[110]

Senator Hatfield's intervention was followed two days later by that of
Senator Jesse Helms, of North Carolina, who also deplored both Kissinger's
statements and the President's repeated endorsements: "These comments,"
Helmes said, "have come against a background of military manoeuvres in the
Indian Ocean and the Mediterranean that will be undoubtedly interpreted
by the Middle East nations as sabrerattling to match the rhetoric."[111] He
described the dispatch of the Seventh Fleet Task Force to the Indian Ocean
as "a rather clumsy attempt to pressure the oil-producing nations."[112] As
for the US Marines' beach-landing exercises in the Mediterranean, these
"will not fail to be interpreted by the oil-producing nations as practice for
landings on their soil."[113] And he went on to underline the Arab reactions
to the American moves. Egypt saw them as undermining American-Arab
relations and the cause of peace. Algerian President Houari Boumedienne
declared that "the occupation of one Arab state would be regarded as an
occupation of the entire Arab world," and added that such action would
cause the destruction of oil installations.[114]

Senator Helmes was joined by Senators Hansen and McClure, who both
denounced the Administration's tactics. McClure spoke out against the
moral bankruptcy of those who advocate the seizure of oil:

> It is disturbing to me personally that it is even necessary for an
> American to stand up and publicly state he is opposed to invading
> an Arab nation and stealing their oil. The immorality of such a
> proposal is so evident that I would have expected an outpouring
> of protests from Government leaders and those in private life who
> have so violently protested against war in the past. That such
> an outpouring has not occurred is a serious disappointment.[115]

However, the Administration had its own reasons for inventing the myth
of strangulation and then reacting to it by a loud campaign of saber-rattling.
To begin with, this would shift the responsibility for the oil crisis on to a

---

[110] *Congressional Record* (Senate), 21 January 1975, p. S529.
[111] *Ibid.*, 23 January 1975, p. S790.
[112] *Ibid.*
[113] *Ibid.*, p. S792.
[114] *Ibid.*
[115] *Ibid.*, p. S794.

convenient scapegoat who could be threatened with punishment through military intervention. At the same time, many analysts have confirmed that a favorite device of Kissinger is to heighten apprehension and disorientation among the parties so that negotiations become, in his view, productive. Besides, history tends to show that gunboat diplomacy is popular on the domestic scene and serves to unsettle the target of the diplomatic action.

As to why several influential organs of the American Jewish establishment and the pro-Israel lobby joined in with evident relish, here also the answer is hardly a mystery. For years, one of the cardinal points in Israel's propaganda routine has been to stress the strategic value of the Zionist state as a anti-Soviet ally and as a policeman for the United States in an oil-rich region. However, this myth was exploded with the October 1973 war. The so-called strategic value of Israel was greatly diminished—in fact, from a strategic point of view it was increasingly perceived as a embarrassment. The problem facing the lobby and its supporters was how to restore the old perception and make it credible. Joining the "seize Arab oil" bandwagon offered a chance. The link with the "Cold Warriors" in America, those who believe in the politics of confrontation rather than of détente with the Soviet Union, would be strengthened. Therefore, in the words of Michael Hudson, "the recent far-fetched attempts to argue why the United States should invade the Arab oil states, now look like self-serving attempts to revive this tarnished perception of Israel's strategic value."[116]

Requirements and Costs of Intervention

In August 1975 *Oil Fields as Military Objectives: A Feasibility Study* was published. Prepared jointly by Colonel John Collins, a senior specialist in National Defense with eighteen years experience in contingency planning in the Pentagon, and by Clyde Mark, analyst in Middle Eastern Affairs for the House Committee on International Relations, the study was a careful analysis and documentation of what military intervention in various locations would involve by way of requirements, costs, and risks. In Part I the authors dealt with "Primal Problems": a) the vital interests of the US and its allies, related to oil; and b) key decisions by the US (and by OPEC) regarding the use of armed force and its justification in terms of "international law, constitutional responsibilities, and public opinion at home and abroad."[117] Part II, entitled "Global Perspective," examined: a) the condi-

---

[116] Lawrence Mosher, "Changing Perspectives in Washington," *Middle East International* (London), June 1975, p. 8. [On the "Cold Warriors," cf. above, pp. 194–95.]

[117] Collins and Mark, *Oil Fields as Military Objectives*, p. 8.

tions ("the irreducible minimum") required for successful missions to seize OPEC oil targets; and b) the counter-intervention threats by OPEC states and the Soviet Union. In Part III the authors selected a sample option, "the Saudi Core," for in-depth examination. This included the "General Geography" (space relationships, topography, water resources, climate, vegetation, and people); the "Petroleum Production Plant" (oil fields, terminals, and control facilities); the "Lines of Communication" (sea, air, and land LOCs) involved both to and within the "Saudi Core;" and the so-called "Critical Terrain," i.e., the key well-heads, choke points, terminal facilities, pumping installations, and bases.[118] This was followed by a detailed discussion of the military, naval, and air force requirements as well as the civilian contingents needed to restore and operate the "Saudi Core." Part IV was a short one-page wrap-up of conclusions. The study also contained a comprehensive section of annexes, numerous and valuable tables on oil consumption, petroleum imports, refinery statistics, and Saudi oil well production, and fifteen maps.

The work of Collins and Mark was in part an answer to the optimistic scenarios constructed by Tucker and Ignotus. Even if the non-military facets (political, legal, and moral) outlined in Part I were entirely favorable, concluded the authors, successful operations

> ...would be assured only if this country [the US] could satisfy
> all aspects of a five-part mission:
> —Seize required oil installations intact
> —Secure them for weeks, months, years
> —Restore wrecked assets rapidly
> —Operate all installations without the owner's assistance
> —Guarantee safe overseas passage for supplies and petroleum
> products.[119]

The authors felt that while the US could defeat the armed forces of a given OPEC country, the element of surprise could not be counted on. Seizing oil fields intact would therefore "be a chancy proposition under ideal conditions."[120] Moreover, there was serious doubt as to whether restoration of oil production could proceed quickly: "one well-blown pump station can shut a pipeline down for 90 days minimum," and, as far as the actual oil

---

[118] *Ibid.*, pp. 46–49.
[119] *Ibid.*, pp. xl, 15.
[120] *Ibid.*, p. 75.

wells were concerned, whereas the average production of one US well is only 18 barrels a day, by contrast, the average production of one Saudi well is 12,000 barrels a day, with some wells pumping 45,000 to 60,000 a day.[121] Much of the specially designed equipment would be virtually impossible to replace. Besides, specialized manpower was in very short supply. To replace the 10 to 15,000 Arab oil men in the "Saudi Core," the United States would have to draft "US oil workers en masse."[122]

* * * *

By mid-1975 the campaign of threats had subsided: President Ford announced on 23 May that he would not use force to respond to a new oil embargo by Arab states.[123] Led by Henry Kissinger, the Administration's brinkmanship had not broken OPEC, forced prices down, or helped to fashion a consumers' block.[124] The firm resolve of the Arab states to blow up their oil installations in response to military intervention was tempered with responsible restraint. This was widely noted. The use of threats as a deterrent against fancied oil embargoes and boycotts risked provoking the very event it was supposed to guard against.

Another important constraint was American public opinion, whose opposition to military intervention in distant places had been revealed on numerous occasions in the post-Vietnam period. In a January 1975 Gallup Poll only ten percent of those interviewed supported military action in the Middle East.[125] In April a Harris survey indicated that 58 percent of Americans were opposed to the seizure of Arab oil fields (while 25 percent approved).[126] Furthermore, a study by Russett and Nincic concluded that, partly because of Vietnam, public opinion was "much less favorably disposed toward the use of American military force than at any time since the beginning of the cold war."[127] Persuading the public to endorse interventionist action in the Gulf would not have been easy.

---

[121] *Ibid.*, p. 70, and Table 14 on p. 68.

[122] *Ibid.*, p. 75.

[123] John Collins and Clyde Mark, "Petroleum from the Persian Gulf: Use of US Armed Force to Ensure Supplies," Library of Congress, Issue Brief IB 79046, 18 September 1979, p. 24.

[124] Emile Nakhleh, *The United States and Saudi Arabia* (Washington: American Enterprise Institute, 1975), p. 59.

[125] *Ibid.*, quoting "Mideast Invasion by US Opposed," *Washington Post*, 23 January 1975.

[126] "Oil or Israel," *New York Times Magazine*, 6 April 1975.

[127] Bruce Russett and Miroslav Nincic, "American Opinion on the Use of Military Force Abroad," *Political Science Quarterly*, Fall 1976, p. 411.

Both factors of constraint—Arab resolve and American public opinion—came out in the open in the course of a major hearing conducted in mid-1976 by the Senate Foreign Relations Committee on the subject of "Middle East Peace Prospects."[128] At one point in the proceedings, Senator McGovern put the following question to Dr. Edward Luttwak, a leading interventionist among the academic hawks: "Are you suggesting an American invasion of the Saudi Arabian oil fields? What do you have in mind?" Luttwak's answer was: "The last resort, the final sanction, the last instrument, the most fragile, the most costly, the most risky instrument for state action is, indeed, force."[129] In reply, Senator Percy argued that he was visiting the Middle East "at the time of the *Business Week* [Kissinger's January interview] article on the pressure and the ultimate threat." His conclusion: "It backfired terribly."[130] Furthermore, Senator McGovern testified that he too had been in the Middle East when the various scenarios appeared in the American press: "There was an article in *Harper's* that broke exactly at the time I was in Saudi Arabia where there was a scenario proposed by the author for a military invasion, a take-over of the Saudi Arabian oil fields. It was a political catastrophe....It strikes me that it is not very helpful for us to be preparing the American public or the world public for a possible American move to take over those oil fields. I think that sets back the whole cause and accommodation with these peoples whose goodwill we need and they need our help."[131]

As to the credibility of the threats issued by the Ford administration, Luttwak felt that they were not backed by the indispensable preparation in the areas of logistics and public information:

> ...the threats that were issued by the President and the Sec-
> retary of State were completely hollow. Behind these threats
> there was no preparation of a physical logistic nature. And ten
> times more important there was no informed public. There was
> no public that was informed and which accepted the need of the
> threat; and public support is nine-tenths of your credibility.
>
> A good threat is a threat that need not be carried out...the
> first need is an informed public, a public that does not see the

---

[128] US Senate, Committee on Foreign Relations, Hearings, *Middle East Peace Prospects* (Washington: Goverment Printing Office, 1976), pp. 213–31.

[129] *Ibid.*, p. 223.

[130] *Ibid.*, p. 226.

[131] *Ibid.*, p. 227.

whole oil business in terms of guilt feeling about overuse of energy but rather in terms of a political problem, a confrontation.

Once you have an informed public then you can do it. If you don't have an informed public, you cannot do it.

As for the specific question—is it ultimately physically possible whether or not you have public support—the answer there is not simple. I have studied this question in a superficial sort of way. I know that a gentleman at the Brookings Institution wrote a detailed study of this. He came to the conclusion it was not easy but it was feasible.[132]

Senator McGovern's very apt rejoinder was: "Those are the same people who told us how easy it was going to be in Vietnam...."[133]

Carter, Camp David, and the Intervention Issue

The First Two Years

There were many indications in early 1977 that, in sharp contrast with his immediate predecessors in the White House, President Carter would seek to avoid confrontation and promote accommodation in foreign affairs. His stress on human rights and on America's moral leadership, his declared intention of withdrawing US troops from South Korea and of negotiating new Panama Canal treaties, his deep attachment to the concept of strategic arms limitations, and his non-interventionist stance in the face of Soviet and Cuban gains in Ethiopia, Angola, Afghanistan, and South Yemen, provided the necessary proof. His response to those critics who felt he should be more forceful in handling crisis situations was that his nation did not have the ability to intervene in the "internal political structure of any nation...unless the [US] wanted to get another Vietnam going."[134] In the words of one analyst writing in April 1979, President Carter could "rightly boast that in his entire term so far not a single American had died in combat anywhere in the world."[135]

On the issues of the Arab-Israeli conflict and of Palestinian rights, Carter appeared to be following the general guidelines of the Brookings Report, at

---

[132] *Ibid.*

[133] *Ibid.*

[134] Don Oberdorfer, "The Paradoxes of Carter's Foreign Policy," *The Guardian Weekly* (Manchester), 4 March 1979, pp. 17–18.

[135] Jonathan Steele, "Goodbye America," *The Guardian Weekly*, 8 April 1979, p. 7.

least during his first year in office. His statement regarding a Palestinian homeland, his recognition in September 1977 that "the PLO represented a substantial part of the Palestinians" (widely interpreted as an evolution from the position of the 1975 Saunders Document),[136] and his clear intention to abandon Kissinger's step-by-step approach in favor of a comprehensive settlement that would take into consideration the Soviet Union's role (the American-Soviet joint statement of 1 October 1977) were generally well received by the Arabs, and with unconcealed hostility by the Israelis.

Rather than seek confrontation in the Indian Ocean, one of the few "uncommitted" zones of peace of the planet Earth, Carter in fact proposed that this ocean be completely demilitarized. In response, the Soviet Union apparently signaled that it was prepared to open negotiations on the subject.[137] On the other hand, Carter issued a secret Presidential Directive PD 18 on 25 August 1977 (which was leaked to the press) calling for the preparation of an adequate strike force of several "light divisions" capable of rapid intervention in the Middle East, especially in the oil-producing areas of the Gulf.[138] Moreover, on 20 February 1978, Defense Secretary Brown fired the Administration's first warning shot in the direction of Arab oil producers. In his address to the Los Angeles World Affairs Council, he said: "Because the area is the world's greatest source of oil, the Middle East and the Persian Gulf cannot be separated from our security and that of NATO and our allies in Asia." And he added: "We intend to safeguard the production of oil and its transportation to consumer nations without interference by hostile powers."[139] In the political climate of early 1978 such strong language was aimed at pressuring the Arab oil producers into acceptance of the new Sadat-Israel initiative, duly blessed by the United States. At this point, as suggested in the pages of the *Nation* (4 February 1978), US policy was embarking on a "Pax Americana for the Middle East."[140] In a misguided and somewhat puzzling volte-face, the Geneva option and the American-Soviet

---

[136] [On the Saunders Document, see below, pp. 417–30.]

[137] Bard E. O'Neill, "Petroleum and Security: The Limitations of Military Power in the Persian Gulf," *National Security Affairs Monograph 77-4*, October 1977, p. 20, note 25. The littoral states of the Indian Ocean, together with the UN, favored the transformation of the ocean into a "Zone of Peace." See Terence Lewin, "The Indian Ocean and Beyond: British Interests Yesterday and Today," *Asian Affairs*, October 1978, pp. 256–57.

[138] "Oil and Policemen," *Mideast Observer* (Washington), 1 March 1978.

[139] *Ibid.*

[140] A. J. Khouri and Paul Saba, "Pax Americana for the Middle East," *Nation* (New York), 4 February 1978, p. 101.

Joint Statement of 1 October 1977 were unceremoniously dumped by the decision-makers in the White House.

A month later, the United States accepted in silence Israel's massive invasion of South Lebanon, despite the obvious fact that this was no quick "strike and withdrawal" operation and that Zionist "economic studies in the past had pointed to the advantage of drawing Israel's northern border so as to embrace the Litani River, and [that] the general complexion of the Begin government aroused apprehension that Israel might be tempted to annex the occupied territory."[141] The road to Camp David was clearly not to be paved with the best of intentions.

What happened at Camp David in the summer of 1978? In addition to an understanding regarding future close coordination on regional security, there was, in essence, a tripartite agreement between Sadat, Begin, and Carter on two frameworks: 1) "A Framework for Peace in the Middle East Agreed at Camp David," 2) "Framework for the Conclusion of a Peace Treaty Between Egypt and Israel." The first related to the question of "the self-governing authority (administrative council) in the West Bank and Gaza,"[142] pending eventual accord within five years. The second was bilateral and concerned specific negotiations that had been under way for some time.

The Camp David agreements never resolved the issue of linkage between the frameworks. Whereas Sadat maintained he had ratified an agreement that referred to specific steps regarding a West Bank and Gaza accord, Begin insisted that the two frameworks were separate, and he adamantly refused to entertain any linkage. As to the Carter administration, it appeared to side with the Israeli view that there was no legal or direct linkage, but also empathized with Sadat and sought to find a way of enshrining some reference to linkage in separate letters.

Clearly, Begin wanted the first framework because of the signal advantages to Israel in detaching Egypt from the Arab camp. But there was little pressure placed on him to do anything in the Palestinian West Bank and Gaza except to sit tight and order more Jewish settlements. The mild rebukes of Vance would hardly stop him. Or as Moshe Dayan put it to the *International Herald Tribune* (28 March 1979): "I know you Americans think you're going to force us out of the West Bank. But we're here and you're in Washington. What will you do if we maintain settlements? Squawk? What

---

[141] Robert Stookey, "The United States," in P.E. Haley and L.W. Snider, *Lebanon in Crisis* (Syracuse: Syracuse University Press, 1979), pp. 246–47.

[142] Department of State, *The Camp David Summit* (Washington: Government Printing Office, September 1978), p. 8.

will you do if we keep the army there? Send troops?" There was probably no American rejoinder.

Besides, the Western media tended to see new opportunities everywhere in the region. In an article on Camp David, the journal *Armies and Weapons* issued an open invitation to Egypt to conquer Libya, dwelling on the so-called ease of such military intrusion. Thereafter, the country would be properly exploited with the help of Israeli talent: "By taking control of Libya, Egypt would acquire control of enormous financial resources and raw materials, huge areas for development and partly for cultivation, possibly with help from Israeli agronomists who have specialized in cultivating the desert....it would be possible to start profitable mining operations, using Arab capital and Israeli and Western technics [sic.]."[143]

Whereas the Carter administration up to this point was careful not to exacerbate relations with Saudi Arabia, other influential circles, particularly in Congress, were prepared to dispense with such niceties. A December 1977 report prepared for Senator Henry Jackson, chairman of the powerful Senate Committee on Energy and Natural Resources, and an ardent backer of both the Shah and Israel, implied very strongly that the United States should support the Shah against Saudi Arabia even to the extent of invasion: "If Iran is called upon to intervene in the internal affairs of any Gulf state, it must be recognized in advance by the United States that this is the role for which Iran is being primed and blame cannot be assigned for Iran's carrying out an implied assignment."[144]   And the study, echoing Senator Jackson's traditional anti-Saudi stance, went on to add: "Historically the Persian Empire occupied a far larger geographic area than does present-day Iran. When Persian leaders were strong their ambitions were great....as Iran's oil reserves peak and decline, across the Gulf will be Saudi Arabia with plentiful oil reserves, enormous wealth, and little to spend it on in terms of native population."[145]

By mid-1978, all the same, there were signs of increased interest in strengthening America's position in the Indian Ocean, Arabian Sea, and Gulf. There was also news that intervention studies were in vogue once more in some academic circles in the USA. Admiral Thomas Moorer, chairman of the Joint Chiefs of Staff from 1970 to 1974, called for the "intermittent de-

---

[143] *Armies and Weapons* (Monte Carlo), 49 (December 1978), p. 11.

[144] Fern Racine Gold and Melvin Conant, "Access to Oil—The United States Relationships with Saudi Arabia and Iran," US Senate, Committee on Energy, Publication 95–70 (December 1977), p. 84.

[145] *Ibid.*

ployment of two carrier forces to the Eastern African littoral and Arabian
Sea, conducting selected exercises inside the Gulf on a random basis."[146]
In making his political and military strategy explicit, he argued that in the
absence of American land bases in the region, "the carriers would provide a
visible presence and timely manifestation of United States resolve."[147] And
in the wake of Camp David, Senator Frank Church warned Saudi Arabia on 5
October to cooperate fully with the new peace initiative: "It is imperative,"
he said, "that we make clear to the Saudi government that our strategic
concerns are mutual, that our interests are intertwined and, in the last analysis, it is the American security umbrella which shields the Kingdom."[148] A
few days earlier Senator Jackson had called for a "New Marshall Plan for
the Middle East" and a "partnership of unprecedented proportions between
Israel, Egypt, and the United States."[149] The pressure on the Arab world
was building up amid signs that all was not well between Washington and
Riyad.

A comprehensive study published in late 1978 by the Brookings Institution provided a detailed analysis of the frequency of US military interventions
during the thirty-year period between 1946 and 1975. It bore the revealing
title *Force Without War: US Armed Forces as a Political Instrument* and
was written by Barry Blechman and Stephen Kaplan (and other contributors including William Quandt); the project was supported by the Defense
Department's Advance Research Projects Agency. The authors' definition
of intervention made a point of excluding actual participation in war. Thus
the Korean or Vietnam conflicts were not dealt with because "US armed
forces were used in these conflicts primarily as a martial instrument—that
is to wage war."[150] Instead the study was concerned with instances "in
which the armed forces were used in a discrete way for specific political objectives in a particular situation."[151] Discrete was a keynote term in the
study, and the list of instances was a long one—215 times between 1946 and
1975—including civil wars in the Dominican Republic, Cambodia, and Laos.

---

[146] Thomas Moorer, "Countering Soviet Global Claims," *International Herald Tribune*, 4
June 1978.

[147] *Ibid.*

[148] *Mideast Observer*, 15 October 1978, p. 1.

[149] *Ibid.*

[150] Barry Blechman and Stephen Kaplan, *Force Without War: US Armed Forces As a
Political Instrument* (Washington: The Brookings Institution, 1978), p. 14.

[151] *Ibid.*, p. 4.

In general the conclusions, although cautious, were nonetheless favorable rather than critical, reflecting perhaps the new mood of "realism" and the "revision" of the Vietnam experience.[152]   According to the study, policy goals were apparently achieved in the first six months following discrete armed intervention, with success eroding somewhat thereafter.[153] The great value of such operations was "to provide a respite, a means of postponing adverse developments long enough to formulate and implement new policies that may be sustainable over the longer term."[154]   Success appeared to be great when the goal of intervention was the maintenance of friendly regimes and much less frequent when the Soviet Union also used or threatened to use force.   In this respect the dramatic increase of Soviet naval presence in the Mediterranean, both in terms of ships and ship-days, was of special significance. Between 1946 and 1971, the number of ship-days (a ship-day is the equivalent of one naval vessel spending one day in a given zone) spent by the Soviet's Fifth Eskadra in the Mediterranean increased from 1,500 to 19,000.   And although Blechman and Kaplan assessed its combat role merely as "a counter to the US force and not as a force to secure sea control or to project power ashore," they nevertheless did recognize its "inhibiting influence on US crisis behavior."[155] In fact, in the last ten years or so, the two superpowers were drawn into military confrontation with each other most frequently in the Mediterranean arena of the Arab-Israeli conflict. The study also concluded that US threats to utilize the strategic nuclear arsenal were made 19 times, notably during the Suez War of 1956, the intervention in Lebanon in 1958, the Cuban missile crisis of 1962, and the Arab-Israeli War of 1973.

In short, between 1946 and 1975 American armed forces were utilized discretely on an average of 7.2 times a year, and 12 times a year (or once a month) during the period 1956–65, which was seen as a time of great activism. The authors predicted another period of increased interventionist activity:

---

[152] Walter La Feber, "Empire Begins at Home," *Nation*, 9 June 1979, p. 658.

[153] Drew Middleton, "US Use of Force Found to Be a Relative Success," *International Herald Tribune*, 20 December 1978, p. 5.

[154] Blechman and Kaplan, *Force Without War*, p. 518. "Was it worthwhile to use armed forces to obtain positive outcomes that could be sustained only temporarily, whether the duration was of several months, or several years? We believe the answer is yes, insofar as an opportunity was gained for diplomancy." *Ibid.*

[155] Barry Blechman and Stephen Kaplan, "The Political Use of Military Power in the Mediterranean by the United States and the Soviet Union," *Lo Spettatore internazionale* (Rome), 13 (January-March 1978), pp. 37–39.

As the Vietnam War fades from the nation's consciousness, and
as other recent blows to the nation's confidence—Watergate, the
1974–75 recession—likewise recede, voices urging a more active
US role in world affairs are being heard more clearly, particularly
as the international system presents a large number of "opportunities." More frequent political uses of the armed forces may
be one result.[156]

The overall implications of *Force Without War* were clear: military intervention was perceived as a profitable enterprise, which could be carried out at
various levels of commitment, with a high once-a-month frequency if necessary, with a reasonable chance of achieving political objectives, and without
leading to war. The message was an ominous one.

Likewise, William O'Brien's recent study *US Military Intervention: Law
and Morality* noted the shift toward active interventionism and the erosion
of the "no more Vietnams" attitude prevalent in the late sixties and early
seventies:

Today we are on the brink of emergence from a period of reaction against intervention, particularly military intervention. The
need to reconsider military interventionary options, notably in
the Middle East, is increasingly urged in American national security debates. In such a time it is important to rethink the legal
and moral guidelines that ought to govern decisions to engage in
or abstain from military intervention.[157]

O'Brien's suggested "guidelines" for future interventions are based on his
study of the Dominican and Vietnamese examples. He did note the ambiva-
lent and risky nature of intervention, even when it was done by invitation.
Nonetheless, in the event that intervention met the requirements of the *jus
ad bellum* and the *jus in bello* (a just war and a justly conducted war), the author proposed yet another criterion. "As the Vietnam experience indicates,"
he wrote, "the proportion of means to a just end must be conscientiously
calculated in the light of a realistic appraisal of the probability of success.
If the costs appear to be high and the probability of success low or highly
uncertain, morality would counsel against military intervention."[158]

---

[156] Blechman and Kaplan, *Force Without War*, p. 533.

[157] O'Brien, *US Military Intervention*, p. 7.

[158] *Ibid.*, pp. 83–84.

To O'Brien, military intervention was warranted in three situations: 1) armed intervention by another international actor; 2) clear danger to local and foreign population because of a civil war or collapse of authority; 3) massive violations of human rights within a given state.[159]

The Iranian Crisis and the Reassessment of the Nixon Doctrine

It is indeed one of the many expressions of the irony of history that while the Camp David summit was in progress an astounding revolution of a new type broke out against the Shah of Iran, whose regime had been toasted only a few months earlier by Carter as representing "an island of stability in an unstable world." As the US was busy propping up Israel, one of the twin pillars of its shaky Middle Eastern policy, by involving it in a Sadat-Israel axis bristling with question marks, the second pillar, the Shah, was shaken by the Iranian earthquake.

The year 1979 opened with alarm and despondency in Washington: alarm over the crumbling positions in Iran and Turkey in addition to the possible repercussions in Saudi Arabia, despondency over the fact that the much-heralded peace treaty between Egypt and Israel had not been signed on 17 December and had led to bitter recriminations in the domestic arena. The overall economic outlook indicated a combination of rapidly rising prices and unemployment matched by rapidly falling economic activity. In addition, the specter of oil shortages was looming larger. The disruption of Iran's oil supplies was seen as having a negative impact on the industrial allies of the United States despite the raise in Saudi production aimed at covering the Iranian shortfall. Carter faced a bleak remainder of his first term and the danger of slim prospects for a second.

On the Senate front, there were unmistakable signs that Senator Frank Church (helped along by Senator Jacob Javits) would lead a revived Senate Foreign Relations Committee into clashes with the Carter administration.[160] Besides, Henry Kissinger was still very much in the limelight as director of the Council on Foreign Relations and as a member of the executive committee of the Trilateral Commission, and was receiving on average a briefing a week by the State Department. In fact, he could be described as a shadow Secretary of State, and one who did not mince his words about America's need to project power more forcefully everywhere, particularly in the Gulf

---

[159] *Ibid.*, p. 82.
[160] *Washington Post*, 31 December 1978.

and the Indian Ocean. In an important interview with *The Economist*, Kissinger was quite explicit:

> We cannot resign from the problem [of Gulf Security] by renouncing the role of policeman....It is a responsibility we cannot avoid. So we need a complex of policies. We need a visible presence of American power in the Indian Ocean, in part as a substitute for the declining Iranian power....We surely should not exclude it [military force] publicly—though of course it can only be a last recourse.[161]

And later in the interview he stressed the significance of the current negotiations: "Until a few years ago an Arab-Israeli policy could act as a symbol of the American strategic and political dominance of the area. Now the Egyptian-Israeli agreement is an admission card to dealing with other even deeper issues."[162] He would have preferred to have seen Camp David "carried to a conclusion rapidly and in a dominant fashion."[163] The failure of the current initiative would spell disaster: "Under the present circumstances the failure of Camp David must be perceived as a sign that the United States and all those who have bet on the United States are incapable of shaping events."[164]

The appropriate response to the situation brought about by the collapse of the Shah's regime was of course the subject of fierce debate in the various power centers of the United States. Doubt was being raised as to the willingness and ability of the President to act decisively in foreign affairs. The rift between Brzezinski's aides on the National Security Council and State Department officials loyal to Cyrus Vance was out in the open and the subject of extensive commentary and gossip.[165] But there were also clear signs that a drastic reassessment of the Nixon Doctrine was under way. Local or proxy forces could no longer be relied upon to police the vital oil flow. The Pentagon was muttering that it wanted to do the job itself. The aircraft carrier *Constellation*, escorted by two cruisers, two guided-missile destroyers, one conventional destroyer, and three support ships, left Subic Bay on New Year's Eve bound for the Indian Ocean and Arabian Sea. However, it was soon ordered back in a puzzling change of mind.

---

[161] *The Economist*, 10 February 1979, pp. 35–36.
[162] *Ibid.*
[163] *Ibid.*
[164] *Ibid.*
[165] *New York Times*, 12 January 1979.

On 12 January, a State Department spokesman announced that a formation of 12 Eagle F-15 jet fighters would fly to Saudi Arabia to demonstrate the importance of America's interest in the security of the region during the revolutionary upheaval in Iran. This "fly-in" and subsequent "fly-out" of sophisticated, albeit unarmed, aircraft was a calculated act of political and military symbolism. Paradoxically, it also helped to remind the Arabs that whereas the F-15 was fully operational in the Israeli air force, notably since the March 1978 invasion of Lebanon in which they were employed, the delivery of the F-15 to Saudi Arabia was not scheduled even to start for another three years.[166]

As analyst Lawrence Mosher wryly put it, the alternative to the Nixon Doctrine in many Washington corridors:

> ...is what military people call the *US 100,000-man Quick Strike Force,* which consists of three divisions rapidly deployable anywhere by air. But as one Defense official said, "One needs a real bogeyman to come in and have to be stopped before you can talk of using the quick strike force." It may turn out that bogeyman may not be defined the same in Arabic as in English.[167]

On the level of grand strategy there was plenty of scope for addressing the geopolitical implications of the decline of American influence in Iran. Zbigniew Brzezinski, in a speech to the Foreign Policy Association, evoked an "arc of crisis...along the shores of the Indian Ocean, with fragile social and political structures in a region of vital importance to [the US] threatened with fragmentation." He felt that the resulting chaos could very well work out to the advantage of "elements hostile to [US] values and sympathetic to [US] adversaries."[168] In some circles, the old Domino Theory was brought once more into play—after being dusted off—and was used to justify intervention aimed at blocking a chain reaction in so-called sensitive regions. Testifying before the Senate Energy and Natural Resources Committee on 17 January, James Schlesinger cautioned that the balance of power in the Gulf region had changed and that the United States "will have to take steps to shore-up the nations around the Gulf...."[169]

---

[166] *Mideast Observer,* 15 January 1979, p. 3.

[167] Lawrence Mosher, "After Iran, US Is Its Own Policeman," *Middle East International,* 19 January 1979, p. 7.

[168] *New York Times,* 7 January 1979.

[169] *Mideast Observer,* 15 January 1979, p. 3. See also *Wall Street Journal,* 18 January 1979, quoting Schlesinger's warning of the "encirclement" of the oil-producing region, and

One more area in the Western regional defense perimeter was heating up. "So it is," concluded columnist Stephen Rosenfeld (reflecting the powerful conservative, neo-Hawk, and pro-Israel wing of the Establishment) in early February 1979, "that the Persian Gulf is now routinely bracketed with Korea as the place where the United States must be ready to fight the "half-war" or the "one-and-a-half wars" for which it has planned its forces since Vietnam."[170] Nor were diplomatic implications neglected: "The triumph of an unarmed mass movement over a heavily armed regime linked closely to the United States has forced a rethinking of the uses of raw military power—the client's and the patron's—in civil conflicts....The old-style diplomacy involved fronting for military power. The new-style diplomacy must anticipate and manage emerging political currents."[171]

The Israelis seized the opportunity provided by events in Iran to argue that, with the collapse of the Shah, they remained the sole strategic asset of the Western alliance in the region and must therefore be suitably rewarded and placated. But the Iranian crisis—much to the disquiet of Israel—also signaled the search for other possibilities. Hence Sadat's candidacy as a surrogate through whom US strategic potency would be partially recovered in the area with other possible benefits: the Egyptian president could also be given a greater role to play in the Red Sea and African scenes. Nor did he require much persuading. Having made the decision to abandon Arab solidarity and to forget about substantive progress on the question of Palestinian national rights, Sadat could only play as though he had taken a quantum leap in strategic importance. According to the *Washington Post,* authoritative US sources reported an offer made by President Sadat to Defense Secretary Harold Brown in person "to play a major pro-Western military role in the Middle East in exchange for the United States equipping his armed forces with billions of dollars of modern weaponry."[172] On the other hand, Israel's role as America's gendarme was repeatedly emphasized during the first weeks of 1979. Shmuel Katz, Israel's former Information Director, wrote in the *Jerusalem Post* (5 January 1979): "There is no nation in this area but Israel... which can ensure a viable security doctrine for the Middle East." A month later he again underlined the importance of his country

his fear that "the texture of strategic relationships in the preeminent oil-producing region is in the process of change...."

[170] Stephen Rosenfeld, "The Uses of Power in the Persian Gulf," *Washington Post,* 2 February 1979.

[171] *Ibid.*

[172] *Washington Post,* 21 February 1979.

"as a crutch" to the United States: "an unweakened Israel *with room for manoeuvre* is the only means in the final analysis, for ensuring the safety even of the Arabian oil field."[173]

In the new triangular relationship fashioned by the United States, two sides of the triangle were, from the very start, at odds with each other and with the third as to who was more useful to the third, and therefore more worthy of preferential treatment.

The Iranian crisis, in addition to precipitating discussions regarding the Pentagon's regional defense perimeter, also provided a new urgency for the peace talks. In mid-January, on the eve of US special envoy Alfred Atherton's visit to the area (16–29 January), Begin is reported to have informed Canada's Conservative Party leader, Joe Clark, of Israel's anxiety regarding the situation in Iran, South Yemen, Ethiopia, and Afghanistan and therefore the need to resume negotiations with Egypt soon and to bring them to a swift conclusion.[174] Likewise, Sadat's eagerness to resume negotiations was evident in his 2 February press statement in which he indicated a readiness to meet Israel's petroleum needs with Egypt's Sinai oil.

The true character of the contemplated Sadat-Begin treaty did not escape Arab observers. Far from being a peace settlement, it was, in fact, in the tradition of the imperial *Pax*; it is in this light that the American intention of defending the treaty against all comers has to be seen. The Arab daily *Al-Thawra* viewed it as "an alliance of Egypt and Israel under the American umbrella to threaten the peace and security of the Middle East."[175]

Interventionist Threats and the Deterioration Of Relations with Saudi Arabia and Jordan

As the year 1979 opened, there were question marks regarding relations between Washington and Riyad. By the end of February, the full extent of the deterioration was out in the open, and the succeeding months brought further strains. The Saudi authorities and press were particularly incensed at some of the actions of the Carter administration and of prominent Senators. To take the reasons for this growing Saudi malaise in chronological

---

[173] *Jerusalem Post*, 16 February 1979, p. 7. The italics are Shmuel Katz's.

[174] *Jerusalem Post*, 16 January 1979, p. 1.

[175] *Al-Thawra*, 7 March 1979. For a particularly perceptive analysis of the significance of the Sadat-Begin treaty, see Elias Shoufani, "Al-Taqsīr wa-l-muʿāhada," *Shuʾūn filasṭīnīya* (Beirut), 90 (May 1979); excerpted (in English) in the *Journal of Palestine Studies*, 32 (Summer 1979), pp. 137–45.

order, there was, to begin with, the anti-Saudi campaign waged by Senator Frank Church in early February. For his first major foreign policy statement as chairman of the Senate Foreign Relations Committee, Church had selected as forum a B'nai B'rith convention. "It was necessary," he stressed in his speech, "for the US to lay it on the line with the Saudis," and it was important that the kingdom's "resistance to the [Camp David] accords be neutralized by the US." In another reference he thought it was "time for plain speaking with the government of Saudi Arabia."[176]

Frank Church called for a review of the whole relationship with Saudi Arabia, including the sale of F-15s, and for strong pressure to be applied on the Kingdom. Moreover, he commissioned a special study entitled "United States Foreign Policy Objectives and Overseas Military Installations," which envisioned the construction of new US bases in the Middle East under three possible conditions: 1) in Israel, Egypt, or perhaps elsewhere in the region as a guarantee of an Arab-Israeli settlement; 2) by invitation of smaller states eager to thwart a "long-term threat from one or more of its neighbors;" and 3) in the event of a "serious threat to regional security posed by another great power."[177]

A second and more serious cause for the growing malaise was the renewed campaign of public threats of intervention by Washington. In separate TV interviews during the last weekend of February 1979, two key members of the Administration, Defense Secretary Harold Brown and Energy Secretary James Schlesinger issued clear warnings of US determination to intervene in the Gulf region to protect vital interests. "We will take any action," Brown said, "that is appropriate, including military force." And Schlesinger (himself a former Defense Secretary) went further: "The United States must move in such a way that it protects those interests [in the Gulf], even if that involves the use of military strength or military presence."[178] This specter of a US *military presence,* appearing as it did in the context of suggestions made a day earlier by Senator Jackson that a joint US-Egyptian strike force was being put together for intervention in the Gulf, did not fail to impress observers in the region. Nor were the wider implications of such moves neglected. The Mecca daily *Al-Nadwa* observed on 8 March: "The Arabs will succeed in barring foreign intervention in the area, and in preventing the

---

[176] *Jerusalem Post,* 2 February 1979, p. 16.

[177] "A Base Decision in the Mideast," *Mideast Observer,* 15 June 1979, p. 2.

[178] TV remarks by Brown (24 February) and by Schlesinger (25 February), *Middle East International,* 2 March 1979, p. 9; see also Alex Brummer, "US Ready to Use Force for Oil," *The Guardian Weekly,* 4 March 1979, p. 6.

international superpower club from practicing its favorite chess game, which it would like to transfer now to the Arab nation. We reject the turning of our territory into a sports ring for world strategies."[179]

Thirdly, one must recall that in mid-February President Carter dispatched Harold Brown on an extended mission to Saudi Arabia, Jordan, Egypt, and Israel. His task was to do something about the region's security in the wake of the Shah's fall from his peacock throne and the dangers posed by the Yemeni crisis, likewise to persuade Saudi Arabia and Jordan to join the Camp David process.

According to Saudi sources, the proposals were appalling: Brown offered "in effect, the establishment of American bases" in return for a near doubling of Saudi oil production (from 8.5 million barrels to 16 million barrels a day), increased purchases by Saudi Arabia of US Treasury certificates, and active support for the Camp David process.[180] It came as no surprise, therefore, that the Saudi government rejected Brown's ideas regarding America's direct participation in regional security and refused to support the American role in the treaty-making process. The American-sponsored Sadat-Israel axis was particularly distasteful to the bulk of Arab opinion; it was seen as an aggressive alliance aimed at the very heart of Arab resistance to expansionism in the region. Washington's heavy-handed pressure to detach Saudi Arabia and Jordan from the Arab consensus only succeeded in drawing Arab ranks closer. In addition, with Muslim revivalism emanating from across the narrow Gulf, it was very naive of American decision-makers to think that Arab governments could be prodded into acceptance of the Camp David heresy. In the words of a perceptive analyst, in such moments "the Saudis are far more likely to take refuge in the *Umma*—in Islamic orthodoxy at home, in efforts towards Arab solidarity, and in support for Palestinian nationalism."[181] One obvious consequence of the Brown mission was the cancellation of Crown Prince Fahd's trip to the United States (scheduled for 12 March). There were also widespread reports that opinion in the Saudi Council of Ministers favored cutbacks in oil production, increased Arab solidarity, and even low-key diplomatic initiatives with the Soviet Union.

According to the Beirut press, President Brezhnev had sent messages to the Saudi government in late 1978 proposing diplomatic relations and indicating an intention to purchase Saudi oil. As relations between the

---

[179] *Middle East International*, 16 March 1979, p. 14.
[180] *The Guardian Weekly*, 13–20 May 1979, p. 15.
[181] Seth Tillman, "Contagion in the Middle East," *Washington Post*, 7 February 1979.

US and the Peninsula worsened, it was announced that Aeroflot had been granted permission in March to use Saudi airspace in passenger flights between Moscow, Kuwait, and Sanaa. A month later, the Saudi Arabian Foreign Minister acknowledged the Soviet Union's role in Arab affairs: "We had relations with the Soviet Union in the past," he said, "but they suspended these. We want to stress, however, that lack of diplomatic relations does not mean that we do not recognize the Soviet Union or the significant role it plays in world politics." Prince Sa'ūd also said that the Kingdom had expressed its gratitude "more than once over the positive stands the Soviet Union has adopted towards Arab issues."[182]

One more indication of a thaw in Saudi-Soviet relations was reflected in a mid-May interview with *Le Monde* in which Crown Prince Fahd said: "We are aware of the important role played by the Soviet Union in international politics and want this role to support the just causes of the Arabs....As for the establishment of diplomatic relations, that is a question which will be reached in the light of events which will contribute to a decision."[183]

One final remark concerning the Brown mission. Whereas the Saudi government turned down his proposals on regional security, Israel, on the other hand, made a point of taking Brown and his party to "two air bases in the Sinai peninsula...[and] signalled to Brown they would feel much more comfortable in having an American presence on the bases."[184] Also, according to the *Economist,* the Secretary of Defense made a controversial tour of the West Bank: "The Israeli generals accompanying him argued that in any West Bank settlement Israel would want to keep at least two divisions of troops (25,000 men) in the West Bank; Mr. Brown apparently accepted the principle but thought one division was enough."[185]

Anti-Saudi mutterings and the increased leaks of oil-grab scenarios in the United States, coming as they did in the context of the signing of the Sadat-Israel peace in March, were exemplified in Senator Henry Jackson's

[182] *Voice* (London), 15 April 1979, p. 6, quoting interview with *Al-Hawadess.* For an analysis of the Soviet critique of the Camp David process, see Rashid Khalidi, *Soviet Middle East Policy in the Wake of Camp David,* IPS Papers, 3 (Beirut: Institute for Palestine Studies, 1979). For an analysis of the strategic and military dimensions, see Riyad al-Ashkar, *The Egyptian-Israeli Treaty and Its Strategic and Military Dimensions,* IPS Papers, 2 (Beirut: Institute for Palestine Studies, 1979), in Arabic.

[183] *Arab Report* (Middle East Economic Digest), 20 June 1979, p. 28, quoting *Le Monde* of 15 May 1979.

[184] Jim Hoagland, "President Seeking to Stem Foreign Policy Reverses," *Washington Post,* 6 March 1979.

[185] *The Economist,* 24 February 1979, p. 58.

11 March 1979 TV interview and constituted a fourth reason for Saudi Arabia's disenchantment. Likewise, the Gulf states and Jordan shared this deep disillusionment with American policies.

Henry Jackson, chairman of the Senate's powerful Energy Committee, argued that the Gulf oil fields were "undefended, wide open" and that an American military presence was therefore "essential on a contingency basis."[186] He thought the Carter administration had made serious mistakes in first announcing the dispatch of an aircraft carrier to the Arabian Sea early in the year and then calling it back, or in sending only unarmed F-15s to Saudi Arabia. His contingency plan emphasized the use of "local forces, Egyptians and Israelis, or a combination of both" with the essential ingredient of an American back-up: "A fleet available in the Persian Gulf and the Indian Ocean and the Arabian Sea." He felt that the Israelis on their own could do the job of intervention, but seemed to prefer the option of a combined Israeli-Egyptian force that "would move right into the oil fields."[187] In addition, Henry Jackson raised the possible use of the Sinai air bases. When asked if the US take-over of the "air bases in the Sinai [was] being actively discussed beyond what Mr. Begin said," he replied: "I think it has been noted and discussed from time to time and it could be the linchpin to bring the two parties together in a final agreement."[188]

The reference to this Begin plan was significant. Israel's prime minister had proposed to President Carter that the United States Air Force take control of the large Etzion air base and possibly other bases in the Sinai, and also suggested the establishment of a US naval base at Haifa. The Washington correspondent of the *Jerusalem Post* (7 March 1979) claimed that Carter reacted positively to such proposals and that "Pentagon officials, especially those in the Air Force and at the Joint Chiefs of Staff, [were] anxious to take control of the Etzion air base...strategically located near the Saudi oil fields....The news, released on the eve of the American president's personal mission to Egypt and Israel, was an obvious attempt to enhance the fading image of Israel as guardian of US national security interests.[189]

---

[186]Transcript of a television interview on ABC News' "Issues and Answers," 11 March 1979.

[187]*Ibid.*

[188]*Ibid.* Similarly, Thomas "Tip" O'Neill, Speaker of the House of Representatives, welcomed the prospect of combined US-Israeli-Egyptian interventions in the Gulf region. See *Mideast Observer*, 15 June 1979, p. 1.

[189]*Jerusalem Post*, 7 March 1979.

Washington also showed a surprising lack of tact with Jordan. National Security Advisor Zbigniew Brzezinski, in his mid-March mission to the Middle East, failed to influence Riyad into softening its opposition to the Begin-Sadat treaty. He next turned his attention, with equal lack of success, to Amman.[190] In fact, King Hussein accused America openly of using "arm twisting" tactics to secure his acceptance of the Camp David process. His top officials also made it clear that Jordan "does not agree with the recent US thesis that the Middle East is threatened by Soviet or radical Arab threats."[191] The principal threat, they insisted, was Israeli occupation and expansion. Relations between Amman and Washington cooled noticeably, and the US House of Representatives passed a resolution making future military aid contingent on Jordan's cooperation with the peace plan.

Following the signing of the Sadat-Begin treaty in March and the Arab counter-decision to impose far-reaching sanctions on Sadat's regime, the United States embarked on what can only be described as a "dirty tricks" campaign coupled with the familiar incidence of threats of intervention: a fifth reason for the Saudi malaise.

In April there were startling leaks in the press regarding the Saudi leadership. One report in the *Washington Post* said: "Recent copies of the *Morning Digest*, a secret daily intelligence summary produced for senior administration officials, have reported that new health problems appear to be keeping Fahd, 57, from functioning as the day-to-day head of government."[192]

Likewise, there was the spreading of persistent reports about the health of other leading Saudi figures and about a struggle for power within the royal family. Saudi annoyance with such practices eventually reached an unprecedented level; the formal expulsion of the CIA station chief from Jedda was contemplated. According to American press reports, the Carter ad-

---

[190]Throughout the campaign of threats and the Sadat-Israel peace negotiations, the Palestinian press in Lebanon devoted considerable attention to the issue of US intervention. See *Filasṭīn al-thawra*, 12 and 21 March 1979, for articles on the new US strategy and military alliances in the region. Articles emphasizing the oil dimension appeared in *Al-Ḥurrīya*: Muṣṭafā Salāma, "Amīrikā tastaʿidd li-l-tadākhul al-ʿaskarī al-mubāshir," 11 June 1979; Wāʾil Zaydān, "Silāḥ al-nafṭ mā zāla ḥaddan," 3 July 1979; Ṭāriq Khalīl, "Al-Nafṭ bayna l-azma al-amīrikīya al-dākhilīya wa-l-sharq al-awsaṭ," 16 July 1979. Likewise, *Al-Hadaf* published several articles on Gulf security following the fall of the Shah (24 February, 10 March, 2 June, and 23 June 1979).

[191] *Washington Post*, 19 March 1979, p. A20.

[192] *Washington Post*, 15 April 1979, p. A6. As reported in the US press, US intelligence organizations were also leaking their predictions of the expected fall of the Saudi-backed North Yemen government. See, for instance, Jim Hoagland, "US Reported to Expect Yemen to Fall," *International Herald Tribune*, 13 April 1979, p. 1.

ministration recalled the station chief "to avoid a public dispute with Saudi Arabia."[193]

In the same month there was yet another sniping incident by Frank Church, chairman of the Senate Foreign Relations Committee, against his favorite Arab target. The design was to create a climate of confusion and suspicion regarding Saudi Arabia's oil-producing capabilities. American oil companies in the Aramco consortium were forced by this Senate body— despite Vance's personal appeal—to release highly sensitive information on the condition of the oil fields, information that was then widely circulated in a controversial report. One obvious aim was to reduce the perception of the strategic importance of the Kingdom in terms of its ability to meet future world demand by claiming that there were "technical" reasons why the oil fields would not be able to meet the projected target of 16 million barrels a day in the eighties. On the other hand, former US ambassador to Saudi Arabia James Akins observed that this target was never agreed upon by the Saudi state, whose policy has since 1973 explicitly linked politics to oil production.[194]

Assessing Saudi-US relations in May, US Secretary of State Vance recognized the damage caused by the peace treaty: "There are very sharp and clear differences between us," he said.[195] He also reported to the House Foreign Affairs Committee that the Saudi position had changed after the Baghdad summit to one of radical opposition to the American initiative, and that "nobody should gloss over that fact."[196]

Throughout the whole process of putting the *Pax Americana* into place in the first months of 1979, and in which, it is recalled, the policy of threats was used freely, the Western allies stuck to their traditional posture of offering the least possible target for controversy. Perhaps much of what was being privately contemplated in influential circles in Europe was expressed

---

[193] *Washington Post*, 15 April 1979, p. A9.

[194] *Ibid.* One might also mention the grilling of Secretary of State Vance and Defense Secretary Brown during a meeting of the Senate Foreign Relations Committee at which time Church asked whether the Carter administration strategists were measuring President Sadat "for the mantle in which the deposed Shah of Iran had tried to wrap himself, that of a pro-Western gendarme for the turbulent Middle East." Church reportedly went on to repeat the joke in vogue at the time as to "whether Washington wanted Sadat to change his name to Shahdat." This kind of humor was not appreciated by Vance and Brown. See *Washington Post*, 16 April 1979, p. A1.

[195] *International Herald Tribune*, 9 May 1979, p. 2.

[196] *Ibid.*

by the *Economist*: "The West's need to keep the Gulf oil flowing may call for military means as a last resort—but please don't shout it loud."[197]

As to public opinion in the Arab world, the tough tone of Saudi press attacks on the United States was a noteworthy indication. The threats of intervention were described as a reversion to the law of the jungle: "We thought," said *Al-Nadwa*, "that the age that produced such an abominable mentality...the time when rapacious Western imperialists used brute force, had gone for ever."[198] In fact, the editorial added, "Talking about using force to secure vital interests is strongly reminiscent of Hitler's vital 'sphere' in rationalizing his aggressions."[199] And after underlining the Arab intention to defend their oil against aggression, *Al-Nadwa* wrote: "Those who talk of vital interests should realize that their statements are causing a great deal of instability in the area, which truly stands on the brink of a volcano, because of their policies."[200]

The pressure on Arab oil states was also kept up elsewhere. The international media mounted an intense campaign against Libya in the first half of 1979. According to Claudia Wright, the *New Statesman's* correspondent in Washington, "In April, for example, the CIA was putting out stories that the Libyan leader had tried to buy a nuclear bomb from Peking in 1971."[201] Stories of nuclear links with Pakistan and involvement with Idi Amin were also circulated. Columnists close to the Defense Department were suggesting that "if Sadat attacked neighbouring Libya...Carter [might] be compelled to back him all the way. Sadat's total dependence on the United States today...makes the United States as much a hostage to Egypt's policy as it long has been to Israel's policy."[202] Likewise, academics with connections in the Administration echoed similar views. Edward Luttwak in his "Strategic Implications of the Camp David Accords" spoke of Egypt "disciplining" Libya and stressed the fact that "American and Egyptian interests are now largely parallel in this area at least, and what serves one serves the other."[203]

By June, however, there were indications of American rethinking on the subject. David Newsom, Under-Secretary for Political Affairs, made a trip

---

[197] *The Economist*, 3 March 1979, p. 13.

[198] As reported in *Ike* (Beirut), 11 April 1979, p. 4.

[199] *Ibid.*

[200] *Ibid.*

[201] Claudia Wright, "Will Egypt Invade Libya?," *New Statesman* (London), 22 June 1979, p. 904.

[202] *Ibid.*

[203] "Egypt and Israel: Prospects for a New Era," *Washington Quarterly*, Special Supplement, Spring 1979, p. 43.

to Libya in a bid to improve relations and to defuse the explosive situation along the Libyan-Egyptian border.

Another observation is in order. During this period Washington and the media made a supreme effort to agitate the Red menace in the Gulf. However, this kind of tactic was wearing thin. On the eve of the signing of the Israel-Sadat peace treaty in Washington, Kuwait's ambassador to Lebanon, 'Abd al-Ḥamīd Būʿayjān, emphasized that the real threat came from Tel Aviv, not Moscow:

> This idea of using the Soviets as a "scare" is an old game. ...Israel is the expansionist state which is occupying Arab territories, and not the Soviet Union. We have not seen the Soviet Union occupy any Arab country, but we have witnessed Israel's occupation of territories belonging to several Arab countries. We have not seen the Soviet Union lay its hand on the petroleum of any Arab country, but we see Israel still occupying the oil fields of Egypt....When Israel took over the Arab oil fields in Sinai, the West remained tight-lipped.[204]

A few months later, Arab public opinion would echo similar feelings to American attempts at mobilizing Muslim sentiment against the Soviet intervention in Afghanistan. It was widely noted that when Israel conquered Jerusalem, one of Islam's three holiest cities and the pride of Arab Muslim architecture, the West did not object. Why then this sudden interest in the defense of Islam?

The Genesis of Carter's Doctrine

In mid-June, the Carter administration's strategists were called together to discuss "the implications of and options for US policy in the Middle East and Indian Ocean:" in other words, to work out the broad outline of a Carter Doctrine to replace the aging Nixon Doctrine. Officials of the Administration said they were searching for an approach that would "avoid the extremes of Vietnam, where we tried to do everything ourselves, and the post-Vietnam

---

[204] *Monday Morning* (Beirut), 26 March-1 April 1979, p. 33. In the same interview the Ambassador described his country's relations with the Soviet Union as being good. He also said: "It is an insult to believe that the Gulf is naive and that it can be misled by arguments of an imminent Soviet threat to the oil fields. This is what prompted our foreign minister to deplore statements to this effect by United States officials." Far from being a threat, he saw the Soviet Union as "helping a number of Arab countries."

period when we wouldn't do anything. ....We're not talking about permanent bases or formal alliances [in the Gulf] but we have to be able to protect our interests in a region far more vital to us than Vietnam ever was."[205]

In actual fact, there was more than a hint that the Carter Doctrine was born even earlier, with the Yemen crisis, when the aircraft carrier *Constellation* and escort vessels were dispatched into the Arabian Sea, with authorization to engage in combat "if Soviet or Cuban pilots stationed in Southern Yemen joined the conflict."[206] The view of Washington, as reflected in the testimony of US Acting Assistant Secretary of State William Crawford, was that South Yemen had carried out "a carefully planned, coordinated and amply supported campaign with the apparent intention of seizing and occupying North Yemeni territory and destabilizing the North Yemen government."[207] President Carter judged that an emergency situation existed that justified the by-passing of Congress in airlifting arms rapidly to North Yemen, sending two AWACS radar aircraft to Saudi Arabia, and dispatching a carrier task force to the area. This response, according to some officials, was the watershed separating the old, cautious Carter policy from the new, more assertive doctrine.[208]

What were the features of the Carter Doctrine as it took shape in the months before the Soviet intervention in Afghanistan? To begin with, stress was placed on enhancing the offensive and rapid deployment capabilities of conventional forces to meet contingencies in the Middle East, Gulf, Indian Ocean, and Horn, now designated as a single interlocking zone of confrontation with the Soviet Union. In this respect the zone was promoted from a "half-war" to a "full-war" status, with significant repercussions on the overall global strategic and capabilities picture. President Carter appeared to have accepted the "counterforce" concept of strategic planning by proposing the introduction of the MX mobile missile.[209]

Other features included the rapid upgrading of the joint British-American base at Diego Garcia, the search for other bases in the new zone, and the

[205] Jim Hoagland, "Carter Ponders Intervention as Instrument of US Policy," *International Herald Tribune*, 23–24 June 1979, p. 7.

[206] Although there was no public acknowledgment of it, "the White House was prepared to authorize the carrier's 85 warplanes to engage in combat if Soviet or Cuban pilots stationed in Southern Yemen joined the conflict." *Ibid.*

[207] "US Arms to North Yemen," *Mideast Observer*, 1 March 1979, p. 1.

[208] *International Herald Tribune*, 23–24 June 1979, p. 7.

[209] *International Herald Tribune*, 9 December 1979, p. 3. For a useful summary of interventionary forces see *Strategic Survey 1978* (London: International Institute for Strategic Studies, 1979), pp. 12–17.

extension of NATO's naval arm into the zone, with Australian participation. With the Conservatives in power in the UK, more British involvement could be counted upon. Defence Secretary Francis Pym's discussions in Washington in July 1979 were widely seen as a step in this direction.[210]

There was also talk of establishing a permanent "Fifth Fleet" for the Indian Ocean from units of the Atlantic and Pacific fleets, increasing the number of American warships on location in Bahrain from three to five, and installing advanced monitoring equipment in Oman and the Strait of Hormuz.[211] Deploying a Fifth Fleet into the Indian Ocean would include the Navy's new LHA-type amphibious assault ships, specifically the 39,000 ton *Tarawa* and the 18,000 ton *Tripoli* carrying about 1800 marines and British-built Harrier vertical take-off jet aircraft.[212]

Another feature was the creation of floating bases—stockpiles of war material on roll-on roll-off ships operating from Diego Garcia. These floating bases could act as alternatives to land bases in the event that political penalties for establishing land bases in the region were judged too high by the US and the host countries.

An alarming angle, persisting until such time as the US could build sufficient conventional capability to "project power" into the zone, is the symbolic nature of the small garrison of marines afloat. A lengthy and secret study prepared by a top Pentagon planner, the so-called "Paul Wolfowitz Report," was recently leaked. The central point of the study was that, for the present, "to prevail in an Iranian scenario, [the US] might have to threaten or make use of tactical nuclear weapons."[213] Or as one analyst put it: "Like the garrison in Berlin, the floating 1800 will be the 'tripwire' to ignite a conflict leading to World War III."[214]

In short, on the eve of the Soviet intervention in Afghanistan, the Carter administration, albeit with characteristic ambiguity, was moving from a strategic doctrine of "minimum deterrence" to one of "extended deterrence" aimed at maintaining strategic superiority over the Soviet Union. Donald Rumsfeld, former Secretary of Defense (1975–77), has described "extended

---

[210] *Sunday Telegraph* (London), 22 July 1979; *Arab Report* (Middle East Economic Digest), August 1979, p. 13.

[211] Robert Manning, "A Move for Military Might," *The Middle East* (London), August 1979, pp. 30–31.

[212] John Cooley, "Use of Force in Iran Crisis Impossible: Pentagon," *Christian Science Monitor*, 9 November 1979.

[213] *International Herald Tribune*, 15 February 1980, p. 4.

[214] *Ibid.*

deterrence," quoting the Hudson Institute, as premised on the idea that "American strategic forces are about the business of posing non-incredible negative sanctions in Soviet minds, and, if need be, imposing such sanctions in actions."[215] Moreover, America's "strategic-nuclear posture should reinforce and be seen to reinforce deterrence at the regional level, including theater-nuclear, conventional, and naval forces."[216]

Yet, is it not remarkable that, despite five US aircraft carrier task forces poised within striking distance of Tehran by Christmas 1979–*Kitty Hawk* and *Midway* in the Arabian Sea, and *Forrestal, Independence,* and *Nimitz* in the Mediterranean—the Soviet Union did not hesitate to launch a massive intervention in Afghanistan?[217]

Conclusion

One of the more obvious conclusions to be drawn from a study of the frequency of the use of threats during the Administrations of Presidents Nixon, Ford, and Carter is their close relationship with the diplomacy of the Arab-Israeli conflict: e.g., Arab linkage strategy and the oil embargo, Kissinger's step-by-step diplomacy, the Rabat Arab Summit, the preparation for Sinai II, the aftermath of Camp David, and the Sadat-Begin peace treaty. The policy of threats was also in use against OPEC and particularly OAPEC—for instance in late 1974—in the hope of sowing dissension in their ranks and breaking oil prices. In 1979, it was also used during the uncertain period following the fall of the Shah. The targets of intervention most frequently cited in the various scenarios were Saudi Arabia, Kuwait, the United Arab Emirates, and Libya. For the latter, a special role was assigned to Egypt throughout 1979.

With respect to public opinion in the United States, whereas in 1975 there was a great deal of opposition to plans and threats of US intervention in Arab oil fields—and indeed elsewhere in the world—by 1979 such opposition appears to have declined significantly. Edward Said has noted that "there has been little public outcry over the well-advertised Pentagon plans

---

[215] Donald Rumsfeld, "The State of American Defence," *Orbis*, Winter 1980, p. 902. This is not to imply that Rumsfeld endorsed Carter's defense strategy, which he criticized as being too timid.

[216] *Ibid.*

[217] *International Herald Tribune*, 1–2 December 1979, p. 2.

to prepare a force for military intervention in the Gulf...."[218] There has been a noticeable growth in advocacy of what may be termed prescriptive interventionism: the conviction that American forces aided by allies and regional proxies should be prepared to seize Arab oil fields at a moment's notice, not only to safeguard production and transport, but also to help cure the economic ills of the Trilateral world. One of the few respected platforms of opinion to speak loudly against this trend has been the *Nation*, which devoted an entire issue to the question of intervention (9 June 1979), with papers by such critics of US policy as William Appleman Williams, Walter La Feber, and Richard Falk; a similar forum has been the Institute for Policy Studies (Washington).

As far as the military establishment is concerned, in 1979 (as was the case during the 1975 intervention debates) there were several indications of dissatisfaction with intervention scenarios and threats. To cite one example, Major Robert R. Ulin, an instructor in the Department of Unified and Combined Operations, USACGSC (US Army Combined General Staff College), argued that "diplomacy must prevail over the use of military force."[219] In this respect:

> Technical hazards, destruction of production facilities likely, and growing concern over Soviet air and sealift capability dictated caution. There seems to be a lingering tendency in the United States to reach for a weapon whenever trouble erupts. In the case of the Middle East the use of force was not a viable alternative for many of the reasons cited above. However, probably the most ominous was the possibility of touching off a superpower confrontation.[220]

It is fair to say that compared to such figures in Congress as Javits, Church, Jackson, and O'Neill (not to mention intellectuals such as Tucker and "Ignotus"), military men and State Department officials appear more cautious about intervention in the Gulf. In fact, as the Iranian crisis moved from one peak of tension to another—and as the threats of military action on behalf of the American hostages multiplied—top US defense officials underlined the difficulties involved in all such operations. In addition to the very

---

[218] Edward Said, *The Palestine Question and the American Context*, IPS Papers, 1 (Beirut: Institute for Palestine Studies, 1979), p. 22.

[219] Robert R. Ulin, "US National Security and Middle Eastern Oil," *Military Review*, May 1979, p. 47.

[220] *Ibid.*

real logistical problems involved, the allies would not cooperate: France, for instance, had for some time the largest naval force in the Indian Ocean.[221] According to one military correspondent, the Carter administration had explored all options and was "virtually unanimous, at top levels, that military intervention [was] not only impossible for human and political reasons, but unworkable in a practical military sense."[222]

As Peter Mangold observed in his *Superpower Intervention in the Middle East,* US policy-making was deeply influenced by a Middle Eastern domino theory:

> More important [than direct Soviet seizure of Middle Eastern oil fields], since it underpinned much of American crisis thinking, was a Middle Eastern domino theory, according to which the overthrow of any one conservative regime in the Middle East, including those in the Eastern Mediterranean, risked a chain reaction in the Gulf and the establishment of a series of radical regimes in the oil-producing areas which would be subject to Soviet influence, if not control.[223]

There is, of course, some doubt as to the validity and veracity of this favorite US geostrategic construct. In any case, is it not incongruous that the United States embarked on courses of action (Camp David and threats of intervention) that in fact tend to provoke increased political and military tension, confusion, and instability?

With the Iranian hostages crisis and the Soviet intervention in Afghanistan, the situation is vastly more complicated in terms of actors, targets, and scope. As one retired Lebanese journalist wryly put it to this writer in late December 1979, in connection with this study:

> The Americans have been threatening friends and non-friends alike with grab scenarios of the "seizing oil, guns blazing" variety. But it is the Russians who actually intervened [Afghanistan]. If a wolf cries wolf, he attracts other wolves. At any rate, the Arab Little Red Riding Hood is now caught between two wolves.

---

[221] John Cooley, "Use of Force in Iran Crisis Impossible."

[222] *Ibid.* In the August issue of *United States Naval Institute Proceedings,* Captain John E. Lacouture (USN, ret.) remarked: "In spite of the importance of maintaining the flow of oil, there is no agreed-upon joint plan within NATO to react to any emergency that might interrupt that flow." *Ibid.*

[223] Mangold, *Superpower Intervention in the Middle East,* p. 77.

However, I am also reminded of 'Abd al-Ḥamīd and the Ottoman Empire. With all kinds of wolves at his door, he kept going for thirty-five years.

* * * *

One of the more consequential miscalculations of the Carter administration in 1978 and 1979 concerned the reactions of Saudi Arabia and Jordan to the Camp David agreements and the subsequent Sadat-Begin treaty. Another significant failure was in the long-standing policy of excluding the Palestinian people, represented by the PLO, from Middle East peace-making. American officials believed that after a short interval Saudi Arabia and Jordan would have to accept the treaty as a *fait accompli*. They were proved wrong. To begin with, the Saudis, in line with the Arab consensus, saw Carter's moves as a further blow to Arab solidarity and as an invitation to regional turbulence. In fact, Foreign Minister Prince Sa'ūd ibn Fayṣal called the treaty "destabilising" and a scenario for "war and destruction."[224] The American *Pax* had provided an escape route for Israel on the issue of the creation of a Palestinian state, thus sowing the seeds of even greater instability. The Carter administration was the prisoner of its own tunnel vision that the so-called distinction between Arab moderates and radicals would serve to throw the Saudis and Sadat into each other's arms—another illusory hope. For how could the Arab consensus accept a settlement that not only held no prospect of leading to the creation of a Palestinian state and the restoration of Jerusalem, but encouraged, instead, Begin's annexationist *pleonexia* under the guise of a limited autonomy?

Not that the Saudis were prepared to see their strategic relations with the United States suffer. Nevertheless, the offer of an American military and naval presence in the region was rejected despite the uncertainty caused by the revolutionary upheaval in Iran, and despite the acute crisis between North and South Yemen, not to mention the Soviet and Cuban presence in the region. In fact, there were signs of discreet Saudi normalization with the Soviet Union. Saudi public criticism against American pressure politics was voiced with increasing vigor. On the oil front, hints were dropped that the increase in Saudi oil supplies would not necessarily be made available for sale through the Aramco consortium of Exxon, Mobil, Texaco, and Standard Oil of California, but would be sold directly to the Third World and to

---

[224] *The Economist*, 9–15 June 1979, p. 73.

European oil companies. In addition, the Saudis made it clear that a conservation policy was in the national interest to insure adequate supplies for their contemplated petro-chemical industries. Not only were the principal consuming nations advised to cut down on oil energy, they were warned that future increase in oil supplies would be linked to savings in consumption by the West and Japan.

Similarly, more than ever before, the leading oil-producing states of the Arabian Peninsula linked oil supplies to progress on the issue of the creation of a Palestinian state and recognition of the PLO.[225] The importance of the Palestinian presence in the Gulf and its loyalty to the PLO is recognized by decision-makers in the West, although this significance has been traditionally down-played by the media. There are close to half a million Palestinians in that crucial strategic region, representing 20 percent of the total population of Kuwait, about 22 percent of that of Qatar, and perhaps 30 percent of that of the United Arab Emirates. Many hold key positions in the administration, banking, oil, education, and the army.[226] It is, therefore, not surprising that Shaykh Aḥmad Zakī Yamānī went out of his way to articulate in *Newsweek* (9 July 1979) a potential situation that must have been present in many decision-makers' minds all round the world: "The Israelis are looking for pretexts to avoid facing the inevitability of a Palestinian homeland and withdrawal from the West Bank. The Palestinians are growing ever more desperate, and I wouldn't be surprised if one day they sank one or two supertankers in the Strait of Hormuz, to force the world to do something about their plight and Israel's obstinacy."[227] Nor were scenarios of oil-grabs by the US, its allies, and proxies realistic: "If some people are thinking of a possible physical occupation of the oil fields, they can forget it. It cannot be done. The people would never stand for it. Sabotage and a few key parts could halt production for a couple of years. And then where would we all be?"[228]

* * * *

Gazing into the regional crystal ball is a hazardous venture. However, three possible developments can be suggested: collusion between the super-

[225] This was particularly true of the OAPEC-EEC dialogue. See *Ike* (Beirut), 10 May 1979, p. 16.
[226] For a perceptive analysis of the Palestinian dimension in the politics, economics, and security of the Gulf, see John Cooley, "Iran, the Palestinians, and the Gulf," *Foreign Affairs* (New York), 57.5 (Summer 1979), pp. 1017–34.
[227] *Newsweek*, 9 July 1979, p. 10, interview of Yamani with De Borchgrave.
[228] *Ibid.*

powers, collision of the superpowers, and exclusion of the superpowers. The first may seem unlikely, but should be considered.

In the 1880s the "Great Game," as it was then called, was being played between the Empire of the Tsars, pushing southward in the Afghanistan-Indian border region, and the British Empire, bent on consolidating valuable gains in the same region. A hundred years later this "Great Game" appears to have started once more in earnest, played this time by the Soviet and American superpowers on an expanded checkerboard, and with their respective allies one step behind.

The "Great Game" of the 1880s, which was (as it remains till today) an imperial game involving the projection of power and the seizure of material and geostrategic advantages, did not lead to open war, although the British and Russians came close to it in 1885 over Afghanistan. By 1907 the two empires had negotiated a settlement through the Iswolski-Nicolson talks, wherein it was agreed "to settle by mutual consent the questions relating to their interests in the Asiatic continent."[229] There were in fact three separate agreements: 1) Persia, 2) Afghanistan, 3) Tibet. In the first, Britain and Russia, while pledging respect for the independence and integrity of Persia, proceeded to carve it up into three zones of influence: a Russian zone in the north, a British zone in the south, and a middle zone including Tehran open equally to both. As for Afghanistan, Russia recognized it as a British sphere of influence, in return for a British pledge not to annex the state. With respect to Tibet, both powers acknowledged Chinese suzerainty over the country, and pledged non-interference in its domestic questions. This Anglo-Russian agreement caused much surprise and was widely debated in diplomatic circles at the time. It was variously interpreted as a purely localized colonial affair aimed at removing points of friction in strategic border zones in Asia, or a part of a design to further isolate Germany diplomatically in Europe, or both.[230]

Deals of this type have been a feature of modern diplomacy. To cite another example, during the Molotov-Ribbentrop negotiations of 1940, which divided vast portions of Eastern Europe into spheres of influence, there was a German attempt to direct Soviet aspirations towards the area south of Baku in the general direction of Persia and the Gulf.[231] The possibility, therefore, of an entente between the two superpowers—"an energy Yalta"—although

---

[229] Oron Hale, *The Great Illusion: 1900–1914* (New York: Harper, 1971), pp. 250–51.

[230] *Ibid.*

[231] R.H. Burrell and Alvin Cottrell, "Iran, Afghanistan, Pakistan: Tensions and Dilemmas," *Washington Papers*, 20 (London: Sage Publications, 1974), p. 4; K.D. McLaurin and

remote, cannot be entirely ruled out. American intelligence studies stress the Soviet Union and Comecon's increased dependence on external sources of energy and predict a crisis situation beginning with the mid-eighties.[232] Recent reports in the Soviet press acknowledging shortfalls in energy production targets in the USSR have come as no surprise.

If such projections are not groundless and Middle Eastern energy becomes a matter of vital interest to the Soviet Union and Comecon, as it already is to the United States and its allies, then a Yalta-type arrangement is not all that farfetched. Who would have thought that the Tsarist and British empires could resolve their differences in the arc of crisis stretching from Iran to Tibet in 1907? Likewise, who would have thought that a Nazi-Soviet pact (the Molotov-Ribbentrop talks) and the partition of Eastern Europe between the two was possible in 1939–40?

In any case it is important to note that Arab opinion tends to perceive collusion between the superpowers as within the realm of probability.

It is difficult and premature to speculate on what a collision between the superpowers might lead to in the context of a revival of the Cold War and a return to the doctrine of containment. More than ever before, the Soviet Union and the United States appear to be firmly locked in a "zero-sum" game situation, particularly in the new zone of confrontation, i.e., a situation where the losses of one superpower represent the gains of the other and vice versa. For the foreseeable future, and until such time as America is capable of providing the necessary sea-lift, airlift, helicopter-lift, and base support for rapid deployment forces of 200,000 men, the risk of escalation into nuclear war is very real. The weakness of the US conventional

---

James M. Price, *Soviet Middle East Policy Since the October War* (Alexandria, Virginia: Abbott Associates, September 1976), p. 11.

[232] The controversial CIA report in question was "The International Energy Situation Outlook to 1985" (April 1977). See also Tyrus W. Cobb, "The Soviet Energy Dilemma," *Orbis* (Summer 1979), p. 381, where it is argued that "as the Soviet Union's impending energy crunch enhances the existing political attractiveness of the region [from the Gulf to the Horn], the temptation to turn the entire area into a Soviet protectorate will grow." There may have been other motivations for the CIA report. B. Schemmer, editor of the *Armed Forces Journal*, has suggested that the CIA had in fact fabricated an oil crisis for President Carter: "When the Energy Secretary, Mr. James Schlesinger, needed an oil crisis to dramatise President Carter's energy goals in 1977 and 1978, Admiral Turner (Director of the CIA) helped him create one by understating uncertainty and using the most pessimistic projections of Soviet demand." See B. Schemmer, "American Intelligence Loses Its Brains," *The Guardian Weekly*, 22 April 1979, p. 17. For a Soviet critique of the CIA report, see Boris Rachkov, "CIA's Prophecies About Soviet Oil Will be Wrong Again," *Soviet News* (London), 12 July 1978, p. 250.

forces currently deployed and potentially deployable in the Gulf and Indian Ocean raises the specter of a US resort to tactical nuclear weapons under certain circumstances. It must, however, be stressed that the development of enhanced US conventional intervention capability, combined with new bases in the region, might encourage adventurism. In any case, such collision, like collusion, would not serve the area well.

The third possibility is the exclusion of the armed strength of the super-powers from the region; or, put differently, the taming of the superpowers through concerted action by the littoral and hinterland states of the Indian Ocean and Mediterranean. The paradox is that power is needed to tame power. This the littoral and hinterland states have in abundance in the form of energy resources and the politics of non-alignment. Mobilizing this power in the service of a true Zone of Peace, not of historical *Pax,* is the greatest challenge currently facing the Third World. One important consequence of the current behavior of the superpowers has been the intensification of Arab effort to establish a collective security arrangement for the region, with the stress on self-reliance.

15

The United States, the Arab-Israeli Conflict, and the Palestine Question in 1974*

Introduction

IN THIS SURVEY of the United States, the Arab-Israeli conflict, and the Palestine question for the year 1974, attention has been focused on the following areas: the disengagement diplomacy in connection with the Sinai and Golan accords, President Nixon's visit, the oil dimension for 1974, the diplomatic stalemate on the Jordan, and the United States and the Palestine Liberation Organization. The survey ends with two brief case studies of the pro-Israel lobby at work during the year.

During the first half of 1974 the center of gravity of American diplomacy tended to be located in the Near East, where the Secretary of State shuttled back and forth between the various capitals to fashion two widely acclaimed disengagement agreements. These were followed by President Nixon's historic visit to the area. Thereafter, and especially after the denouement of Watergate, the center of gravity returned to Washington, with a brief interlude at the UN in New York on the occasion of Yasir Arafat's appearance. With regard to momentum, American diplomatic initiatives were conducted

*From the original English typescript for the study abridged and translated and published as "Al-Wilāyāt al-muttaḥida al-amīrkīya," in *Al-Kitāb al-sanawī li-l-qaḍīya al-filasṭīnīya li-'ām 1974*, edited by Camille Mansour (Beirut: Institute for Palestine Studies, 1977), pp. 345–91. The section on the Rockefeller affair (pp. 362–64 below) was missing in the English text, and quotations from Arabic statements and documents were cited in the original Arabic. These passages have been retranslated from the published Arabic text and from the documents referred to therein.

with great energy during the first half of the year, then gradually petered out to reach a position of relative stalemate as the year came to a close.

The introductory section will briefly consider the Nixon-Kissinger administration of foreign policy, the effect of Watergate, the concept of step-by-step diplomacy and Israel's peace intentions, as well as the bare outline of the American aid bill voted in 1974.

The Nixon-Kissinger Administration of Foreign Policy

In his *American Foreign Policy in the Nixon Era*, A. Hartley has underlined the joint aspect of the Nixon-Kissinger formulation of American foreign policy: "Theirs has been an altogether exceptional partnership, based on a compatibility of mind and temperament rare between a politician and his advisers."[1] Traditionally, American diplomacy has been characterized by two features: "the public nature of decision-making and also its diffusion."[2] However, to Hartley, "the principal innovations into the methods of American foreign policy by the Nixon-Kissinger conjuncture can be defined as *centralization* and *secrecy*."[3] The growth of the National Security Council in the early 70s under the effective leadership of Dr. Henry Kissinger, and then his appointment in 1973 as Secretary of State while retaining his former powerful position as the President's assistant on the National Security Council, were obvious reflections of the centralization process.

Another feature of the combined Nixon-Kissinger conduct of foreign policy was a predilection for personal diplomacy, the direct interaction with other leaders. In short, this meant the cultivation of "summit" diplomacy. As one analyst has put it: "The emphasis on intense involvement in the day-to-day conduct of certain aspects of foreign policy reached its apogee in Mr. Kissinger's supervision of the disengagement negotiations between Israel and Egypt, and later between Israel and Syria."[4] From the point of view of centralization, "summit" diplomacy had a further advantage, "for it is only at the highest level that package deals cutting across bureaucratic responsibilities for separate topics on geographical areas can be formulated."[5]

---

[1] A. Hartley, *American Foreign Policy in the Nixon Era* (London: International Institute for Strategic Studies, 1975; *Adelphi Papers*, no. 110), p. 1.

[2] *Ibid.*, p. 9.

[3] *Ibid.*

[4] Linda B. Miller, "America in World Politics: Linkage or Leverage?," *The World Today*, July 1974, p. 272.

[5] *Ibid.*, p. 271.

There was, however, the popular and public aspect of the Nixon-Kissinger administration of foreign policy which was deliberately sustained to counterbalance centralization and secrecy. Jet diplomacy, with the Secretary of State holding court high in the skies before a grateful news media, and the deliberate portrayal of diplomatic moves as *tour de force* tricks in the repertoire of the Super Magician, Henry Kissinger, provided the widely reported grandstand acts—and the counterbalance. This aspect of Kissinger's disengagement diplomacy—the staging aspect and media extravaganza—was as characteristic of the 1974 diplomatic scene as was the "ballroom" spectacular of the Congress of Vienna in 1815. A reflection of the State Secretary's own personality—it is difficult to conceive of Mr. Dulles or Mr. Rogers engaging the media in the same manner—the staging may also have been a ploy to shift the spotlights away from the White House and Watergate to where the glamor was.

To what extent did the specter of Watergate affect both the decision-making process and the conduct of US foreign policy? This question and its corollary, the impact of Watergate on the foreign policy of other nations (USSR, the Arab states, Israel), retained the attention of many observers. Apart from the destruction of his credibility, could the President devote the necessary time and attention to foreign affairs, notwithstanding the presence of Henry Kissinger? More specifically, did Watergate add to the momentum of American moves in the Arab-Israeli conflict, or did it halt it? The answer to this last question is a dual one: during the Sinai and Golan negotiations Watergate undoubtedly provided an impetus to secure results: the President, as will be seen, leaned hard on Golda Meir to keep the talks going. However, in the immediate period of the denouement it probably served to halt the momentum.

To be sure, many American analysts suspected that the President was manipulating foreign policy in order to reduce the pressure of Watergate on his domestic front. And this may very well be true. At any rate, during the intensive diplomatic peregrinations of Henry Kissinger in the Near East, Watergate probably served to give him more scope and latitude to do his own thing, to free him from the White House connection.

The American Concept of Step-by-Step Diplomacy and Israel's Peace Intentions

The specifics and rationale of this particular American contribution have been the subject of debate and controversy. It is therefore important at the outset to establish the official American view of it. In this respect, its articulation by Assistant Secretary of State Alfred Atherton, one of the foremost experts of the Arab-Israeli conflict, is particularly revealing:

> We have moved steadily forward in accordance with a concept which the Secretary has explained many times and which I think is accepted by the principal parties to the conflict—that if there is to be progress there has to be a negotiating forum, there has to be a means for the two sides to exchange views with each other, and there has to be a pragmatic step-by-step approach. You take a problem at a time, recognizing that solving each step along the way is not the end of the road but simply a beginning or one more step down the road....This concept underlies our whole approach—the commitment to continue the process, but at the same time the recognition that realistically one can't go to the end of the road without travelling down the road step by step....I think it's inherent in the concept of the step-by-step approach that it's not possible to say now in every detail where we are going....We have no blueprint; we assume others have ideas that we want to hear. We will attempt to identify common areas of agreement about what the next procedures ought to be. All of this is pointing towards a reconvening of the Geneva Conference this fall.[6]

From an Arab point of view, however, step-by-step presented many difficulties. For a start, there was the perennial problem of trying to distinguish where Israeli policy ended and American policy began: the continuum has always been striking and the differences, in practice, almost imperceptible. In addition, step-by-step could also signify little-by-little or country-by-country; i.e., the Arab front, so painstakingly constructed, would become especially vulnerable to dissolution. Traditionally, US policy had never promoted the construction of a common Arab front. Besides, step-by-step to where? As *The Economist* wryly remarked, why should the Arabs accept the step-by-step approach if the end of the road is not clear, "if the step that most affects them [is] obscured by distance."[7] Furthermore, what about the Israelis; were they really interested in a process of settlement or was the Cabinet merely

---

[6]Transcript of the interview with US Assistant Secretary of State Alfred Atherton, published by the US Embassy in Beirut on 1 August 1974.

[7]*The Economist*, 19 October 1974, pp. 41–42.

buying time? The opinion of Senator William Fulbright, chairman of the Foreign Relations Committee, on Israel's intention with regard to peace is sobering. In his Fulton, Missouri speech of 2 November 1974 he remarked: "Israel, it appears, is stalling, and with nothing concrete in mind except to get all the arms and money she can get from the United States so as to try to hold off the inevitable."[8]

At about the same time, Prime Minister Yitzhak Rabin gave his famous *Haaretz* interview, where he enunciated his "seven lean years" theory of Israeli politics. To Rabin the object of Israel was to gain time: periods of stalemate were to its advantage. The implication is that the Zionist state must work to that end. How much time? Seven years, "seven lean years"—the length of time needed, in his view, for the world to become independent of Arab oil.[9] In this interview Rabin declared that Israel had to pay "a reasonable price—another interim settlement with Egypt"[10] simply to ensure the breakup of the Egypt-Syria common front and to keep Egypt away from the Russian camp. Clearly, then, the Israeli cabinet was stalling, whereas Henry Kissinger assumed—although this is not at all certain—that Israel still wanted a settlement on the Jordan after the two settlements on the Sinai and Golan fronts achieved during the first five months of the year 1974.

The US Foreign Aid Bill

In December the United States Senate approved a $2670 million foreign aid bill that included $230 million in economic aid for Egypt, $203 million for Jordan, $100 million for Syria, and $639 million to Israel ($339 million in economic aid, $100 million in weapons grants, and $200 million in weapons loans). Allocation to Israel was reduced by the House of Representatives to $550 million.[11] However, there were reports circulating of long-term package deals involving $7.5 billion over five years,[12] and even of $12 billion,[13] requested by Israel and approved in principle by the American administration,

[8]Senator Fulbright's Fulton, Missouri speech of 2 November 1974, text supplied, on request, by the Senator. [For this text, see *International Documents on Palestine, 1974*, edited by Jorgen S. Nielsen (Beirut: Institute for Palestine Studies, 1977), p. 346, doc. 168.]

[9]*Haaretz* (Tel Aviv), 3 December 1974, interview conducted by Yoel Marcus.

[10]*Ibid.*

[11]*Arab Report and Record*, 1–15 December 1974, p. 561.

[12]Interview with Senator James Abourezk, *Journal of Palestine Studies*, IV.1 (Autumn 1974), p. 7.

[13]Interview with Prime Minister Rabin, *Newsweek*, 8 July 1974, p. 26.

although such long-term commitments of public funds have no basis under US laws. In addition, there was a $50 million allocation of aid for Russian Jews emigrating to Israel from the Soviet Union, an allocation which is administered by the United Israel Appeal.[14]

Disengagement Diplomacy and Nixon's Middle East Visit

The Sinai Disengagement Agreement

As the year opened, Egyptian and Israeli military delegations were still conducting low-level talks at Geneva with both sides reporting only slight progress. Geneva was more in the nature of a ritual, since no one really expected anything spectacular from this forum at this time—and with low-level delegations. The general hope was for a convening in January of the plenary session, at the foreign ministers' level, after the results of the Israeli elections.

When the dimension of the defeat of Israel's Labor Party became known on the opening day of the year, with the Likud bloc significantly improving its position in the Knesset, Mrs. Golda Meir urgently dispatched Moshe Dayan to Washington with instructions to get the negotiating process moving again. This time the Labor Party was in a hurry, as was, apparently, President Sadat. Both were interested in another early visit by Dr. Kissinger to the area.[15]

Moshe Dayan's visit to Washington was regarded as important from Dr. Kissinger's point of view as well. The general had brought with him a plan known as the "five zone" concept, which conceded Israeli withdrawal across the Canal and into Sinai short of the strategic passes. According to Sheehan's description, the area of disengagement would cover the following five zones:

> Zone one, a buffer zone between the Israeli and Egyptian armies, whose forces in zones two and three respectively would be severely limited. Beyond zones two and three there should extend on either side of the Suez Canal zones four and five, respectively, each

---

[14] *Hearings Before a Subcommittee on Appropriations, House of Representatives, 93rd Congress* (Washington: Government Printing Office, 1974), p. 150.

[15] Edward Sheehan, "Step by Step in the Middle East," *Journal of Palestine Studies*, V.3–4 (Spring-Summer 1976), p. 24; Matti Golan, *The Secret Conversations of Henry Kissinger* (New York: Bantam Books, 1976), p. 156.

30 kilometers deep, where surface-to-air missiles would likewise be forbidden.[16]

In Washington the Israeli general also conducted talks with Defense Secretary James Schlesinger on arms supplies described as satisfactory, which probably meant that Israel was going to get its shopping list taken care of fully. The stage was set for the resumption of Kissinger's shuttle diplomacy.

At this stage, the aims of the Secretary of State appeared modest: he hoped to receive concrete proposals leading to negotiations by both sides and to help narrow the differences.[17] On the eve of his opening flight of the year to the Near East, he commented in his very own convoluted style: "The more likely outcome of this [trip] would be not that there would be an agreement but that there would be a negotiation which would be conducted at Geneva."[18] He further stressed that he was making the trip not at his own initiative, but at the request of the concerned parties. "I want to grease the wheels at Geneva," he reportedly told the reporters, "That's my goal."[19]

In Aswan, where he met with President Sadat, then recovering from bronchitis, it became clear that he was being invited to mediate a separation of forces and to conclude an accord while he was still in the area, instead of at Geneva.[20] This must have delighted the Secretary of State: at Geneva he would have to share the sponsorship—and the limelight—with the USSR; in the Near East he might be able to pull it off alone without appreciable danger to détente. The risk in his view seemed worth it.

Adopting a feverish pace of diplomatic rounds, and shuttling back and forth from Egypt to Israel, Kissinger made rapid progress in forging a disengagement agreement acceptable to both sides. On his return to Aswan from the Israeli capital he told reporters: "The Israeli plan takes the Egyptian point of view into account, and I now think chances are pretty good that this Israeli proposal and the map will trigger a negotiation."[21] One impor-

---

[16]Sheehan, "Step by Step in the Middle East," p. 24.

[17]*Department of State Bulletin*, LXX, 1806 (4 February 1974), pp. 120–22.

[18]*Ibid.*

[19]Marvin and Bernard Kalb, *Kissinger* (New York: Dell, 1975), p. 598.

[20]Sheehan reports ("Step by Step in the Middle East," p. 25): "Why Geneva?," Sadat asked, "You can do it all here?" Matti Golan reports (*Secret Conversations*, p. 158): "Wouldn't it be better if Kissinger stayed in the area so they could finish the affair quickly?," asked Sadat. "Instead of Geneva?," asked an amazed Kissinger. "Absolutely," replied the Egyptian president. The Kalbs report (*Kissinger*, p. 601): "Mr. Secretary," Sadat suggested, "why confine your objective merely to getting proposals? Why not try to finish the negotiation while you're out here?"

[21]Marvin and Bernard Kalb, *Kissinger*, p. 602.

tant stumbling block was the reconciliation of the limitations of forces and armaments with the concept of sovereignty; another was the preference of President Sadat for a "three zone" concept instead of Dayan's five zones;[22] a third involved the highly sensitive issue of the modality and content of the final disengagement document. At this point the Secretary of State reportedly had recourse to "some innovative diplomacy."[23] In effect, this was an American plan to "enshrine the disengagement in two documents—a formal agreement to be signed by Israel and Egypt, and a separate letter from the United States to each government stating its understanding of the limitation of forces."[24] The second document, also referred to in some sources as the "Memorandum of Understanding," would embody mutual assurances bordering on guarantees, sensitive details concerning the limitation of forces, the acceptance of American aerial monitoring of the disengagement area, and the passage of Israeli cargo, but not ships, through the Suez Canal.

Such supposedly secret provisions were not likely to remain so for very long. Throughout the entire course of Kissinger's negotiations, leakages by American and Israeli officials were commonplace. Matti Golan, chief correspondent for *Haaretz* and military correspondent for the Israeli army—the recipient of many leaks—reports an angry exchange between Yigal Allon and Kissinger, each accusing the other of premature and unauthorized leakages.[25]

At any rate, having smoothed over the remaining differences in a surprisingly short time, Dr. Kissinger was in a great hurry to break the news of a successful disengagement agreement. This was important for both personal and US domestic reasons: the shadow of Watergate was growing longer on the White House and its occupants. After some haggling, it was finally agreed that the news of a successful disengagement and separation of forces would be released simultaneously in the US, Egypt, Israel, and the USSR on 17 January, and that the agreement itself would be signed the following day at Kilometer 101 on the Cairo-Suez road with General Ensio Siilasvuo, the Commander of the UN Emergence Force, as witness.[26] Egypt accepted a reduction of its forces on the east bank of the Suez Canal; Israel accepted to withdraw from all positions held on the west bank of the Canal and to effect a 20-mile pullback of its troops into the Sinai.

---

[22] Sheehan, "Step by Step in the Middle East," p. 25.

[23] Marvin and Bernard Kalb, *Kissinger*, p. 603.

[24] Sheehan, "Step by Step in the Middle East," p. 25.

[25] Golan, *Secret Conversations*, p. 170.

[26] *Department of State Bulletin*, LXX, 1807 (11 February 1974), pp. 145–46.

The UNEF was given the task of controlling a special zone separating the two armies. The whole process of disengagement was to take no longer than 40 days. The final clause (Clause D) declared: "This Agreement is not regarded by Egypt and Israel as a final peace agreement. It constitutes a first step toward a final, just and durable peace according to the provisions of Security Council Resolution 338 (1973) and within the framework of the Geneva Conference."[27]

How did the US government explain both the significance of the accord and its own role in the negotiating process? Breaking the news of a successful agreement on 17 January, President Nixon underlined the long history of wars and of uneasy truces in the area, then went on to remark: "This, I would say, is the first significant step toward a permanent peace in the Mideast...this is a very significant step reached directly as a result of negotiations between the two parties."[28] As to the role of the United States, he saw it as essentially that of an intermediary helping to narrow differences. And in this connection he paid tribute to his Secretary of State. No guarantees to either party to the conflict were mentioned in the Presidential announcement.[29]

As to Dr. Kissinger's view, following his return to the US the principal architect of shuttle diplomacy provided further explanation—adding a few important nuances—of the American role in the Egypt-Israel disengagement agreement. Questioned on whether any commitments by the US were made, or beyond that, "whether there were any unpublished understandings which put the United States in the position of being a diplomatic guarantor,"[30] the Secretary of State affirmed, in effect, that the final agreement was the result of an acceptance by both sides of the American proposal, that there was no actual US guarantee, but that at the request of both sides the details of their acceptance of certain limitations on armaments were not published. Kissinger spoke in terms of "assurances" rather than of "guarantees." In the same interview he also spoke against the Arab oil embargo, intimating that "failure to end the embargo in a reasonable time would be highly inappropriate and would raise serious questions of confidence in our minds with respect to the Arab nations."[31] Was he playing to the gallery, or was he bent

---

[27] *Official Record of the Security Council, 29th Year, Supplement for January, February and March 1974* (New York: United Nations, 1974), pp. 84–85.
[28] *Department of State Bulletin*, LXX, 1807 (17 February 1974), pp. 145–46.
[29] *Ibid.*
[30] *Department of State Bulletin*, LXX, 1807 (11 February 1974), pp. 137–39.
[31] *Ibid.*

on throwing the Arabs off balance, or both? Finally, Kissinger voiced hopes about a future Syria-Israel disengagement agreement: "It's the first time," he said, "that the Syrian Government put forward concrete suggestions on any phase of the negotiations."[32]

It is clear from the above that Kissinger's own personal initiative, with the stress on bilateral accords, ran the risk of superseding the Geneva Conference. Not that Geneva remained a favored option after his January achievement. An opportunity to shut out the Russians had presented itself; this temptation, as it turned out, was irresistible. However, the Secretary of State was careful to portray his diplomacy as being within the framework of the Conference chaired by two co-chairmen, the US and USSR. Finally, reflecting on his own personal role, the Secretary of State justified in somewhat flattering terms what he had done:

> My personal role has been produced by the fact that both parties found it easier to convey certain ideas through an intermediary and because, given the hostility in the area, it was useful to have a more impartial third party convey certain considerations and particular assurances. It is to be hoped that as these negotiations develop, and as the parties gain confidence in each other, the role of a mediator will become less crucial. But given the importance to the peace of the whole world of making progress toward a settlement in the Middle East, I don't want to take a dogmatic position on that issue.[33]

In other words, he was virtually saying that the world needs Henry Kissinger as mediator. On that he could be dogmatic.

A third American explanation, that of Assistant Secretary of State Joseph Sisco, expressed three days after Kissinger's interview of 22 January, would help to further clarify the US government's assessment of the disengagement agreement. To Sisco, as to Nixon and Kissinger, it was in the nature of a turning point and a first step on the step-by-step road to further negotiations; he felt the growing importance of his nation as the acceptable mediator to both sides. Questioned on US guarantees and the possibility of intervention, he replied:

> We are not a guarantor of this agreement in the sense that we have undertaken any specific legal obligations to intervene. We

---

[32] *Ibid.*, pp. 141–42.
[33] *Ibid.*

have in certain instances had to interpret one side to the other. We have had to convey, for example, assurances from one side to the other....In my judgment, we are involved because of our overall political, economic, and strategic interests in the area. We are involved in the sense that I have described by way of having been the principal intermediary in bringing about the agreement.[34]

Although he did not actually express it, the US was further involved in that the agreement itself was an American product. By the first week of February, some aspects of the unpublished annex to the agreement were becoming clear: for instance, that the US would use satellites and aircraft to monitor the disengagement, thereby underlining the involvement. Moreover, the oil embargo and the energy crisis had made the US a party in the negotiations and not a mere "honest broker" as it officially liked to portray itself.

One direct outcome of the American role was the restoration of full diplomatic relations between Egypt and the US beginning on 28 February. Egypt appointed Ashraf Ghorbal as ambassador to Washington, and President Nixon nominated Hermann Eilts as ambassador to Cairo.[35] The Egyptian president also announced his invitation to President Nixon to visit Egypt. Another direct outcome was a massive American undertaking to help clear the Suez Canal—one more sign that a new American policy had emerged. But how different it would be from the old remained to be seen. On the level of economic aid, the promise of increased US commitment was held out.

The extent to which the Soviet Union was discomfited by this surge of American prestige—not to mention the bypassing of Geneva—is difficult to determine. Its public reaction was relatively mild and limited to a denunciation of Kissinger's efforts and a call urging the Arabs to maintain the embargo against the US.[36] As to the Palestine Liberation Organization, the news of the disengagement was not a cause for rejoicing. A deep split occurred within its ranks with the Chairman of the Executive Committee, Yasir Arafat, adopting a noncommittal attitude, whereas many representatives bitterly denounced the bilateral and partial nature of the accord.

---

[34] *Department of State Bulletin*, LXX, 1808 (18 February 1974), pp. 176–78.

[35] *Department of State Bulletin*, LXX, 1814 (1 April 1974), p. 338.

[36] "Reflections on the Quarter," *Orbis*, 18 (Spring 1974), p. 4; F. Kohler, L. Gouré, and M. Harvey, *The Soviet Union and the October 1973 Middle East War* (Miami: Center for Advanced International Studies, 1974), pp. 113–15.

The Golan Disengagement Agreement

Meanwhile, in Syria the situation on the Golan front was far from quiet, with tank and artillery battles being fought on almost a daily basis. Fighter planes frequently joined in the action. The casualty toll mounted steadily. On the negotiating front the Americans were having a hard time convincing the parties concerned of the need for a disengagement agreement in the wake of the Egypt-Israel accord. The Syrian position had called for a simultaneous withdrawal of Israeli forces from the Sinai and the Golan. Signs of a growing tension between Egypt and Syria were becoming apparent, despite President Sadat's denials.[37] The Arab oil embargo was still in force.

For its part, Israel had insisted that it would not conduct talks until a list of Israeli prisoners held in Syria was handed to the International Red Cross. Furthermore, the Israelis would not allow the return of Syrian civilians to their homes in newly occupied Golan villages; in fact, the Israeli government announced vast colonization projects and the building of new towns in the area, measures regarded as particularly hostile by Syria.

Clearly, progress on the road to Geneva (if there was anything left of that option), on the lifting of the Arab oil embargo, on some sort of West Bank accord, and on further disengagements in Sinai, depended on progress toward a separation accord in the Golan. The State Department was therefore eager to get a negotiating process started between Syria and Israel, with Dr. Kissinger acting once more as mediator.

In fact, some preliminary diplomatic reconnaissance had been done within the framework of the Egypt-Israel shuttle. On 20 January Dr. Kissinger had paid a quick visit to Damascus and had apparently prevailed on President Asad to conduct some quiet diplomacy in the Washington setting. Upon his return to the State Department in late January, he worked on a formula reconciling the Israeli preconditions regarding the prisoners issue and the Syrian position on disengagement. According to Matti Golan, Washington informed the Israeli government on 3 February that "an understanding had been reached with Syria on the following procedure: Syria would give Kissinger the list of prisoners; Kissinger would turn the list over to Israel and would receive for transmittal to Syria a proposal for a disengagement of forces on the Golan front; Syria would then allow Red Cross visits to the prisoners."[38]

---

[37] *Arab Report and Record*, 16–31 January 1974, pp. 24, 36.
[38] Golan, *Secret Conversations*, p. 182.

Between 18 and 24 February, Arab diplomatic activity in Washington was stepped up with visits by both the Egyptian and Saudi foreign ministers to discuss progress on the Golan disengagement and the oil embargo.[39] On 26 February, the State Secretary arrived in the Syrian capital on the first leg of another Near East tour. The next day Washington and Damascus announced that Syria had authorized Dr. Kissinger to transmit a list of 65 Israeli prisoners of war and that the Red Cross would begin visiting the prisoners on 1 March.[40] The announcement also specified that Israel would present its own proposals on disengagement to Dr. Kissinger for transmission to Damascus in person on 1 March. The Israeli proposal for a limited withdrawal was promptly rejected by the Syrian government. Meanwhile, Dr. Kissinger visited Saudi Arabia and Jordan, where his meeting with King Hussein was described as cool. A negotiating process had begun, but no one was left in any doubt as to its length and difficulty.

The month of March also saw other diplomatic activities: a visit by Soviet Foreign Minister Andrei Gromyko to the Near East in early March; King Hussein's visit to Washington, reportedly in connection with talks concerning the establishment of a Palestinian state in the West Bank;[41] Abba Eban and Moshe Dayan's Washington visits; and Dr. Kissinger's visit to Moscow.[42] Israeli Foreign Minister Eban brought hardly any change in the Israeli negotiating position: Israel would not retreat beyond the lines held on the eve of the October 1973 war. And another visit to Washington, this time by Moshe Dayan, only served to affirm Israel's unyielding position on the question of a retreat to the city of Quneitra.

One factor during this episode requires stressing: Israel's loudly proclaimed reluctance to negotiate on matters of substance when faced with domestic and cabinet crises. This type of logic was accepted with uncommon haste and eagerness by Dr. Kissinger, who used it rather frequently to serve his own ends during negotiations with Arab leaders. One wonders whether the internal crises of March and April were not deliberately sustained to provide convenient excuses for delaying tactics and to support inflexible positions.

During April it became abundantly clear that Israel had compelling reasons for reaching a separation of forces accord: to discharge the many re-

---

[39] *Arab Report and Record*, 15–28 February 1974, p. 73.

[40] *Department of State Bulletin*, LXX, 1814 (1 April 1974), p. 338; BBC Monitoring Service, *Summary of World Broadcasts*, ME/4539/A/1.

[41] *Arab Report and Record*, 1–15 March 1974, p. 83.

[42] *Department of State Bulletin*, LXX, 1817 (22 April 1974), pp. 417, 418.

servists called to the Golan front; to get back the prisoners of war captured during 1973 and in the renewed battle of 1974; and to restore the economy to peacetime conditions. In addition, the Palestinian guerrilla attack on Qiryat Shmona indicated the difficulty of coping with more than one front at a time and highlighted the vulnerability of Israeli settlements to Palestinian action in spite of Israel's mobilization along its entire northern front. Yet years of military and diplomatic successes had conditioned Israel's ruling elite into an unyielding arrogance and the belief that a disengagement could be had without relinquishing substantial territory.

Syria, on the other hand, showed every intention of maintaining and even escalating the war of attrition; the grave implications were acknowledged by Israeli military leaders and correspondents.[43] On 9 April, President Asad dispatched a delegation led by General Ḥikmat Shihābī to Washington to underline the Syrian position on disengagement, and himself flew to Moscow with his foreign minister. Despite the disengagement accord on the Suez Canal (Sinai I) and the lifting of the oil embargo, Syria's overall position remained strong. The June deadline for a reconsideration of the oil embargo was not too far off. Moreover, Syria could count both on Arab economic backing to sustain the war of attrition and on the recent promise of Soviet military equipment given to President Asad in Moscow. In the event of the attrition war escalating to full-scale war, the reimposition of the Arab oil embargo and the participation of Egypt and Jordan on the battlefield were factors that could not be ignored. The Americans could not afford a second surprise so soon after that of October 1973.

In short, Syria retained a viable war option to back its negotiating position, which included the demand for a significant Israeli pullback into the Golan beyond the 1967 lines and Quneitra. The whole situation was fraught with danger for a US seeking to consolidate its new policy on the Arab-Israeli conflict: a slight shift from a position of all-out support to Israel to one which would also increasingly weigh the advantages of better relations with Arab countries, including the possibility of some influence in traditionally hostile Syria. The unexpected American support for the UN Security Council vote of 12 April, censuring Israel for attacks on Lebanese villages—a position that raised bitter disappointment in Israel—may be seen in this light. From the vantage point of Washington it was time for the Secretary of State to resume his diplomatic initiative on the actual scene of the conflict.

---

[43] Hirsh Goodman, "Portents of War," *Jerusalem Post* (Weekly Overseas Edition), 26 March 1974, p. 11.

Dr. Kissinger arrived in the Near East at the end of April, stopping first at Alexandria to visit President Sadat. On 1 May 1974 he announced to no one's surprise: "I expect that the talks will be very difficult and that we will not have an easy passage."[44] And in commenting on the nature of the forthcoming round of negotiations, he said:

> I will proceed as I did in the case of Egypt; that is to say, the ultimate responsibility is that of the parties concerned. After I have seen the next position of the two sides, I may then perhaps suggest some ideas of my own when I may urge the two sides to rethink their positions. But as I said, I am not going to either Damascus or Tel Aviv with an American proposal.[45]

But at the very first meeting with a new Israeli negotiating team, which in addition to Mrs. Meir, Dayan, Eban, and Allon now included Rabin, Shimon Peres, and General Mordechai Gur, it would appear that Dr. Kissinger quickly abandoned his role of persuasive mediator and pressed the Israeli leaders—at first without much success—to offer a pullback beyond the 1967 cease-fire line.[46] At this point he was building momentum but not getting any movement. Shimon Peres, Israel's minister of information, warned that meaningful negotiations could not be held without a Syrian cease-fire on the Golan front, but he also made it clear that he "was not issuing an ultimatum."[47] The next day (3 May) President Asad in Damascus rejected outright the proposals carried by Dr. Kissinger and maintained the military pressure in the war of attrition; the State Secretary flew back to Israel, urged Mrs. Meir to be realistic, and apparently received proposals for a new line of retreat.[48]

So far the US was playing the role of the principal Big Power on the scene unhindered, orchestrating the moves on the complex negotiations checkerboard virtually alone. The co-chairman of the Geneva Conference seemed far away—and perhaps discomfited. It is therefore not surprising that Foreign Minister Andrei Gromyko flew to Damascus on 5 May to indicate the Soviet Union's intention not to be shut out from the current round of negotiations. Two days later, in an unexpected move, he conferred with Dr. Kissinger in

---

[44] *Department of State Bulletin*, LXX, 1826 (24 June 1974), p. 678.

[45] *Ibid.*

[46] Golan, *Secret Conversations*, p. 190.

[47] *New York Times*, 3 May 1974, p. 1.

[48] Sheehan, "Step by Step in the Middle East," p. 29.

Cyprus, an episode that caused apprehension in Israel's ruling circles that the two Big Powers were planning an imposed solution. But no special significance was attached to the meeting by the State Secretary himself—Cyprus was chosen because he did not want to meet with his Soviet counterpart in the Syrian capital.[49] In fact, his entourage tended to dismiss the exercise as a face-saving device for the Russians. Nonetheless, it would seem from reports emanating from American pressmen on the shuttle service that Dr. Kissinger was given new proposals for a troop separation upon his return to Israel from Cyprus.[50] Moreover, American officials were acknowledging the presence of flexibility in Israel's negotiating position. Perhaps Henry Kissinger, in search of leverage to nudge Israel, had contrived this interlude with Gromyko in order of serve his own ends.

Meantime in Washington, in addition to the problem of Watergate, there was more trouble brewing. On 8 May, William H. Donaldson, Under-Secretary of State for Security Assistance and one of Dr. Kissinger's top aides, resigned "over what his associates said was his despair over the way Mr. Kissinger was running the State Department and dealing with the Pentagon."[51] There was some on-the-spot trouble as well. US Ambassador James Akins in Riyadh had clashed with the State Secretary over sensitive matters pertaining to relations with Saudi Arabia, and had in fact threatened to resign.[52]

But to return to the scene of the negotiations, the new "flexibility" noted in the Israeli position fell short of Henry Kissinger's expectations, let alone those of Syria. What was being proposed was a division of Quneitra into three zones: a) one under complete Israeli sovereignty and control; b) a central portion under a civilian administration run jointly by Israel and the UN; and c) one under a joint Syrian and UN administration. The minimum acceptable Syrian position on this aspect of the negotiations was the return of the whole city and some breathing space including the strategic hills overlooking it. According to Matti Golan, "Kissinger bluntly informed the Israeli negotiator that he supported President Asad's position," and as the heated negotiating session went on, he finally burst out:

> Such bargaining is not dignified for an American secretary of
> state. I am wandering around here like a rug merchant in order

[49] *New York Times*, 7 May 1974, p. 6.
[50] *Ibid.*, 8 May 1974, pp. 1, 5.
[51] *New York Times*, 9 May 1974, p. 5.
[52] Sheehan, "Step by Step in the Middle East," p. 27.

to bargain over 100 to 200 meters! Like a peddler in the market! I'm trying to save you, and you think you are doing me a favour when you are kind enough to give me a few more meters. As if I were a citizen of El-Quneitra. As if I planned to build my house there.[53]

Henry Kissinger also showed his exasperation at the fact that Israeli officials were leaking proposals to the press. But in this respect, so was he.

Progress was painfully slow: the talks were turning out to be more difficult than Dr. Kissinger had anticipated. Compared to the later stages in the negotiations, he was not leaning as hard on the Israeli government to make the required concessions. Predictably, Syria's response to this stalemate situation remained firm. In a quiet but significant move, Damascus announced on 8 May that "a meeting of Arab chiefs of state might be necessary,"[54] a move that Israel, eager to preserve the sector-by-sector approach, would have regarded with some concern. Similarly, to the Americans an Arab summit would have signified support for a hard-line position on negotiations. The strategy of "step by step," to which the State Department was strongly committed, was clearly in danger.

During the first two weeks of his peregrination the State Secretary also paid various visits to Arab capitals. On 5 May in Amman, he did not appear to progress very far with King Hussein on the thorny West Bank disengagement negotiation: the proposals he submitted were unacceptable to Jordan. In an important press interview Prime Minister Zayd al-Rifāʿī asserted:

> We have firmly rejected the Israeli proposal, and on our part have insisted that there begin an Israeli withdrawal westward from the Jordan River and along the entire confrontation line, for in no case can Israel be allowed to maintain military posts or civilian settlements anywhere in the West Bank. Nor can there be any bargaining over the future of Jerusalem: it is essential that Arab sovereignty be restored over all of Arab Jerusalem.[55]

Visits on 9 and 10 May to both Egypt and Saudi Arabia were also included. In Riyadh, Dr. Kissinger sought and received endorsement for his current efforts from King Faysal. He also invited Prince Fahd to Washington for

---

[53] Golan, *Secret Conversations*, pp. 194, 195.
[54] *New York Times*, 9 May 1974, p. 7; *Al-Nahār* (Beirut), 9 May 1974.
[55] *Al-Nahār*, 12 May 1974.

bilateral discussions on technological, defense, and economic matters.[56] According to press reports, however, the atmosphere in Riyadh was a little more tense than it would appear: the Saudi monarch warned his visitor that "unless some settlement was achieved, Saudi Arabia would reimpose its oil embargo on the USA."[57]

At this point the Secretary of State had spent a fortnight on the shuttle and his progress report, as related to a retinue of attentive pressmen, may be summed up as follows. The process of narrowing the gap was making progress; there was more willingness by parties concerned to reach an agreement, but the gulf was still wide and agreement far off. Perhaps an accord would not be reached in the present tour, yet the shuttle would go on as long as there was hope; the chances were 50–50, the talks could go either way.[58]

The principal areas of discord remained the location of the new demarcation line in the Golan, particularly in connection with the strategic hills in the vicinity of Quneitra which Israel insisted on retaining. Other problems, to be tackled later, involved the dimension of the buffer zone separating the two armies, the size and equipment of forces in the zones of limitation, the size and role of the UN supervisory contingent, and the various assurances demanded by and from the US. But the first priority was the location of the demarcation line. By 13 May American officials assessed that the talks had reached a crucial stage; they pointed to the participation of the two additional military leaders in the Syrian negotiating team: Generals Muṣṭafā Ṭlās and Nājī Jamīl. Another indication was the official news from the State Secretary's Boeing that the differences over the demarcation line had been reduced to a few kilometers.[59]

In actual fact the Israeli position was still obdurate; this may be judged from the dramatic appeal of Dr. Nahum Goldman, President of the World Jewish Congress, who urged Israel to "stop bickering over a settlement or two" and to reach an accord with Syria.[60] Kissinger was speaking openly of ending his tour and announcing that his aides were preparing an appropriate announcement leaving the door open for the resumption of the negotiating process at a later date. Then on 15 May Palestinian guerrillas attacked Maalot, demanding the release of certain prisoners held in Israeli jails. This

---

[56] *New York Times*, 10 May 1974, p. 9.

[57] *Arab Report and Record*, 1–15 May 1974, p. 178.

[58] "Reporter's Notebook: Life on the Kissinger Shuttle," *New York Times*, 10 May 1974, p. 8.

[59] *Ibid.*, 13 May 1974, p. 8; 14 May 1974, p. 1.

[60] *Jerusalem Post* (Weekly Overseas Edition), 14 May 1974, p. 2.

action was considered by the Americans on the Boeing as a blow to the negotiations. It would no longer be possible, in their view, to extract additional concessions from Israel.[61] Yet the talks went on. By 17 May the American party was claiming that to break the deadlock Kissinger was proposing his own ideas, apparently with some success because there was a last-minute cancellation of his announced return to Washington.[62] The crucial breakthrough probably occurred on 18 May, when the Americans referred to the location of the demarcation line as "buttoned up."[63]

But other issues remained. During the next 11 days, the State Secretary conducted a frenzied round of negotiations to break the deadlock over the limitations of forces and armaments and over the size of the UN force. On 23 May the situation appeared hopeless—as it had appeared also five days earlier on 18 May. In fact, at a lunch in honor of Foreign Minister Khaddām in Damascus on 23 May, Dr. Kissinger hinted strongly at the current deadlock:

> It is my judgment that we have made great progress in this negotiation and, even if we should for some reason not complete it on this trip, we will surely bring it to a conclusion in the near future. But we will continue to persevere in the next few days, and I want to pay tribute to the constructive and positive spirit that has been displayed by the Syrian side.[64]

The American negotiating team reported that the two major issues remained unresolved.[65] At this point Professor Kissinger appears to have utilized the intensive "seminar" method, helped by his top aides Joseph Sisco, Alfred Atherton, Harold Saunders, Carlyle Maw, Ellsworth Bunker, and Robert McCloskey. Such American-led seminars were reportedly being conducted both in Israel and Syria: questioning the Israelis "on what they wanted to accomplish by the thinning out of forces and what it was that really worried them,"[66] then conducting the same with the Syrians. In the meantime, some of the heaviest fighting was reported all along the 80-kilometer Golan front, with fierce tank, artillery, and aircraft duels. Nonetheless, the intense seminars over the thorny military specifics to the limitation zone proved helpful: the issue was resolved by subdividing the zone, with the limitations

---

[61] *New York Times*, 16 May 1974, p. 1.

[62] *New York Times*, 18 May 1974, p. 1; 20 May 1974, p. 1.

[63] *Ibid.*

[64] *Department of State Bulletin*, LXX, 1826 (24 June 1974), pp. 688–89.

[65] *New York Times*, 23 May 1974, p. 1.

[66] *Ibid.*, 24 May 1974, p. 2.

most severe in the areas closest to the UN buffer zone.[67] In this manner Syria's offensive and defensive capability was preserved.

Even this was not enough: a new impasse was to tax the Secretary of State's ingenuity on 27 May. The accompanying press was reporting that the talks had virtually collapsed, whereas the officials—more cautious—were speaking in terms of a few remaining stumbling blocks. The Israelis were insisting on guarantees against guerrilla activity emanating from Syria, which President Asad refused to give. On 27 May Gromyko flew to Damascus, where he expressed the Soviet Union's determination to stand firm on Syria's side in the negotiations.[68]

This is how Edward Sheehan described the last round of talks:

> The haggling went on—about the location of the line, the cultivation of the fields, a village here, a crossroads there, the width of the buffer zone, the limitation of forces and artillery (another American letter to resolve that!), the length of the UN mandate, the exchange of prisoners wounded and unwounded, the quantity of Syrian police to be permitted in Qunaitra. The Syrians wished only observers in the buffer zone; the Israelis insisted on an armed force; the issue was resolved by calling them both—the United Nations Disengagement Observer Force (UNDOF). The talks nearly collapsed again at least twice, and Kissinger kept threatening to go home. Nixon—who needed the agreement as much as anybody—told him to stay, and started calling up Golda Meir. An audacious poker-player, constantly bluffing to improve the pot, Asad retracted his previous assent to the Israeli line. On May 27, Asad and Kissinger composed a communiqué announcing the collapse of the negotiations. On the way to the door, Asad touched Kissinger's hand and said, "What a pity. We've come so far and we've not succeeded. Can't anything be done about the line? Go back to Jerusalem and try again."[69]

Dr. Kissinger was glad to take up the invitation; two days later, on 29 May, a jubilant President Nixon went on the air to announce the successful conclusion of a Syria-Israel disengagement agreement. The guns on the Golan front became silent.

---

[67] *Ibid.*, 31 May 1974, p. 8.

[68] *Ibid.*, 28 May 1974, p. 6.

[69] Sheehan, "Step by Step in the Middle East," p. 31.

According to the *New York Times*, quoting Israeli official sources, Israel made the last compromise, "dropping a previous demand that Syria agree in writing to bar guerrilla forces from using her territory against Israel, in return for an American letter of support for Israel's right to protect herself against such incursions and to retaliate if necessary."[70] In addition, support would be extended to the UN arena where the US would veto UN sanctions following Israeli retaliation against such guerrilla action.

On 31 May, a joint Syrian-Egyptian military delegation and an Israeli military delegation signed the accord at the Palais des Nations in Geneva. Syria, it is recalled, had not participated in the Geneva Conference. But even before the long-awaited agreement was signed, Israel's Defense Minister, Moshe Dayan, had gone on television to interpret it "not as a stage toward a further development but as an agreement in itself," recommending that "the impending agreement be seen as one that did not entail a further step."[71] This, of course, was hardly in keeping with Clause H, which affirmed: "This Agreement is not a Peace Agreement. It is a step towards a just and durable peace on the basis of Security Council Resolution 338 dated 22 October 1973."[72] General Dayan's position, if truly representative of Israel's ruling elite, would not augur well for America's step-by-step diplomacy.

How did the US administration view the significance of the accord? On 30 May Dr. Kissinger said in Cairo that his country was "dedicated to achieving a permanent peace based on justice," and that he regarded both disengagements as representing "a necessary first stage toward that objective."[73] He also indicated that a process of rapid improvement in relations between the US and Syria was being inaugurated. A few days later, in a televised reply on "How did Mr. Kissinger do it?" Joseph Sisco offered his own comments:

> I think President Sadat took the lead; I think it is significant
> that the Syrians have followed. Hopefully, this could be a very
> significant turning point in the area. In so far as our Secretary
> of State is concerned, a remarkable rapport was established with
> both sides—confidence of both sides in the kind of personal diplo-
> macy that he has pursued throughout this last six months.[74]

---

[70] *New York Times*, 30 May 1974, p. 1.

[71] *Jerusalem Post* (Weekly Overseas Edition), 29 May 1974, p. 1.

[72] *International Documents on Palestine, 1974*, p. 291, doc. 115.

[73] *Department of State Bulletin*, LXX, 1826 (24 June 1974), pp. 696–97.

[74] *Ibid.*, LXXI, 1827 (1 July 1974), pp. 11–14.

Joseph Sisco went on to analyze the American role, which he preferred to characterize as a communicator of assurances rather than as a guarantor:

> We did communicate assurances between the two sides. There were instances where one side or the other preferred to give an assurance directly to the United States rather than to the other side, and we did that. We also interpreted various aspects of the agreement. We also made a US proposal that both sides found to be the right compromise. This is analogous to the situation at the time that we negotiated the Egyptian-Israeli agreement.[75]

For 33 whirlwind days Dr. Henry Kissinger had shuttled back and forth between Damascus, Israel, and various other locations, narrowing down differences, setting deadlines aimed at pressuring the parties to overcome difficulties rapidly, proposing his own plan on at least three major deadlock situations, and in general breaking new ground in the field of international relations. His reputation as the Odysseus of diplomacy was consecrated. Upon his return to Washington he was met with the highest praise. For a brief moment, even Watergate was eclipsed.[76] The news media went overboard: "*Time* put a beaming Kissinger on its cover, with 'Mideast Miracle' emblazoned on his forehead; *Newsweek* featured him on its cover as a pop-art 'super K'; his face turned up nightly on all three television network news broadcasts."[77] Step-by-step appeared to be working. But as Edward Sheehan put it: "The Israeli-Syrian disengagement marked the high noon of Kissinger's gradualist diplomacy in the Middle East. Thereafter we begin to observe lengthening shadows, faltering steps, frustration, recrimination, paralysis, and doubt."[78]

President Nixon's Visit to the Region

Before October 1973 hardly anyone would have seriously admitted the possibility of an American president visiting such places as Cairo and Damascus during the first half of 1974. Nonetheless, following in the footsteps of his Secretary of State President Nixon made a grand if rapid tour of the Near East that included visits to states never visited by an American president.

---

[75] *Ibid.*

[76] Marvin and Bernard Kalb, *Kissinger*, p. 615.

[77] *Ibid.*

[78] Sheehan, "Step by Step in the Middle East," p. 32.

The tour involved five states: Egypt (12–14 June), Saudi Arabia (14–15 June), Syria (15–16 June), Israel (16–17 June), and Jordan (17–18 June).

How significant was President Nixon's visit to the scene of the Arab-Israeli conflict? Was it a desperate attempt to escape impeachment, as so many analysts have claimed, or was it an act of statesmanship aimed at consolidating the change in US policy and the new relationship with the Arab world that the Administration had painstakingly constructed. It is of course clear that in the final analysis the Watergate scandal cast a shadow on Nixon's foreign policy record. Yet in his resignation speech he "based his claim to appear in history on his achievements in foreign policy"[79]—a not unreasonable claim. With respect to the Near East, his policy had placed the US in a position of unprecedented influence. If eluding Watergate was an objective, it was certainly overshadowed by the historical significance of the tour.

On 6 June Dr. Kissinger, commenting on the reasons for the Presidential tour, underlined the emergence of a new long-term relationship between the US and some Arab countries and the need "for the President to symbolize the American commitment to this new relationship."[80] In his view, prior to the disengagement agreements there was a clear situation of polarization in which "every conflict had the insoluble quality of a superpower confrontation."[81] As the visit was nearing its end Dr. Kissinger once more assessed the reasons and significance of President Nixon's tour:

> [The] process leading to disengagement negotiations culminated in the Presidential trip, which had to be seen on many levels— on the one level, as a symbolic affirmation of a dramatic reversal in the whole historic evolution of this area, at the same time as enabling the United States to begin a relationship with all of the countries in the area not based on exigencies of a particular crisis but based on the long-term prosperity and progress of the area. The President's visit and conversation in all of these countries has served to crystallize and to put into a focus this direction of the relationship between the United States and all of the countries in the area. And thirdly, it has enabled the President to engage in preliminary conversation, not about the tactics of how peace should be made but about the general direction of the peace

[79] Hartley, *American Foreign Policy in the Nixon Era*, preface.
[80] *Department of State Bulletin*, LXX, 1826 (24 June 1974), pp. 705–707.
[81] *Ibid.*, LXXI, 1829 (15 July 1974), p. 125.

efforts. I therefore think that the Middle East policy, if we stay on this course—and we all recognize that this is a very tricky and complicated area—could mark one of the turning points in the postwar diplomatic history.[82]

The tour began in Cairo with cheering millions to greet the American president with unrestrained enthusiasm. There he heard from President Sadat that "the political solution and the national aspirations of the Palestinians are the crux of the whole problem....There is no other solution and no other road for a durable peace without a political solution to the Palestinian problem."[83]

In the past, with President Nasser, the US had let an opportunity slip—by waffling over the Aswan Dam project. This time Nixon was bent on closing that chapter and setting the tone of what both Americans and Egyptians agreed was the new relationship. To this effect, a Joint Cooperation Commission headed by the US and Egyptian foreign ministers was set up to implement programs in the economic, scientific, and cultural fields. In addition, a most important and politically significant agreement was signed in the nuclear field, involving the sale of "nuclear reactors and fuel to Egypt which will make it possible for Egypt by the early 1980s to generate substantial additional quantities of electric power to support its rapidly growing development needs."[84]

The two governments also agreed to establish several Joint Working Groups for the reconstruction and development of the Suez Canal, for the promotion of trade and of private investments, for agriculture, for science and technology, for medical cooperation, and for cultural exchange.[85] And there was mention, in the "Principles of Relations and Cooperation" signed by Presidents Nixon and Sadat, of the Palestinian people: "A just and durable peace...should take into due account the legitimate interest of all the peoples in the Mid East, including the Palestinian people, and the right to existence of all states in the area."[86] Though the wording of this reference was almost identical to the Brezhnev-Nixon San Clemente summit communiqué of 24 June 1973, and therefore could not be regarded as an evolution of the American position on the status of the Palestinians, the inclusion of such

---

[82] *Ibid.*

[83] *Ibid.*, p. 81.

[84] [*Ibid.*, p. 93.]

[85] *Ibid.*

[86] [*Ibid.*, p. 92.]

a statement in a joint American-Arab declaration signed by the respective presidents is nevertheless significant.[87]

What did Egypt get out of the Presidential visit besides the nuclear reactor promise, the joint commissions, the promise of substantial economic and technical aid, the specially equipped helicopter, and a repetition of the San Clemente statement regarding the Palestinians? On the all-important question of the American interpretation of Resolution 242 there seems to have been some shift in the Arab direction. Edward Sheehan in his book affirms: "Nixon did tell his host that the American objective in the Sinai was to restore the old Egyptian international border. Dr. Kissinger was sitting there when Nixon said it."[88]

Next on the agenda was the visit to Saudi Arabia. In Jedda on 14 June, King Faysal reminded his guest of the injustice committed to the Palestinian people and of the crucial importance of Jerusalem:

> The injustice and aggression suffered by the Palestinian Arab people is without precedent in history, even in the Dark Ages. An entire people has been expelled from its land and home so that another could take its place....In our view, there will never be a true and lasting peace in the region unless Jerusalem is liberated and restored to Arab sovereignty, all occupied Arab lands are liberated, and the Palestinian Arab people regain its right to return to its homeland and to decide its own destiny.[89]

In reply, President Nixon explained that while the US was playing a helpful role in bringing about a permanent peace, it could not "produce an instant formula to solve all longtime differences."[90] He emphasized that the American and Arab nations were now bound by the ties of cooperation and interdependence, and he pledged US assistance in maintaining the Saudi military potential "consistent with its role as a leader in this part of the world."[91]

In Damascus President Nixon appeared to be enjoying his Near Eastern tour. He complimented the Syrian head of state on his statesmanship and negotiating skills, and on the merits of Syrian food, remarking:

---

[87] *International Documents on Palestine, 1973,* edited by Jorgen S. Nielsen (Beirut: Institute for Palestine Studies, 1976), p. 260, doc. 102.

[88] Edward Sheehan, *The Arabs, Israelis, and Kissinger* (New York: Reader's Digest Press, 1976), p. 132.

[89] [*Al-Bilād* (Jedda), 15 June 1974.]

[90] *Department of State Bulletin,* LXXI, 1829 (15 July 1974), p. 95.

[91] *Ibid.,* p. 96.

I can now see why Henry Kissinger gained seven pounds in his 13 trips to Damascus in the past 30 days. And whenever we wear him out on his other travels throughout the world, we will send him back here to build him up.[92]

President Asad, in his turn, stressed that a new and better page in the history of Syrian-American relations had been inaugurated, but emphasized that his country would never accept Israeli presence in the Golan Heights. He insisted on the importance of strict implementation of UN resolutions, and on the national rights of the Palestinian people. He made a complimentary reference to the Americans of Syrian origin:

It gives me pleasure to note that in the United States there are many citizens of Syrian Arab descent who have been living in their new homeland as decent citizens in all walks of life. This in itself is an incentive for strengthening the friendship between our two peoples.[93]

One of the highlights of the visit was the resumption of diplomatic relations between the two nations at ambassadorial level as of 16 June 1974.[94]

From Syria the Presidential party went to Israel, where the newly installed Rabin cabinet was eager to extend the warmest possible welcome, but where also many misgivings were being entertained concerning the next step in the disengagement process and the long-term effects of the sale of nuclear reactors to Egypt. According to Matti Golan, it was made clear to the Cabinet by Dr. Kissinger that the choice confronting Israel was not simply whether to negotiate with King Hussein. It was "whether to negotiate with Hussein now or be forced to negotiate with Yasir Arafat or the PLO later."[95] But it would seem that the Israelis were playing for time: "to forestall the Jordanian option [Rabin] started manoeuvring almost obsessively for another step with Egypt."[96]

Israel was out to get as much out of President Nixon as possible, and it certainly succeeded. The final joint communiqué spoke of the visit symbolizing "the unique relationship, the common heritage and the close and historic

---

[92] *Ibid.*, p. 100.
[93] [*Al-Ba'th* (Damascus), 16 June 1974.]
[94] *Ibid.*
[95] Golan, *Secret Conversations*, p. 217.
[96] *Ibid.*, p. 219.

ties"[97] existing between the two states. The President "affirmed the continuing and long-term nature of the military supply relationship between the two countries."[98] The communiqué also announced that a Defense Ministry delegation would pay an early visit to Washington "in order to work out the concrete details relating to long-term military supplies."[99] In the months ahead these promises and commitments were to materialize, and Israel was showered with economic and military aid.

One curious episode during the Nixon visit was the reported request by Rabbi Amram Blau, head of the anti-Zionist *Neturei Karta* (Guardians of the City), that their Mea She'arim area in West Jerusalem "be placed under Arab rule in any future peace settlement."[100]

The last phase of the Presidential tour was the visit to Jordan. Expectations in Amman ran high: after Sinai and the Golan the next step, according to Kissinger's scenario, involved the West Bank. Here again the American visitors heard what they had heard in every Arab capital: the crucial importance of Palestinian rights in any peace settlement. In a dinner honoring his guest, King Hussein warned:

> Disengagement of forces can be arranged, truce lines can be drawn, and political settlement can be negotiated, but there can be no peace until the major issue in the conflict between Israel and the Arab world is resolved and resolved justly. That is the problem of Palestine. There can be no peace until the legitimate rights of the Palestinian people are recognized and restored. The Palestinian problem has never been a refugee problem, but one of the inherent rights of a people to return to their homeland and to determine their own future. Once the occupied territory has been evacuated by the Israelis, only Palestinians can decide what its future is to be. They can choose continued union with Jordan, a new form of federation, or the creation of a separate state. The choice is theirs and theirs alone, and whatever their choice, it will enjoy our full acceptance and support.[101]

As to disengagement on the Jordan, the joint communiqué cautiously stated:

---

[97] *Department of State Bulletin*, LXXI, 1829 (15 July 1974), p. 110.
[98] *Ibid.*
[99] *Ibid.*
[100] *Jerusalem Post* (Weekly Overseas Edition), 18 June 1974, p. 5.
[101] [*Department of State Bulletin*, LXXI, 1829 (15 July 1974), p. 113.]

His Majesty and the President discussed the strategy of future efforts to achieve peace, and the President promised the active support of the United States for agreement between Jordan and Israel on concrete steps toward the just and durable peace called for in United Nations Security Council Resolution 338 of 22 October 1973.[102]

But if in the disengagement issue the promises were somewhat vague, Nixon was more forthcoming in the area of economic and military assistance: "The President explained to His Majesty in detail the proposal he has submitted to the Congress of the United States for a substantial increase in American military and economic assistance for Jordan in the coming 12 months."[103] Finally, an invitation to visit Washington at an early date for peace talks was extended to King Hussein.

However, in the months ahead the American momentum toward disengagement in the West Bank—assuming there was any—failed to nudge the Rabin cabinet in that direction.

The Oil Embargo

On the oil front, the year 1974 opened ominously, with the storm clouds that had formed in November and December 1973 still overhead. These were caused by Dr. Kissinger's and especially by Defense Secretary Schlesinger's warning regarding the strengthening of the American naval presence in the Indian Ocean to better protect US interests in the Gulf in the wake of the Arab oil embargo.[104] The year 1974 began on a grave keynote of warning, and, in the words of Edward Sheehan, "the warning was buttressed by murky hints of American military intervention in the Gulf."[105] The Arab response to another thinly veiled threat made by Schlesinger on 7 January was swift and clear to everyone: Saudi Arabia and Kuwait announced on 8 January their determination to blow up their oil fields in the event of a military intervention.[106] As the year came to a close, the keynote grew graver still.

In this brief analysis of the oil question, attention will be focused on its growing dimension in the Arab-Israeli conflict as well as in its resolution.

---

[102] [*Ibid.*, p. 119.]

[103] [*Ibid.*, p. 118.]

[104] *New York Times*, 1 December 1973.

[105] Sheehan, "Step by Step in the Middle East," p. 27.

[106] *Arab Report and Record*, 1–15 January 1974, pp. 6, 18.

Two topics will be singled out: 1) Arab linkage strategy and the response of the US; 2) tensions of the last quarter of 1974: the threat of military intervention.[107]

Arab Linkage Strategy and the US Response

High on the list of priorities of the Nixon-Kissinger administration was the early lifting of the oil embargo. This was dictated by several crucial factors: a) domestic grandstand considerations in the wake of Watergate; b) the need to restore a badly shaken Western alliance; and c) the national interest of the US in the context of Big Power rivalry. And the closer Dr. Kissinger got to an agreement on the disengagement of forces in the Suez Canal area, the more King Faysal was pressed to persuade the Organization of Arab Petroleum Exporting Countries (OAPEC) to lift the embargo in recognition of the American effort.

The Saudi monarch made it clear that he was interested in seeing progress toward disengagement equally on other fronts.[108] What would happen, for instance, if with the embargo lifted the ardor of Kissinger were to sag and Israel's posture were to grow even more obdurate? Syria, Jordan, and the Palestinians would be left, so to speak, out in the cold; the unity of the Arab front—a key card—would probably erode. Once lifted, the reimposition of the embargo would obviously be a risky undertaking; the element of surprise would no longer be present. Nevertheless, the Arab position was sufficiently flexible and conciliatory to indicate a fair measure of progress toward an easing—or even a lifting—of the embargo at the forthcoming February meeting of OAPEC. Yet both President Nixon and Dr. Kissinger virtually ensured the failure of such progress by characterizing the projected OAPEC meeting as yielding to the logic of American pressure and by suggesting that failure to put an early end to the embargo would be interpreted as a form of blackmail. Predictably, the February OAPEC meeting was postponed at the request of King Faysal and President Sadat.[109] In this whole diplomatic episode an additional Arab move requires stressing: President Asad's trip in early February to Saudi Arabia and Kuwait, where he is believed to have received firm pledges linking the lifting of the embargo with successful disengagement in the Golan and assurances regarding Palestinian rights.[110]

---

[107] [These topics were also discussed by Buheiry in a later study. See pp. 249–310 above.].

[108] *The Economist*, 26 January–1 February 1974, p. 36.

[109] Joe Stork, *Middle East Oil and the Energy Crisis* (New York: Monthly Review Press, 1975), pp. 240–41.

[110] *Ibid.*; *Arab Report and Record*, 1–14 February 1974, pp. 51, 53.

Perhaps for the first time in the annals of the Arab-Israeli conflict, Arab diplomacy was trying out a sophisticated form of linkage strategy—and with some measure of success. Of course the conjuncture of events was of great help. The world energy crisis, the Arab embargo, and the organized drive by a united front of oil producers to keep the price of crude from falling impacted directly on the US scene and even more dramatically on that of its allies. Undoubtedly, the US displayed annoyance at the use of its favorite strategy by others: superpowers have a tendency to regard linkage strategy as their own very private possession. Hence the strenuous, and often strained, attempts by the Administration to deny the existence of linkage between oil and disengagement diplomacy. Yet it is clear that although Dr. Kissinger denied linkage, "his Syrian shuttle was the price he paid to end the embargo."[111] On 6 March President Nixon acknowledged that "progress on the diplomatic front, while it is not linked to lifting of the embargo, inevitably has an effect on it."[112] And in sharp contrast to the tough language he had earlier used to indicate that American pressure would force a lifting of the embargo, he now said that he had decided "to leave that decision to them (the Arabs), because indicating what they will do might lead them to do otherwise."[113] This was obviously a more cautious statement to make.

By mid-March sufficient progress had been made in the Golan disengagement talks to warrant a reconsideration of the embargo. Thus, in the 18 March Vienna meeting the oil ministers of OAPEC outlined the linkage between oil measures, the drawing of world attention to the Arab cause, and encouragement to be granted to "countries which showed readiness and willingness to work for a just remedy to the cause which would lead to the complete termination of the Israeli occupation and to the restoration of the legitimate rights of the Palestinian people."[114] The meeting also expressed recognition of the emergence of a new American policy more compatible with justice toward Arab and Palestinian rights. Furthermore, two crucial decisions were taken: first, "to treat Italy and the West German Republic as friendly states and to meet their petroleum needs,"[115] and second, to lift the embargo on oil supplies to the US. The decision on the embargo was subject to review at the next OAPEC meeting in June 1974, with Egypt and Saudi Arabia providing assurances against its reimposition—a point duly noted by

---

[111] Sheehan, "Step by Step in the Middle East," p. 27.

[112] *Department of State Bulletin*, LXX, 1813 (25 March 1974), pp. 294–95.

[113] *Ibid.*

[114] *Middle East Economic Digest*, 22 March 1974, pp. 324, 342.

[115] *Ibid.*

the American Secretary of State.[116] On the other hand, the embargo on Holland, Portugal, South Africa, and Rhodesia was maintained.

Arab linkage strategy had made a convincing debut. The careful planning, the avoidance of the many pitfalls strewn along its paths, and the selection of the appropriate forums did not fail to impress international opinion. Not that the Arab states were enduringly united. However, sufficient consensus was maintained to ensure the credibility of the strategy.[117]

The US showed repeated annoyance at this Arab move—even explicitly asserting, as President Nixon had done, that oil pressure would have "a counter effect on our effort to go forward on the peace front, on the negotiation front."[118] Yet the recognition that it was an important factor, that there was no longer room for the old complacency, may be gauged by the following Presidential assessment made just after the lifting of the oil embargo.

> It is in the interest of those countries that imposed it as well as the United States that it be lifted. The two should go parallel. Inevitably, what happens in one area affects the other, and I am confident that the progress we are going to continue to make on the peace front in the Mideast will be very helpful in seeing to it that an oil embargo is not reimposed.[119]

In short, the Arabs had left it to the Americans to choose between having the embargo as a semi-permanent imposition or as an Arab tactical weapon. The first alternative was particularly intolerable. Predictably, the US chose the second, especially as it presented certain advantages stemming from the limitations of the embargo as a tactical weapon when lifted and therefore the element of surprise gone, and in the absence of a state of war.

Tensions of Late 1974: the Threat of Military Intervention

In late September the recently installed Ford administration launched a tough policy on oil prices. Believed to have been orchestrated by Dr.

---

[116] Stork, *Middle East Oil*, p. 242.

[117] One of the best studies of the Arab oil weapon is Fuad Itayim, "Strengths and Weaknesses of the Oil Weapon," in *The Middle East and the International System*, II: *Security and the Energy Crisis* (London: International Institute for Strategic Studies, 1975; *Adelphi Papers*, no. 115), pp. 1–7.

[118] *New York Times*, 16 March 1974, p. 12.

[119] *Ibid.*, 20 March 1974, p. 28.

Kissinger himself, with a public warning before the UN that "what has gone up by political decision can be reduced by political decision,"[120] the campaign aimed at attracting support from hesitant allies for a united front. The Administration may have also aimed at making a splash on the domestic scene in support of a much-weakened Republican Party on the eve of elections involving 34 out of 100 Senate seats, all of the 435-seat House of Representatives, and 35 out of 50 state governorships.

In addition, the question of projected military action against Arab producers was being repeatedly raised and attracted wide attention; the press, of course, participated fully in the campaign. Early in October, *Newsweek* magazine ran a lengthy article entitled "Thinking the Unthinkable," based on interviews "with a number of government officials, military strategists, and experts on the Mideast."[121] The editor concluded that the three most talked-about options were 1) psychological warfare aimed at "unnerving the enemy;" 2) covert operations aimed at terrorizing Arab shaykhs; and 3) military intervention in the form of American parachute assaults—supported by similar Israeli units—to quickly seize the major Arab oil fields. According to *Newsweek* the idea of military intervention was gaining respectability in the Western world.[122] And the journal *Business Week*, in a controversial interview with Dr. Kissinger, supplied further confirmation: "One thing we also hear from businessmen," said the interviewer, "is that in the long run the only answer to the oil cartel is some sort of military action."[123]

The press campaign against Arab oil interests, suggesting military seizure, continued throughout November and December. Jack Anderson, who is believed to have important leads to the corridors of power in Washington, wrote in the *Washington Post* of 8 November that a military takeover of Libyan oil fields would not require more than a couple of US Marine divisions.[124] This recipient of many timely official leaks claimed the role of seizing Kuwait's rich oil fields for Israel,[125] where early in the year the press had called for military action against the Arab oil-producing states.[126] And Paul Seabury contributed his "Thinking About an Oil War" to the *New Leader* of 11

---

[120] *Newsweek*, 7 October 1974, pp. 15–17.
[121] *Ibid.*
[122] *Ibid.*
[123] *Business Week* (New York), 13 January 1975, p. 69.
[124] *Arab Report and Record*, 1–15 November 1974, p. 486.
[125] *Jerusalem Post*, 10 November 1974, p. 5.
[126] *Haaretz*, 18 April 1974.

November.[127] In short, seizing Arab oil was portrayed as a patriotic duty, a necessary action in the defense of the West.

Whether the implied threats were real or not is of course a moot point. For their part, the Arab oil producers, as exemplified by the Saudi Arabian oil minister, Shaykh Aḥmad Zakī Yamānī, were not unduly alarmed. "The era of using military force is gone," he announced, adding that the risk involved could be too great and that "the danger of reducing the oil supply [was] very clear."[128] Similarly, George W. Ball, who was US Under-Secretary of State between 1961 and 1966, criticized the fact that "not only the Secretaries of State and Treasury but the President himself made harsh, brooding speeches, overlaid with frustration, anxiety and shadowy threat but empty of content or any reasoned program."[129] To Ball the military seizure option was clearly impossible, and he spoke out sharply against the practice of thinly veiled threats:

> Such talk is archaic fantasy, for this is no longer the nineteenth century. It is a period of nuclear parity and strategic stalemate. There is a powerful Soviet fleet in the Mediteranean, Soviet missiles are targeted on Western capitals, and the USSR clearly has a compelling interest in the Middle East. That a military move by one superpower in that area would automatically be countered by the other was vividly demonstrated last October at the time of the American worldwide military alert....We had better stop muttering under our breath. Great nations should not even hint at threats they have no intention of carrying out.[130]

In actual fact the campaign of threats appears all the more surprising in the context of an Arab policy of calculated moderation. In general, Arab oil producers led by Saudi Arabia had worked out the consequences of the dramatic geopolitical and energy changes in the wake of the 1973 war and had embarked on a giant recycling of petrodollars to prop up the flagging economy of the Western world. In November Saudi Arabia, the United Arab Emirates, and Qatar even lowered oil prices a little, while increasing taxes and royalties paid by the oil companies.[131] The option selected was cooperation not confrontation, but a cooperation between equals with the

---

[127] Paul Seabury, "Thinking About an Oil War," *The New Leader*, 11 November 1974.

[128] *Newsweek*, 7 October 1974, p. 19.

[129] George W. Ball, "No Times for Threats," *Newsweek*, 7 October 1974, p. 19.

[130] *Ibid.*

[131] *New York Times*, 12 November 1974, p. 60.

clear understanding that oil prices and recycling would be linked to political issues, such as progress toward Israeli withdrawal from Arab territory, including East Jerusalem, and the recognition of the legitimate rights of the Palestinians as a people. Nevertheless, Arab moderation and cooperation were not granted recognition by the Western media, who persisted in their campaign of character assassination and deliberate provocation, while responsible officials in Washington provided indirect (or sometimes direct) help to the campaigns of provocation by, for instance, suggesting that Arab petrodollars could be made available in the form of aid to Israel. Gerald L. Parsky, Deputy Secretary of the US Treasury, stated the possibility of "even providing Israel with Arab oil money under a three-party agreement."[132]

The magnitude of Arab recycling potential—and its political and diplomatic implications—was, of course, the subject of intense speculation. One estimate reckoned that Saudi Arabia had about $4 billion on deposit in October 1974 at the Chase Manhattan Bank alone.[133] According to Prime Minister Rabin, Arab investments in the US and Europe stood at some $27 billion in November 1974.[134]

With the embargo lifted back in March, there remained the issue of the reduction of oil prices, also that of the linkage between the supposedly high level of prices and the resolution of the Arab-Israeli conflict. The principal figures of the State Department took pains to make the separation clear. Thus, on the eve of his October departure to yet another round of talks in the Near East, Dr. Kissinger asserted:

> The impact of the high oil prices is not inevitably linked to the Arab-Israeli negotiations. And we are negotiating these two issues separately...we are conducting them in separate forums.[135]

A month later the Under-Secretary, Joseph Sisco, also reflected the US position on this thorny question. In response to a statement that affirmed the existence of a link between Kissingerian peace diplomacy and oil sanctions, Sisco said:

> Well, we certainly do not make this link. But as the Secretary has said quite recently in a press conference, obviously oil is a

---

[132] *Daily Star* (Beirut), 6 September 1974, p. 6.
[133] Arnaud de Borchgrave in *Newsweek*, 7 October 1974, p. 20.
[134] *Haaretz*, 3 December 1974, interview with Yoel Marcus.
[135] *Department of State Bulletin*, LXXI, 1844 (28 October 1974), pp. 565–67.

factor. The threat of embargo is one that we always have to bear
in mind and take into account.[136]

Why this caution with regard to the linkage, since no one in the area or in
the know was really fooled? Perhaps the best explanation came from Senator
Fulbright, who stressed the central fact that "for domestic political reasons
the [US] is exceedingly reluctant to acknowledge the close relationship between the Arab-Israeli conflict and the price and availability of oil."[137]

In the final weeks of the year 1974, the threat of oil seizure— whether
real or a mere diplomatic ploy—loomed larger. An American aircraft carrier,
the *Constellation*, escorted by two guided-missile destroyers, appeared in
the waters of the Gulf on what was officially described as a "familiarization"
tour, raising speculation on a possible action against certain oil installations.
This was clearly an ominous move both because of the general context of
harrassment policy and because no American aircraft carrier had penetrated
the waters of the Gulf since 1948.[138] The US press continued to echo the
likelihood of a move against Arab oil producers.[139]

On 13 December Dr. Kissinger denied reports of US military training
for intervention in Arab oil-producing countries: "There is no American
army," he said, "that is being trained to take over Arab oil fields."[140] Yet
ten days later he did not entirely rule out this possibility in the course of a
controversial interview accorded to *Business Week*. In response to a question
on military action against oil, the State Secretary remarked:

> A very dangerous course. We should have learned from Vietnam
> that it is easier to get into a war than to get out of it. I am
> not saying that there's no circumstance where we would not use
> force. But it is one thing to use it in the case of a dispute over
> price, it's another where there's some actual strangulation of the
> industrialized world.[141]

---

[136] Text of US Under-Secretary of State Joseph Sisco's USIS interview (Washington, 18
November 1974), published by the US Embassy in Beirut on 20 November 1974.

[137] Senator Fulbright's Fulton, Missouri speech of 2 November 1974, in *International
Documents on Palestine, 1974*, p. 346, doc. 168.

[138] Michael Klare, "La Stratégie américaine dans le Golfe Arabo-Persique," *Le Monde
diplomatique*, March 1976, p. 6.

[139] *Christian Science Monitor*, 26 November 1974; *US News and World Report*, 2 December 1974, pp. 18–20.

[140] *Department of State Bulletin*, LXXII, 1854 (6 January 1975), p. 2.

[141] *Business Week*, 13 January 1975, p. 69.

And in another reference in the same interview—normally one such reference is one too many—he went on to affirm "that the use of force would be considered only in the gravest emergency."[142] Yet in the same interview he had remarked: "I don't anticipate an oil embargo in the absence of war. I am not even sure of an oil embargo in the event of a war. It would now be a much more serious decision than it was the last time."[143] Why then the campaign of warnings and threats?

Until Dr. Kissinger chooses to provide the answer, perhaps in his forthcoming memoirs, or until US diplomatic and military archives are made available, any explanation will of course remain speculative. However, at least three factors could be retained. Firstly, Big Powers have an inordinate tendency to flex their muscles before an adoring public, especially when domestic considerations are at stake: in addition, gunboat diplomacy is the normal practice of nations that maintain large fleets of gunboats, or of aircraft carriers. Second, many analysts of the Kissingerian style—Edward Sheehan, Matti Golan, Marvin and Bernard Kalb, to mention a few—share the view that the Secretary of State likes to operate best under conditions of extreme tension: the war of nerves over oil in the last quarter of 1974 may thus be seen as a deliberate tactic to keep the Arabs off balance while the deadly game of negotiating a settlement went on. Third, the whole campaign may also be seen in the context of and as a response to the Rabat summit: it was set in motion as a warning shot on the eve of this crucially important conference, and when the resolutions failed to please Dr. Kissinger, a couple of turns of the screw may have been applied.

Difficulties of the Ford Administration: Jordan and the PLO

Stalemate on the Jordan

If Washington had an abiding interest in strengthening King Hussein's position by arranging for a third disengagement, it certainly failed to follow through. The point is, why? Conjectures abound. To Edward Sheehan the answer lay in Jordan's lack of manipulative power: "Kissinger, like Nixon and President Johnson before him, took Hussein for granted. Jordan, after all, was nearly an American protectorate; but unlike Israel it possessed no American constituency and thus had to be content with whatever scraps

---

[142] *Ibid.*
[143] *Ibid.*

Washington might care to cast its way."[144] There were, of course, other reasons as well. Prime Minister Rabin, perhaps deliberately, had pushed himself into a corner by tying any West Bank moves to general elections. This gave him plenty of scope for dragging the issue. He could wave the dismal prospect of a Likud victory in the elections. Basically he stuck to the Israeli hard-line negotiating strategy by offering the humiliating final peace settlement which Jordan had already rejected. The Americans and the King, on the other hand, favored an interim disengagement of forces.

When Foreign Minister Allon arrived in Washington in July, Kissinger immediately tried to float two versions of the so-called Jericho plan: a) Jordanian civil administration over Jericho without an Israeli military retreat; or b) UN civil administration over Jericho with an Israeli military retreat. Kissinger reportedly favored the latter; and Allon, who was more eager for a settlement than Rabin or Peres, led him to believe that this might be possible without an Israeli general election. He checked with Rabin, the Israeli prime minister thought otherwise, and instructed him to inform a now furious Kissinger that Jericho was definitely out of the question.[145]

Nevertheless, Allon brought back with him an invitation for Rabin to visit Washington in September and, if Matti Golan's report is correct, a significant commitment: the US would not come "to any final conclusion on the Jordanian question without further consultations with Israel."[146] Kissinger did not seem willing or able to prod the Israeli cabinet from its position of final peace settlement to his own interim disengagement of forces position.

In the meantime there was the denouement of Watergate, and Gerald Ford became the new President of the United States. This was not the most auspicious time for active diplomacy, yet during King Hussein's mid-August visit Ford and Kissenger "assured him that disengagement in the Jordan Valley was their next priority."[147] In fact, the joint communiqué indicated that consultations between the US and Jordan "will continue with a view to addressing at an appropriately early date the issues of particular concern to Jordan, including an Israeli-Jordanian agreement for disengagement of forces."[148] Clearly the Ford administration's position differed from Rabin's.

---

[144] Sheehan, *The Arabs, Israelis, and Kissinger*, p. 136.

[145] Golan, *Secret Conversations*, p. 222.

[146] *Ibid.*, p. 223.

[147] Sheehan, *The Arabs, Israelis, and Kissinger*, p. 148.

[148] *Department of State Bulletin*, LXXI, 1837 (9 September 1974), p. 362; *Al-Dustūr* (Amman), 18 August 1974.

The deadlock persisted even after the Israeli prime minister's September visit to Washington and after Kissinger's October visit to the Near East.

Unlike his earlier handling of deadlock situations, this time the Secretary of State was very reluctant to propose his own formula with the appropriate backing making it difficult for the other party to refuse outright. Yet in the Jordanian situation he did not make use of the immense leverage at his disposal to back his own policy of disengagement. By the end of October it was too late. The Rabat Conference had put forward another candidate for West Bank negotiations.

Senior officials of the State Department, of course, have expressed surprise and disappointment at the Rabat summit decision. There was, however, an element of sanctimonious hypocrisy in such expressions. The Americans were perfectly aware of what was happening to Jordan and had warned the Israelis of the danger of dilly-dallying on a West Bank withdrawal. Although Kissinger made a final attempt to rally Arab support for Hussein on the eve of Rabat, in the event he had not tried very hard. In November Joseph Sisco stated during an interview: "Our hope had been that the [Rabat] Conference would have given support to King Hussein's efforts to negotiate with the Israelis with respect to the West Bank. That, I think we ought to say quite candidly, was our hope."[149] Not only was it a hope, it was one of the cardinal points of US policy, which Kissinger had failed to push through with customary zeal. The obvious question is why? Was it merely because the King had no manipulative power in Washington?

The United States and the PLO: Hesitation and Confusion

The year 1974 was a particularly important year for the Palestine question and the growing political role and international recognition of the Palestine Liberation Organization. The principal highlights of the year included the Palestine National Council's decision on sovereignty, the Rabat summit's decision, and PLO Chairman Yasir Arafat's dramatic address at the UN General Assembly. Similarly, the Palestine issue was an important factor, as has already been seen, in the disengagement agreements and the Nixon visit. Clearly this was a time for decision for the United States, for a United States eager to implement its new Near Eastern policy. Yet in lieu of decisiveness, one is confronted with hesitation and confusion.

---

[149] Text of Sisco's 18 November interview, published by the US Embassy in Beirut on 20 November 1974.

Before considering the American administration's thinking and action vis-à-vis the PLO and the Palestine question during 1974, two events of the previous year will be considered in brief and as background: the San Clemente summit statement of June 1973, and Henry Kissinger's reported promise to President Sadat, made in early November 1973, to arrange some form of Palestinian participation at Geneva—a promise that was soon retracted at Israeli insistence.[150]

The Nixon-Brezhnev joint communiqué issued at the San Clemente summit of 24 June 1973 had specified: "This settlement [in the Middle East] should be in accordance with the interests of all states in the area, be consistent with their independence and sovereignty, and should take into due account the legitimate interests of the Palestinian people."[151] The last clause constituted a further step in the evolution of US foreign policy regarding the Palestinians. It was acknowledged clearly for the first time that the Palestinian people—as a people and not as individual refugees—represented a political force to be considered in any future settlement. The joint communiqué failed to specify how the Palestinians were to be represented in the negotiations, nor did it define their legitimate interests. Nevertheless, in the aftermath of the October War, the peace initiatives of 1974, and in the perspective of the much-heralded new American policy, some clarification to these crucial questions was generally expected.

As to Kissinger's reported promise of Palestinian participation, not only was it retracted, it was—in effect—torpedoed by the State Secretary himself. According to Edward Sheehan, on 20 December 1973, the day before the Geneva Conference, "Kissinger passed to the Israelis a secret and very significant 'Memorandum of Understanding' promising that no other parties would be invited to future meetings at Geneva 'without the agreement of the initial participants'—which meant an Israeli veto on participation by the PLO."[152] If this report is correct, it would explain many of the 1974 actions and reactions.

Phase I: Hesitation

Typical of the American administration's thinking on the Palestinians early in the year was Joseph Sisco's 25 January observation at the White House energy conference:

---

[150] Sheehan, *The Arabs, Israelis, and Kissinger*, pp. 49, 84–85.

[151] *International Documents on Palestine, 1973*, p. 260, doc. 102.

[152] Sheehan, *The Arabs, Israelis, and Kissinger*, p. 108.

What the eventual [Geneva] settlement will be as far as Palestinians specifically are concerned is very hard to say: the Palestinians are divided. When one talks about Palestinian representation, you have to ask who speaks for the Palestinians. Certainly King Hussein's answer to that is different from that of [Yasir] Arafat. So it is an issue which at the moment does not arise in a very concrete sense....[153]

Inasmuch as it was overshadowed by the intense disengagement negotiations that absorbed the first half of the year, this issue may not have presented itself "in a very concrete sense," to use Sisco's characterization. Yet it did hang as a backdrop to the whole peregrination's scene, a position that the State Secretary was determined to maintain. In answer to repeated questions concerning possible contacts between the American administration and the PLO, the spokesmen invariably denied that these had taken place or were envisaged.[154] It would seem, from the published record, that American diplomacy shied away from the PLO issue during the first five months of the year, except for obvious allusions—pleasant to Israeli ears—concerning so-called terrorist activities.

During President Nixon's tour of Arab states in June, the Palestine question in general and the PLO in particular arose "in a very concrete sense." Sheehan reports that President Nixon, in cautious response to Anwar Sadat's probes, promised that "at some appropriate future time, the United States would endeavor to bring the PLO into the negotiation process."[155] If true, this could be interpreted as a slight shift from Kissinger's "Secret Memorandum to Israel" position of 20 December 1973. But then what does the term "endeavor" really mean in diplomacy?

Phase II: Mellowing?

By early June—that is, soon after the Golan disengagement agreement—there were indications that the American position on the matter of Palestinian representation had mellowed somewhat. On nationwide TV and in answer to a question that stressed Rabin's refusal to accept PLO representation at Geneva, Joseph Sisco had replied: "Well, I think that we will have to

---

[153] *Department of State Bulletin*, LXX, 1808 (18 February 1974), pp. 176–78.

[154] Sisco's decrial of 3 June 1974, in *Department of State Bulletin*, LXXI, 1827 (1 July 1974), p. 12.

[155] Sheehan, *The Arabs, Israelis, and Kissinger*, p. 132.

wait and see....I think it is premature to tell as to with whom negotiations will be conducted in the future, and I think we will just have to wait and see how it evolves. I think none of us would have predicted, for example, the amount of progress that has been made in the last six months."[156] More significantly, in answer to whether the US favored the presence of a Palestinian delegation in Geneva, he explained: "We have not taken any concrete position on this, for the following reasons. In the first instance, this is a matter for the Arab states and the Palestinians to determine."[157] Sisco did not offer any other reasons, and on this occasion did not tie the question to Israeli acceptance.

Two weeks later in Jerusalem, in answer to the query of how the Palestinians could be brought into the negotiating process, State Secretary Kissinger replied: "Of course, the most efficient way for the Palestinians to be brought into the process is through a Jordanian negotiation, in which there is the historical background and for which Israel has always declared its readiness in principle."[158]

As to the proposed federal links between Jordan and Palestine, the matter was being discussed in the US as early as March. At a University of Chicago roundtable discussion between Under-Secretary of State Joseph Sisco and some American Middle East experts, the federal solution was seen in positive terms. Sisco informed the participants that this was basically King Hussein's approach also.[159]

But perhaps one of the most comprehensive statements on the Palestinian policy of the Nixon-Kissinger administration was articulated by Assistant Secretary of State Alfred Atherton in late July. To the question, "Would the United States be in favor of the establishment of a Palestinian state, say on the West Bank, and as a corollary to that is the United States or has the United States been engaged in discussions with Palestinian groups?," he replied:

> I welcome a chance to clarify our policy—the United States Government policy—on the Palestinian problem, because I have the impression that perhaps there is some misunderstanding what that policy is. I would say several things. First of all, there is a great deal of sympathy in the United States for the Palestini-

---

[156] *Department of State Bulletin*, LXXI, 1827 (1 July 1974), p. 13.
[157] *Ibid.*
[158] *Ibid.*, LXXI, 1829 (15 July 1974), p. 125.
[159] *Ibid.*, LXXI, 1834 (19 August 1974), p. 299.

ans, for their plight over the years. I should add, I think, that this sympathy tends to be undermined sometimes when acts of violence are committed in the area in the name of the Palestinians. Some way must be found to involve the Palestinians in the process and to see that their interests are taken into account in the final settlement. Now at the present time and during this summer of preparation for Geneva, there are discussions in the Arab world of exactly how the Palestinians will be involved in the process. I think also a great deal of discussion of this is going on in Israel. For our part, I think it would be premature for me to say what our specific ideas are as to how the answer to this problem can be found. But that an answer must be found is very clear to us. The question of how the Palestinians will be represented or will participate in the Geneva Conference is obviously one that is very much in everybody's mind. In that connection our position is—and this is a position that we and the Soviet Union have jointly enunciated in the communiqué in Moscow at the end of the last summit meeting—that the question of additional participants in the Geneva Conference, that is, additional to the original participating governments, is something the Conference itself is going to have to decide, and I would not try to prejudge or foreshadow what that decision will be, because it has to be made by all the participants jointly.[160]

As the stalemate on the Jordan set in, principally because of Israel's intransigence and Kissinger's unwillingness to pressure the Rabin cabinet, and as the Arab states prepared for the Rabat summit, the international stature of the PLO continued to grow. The State Secretary once again visited the Near East in the first half of October to float a possible Sinai II disengagement and to convince President Sadat to back King Hussein rather than the PLO at the impending Arab summit.[161] This aspect of the Kissinger scenario is most unclear. One is tempted to think that he could not have been serious; he had done virtually nothing to enhance the Jordanian king's position. On the other hand, perhaps he no longer thought in terms of a disengagement on the Jordan; the Rabat summit decision would then bring him relief and an occasion to shed crocodile tears.

---

[160] Transcript of the interview, published by the US Embassy in Beirut on 1 August 1974.
[161] Sheehan, *The Arabs, Israelis, and Kissinger*, p. 148.

Meanwhile, at the UN the United States showed how out-of-phase it had become with respect to the world community. On 14 October Ambassador John Scali cast his vote against the UN General Assembly resolution to invite the PLO to its plenary meetings. The resolution was adopted with 105 in favor, 4 against, and 20 abstentions. In explaining his country's decision, Scali said: "Our vote today in no way reflects a lack of understanding or sympathy for the very real concerns and yearning for justice of the Palestinian people."[162] He also recognized that the Palestinian problem was the very heart of the Arab-Israeli conflict. Nonetheless, the blind spot concerning the PLO remained.

And then there was the Arab summit at Rabat, which many analysts have interpreted as a major setback for US diplomacy in the Arab-Israeli conflict. However, there is more than a hint that it had merely confirmed a decision already taken by Henry Kissinger to abandon his disengagement on the Jordan initiative, in line with and to the great relief of the Israeli triumvirate of Rabin, Peres, and Allon. This does not mean, however, that Rabat did not reflect the realities of the Arab situation. Nor does it mean that the two decisions to commit Egypt to a joint Arab position on the Syrian and Jordanian fronts and to recognize the PLO as the sole sovereign representative of the Palestinians were not in themselves significant achievements in the long and complex Arab-Israeli struggle.

Phase III: Post-Rabat Retrenchment and Confusion

In the aftermath of the Rabat summit, the State Secretary paid a quick visit (5–7 November) to the capitals of Egypt, Saudi Arabia, Jordan, Syria, and Israel to assess for himself whether Egypt was now obligated to negotiate as part of a united Arab diplomatic front that included the PLO, or whether enough flexibility was retained for Egypt to pursue separate talks on a second-stage disengagement. It would seem that Kissinger got the impression that there was wide Arab support for his continued diplomatic effort and that the Rabat summit would not stand in the way of President Sadat's willingness to seek further progress in the Sinai.

In Riyadh, he heard from Foreign Minister 'Umar al-Saqqāf that Saudi oil policy sought to keep oil prices stable and even to work for a symbolic reduction. This was immensely pleasing, and he called Saqqāf "a voice for moderation and wisdom in the area."[163]

---

[162] *Department of State Bulletin*, LXXI, 1845 (4 November 1974), p. 622.

[163] *New York Times*, 7 November 1974, p. 3.

In Jordan, where he conferred with King Hussein, a differentiation was suggested between the West Bank as a diplomatic and as an administrative question. As to the former, the King reportedly claimed that in accordance with the Rabat decision he could not involve Jordan. On the other hand, with regard to the West Bank as an administrative and economic question, the King affirmed Jordan's continued involvement.[164] On his departure from Amman airport to the Syrian capital, Kissinger declared that the Arab summit decisions "had complicated the problem" of seeking a solution, a view that the American administration would repeat thereafter on numerous occasions.

In Syria, according to the *New York Times*, Kissinger told President Asad: "By giving the PLO the authority to administer any West Bank areas Israel may yield, the Arab leaders were in effect ruling out the recovery of any of that land, because Israel could not be expected to deal with a group that has consistently called for the destruction of Israel."[165] Clearly, the American Secretary of State was only repeating Israel's hard-line position.

What had the rapid visit of Kissinger accomplished? Probably not very much in terms of substantive gains. But the clarification in the aftermath of Rabat was important. He had also ensured that the door to negotiation was not slammed shut, and had therefore allayed fears of a possible resumption of an Arab-Israeli war, and an ensuing oil embargo. Finally, his diplomacy— with all its shortcomings—was still very much in the picture. He had received a public endorsement from President Sadat for his continuing step-by-step approach to negotiations.

Even before the State Secretary's rapid tour of the Near East, in fact on the very day that the Rabat decisions were announced, one of the first official reactions to the implications of the Arab summit regarding the increased diplomatic stature of the PLO came from President Ford. In a news conference at the White House on 29 October, he remarked: "The decision by the Arab nations to turn over the negotiating for the West Bank to the PLO may or may not—at this stage we aren't certain what impact it will have on our role in the Middle East." And he went on to add: "We of course feel that there must be movement toward settlement of problems between Israel and Egypt on the one hand, between Israel and Jordan *or the PLO* on the other, and the problems between Israel and Syria in the other category."[166]

---

[164] *Ibid.*, 8 November 1974, p. 3.

[165] *Ibid.*

[166] *Department of State Bulletin*, LXXI, 1848 (25 November 1974), p. 738 (italics added by this writer).

This reference to the PLO as a party in the negotiating process, coming as it did from the President himself, was bound to cause a stir. At first sight it appeared as a radical departure from the US position regarding the PLO and raised the question of its recognition with more positive implications. In any case, the President's reference was open to a wide range of interpretation.

In Israel the President's remarks were received with some concern, in spite of Ron Nessen's (the President's press secretary) prompt denial that the statement regarding the PLO represented any change in US policy.[167] The confusion in Washington was noted by the Israeli press, although both American and Israeli officials apparently insisted in private that the President, being a newcomer to foreign affairs, "misstated a delicate diplomatic phrase."[168] According to the *Jerusalem Post*, Israel was informed that the President's remark was a slip of the tongue. But the paper also noted that there was no amendment or retraction because the PLO statement "went over well in the Arab world."[169] However, to Matti Golan, the President's statement was a deliberate move planned by Kissinger to use the Rabat decision "as leverage with Israel for an agreement with Egypt."[170]

Whatever explanation one may wish to give to this unexpected incident, the State Department repeatedly underlined that there was no change in American policy regarding the PLO, and that the Rabat summit had complicated the situation.[171] The President himself, at a press conference in Phoenix, Arizona, on 14 November 1974, appeared to backtrack on his 29 October statement, insisting that only Israel could decide whether to negotiate with the PLO. However, here too the President's statements led to some confusion. In one passage he said: "Our plans are aimed at trying to get the Israelis to negotiate a settlement or additional settlements with the Egyptians and the other Arab nations."[172] Then, in response to a clarification question, he went on to add:

> I did say that the Israelis should negotiate with the Egyptian and other Arab parties. The Israelis have said they will never negotiate with the PLO. We are not a party to any negotiations.

---

[167] *Jerusalem Post*, 31 October 1974, p. 1.

[168] *Ibid.*, 1 November 1974, p. 1.

[169] *Ibid.*, 8 November 1974, p. 1.

[170] Golan, *Secret Conversations*, p. 227.

[171] *Department of State Bulletin*, LXXI, 1849 (2 December 1974), pp. 761–62.

[172] *Department of State Bulletin*, LXXI, 1850 (9 December 1974), p. 789.

I think we have to let the decision as to who will negotiate to be the responsibility of the parties involved.[173]

This discrepancy in the use of the terms "states" and "parties" virtually in the same passage was noted by observers: for instance, during Henry Kissinger's press conference in Tokyo, shortly after the President's Phoenix statement. Presumably "states" would exclude the PLO, whereas "parties" might include it.

One more attempt at "clarification" needs to be mentioned. In an interview conducted for the United States Information Service on 18 November 1974 by Marie Koenig (USIS diplomatic correspondent), Dean Milles (*Baltimore Sun*), and George Sherman (Public Affairs Officer in the Near East and South Asia Bureau of the State Department), Under-Secretary of State Joseph Sisco added his own contribution to the confusion regarding the PLO:

> *Question*: Does the United States now regard the PLO as a party?
> *Sisco*: The PLO, we regard the PLO as the overall umbrella organization of the Palestinians. We also believe that in order to achieve any kind of a durable peace the legitimate interests of the Palestinians have to be taken into account. I think we've made this very clear indeed. Insofar as the parties to the negotiations are concerned, I would recall to you what was agreed to at the time of the convening of the Geneva Conference: specifically what was agreed to by the participants at the Geneva Conference—ourselves, the Soviet Union, the others—that the question of any other participants, the question of anyone else being involved in the Geneva negotiations, and in that process, that was a decision that had to be made by the Geneva participants. And there is no change in American policy in that regard.[174]

The far-reaching importance of the Under-Secretary of State's formulation—"The PLO, we regard the PLO as the overall umbrella organization of the Palestinians"—is obvious; it represented a significant evolution in US policy. But here again confusion was compounded, for two days later, he made an equally significant retraction on a widely publicized American television program. The interviewer, Richard Valeriani, asked: "Mr. Sisco,

[173] *Department of State Bulletin*, LXXI, 1852 (23 December 1974), p. 890.
[174] Excerpted from the transcript of the USIS interview, published by the US Embassy in Beirut on 20 November 1974.

you said on Monday in an interview to be published outside the country that the United States now regards the Palestine Liberation Organization (PLO) as the umbrella organization for all Palestinians. Now, that seems to go further than you've ever gone before."[175] Joseph Sisco's answer was, to say the least, odd:

> I think that was an unfortunate way to put it. Actually what I was trying to reflect was that the Arabs consider the PLO as the umbrella organization. Now, let me make very clear that our policy is as stated by the President and the Secretary of State. We've accorded no recognition of any kind; our position remains unchanged. I think some people have read something into that—I was really trying to state a fact as conceived by the Arabs, that the Arabs do conceive of the PLO as the umbrella organization.[176]

In actual fact, the Under-Secretary of State had said no such thing in the USIS interview conducted two days earlier. He had clearly stated at the time that "we" (i.e., the US) regarded the PLO as the overall umbrella organization of the Palestinians. There is no reference in the question or in Sisco's answer to any Arab view or conception of the PLO. On the contrary, there is every indication that he was referring to the US view or conception. The question had specifically asked: "Does the United States now regard the PLO as a party?" And his answer was: "The PLO, we regard the PLO as the overall umbrella organization of the Palestinians. We also believe that in order to achieve any kind...etc." The "we" in both instances could not possibly mean the Arabs.

The Sisco statement was received with consternation by the Israeli press, especially as it had coincided with a Palestinian guerrilla attack on Beisan aimed at releasing Arab prisoners held in Israeli jails, including Archbishop Hilarion Capucci. David Landau, diplomatic correspondent of the *Jerusalem Post*, claimed that "Joseph Sisco has been known for some time to be further advanced than Dr. Kissinger himself in advocating a revision of US thinking vis-à-vis the PLO."[177] Joseph Sisco had to retract in an interview he accorded to an Israeli journalist. But the transcript of the original Sisco statement of 18 November regarding the PLO was published unedited. In

---

[175] Interview conducted by Richard Valeriani and Barbara Walters for NBC's "Today" show; *Department of State Bulletin*, LXXI, 1850 (9 December 1974), p. 790.

[176] *Ibid.*

[177] *Jerusalem Post*, 20 November 1974, p. 1.

Israel both the *Likud* and the *Aguda* blocs requested debates in the Knesset on Sisco's remarks.[178]

Undoubtedly, both the importance of the President's 29 October statement and the frequency and intensity of the denials and clarifications—often leading to further ambiguity, as in the Sisco PLO episode—raise serious questions. Was President Ford's reference a calculated attempt by a new President to assert his prerogatives in matters of foreign policy in the face of a controversial Secretary of State who was then on one of his periodic absences from the country? Were the Ford and Sisco statements in the nature of trial balloons designed to test both domestic and international reaction? Were they a reflection of the often-cited differences within the State Department between the conventional "Establishment" and a "pushy" Secretary of State prone to strike out on his own and to keep his colleagues in the dark? Or in the case of the President was it merely a *lapsus linguae* combined perhaps with insufficient briefing by his staff?

The first hypothesis—namely, a deliberate move on the part of the President—seems highly improbable. Gerald Ford was then in the Presidential seat vacated by Richard Nixon for only a couple of months and would hardly be in a position for such a major initiative. Besides, he was never much of an expert on foreign policy and appeared to be happy to leave such tortuous matters to the discretion of his powerful Secretary of State. The second and third hypotheses are more plausible and would tend to explain the retreat into confusion as a possible way out of a sticky situation produced by the trial balloons. Perhaps the most plausible is the *lapsus linguae* hypothesis, especially as President Ford is known for such slips of tongue and memory. Yet one must attempt to explore the circumstances and context of the *lapsus*. It is, as Freud tells us, seldom a mere accident. Rather, in political life it is more often a reflection of intense preoccupation and indecisiveness: in this particular case, the preoccupation of the Washington scene with the PLO issue.

However, in the case of Joseph Sisco, if it was at all a *lapsus*, it was probably deliberate. In the aftermath of the Rabat decisions this seasoned diplomat and experienced spokesman "zigged and zagged in talking about Washington's view of the PLO."[179] With this kind of diplomatic upmanship he was intimating a change in Washington's position without actually having to say it aloud and explicitly. Besides, this may have also been a signal to

---

[178] *Ibid.*, 21 November 1974, pp. 1, 2.

[179] Erwin Frenkel, "Changing the Gears of Policy," *Jerusalem Post*, 22 November 1974.

the Arabs that Washington was to some extent coming round to their Rabat position on the status of the PLO, yet that the shift would have to take time and preparation.[180]

Whatever the explanation of this series of real or simulated lapses, the picture that emerges is one of confusion.

Phase IV: Yasir Arafat at the United Nations

The growing recognition of the PLO by the international community was symbolized by the appearance of Yasir Arafat before the United Nations in New York on 13 November. To say the least, the American administration had shown no enthusiasm for this historic initiative: in fact, its UN delegation had voted against it. The carefully prepared address before the General Assembly was widely seen as moderate and statesmanlike. It was the dramatic speech of a revolutionary leader who pleaded: "I have come to you bearing an olive branch and the freedom-fighter's gun. Do not let the olive branch fall from my hand."[181]

Nevertheless, the American administration chose to ignore the olive branch. It wanted to see him only in terms of the gun. On the eve of his departure with President Ford to the much-heralded Vladivostok summit, Henry Kissinger reflected on the PLO phenomena. Questioned on whether Israel was going to have to negotiate with the PLO in view of the recognition accorded by Rabat and the UN General Assembly, the Secretary of State insisted: "The proper negotiation, or the best negotiation for the future of the West Bank, was between Jordan and Israel...the US had used its influence to bring about such a negotiation."[182] He then added: "As to any other parties that might negotiate, this is entirely a decision for Israel and for any of the other parties that may be involved, and it is not a matter on which the United States will give advice as to the conditions in which such negotiations may be appropriate, if indeed it is appropriate."[183] In the same interview Kissinger commented on the two-day-old speech of Yasir Arafat. "Our reading of it," he said, "is that it called for a state which really did not include the existence of Israel and therefore was dealing with a successor state, and we do not consider this a particularly moderate position."[184]

---

[180] *Ibid.*

[181] [See the English translation in *Journal of Palestine Studies*, IV.2 (Winter 1975), p. 194.]

[182] *Department of State Bulletin*, LXXI, 1850 (9 December 1974), p. 782.

[183] *Ibid.*

[184] *Ibid.*, p. 783.

On this occasion, the Secretary of State also indicated that he had no immediate plans for another visit to the Near East: "We think that this is now a period of quiet diplomacy, and I do not expect to return to the Middle East in the near future."[185] The disenchantment of Dr. Henry Kissinger was plain.

A few days later, Under-Secretary of State Joseph Sisco confirmed in greater detail the remarks of his superior. He denied that there was any preparation for bringing the PLO into the negotiating process. His attitude to Arafat's speech was entirely negative:

> I found no openings in that speech. As the Secretary of State said in his press conference last Friday, he hardly saw that as a moderate approach. There was no, for example, explicit or implicit implication of giving up terrorism as a matter of policy. The proposal for a secular state would really have the effect of negating the existence of the state of Israel as we know it.[186]

Likewise, Sisco had nothing positive to say about the Rabat decisions. They had complicated the American peace effort, in his view. And he went on to repeat Kissinger's statement that the coming weeks would be "a period of quiet diplomacy, largely within the confines of diplomatic channels."[187]

At the Vladivostok summit Brezhnev and Ford reaffirmed their intention to uphold UN Security Council Resolution 338 "with due account taken of the legitimate interests of all peoples of the area, including the Palestinian people, and respect for the right of all states of the area to independent existence."[188] Apart from the fact that it seemed to bring the Soviet Union back into the picture as co-chairman of the Geneva Conference, and apart from the obvious value of repetition, there was no significant progress in the Palestinian direction: the term "interests" instead of "rights" was still in usage. Perhaps the Vladivostok accord limiting the number of strategic nuclear weapons and delivery vehicles through 1985 was an important breakthrough in efforts to halt the arms race, and a gain for détente. But from the point of view of the Palestinians it was hardly a revelation: on the contrary, the loosely worded summit communiqué could be interpreted as an implicit backing for Henry Kissinger's step-by-step approach to peace.

---

[185] *Ibid.*

[186] *Ibid.*, p. 790.

[187] *Ibid.*

[188] *Soviet News* (London), no. 5763, 26 November 1974, p. 442.

As the end of the year loomed in sight, the official position of the American administration, after hesitation and confusion, was back essentially to the Israeli hard line. In a 9 December interview with *Newsweek*, President Ford said that at this point the US should not have any diplomatic contacts with the Palestine Liberation Organization. The whole question, for him, was still premature. Nor did he think that the PLO's recognition by the UN was anything really positive; in terms of a peace settlement, he like Kissinger assessed that it had "complicated the situation."[189] As to the Secretary of State, he was asked on 18 December: "What would be the necessary condition before the PLO and Israel could sit down together and talk?" His answer was:

> It is impossible for the United States to recommend negotiation with the PLO until the PLO accepts the existence of Israel as a legitimate state. As long as the PLO proposals envisage, in one form or another, the destruction of Israel, we don't see much hope for negotiation with the PLO.[190]

Nonetheless, in contrast to the intransigent attitude of their Administration regarding the non-contact with the PLO, a group of Senators and Congressmen did meet with the PLO delegation at the United Nations in November. This perhaps historic event was believed to have been sponsored by Senator James Abourezk, and included the following Senators and Congressmen: Senators James Abourezk (D. South Dakota), Dewey F. Bartlett (R. Oklahoma), Walter F. Huddleston (D. Kentucky), Gale W. McGee (D. Wyoming), and Frank E. Moss (D. Utah); and Congressmen Tom Bevill (D. Alabama), Donald Clancy (R. Ohio), Cardiss Collins (D. Illinois), Paul Cronin (R. Massachusetts), Clarence Long (D. Maryland), George O'Brien (R. Illinois), Edward Derwinski (R. Illinois), and Joseph Vigirito (D. Pennsylvania). According to the *New York Times*, the thrust of the American interest during the meeting was the impact of a possible West Bank Palestinian state on Israel, whether such a nation would signify the destruction of Israel. Some Americans later expressed the opinion that the PLO delegation had shown moderation, were interested in an "interim accommodation," and "were ready for a compromise on their proclaimed goals of struggle."[191]

---

[189] *Newsweek*, 9 December 1974, p. 33.
[190] *Department of State Bulletin*, LXXII, 1856 (20 January 1975), pp. 58–59.
[191] *New York Times*, 15 November 1974, p. 17.

Pressure Group Activity: the Cases of Rockefeller and Brown

The Questioning of Vice-Presidential Designate Nelson Rockefeller

In November, while the Administration was busy making ambiguous statements concerning its policy toward the PLO, Nelson Rockefeller, the President's nominee for the office of Vice-President, was subjected to close questioning by Congressman Joshua Eilberg (D. Pennsylvania) during the Congressional hearings convened by the Judiciary Committee of the House of Representatives to confirm this nomination. American law provides for public discussions of the competence and qualifications of such nominees; and where Governor Nelson Rockefeller was concerned, one of the main topics was the impact of his immense wealth, and consequently, his influence on Vice-Presidential and Presidential policies, especially in light of his immediate succession in the event of the President's death.

Eilberg put the following questions to Rockefeller: "What are your feelings about the current situation in the Middle East, and would you as President, without a mutual agreement with Israel, recognize the Palestine Liberation Organization as the spokesman for the Palestinian people?" Rockefeller ducked the question, saying:

> We cannot deal with problems with simplified headlines, or a half a minute on television, and have the American people understand the complexity....Now, this situation has now come to a point where other possible solutions that might have taken place earlier were passed up, and now this has come to the confrontation which many people feared, which is should this organization be recognized.

Eilberg cut him off and said: "What is your answer? What would your answer be?" Rockefeller tried to leave the subject of recognition open, and replied: "I would have to talk with the Israelis about how they feel and what are the possibilities of getting some solution....I don't know what the answer is."

Although Ford, Kissinger, and Sisco—each in his own special way—had all given rather definitive answers concerning any American recognition of the PLO, the vice-presidential designate seemed to waver on the subject and refused to say unequivocally, "Of course not." Eilberg pursued his question and said: "Israel does not recognize or would not recognize or would not deal with the Palestine Liberation Organization." This time Rockefeller interrupted and said, "Not yet." But this did not deter the Democratic Congressman from Pennsylvania, who continued: "And so I am asking you, if you had to face this question at this time, what would your answer be?" Not interested in placating the Israelis, their American constituencies, or the powerful pro-Israel lobby in the US, Governor Rockefeller replied:

> My answer would be I would sit down with the leaders of the Israeli Government and I would say, all right, here is the reality and how are we going to deal with it? If you will forgive me, sir, this happens to be their problem. This is not our problem. This is their problem. They live over there. These people were on their land, and they took the land.

To this Eilberg replied: "Governor, I think your position and my position are somewhat different. I think it is more our problem than you think it is."[192]

The story did not end here. Predictably enough, several powerful Jewish-American organizations reacted with hostility to Rockefeller, for he had failed to express the blind commitment to Israel generally expected from American political figures. Furthermore, he had raised a sensitive subject— that of the expulsion from Palestine of its original inhabitants. The campaign precipitated by Rockefeller's position was in many ways typical of the pressure tactics collectively pursued by these groups. Rabbi Israel Miller, president of the Conference of Presidents of Major American Jewish Organizations (the umbrella organization for 33 Jewish groups), demanded that Rockefeller give a "prompt clarification" of his observations concerning the PLO and of his statement that "these people (i.e., the Palestinians) were on their land, and they (the Zionists) took the land." In an open letter, he also attacked Rockefeller for failing to "support the present position of our (the American) government."[193] Rabbi Arthur Hertzberg, president of the American Jewish Congress, also mounted a bitter attack on the vice-presidential designate for failing to condemn the PLO during the public hearings.[194]

Such tactics of repeated attacks usually end in unqualified success. Forced to yield to this mounting pressure, the American vice-presidential designate

---

[192] *Confirmation Hearings before the Judiciary Committee of the House of Representatives*, preliminary transcript (1974), pp. 137–40. [See the relevant extracts reprinted in *International Documents on Palestine, 1974*, p. 358.]

[193] *Jerusalem Post*, 1 December 1974, p. 4.

[194] *Ibid.*

issued a corrective statement representing the "prompt clarification" demanded by Rabbi Miller. Printed on the first page of the *New York Times*, it stated:

> In no portion of my reply did I intend to modify in any way the position of the President or the Secretary of State regarding the PLO, or to urge the State of Israel to negotiate with the PLO, an organization that has called for the elimination of the Jewish state. Neither did I, in my statement, in any way intend to weaken the enduring commitment of the United States for a strong and independent Israel, which is, and has been, a cardinal principle of United States foreign policy.[195]

This incident was yet another clear example of the continuing inability of any high-ranking American official to take a position, or even to utter a sentence, no matter how innocuous, that does not express blind support for Israel.

The General Brown Affair

On 10 October 1974, General George Brown, Chairman of the Joint Chiefs of Staff (the highest military figure in the US), addressed a group of students at Duke University. He made certain off-the-record remarks concerning the powerful Jewish influence in US politics that went unnoticed until a recording of his statements was leaked to the *Washington Post*. Over a month later, as the Arabs were conducting their UN campaign, which included speeches before the General Assembly on the Palestine question by PLO leader Yasir Arafat and Lebanese President Suleiman Franjieh (13 and 14 November), the *Washington Post* released General Brown's statements in an obvious attempt to steal the headlines from the well-coordinated Arab campaign to bring American and world attention to the Palestine question.

The general had allowed himself to be drawn by a student at Duke University into sensitive ground watched over by one of the most powerful and organized of pressure machines. In answer to a question regarding the possibility of another oil embargo, he had observed: "The American people might get tough-minded enough to set down the Jewish influence in this country and break that lobby."[196] He also remarked that this influence "is so strong

---

[195] *New York Times*, 1 December 1974.
[196] *New York Times*, 14 November 1974, p. 1.

you wouldn't believe it; now they own, you know, the banks in this country, the newspapers. Just look at where the Jewish money is."[197] He also remarked that Israel had undue influence in the Congress, particularly over such matters as the supply, in terms of quantity and quality, of the latest military equipment. General Brown had dared to expose the pro-Israel lobby in the United States, thus bringing "a heavy thud of rebukes down on his head."[198] The Jewish War Veterans of America demanded that the general be fired for what they called his "undeniable anti-Semitic venom."[199] Pro-Israeli Senators and Congressmen also asked for his removal, accusing him of anti-Semitism (Senator William Proxmire) and even of acting like a Nazi (Representatives Bella Abzug and Edward Koch).[200]

On 13 November, as Yasir Arafat spoke in New York, General Brown publicly recanted, expressing his regrets in a statement issued by the Department of Defense and characterizing his comments as having been unfounded, ill-considered, and as not representing his convictions.[201] This apparently was not sufficient. President Ford called the nation's top military officer to the White House and personally administered a severe—and much publicized—reprimand, thus lowering the prestige of his own chief-of-staff. The witch hunt continued with Jewish American groups pressing for this distinguished soldier's dismissal. Then all of a sudden the campaign was switched off. A backlash in favor of Brown was visibly emerging. He had, after all, expressed feelings shared by a large American public. Moreover, he was being victimized. There is a suggestion that the campaign against him was called off because his dismissal would have only served to reinforce the thought present in many American minds that the Jewish lobby is all-powerful.

In actual fact, the context of General Brown's remarks at Duke University concerning the role of Israelis and Jews in American politics reflected a deep-seated resentment in the US defense establishment against the priority accorded to Israel in military needs. The Pentagon was finding its own defense requirements affected by the flood of American arms shipments to Israel. Pentagon officials openly voiced that weapons in short supply—particularly tanks, TOW anti-tank missiles, "smart" bombs, and fighter aircraft—were being siphoned off in response to pressures exerted by the pro-Israel lobby in

---

[197] *Ibid.*
[198] *The Economist*, 23 November 1974, p. 56.
[199] *Ibid.*
[200] *Near East Report*, 47 (20 November 1974), p. 244.
[201] *New York Times*, 14 November 1974, p. 1.

Washington and its power over Congress. The dimension of this lobby was vividly exposed by General Brown: "We have the Israelis coming to us for equipment. We say we can't possibly get the Congress to support a program like this. And they say, don't worry about the Congress, we will take care of the Congress."[202]

It is this exposure—more than the remarks concerning Jewish wealth in America—that was particularly galling to the pro-Israel lobby and its supporters in Congress. It showed that the representatives of the nation were in a sense subservient to a lobby working on behalf of a foreign state. Apart from Senators Fulbright and Abourezk, very few public figures had ever decried Israeli and Jewish influence on Congress. Now the Chairman of the Joint Chiefs of Staff had added his remarks regarding this all-persuasive and powerful influence. Predictably, "the plethora of vociferous and well-organized Jewish lobbies"[203] were after his head, but stopped short when the backlash of "middle America" developed.

In fact, Israeli Prime Minister Rabin found it advisable to pay a compliment to the general. "General Brown," he said, "probably helped Israel during the last war more than anyone else." He also went on to warn the public "not to talk too much about the power of the Jewish lobby in the US. Too much stress here on Jewish pressure in Washington will finally boomerang."[204]

Conclusion

By the end of the year the warm relationship established between the US and some of the Arab states was showing signs of strains. The promises that the American step-by-step approach had evoked were only partially fulfilled. President Ford was rushing to Israel a massive supply of ultra-sophisticated weapons, which included the Lance missile in a version capable of modification for nuclear warheads, and advanced fighter aircraft. The press continuously spoke of impending moves against Arab oil producers, including military action; it was believed that such reports were emanating from the corridors of power in Washington. It is true that some initial exploration toward a second-stage disengagement in the Sinai had started, but it was also clear that the Israelis were intent on dragging the issue to the

---

[202] *The Economist*, 23 November 1974, p. 56.
[203] *Jerusalem Post*, 6 December 1974, p. 2.
[204] *Ibid.*

maximum and obtaining, in the meantime, several billions of dollars worth of American economic and military aid.

There was a general mood of disappointment in the Arab world. President Sadat's Washington trip, scheduled to take place in November, was postponed indefinitely. There were signs that Congress was going to block the $25 million assistance program to Egypt. Furthermore, a letter to President Ford dated 9 December and signed by 71 Senators, denounced the growing prominence of the PLO and reaffirmed American commitment to Israel.[205]

The improvised pragmatism of Henry Kissinger had yielded some results at first, but by the end of the year it was clearly in trouble. In conclusion, perhaps George Ball's criticism of the Kissingerian approach during 1974 is worth keeping in mind:

> Highly personalized diplomacy is effective only in a bilateral setting; it has limited value in a complex situation involving many countries. Thus the attempt to settle the Arab-Israeli issue by shutting out both the more activist Arab states and the Soviet Union was predestined to failure. "Shuttle diplomacy" could be used to adjust minor technical issues...but there was no practical way to apply the technique to the hard substantive issues that involve all Arab states.[206]

[205] *International Documents on Palestine, 1974*, p. 371, doc. 193.
[206] George Ball, "The Looming War in the Middle East and How to Avert It," *Atlantic Monthly*, January 1975, pp. 10–11.

16

The United States, the Arab-Israeli Conflict, and the Palestine Question in 1975*

IN THIS SURVEY of United States policy toward the Arab-Israeli conflict and the Palestine question for the year 1975, attention has been focused on six topics presented in chronological order: 1) the threat of military seizure of oil; 2) the negotiations for a second-stage Sinai agreement, January to March; 3) reassessment: how real was it?; 4) the Sinai II accord; 5) Kissinger's and Fulbright's assessment of the Sinai accord; 6) the Ford administration and the PLO; the Saunders Document.

During the first quarter of the year, the center of the stage was occupied by the well-coordinated campaign of American threats of military intervention to seize Arab oil fields, which was coupled with moves by the Ford administration to place maximum pressure on the Arab boycott of American firms dealing with Israel. The campaign acted as a backdrop to State Secretary Kissinger's attempts to fashion a second-stage accord between Egypt and Israel, which brought him to the Near East in February on an exploratory mission and again in March with reasonably high hopes to achieve an accord.

In the meantime, on the Lebanese front, Israel was conducting a systematic bombardment of towns, villages, and economic targets in southern Lebanon, combined with infantry assaults across the border, such as at Kfar Shūbā, thus provoking an exodus of the rural population to ur-

---

*From the original English text translated and published as "Al-Wilāyāt al-muttahida al-amīrkīya," in *Al-Kitāb al-sanawī li-l-qadīya al-filastīnīya li-'ām 1975*, edited by Camille Mansour (Beirut: Institute for Palestine Studies, 1978), pp. 455–95.

ban centers and eroding the already fragile demographic fabric of Lebanese society. This scorched-earth policy, openly espoused by General Moshe Dayan, was brought to the attention of the US Senate by Senator James Abourezk.[1]

By the end of March, Kissinger's diplomatic initiative had ended in a deadlock situation and was therefore described as a failure. Amerian diplomacy, especially seen in the context of failures in Vietnam and elsewhere, suffered an additional and serious setback. Thereafter, the focus of attention shifted to the American capital, with the shuttle going, so to speak, in reverse gear.

During the next three months—April to June—the Ford administration, in response to the deadlock, embarked on a loudly advertised "reassessment" of its entire Near Eastern policy. The implication was that Israel should no longer expect privileged treatment in terms of military, financial, and diplomatic support. Ford and Kissinger publicly blamed Israeli intransigence for the March collapse and hinted that Geneva would have to be taken seriously as an option, in which case the United States would probably have to reveal its own plans for a comprehensive settlement, an initiative that Israeli strategy has sought to negate ever since the Rogers Plan. The Administration also hinted that "reassessment" would include a reexamination of Palestinian participation.

During this period the pro-Israel lobby in the United States mounted an unprecedented campaign of pressure against the Ford administration that culminated in a letter to the American President, signed by 76 Senators on 21 May, reminding him of the "special relationship" between Israel and the United States and urging that the military and financial aid requirements of Israel be fully met. At the same time, the tenors of the lobby led the attack against the Administration's proposal to supply Hawk missiles to Jordan and fighter aircraft to Saudi Arabia.

In the end, a hesitant Ford retreated in the face of such determined opposition. Reassessment was quietly dropped and with it the Geneva option. Shuttle diplomacy aimed at achieving a second-stage accord between Israel and Egypt was revived, which is probably what the Ford administration wanted anyway. The meeting in Salzburg betwen Presidents Ford and Sadat on 1 and 2 June seemed to indicate that a limited agreement in Sinai was attainable. An American civilian presence in the strategic Giddī Pass, particularly at the electronic surveillance station at Umm Khushayba to monitor

---

[1] *Congressional Record* (Senate), 25 February 1975, p. S2586.

violations, seemed to offer a compromise between the Israeli insistence on remaining in the passes and the Egyptian insistence that Israel evacuate the passes.

Thereafter, the road to the Sinai II accord was much smoother, particularly after Israel obtained the promise of unprecedented financial, military, and diplomatic support in return for a more flexible position during the renewed negotiations with Egypt through the State Secretary. By the time Kissinger left on his 20 August shuttle, agreement was within reach.

The specific details of the agreement and its far-reaching implications, as well as its assessment by Kissinger and Fulbright, feature prominently in this chapter. It is clear that American diplomatic flexibility was lost following the "secret pledge" made to Israel. Instead, the Ford administration was tied down more closely than ever to Israel's strategy of stalemate politics, and therefore was incapable of working for further accords on other sectors of the conflict, as called for by UN Security Council Resolution 242.

The last section of the chapter deals with the Saunders Document, one of the most comprehensive statements ever made by any US administration on the Palestine issue. Released during the heated debate of the United Nations vote that described "Zionism as a form of racism and racial discrimination" (10 November 1975), which was bitterly opposed by the United States, the Saunders Document aimed to keep certain Arab options open. However, although observers could detect a minor shift in American policy toward the Palestinian equation, it was hardly substantive. Besides, Kissinger deliberately took his distance from it in public when faced with Israeli and lobby pressure.

Finally, late in 1975 a report of the Middle East study group of the prestigious Brookings Institution was published. It was entitled "Toward Peace in the Middle East" and reflected an American consensus on the broad lines of a comprehensive Arab-Israeli peace agreement.[2] However, its impact, coming as it did during the last days of 1975, was very little in terms of that year, and will therefore be discussed in the context of 1976.[3]

---

[2] *International Documents on Palestine, 1975*, edited by Jorgen S. Nielsen (Beirut: Institute for Palestine Studies, 1977), pp. 328–38, no. 194.

[3] [See p. 432 below.]

The Threat of Military Seizure of Arab Oil

The Ford Administration and the Threat of Intervention

On the all-important oil crisis front, the year 1975 opened with the late-December provocative remarks of State Secretary Henry Kissinger regarding the possible use of military force against Arab oil-producing states holding the center of attention. In the *Business Week* interview he had said: "I am not saying that there is no circumstance where we would not use force. But it is one thing to use it in the case of a dispute over price, it is another when there is some actual strangulation of the industrialized world."[4] And he had gone on to affirm—normally one such reference is one too many—that the "use of force would be considered only in the gravest emergency."[5]

In actual fact, the Secretary's remarks were a continuation of the saber-rattling campaign against Arab oil that had begun in the last quarter of 1974.[6] Only this time, both in terms of scope and intensity, the campaign reached new heights. Scholars, analysts from various think-tanks, and sensational journalists joined the Ford administration in the "seize Arab oil" bandwagon.

Following the release of the "strangulation" remarks by Kissinger, President Ford was questioned on the prospect of America using force in the Near East:

> I stand by the view that Henry Kissinger expressed in the *Business Week* [interview]. Now, the word "strangulation" is the key word. If you read his answer to a very hypothetical question, he didn't say that force would be used to bring a price change. His language said he wouldn't rule force out if the free world or the industrialized world would be strangled. I would affirm my support of that position as he answered that hypothetical question.[7]

In the same interview the President regarded the prospects of renewed fighting between the Arabs and Israelis as being very serious.

---

[4] *Business Week*, 13 January 1975, p. 69.

[5] *Ibid.*

[6] For details of the campaign and its repercussions, see Marwan Buheiry, "Al-Wilāyāt al-muttahida al-amīrkīya," in *Al-Kitāb al-sanawī li-l-qadīya al-filasṭīnīya li-'ām 1974*, edited by Camille Mansour (Beirut: Institute for Palestine Studies, 1977), pp. 365–71 [= pp. 338–46 above.]

[7] *Time*, 20 January 1975, pp. 27–28.

This was hardly the end of the "strangulation" affair. In a Washington press conference on 21 January, the President, far from ducking questions concerning the prospect of intervention, took his time to field them.[8] Such desire on the part of the Administration to encourage questions and speculation on the subject of military force was noted by observers. On 23 January the President, in a televised interview, was asked:

> The other day at your press conference, you were asked about Dr Kissinger's quote and the possibility of military intervention and something surprised me, Sir. You have been in politics for a long time and you are as expert a question-ducker as anybody in that trade. Why didn't you duck that question? Why didn't you just say that's hypothetical? You did go into some detail on it.[9]

And the President's answer is revealing:

> I did. In part, I reiterated what I had said, I think at a previous conference. I wanted it made as clear as I possibly could that this country, in case of economic strangulation—and the key word is "strangulation"—would take the necessary action for our self-preservation.[10]

The President was also asked whether, even under such circumstances, it was moral to take another nation's natural resources. And once more his answer was revealing. While recognizing that it was a troublesome question and that he hoped such action would not be necessary, he nevertheless remarked:

> It may not be right, but I think if you go back over the history of mankind, wars have been fought over natural resources from time immemorial....History, in the years before us, indicates quite clearly that that was one of the reasons why nations fought one another.[11]

This "saber-rattling" has to be seen in the context of a leak—confirmed by the Pentagon—that three American divisions were either being sent to or

[8] *Department of State Bulletin*, LXXII, 1859 (10 February 1975), p. 179.
[9] *Department of State Bulletin*, LXXII, 1860 (17 February 1975), p. 220.
[10] *Ibid.*
[11] *Ibid.*, p. 222.

being prepared for the Near East: one airborne, one armored, and one air mobile.[12]

Just as ominous were the Defense Secretary's remarks. On 14 January 1975 he indicated that the US would have recourse to force in the gravest emergency and that from a military point of view military intervention both in the Near East and the Gulf was practical: "It is indeed feasible to conduct military operations if necessity should arise."[13] To him, gravest emergency meant "the likelihood of the strangulation of the industrial economies of the West."[14] In the same interview, he said that there was nothing unusual about American marine amphibious exercises in the Mediterranean, and he refused to comment on whether the US carrier *Enterprise*, which was in the Indian Ocean, was heading to the Gulf. And yet in almost the same breath he insisted that the United States aimed at maintaining "friendly relations with the nations of the area." However, one reporter remarked:

> Mr. Secretary, I must say, Sir, you sound rather Delphic this morning. As far as I'm concerned, I am trying to sort out some of the enigmas you pose. On one hand you say we desire friendly relations with all the nations of the Middle East, but you are not hesitant, nor was Secretary Kissinger, nor was the President, about tossing about the necessity to take military actions should the gravest of circumstances arise. I have trouble putting together these two, if I may use the term, "saber-rattling" expressions.[15]

These examples of statements made by Kissinger, Ford, and Schlesinger were only part of the campaign. Equally important were the contributions by various individuals and pressure groups that added fuel to the near-hysteria surrounding the topic of the oil crisis and military intervention to seize Arab installations and fields.

Robert Tucker's "Oil: The Issue of American Intervention"

In the January issue of *Commentary*, an influential journal published by the American Jewish Committee and regarded as one of the principal

---

[12] *Ibid.*, p. 220.

[13] Excerpted from the transcript of US Secretary of Defense James Schlesinger's press conference published by the US Embassy in Beirut on 15 January 1975.

[14] *Ibid.*

[15] *Ibid.*

forums of the American Jewish intellectual establishment, Professor Robert Tucker (a leading figure among educators in political science) took up the technical feasiblity of seizing Arab fields by means of military intervention. He began by emphasizing that the oil crisis was one of the turning points of history and that until recently it would never have occurred, "because of the prevailing expectation that it would have led to armed intervention."[16] He argued that without intervention there was a "distinct possibility" of an economic and political disaster bearing more than a superficial resemblance to the economic disaster of the 1930s.[17] Therefore, to Tucker, this led to the question of "employing extraordinary means" to deal with the oil crisis. "Is military intervention technically feasible?," he asked. The answer was "yes," and it depended in the first place on "geography." This is how this expert on international relations at Johns Hopkins University put his inflammatory proposal:

> Since it is impossible to intervene everywhere, the feasibility of intervention depends upon whether there is a relatively restricted area which, if effectively controlled, contains a sufficient portion of present world oil production and proven reserves to provide reasonable assurance that its control may be used to break the present price structure by breaking the core of the cartel politically and economically....[18]

Such an area, to his mind, there was. And it happened to be the Arab shoreline of the Gulf:

> The one area that would appear to satisfy these requirements extends from Kuwait down along the coastal region to Qatar. It is this mostly shallow coastal strip less than 400 miles in length that provides 40 percent of present OPEC production and has by far the world's largest proven reserves (over 50 percent of total OPEC reserves and 40 percent of world reserves). Since it has no substantial centers of population and is without trees, its effective control does not bear even remote comparison with the experience of Vietnam.[19]

---

[16] Robert Tucker, "Oil: The Issue of American Intervention," *Commentary*, 59 (January 1975), p. 22.

[17] *Ibid.*

[18] *Ibid.*, p. 25.

[19] *Ibid.*

He was prepared to dismiss the possibility of Russian counter-intervention, principally because the Soviets did not possess the necessary naval capabilities for such action in the Gulf; and even if they did, "the balance of perceived interest" was against them: they simply did not have, in his view, the interest that the Americans had in the area.[20] He recognized that intervention would have to be undertaken by the United States unilaterally, "and, initially at least, in the face of condemnation by most of the world." This did not seem to worry him. What mattered was Western Europe and Japan; and these, later on, would be won over to the American action because there would be something in it for them too: namely oil, allocated "evenhandedly."[21] Significantly, he also argued that American seizure of Arab oil fields would "markedly improve Israel's position," adding: "It would be both useless and insincere to deny the benefits accruing to Israel from intervention, just as it is both useless and insincere to deny the present linkage between the oil crisis and the steady erosion of Israel's position."[22] As to the reaction of American public opinion, "if intervention were to promise success at relatively modest cost, opinion might well move in the direction of support."[23] In short, nothing does it like success. One might mention in passing that in the November issue of *Commentary* once again, Professor Tucker urged Israel to adopt a defense policy "based on a known nuclear deterrent."[24]

The Debate Over Seizure in the Press and in Congress

The remarks of Kissinger, backed by Ford and Schlesinger, together with the much-advertised and commented article of Professor Tucker, stimulated military discussion. The consensus among senior naval and infantry officers, as reported by the *New York Times*, was that the operation was "militarily feasible but politically disastrous."[25] However, there was disagreement as to the preferred target. Tucker's preference, as mentioned earlier, was for the 400-mile stretch from Kuwait down the Saudi Arabian coast to Qatar. This terrain, containing no large population and "no trees," appeared to have significant advantages from the point of view of seizure and control. However, other military strategists preferred the Libyan target, arguing that the factor

---

[20] *Ibid.*, p. 26.

[21] *Ibid.*, p. 28.

[22] *Ibid.*, p. 29.

[23] *Ibid.*

[24] *Time*, 17 November 1975, p. 23.

[25] Drew Middleton, "Military Men Challenge Mideast Force Strategy," *New York Times*, 10 January 1975, p. 3.

of surprise would be difficult to achieve in the Gulf area, where the airborne troops would have to be flown either from Mediterranean bases or from a naval task force in the Indian Ocean. Detection would be inevitable and the element of surprise gone. On the other hand, surprise, it was argued, would be more easily achieved in Libya through a combined air and sea strike.[26]

Blueprints for such takeovers remained the subject of open discussion. In an article entitled "Kissinger Views Make Serious Speculation of Idle Talk," Clifton Daniel of the *New York Times* affirmed: "Military action to solve the oil problem, once a matter for cocktail-party conversation in Washington, has become the subject of serious speculation."[27] And Senator J.W. Fulbright, who had just retired as chairman of the Senate Foreign Relations Committee, said he had "heard intervention discussed at dinner tables and in Capitol cloakrooms."[28] The pro-Israel lobby also joined in the game, but geared it to the campaign against arms supplies to Saudi Arabia. Thus the *Near East Report* remarked in mid-January: "Didn't Kissinger warn that we might have to take over oil-producing countries to avert 'strangulation'? Then why arm them against us?"[29]

Just as self-seeking and repugnant as Tucker's article was that of Miles Ignotus (presumably the pseudonym of Edward Luttwak, according to William Quandt) entitled "Seizing Arab Oil" and published in the March issue of-*Harper's*.[30] Ignotus, identified also as a Pentagon adviser, developed a rapid deployment strike scenario in which airborne divisions would embark on giant transport planes, refuel at Israeli bases, and proceed to drop some paratroopers who would seize key Saudi oil fields and guide the bulk of the American forces in.[31]

A similar scenario was reported in the *Sunday Times* on 9 February and was quoted in the *Arab Report and Record* as follows:

> The US National Security Council has completed a detailed review of top-secret Department of Defense plans to invade Saudi Arabian oil fields in the event of another Middle East war resulting in a further Arab oil embargo, the London *Sunday Times*

---

[26] *Ibid.*

[27] *New York Times*, 7 January 1975, p. 2.

[28] *Ibid.*

[29] *Near East Report*, 19.3 (15 January 1975), p. 9.

[30] William Quandt, *Decade of Decisions* (Berkeley: University of California Press, 1977), p. 260 n.

[31] Michael Klare, "La Stratégie américaine dans le Golfe Arabo-Persique," *Le Monde diplomatique*, March 1976, p. 6.

reported on February 9. The paper said that the plan, code-
named Dhahran Option Four, had been drawn up by the Pentagon and provided for a US attack on the oil field of Ghawar,
which contains 40 percent of the world's known oil reserves. The
attack would be led by nine airborne infantry battalions based in
North Carolina, which would be flown under escort to Dhahran
in the Gulf by way of the Israeli air base at Hatserim. The infantry battalions would seize the oil field at Dhahran, evacuate
US personnel, and move inland to Ghawar after capturing landing jetties and storage tanks at Ras Tanura. They would be
joined three days later by a Marine division of some 14,000 men
who would be sent to the Gulf by sea.[32]

Another contribution to this infamous literature came from the pen of
Walter Goodman. In an article entitled "Fair Game," published in the journal *The New Leader* (which incidentally had earlier published, in November
1974, Paul Seabury's article "Thinking about an Oil War"), Goodman argued: "Should [military intervention in the Gulf] be successful, should the
troops move in, quickly take over the fields and get the oil flowing again
without much delay or opposition, my guess is that the polls would show
overwhelming support for the action." And he added: "We should see a
flowering of friendship for the Israelis, who would then, willy nilly, be our
main allies in the area. At home, American Legionnaires and Zionists would
be trading plaques at patriotic banquets."[33] On the other hand, if this scenario did not work and the military situation became messy, "it could be
bad for the Jews here at home."[34]

The close connection between pro-Israeli stands and American intervention to seize Arab oil that was expressed by so many American Jews and
in their press was denounced by I.F. Stone, a prominent Jewish intellectual
and critic of Israel. He warned American Jews against proposing solutions
through war or stimulating "hate the Arabs" campaigns. He was troubled
by Tucker's article. "*Commentary* is published by the American Jewish
Committee," he wrote. "Nothing could be more dangerous for American
unity, for the future of the American Jewish community, and for Israel itself
than to have it look as if Jewish influence were trying to get the US into

---

[32] *Arab Report and Record*, 1-14 February 1975, p. 116.
[33] Walter Goodman, "Fair Game," *The New Leader*, 17 March 1975, p. 15.
[34] *Ibid.*

war with the Arabs, and take their richest resource from them."[35] However, it is significant that I.F. Stone's article was criticized in turn by Walter Goodman.[36]

On the other side of the debate, many articulate voices were heard against intervention, either on moral gounds or because it would not work. Arnaud de Borchgrave's article "Intervention Wouldn't Work" was one such contribution. After a visit to the scene of the proposed intervention, he concluded: "The notion is considered too absurd to contemplate; intervention would precipitate the very event it is supposed to prevent: the economic strangulation of Western industrialized society."[37] The opinion of Frank Jungers, chairman of the Saudi-owned Arabian American Oil Company (ARAMCO), as reported by Borchgrave, was equally emphatic: "If anyone were mad enough to commit such an act of folly, Aramco's production—a quarter of the world's oil exports, requiring the service of one-third of the world's tanker fleet—would be out of commission for at least two years."[38] Borchgrave was told by Saudi experts on the spot that the whole oil operation could be knocked out of action without having to blow up wells and cause widespread damage. This was a technical problem involving the destabilization of water or gas injection plants, to cite one example.

On the floor of the Senate, there was some criticism in January of the Ford administration's repeated statements regarding military intervention. A few Senators denounced the fact that oil seizure was being presented to the nation as a viable policy option. In this respect, Senator Mark Hatfield's reaction to the State Secretary's threat of intervention was particularly sharp. On 21 January in the Senate, he decried the mounting campaign of reports concerning direct military intervention against oil producers and deplored the threat to the fragile peace caused by such unwarranted tactics. In his address, Hatfield remarked:

> I will not stand before you today and pretend to understand the nuances and subtleties of Dr. Kissinger's moral juxtaposition, or what possible purpose he hopes to achieve by threatening overtly the countries of the Middle East and the fragile peace of a troubled world. For I can sense little reason for hope in the Secre-

[35] *Ibid.*, p. 14.
[36] *Ibid.*
[37] Arnaud de Borchgrave, "Intervention Wouldn't Work," *Newsweek*, 31 March 1975, p. 21.
[38] *Ibid.*

tary's remarks. Let me speak plainly. As every American real-
izes, Dr. Kissinger is not talking in the abstract about imaginary
crises, or hypothetical situations. He is talking and threatening
military action.[39]

Senator Hatfield's intervention was followed two days later by Senator
Jesse Helms, who also deplored both Kissinger's statements and the President's repeated endorsements: "These comments," Helms said, "have come
against a background of military manoeuvers in the Indian Ocean and the
Mediterranean that will be undoubtedly interpreted by the Middle East nations as saber rattling to match rhetoric."[40] He described the dispatch of the
Seventh Fleet Task Force to the Indian Ocean as "a rather clumsy attempt to
pressure the oil-producing nations."[41] As for the US marines' beach-landing
exercises in the Mediterranean, these "will not fail to be interpreted by the
oil-producing nations as practice for landings on their soil."[42] And he went
on to underline the Arab reactions to the American moves. Egypt saw them
as undermining American-Arab relations and the cause of peace. Algerian
President Houari Boumedienne declared that "the occupation of one Arab
state would be regarded as an occupation of the entire Arab world," and
added that such action would cause the destruction of oil installations.[43]

Senator Helms was joined by Senators Clifford Hansen and James Mc-
Clure, who both denounced the Administration's tactics. McClure spoke
out against the moral bankruptcy of those who advocate the seizure of oil:

> It is disturbing to me personally that it is even necessary for an
> American to stand up and publicly state he is opposed to invading
> an Arab nation and stealing their oil. The immorality of such a
> proposal is so evident that I would have expected an outpouring
> of protests from government leaders and those in private life who
> have so violently protested against war in the past. That such
> an outpouring has not occurred is a serious disappointment.[44]

The Administration had its own reasons for inventing the myth of strangulation and then reacting to it by a loud campaign of saber-rattling. To

---

[39] *Congressional Record* (Senate), 21 January 1975, p. S529.
[40] *Ibid.*, 23 January 1975, p. S790.
[41] *Ibid.*
[42] *Ibid.* p. S792.
[43] *Ibid.*
[44] *Ibid.*, p. S794.

begin with, this would shift the responsibility for the oil crisis onto a convenient scapegoat who would be punished through military intervention. At the same time, many analysts have confirmed that it is part of the Kissinger style to create sufficient apprehension and disorientation among the parties so that negotiations become productive. Besides, any student of history knows that "gunboat" diplomacy, as practiced by the Big Powers, is popular on the domestic scene and serves to unsettle the target of the diplomatic action.

As to why several influential organs of the American Jewish establishment and the pro-Israel lobby joined in with evident relish, here also the answer is hardly mysterious. For years, one of the cardinal points in Israel's propaganda routine has been to stress the strategic value of the Zionist state as an anti-Soviet ally and as a policeman for the United States in an oil-rich region. However, this myth was exploded with the October 1973 war. The so-called strategic value of Israel was greatly diminished—in fact, from a strategic point of view it was increasingly perceived as an embarrassment. The problem facing the lobby and its supporters was how to restore the old perception and make it credible. Joining the "seize Arab oil" bandwagon offered a chance. The link with the "Cold Warriors" in America (i.e., those who believe in the politics of confrontation rather than of détente with the Soviet Union) would be strengthened. Therefore, in the words of Michael Hudson, "the recent far-fetched attempts to argue why the United States should invade the Arab oil states now look like self-serving attempts to revive this tarnished perception of Israel's strategic value."[45]

The Negotiations for a Second-Stage Sinai Agreement

The Respective Positions in January

On the negotiations front for a second-stage accord, the year opened with an apparent deadlock. In the closing weeks of 1974 there was a general agreement, particularly between the United States and Israel, that a disengagement accord with Jordan in the West Bank would not be pursued. The official rationale for this joint position was that the Rabat summit decisions had foreclosed the Jordan option. But in actual fact, Israel was determined to break Arab solidarity by creating a rift between Egypt and Syria, as was publicly announced by Premier Yitzhak Rabin in his 3 December interview

---

[45] L. Mosher, "Changing Perspectives in Washington," *Middle East International*, June 1975, p. 8.

with *Haaretz*.[46] And the least that can be said about Kissinger is that he went along with this cardinal strategy of the Zionist state. Thus the Israeli cabinet was invited to present its bargaining position. On 9 December 1974, Foreign Minister Yigal Allon arrived in Washington and submitted a ten-point proposal:

> 1) Israel and Egypt would commit themselves publicly to ending the state of belligerency; 2) demilitarization of evacuated territories; 3) Egypt would have to stop economic and propaganda warfare against Israel; 4) the accord to be signed would be called an "agreement," not an "interim agreement;" 5) Egypt would commit itself not to assist guerrilla activities against Israel; 6) the agreement would include a clause stating that it was part of a peace agreement to follow; 7) Egypt would commit itself not to join in any war started against Israel by any other country in the area; 8) a duration of twelve years for the agreement; 9) an Egyptian commitment to implement the disengagement of forces before the implementation of the rest of the agreement; 10) the means for efficient supervision of the demilitarized areas would be determined.[47]

In return for all this, Israel would be prepared to pull back 30 to 50 kilometers, but without giving up control of the Miṭla and Giddī passes and the Abū Rudays oil fields.

The reaction of President Ford and Henry Kissinger to the proposals was cool. They pointed out that this was hardly a basis for an accord. Allon apparently hinted that Israel would be satisfied with a five-year instead of a twelve-year agreement, but insisted on the demand for nonbelligerency, which to Kissinger represented "the main problem with the Israeli proposal."[48] Nevertheless, the package was forwarded to President Sadat and was rejected; thereupon, the Rabin cabinet was notified by Washington that it would have to come up with a new package.[49] And as the first week of January came to a close, it was reported that the Israeli government was reacting by urging State Secretary Kissinger to "stop seeking further

[46]See Marwan Buheiry, "Al-Wilāyāt al-muttaḥida al-amīrkīya," pp. 347–48 [= p. 315 above.]

[47]Matti Golan, *The Secret Conversations of Henry Kissinger* (New York: Bantam Books, 1976), pp. 229–30.

[48]Quandt, *Decade of Decisions*, p. 262.

[49]*Ibid.*

territorial concessions from Israel and fly instead to the Middle East to find out what President Anwar Sadat would give up in return for a new Sinai withdrawal."[50] This, at least, is what the Ford administration was saying; but it was also revealing that Kissinger would not undertake another trip unless there was a narrowing of the gap separating the Israeli and Egyptian positions.[51] The Secretary of State was eager to maximize the chances of progess toward a second-stage accord and was not interested in mere, and perhaps fruitless, probing operations on the spot in the Near East. The negotiating situation seemed deadlocked.

In the meantime, there had been important developments on the scene. Leonid Brezhnev's expected visit to Egypt was indefinitely postponed on 30 December 1974—an obvious indication of the severe strain in Soviet-Egyptian relations. And this had significant implications when seen in the context of worsening Soviet-American relations, culminating in mid-January with the Russian rejection of the American offer of most-favored-nation trading status, predicated, however, on an unacceptable requirement regarding the emigration of Soviet Jews.[52] In one sense, therefore, Cairo and Washington were moving closer, as indicated by the Egyptian president's remarks that the United States now held virtually all the trump cards in the settlement of the Arab-Israeli conflict and that he could not exclude the possibility of renouncing the friendship treaty with the Soviet Union.[53] And when it is remembered that President Sadat was experiencing domestic pressures, including serious demonstrations and riots in Cairo as the year opened, it became clear that a new situation had been created, providing an opportunity as well as a pressure for renewed American diplomatic initiatives aimed at taking advantage of the Soviet setback.

What were the prospects for a second-stage Sinai accord in the wake of the Cairo-Moscow crisis as seen in Israel? Political circles assessed the deterioration in Soviet-Egyptian relations as a positive factor toward negotiations, but also predicted that the American administration would seek "to coax Israel towards further concessions in order to 'compensate and encourage' President Sadat in his dispute with the Soviets."[54]

---

[50] Bernard Gwertzman, "Israelis Bid Kissinger Sound Out Sadat," *New York Times*, 10 January 1975, p. 3.

[51] *Ibid.*

[52] Quandt, *Decade of Decisions*, p. 261.

[53] *Le Monde*, 22 January 1975, p. 2.

[54] *Jerusalem Post* (Weekly Overseas Edition), 7 January 1975, p. 1.

In short, the respective negotiating positions during January could be described as firm. In Sadat's view, and as he himself explained to *Le Monde* correspondent Eric Rouleau, a minimum for another accord signified a substantial Israeli withdrawal beyond the lines of the strategic passes and the return of the Abū Rudays oil fields and installations.[55] In addition, there was no question of political concessions to Israel. The rift in the Arab ranks was bad enough. The Israelis, on the other hand, were insisting that in return for Egyptian political concessions, which would, in effect, detach Egypt from Syria, it would withdraw a distance varying from 30 to 50 kilometers, without, however, giving up the strategic passes or the oil fields. In Washington, it was generally agreed that the Israeli proposal was short of what the Egyptian president could even consider as a basis. The Ford administration was therefore urging the Israeli cabinet to add more flexibility to its position, specifically on the questions of territory and non-belligerence.

Kissinger's Diplomatic Pulse-Taking in February

The ball was now, so to speak, in Israel's court. On 7 February, Prime Minister Rabin accorded an interview to former Mayor of New York John Lindsay in which he stated, to everyone's surprise, that "in exchange for an Egyptian commitment not to go to war, not to depend on threats of use of force, and an effort to reach true peace, the Egyptians could get even the passes and the oil fields."[56] According to Matti Golan, this move was prompted by Rabin's personal feud with Shimon Peres—a desire to project the image of tough realism and control at a time when public opinion polls favored his ambitious rival.[57] And although Rabin's move was interpreted in Washington as a sign of a new Israeli flexibility, the Secretary of State himself was furious. From his own point of view, not only had Rabin made the "big concession" without an Egyptian *quid pro quo*, he had negated Kissinger's big chance of appearing as the one responsible for extracting it from Israel.[58] A personal assessment on the spot had become all the more urgent.

How did Henry Kissinger view his forthcoming Middle East trip in early February? In answer to inquiries concerning the possible failure of his mission and of his step-by-step diplomacy, the State Secretary appeared

---

[55] *Le Monde*, 22 January 1975, p. 1.

[56] Golan, *Secret Conversations*, p. 232.

[57] *Ibid.*, p. 233.

[58] *Ibid.*; Quandt, *Decade of Decisions*, pp. 263–64.

rather sure of himself: "First of all, I don't expect the mission to fail. Secondly, I have never looked at Geneva as an alternative to the step-by-step approach."[59] He also added that his forthcoming trip was exploratory, "to get a feel for the real convictions of the chief protagonists who might be reluctant to put their thoughts in writing."[60] "After I've had this," he said, "I will come back here (Washington), formulate an American view on the matter, and then return to the Middle East and conclude the negotiations."[61]

This was part of the Kissinger technique—well tested by now—for conducting limited agreements in the Arab-Israeli conflict: a technique described by William Quandt as follows:

> It began by eliciting proposals from each side, getting preliminary reactions, identifying obstacles, and then starting the diplomatic process that would eventually bridge the substantive gaps. This process would include a heavy dose of reason and persuasion, as Kissinger would explain the dire consequences internationally of failure to reach an agreement; it involved marshalling forces that might influence the parties, such as other countries or the United States Congress; then Kissinger would commit his own prestige to bringing about an agreement, shuttling back and forth between the two sides. At this last stage, Kissinger was likely to involve the President if additional pressure on Israel or commitments on future aid were needed.[62]

On 9 February the State Secretary began his exploratory trip to the Near East (Israel, Egypt, Syria, Jordan, and Saudi Arabia in that order), and also to Europe where he saw, among others, Soviet Foreign Minister Andrei Gromyko in Geneva and the Shah of Iran in Zurich, before returning to Washington on 19 February. In Israel he affirmed the need for a suitable Egyptian *quid pro quo* to any Israeli withdrawal. He sought to convince the Israelis to give up non-belligerence at this stage. It would come, he argued, later with formal peace. Security, he argued, "had to be a process—not a precondition."[63] The Rabin cabinet remained unconvinced. In Egypt, President Sadat "indicated a willingness to end some hostile action towards

[59] *Department of State Bulletin*, LXXII, 1862 (3 March 1975), p. 262.

[60] *Ibid.*

[61] *Ibid.*

[62] Quandt, *Decade of Decisions*, p. 260.

[63] Edward Sheehan, *The Arabs, Israelis, and Kissinger* (New York: Readers' Digest Press, 1976), p. 155.

Israel."[64] There was, however, no question of yielding on non-belligerence. In Syria, President Asad stressed the need for a significant withdrawal on the Golan front and asked for a definite date for the reconvening of the Geneva Conference. According to Quandt, Kissinger could not get the Syrian government "to drop their opposition to a second step in Sinai."[65] In Aqaba and Riyadh, the Secretary of State briefed King Hussein and King Faysal on his exploratory mission.

It would seem, in retrospect, that the February trip to the Near East did not achieve any significant narrowing of Egyptian and Israeli positions. A wide gap still remained. With one important exception, the Zurich meeting where the Shah of Iran accepted to supply Israel with oil provided she returned the Abū Rudays oil fields to Egypt, the exploratory tour did not reveal anything particularly new.

The March Shuttle Ends in Failure

Henry Kissinger may have violated his own favorite technique for conducting negotiations in that he proceeded on the shuttle in March with insufficient preliminary preparation. However, the Ford administration was experiencing domestic pressures at home as well as foreign policy setbacks in Vietnam, Cambodia, Portugal, and Turkey. Some success somewhere was in order, and Kissinger may have taken a calculated risk in trying to reverse the Administration's fading image by achieving a success—with the usual accompanying mass media fanfare—in the one area where there was still a chance: the Arab-Israeli conflict. It is also likely that he overestimated his own ability in pressuring the Egyptians and Israelis to bridge the gap between their respective negotiating postures. On 6 March he departed to the Middle East on a momentous 17-day tour of arduous negotiations that began on a hopeful note, but finally ended in deadlock, frustration, loss of his prestige, and a declaration of a reassessment of US policy vis-à-vis the Israelis and the Arabs, with the implication that it would favor the latter.

Upon his arrival in Israel on 9 March from Aswan and Damascus, "he received from Premier Rabin a formal document in seven points. This "Proposed Main Elements of Agreement Between Israel and Egypt," as it was called, included in brief the following: a separate and independent formal agreement with Egypt associated with a declaration of intent that Israel would "be ready to negotiate with each of its neighbors;" the agreement had

---

[64]Quandt, *Decade of Decisions*, p. 264.
[65]*Ibid.*

to be a "step toward peace in some practical measure," such as the passage of Israeli cargo through the Suez Canal, the end of economic boycott, and the free passage of people across the borders; the agreement had to terminate the use of force through "a renunciation of belligerency clearly and in the appropriate legal wording." In addition, the remaining points emphasized the creation of a real buffer zone between the military forces; the duration of the agreement; the definition of the link between this agreement and subsequent negotiations in Geneva; and finally, the proposal indicated that Israel would discuss the new Israeli line of withdrawal in the Sinai only after Egypt "had responded to the first six points."[66]

The mood was gloomy. Israel was still insisting on formal non-belligerency, which Kissinger knew to be unacceptable to President Sadat. According to American reporters on the shuttle: "Egyptian officials hinted privately that an accommodation on this point could be found if Israel settled for some sort of general declaration rather than a formal statement of non-belligerence."[67] The Israelis were expressing concern over the need to receive significant concessions in the political sphere. Kissinger was appealing to the media for cooperation and not to expect a daily progress report on the negotiations. Apparently he wanted to obtain compromises from the two parties without their being afraid of close scrutiny by their respective opponents.[68] In short, Kissinger was pleading for "quiet diplomacy," almost a contradiction given the style of his staging. Clearly the negotiations were at the point of the big hurdle. And Kissinger's task was to try to find an acceptable formula that would give Israel the "functional equivalent" of non-belligerency.

In the next few days he apparently got the Israelis to accept a "non-use of force" formula to replace "non-belligerence," but this was coupled with an insistence that there would be no withdrawal from the passes for anything less than non-belligerency. In other words, the Israelis would remain deep within the passes—at least halfway—and would not give a map indicating the line of withdrawal. And there was a further stumbling block. According to Quandt, Israel insisted on "maintaining control over an electronic intelligence station at Umm Khushayba at the western end of the Giddī Pass, [whereas]

---

[66]Sheehan, *The Arabs, Israelis, and Kissinger*, p. 156; Quandt, *Decade of Decisions*, p. 265.

[67]*New York Times*, 11 March 1975, p. 9.

[68]*Ibid.*, p. 1.

Sadat would not agree to Israel keeping the station even if it were formally placed in the UN zone."[69]

A week of arduous shuttling between Egypt and Israel, as well as over the Near East, failed to break the deadlock over non-belligerency, the passes, the oil fields, and the electronic station at Umm Khushayba. On 21 March the negotiating situation appeared to be hopeless, with Rabin refusing to make further moves. It was at this point that a controversial message from President Ford was sent to the Israeli cabinet expressing disappointment with Tel Aviv's inflexibility and threatening that the United States would drastically reassess its policy towards Israel. Sheehan has described it as "the severest American reprimand to the Israelis since President Eisenhower's...,"[70] and Matti Golan called it "tough, even brutal."[71] Most analysts, at any rate, believe that Ford's message only hardened Israeli refusal. One more attempt was made on 22 March to break out of the deadlock, but it was clear that Kissinger had this time failed to repeat his 1974 successes. His final session with the Israeli cabinet was dramatic, and the notes of his remarks have been made available:

> *Kissinger:* There was no ultimatum....In the absence of new Israeli ideas, we received no new Egyptian ideas. We have no illusions....The Arab leaders who banked on the United States will be discredited....Step-by-step has been throttled, first for Jordan, then for Egypt. We're losing control. We'll now see the Arabs working on a united front. There will be more emphasis on the Palestinians, and there will be a linkage between moves in the Sinai and on Golan. The Soviets will step back onto the stage. The United States is losing control over events, and we'd all better adjust ourselves to that reality....We just don't have a strategy for the situation ahead. Our past strategy was worked out carefully, and now we don't know what to do. There will be pressures to drive a wedge between Israel and the United States, not because we want that but because it will be the dynamic of the situation. Let's not kid ourselves. We've failed.[72]

At this point Allon stepped in to suggest that the negotiations could perhaps be resumed in a few weeks. Kissinger's answer indicated his pessimism:

---

[69]Quandt, *Decade of Decisions*, p. 266.

[70]Sheehan, *The Arabs, Israelis, and Kissinger*, p. 159.

[71]Golan, *Secret Conversations*, p. 237.

[72]Sheehan, *The Arabs, Israelis, and Kissinger*, p. 160.

Kissinger: Things aren't going to be the same again. The Arabs won't trust us as they have in the past. We look weak—in Vietnam, Turkey, Portugal, in a whole range of things. Don't misunderstand me. I'm analyzing the situation with friends. One reason I and my colleagues are so exasperated is that we see a friend damaging himself for reasons which will seem trivial five years from now....I don't see how there can be another American initiative in the near future. We may have to go to Geneva for a multilateral effort with the Soviets—something which for five years we've felt did not offer the best hope for success....An agreement would have enabled the United States to remain in control of the diplomatic process. Compared to that, the location of the line eight kilometers one way or the other frankly does not seem very important. And you got all the military elements of non-belligerency. You got the "non-use of force." The elements you didn't get—movement of peoples, ending the boycott—are unrelated to your line. What you didn't get has nothing to do with where your line is....This is a real tragedy....We've attempted to reconcile our support for you with our other interests in the Middle East, so that you wouldn't have to make your decisions all at once....Our strategy was to save you from dealing with all those pressures all at once. If that was salami tactics—if we wanted the 1967 borders, we could do it with all of world opinion and considerable domestic opinion behind us. The strategy was designed to protect you from this. We've avoided drawing up an overall plan for a global settlement....I see pressure building up to force you back to the 1967 borders—compared to that, ten kilometers is trivial. I'm not angry at you, and I'm not asking you to change your position. It's tragic to see people dooming themselves to a course of unbelievable peril.[73]

In analyzing the complex causes of the March failure, several factors have to be retained. It has already been mentioned that Kissinger proceeded on his negotiations shuttle with insufficient initial preparation and with the gap still wide. In addition, it is also possible that he forced the pace on a weak Israeli cabinet, torn by internal rivalries and struggle for power, to such a degree as to cause it to dig in hard. In particular, Rabin did not want to emerge from the negotiations domestically weaker than when

---

[73] *Ibid.*, pp. 161–62.

he started. There may also have been an additional factor. According to Matti Golan, Kissinger informed Tel Aviv around 19 March—i.e., at the height of the impasse—that even if it signed the agreement there would be no respite. "Within three months of the signing," he reportedly said, "the Israelis would have to make further proposals to Syria and Egypt."[74] Seen in the perspective of Rabin's avowed imperative of gaining time, Kissinger's remarks may have caused him to harden his posture further. The more he could postpone signing an agreement with Egypt—preferably until the end of the year 1975—the more he would be able to take advantage of the factor of the American Presidential elections, at which time the pressure would not only be off, but in fact reversed, for at that point the lobby would be expected to do its job of influence under ideal conditions.

When President Ford's message was received, Rabin made it known that he was being pressured by the United States. He portrayed it as something of an ultimatum, which it never was. And it gave him the opportunity to appear as the strong figure in the Cabinet who had stood up to Ford and Kissinger by daring to say no: this made him immensely popular in Israel. "Temporarily at least it was Rabin who scored," as Matti Golan pointed out. "In Israel his political stock went sky-high; he had said no to the United States, and that was enough to make him a national hero in most circles."[75]

Reassessment: How Real Was It?

Less than 24 hours after Kissinger's return and his report to the White House on the failure of the talks, President Ford gave an interview to Randolph Hearst Jr. in which he blamed Israeli inflexibility for the collapse of the Sinai talks. He was asked: "Do you think that Israel should be prepared to take greater risks for peace?;" and he replied: "I would like to refer to the unfortunate developments of the last 72 hours. If they had been a bit more flexible, you can say a greater risk, I think in the long run it would have been the best insurance for peace."[76] In the meantime, the Secretary of State also added his weight to the campaign of reassessment loudly proclaimed by the Ford administration. On his way home, he had left a clear impression with newsmen of an intransigent Israel unable or unwilling to make the necessary concessions and therefore precipitating a reconvening

---

[74] Golan, *Secret Conversations*, p. 236.

[75] *Ibid.*, p. 242.

[76] *San Francisco Examiner*, 27 March 1975, p. 8.

of the Geneva Conference.[77] In actual fact, the term reassessment had first been used in President Ford's cable to the Israeli government on the eve of the breakdown of the talks as an instrument of pressure.[78]

Kissinger announced on 26 March: "With the end of the step-by-step approach, the United States faces a period of more complicated international diplomacy. Consequently, a reassessment of policy is essential. This reassessment has been ordered by the President."[79] And in answer to the inevitable follow-up questions concerning the meaning and aim of reassessment, he clarified that reassessment was now necessary. US policy was designed "to segment the issues into individual elements, to negotiate each element separately."[80] However, this approach was to be abandoned. From now on, he claimed: "All problems will have to be negotiated simultaneously, and, instead of a forum in which Israel deals with one Arab country through the mediation of the United States, the strong probability is that Israel will have to deal with all Arab countries in a multilateral forum."[81] Kissinger strongly hinted that the "obvious forum now open was Geneva."[82]

Both Ford and Kissinger seemed personally affected by the breakdown of the talks. According to Edward Sheehan, for weeks following his return to Washington the Secretary of State "sulked and raged, castigating Israeli blindedness to aides and visitors alike, compulsively telephoning distinguished Jews all over the country to complain of Israel's intransigence."[83] With serious problems and setbacks in Vietnam, Cambodia, and Portugal, President Ford was in no mood to digest a major upset in American Near East policy. This was one area in which he had high hopes of asserting his leadership and obtaining luster. According to Matti Golan, he observed to people close to him: "All my life I fought for Israel and now when I need understanding from them I get refusal."[84] *Newsweek* reported:

> The President, frustrated and angry, blamed Israel for the collapse of Kissinger's mission—and touched off the most serious

---

[77] *New York Times*, 28 March 1975, p. 2.

[78] "Reflections on the Quarter," *Orbis*, 19.2 (Summer 1975), p. 307; *Jerusalem Post* (Weekly Overseas Edition), 25 March 1975, p. 1.

[79] Kissinger's news conference on 26 March in *Department of State Bulletin*, LXXII, 1868 (14 April 1975), p. 461.

[80] *Ibid.*, pp. 463–64.

[81] *Ibid.*

[82] *Ibid.*, p. 464.

[83] Sheehan, *The Arabs, Israelis, and Kissinger*, p. 164.

[84] Golan, *Secret Conversations*, p. 242.

breach between the two allies since Dwight Eisenhower forced Israel to turn back the occupied Sinai to Egypt nearly twenty years ago.[85]

The immediate effect of reassessment included a temporary and selective freezing of American commitments to Israel, particularly the current proposal of over $2.5 billion in economic and military aid, and the suggestion that the visits of Allon and Peres to Washington be postponed until the reassessment was completed. The Ford administration also "suspended negotiations on new F-15 fighter planes for Israel, and delayed delivery of already committed Lance ground-to-ground missiles."[86] To underline his displeasure, Kissinger issued instructions to have the special line connecting his office to Israel's embassy removed. He also made it widely known that he had been misled by the Israeli cabinet.[87] The Administration conveyed the impression that "a more ambitious strategy was needed [and that] the Palestinians could no longer be ignored."[88]

Within the framework of the reassessment campaign, the State Secretary conferred with all kinds of personalities and experts in the fields of foreign policy and defense. This seeking of advice was loudly advertised. He also met with Senators, Congressmen, and leading spokesmen of the American Jewish community. The Administration wanted to convey the impression that it was taking reassessment very seriously.

On 21 April, President Ford appeared on television to discuss the reassessment of Middle East policy and attitude toward the Palestinians. In answer to a question on whether he still favored the step-by-step approach, he replied:

> I think, following the very serious disappointment of the last negotiations between Israel and Egypt, we are committed, at least in principle, to going to Geneva. Now in the meantime we are going through this process of reassessment of our whole Middle East policy....There are really three options. You could resume the suspended negotiations without making a commitment to go to Geneva. You could go to Geneva and try to get an overall settlement—which is a very complicated matter. People advocate it however. But while you were going through this negotia-

---

[85] *Newsweek*, 7 April 1975, p. 10.

[86] Sheehan, *The Arabs, Israelis, and Kissinger*, p. 165.

[87] Golan, *Secret Conversations*, p. 242.

[88] Quandt, *Decade of Decisions*, p. 270.

tion for an overall settlement, as a third option you might have an interim negotiated settlement between two of the parties, such as Israel and Egypt. Those are basically the three options. We have not made any decision yet.[89]

There was little public indication at this point of which one the White House favored.

According to one translation—that of Edward Sheehan—the three options (in the order presented by Ford) meant the following. Option I involved the resumption of step-by-step diplomacy. Option II was Geneva and the overall settlement, in which case:

> The United States should announce its conception of a final settlement in the Middle East based upon the 1967 frontiers of Israel with minor modifications, and containing strong guarantees for Israel's security. The Geneva Conference should be reconvened; the Soviet Union should be encouraged to cooperate in this quest to resolve all outstanding questions (including the status of Jerusalem), which should be defined in the appropriate components and addressed in separate subcommittees.[90]

Ford's third option—the interim—is translated by Sheehan as: "The United States should seek a quasi-settlement for the near future, with Egypt the beneficiary. Israel should withdraw from most of Sinai in return for nonbelligerency, her final frontiers with Egypt to be determined at a later stage."[91]

Asked whether the reassessment also included a reassessment of the position toward the Palestinians, Ford answered:

> If you take the path of an overall settlement and going to Geneva, I think you have to have an analysis of what is going to happen there because the Palestinians are going to demand recognition. But I don't mean to infer that we have made any decision. But the Palestinians have to be examined as part of the overall Middle East situation. I am not making any commitment one way or another, but it has to be part of the problem that we are analyzing.[92]

---

[89] Interview conducted by Walter Cronkite and Eric Severeid, broadcast by CBS: partial transcript published by the US Embassy in Beirut on 23 April 1975.
[90] Sheehan, *The Arabs, Israelis, and Kissinger*, p. 166.
[91] *Ibid.*
[92] *Ibid.*

Ford also suggested that the US would proceed much more cautiously and evenhandedly because of the danger of war and the inevitable oil embargo. The Ford remarks were interpreted as implying the end of the favored nation treatment of Israel.

Under-Secretary of State Joseph Sisco added a nuance to the reassessment. Speaking before the third annual convention of the National Association of Arab-Americans in May, Sisco left the clear impression that Geneva would force the attention of the US away from interim agreements. The concentration would have to be instead on a comprehensive accord including Israel's final borders. He also left the impression that while the US would withhold recognition as long as the PLO refused Israel's right to exist, it might very well have to consider recognition if the PLO were to moderate its stand.[93]

The Ford administration's reassessment campaign was met with an unprecedented counter-campaign by the Israelis, aided by the powerful pro-Israel lobby in the United States. Tel Aviv lost no time in alerting American Jewish organizations. This is how *Newsweek* reported the alert:

> Even before Kissinger left, the Israeli government launched a campaign to head off an anti-Israel backlash in the U.S. From Rabin's office a telephone call was made to a prominent Jewish leader in New York. The message: convene an urgent session of the Conference of Presidents of Major American Jewish Organizations to bring "pressure and persuasion" to bear on the Administration and Congress. Early last week, the meeting was held, and in the days that followed pro-Israeli lobbyists buttonholed congressmen all over Capitol Hill.[94]

This is confirmed by the fact that Ambassador Simcha Dinitz, who had been in Israel during Kissinger's mission, flew back to the United States when the negotiations broke down, and upon his arrival in New York he scheduled an extraordinary meeting with the heads of the Conference of Presidents of Major American Jewish Organizations, the active vanguard together with AIPAC (American-Israel Public Affairs Committee) of the pro-Israel lobby. The chairman of the powerful coordinating Conference, Rabbi Israel Miller, immediately issued a statement fully supporting Israel and blaming Egypt for the breakdown.[95] The swiftness of the Israeli move was noted: according

[93] *Jerusalem Post* (Weekly Overseas Edition), 13 May 1975, p. 1.
[94] *Newsweek*, 7 April 1975, p. 20.
[95] *Jerusalem Post* (Weekly Overseas Edition), 25 March 1975, p. 1.

to the *Jerusalem Post's* Washington correspondent, "Observers could not recall a precedent when an Israeli Ambassador had called for such a quick meeting with the American Jewish leadership."[96]

The efficient campaign against Ford's reassessment policy gathered speed quickly. The *Near East Report*, an influential instrument of the lobby, warned that reassessment would increase the hostility of the Congress and the American people towards the Administration, emphasizing that the Harris Poll indicated a more solid support of American public opinion toward Israel than ever.[97] President Ford was having some difficulties with Congress, and the lobby was doing its best to erode his position further. This sniping was also taken up in the leading newspapers. William Safire, in a short essay entitled "Henry's Two Faces," bitterly attacked the State Secretary and called reassessment the clearest and cruelest implied threat to Israel.[98] He accused Kissinger of wanting to punish the Israelis, of undermining the support they had with American public opinion.[99] Other editorials called for his retirement or at least speculated on who would be his likely successor.[100] Similarly, the President himself came under fire. A group calling itself American Jews Against Ford (AJAF) was formed and loudly threatened retribution during the forthcoming Presidential election year, calling on "American Jewry to work tirelessly to change the Administration."[101]

As might be expected, the heavy guns among the traditional supporters of Israel in the Congress turned against reassessment. In an address entitled "The Enduring Partnership: United States-Israel," Senator Jacob Javits remarked:

> I have been given to understand that the "reassessment" is tactical rather than strategic and that its primary focus is upon the next steps to be taken into continuation of the US policy initiative to promote negotiations between the parties to the Arab-Israeli conflict. Hence, I deplore the exaggerated publicity which is being given to reassessment. The very nature and prominence of the publicity suggests that it is itself a diplomatic tactic of potentially dangerous and unintended consequences. This is clearly

---

[96] *Ibid.*

[97] *Near East Report*, 19.15 (9 April 1975), p. 61.

[98] *New York Times*, 27 March 1975, p. 31.

[99] *Ibid.*

[100] *Time*, 28 April 1975, p. 29.

[101] *Time*, 12 May 1975, p. 28.

no time to be sending misleading signals to the Arab capitals and
to the Kremlin.[102]

And when the Ford administration had let it be known earlier that reassessment could affect the high levels of aid to Israel, prominent Congressional figures, prodded by the lobby, reacted by affirming that Israel could
count on Congress for the military and financial aid it needed.[103] The well-
orchestrated pressure against the Ford administration on the domestic front
was yielding results, undermining the relations between the White House
and Congress, and disorienting a President who in any case seemed to lack
the necessary will to back his own policy.

So much for the reaction in the United States. Meanwhile, in Israel
the public posture adopted by the government in answer to reassessment
was tough. Top officials affirmed to the Western press on 20 April that
Israel would not offer new proposals to Egypt until there were "practical
signs" that the current negative position adopted by the Ford administration
toward Israel was ended. The practical signs in question were defined as "a
resumption of discussions of arms requests, which were suspended [following]
the announcement of reassessment."[104] Terence Smith of the *New York
Times* reported that Rabin viewed "the whole of reassessment as something
of a diplomatic sham...a maneuver through which President Ford and Mr.
Kissinger hope to test the sentiment of Congress and the American public
for more pressure on Israel."[105] There was a relentless campaign to present
to the Congress and to American public opinion at large the image of an
embattled and victimized Israel undergoing intolerable pressures by the Ford
administration.

But to return to the fate of the three options articulated by the President, there was indication that most of the experts from the universities,
together with the prominent figures of the Foreign Service establishment
who were called upon to express their views, favored the Geneva and comprehensive settlement option.[106] This was echoed quite strongly in the State
Department during April. But in early May it was also becoming clear that
Kissinger would favor precisely the kind of option that would not have to
bring the Soviets and the Palestinians into the negotiations—at least in the

---

[102] *Congressional Record* (Senate), 1 May 1975, p. S7327.

[103] *Newsweek*, 7 April 1975, p. 12.

[104] *New York Times*, 21 April 1975, p. 1.

[105] *Ibid.*

[106] Sheehan, *The Arabs, the Israelis, and Kissinger*, p. 167.

short run. Kissinger's "explanation" for excluding the Russians was that the moderate Arabs wanted it that way.[107] As for excluding the Palestinians, one can infer that he himself wanted it that way, for domestic reasons and perhaps for personal reasons as well. This aspect—Kissinger's own standpoint regarding the Palestinians and the PLO—remains one of the most obscure. It is clear that he had sought, ever since the early stages of the disengagement negotiations in November-December 1973, to exclude or indefinitely postpone their participation. However, it is not clear why he did it.

It seemed for a moment that, urged by the advice he received from George Ball and William Fulbright, the President toyed with the idea of confronting the pro-Israel lobby by appealing directly to the silent majority: to Mid-America as it is sometimes known. This majority Ford knew instinctively: he was one of its sons, so to speak. It would have meant "going to the American people, explaining lucidly and at length on television the issues of war and peace in the Middle East, pleading the necessity of Israeli withdrawal in exchange for the strongest guarantees..., appealing over the heads of the lobby and of Congress."[108] It would have been a risky affair with unpredictable results, and in the end Ford abandoned the Geneva option and played it safe.

The final nail in the coffin of reassessment came in the form of a letter to Ford signed by 76 Senators on 21 May—an unmistakable sign of the lobby's power. In it the President was reminded of the "special relationship" between Israel and the United States and was urged to give Israel virtually all that it wanted:

> Recent events underscore America's need for reliable allies and the desirability of greater participation by the Congress in the formulation of American policy....We believe that a strong Israel constitutes a most reliable barrier to domination of the area by outside parties. Given the recent heavy flow of Soviet weaponry to Arab states, it is imperative that we not permit the military balance to shift against Israel.
>
> We believe that preserving the peace requires that Israel obtain a level of military and economic support adequate to deter a renewal of war by Israel's neighbors. Withholding military

---

[107] *Ibid.*

[108] *Ibid.*, p. 174.

equipment from Israel would be dangerous, discouraging accommodation by Israel's neighbors and encouraging a resort to force.

Within the next several weeks, the Congress expects to receive your foreign aid requests for fiscal year 1976. We trust that your recommendations will be responsive to Israel's urgent military and economic needs. We urge you to make it clear, as we do, that the United States acting in its own national interests stands firmly with Israel in the search for peace in future negotiations, and that this premise is the basis of the current reassessment of US policy in the Middle East.[109]

The extent to which "reassessment" also included a comprehensive reexamination of American policy in the light of new developments in the Arab world is difficult to determine. The assassination of King Faysal of Saudi Arabia, the outbreak of a bitter internal war in Lebanon, the estrangement between Syria and Egypt, and the signs of a rapprochement between Syria, Jordan, and the PLO had created new conditions whose consequences were yet to come and whose impact were as yet difficult to measure. In any case, the thinking of the Ford administration on these issues was not being revealed in public, in sharp contrast with the loudly advertised reassessment initiatives with respect to Israel.

On the specific subject of Egypt, despite the March failure President Sadat's relations with the United States remained warm. His unexpected announcement that the Suez Canal would be reopened on the symbolic date of 5 June was widely interpreted as an invitation of a negotiating formula. On 1 and 2 June, Presidents Sadat and Ford, accompanied by Ismail Fahmy, Husni Mubarak, Henry Kissinger, and Joseph Sisco met in the Austrian city of Salzburg. Few substantive details of the talks were made known. However, it would seem that the Egyptian president pressed Ford to issue a public statement that Israel should withdraw to the borders of 1967. However, Ford did not wish to go along with this request and reportedly preferred to repeat Nixon's private commitment "to work for that goal."[110] Nonetheless, at the Salzburg talks one major obstacle in the negotiations between Israel and Egypt was smoothed over by a compromise suggestion involving an American civilian presence at the Umm Khushayba electronic surveillance station located in the Giddī Pass.[111] This was an indication—especially when it

---

[109] *International Documents on Palestine, 1975*, pp. 213, 214, docs. 100, 101.
[110] Quandt, *Decade of Decisions*, p. 271.
[111] *Ibid.*

was issued in the context of further deterioration of Egypt-Soviet relations following President Anwar Sadat's May Day speech—that an interim accord in the Sinai was attainable.

To return to the topic of reassessment, with it had come the threat— or at least the implication—of an American-imposed solution in a Geneva forum. To what extent the threat was serious is not a question that is easily answered. It is doubtful that Henry Kissinger intended to travel that road. At any rate, the Israelis and the pro-Israel lobby in the US were not prepared to take any chances. So it would seem that the Geneva option in the reassessment was a non-starter in terms of American domestic politics.

But there may have been other reasons as well. It has always been argued in Washington that the Geneva Conference would bring the "militant" Arabs (as opposed to the "moderate" Arabs) into the political limelight or forefront by providing them with a forum backed by the Soviet Union. Why then should the United States sponsor an initiative that would promote the militants and by the same token weaken the moderates, its allies? Another reason for US hesitation could be described as psychological. In April, a White House aide had remarked in *Newsweek*: "We would be going there (Geneva) under the worst possible circumstances, with our strategy having failed."[112] Could it be that the deadly game played by the superpowers is sometimes colored by children's tantrums? It was failure in the first place that prompted the talk about a Geneva option. Yet the decision to go there is quickly brushed aside because one is angry and has lost face. Presumably then, Geneva is possible only if the superpowers are equally happy or equally discontented.

The Sinai II Accord

By mid-June the Ford administration had opted for the continuation of the step-by-step diplomacy. Upon Prime Minister's Rabin visit to Washington on 11–12 June, he was apparently warned that the unavoidable alternative to a renewed step-by-step (during which Israel would be expected to show more flexibility) would have to be the revival of Geneva, at which time, the Ford administration hinted, it would have to favor a return to the 1967 frontiers. According to Sheehan, "Rabin got the message."[113] According to Matti Golan, President Ford had been unusually tough, warning Rabin that "the

---

[112] *Newsweek*, 7 April 1975, p. 20.
[113] Sheehan, *The Arabs, Israelis, and Kissinger*, p. 177.

approaching American elections would not get Israel off the hook. . . . If there was no agreement with Egypt, the United States would go to Geneva with a plan of its own, even if it lost him (Ford) votes and stirred up oppositon in Congress."[114] However, it was also clear that the Ford administration was anxious to secure an agreement. It was not doing well with Congress over the proposed Hawk missile sale to Jordan, and was getting nowhere regarding the lifting of the embargo on arms delivery to Turkey. Congress was in no mood to listen to the Administration's arguments on overall strategy in the Mediterranean and Near East. Rabin was therefore well-placed to extract colossal advantages and strategic concessions from Washington in return for resuming the step-by-step negotiations. One such strategic concession, crucial to the Israelis, and which the Ford administration (i.e., Henry Kissinger) presented to them on a silver platter, was the end of American formulations of schemes for a final settlement, particularly the public formulation of such schemes. This, for instance, had been one of President Sadat's objectives at his meeting with President Ford in Salzburg on 1–2 June: a public statement from Ford that Israel should withdraw to the 1967 lines.[115] Rabin therefore sought to negate such a possibility for the future and to secure massive financial and military advantages in return for saying yes. He merely needed a few face-saving devices: to be able to claim, for instance, that he would not have to completely evacuate the passes; and an American presence in the buffer zone to man an early-warning system would certainly help.[116] Henry Kissinger, at this point, did not require much persuasion.

At the end of the month of June the leading American media generally expressed that the Egyptian and Israeli stands were still far apart. However, it was emphasized that the step-by-step approach to achieve a limited Sinai agreement was supported by the United States, Israel, and Egypt, and that all recognized that Geneva would be an invitation to a stalemate.[117] According to Quandt, the careful preparations for the resumption of Kissinger's shuttle went on for the most part of July. Early in July, Henry Kissinger on vacation met with Israeli Ambassador Dinitz in the Virgin Islands, and it would appear that Israel extracted far-reaching political and diplomatic concessions from the State Secretary. An aid package of about $2 billion was promised, plus a commitment—later watered down somewhat—that

---

[114] Golan, *Secret Conversations*, p. 244.

[115] *Ibid.*, p. 271.

[116] *Ibid.*, pp. 246–47.

[117] *New York Times*, 28 June 1975, p. 1.

the US would prevent Russian intervention in the Near East.[118] In addition, Kissinger agreed not to work for an interim agreement on the Jordan front and to accept the principle of "cosmetic" changes only on the Golan.[119] The Virgin Islands was described by Matti Golan as the big breakthrough for Israel: the US would provide massive financial aid, additional military hardware, and most important, "would agree to forget about an interim agreement with Jordan."[120] In effect, Israel had neutralized American diplomatic efforts to implement Resolution 242. For the foreseeable future—and with a Presidential election coming up—there would be no pressure on Israel to negotiate on any other front.

The remainder of the month was used to refine the American-Israeli position and to respond to Egypt's reaction. By mid-August the heavy work had been done, and there remained a few details to pin down. Kissinger was ready to resume the shuttle, which this time would amount to little more than a ritual.[121]

The State Secretary, accompanied by Sisco and Atherton, left for his shuttle tour on 20 August and was received with violent right-wing demonstrations in Israel. But unlike the March shuttle, this one had been much better prepared and the risk of failure was minimal. According to Quandt: "By the time Kissinger departed, an agreement was within reach. Only the exact location of the Israeli line, the levels of United States aid, and the technical aspects of the American civilian presence in the passes remained to be negotiated."[122] Another analyst described the final stages of the negotiations as follows:

> Until very late in the negotiation, the great issue remained the passes. The Israelis claimed their line took them out, but Kissinger examined aerial photographs and told them it did not. By August 28, the Egyptians had agreed to Israeli and American monitoring stations, but the Israeli maps were unsatisfactory and their line was still in doubt. At the eleventh hour, the Israelis capitulated—though not completely. In the Mitla, it was difficult to define where the eastern entrance was, but essentially they

[118] Quandt, *Decade of Decisions*, p. 273.
[119] *Ibid.*
[120] Golan, *Secret Conversations*, p. 248.
[121] *Department of State Bulletin*, LXXIII, 1890 (15 September 1975), pp. 405–407. At this press conference in Vail, Colorado, on 17 August, the Secretary of State was particularly optimistic.
[122] Quandt, *Decade of Decisions*, p. 273.

were out of that pass. In the Giddi, they relinquished the road, but clung to some high ground on the northern perimeter, and bent their line westward slightly between the passes to retain some hills.[123]

The promises made at the Virgin Islands meeting had included an American military commitment on the side of Israel in case of a Soviet intervention. The Israelis wanted this undertaking as well as others to figure prominently in the "Memorandum of Agreement." Kissinger acquiesced, but watered down the provisions to read that the US and Israel would "consult promptly" in the event of such action by a "world power" (i.e., the Soviet Union).[124] Furthermore, Israel did not receive the specific formal promise of non-belligerence it had consistently insisted upon. Kissinger nonetheless claimed that it had received its "functional equivalent."

The Sinai II agreements provided for an Israeli withdrawal from Sinai territory including the strategic passes of Miṭla and Giddī and the Abū Rudays oil fields. Both Egypt and Israel agreed to observe the cease-fire, to refrain from the use of force or the threat of force in the settlement of disputes, and to continue negotiations aimed at a comprehensive peace settlement. Moreover, Egypt agreed to allow non-military Israeli cargo to transit through the Suez Canal in both directions. Much of the package of agreements was a continuation of the previous disengagement accord negotiated in 1974. The UN would retain its role, would move to a new buffer zone located further east, and would have its mandate renewed annually. A redeployment of Egyptian and Israeli forces, specified on detailed maps, would take place in the Sinai in zones of limited armaments. The forces would be slightly larger than in the January 1974 accord: 8000 men in eight infantry battalions, 75 tanks, and 72 artillery pieces with ranges not exceeding 12 kilometers.[125]

There was also a significant novelty. For perhaps the first time, the United States was given a formal presence on the terrain as a sophisticated monitor in the zone separating the combatants: a presence with obvious political overtones, the object of controversy on the domestic scene, but also representing an unmistakable increase in the American commitment to the consolidation of the cease-fire on the Sinai front.

---

[123] Sheehan, *The Arabs, Israelis, and Kissinger*, p. 188.

[124] *Washington Post*, 16 September 1975; text of the "Memorandum of Agreement," Clause 10.

[125] *Department of State Bulletin*, LXXIII, 1892 (29 September 1975), p. 469.

The whole package of agreements was quite complicated, consisting of three public documents: 1) Agreement Between Egypt and Israel, 2) Annex, and 3) Protocol. There were also a number of secret agreements—four according to William Quandt—signed by the United States.[126] Three of these were with Israel and one was with Egypt: "A sixteen-point US-Israeli memorandum of understanding dealt with military assistance, oil supply, economic aid, and a number of political points."[127] Then in an Addendum (which apparently was not mentioned by Kissinger to President Sadat) the United States promised to be responsive to Israel's requests for F-16 aircraft and the Pershing missile. In addition, there was a special Memo given to Israel on the subject of Geneva and the PLO, which will be discussed below. On the other hand, to Egypt "the United States merely committed itself to try to bring about further negotiations between Syria and Israel, to provide assistance for the Egyptian early-warning system in the buffer zone, and to consult with Egypt on any Israeli violations of the agreement."[128] Many observers noted the discrepancy between the far-reaching, detailed, and comprehensive nature of the American secret pledges to Israel and the vague limited assurances given to Egypt.

As to the public document of agreement, the Basic Agreement Between Egypt and Israel was composed of nine articles. The Annex to the agreement specified the limitation of the forces, and also a five-month period for the execution of the agreement. Further details would have to be negotiated by an Egyptian and Israeli Military Working Group at Geneva, which would follow already agreed-upon principles regarding deployment lines, buffer zones, and the separate manning of Egyptian and Israeli early-warning stations in the area of the passes. These details would be incorporated in the Protocol for the implementation of the Agreement; and when concluded, the Protocol would become an integral part of the Agreement itself.[129]

Expanding on the early-warning system referred to in Article IV of the Basic Agreement signed by Israel and Egypt, the United States proposed its own participation in a separate document signed this time by Kissinger and the Prime Minister of Egypt, Mr. Mamdūḥ Sālim. This detailed the American involvement in an early-warning complex of its own composed of three watch stations manned by a maximum of 200 American technicians armed with handguns, as well as three unmanned special sensor fields. The Ameri-

---

[126] Quandt, *Decade of Decisions*, p. 275.

[127] *Ibid.*

[128] *Ibid.*, p. 276.

[129] Sheehan, *The Arabs, Israelis, and Kissinger*, p. 246.

cans could be withdrawn by US decision or if both Israel and Egypt requested it. The document was, of course, subject to the approval of Congress.

As mentioned earlier, there were also "secret" pledges contained in the special Memo on Geneva on crucial political issues that dealt a mortal blow to American diplomatic flexibility, tying the Ford administration instead more closely than ever to the Israeli position and impairing its ability to work for other accords elsewhere on the Arab-Israeli scene. Israel secured what amounted to a veto over the reconvening of the Geneva Conference, the participants, and the modality of the negotiations: "The United States will make efforts to insure at the conference that all the substantive negotiations will be on a bilateral basis."[130] As was pointed out by Senator Fulbright in his critique of the Sinai II accord, Israel was given to understand, in writing, that it did not need to make disengagements on other fronts—that, in fact, the accord stood on its own.

In other words, Henry Kissinger had wittingly or unwittingly given the Israelis the "functional equivalent" of a repudiation of Resolution 242 in the form of a "secret" memorandum that was not at all secret. He had failed to raise the crucial issue of Israeli settlements in the Sinai, the West Bank, and the Golan, giving the Israelis even greater opportunity for further expansion of their settlement policy. It is not surprising, therefore, to find a senior Israeli government official observing soon after the signing of Sinai II:

> We have been maneuvering since 1967 to gain time and to return as little as possible. The predominant government view has been that stalemates are to our advantage. Our great threat has been the Rogers Plan—and American policy to move us back to the old [pre-1967] armistice lines. The current agreement with Egypt is another nail in the coffin of that policy.[131]

It is, of course, widely reported that Henry Kissinger had opposed the Roger's Plan of 1969–70. He had taken the view (which must have suited the Zionist state fine) that Isreali reasonableness was preconditioned on massive American financial and military support, that the stronger Israel was, the more it would be prepared to make concessions. Rogers and the State Department had contended the opposite: "Israel could be persuaded to mod-

---

[130] *Ibid.*, p. 257; also *Middle East International*, October 1975, p. 3.
[131] Interview accorded to Martin Levin, *Time*, 22 September 1975, p. 13.

erate her negotiating stance if arms were withheld."[132] Viewed in retrospect, Kissinger in 1975 perhaps contributed his own nail to the coffin as well.

The Kissinger and Fulbright Evaluations of Sinai II

How did Secretary of State Kissinger view the Sinai II accord? Speaking before the Cincinnati Chamber of Commerce on 16 September, he outlined the US diplomatic involvements, the strategy pursued and the significance of the agreement, and US expectations as to the immediate future. Stressing the often-repeated strategic importance of the region and the fact that it "provides the energy on which much of the world depends," the Secretary characterized the US role not as a matter of "preference, but as a matter of vital interests" because of 1) commitment to Israel; 2) the presence in the region of the world's largest oil reserves; 3) the negative impact of crisis in the Middle East on US relations with Europe and Japan; 4) the threat of world instability; and 5) the "prospect of direct US-Soviet confrontation with its attendant risk."[133]

Kissinger emphasized that the October War had "set in train a momentum that is now irreversible," that progress toward peace depended, as he put it, "crucially—even decisively—on the United States," and that stagnation invited disaster. As to the strategy pursued by this Administration, the Secretary first outlined the basic premise "that all issues pertaining to all the countries involved had to be addressed comprehensively: the final frontiers of Israel and the reciprocal guarantees of peace of the Arab states, the future of the Palestinians, the status of Jerusalem, and the question of international guarantees should all be considered together."[134] However, in his view it had been impossible for the past 30 years even to begin the process of negotiation of the comprehensive solution. Hence the step-by-step approach, where agreements achieved "could become building blocks for a final peace...for the overall settlement called for by Security Council Resolution 338."[135] And this approach had apparently yielded positive results: separation of forces agreements first with Egypt, then with Syria, in January and May of 1974. Thereafter, as he explained it, progress had been interrupted "first by the presidential succession (the reference here is to Wa-

---

[132] Quandt, *Decade of Decisions*, p. 145. Edward Sheehan (*The Arabs, Israelis, and Kissinger*, p. 17) goes as far as to say that "Kissinger was contemptuous of Rogers."

[133] *US Policy Documents*, text released by the US Embassy in Beirut, 17 September 1975.

[134] *Ibid.*, p. 5.

[135] *Ibid.*, p. 6.

tergate), then by the decision of the Arab Summit at Rabat, which made negotiations over the West Bank impossible." It is interesting to note in this connection that Kissinger put the blame exclusively on American domestic politics and the Arab summit, absolving Israel of all responsibility—one more glaring example of his bias in favor of Israel.

The Secretary of State explained that the reassessment following March had led to the conclusion that a comprehensive settlement was still premature; bringing all parties together was, in his view, "an invitation to a deepened stalemate."[136] "Therefore," he added, "at the request of both sides the US resumed its step-by-step effort," which finally led to a new agreement signed in Geneva on 4 September.

The agreement was described by Kissinger as "fair and balanced" territorially, militarily, and politically. "For the first time," he emphasized, "Israel and an Arab state have taken a step, not just to halt fighting or to disentangle the forces, but to reduce the danger of future war and to commit themselves to a peaceful settlement of the conflict."[137] Tackling the thorny question of the 200 American civilians involved in the early-warning system in the passes (this in the aftermath of Vietnam), Kissinger argued that it was not a role sought by the US and that it "was accepted at the request of both sides only when it became totally clear that there would be no agreement without it." He also tried to pass it off as not representing a completely new American involvement: "Thirty-six Americans have served with the UN truce supervision organization in the Middle East for more than twenty-five years." He stressed the American move not as an "involvement in war but as an investment in peace."[138]

As to the immediate future, he promised: "We will not move precipitously, because we want confidence to build."[139] He claimed that the US would seriously encourage negotiations between Syria and Israel, and would consult with the Soviet Union "about the timing and substance of a reconvened Geneva Conference," adding that "we are fully aware that there will be no permanent peace unless it includes arrangements that take account of the legitimate interests of the Palestinian people."[140]

The next day at a news conference, also in Cincinnati (17 September), the State Secretary was questioned more closely on the significance of the

---

[136] *Ibid.*, p. 8.

[137] *Ibid.*, p. 10.

[138] *Ibid.*, p. 12.

[139] *Ibid.*, p. 13.

[140] *Ibid.*, p. 14.

undertaking given to Israel regarding the PLO. A day earlier the *Washington Post* had published the supposedly secret "Memorandum of Agreement" between the United States and Israel. The question and the Secretary of State's answer are quoted in full:

> *Question:* Dr. Kissinger, did you sign with Israel an agreement refusing to allow the Palestine Liberation Organization to take part in the Geneva peace talks unless Israel approved? And did you agree not to have the United States recognize the PLO unless the PLO recognized Israel's right as a sovereign nation? *Secretary Kissinger:* Technically we have not signed any agreement with Israel. We have agreed on some documents that we might agree to.
>
> Secondly, you have to remember that in every previous negotiation and at every previous critical point we have had what are called memoranda of understanding between us and Israel that up to now have guided our policies and have not been made public. In this particular case, because of the American presence that we have recommended, we felt morally obliged to submit to the Congress the whole record of our commitments, and this is why these things are becoming public in a more absolute way than would otherwise be the case.
>
> Our position vis-à-vis Israel is exactly the one I have publicly stated today; that is, vis-à-vis Israel and the PLO. Our position is exactly what I have stated; it is neither more nor less. Unless the PLO recognizes the existence of Israel and the relevant resolutions, we cannot make a decision. After that, we will see. That is not a secret agreement; that is a public statement. We have also expressed it as a formal statement to the Israelis, but it is merely codifying what we have repeatedly said publicly and what I have said again publicly this morning.[141]

However, in view of the political concessions made to Israel in the Memorandum, it is clear that despite Kissinger's clever interpretation of the Memorandum's status in international relations (or in bilateral relations with Israel), the United States had forestalled the possiblity of progress in the West Bank and PLO issues. Never had the US position been closer to Israel's than with the signing of the Memorandum.

---

[141] *Department of State Bulletin*, LXXIII, 1894 (6 October 1975), pp. 510–11.

Not everyone in American political life greeted the Sinai accord enthusiastically. In his assessment of it, Senator William Fulbright injected a note of caution. He warned that if the agreement is utilized to advance Israeli intransigence (which he suspected) or as an excuse for the US to take "a holiday from statesmanship during the forthcoming American political season" (i.e., the Presidential election campaign), the accord will stand "as something between a futile exercise and an outright disaster."[142] As he saw it: "The artful generalities in the Sinai agreement are fraught with peril for the future—and not necessarily the far distant future."[143] "Our job" he said, "is to get Israel to withdraw...to persuade her to a course consistent with United Nations resolutions, with the United Nations Charter itself, with declared American objectives such as the Rogers Plan of 1969, and with our own traditional principle of the right of peoples to self-determination."[144] Time was not on America's side. "If the interim Sinai agreement is not soon followed by other, more substantial steps, especially with respect to the central question of Palestinian rights, frustrations will increase and tensions will rise. Moderate Arab leaders will either be radicalized or displaced, and a fifth war will follow." And Fulbright went on to add:

> As we concentrate our attention on the interim agreement we should not overlook the seriousness of the tragedy unfolding in Lebanon....The seriousness of the situation in Lebanon emphasizes the urgency of a comprehensive peace settlement between Israel and her neighbors and the fact that we cannot afford to delay that settlement.[145]

Fulbright knew that his views were not shared by the Israeli lobby in the United States, "with its *extraordinary* influence on our politics," who defined American policy in the Near East in terms of Israeli security "as judged by the Israelis themselves."[146] But he felt that his view—although a minority one in terms of Congress and the press—"was more widely shared among the people at large."[147]

Focusing more directly on the shortcomings of the Sinai accord, he wrote:

---

[142] J.W. Fulbright, "Beyond the Sinai Agreement," *World Review*, December 1975, p. 9.
[143] *Ibid.*
[144] *Ibid.*, p. 11
[145] *Ibid.*, p. 12.
[146] *Ibid.*, p. 9 (italics by Fulbright).
[147] *Ibid.*

My more serious apprehensions are directed toward two basic and potentially dangerous shortcomings in the overall agreement. One is the excessive, sweeping United States commitment to Israeli military, energy, and economic needs as these are perceived by Israel. The other is what could be a *de facto* American acquiescence in the new status quo for an indefinite period, masked behind several less-than-constructive ambiguities.[148]

Fulbright deplored the asymmetry in US military aid policy in the Near East; the gift to Israel of powerful ground-to-ground missiles designed to carry both conventional and nuclear warheads, and also the most sophisticated aircraft in the world, while at the same time showing little response to the much smaller and less sophisticated arms requests by the Arab states of Saudi Arabia, Jordan, and Egypt. Then turning to the question of the cost involved in getting Israel to withdraw in the Sinai, he wrote: "This turns out to be $7.5 million to every square mile of sand to be given up by Israel, more per square mile than we paid for all of Alaska back in 1867."[149]

As to the second grave shortcoming of the Sinai accord, he deplored the double talk that led to substantive inconsistencies—not technical ones as claimed by its defenders. Egypt points to the US assurance that "it intends to make a serious effort to help bring about further negotiations between Syria and Israel." The Israelis, on the other hand, are entirely satisfied that according to the US assurance the agreement with Egypt stands on its own and that the Egyptian commitments are "not conditional upon any act or developments between the other Arab states and Israel."[150]

In short, Fulbright reflected, the "American assurances to Egypt and to Israel regarding Syria are scarcely reconcilable in their substance. Behind the artful diplomatic language we seem to have come perilously close to having promised one thing to one side, something quite different to the other."[151] And of course, the Israeli government was exploiting this double talk to the maximum by openly declaring that there was "virtually no chance" for an interim agreement with Syria, giving as one of the reasons the fact that the extensive settlements on occupied land "were not established in order to be evacuated."[152]

---

[148] *Ibid.*, p. 12.

[149] *Ibid.*, p. 13.

[150] *Ibid.*, p. 14.

[151] *Ibid.*

[152] *Ibid.* Fulbright is quoting a statement made by Prime Minister Rabin on 5 September 1975.

Fulbright, in conclusion, discerned in the whole package of Sinai agreements "a *de facto* American acceptance of the new status quo" in which there was no real need (and no real pressure) for Israel to move in the direction of further negotiations.

The US and the PLO: The Saunders Document

In November 1975 the State Department came out with one of the most comprehensive statements ever made by any US administration on the Palestine issue. Deputy Assistant Secretary of State for Near Eastern and South Asian Affairs Harold Saunders discussed this subject at length before the House of Representatives Subcommittee on International Relations and presented a carefully prepared paper which caused concern in Israel and among Israel's supporters in the United States. The Saunders Document—as it came to be known—came at the end of a two-month-long series of Congressional hearings that saw this hotly contested issue discussed at considerable length and detail.[153] In the short presentation that preceded the reading of the actual paper, Saunders began by stressing: "We have repeatedly stated that the legitimate aspirations or interests of the Palestinian Arabs must be taken into account in the negotiations of Arab-Israeli peace. The issue is not whether this should be done but how it can be done." He outlined the fact that initially the US saw the issue in terms of refugees and displaced persons. Now, however, there was the recognition that the Palestinians desired a voice in determining their political future: "The Palestinians collectively are a political factor which must be dealt with if there is to be a peace between Israel and its neighbors."[154] There were, in the view of the State Department, major problems: definition of Palestinian aspirations, the development of a negotiating framework acceptable to both Israelis and Palestinians, and "the question of who negotiates for the Palestinians."[155] Saunders further argued for the need of evolution from all the parties concerned with respect to the Palestinian factor in the Arab-Israeli conflict; and as this evolution occurs, "what is not possible today may become possible."[156]

---

[153] [This document was discussed by Buheiry in greater detail in a subsequent study. See below, pp. 417–30.]

[154] House of Representatives, "The Palestine Issue in the Middle East Peace Efforts" Hearings, Committee on International Relations, 94th Congress, (Washington, D.C.: Government Printing Office, 1976), p. 176.

[155] *Ibid.*, p. 177.

[156] *Ibid.*

In the prepared statement Saunders had noted that "the Palestinian dimension of the Arab-Israeli conflict was the heart of that conflict, [and that] final resolution of the problems arising from the partition of Palestine, the establishment of the State of Israel, and Arab opposition to these events will not be possible until agreement is reached defining a just and permanent status for the Arab peoples who consider themselves Palestinians."[157] This argument was to cause a storm in Israeli and pro-Israeli American circles, which criticized Saunders for describing the Palestinian dimension as the heart of the conflict, whereas, in their own much-publicized view, the heart was rather Palestinian determination to destroy Israel. Tel Aviv regarded it as a violation of the policy of close coordination between US and Israeli policies in the Middle East, particularly on such sensitive issues as the PLO.[158] Another cause for concern was the "factual" presentation of the various Palestinian viewpoints regarding the shape of a settlement, and Saunders' broad hint that the Palestine Liberation Organization (PLO) had indicated "that coexistence between separate Palestinian and Israeli states might be considered."[159] In fact, Saunders took the unusual step of describing the organizational, representational, and popular character of the PLO: "Affiliated with the PLO are a number of 'popular organizations'—labor and professional unions, student groups, women's groups, and so on."[160] He even talked about the welfare apparatus of Fatah. Likewise, he stated that "an unusually large number of Palestinians have completed secondary and university education," adding that "one finds Palestinians occupying leading positions throughout the Arab world as professionals and skilled workers in all fields."[161]

But he also articulated the habitual American theses and images regarding the PLO: its divisiveness, ambivalence on objectives, the use of terror as a means to gain attention, and its rejection of UN Security Council Resolutions 242 and 338. Nevertheless, what struck observers was the factual tone and the desire to be open-minded about the PLO and the whole Palestinian representation issue. The chairman of the Subcommittee on International Relations, L. Hamilton, called it "probably the most important policy statement on the Palestine issue that has occurred," and went on to add: "It appears to me the process of rethinking of the Palestinian issue is under-

---

[157] *Ibid.*, p. 178.

[158] *Near East Report*, 19 (26 November 1975), pp. 203, 206.

[159] House of Representatives, "The Palestine Issue," p. 179.

[160] *Ibid.*, p. 180.

[161] *Ibid.*, p. 178.

way and that the [State Department] is now seeking ways and means of opening up what had been a part of the Middle East problem that had not been discussed to any very great degree."[162] He characterized the Saunders statement as "conciliatory in tone toward the PLO and the Palestinians," reflecting no hostility, and hopefully one that "will open doors."[163] However, in the succeeding months and in the aftermath of Kissinger's cold shoulder to the statement, it would seem that Hamilton's expectations did not materialize.

In the questions period immediately following the reading of the statement, Hamilton significantly took exception to the official reasoning behind the American refusal to talk to the PLO: the issue of the recognition of Israel and the issue of terrorism. "We have talked," he pointed out by way of analogy, "and we have dealt with North Vietnam and with the People's Republic of China at a time when they refused to recognize the existence of our friends, South Vietnam and Taiwan, and each of those countries were dedicated to the destruction of states that were friendly to us. If we can talk with those countries, why is the PLO different?"[164] And again he inquired: "Why do we raise the question of terrorism in this case when it has not bothered us with our dealings with many governments in the world which practice terrorism today?"[165] Hamilton also observed: "Why do we use the word interests and not rights; does that suggest that the Palestinians have no rights?" In fact, Hamilton warned that this American posture was "actually increasing the rejectionist group of the Palestinians and making it more difficult for the moderates among the Palestinians....It was playing into the hands of the radical element and making their case stronger."[166] He wanted to find out what the State Department's thinking was on the question of Palestinian self-determination. Saunders avoided being drawn into the discussion and spoke in general terms about the lack of consensus among Palestinians on this specific issue. He was reminded by Congressman Larry Winn that President Anwar Sadat, on his recent visit to the United States, had said he would urge acceptance by the PLO of a Palestinian state on the West Bank and Gaza. Would this acceptance by the PLO be regarded "as a positive development and a start of negotiations."[167] Saunders' re-

---

[162] *Ibid.*, p. 181.
[163] *Ibid.*
[164] *Ibid.*, p. 182.
[165] *Ibid.*, p. 183.
[166] *Ibid.*, p. 184.
[167] *Ibid.*, p. 187.

ply suggested that the US has to be careful about stating a position on the substance of negotiations. And when pressed more closely on whether the United States would support the creation of such a state if the "Palestinians recognized Israel," the Assistant Secretary of State finally replied: "We do a great deal of thinking about those subjects as you can well imagine. Our problem here is that (a) the statement of US position is not something that we want to provide publicly at this point and (b) what is really important is to know what the parties themselves are prepared to do."[168]

Hamilton's probing continued on other issues: the American attitude toward the Rabat decision, the representativeness of the PLO, and the problem of the PLO in US relations with Jordan. The questioning had established that the PLO was receiving increased recognition in the world and at the UN and that there appeared to be no alternative to it as spokesman for the Palestinians, although Saunders was very uncomfortable with this line of exploration. When asked what the American view of the Rabat decision was, Saunders replied: "That, of course, is a judgment by Arab leaders that the PLO does in effect represent the Palestinian people, and we do not deny the fact that the PLO is the principal organization of Palestinian groups."[169] But he did not want to be drawn on the questions of whether there were other groups representing the Palestinians, their importance, and "what percentage of the Palestinians the PLO spoke for."[170] At this point in the hearings he sought the assistance of Arthur Day, a senior official of the State Department and an expert on the West Bank, who took the position that the great mass of the people are generally inarticulate, that "some of the leading personalities on the West Bank did not accept the PLO as their spokesman."[171] But he also stated that the PLO being "the only organization that had the eye of the world" did incline most of the West Bank to view it as a spokesman and that there was no opposition to it in any organized sense.[172]

On the subject of US relations with Jordan, Mr. Hamilton asked: "What would be the effect on US relations with Jordan if we tried to talk with and meet with and negotiate with the PLO?" Saunders answered that Jordan "could be quite sensitive to it...very concerned about the implications for

---

[168] *Ibid.*, p. 188.
[169] *Ibid.*, p. 192.
[170] *Ibid.*, p. 193.
[171] *Ibid.*, p. 194.
[172] *Ibid.*

Jordan and for its future relationship with the West Bank."[173] Furthermore, Saunders was closely questioned on the "Memorandum of Agreement" between the USA and Israel of September 1975, which states that the US will "consult fully and seek to concert its position and strategy with Israel with regard to the participation of any other additional states at that conference."[174] Hamilton felt that this undertaking had tied US hands and wanted Saunders to interpret the language of that document. The Deputy Assistant Secretary of State felt that full flexibility was retained and that there was nothing new in this declaration. Finally, in defense of the US vote against two UN resolutions, one recognizing the PLO as the representative in all UN-sponsored dealings in negotiations on the Arab-Israeli conflict, and the other setting up the UN Committee on the Exercise of the Inalienable Rights of the Palestinian People, Saunders suggested that such votes did not place any obligations on the US and repeated the traditional argument that the subject of additional participants at the Geneva Conference (i.e., the PLO) is something which would have to be discussed at the conference itself.[175]

The context and timing of the Saunders Document is most significant. It came in the wake of Sinai II when the US was faced with the problem of deciding what else could be done on the negotiating front. Kissinger had indicated to the Arab representatives at the United Nations on 29 September that he was prepared to work for a Syria-Israel second step, if that was their desire. He had stated, to use the words of Quandt, "that he would begin to refine his thinking on how the legitimate interests of the Palestinian people could be met."[176] The document came in the uncertain period just prior to Syria's renewal of the United Nations Disengagement Observation Force in late November. Yet another important dimension of the context was American UN Ambassador Daniel Moynihan's violent denunciation of the General Assembly 10 November vote defining Zionism as a form of racism or racial discrimination. There were also persistent reports that President Ford was seeking a meeting with President Asad, and some indication that the US was seeking to align itself with the West European position on peace moves in the Arab-Israeli conflict, particularly the move away from the consideration of the Palestinians as refugees to that of a people with a definite political identity.

---

[173] *Ibid.*

[174] *Ibid.*

[175] *Ibid.*, pp. 196–97.

[176] Quandt, *Decade of Decisions*, p. 276 n.

It is clear, therefore, that the Ford adminstration was caught between several fires: having to show publicly a commitment to further negotiations, having to maintain a hard-line attitude of support to Israel at the United Nations at the start of the Presidential campaign period, and having to "refine" thinking on the PLO issue. For this reason, perhaps, the State Department had chosen a "low-key presentation and had made no effort to publicize the hearing."[177] The big question is whether the Saunders episode represented an evolution in US policy regarding the Palestinian component of the Arab-Israeli conflict. There is also the question of Kissinger's own role in the formulation of the document.

In response to close questioning by Israeli reporters in Washington follow-ing the Saunders statement, which was seen as bending toward acceptance of the PLO, Henry Kissinger replied: "Three times a week I announce there is no change. Just relax and have a nice weekend."[178] A few days later, ap-pearing before the Senate Foreign Assistance Committee chaired by Hubert Humphrey, he was asked about the significance of the Saunders Document. He replied:

> This was a paper delivered by a Deputy Assistant Secretary to a subcommittee of the House International Relations Committee, which was a somewhat academic exercise explaining in a purely theoretical manner several aspects of the Palestine problem as Mr. Saunders saw them. I have stated innumerable times our position on the Palestinian question. The United States will not deal with the PLO, until the PLO accepts the existence of the State of Israel and Security Council Resolutions 242 and 338. That has been our position, remains our position, and if we were to change that position it could not be announced by a Deputy Assistant Secretary of State before a subcommittee of the Congress. It would be announced at the Presidential or my level and only after the fullest consultation with Israel.[179]

Hamilton wrote to Kissinger asking if he had approved the Saunders state-ment and received a very evasive answer: merely that Saunders had spoken for the Administration. Kissinger also repeatedly informed the Israeli em-bassy in Washington that he had not seen the Saunders statement ahead of

---

[177] Bernard Guertzman, "US Seeks Talks on PLO," *New York Times*, 31 December 1975, p. 3.

[178] *Jerusalem Post*, 16 November 1975, p. 1.

[179] *Ibid.*

time.[180] Therefore, to Kissinger, the statement did not represent a change in US policy.

Recently, William Quandt had this to say about the Saunders episode:

> There was little new in the statement, but its timing was sig-
> nificant. It was meant to symbolize a continuing willingness
> on the part of the Administration to work for a peace settle-
> ment. Kissinger had gone over the draft carefully, had checked
> the wording, and had reportedly cleared it with President Ford.
> When confronted with the hostility of Israel's reaction, however,
> he dismissed the Saunders statement as an academic exercise.
> Nonetheless, the United States seemed to take a somewhat more
> flexible position than in the past when the issue of the PLO par-
> ticipation in the UN debate scheduled for January 1976 came up.
> Briefly, Arab hopes were raised, but they were soon to be dis-
> appointed. Behind the symbolic shift in American policy, there
> was no real substance.[181]

William Quandt ought to know. For two years, and until 1974, he had worked as Harold Saunders' deputy in the Middle East office of the National Security staff. It is difficult to disagree with his assessment: "There was no real substance."

So far as the Arab reaction to the Saunders Document was concerned, the Egyptian press was inclined to regard it as a constructive step forward.[182] The news media of the Palestinian resistance, however, viewed it as an effort to induce it to give up armed struggle in favor of the Geneva Conference.[183]

---

[180] *Ibid.*

[181] Quandt, *Decade of Decisions*, pp. 278–79.

[182] *Al-Ahrām*, 14 November 1975.

[183] *Ilā l-amām* (Beirut), 28 November 1975, p. 20; *Filasṭīn al-thawra* (Beirut), 30 November 1975, pp. 30–31.

17

The Saunders Document*

ON 12 NOVEMBER 1975 the State Department released the Saunders Document, one of the most comprehensive statements ever made by any US administration on the Palestine question. The forum selected was one of the "Hearings" before a House of Representatives subcommittee on international relations in session since 30 September to discuss[1] specifically this hotly contested issue of American foreign policy. The chairman, Lee H. Hamilton, opened the proceedings by informing those present that the object was to review with the State Department such questions as: "Who represents the Palestinians? What contacts, if any, [does the US] have today

---

*From *Journal of Palestine Studies*, 8.1 (Autumn 1978), pp. 28–40. © 1978 by the *Journal of Palestine Studies*. Reprinted courtesy of the Institute for Palestine Studies. An Arabic version of this study, "Wathīqat Saunders: al-qaḍīya al-filasṭīnīya fī l-siyāsa al-amīrkīya," appeared in *Al-Siyāsa al-amīrkīya fī l-Sharq al-Awsaṭ,* edited by Laila Baroody and Marwan Buheiry (Beirut: Institute for Palestine Studies, 1984), pp. 41–60.

[1] House of Representatives, "The Palestine Issue in the Middle East Peace Efforts" Hearings, Committee on International Relations, 94th Congress (Washington, D.C., 1976). The witnesses included I. Abu-Lughod and Edward Said (30 September), M. Abir and I. Rabinowich (1 October), G. Assosa and J. Ben-Dak (8 October), and Harold Saunders and Arthur Day (12 November), representing the Department of State.

Harold Saunders joined the National Security Council staff in 1961, became an expert in the general area of the Near East, and rose to the position of senior staff member in 1967. Henry Kissinger brought him to the State Department as Deputy Assistant Secretary for Near Eastern and South Asian Affairs. He was considered to be one of Kissinger's top aides and was a constant companion on his trips to the Near East. Edward Sheehan wrote about him: "Laconic, cautious, bland of aspect, Saunders was very competent and shrewd. He was renowned in the department for the tightness and lucidity of his prose, for his cogency of analysis in strategic papers." See Edward Sheehan, *The Arabs, Israelis and Kissinger* (New York: Reader's Digest Press, 1976), p. 169. The policy paper that bears his name is commonly known as the Saunders statement or the Saunders Document.

with Palestinian individuals or organizations? How do we expect this issue to be addressed in the months and years ahead? Why won't we or can't we deal with the PLO? Under what circumstances might we deal with the PLO? How do we expect to help break the current impasse over the role of the PLO or Jordan in negotiations? What do we think can be done in the next few months to defuse this issue at a Geneva conference or through bilateral contacts? What are our views on the Palestinians' right to self-determination in areas of the West Bank and Gaza?"[2]

The context and timing of the Saunders initiative are significant. It came in the wake of the Sinai II accord when the US was faced with the problem of deciding what else could be done on the negotiating front. Kissinger had indicated to the Arab representatives at the United Nations on 29 September that he was prepared to work for a second disengagement step in the Golan, if that was the desire of the parties, and that he would begin "to refine his thinking on how the legitimate interests of the Palestinian people could be met in an overall peace."[3]

On 5 November, President Sadat had addressed a joint session of the US House of Representatives and Senate, urging contacts between the United States and the PLO. Earlier, he had suggested to reporters in Jacksonville, Florida that the moderates in the PLO would agree to a Palestinian state in the West Bank and Gaza.[4]

The document came in the uncertain period just prior to Syria's renewal of the United Nations Disengagement Observer Force in late November. There were also persistent reports that President Ford was seeking a meeting with President Assad, and some indication that the US was seeking to align itself with the West European position on peace moves in the Arab-Israeli conflict, particularly the move away from the consideration of Palestinians as refugees to that of a people with a definite political identity. In addition, there was the Soviet note to the US (9 November) calling for a resumption of the Geneva conference "with the participation on an equal footing of all the directly involved parties: Egypt, Syria, Jordan, representatives of the Arab Palestinian people in the form of the PLO, and Israel, together with the Soviet Union and the United States of America as alternating co-chairman of the Conference."[5]

[2] *Ibid.*, p. 175.

[3] *Department of State Bulletin*, LXXIII, 1895 (20 October 1975), p. 583.

[4] *Arab Report and Record*, 1–15 November 1975.

[5] *International Documents on Palestine, 1975*, edited by J. Nielsen (Beirut: Institute for Palestine Studies, 1977), p. 310, doc. 183, quoting *Pravda*, 11 November 1975. The

Other important dimensions of the context and timing include the off-on internal war in Lebanon, the persistent Israeli bombing raids and incursions in southern Lebanon, and American UN Ambassador Moynihan's violent denunciation of the General Assembly 10 November vote defining Zionism as a form of racism or racial discrimination.

It is clear, therefore, that the Ford Administration was caught between several fires: having to show publicly a commitment to further negotiations and a reward to President Sadat, having to maintain a hard-line attitude of support to Israel at the United Nations at the start of the Presidential campaign period, and having to "refine" the thinking on the PLO issue within a Jordanian framework. For this reason, perhaps, the State Department had chosen a "low-key presentation and had made no effort to publicize the hearing."[6] The big question is whether the Saunders episode represented an evolution in US policy regarding the Palestinian component of the Arab-Israeli conflict. There is also the question of Kissinger's own role in the formulation of the document.

In the brief summary presentation that preceded the official release of the document in the November session, Saunders began by stressing: "We have repeatedly stated that the legitimate aspirations or interests of the Palestinian Arabs must be taken into account in the negotiations of Arab—Israeli peace. The issue is not whether this should be done but how it can be done." He noted that initially the US had seen the issue in terms of refugees and displaced persons. Now, however, there was the recognition that the Palestinians desired a voice in determining their political future: "The Palestinians collectively are a political factor which must be dealt with if there is to be a peace between Israel and its neighbors."[7] Some of the major problems, as seen by the State Department, included: definition of Palestinian aspirations, the development of a negotiating framework acceptable to both Israelis and Palestinians, and the "question of who negotiates for the Palestinians."[8] Saunders further argued for the need for evolution from all the parties concerned with respect to the Palestinian factor in the Arab—Israeli conflict and noted that as this evolution occurs, "what is not

---

American answer stressed the need for a preparatory conference to pave the way for the Geneva conference and rejected the Soviet attempt to alter "the definition of the participants in the Conference initially agreed to by the original participants," thus ruling out the PLO. See *Department of State Bulletin*, LXXIV, 1906 (5 January 1976), pp. 12–13.

[6] Bernard Gwertzman, "US Seeks Talks on PLO," *New York Times*, 31 December 1975.
[7] House of Representatives, "The Palestine Issue," p. 176.
[8] *Ibid.*, p. 177.

possible today may become possible." He indicated that the US would not close its mind to "any reasonable solution." Finally, he said that the US had to work for a settlement "because the issues of concern to the Palestinians are important in themselves and because the Arab governments participating in the negotiations have made it clear that progress in the overall negotiations will depend in part on progress on issues of concern to the Palestinians."[9]

As to the comprehensive document prepared by Harold Saunders, it contained, in addition to the above points in expanded form, a public recognition that "the Palestinian dimension of the Arab-Israeli conflict was the heart of that conflict and that final resolution of the problems arising from the partition of Palestine, the establishment of the State of Israel, and Arab opposition to those events will not be possible until agreement is reached defining a just and permanent status for the Arab peoples who consider themselves Palestinians."[10] This argument caused an immediate storm in Israeli and pro-Israeli American circles, who bitterly attacked Saunders for this unprecedented public acknowledgment of the Palestinian dimension as the core of the conflict.

The document presented a factual outline of the various Palestinian positions regarding the shape of a peace settlement. It mentioned a reported PLO indication "that coexistence between separate Palestinian and Israeli states might be considered."[11] In addition, it took the unusual step of describing the organizational, representational, and popular character of the PLO: "Affiliated with the PLO are a number of 'popular organizations'— labor and professional unions, student groups, women's groups, and so on."[12] There was a reference made to the welfare apparatus of Fatah, the largest resistance organization within the PLO. The document also acknowledged the high level of Palestinian talent and educational attainment: "An unusually large number of Palestinians have completed secondary and university education. One finds Palestinians occupying leading positions throughout the Arab world as professionals and skilled workers in all fields."[13] The distribution statistics for the more than 3 million Palestinians were quoted as: 1 million in the occupied West Bank, Gaza, and East Jerusalem, about 1

---

[9] *Ibid.*, pp. 177–78.

[10] *Ibid.*

[11] *Ibid.*, p. 179: "Officially and publicly, its [PLO] objective is described as a binational secular state, but there are some indications that coexistence between separate Palestinian and Israeli states might be considered."

[12] *Ibid.*, p. 180.

[13] *Ibid.*, p. 178.

million in Jordan, 450,000 in Israel, about 500,000 in Syria and Lebanon, and 200,000 elsewhere, primarily in the Arabian Gulf states. The total figure of Palestinians living in camps was given as 650,000.

With the Palestinian dimension constituting the "heart of the Arab-Israeli conflict," what was needed as a first step was a "diplomatic process which would help bring forth a reasonable definition of Palestinian interests—a position from which negotiations on a solution of the Palestinian aspects of the problem might begin."[14] Another requirement was the development of a negotiating framework, an undertaking that would face the following problems as seen by Saunders:

> The major problem that must be resolved in establishing a framework for bringing issues of concern to the Palestinians into negotiation, therefore, is to find a common basis for the negotiation that Palestinians and Israelis can both accept. This could be achieved by common acceptance of [Security Council Resolutions 242 and 338], although they do not deal with the political aspect of the Palestinian problem.
>
> A particularly difficult aspect of the problem is the question of who negotiates for the Palestinians. It has been our belief that Jordan would be a logical negotiator for the Palestinian-related issues. The Rabat Summit, however, recognized the Palestinian Liberation Organization as the 'sole legitimate representative of the Palestinian people.'[15]

However, Saunders' policy paper also articulated the habitual American theses and images regarding the PLO: divisiveness, ambivalence on objectives, the use of terror as a means to gain attention, and the rejection of UN Security Council Resolutions 242 and 338. He saw divisiveness, but failed to recognize the democratic pluralism of the resistance movement. Nonetheless, many observers were struck by the factual tone, and by what was seen as a desire to be open-minded about the PLO and the whole issue of Palestinian representation. The Chairman of the Subcommittee on International Relations, Lee Hamilton (Democrat, Indiana), called it "probably the most important policy statement on the Palestine issue that has occurred," and went on to add: "It appears to me the process of rethinking of the Palestinian issue is underway and that the [State Department is] now seeking

---

[14] *Ibid.*, p. 179.
[15] *Ibid.*

ways and means of opening up what had been a part of the Middle East problem that had not been discussed to any very great degree."[16] He characterized the Saunders statement as "conciliatory in tone toward the PLO and the Palestinians," reflecting no hostility, and hopefully one that "will open doors."[17]

* * * *

In the questions period, immediately following Deputy Assistant Secretary of State Harold Saunders' presentation, Lee Hamilton took exception to the official reasoning behind the American refusal to talk to the PLO: the issue of the recognition of Israel and the issue of terrorism. "We have talked," he pointed out by way of analogy, "and we have dealt with North Vietnam and with the People's Republic of China at a time when they refused to recognize the existence of our friends, South Vietnam and Taiwan, and each of these countries were dedicated to the destruction of states that were friendly to us. If we can talk with those countries, why is the PLO different?"[18] And again he inquired: "Why do we raise the question of terrorism in this case when it has not bothered us with our dealings with many governments in the world which practice terrorism today?"[19] Hamilton also observed: "Why do we use the word interests and not rights? Does that suggest that the Palestinians have no rights?" In fact, Hamilton warned, this American posture was "actually increasing the strength of the rejectionist group of the Palestinians and making it more difficult for the moderates among the Palestinians ... [it was] playing into the hands of the radical element and making their case stronger."[20] Furthermore, he sought clarification of the State Department's thinking on the question of Palestinian self-determination. But at this point, Saunders avoided being drawn into the discussion and spoke in general terms about the lack of consensus among Palestinians on this specific issue. He was reminded by Congressman Winn that President Anwar Sadat, on his recent visit to the United States, had said he would urge acceptance by the PLO of a Palestinian state on the West Bank and Gaza. Would this acceptance by the PLO be regarded "as a positive development and a start of negotiations?"[21] In response Saunders said that the US had to be careful

---

[16] *Ibid.*, p. 181.
[17] *Ibid.*
[18] *Ibid.*, p. 182.
[19] *Ibid.*, p. 183.
[20] *Ibid.*, p. 184.
[21] *Ibid.*, p. 187.

about stating a position on the substance of negotiations. And when pressed more closely on whether the United States would support the creation of such a state if the Palestinians recognized Israel, he finally replied: "We do a great deal of thinking about those subjects, as you can well imagine. Our problem here is that (a) the statement of US position is not something that we want to provide publicly at this point, and (b) what is really important is to know what the parties themselves are prepared to do."[22]

Hamilton's probing continued on other issues: the American attitude toward the Rabat decision, the representativity of the PLO, and the problem of the PLO in US relations with Jordan. The questioning had firmly established that the PLO was receiving increased recognition in the world and at the UN, and that there appeared to be no alternative to it as spokesman for the Palestinians, although Saunders was very uncomfortable with this line of exploration. When asked about the American view of the Rabat decision, Saunders replied: "That, of course, is a judgment by Arab leaders that the PLO does in effect represent the Palestinian people, and we do not deny the fact that the PLO is the principal organization of Palestinian groups."[23] But he did not want to be drawn on questions of whether there were other groups representing the Palestinians, their importance, and "what percentage of the Palestinians" the PLO spoke for.[24] At this point in the Hearings he sought the assistance of Arthur Day, a senior official of the State Department and an expert on the West Bank, who argued that the great mass of the people were generally inarticulate (he may have changed his mind after the West Bank municipal elections of 12 April 1976, which elected to power candidates publicly expressing support for the PLO), and that "some of the leading personalities on the West Bank did not accept the PLO as their spokesman."[25] But he also stated that the PLO, as "the only organization that had the eye of the world," did incline most of the West Bank to view it as a spokesman and that there was no opposition to it in any organized sense.[26]

On the subject of US relations with Jordan, Mr. Hamilton asked: "What would be the effect on US relations with Jordan if the US tried to talk with and meet with and negotiate with the PLO?" Saunders answered that Jordan "could be quite sensitive to it [and] very concerned about the implications for

---

[22] *Ibid.*, p. 188.
[23] *Ibid.*, p. 192.
[24] *Ibid.*, p. 193.
[25] *Ibid.*
[26] *Ibid.*

Jordan and for its future relationship with the West Bank."[27] Furthermore, Saunders was closely questioned on the Memorandum of Agreement between the US and Israel of September 1975, which stated that the US will "consult fully and seek to concert its position and strategy with Israel with regard to the participation of any other additional states at that conference."[28]

Hamilton felt that this undertaking had tied US hands and wanted Saunders to interpret the language of the Memorandum. In response, Saunders claimed that full flexibility was retained and that there was nothing new in this declaration. Finally, in defense of the US vote against two UN resolutions, one recognizing the PLO as the representative in all UN-sponsored dealings in negotiations on the Arab-Israeli conflict, and the other, setting up the UN Committee on the Exercise of the Inalienable Rights of the Palestine People, Saunders suggested that such resolutions did not place any obligations on the US. He also reiterated the traditional argument that the subject of additional participants at the Geneva conference (i.e., the PLO) is something which would have to be discussed at the conference itself.[29]

It is certain that Secretary of State Henry Kissinger played a central role in the whole affair.[30] Questioned closely by a nervous group of Israeli newsmen in Washington soon after the release of the policy paper, he replied: "Three times a week I announce there is no change. Just relax and have a nice weekend."[31] Amid growing (and deliberately exaggerated) manifestations of concern and hostility, he appeared a few days later before the Senate Foreign Assistance Committee chaired by Hubert Humphrey, and was asked about the significance of the Saunders Document. His appeasement performance was characteristic:

> This was a paper delivered by a Deputy Assistant Secretary to a subcommittee of the House International Relations Committee, which was a somewhat academic exercise explaining in a purely theoretical manner several aspects of the Palestine problem as Mr. Saunders saw them. I have stated innumerable times our position on the Palestinian question. The United States will not deal with the PLO, until the PLO accepts the existence of the state of Israel and Security Council Resolutions 242 and 338.

---

[27] *Ibid.*, p. 194.
[28] *Ibid.*
[29] *Ibid.*, pp. 196–97.
[30] Sheehan, *The Arabs, Israelis and Kissinger*, p. 213.
[31] *Jerusalem Post*, 16 November 1975.

That has been our position, remains our position, and if we were to change that position it could not be announced by a Deputy Assistant Secretary of State before a subcommittee of the Congress. It would be announced at the Presidential or my level and only after the fullest consultation with Israel.[32]

Lee Hamilton wrote to Kissinger asking if he had approved the Saunders statement and received a very evasive answer: merely that Saunders had spoken for the Administration. Kissinger also reportedly informed the Israeli embassy in Washington that he had not seen the statement ahead of time.[33] Therefore, to Kissinger, it did not represent a change in US policy.

* * * *

The response in Israel to Saunders' policy paper was predictably violent. According to *Haaretz* (14 November 1975), the fact that the Israeli embassy in Washington was not informed of its content or had not got wind of its preparation constituted a grave shortcoming, casting doubt on the pretended intimate relationship between Ambassador Dinitz and Henry Kissinger.[34] According to *Davar* (17 November 1975), the Israeli government, during a special session, severely criticized the document for containing "many mistakes and distortions—particularly relating to facts and policies—that could not be ignored."[35] Saunders was accused of having misrepresented the true objectives of the PLO and of having reduced the role of Jordan in negotiations with Israel regarding the Palestinian issue. Some sources also estimated the action as an offer to the PLO to define its objectives and demands in such a way as to permit the United States to initiate contacts with it. Yet for all this *Davar* did not think that "Saunders would enter Near East history as the Lord Balfour of the Palestinians."[36]

The Israeli cabinet regarded the whole episode as a violation of the policy of close coordination between American and Israeli positions on the Arab-Israeli conflict, particularly on such sensitive issues as the PLO.[37] The powerful machinery of the Israel lobby was mobilized to exert pressure on the

---

[32] *New York Times*, 31 December 1975.

[33] *Ibid.*

[34] Institute for Palestine Studies, *Al-Nashra*, 1–16 December 1975, p. 567. This source surveyed Israeli press reactions to the Saunders initiative, pp. 567–72.

[35] *Ibid.*, p. 569.

[36] *Ibid.*

[37] *Near East Report*, 19 and 26 November 1975, pp. 203, 206.

Ford Administration to reverse what was seen as a trend toward acceptance of the PLO as a party in future negotiations.

Not unexpectedly, the Saunders Document and its repercussions received much attention in the Arab press. The semi-official *Al-Ahrām*, reflecting the view of the Egyptian government, expressed approval. It stressed on two occasions that the document was being interpreted widely as a vindication of Sadat's policy.[38] Foreign Minister Ismail Fahmy had stated that it was a positive evolution in the US position following President Sadat's visit to the United States.[39] *Al-Ahrām* also gave prominence to the bitter attacks launched against the Saunders episode by the Israeli government and press.[40]

In Lebanon, the independent *Al-Nahār* focused attention on this new initiative by the Ford Administration. Pointing out that the Saunders Document was widely distributed by the US embassy's press office in Beirut, this daily went on to print virtually the whole text, selecting such passages as "[the US] has not closed its mind to any reasonable solution," and "What is not possible today may become possible" for descriptive headlines.[41] Subsequent articles described Israeli rejection and Egyptian endorsement of the Saunders initiative.[42]

The Palestinian press also commented at length on the initiative, highlighting the dangers it represented to the resistance movement. The twenty or so articles and editorials consulted for this study, representing virtually the whole spectrum of Resistance opinion, were critical of the document's contents, intentions, and the endorsement it received from Egypt.

Filasṭīn al-thawra, organ of the PLO, interpreted the Saunders statement as a maneuver aimed at blunting the revolution, in preparation for an American-Israeli imposed peace settlement.[43] It is worth remarking that the PLO position on the peace settlement emphasized the participation of the Palestinian people represented by the PLO "on an equal basis with other interested parties in efforts—including the Geneva peace conference on the Middle East—to reach a Middle East settlement."[44] Moreover, there was the stress on the Palestinian people's right to form their

---

[38] *Al-Ahrām*, 14 and 15 November 1975.

[39] *Al-Nahār*, 18 November 1975.

[40] *Al-Ahrām*, 18 and 29 November 1975.

[41] *Al-Nahār*, 14 November 1975.

[42] *Ibid.*, 15, 16, 17, 18 and 26 November 1975.

[43] Ghāzī Khalīlī, "Shahādat Saunders," *Filasṭīn al-thawra*, 30 November 1975, and the editorial of 23 November 1975.

[44] Joint communiqués of 4 May 1975 and 28 November 1975 issued on the occasion of visits to the USSR of Yasir Arafat, Chairman of the PLO Executive Committee. For the

own national state on Palestinian territory. Obviously the Saunders policy paper did not go far enough to meet the mainstream position of the
PLO.

The response of *Al-Ṭalā'i'*, organ of Saiqa, was likewise critical. It reported Egyptian ruling circles as insisting that the Saunders Document was
the direct outcome of the Sadat visit to America. The contents and tone
were described by *Al-Ṭalā'i'* as being "cryptic...and below the level of what
Palestinians could expect even from America,"[45] and it warned that the
PLO was being pressured by Egypt's president to respond favorably to the
Saunders initiative in order that it be dragged along the diplomatic road
of Sinai II.[46] Moreover, Sinai II was achieved only at the expense of the
cause of non-Egyptian Arab parties to the conflict. *Al-Hadaf*, organ of the
Popular Front for the Liberation of Palestine (PFLP), denounced this new
move by the Ford Administration as a further attempt to disarm the Palestine revolution. The analyst also went on to suggest that the PLO was
being dragged gradually into the framework of a negotiated compromise settlement at Geneva, although the exercise was being staged as a valuable
"conquest" for the PLO and the Palestinian nation rather than as a yield to
pressure.[47]

In much the same vein, *Ilā l-amām*, organ of the Popular Front for the
Liberation of Palestine—General Command (PFLP-GC), accorded considerable space to the objectives of this American move on the Palestinian
checkerboard. One source referred to it as the most dangerous of American
initiatives aimed at forcing the hand of the PLO, particularly when seen in
the context of the mediation initiative by President Ceausescu of Romania
between Israel and the PLO.[48] In general, the document was seen as placing
four preconditions on the PLO in return for American recognition: 1) the
abandonment of armed struggle, 2) the recognition of Israel, 3) the accep-

texts in question, see *International Documents on Palestine, 1975*, pp. 204, 327, docs. 88
and 192.

[45] *Al-Ṭalā'i'*, 2 December 1975.

[46] *Ibid.*

[47] 'Adnān Badr, "Wathīqat Saunders, khuṭwa ukhrā...," *Al-Hadaf*, 22 November 1975.

[48] Walīd Naṣṣār, "Wathīqat Saunders, akhṭar mā ṭaraḥathu Amīrikā," *Ilā l-amān*, 28
November 1975. This organ of the radical Rejection Front went as far as to state that
the Saunders document was "cooked up" with the help of certain Arab parties dedicated
to a negotiated compromise settlement (*taswiya*) assisted quietly by the PLO leadership.
Moreover, the Soviet Union was seen as approving it.

Other articles in *Ilā l-amām* include Muḥammad al-Maqdisī, "Ḥawla Mudhakkirat Saunders," 5 and 12 December; and editorials on 21 and 28 November and 19 December 1975.

tance of Resolution 242 as the framework for the Geneva conference, and 4) an understanding with Jordan.[49]

Al-Thā'ir al-'arabī, organ of the Arab Liberation Front (ALF), interpreted the initiative as one of many American moves to neutralize recent successes scored by the PLO in the arena of the United Nations, particularly the condemnation of Zionism as racism, and the setting up of the Committee of Twenty (Committee on the Exercise of the Inalienable Rights of the Palestinian People). Another such move, according to this source, was a leak from the State Department to the *Agence France Presse* suggesting that following his meeting with Henry Kissinger, UN Secretary-General Kurt Waldheim would transmit to Palestinian leaders the latest American thoughts on how to implement Palestinian national demands. It was necessary, therefore, to guard against the dangers inherent in this new American political initiative.[50]

Thus, on the level of the Palestinian press, there was a unanimous rejection of the Saunders Document, with various degrees of emphasis. As to the leadership of the PLO, it treated it with great caution, and there was no public comment released by the official spokesman. *Wafa*, the official news agency of the PLO, merely carried excerpts of a *Filasṭīn al-thawra* editorial denouncing the American initiative. The attitude of the leadership toward the Saunders statement remains undocumented.[51]

---

[49] *Ilā l-amām*, 28 November 1975.

[50] *Al-Thā'ir al-'arabī*, 1 December 1975.

[51] According to *Time* (15 December 1975): "The Saunders testimony, even as it profoundly disturbed Israelis, profoundly intrigued Palestinian moderates, including Yasser Arafat. According to some reports, he is ready to accept a 'half a loaf' solution to the Middle East problem—a state on the West Bank and in Gaza, instead of all Palestine."
Analyzing the Saunders Document and the repercussions on the Resistance scene, Ghāzī Khalīlī wrote in *Filasṭīn al-thawra* (30 November 1975): "Some Palestinian circles viewed the document generally in concordance with the Egyptian line adopted toward the Saunders initiative, whereas other circles rejected it on the grounds that it did not represent anything new in the American policy vis-à-vis the Palestine question."
During an interview conducted by the Committee on the Exercise of the Inalienable Rights of the Palestinian People with Fārūq al-Qaddūmī, head of the PLO's Political Department in 1977, al-Qaddūmī appeared to regard President Carter's 'homeland' statement as a retreat from the Saunders position. In answer to a question on the PLO's attitude toward Carter's statement, al-Qaddūmī said: "We fear that the 'homeland' means merely a refuge for the Palestinian refugees, the settlement proposals once more. For this position to be a positive step, a few words need to be added to make Carter's statements positive. Instead of 'homeland' we must say 'national homeland,' the words 'the Palestinian people' must be used instead of the 'Palestinian refugees.'... If these additions are made to the statement we can consider it positive. But I fear the expression 'a homeland for the Pales-

This reticence was noted by some analysts. The editor of *Ilā l-amām* deplored the fact that the document was not debated publicly by the leadership: "When the PLO Central Council met on 14 November 1975, the Saunders memorandum was in circulation; yet it was not debated during the proceedings of the Council on the grounds that there was insufficient time to study the contents and give an opinion." The editorial went on to declare that the Saunders statement passed without any notable comment, "not even from the official spokesman who is normally generous with his commentaries."[52]

* * * *

Recently, William Quandt had this to say about the Saunders episode:

> There was little new in the statement, but its timing was significant. It was meant to symbolize a continuing willingness on the part of the Administration to work for a peace settlement. Kissinger had gone over the draft carefully, had checked the wording, and had reportedly cleared it with President Ford. When confronted with the hostility of Israel's reaction, however, he dismissed the Saunders statement as an academic exercise. Nonetheless, the United States seemed to take a somewhat more flexible position than in the past when the issue of the PLO participation in the UN debate scheduled for January 1976 came up. Briefly, Arab hopes were raised, but they were soon to be disappointed. Behind the symbolic shift in American policy, there was no real substance.[53]

William Quandt ought to know. For two years, and until 1974, he had worked as Harold Saunders' deputy in the Middle East office of the National Security staff. It is difficult to disagree with his assessment that "there was no real substance." Besides, if one of the objectives of the Saunders testimony

tinians' is a step backwards. The Saunders Document said that a solution in the Middle East was impossible without the Palestinians. Saunders stood up for the legitimate rights of the Palestinian people—that is, he recognized the existence of a Palestinian people. But now there is a retreat, with the use of the word 'refugees.'" See *Journal of Palestine Studies*, 6.4 (Summer 1977), p. 186, quoting *Shu'ūn filasṭīnīya*, June 1977.

[52] *Ilā l-amām*, editorial of 28 November 1975; also Muḥammad al-Maqdisī's articles of 5 and 12 December in the same source.

[53] William Quandt, *Decade of Decisions* (Berkeley: University of California Press, 1977), pp. 278–79.

was to signal to the leadership of the PLO that the door was being kept open (albeit hesitatingly and almost imperceptibly), State Secretary Henry Kissinger, with his remark that it was merely an academic exercise, wasted no time in slamming it shut.

The Saunders affair highlights the fundamental inconsistency of American policy vis-à-vis the Palestine question and the crucial role of the PLO. In September 1975, Secretary of State Henry Kissinger freely accorded Israel carte blanche on the question of future Palestinian participation in negotiations. This carte blanche was enshrined in a controversial Memorandum of Agreement between the United States and Israel that formed part of the Sinai II package: "...the United States will consult fully and seek to concert its position and strategy with Israel with regard to the participation of any other additional states. It is understood that the participation at a subsequent phase of the Conference of any possible additional state, group or organization will require the agreement of all the initial participants."[54]

Two months later the Kissinger-Saunders document openly recognized the centrality of the Palestine issue in the Arab-Israeli conflict ("the Palestinian dimension of the Arab-Israeli conflict is the heart of that conflict"), a truth that the US State Department, like everyone else, knew all along but was unwilling to acknowledge in public because of Israeli susceptibilities. It is difficult to comprehend how a great power could have acted so irresponsibly by foreclosing its options for dealing with the "heart of the conflict" by granting veto power to a client state.

---

[54] *International Documents on Palestine, 1975*, pp. 267–68, doc. 150.

18

The United States, the Arab-Israeli Conflict, and the Palestine Question in 1976*

THE YEAR 1976 WAS DOMINATED by the Presidential election campaigns, at which time, traditionally, the Administration is preoccupied more with domestic than foreign issues. With respect to the Arab-Israeli conflict and American initiatives to maintain the momentum of negotiations, many observers felt that the year would not witness any significant moves, especially following the Sinai II accord. Israel, as usual, played for time and could easily neutralize President Ford's somewhat timid attempts to keep the negotiations option alive while at the same time fighting for his re-election. Besides, there was the Lebanese internal war—a vortex that could draw all the parties to the Arab-Israeli conflict into a controllable arena and provided an ideal rationale or excuse with which the American administration could answer critics. The President, Kissinger, and many State Department spokesmen repeatedly claimed that the reason for the lack of progress in the negotiating picture was the internal war in Lebanon. These two important issues—American peace initiatives in 1976 and the Lebanese internal war—are the subject of our investigation in this chapter.

The year 1976 was also a very active one for the Palestine Liberation Organization on the diplomatic front, as it was in the military field. At the United Nations, the PLO sought to win increased recognition for the

---

*From the original English typescript for the study translated and published as "Al-Wilāyāt al-muttaḥida al-amīrkīya," in *Al-Kitāb al-sanawī li-l-qaḍīya al-filasṭīnīya li-'ām 1976*, edited by Camille Mansour (Beirut: Institute for Palestine Studies, 1979), pp. 347–76.

Palestinian people's right of self-determination and statehood. It was met there by a series of US vetoes. An election year provided ideal conditions for Zionist pressures to bring the United States into the closest alignment with Israeli hard-line policies regarding the PLO. Compared to the end of 1975, when the United States appeared to be moving toward some recognition of the PLO's role through such policy statements as the Saunders Document,[1] the year 1976 represented a backtracking. The United States and the Palestine question at the United Nations is also the subject of our investigation in this chapter.

Finally, we have included a selection of issues and initatives in the American Senate and House of Representatives. Early in the year Senator James Abourezk attempted to amend the Foreign Military Sales Act in a bid to place limitations on Israeli violations, such as the ruthless bombing of South Lebanon. The amendment was defeated, but the Senator had succeeded in drawing attention to the use by Israel of US-supplied Cluster Bomb Units (CBUs) against civilian targets.

Throughout the year, there was a bitter campaign in both the Senate and the House of Representatives against the Arab economic boycott of Israel. The campaign was led by the shining figures of the pro-Israel lobby in the Congress, and it became an issue in the Presidential elections. Another hotly debated issue was the sale of arms to Saudi Arabia and Jordan and the sale of C-130 transport planes to Egypt. Here again the opposition in Congress included many articulate supporters of Israel.

The chapter closes with a description of the hearings conducted by the Senate Foreign Relations Committee on the subject of the prospects for peace, with special sessions devoted to the Palestine question and the internal war in Lebanon.

In 1976 the Brookings Report became the subject of speculation that it might serve as a peace framework for Jimmy Carter if he should win the Presidential elections. It was also felt that some of the leading experts who participated in the drawing up of the report would be invited to serve in the Democratic administration. It may be interesting to note that the Brookings Report, signed by such key figures as Zbigniew Brzezinski and William Quandt, recommended the establishment of an independent Palestinian state.

---

[1][For the author's assessment of the Saunders Document, see pp. 402–408 and 417–30 above.]

How Serious Were American Peace Initiatives During 1976?

Rabin's Visit to the US

Israeli Prime Minister Yitzhak Rabin paid an official visit to the United States between 26 January and 5 February, the first head of government to visit the US during its Bicentennial Year celebration. The peace process, particularly with regard to Jordan, was an item of priority on the agenda. Yet Kissinger, right from the first exchange of toasts on 27 January, hinted very strongly that there was no hurry, no particular "crisis" in the Near East at this time. He used such expressions as peace being a "long-term issue," that Rabin was in Washington at a time "when there isn't any immediate crisis, when there isn't a particular negotiation on which we must achieve a specific result...we can talk in a free atmosphere about what can happen in the years ahead."[2] Presumably, Sinai II had taken care of that. He also stressed that the United States would not accept changes in the framework of peace negotiations: "We will not participate or encourage a negotiating process in which as an entrance price into negotiations the fundamental issues should already be determined by groups of countries that are not parties to the negotiations."[3] This was a reference to the current UN debate over the Palestine issue, and the veto cast on the preceding day by the United States. In an election year, the Israelis and their friends in the US could ensure maximum pressure on the American administration to keep the PLO out of the political framework of peace negotiations.

Prime Minister Rabin addressed the US Congress on 28 January, at which time he compared the American and Zionist revolutions and certain features shared by the two societies: "For both of our new societies, immigration became pioneering."[4] He also talked about peace with the Arabs:

> Peace will come when the Arab leaders finally cross the Rubi-
> con from aggressive confrontation to harmonious reconciliation.
> Then, there is no problem between us that cannot be solved in
> negotiation. That includes too the Palestinian issue within the
> geographic and political context of peace with Jordan. When I
> say Jordan, I do not discount the Palestinian representation in
> the peace delegation of that country. And when I say geography,

---

[2] *Department of State Bulletin*, LXXIV, 1913 (23 February 1976), p. 223.
[3] *Ibid.*
[4] *Ibid.*, p. 230.

I do not discount a negotiation concerning the future final peace boundaries of the territories involved.[5]

How serious was the expression of peace? United States officials were saying that Ford and Rabin had explored the possibility of talks with Jordan on a West Bank accord, a revival of the old Jericho Plan floated back in 1974. However, the chances of success were being described as uncertain because of the Rabat decisions and the Israeli refusal to deal with the PLO.[6] Nonetheless, Rabin asked the United States to use its good offices as mediator. He also made the kind of gesture likely to appeal to the State Department by suggesting the inclusion of Palestinians in the Jordanian negotiating team at a time when relations between Jordan, Syria, and the PLO were improving rapidly. However, Shimon Peres expressed the prevalent mood in Israel better when he said that nothing much could be expected to happen on the negotiations front during an American election year. And we must also remember the remarks of Kissinger quoted above. There was, from his point of view, no hurry and no immediate crisis. Perhaps he had forgotten the Lebanese crisis, or else it was of little consequence. Hence, it is difficult to take the US and Israeli public announcements seriously. The fact is that the Israeli government was determined to sit tight until after the US elections of 1976 (and perhaps even the Israeli elections of 1977), and that this diplomatic stagnation did not seem to bother the Ford administration unduly, despite President Ford's much publicized irritation at Shimon Peres' remarks. As one Israeli source remarked: "After all, all they want this year is movement towards movement towards movement."[7]

The momentum of the diplomatic negotiations in the Near East was going to be kept rather low. In mid-February, the State Secretary indicated that after the Rabin visit, the US would have more exchanges with the Israelis and would then bring the US ambassadors in the Near East to Washington for consultations "to discuss what the next move should be."[8]

The next move appears to have occurred around 8 March, when American officials announced new "explorations" to negotiate a comprehensive settlement between Israel and the Arab states and "conceded that the step-by-step procedure had reached its limit."[9] It was also reported that the

---

[5] *Ibid.*

[6] *International Herald Tribune*, 4 February 1976, p. 1.

[7] David Landau, "American Odyssey," *Jerusalem Post Magazine*, 23 January 1976, p. 5.

[8] *Department of State Bulletin*, LXXIV, 1915 (8 March 1976), p. 287.

[9] *International Herald Tribune*, 9 March 1976, pp. 1, 2.

United States was seeking to include the "non-belligerency" principle in the "end to the state of war" principle as a compromise between limited disengagement and full-scale peace agreements.[10] However, observers quickly noted that this was a US gimmick to keep "negotiations alive while not actually achieving anything."[11] In other words, the objective seems to have been the creation of the illusion rather than the substance of real movement. In any case, the United States did everything to scuttle the issue of PLO representation, thus going back on the promises implied in the Saunders initiative of November 1975.

As the implications of the sweeping victories of the PLO in the West Bank elections became clear, American policy-makers had the necessary proof and indicators to reassess their position toward the PLO. However, there is no published evidence that they did. On the contrary, with the election campaign in full swing, Henry Kissinger appeared before a Jewish audience in a Baltimore synagogue to articulate the traditional hard-line support for Israel, pledging that there "will be no imposed solutions."[12] A few days later, President Ford reaffirmed the "special relationship" with Israel in a special bid to swing more Jewish votes to the Republican camp following the collapse of the Jewish vote's favorite son, Democratic candidate Henry Jackson, at the hands of Jimmy Carter. It was then believed that the swing vote away from the Democratic ticket could be substantial.[13]

President Ford and the Chances for a Geneva Conference

Then came the diplomatic bombshell in early June when President Ford announced, to the delight of Israel and its supporters, that the chances for a Geneva conference for 1976 were remote.[14] The momentum, assuming there was any in the first place, had evaporated. Moreover, in a last-minute bid to win even more Jewish votes, President Ford met on 14 October with a group of editors from the American Jewish press and brought the US position even closer to the Israelis by insisting on direct negotiations.[15]

While photographers and reporters looked on, President Ford, with an obvious eye to political advantages in the last phase of the Presidential cam-

---

[10] *Ibid.*

[11] *Ibid.*

[12] *Jerusalem Post*, 10 May 1976, p. 1.

[13] *International Herald Tribune*, 15–16 May 1976, p. 3.

[14] *Department of State Bulletin*, LXXIV, 1931 (28 June 1976), p. 816.

[15] *New York Times*, 16 October 1976.

paign, informed Rabin, who was on yet another visit to Washington in October, that the ban on the sale of some ultra-sophisticated weapons to Israel would be lifted and the delivery of already approved items speeded up. The ultra-modern equipment included laser-guided bombs and helicopter gunships armed with anti-tank missiles, special night-fighting equipment, radar, and the latest in communications installations. The speeding up in delivery involved primarily items in short supply in the United States army: M-60 heavy tanks, self-propelled artillery, and armored personel carriers.[16] In fact, the quantity and quality of this military hardware, as well as its obvious electioneering dimension, was sharply noted by former Secretary of Defense James Schlesinger, who called it an "abrupt, pre-election reassessment which has not been coordinated either with the Department of State or with the Department of Defense."[17] Moreover, Schlesinger by way of criticism insisted that the sale of advanced military equipment to other countries must not be at the expense of the US's own security requirements. "I was always reluctant," he added, "to use our weapons, particularly advanced technology weapons, as domestic political currency."[18]

In short, the Ford administration was prepared to make every effort, even at the risk of increasing the tensions in the Near East, to please the Israelis and thereby to influence the Jewish swing vote to its side. By May this dangerous deterioration was noted by Congressman Lee Hamilton of Indiana. Speaking before the House, he said:

> Most disturbing in the present deteriorating situation is the apparent paralysis in US diplomatic efforts. Everyone here recognizes that tensions are on the rise in the Middle East, but policy-makers are unable, in this political season, to come forward with an approach or a plan to break the log jam in peace talk efforts.[19]

He stressed that step-by-step had become obsolete and that what was needed was a multilateral forum such as Geneva to revive the peace talks. He also urged Palestinian representation at the talks, and warned against attempts to keep the Soviet Union out of the negotiating process and to undercut "their substantial interests in the region."[20]

---

[16] *New York Times*, 12 October 1976.

[17] *Jerusalem Post*, 18 October 1976.

[18] *Ibid.*

[19] *Congressional Record* (House), 20 May 1976, p. H4772.

[20] *Ibid.*

The Ford Administration and the Lebanese Internal War

Kissinger's Attitude Towards the Internal War

Of the many intriguing questions that will probably remain unanswered for many decades is the attitude and role of Henry Kissinger in the complex events unfolding on the scene of the Lebanese civil or internal war, particularly during the year 1976. Did he, for instance, have a master plan? In the opinion of William Quandt, one of America's leading Middle East experts, the answer is negative: "The United States, rather than having a grand policy for dealing with the Lebanese crisis or the Palestinians, was confused and perplexed by the internecine war in Lebanon."[21] This view is also shared by Thierry Desjardins, *Le Figaro*'s special correspondent in Lebanon:

> There is no Machiavellian plan behind this collective suicide.... Someone could have perhaps played the witch in launching this war, but it would be absurd to believe that everything was planned—even by the CIA computers....The culprits are more in Beirut than in Washington and the causes are part and parcel of the Lebanese realities—much more than in the imagination of an American Secretary of State.[22]

In reference to the Secretary of State's role, William Quandt wrote: "Kissinger dealt with the crisis chiefly as an extension of the Arab-Israeli conflict."[23] And with respect to the Arab-Israeli conflict the Secretary of State has always shown a marked interest and a great deal of self-advertised creativity. It is not yet clear how his creativity was displayed in 1976 in Lebanon; perhaps the veil of secrecy will be lifted one day.

Another analyst, Roger Morris, drawing—as he tells us—on "his own experience in the State Department and White House from 1966 to 1970 and as a Senate aide from 1970 and 1972," and who acknowledges receiving information about Henry Kissinger and his policies from the inside, painted a somewhat different picture than William Quandt. In his critical study, *Uncertain Greatness: Henry Kissinger and American Foreign Policy*, Morris has written:

---

[21] William Quandt, *Decade of Decisions* (Berkeley: University of California Press, 1977), p. 283.

[22] Thierry Desjardins, "Three Acknowledgments," *Monday Morning* (Beirut), 214 (19–25 July 1976), pp. 10–11.

[23] Quandt, *Decade of Decisions*, p. 283.

Ironically, however, it was the most ruthless exploitation of internal weakness that crowned Kissinger's Middle East policy in 1975–76—and this time, his Jewish detractors silent, on the side of Israel. As Lebanon plunged into a bloody civil war, the CIA, with the connivance of the intrepid if short-sighted Israeli intelligence service, was accused by some officials of supporting covertly the fighting that inflicted an awful, temporarily crippling attrition on the PLO. Allegedly conducted by the special Israeli bureau of the CIA, the Lebanese operation proceeded, according to these sources, while unknowing American diplomats (like Korry in Chile) tried to arrange a cease-fire, and while Congressional and executive oversight groups were consistently misled on the scope and purpose of our covert involvement in Lebanon. Perhaps the final irony was that the same officials who were shocked at the CIA role and apparently leaked it could not be quite sure if Kissinger himself even knew the full details or motives of the Agency's operations. Having watched the shuttle diplomacy extract concessions from their clients, having weathered a Congressional and public storm intact, the CIA by 1976 still possessed the bureaucratic capacity and self-defined mission to carry out its own Mideast policy. . . . Whether or not he had any knowledge of such a gruesome intervention by the CIA in Lebanon, Kissinger would leave the Middle East in an uneasy balance. . . .[24]

Thought-provoking as all of the above undoubtedly is, it must be treated with caution until the relevant archives are opened or key participants are willing to shed additional light in their memoirs. In the meantime, one has to consult the public record and examine the prepared and unprepared statements, which in this age of mass media are at least plentiful.

Throughout 1976, the internal war in Lebanon was the subject of frequent commentary by Kissinger. In an interview in Los Angeles in January, the Secretary of State described the conflict in Lebanon as a "terrible tragedy" and as having "absorbed the energies of the surrounding countries,"[25] a theme that he was to repeat on frequent occasions, and as explanation (or was it as excuse) for the stagnation in the general Middle East peace negotiations front. "The problem in Lebanon," he said, "is to keep the situation

---

[24] Roger Morris, *Uncertain Greatness: Henry Kissinger and American Foreign Policy* (New York: Harper and Row, 1977), p. 261.

[25] *Department of State Bulletin*, LXXIV, 1914 (1 March 1976), pp. 267–68.

from involving the surrounding countries and at the same time to end the civil war."[26]

He also maintained that there was a "very serious danger that Lebanon may become a confrontation state, with the large number of Palestinians that live there."[27] This statement has to be seen in the context of the Rabin visit to the US and the common American-Israeli understanding that the PLO would be kept out of a reconvened Geneva Conference, as part of the plan to blunt the Soviet-Syrian-PLO diplomatic offensive of early 1976.

During this first quarter of the year, Kissinger repeatedly warned against military intervention in Lebanon: "We have strongly warned all outside countries, including Israel and including Syria, against rash military moves ....The United States would oppose unilateral intervention."[28] Again, on 29 March, the State Department underlined America's opposition to military intervention.[29]

As to the diplomatic initiative of Syria in arranging for a cease-fire on 22 January, the Department of State appeared to regard it as a positive development. On 29 March a State Department spokesman, Robert Funseth, stated:

> The political compromise worked out with constructive Syrian assistance in connection with the January 22 cease-fire appears to us to provide a fair basis for such a solution (to the Lebanese crisis)....It appears to us, moreover, that a cease-fire and an orderly and constitutional resolution of the Presidential question are necessary if progress is to be made on the more fundamental issues.[30]

Moreover, at this time State Secretary Henry Kissinger was preparing to dispatch a special envoy to Lebanon in the person of L. Dean Brown.

At this time also, King Hussein was making a state visit to Washington, where he reportedly conducted intensive consultations on the situation in Lebanon.[31] During an "Issues and Answers" televised interview (4 April), he declared that Syria would do everything possible to separate the warring factions in Lebanon. He did not rule out the use of armed units, indicating

---

[26] *Ibid.*

[27] *Ibid.*

[28] *Ibid.*, LXXIV, 1920 (12 April 1976), p. 478.

[29] *Ibid.*, LXXIV, 1921 (19 April 1976), p. 507.

[30] *Ibid.*

[31] *Time*, 12 April 1976, pp. 15–17.

that it was sought after by the "Lebanese authorities at the very highest levels."[32] He took his stand on the side of Syria and described the close coordination and cooperation in all aspects, including the political, that has developed between Syria and Jordan.[33]

The Brown Mission to Lebanon

Ever since January 1976, American Ambassador to Lebanon G.M. Godley had been away on sick leave recovering from a grave operation. The cease-fire was still very shaky, despite Syria's mediation. A new situation had been created by General 'Azīz al-Aḥdab's coup d'état of 11 March, and toward the end of the month relations between Kamāl Jumblāṭ and Syria were strained.

L. Dean Brown, a veteran diplomat with a reputation as a troubleshooter, had retired from the American diplomatic service to head the Middle East Institute. He was summoned at very short notice—Kissinger said at 24 hours notice—and dispatched as a special envoy to Lebanon with instructions to make contact with all Lebanese parties, particularly President Franjieh and Kamāl Jumblāṭ, and to offer his good offices as mediator. He was instructed not to make contact with the PLO.[34] Arriving in Beirut on 1 April, Ambassador Brown wasted no time in starting his round of consultations. More information about the mission was made available publicly on 5 April at a hearing before a Senate Committee on the Judiciary, conducted by Senators Edward Kennedy, James Abourezk, and Hiram Fong, with statements given by Under-Secretary of State Joseph Sisco, James Wilson, Coordinator for Humanitarian Affairs in the Department of State, and Dr. Clovis Maksoud, senior editor of Beirut's *Al-Nahār*. The purpose of the hearing was to discuss humanitarian as well as political problems brought about by the escalating crisis in Lebanon.

Thus, during the hearing on 5 April Joseph Sisco declared:

> Brown is under instructions to do everything that he can to not only make this cease-fire stick, but to begin to talk to factions within Lebanon, with a view to trying to find some common understanding on this political adjustment process along the lines of

[32] *International Documents on Palestine, 1976*, edited by Jorgen S. Nielsen (Beirut: Institute for Palestine Studies, 1978), pp. 402–405, doc. 231.
[33] *Ibid.*
[34] *Time*, 12 April 1976, p. 14.

a Syrian proposal. We think, on the whole, the Syrian proposal
makes a certain amount of sense, which would involve Franjieh resigning, and the election of a new President by the Parliament.[35]

The critical problem as seen by the State Department was the disintegration
of the Lebanese army. A UN peace-keeping operation was not regarded as
a serious possibility at this stage. As to the Egyptian proposal for an inter-
Arab force, Sisco's opinion (5 April) was: "It's not that the United States
has taken any position of opposition, *per se*. But with regard to the inter-
Arab force as put forward by Sadat, the reaction was negative throughout
the entire region and within Lebanon."[36] He characterized the Soviet role
as being, on the whole, rather inactive. Early in April the Soviets had made
"a diplomatic demarche in favor of the cease-fire," and Sisco did not think
the Soviets were interested in a confrontation posture at this time.[37]

As expected, Kennedy and Abourezk questioned Under-Secretary Sisco
very closely on the Geneva Conference and PLO representation, and whether
L. Dean Brown's mission would seek to establish contact with the PLO. The
transcript of questions and answers in the Executive Session of the hearings
is almost completely deleted at this point (as it is in many other sensitive
areas of the discussions), but Sisco did insist that Brown had instructions
not to talk to the PLO.

Finally, in answer to a question concerning the French role during this
early April period, Sisco said:

> We have been in close touch with the French. The French have
> obviously a natural affinity in this situation. They are active
> diplomatically and we keep each other informed. They favor
> what we're trying to do at the present time...they are trying to
> exercise a reasonable influence, particularly with the Christian
> community where they have a special relationship.[38]

In actual fact, France did on 7 April send to Lebanon a special envoy, George
Gorse, who announced his country's willingness to host a roundtable conference of the various warring Lebanese parties. At this time also the Vatican
dispatched a Papal delegation.

---

[35] US Senate, Committee on the Judiciary, "Humanitarian Problems in Lebanon," Part
1, *Hearing*, 5 April 1976, p. 17.
[36] *Ibid.*
[37] *Ibid.*, p. 20.
[38] *Ibid.*, p. 21.

On 22 April Kissinger announced in Washington that he would be meeting in London with Ambassador L. Dean Brown the next day, and following
the meeting they both addressed the press. The State Secretary praised
Brown: "Partly as a result of [Brown's] extraordinary efforts, we can now talk
about the beginning of constitutional government in Lebanon."[39] He characterized Brown's role in the diplomatic process as decisive: "probably the only
person in Lebanon who has been in touch with all the factions...and therefore in a position to carry the views of the various parties to the others."[40]
The press conference appeared to indicate that the subject of the creation of
a security force in Lebanon was high on the agenda. He did not want to go
into details, but he did specify that he was talking about "Lebanese forces
drawn perhaps from some of the factions or separately recruited...[which] to
be effective must be acceptable to all of the parties there and all of the parties that feel threatened."[41] He also announced that upon the completion
of Brown's mission in about two weeks' time, Ambassador Francis Meloy
would be sent to replace him.

When Ambassador Brown left Beirut on 11 May, he was asked to explain
his expression of cautious optimism. He attributed it in part to the election
of a new President, Elias Sarkīs, and his belief that the various factions
would rally around him: "It is just an intuitive sense that they (the warring
factions) are in the process of realizing there are no winners and no losers
here."[42] It did not take him long to revise his opinion. On 10 August he
appeared to be pessimistic. He saw no prospect whatsoever for a settlement
"in the few months to come."[43] He seemed to think that eventually the
Swiss canton solution would come out and warned that it would only create
further problems. He saw Lebanon as "a cockpit in which everybody fights
quarrels...Israel itself has played a role in this. It appears that Israel has
become one of the chief suppliers" of one of the sides.[44]

To bring this short survey of Dean Brown's mission to Lebanon to a
close, despite public gestures of harmony—such as during the joint Kissinger-
Brown interview with the press in London on 23 April—the special envoy to
Lebanon was critical of the Administration's handling of the Lebanese crisis.

---

[39] *Department of State Bulletin*, LXXIV, 1925 (17 May 1976), p. 627.

[40] *Ibid.*, p. 628.

[41] *Ibid.*, p. 627.

[42] *International Herald Tribune*, 12 May 1976, p. 1.

[43] Dean Brown, appearing on the "Press Conference, USA" panel. Transcript reproduced
in *Monday Morning*, 23–29 August 1976, pp. 11–15.

[44] *Ibid.*

He felt that the US had "made a mistake" in leaning hard on Syria not to send troops to Beirut in an attempt to separate the combatants and to stop the bloodshed, especially in April. The consequence was that the Syrian leadership remained "deeply suspicious" of America's role and motives.[45] On 27 May he said in an interview: "We reined in the Syrians too much to please the Israelis; it resulted in a lot more killing."[46] William Quandt sees this statement as a critique of Kissinger's policy. It is worth mentioning that Brown paid tribute to Syria's initiatives as well as to the PLO "for playing a calming role" with the Lebanese left, and for helping to rescue US citizens trapped by the fighting.[47] At a conference held at the prestigious Brookings Institution he supported the creation of a Palestinian state, which he felt would be an important step toward the resolution of the conflict in Lebanon.[48]

The Evacuation of US Citizens from Beirut

Despite the election of a new Lebanese president and the missions of Brown and Gorse, the bloodbath in Lebanon did not end. In fact, the whole situation took a turn to the worse. The leaders of the Lebanese National Movement, joined by the PLO, were voicing increased scepticism regarding Syria's role. In the last week of May, following his talks with President Ford, French President Valery Giscard d'Estaing announced that he was prepared to dispatch French troops to Lebanon on 48 hours' notice if requested to do so by President-elect Elias Sarkīs. The move was favored by the Lebanese Right, but denounced by Prime Minister Rashīd Karāmī, joined by the Lebanese National Movement and the PLO.[49] The American reaction to this proposed initiative by France was one of cautious support. Kissinger remarked on 25 May: "If all the interested Middle East parties agree, if the French move does not bring with it the introduction of other outside forces, and if all the parties in Lebanon agree, then the United States would be prepared to consider it."[50] A few days later regular units of the Syrian army entered Lebanon. But the fighting, especially in Beirut, raged on.

---

[45] *International Herald Tribune*, 28 May 1976, p. 7.

[46] Quandt, *Decade of Decisions*, p. 283.

[47] *International Herald Tribune*, 28 May 1976, p. 1.

[48] *Jerusalem Post*, 24 June 1976, p. 3.

[49] *International Herald Tribune*, 24 May 1976, p. 1.

[50] *Department of State Bulletin*, LXXIV, 1930 (21 June 1976), p. 792.

Following the assassination in Beirut of American Ambassador Meloy and Robert Waring, head of the economic section, on 16 June, the Ford administration organized two evacuations of American citizens by sea from Beirut. These operations were done with vast media coverage, and many observers—including American residents who refused to evacuate—saw a link with the American Presidential elections. Ford was out to please the electorate. On 20 June a US Navy landing craft took on about 300 persons, including many non-Americans, and transferred them to the mother ship standing some three miles offshore in a rescue operation labelled "Fluid Drive."[51]   Western diplomats in Beirut criticized the move as an "over-dramatization," as more than 1700 US citizens had chosen to remain in Lebanon.[52]

Following the evacuation, President Ford gave a public expression of gratitude to the PLO. He said: "The PLO and all other parties in Lebanon cooperated completely in making it possible for us to evacuate the Americans and the other nationals without incident."[53]   This episode led to "a stir among Israeli diplomats and their American supporters, who feared that the US may be easing its opposition" to the PLO.[54] As usual, the State Department announced that the President's remarks constituted no change in policy. In explaining the PLO role in the evacuation, Henry Kissinger said: "The United States, of necessity, had to deal through various intermediaries with the PLO. That is to say, other countries that have relations with the PLO contacted the PLO about physical arrangements in an area that was controlled by Palestinians."[55]

What was the PLO attitude toward the State Department message of gratitude addressed indirectly to the PLO following the naval evacuation of US citizens? Fārūq Qaddūmī, head of the PLO Political Department, declared in late June:

> The message was addressed to the Palestinian command and those who assisted in the evacuation of European and American citizens from Lebanon. The message was relayed to the Egyptian Foreign Ministry, which in turn conveyed it to us. It was more of a word than a message. It was not written. It was a verbal

---

[51] *Arab Report and Record*, 16–30 June 1976, p. 385.

[52] *Ibid.*

[53] *Jerusalem Post*, 22 June 1976, p. 1.

[54] *Ibid.*

[55] *Department of State Bulletin*, LXXV, 1934 (19 July 1976), p. 90.

message of gratitude to the Palestinian command and those who assisted in the evacuation effort. We do not consider the message or these words a recognition by Washington of the PLO.[56]

Following this first naval evacuation, there were expectations that a State Department meeting scheduled with American ambassadors serving in Near East countries would lead to a new American initiative. But in response to a question the State Secretary explained:

> It was important to have an opportunity to get a first-hand view from our Ambassadors in those countries in the Middle East that are most concerned with the Lebanese crisis. And also to give us an opportunity to avoid misconceptions about what role the United States may or may not have played in particular events. Out of this meeting today I do not expect an American peace initiative for Lebanon.[57]

In actual fact, this was the phase of the Arab League's attempt to bring about a settlement in Lebanon. There was also the French idea of a round-table in Paris and a French force to assist in the cease-fire. In this respect, the United States, while "not wanting to commit itself to any one particular formula," appeared to lean in the direction of the Arab League initiative. On 28 June Kissinger said: "If the French government were prepared to send one (a force), it could play a potentially useful role, but it is not now being discussed, and our impression is that the Arab League force will be the principal international instrument that is being used."[58]

The conference of Arab League foreign ministers had called for an immediate cease-fire in Lebanon on 1 July, and sent a three-man delegation composed of Secretary General of the Arab League Maḥmūd Riyāḍ and the foreign ministers of Tunisia and Bahrayn. The backdrop to this initiative was the fierce battle raging at the Palestinian camp of Tall al-Zaʿtar. The delegation met with the leadership of the Lebanese Right in Kfūr. It then sponsored a meeting on 4 July at Ṣofar attended by Saudi Foreign Minister Prince Saʿūd al-Fayṣal, Syrian Foreign Minister ʿAbd al-Ḥalīm Khaddām, PLO Chairman Yasir Arafat, and representatives of the Lebanese Right.

---

[56] Fārūq Qaddūmī interviewed by *Monday Morning*, 28 June–4 July 1976, p. 22. He also stated: "We have publicly denounced the criminal assassination of the United States Ambassador."

[57] *Department of State Bulletin*, LXXV, 1934 (19 July 1976), p. 91.

[58] *Ibid.*, LXXV, 1935 (26 July 1976), p. 121.

Kamāl Jumblāṭ refused to attend. A meeting scheduled for the next day, also at Ṣofar, was cancelled, reportedly because of the National Movement's attack on the town of Shekkā in northern Lebanon.[59]

The next episode in the evacuation of Americans from Lebanon took place on 27 July. Ten days earlier, the US Embassy in Beirut announced that it was closing down its consular services and invited American and foreign residents to take advantage of what was described as the last such organized evacuation from Beirut. In a repeat performance, a landing craft took on 309 foreigners, only half of whom were Americans, to the transport ship *Coronado* lying offshore. Athens, the final destination, was reached on 29 July—again amid much publicity.[60]

In late October the long-awaited breakthrough occurred. An urgent conference called for by King Khālid grouped Presidents Asad and Sadat and PLO chairman Arafat in Riyadh. A few days later, an Arab summit in Cairo completed the work of Riyadh, establishing a combined Arab force, with deterrent capabilities, composed for the most part of Syrian units. In the meantime, US policy appeared to increasingly recognize the Syrian role in Lebanon. In August, for instance, Kissinger had declared:

> With respect to Lebanon, our view is that the Damascus formula of earlier this year is the best solution for the problem of Lebanon; that is to say, a certain reapportionment of power as between the Christian and the Moslem communities but nevertheless an essential balance in their political influence.[61]

It is also clear that the United States was supporting Saudi Arabia's role in healing the rift in Arab ranks. On 9 July, in the presence of Prince 'Abdallāh ibn 'Abd al-'Azīz, Deputy Prime Minister of Saudi Arabia, who was on a visit to the US, Henry Kissinger remarked: "We think that the Kingdom, and His Majesty in particular, has taken wise initiatives in bringing together the Prime Ministers of Syria and Egypt and in using the good offices of Saudi Arabia to arrange negotiations among all of the parties in Lebanon."[62] In addition, at this time the US position against the partition of Lebanon was more frequently heard, particularly during September, when US emissaries were sent to the Lebanese Right via Cyprus.[63] On the

---

[59] *Arab Report and Record*, 1–15 July 1976, p. 434.

[60] *Ibid.*, 16–31 July 1976, p. 454.

[61] *Ibid.*, LXXV, 1941 (6 September 1976), p. 325.

[62] *Ibid.*, LXXV, 1936 (2 August 1976), p. 172.

[63] *Ibid.*, LXXV, 1944 (27 September 1976), p. 401.

occasion of the installation of Elias Sarkīs as President in late September, the State Department again reaffirmed its commitment to the integrity and unity of Lebanon: "Solutions based on the partition of Lebanon," it declared, "are invitations to further strife and instability. The states so created would not be viable and would invite external intervention."[64] This was reiterated on 22 December when President Sarkīs' personal emissary, Ghassan Tueini, visited Washington.

As to the question of assistance and reconstruction, the United States had provided emergency aid totalling $7 million to the International Committee of the Red Cross (ICRC) relief work in Lebanon, and $6 million to the American University Hospital in Beirut, plus $1 million to special UN relief programs in Lebanon. A food aid program of $20 million was also planned.

The United States and the Palestine Question at the UN

As the year opened, Israeli Foreign Minister Yigal Allon visited Washington with the aim of obtaining full US support for the Israeli stand in the forthcoming United Nations Security Council debate on Palestine. The Israeli cabinet had issued a statement on 4 January reaffirming its policy of boycotting this UN Security Council debate, rejecting the participation of the PLO at a reconvened Geneva Conference, opposing any change of the site of peace talks from Geneva to the Security Council, and rejecting any changes in the wording of UN Resolutions 242 and 338. As the *New York Times* put it: "Mr. Allon has come to the United States to press for an American commitment to block any Council resolution that gives additional standing to the Palestinians or that seeks to move the negotiating framework from the Geneva conference to the Security Council."[65]

It would seem that he was largely successful. The Saunders Document of November 1975 had been seen by Israel as an indication of a possible shift in the American position on the subject of Palestinian representation and the role of the PLO, although it is also clear that Israel was exaggerating its significance. In any case, Israel was very keen to align the United States even more closely to its own policy of total rejection of the PLO, particularly because of reports circulating that some Western European states were planning to introduce a resolution in the Security Council described as acceptable to all sides. An American election year provided ideal conditions

[64] *Ibid.*, LXXV, 1946 (11 October 1976), pp. 459–60.
[65] B. Gwertzman, "US to Oppose Changing Basis of Mideast Talks," *New York Times*, 8 January 1976, p. 4.

for the pressure tactics required for the task of pushing the United States to exercise the veto power on behalf of Israel.

Allon need not have worried so much. President Ford had summoned his envoys from Egypt, Syria, Jordan, and Saudi Arabia for consultations and was letting it be known widely that the United States would inform the Arab states of her resolve to veto any moves to bring Palestinians into the Geneva talks or to change the framework set by Resolutions 242 and 338. [66]

Daniel P. Moynihan and UN Security Council Draft Resolution S/11940

As the Security Council debate opened, Chaim Herzog, Israel's delegate to the United Nations, boycotted the deliberations and conducted his own highly publicized "show" from across the street.[67] The Council voted overwhelmingly to permit the PLO to attend the debate, despite vehement protests by the United States, which on this occasion was unable to exercise its veto. The seating of the PLO was a procedural not a substantive resolution. The American delegate, Daniel P. Moynihan, displayed his art of violent histrionics to the full, using particularly angry words and describing the Security Council as "totalitarian."[68] And as the debate entered its fourth day, the United States was increasingly isolated: it was, in the words of the *New York Times*, "the only nation that refused to support Arab efforts to obtain recognition for the political rights of the Palestinians."[69] In the corridors of the United Nations, Moynihan was busy repeating that he would veto any resolution that called for recognition of Palestinian "rights."[70]

Finally, on 26 January, the United States vetoed draft resolution S/11940, which included among other things an affirmation of the Palestinian right to establish an independent state in Palestine and a call for total Israeli withdrawal from all Arab territories occupied in 1967.

In explaining the US veto, Moynihan said:

> The US negative vote on the resolution was not based on antipathy to the aspirations of Palestinians but, rather, on the conviction that the passage of that resolution would not ameliorate their condition nor be the most effective way of addressing the

---

[66] *New York Times*, 12 January 1976, p. 1.

[67] *Ibid.*, p. 3.

[68] *Ibid.*, 13 January 1976, p. 1.

[69] *Ibid.*, 16 January 1976, p. 2.

[70] *Ibid.*

long-neglected problem of their future in the context of an overall settlement.[71]

Furthermore, the principal consideration in US policy was "to preserve the framework for negotiations established in Security Council Resolutions 242 and 338," whereas the draft resolution, referring specifically to the Palestinian people's national right of self-determination and statehood, would in his opinion "have been seriously harmful to the future of the peacemaking process."[72]

The veto was also the subject of a lengthly (and more conciliatory) explanation by the Department of State, particularly with reference to the Palestinian people and their future. The statement stressed the importance of developing "a common understanding of this particularly complex issue:"[73]

> The Palestinian question was for many years considered primarily a refugee problem. It is widely accepted today that this is only one aspect of a larger question. The United States has repeatedly affirmed its recognition that there will be no permanent peace unless it includes arrangements for the Palestinian people. The United States is prepared to work with all the parties toward a solution of all the issues yet remaining, including the issue of the future of the Palestinian people. We have no preconceptions as to the nature of such a solution as it involves them, which can only be worked out as part of the negotiating process. But we recognize that a solution must take into account their aspirations within the framework of principles laid down in Resolutions 242 and 338.
>
> This issue, as is the case with the other issues, can be successfully dealt with, however, only by maintaining the momentum of practical progress in the negotiating process. We look to this process to clarify issues and to help develop a reasonable and accepted definition of Palestinian interests, without which negotiation on this aspect of the overall problem cannot be successfully addressed.[74]

---

[71] *Department of State Bulletin*, LXXIV, 1912 (16 February 1976), p. 193.

[72] *Ibid.*

[73] *Ibid.*

[74] *Ibid.*, pp. 195–96.

It is interesting to note that shortly thereafter Moynihan paid his first visit to Israel, where he was presented with an honorary doctorate from the Hebrew University "in recognition of his forceful and articulate defense of Israel."[75]

William Scranton and UN Security Council Draft Resolution S/12022

After the fiery performances of Moynihan in the UN in December, January, and February, everyone expected his successor, William Scranton, to represent the United States at the UN with more reserve in March. There was, in addition, the hope among the Arab delegations that Scranton, who had gotten himself into trouble back in 1968 with Israel and its backers for suggesting an "evenhanded" US diplomacy in the Arab-Israeli conflict, might show some of this evenhandedness in the current UN Security Council debates. This was a period of intense protest activity in the West Bank against continued Israeli occupation and new expropriation of Palestinian land by Jewish religious extremist groups. In addition, there were attempts by Israelis to invade the precincts of the Noble Sanctuary (*Al-Ḥaram al-sharīf*) in Jerusalem. The ensuing protests, as usual, were met with violent repression by the Israeli troops, resulting in many Palestinian casualties.

It was in this context that the debate was called. The participants included PLO representative Zuhdī al-Ṭarazī, invited "to act as a spokesman for the West Bank."[76] The Israeli ambassador to the UN, Chaim Herzog, also attended at the urging of the United States. It was the first time that Israelis and PLO representatives were present together in a Security Council session. During the debates, Scranton figured prominently and drew objections from the Israelis because he insisted on stressing the "interim and provisional" character of the Israeli occupation, which Israel would like to consider as permanent: "Unilateral attempts," he maintained, to predetermine "East Jerusalem's future have no standing."[77] Then referring to Israeli settlements in the occupied territories, including East Jerusalem, Scranton referred to them as illegal and as a violation of the Fourth Geneva Convention (" The Occupying Power shall not deport or transfer parts of its own civilian population into the territory it occupies.") "Indeed," he added, "the presence of these settlements is seen by my government as an obstacle to the success of the negotiations for a just and final peace between Israel and its

---

[75] *Jerusalem Post*, 9 July 1976.

[76] *Time*, 5 April 1976, p. 12.

[77] *Department of State Bulletin*, LXXIV, 1921 (19 April 1976), p. 528.

neighbors."[78] However, when it came to the final vote, and although the draft resolution was specifically watered down to accommodate the United States, Scranton cast a veto on the grounds that the resolution would have a negative impact on the current peace negotiations. Significantly, this draft resolution (UN doc. S/12022) received the votes of such Western nations as France and Britain, which normally would refrain from voting when the United States vetoed a resolution.

Arab and Muslim states were once again disappointed. So were the Israelis, for different reasons. The dispute with the United States over the changes of status in East Jerusalem and the settlement policy was aired openly in a Security Council forum, although there was little cause for worry on the part of Israel since the United States had repeated its stand on Israeli violations on many previous occasions without really doing anything concrete about them. The sanctimonious phrases were designed merely to soothe Arab and Muslim susceptibilities on such sensitive issues as Muslim holy places in Jerusalem and Hebron and the continued colonization of the West Bank. There is no evidence that the United States was ever disturbed by Israeli violations beyond uttering a few pious wishes in the direction of the Arabs. In addition, the Israelis were particularly annoyed at Scranton's casual invitation to "any...and preferably all" present in the chamber during the debate to consult with him about the situation in the Near East. With Zuhdī al-Ṭarazī present in the room at the time, Scranton's invitation could imply some sort of recognition of the PLO. Israel's ambassador to the US was ordered to promptly protest to the State Department, and Kissinger remarked that Scranton's invitation was "an unfortunate formulation."[79] On another level, Rabin's reaction to the American criticisms regarding the colonization of the West Bank was to declare that his cabinet would intensify settlement and construction projects in East Jerusalem and the West Bank. In short, the tactic adopted by the Israelis to confront American criticism in this particular field was escalation: the more America formulates objections about the settlements, the more defiant Israel becomes, and the more it intensifies the colonization process. Eventually, America backs down. Scranton, for instance, let it be known that he might favor some permanent settlements in the occupied territories. "Something along the line of the Allon Plan makes sense," he told the *Chicago Sun Times* in an interview.[80]

---

[78] *Ibid.*

[79] *Time,* 5 April 1976, p. 13.

[80] *Jerusalem Post,* 9 June 1976, p. 1.

One can only conclude that "evenhandedness," especially when applied to Palestinian rights and territory, is a very vague concept indeed.

Activities from June to December

In addition to the negative votes to block progress on issues vital to Palestinians during the first half of the year, the United States went on to repeat much the same performance during the second half. Thus, on 29 June the United States cast its third veto of the year on a draft resolution on Palestine. This resolution, S/12119, had affirmed "the inalienable rights of the Palestinian people to self-determination, including the right of return and the right to national independence and sovereignty in Palestine, in accordance with the Charter of the United Nations."[81]

As this debate in the UN was taking place, a row developed between Israel and the Ford administration over the visit of PLO representative Shafīq al-Ḥūt to Washington, where he met with a number of Senators and also held a press conference. Israeli reactions were sharp. The *Jerusalem Post* reported it as "the first recorded sally by a PLO leader into Washington from the PLO's mission to the UN in New York; Al-Hut apparently received official permission to make the trip."[82] What had exasperated Israel even more was that al-Ḥūt's initiative and his reception in Washington had been preceded by public expressions of thanks to the PLO by President Ford and Secretary of State Kissinger for the help extended in the evacuation of US citizens from Lebanon.

There was a flurry of speculation in the American capital. The *Washington Star* quoted official sources as saying that the PLO had been recognized *de facto*, and that its status was now comparable to that "of the Jewish Agency prior to the establishment of the State of Israel."[83] Moreover, the al-Ḥūt visit, which had been arranged by Senator Abourezk, did score a few points on American public opinion. The PLO leader informed the Senators that the PLO forces had provided security for the Jewish quarter in Beirut during the internal civil war. Senator Abraham Ribicoff, who had accepted the invitation to meet with Shafīq al-Ḥūt, expressed his amazement that no one had ever informed him of this fact before. Predictably, he was severely criticized by the pro-Israel supporters in the United States. As one of the

---

[81] *United Nations Resolutions on Palestine, 1976* (Beirut: Institute for Palestine Studies, 1977), p. 47.

[82] *Jerusalem Post*, 28 June 1976, p. 1.

[83] *Ibid.*

three Jewish Senators, he was accused of having been used to extend "legitimacy to the PLO."[84]

After the defeat of President Ford by Jimmy Carter in early November, a surprising move was made by the Ford administration during a November debate in the Security Council. Egypt had requested this debate as an agenda item entitled "The Situation in the Occupied Arab Territories." After several meetings the Security Council issued an important consensus statement on 11 November, expressing among other things "grave anxiety and concern over the present situation in the occupied Arab territories as a result of continued Israeli occupation." It strongly deplored the establishment of Israeli settlements on occupied Arab territories. It declared illegal the annexations in Jerusalem and called upon Israel to rescind all measures taken in this respect and to refrain from violations of the Geneva Convention. It also affirmed that "any act of profanation of the Holy Places...seriously endangered international peace and security."[85] The consensus statement itself, plus the fact that the United States had joined in to make of it a unanimous expression, after having refused to join in a similar consensus statement by the Security Council on 26 May, infuriated Israel. Herzog called it a "modern international expression of anti-Semitism,"[86] a well-worn accusation repeatedly used by Israelis to harass people in the West who are critical of anything the Zionist state does.

This rare American action drew sharp protests from Israel and its US supporters. In Tel Aviv, Allon accused the United States of "discrimination" during a meeting with the American Ambassador, and made the accusation public. He also went out of his way to publicly snub the American Ambassador.[87] In explaining this surprising move by the US, the *New York Times* saw it as "a shift in diplomatic tactics without changing the substance of US policy."[88] The United States apparently wanted to give public recognition to Arab moderation and to encourage this trend by "rewarding" it. Another example was that Kissinger, with the Presidential elections over, wanted to clear the decks, so to speak, for the Carter administration in its search for new peace initiatives.[89] There is also Henry Kissinger's clarification that has to be taken into account, especially as the criticism from the

---

[84] *Ibid.*, 29 June 1976, p. 1.
[85] *United Nations Resolutions on Palestine, 1976*, p. 48.
[86] *New York Times*, 12 November 1976, p. 6.
[87] *Washington Post*, 13 November 1976, p. 1.
[88] *New York Times*, 13 November 1976, p. 1.
[89] *Ibid.*

Israeli lobby mounted. Answering a question put to him on 16 November which claimed that the US consensus vote "might have been different if it had come before rather than after the last elections," Kissinger said:

> We have before us a [forthcoming] general debate on the Palestine question in the General Assembly...a consensus statement by the Chairman [of the Security Council] as you know, has in itself no legal force; it simply reflects a view.[90]

Effectively, on 24 November William Scranton cast a negative vote on the United Nations General Assembly Resolution No. 31/20 on the Question of Palestine. Of course, being at the General Assembly, the US could not exercise its veto power. Perhaps Kissinger had said "yes" on 11 November so that he could better say "no" on 24 November. Moreover, he took the step (simultaneously) of leaking to the press the fact that the State Department was investigating the status of two PLO representatives, Ṣabrī Jirjīs and 'Iṣām Sarṭāwī, in connection with the opening of a PLO information office in Washington. On 24 November, headlines in the American press announced that the US had ordered the PLO representative to leave the country, and the Department of State announced that "from a foreign policy point of view, we do not believe it is a propitious moment for the PLO to open an office in Washington."[91] And yet it also acknowledged that under US law the PLO could not be prevented from opening an office in Washington.

Initiatives by the Congress

In reviewing issues and initiatives before both houses of the Congress, the Senate and the House of Representatives, during the year 1976, the following were selected for brief treatment: 1) Senator James Abourezk, the bombing of South Lebanon, and the Foreign Military Sales Act; 2) the campaign against the Arab economic boycott of Israel; 3) the question of arms sales to Arab states; and 4) the Committee on Foreign Relations' hearings.

Despite the fact that massive American aid brought Israel's armed forces to a peak situation in early 1976, with strategic stockpiles and the latest arsenal, the Israelis still complained bitterly about Washington's alleged lack of response to her military needs. It is axiomatic that the more the US beefs up Israel with political commitments (such as the ones during Sinai II),

---

[90] *Department of State Bulletin*, LXXV, 1955 (13 December 1976), pp. 706–707.
[91] *New York Times*, 24 November 1976.

economic aid, and military power, the more Israel talks of strained relations with the US and the erosion of American support.[92]

Nevertheless, during an election year Israel's ability to manipulate Congress increases significantly. This was shown in a dramatic move by pro-Israeli leaders in Congress to maintain the high rate of military aid, $1.5 billion a year, during the so-called "transitional quarter," a three-month period between the end of the fiscal year ending 30 June 1976 and the start of the new one under a new accounting system beginning 1 October. President Ford had previously agreed to grant a very high level of $1.5 billion in arms aid on the grounds that Israel had shown flexibility in the Sinai II peace talks, and it was reported that Ford's careful strategy aimed at linking future high levels of aid to continued willingness of Israel to negotiate in good faith. Apparently Ford was not satisfied with Israel's posture and had ordered a major cut in arms aid from $1.5 billion to $1 billion. But Israel and its friends were putting pressure on the Ford administration to maintain the high level intact through the "transitional quarter," and they succeeded in getting Kissinger temporarily on their side. In the end the Administration had to reach a compromise figure high enough to satisfy the pro-Israel lobby during an election year.

Senator Abourezk, the Bombing of South Lebanon, and the Foreign Military Sales Act

From an Arab perspective, one of the more important initiatives undertaken by a member of the Senate in 1976 was Senator Abourezk's attempt during February to amend the Foreign Assistance and Foreign Military Sales Acts. His proposed amendment, as he explained it, "would shut off military aid to any country that violates the air space or territorial sovereignty of another nation...[except when it] is acting in its own defense resulting from an attack by the armed forces of another nation."[93]

As he himself indicated, the amendment was aimed primarily at Israel, which was cited as the prime example of a violator. "The continuing Israeli bombing in southern Lebanon, bombing which has been going on for the last several years," said Abourezk, "has killed and wounded thousands of innocent people, both Palestinians in the Palestinian refugee camps and

---

[92] Wolf Blitzer, "Strained Relations," *Jerusalem Post Magazine*, 2 January 1976, p. 5; David Landau, "Testing Time," *Jerusalem Post Magazine*, 7 January 1976, p. 5.

[93] *Congressional Record* (Senate), 18 February 1976, p. S1878.

Lebanese farmers and villagers in South Lebanon."[94] He went on to add
that the Israelis were practicing a deliberate "scorched earth policy:"

> I want to illustrate what the policy means as southern Lebanon
> is concerned. Israel has dropped napalm, phosphorous bombs,
> cluster bombs, rockets, and regular TNT explosive bombs on the
> fields, in the villages, and in the densely populated Palestinian
> refugee camps in Lebanon—all to no avail. Mostly, what we read
> about in this country as an excuse for this kind of military terror-
> ism is that they are seeking out Palestinian terrorists. . . .Lebanon
> is a country which has nothing to do with anybody's war in the
> Middle East. Yet its civilians are suffering almost every day as a
> result of US arms aid to Israel, which with impunity, continues
> to conduct raids in that country causing the death and suffering
> of thousands of people.
>
> We have furnished to Israel what is known as cluster bombs.
> Cluster bombs are round weapons a little larger than grapefruit
> size. When dropped to the ground, they explode in small metal
> fragments contained inside the cluster bombs, scattering frag-
> ments in every direction which kill, wound, and destroy every-
> thing in their path. Anyone who says they are seeking out a
> terrorist or a guerrilla with that kind of bomb, when that bomb
> is dropped inside a Palestinian refugee camp or dropped in a
> civilian village in Lebanon, is simply not telling the truth. In
> fact, they are conducting the very same savagery that we in this
> country have denounced through the generations.[95]

The Senator was particularly incensed at Israel's use of CBUs (Cluster Bomb
Units) furnished by the United States in their frequent bombing raids in
South Lebanon, as early as 1975. In letters to Secretary of Defense Donald
Rumsfeld, Senator Abourezk requested information on the dates, quantities,
and modality of the shipments of CBUs to Israel. He received only an
interim answer and promises of a full response later. The full response never
came, and he was told that the State Department had intervened to block
the response. "Secretary Kissinger literally has the letter in his briefcase
and refuses to release it," said Abourezk, adding: "I am certain that, if we
got the letter, it would disclose that, indeed, we have been furnishing great

---

[94] *Ibid.*
[95] *Ibid.*

numbers of cluster bombs to Israel and that they, indeed, have been using those cluster bombs on innocent civilians in Lebanon, both in Palestinian refugee camps and in the fields and villages of southern Lebanon."[96] He cited in evidence eyewitness accounts by American newsmen and requested that their reports be printed in the *Congressional Record*. These included a *New York Times* article of 4 December 1975 referring to round and shiny balls about the size of grapefruits, and CBS News stories by Ike Pappas and Mike Lee, who reported "seeing the small softball size so-called cluster bombs unexploded on the ground in the area."[97]

Senator Abourezk had raised several embarrassing issues, including the role of Israel in triggering the Lebanese internal war. The reaction by such all-out supporters of Israel as Senators Jacob Javits and Henry Jackson was quick. After heaping insults at the PLO, they suggested that Abourezk's amendment would favor the PLO and that it was aimed at the "dismantling of Israel."[98] Invoking the right of self-defense, they justified the bombings. Abourezk replied by recalling that Javits during the Vietnam War had eloquently argued precisely the opposite, and had denounced US bombings because they were killing civilians in the process.

Finally the proposed amendment was put to the vote and defeated; 79 Senators voted against it, while the eight who voted for it included Abourezk, Thomas Curtis, Paul Fannin, Barry Goldwater, Mark Hatfield, James McClure, Willy Metcalf, and William Scott. In one sense, the vote against the proposed amendment may be seen as a barometer of support for Israel in the Senate in the wake of growing speculation regarding the possible erosion of such support following the Sinai II accord, President Sadat's visit to Washington, and his address to a joint session of Congress. In fact, the "special relationship" in the Senate during 1976 remained as strong as ever. Nine months earlier (May 1975), 76 Senators had reminded President Ford of the importance of the "special relationship" and had publicly urged him in an open letter to give Israel virtually all that it wanted in sophisticated military equipment and economic aid.[99] In February 1976, 79 Senators defeated an amendment that sought to inhibit Israeli aggression.

It may be interesting to note here another test for the Congressional support to Israel, this time in the House of Representatives. Early in March,

---

[96] *Ibid.*, pp. S1879–80.

[97] *Ibid.*

[98] *Ibid.*

[99] *International Documents on Palestine, 1975*, edited by Jorgen S. Nielsen (Beirut: Institute for Palestine Studies, 1977), p. 213, doc. 100.

Congressman David Obey of Wisconsin attempted to pass an amendment that would have cut the military credit sales portion of the Israel aid bill by $200 million. In his remarks to the House he said that he had no illusions about the amendment's chances of adoption. Nonetheless, he felt that the issue of military aid to Israel should have full and open debate. He was not at all impressed by Israel's obvious strategy of dilatoriness in negotiations in an American election year, and felt that a clear message ought to be delivered by the US regarding the urgency of movement toward peace. He also felt that Israel's military superiority was far too great. As he himself had foreseen, the amendment was defeated. The voting was: Yes 32, No 342, Not Voting 58.[100]

The Campaign Against the Arab Economic Boycott of Israel

On 22 January Congressman Edward Koch of New York indicated his intention to introduce legislation to prohibit by law the participation of American firms in the Arab boycott. His 35 cosponsors included some of the most ardent supporters of Israel among the Jewish members of the House of Representatives. Thus, Congressmen Henry Waxman and Benjamin Rosenthal, representing respectively California and New York, spoke violently against the Arab boycott, intimating that even at the risk of losing the substantial trade with the Arab world the United States must declare the boycott illegal.[101] The momentum of the campaign was kept up in March. Elizabeth Holtzman of New York was furious that so far attempts to oppose the Arab boycott was resulting in the transfer of trade and shipping destined to the Arab world from the port of New York to other American ports.[102] She should have perhaps realized that if the port of New York was not prepared to handle shipments to the Arab world bearing certification that they were not of Israeli manufacture, then other American ports were prepared to step in and take over that portion of a growing business. Holtzman was joined by Bella Abzug, also representing New York, in criticizing the US government for being indecisive about the boycott. Apparently many American firms were only too glad to pick up the business of the few American firms that refused to comply with the regulations.

---

[100] *Congressional Record* (House), 4 March 1976, pp. H1642, H1652.

[101] *Congressional Record* (Extension of Remarks), 9 February 1976, p. E553, and 16 February 1976, p. E626.

[102] *Ibid.*, 25 March 1976, p. E1561.

Meanwhile, in the Senate, Abraham Ribicoff and his cosponsors also introduced legislation aimed at hurting American firms that complied with the Arab boycott. And as in the case of the House of Representatives, the cosponsors included many of the most articulate Jewish defenders of Israel. Using in this case—and perhaps all of a sudden—many moral arguments, the Arab action was described as a national problem to the United States, whereas in strict terms it was a problem only for those firms that for one reason or another did not wish to comply with the Arab trade regulations. Moreover, there were many more American firms which found it particularly attractive to comply with the regulations than firms which did not.

In fact, the moral dimension was a piece of hypocrisy. During the many years of weak Arab economic power there seems to have been little reaction against the Arab boycott of Israel and of American firms with close dealings with Israel. And there was very little attention paid to the other and perhaps more severe boycott exercised in America by Israel against Arab economic interests, a subject that will be discussed below. However, now that the Arab economic position appeared brighter and huge financial resources were now in Arab hands and capable of being used to further Arab interests, American Jewish leaders of both the Senate and the House led the vanguard against the Arab economic boycott of Israel, and did so in the name of a specious morality. The speakers condemning the boycott included Senators Vance Hartke, Clifford Case, Henry Jackson, and Ribicoff.[103]

By the beginning of September the campaign against the Arab boycott had reached its height, coinciding with moves by pro-Israel Senators and Congressmen to block the sale of 650 Maverick air-to-ground missiles (worth $30 million) to Saudi Arabia.[104] Tax penalties on American companies cooperating with the boycott against Israel were approved by a joint Senate and House committee.

A group of Congressmen also unleashed an attack on the Department of Commerce, charging it with virtual complicity with certain American corporations complying with the Arab boycott of Israel. They urged public exposure of such firms and the adoption of legislation that would make compliance illegal. American banks and construction firms were also singled out, especially by the media, for their alleged cooperation with the boycott.[105] Typical of the media attacks was a story by syndicated colum-

---

[103] *Congressional Record* (Senate), 15 March 1976, p. S3377.
[104] *Washington Star*, 29 September 1976.
[105] *Washington Post*, 29 September 1976.

nist Jack Anderson that described a secret business meeting in March at which a Commerce official advised how multinationals "could comply with the boycott—and US regulations—by doing business with the Arabs through their foreign affiliates."[106]

In the face of such mounting criticism the US administration moved to cool tempers by pointing out that US anti-boycott legislation was unnecessary because of increased Arab easing of the boycott. Key figures warned against action that would be viewed by Arab states as unfriendly, and the consequent effect on American foreign policy. And businessmen were clearly opposed to any anti-boycott legislation because of the damaging effects it would have on half a million jobs, oil supplies, and American influence in the Arab world generally.[107]

From the State Department, Alfred Atherton expressed grave concern that the Saudis would view the mounting campaign against the Arab boycott and the missile sale as "a pattern of attacks" on their relationship with the United States.[108] There were reports—denied by Saudi Foreign Minister Saʿūd ibn Fayṣal—of a Saudi threat to embargo oil sales to the US in retaliation to proposed anti-boycott legislation or to the moves aimed at blocking the sale of missiles to the Saudi forces.[109] In Washington the pro-Israel lobby clashed with the business and oil lobbies, and the Senate Foreign Relations Committee voted 8 to 6 to block the sale of 650 Maverick missiles to Saudi Arabia. This brought a quick reaction from the State Department to reverse the decision.

Inevitably, the boycott affair became an issue during the final weeks of the campaign for the Presidential elections. Ford promised that his administration would expose firms that participated in the Arab boycott of Israel, while Jimmy Carter blamed Ford for the continued existence of the boycott and "pledged to put an end to it if he (Carter) is elected."[110] It is significant that during the national convention of the Bnai' Brith Jewish Association in September, both President Ford and Governor Carter appeared successively to declare their firm opposition to the Arab boycott.

Finally, as the year came to a close, an article in the *Washington Star* brought to light details of the little-known Israeli boycott of Arab economic

---

[106] *Ibid.*, 8 September 1976.

[107] Kennan Teslik, "America and the Arab Boycott," *Middle East International*, April 1978, pp. 22–23.

[108] *Washington Post*, 28 September 1976.

[109] *Ibid.*

[110] *New York Times*, 20 October 1976.

interests. A Californian bank, Wells Fargo in San Francisco, reported clauses in letters of credit of American firms dealing with Israel that required certification that vessels carrying the goods would not enter the territorial waters of Egypt, Yemen, Jordan, Saudi Arabia, Iraq, Lebanon, Syria, or Kuwait before unloading in Israeli ports. The bank in question felt that by processing such letters of credit they would be complying with the Israeli boycott against Arab states. It also became known that an Israeli contractor, in a contract with a US firm, "had included a clause that specifically excluded people of Arab origin from taking part in the work covered by the agreement."[111] As usual this dramatic exposure of Israeli practices was quickly squashed; American media seem to have ignored it thereafter.

The Question of Arms Sales to Arab States

On the subject of arms sales to the Arab states, the question of transfers to Saudi Arabia dominated the scene in 1976. It was frequently discussed in Congress, where, in the House, one of the most determined opponents of arms sales to Saudi Arabia, who predictably was also one of the keenest supporters of Israel, turned out to be New York Congressman Benjamin Rosenthal. On 2 March 1976 he launched a bitter attack on Saudi arms purchases assorted with various uncomplimentary remarks about the Kingdom, and argued that the Saudis "should not be permitted to obtain American technology, regardless of their wealth."[112] There followed the usual succession of pro-Israeli Senators and Congressmen who sought to ban the sale of advanced weapons to Saudi Arabia.

During August, Kissinger informed the Senate Foreign Relations Committee that the Ford administration was planning to sell $573 million in equipment, including Sidewinder air-to-air missiles and Maverick TV-guided bombs, to Saudi Arabia. There were reports of other military deals, including the modernization of the Saudi National Guard; the American press disclosed classified information including "construction work at Tabuk air base in the north of the country, an air force headquarters at Riyadh, and a naval training center at Jubayl, near the Gulf oil fields."[113] It was expected that pro-Israel members would attempt to block the sales in the Senate and House. But this was of course a very delicate issue—one which the Ford administration insisted could influence future relations with Saudi Arabia,

---

[111] *Washington Star*, 13 December 1976.

[112] *Congressional Record* (House), 2 March 1976, p. HI473.

[113] *Washington Star*, 4 September 1976.

and, increasingly, with Egypt. Furthermore, there was an important economic dimension to be considered. According to one report, Saudi Arabia was set to purchase weapons and equipment worth \$4.5 billion for the year 1976.[114]

After blocking the sale of US missiles to Saudi Arabia in September, the Senate soon reversed the measure following a personal plea by Henry Kissinger, who showed concern that the ban on the sale would affect the long-standing relationship with the Saudis, including the question of oil supplies.[115] On this question the Ford administration was able to impose its will on the Senate and House.

As to the question of the proposed sale of Hawk missiles to Jordan, which was being viewed with some suspicion by the Congress, it would seem that the Administration reacted by hinting that Congress would be to blame if Jordan purchased Soviet missiles and weapons to replace the Hawk deal.[116] This was a persuasive tactic, which caused the Congress to show more caution.

The other sale that held the attention of the news media during 1976 was the sale of C-130 transport aircraft to Egypt. Here again the opposition in Congress included many articulate supporters of Israel. In introducing his resolution against the sale, Congressman Philip Burton described the aircraft as "combat transport... capable of dropping paratroops into battle," and as symbolizing "a new relationship with the Sadat government and a precedent."[117] Using a rather strange argument for his resolution, Burton, who was joined by the following cosponsors—Jonathan Bingham, Cardiss Collins, Benjamin Gilman, Robert Nix, Donald Riegle, Benjamin Rosenthal, Stephen Solarz, and Lester Wolff—went on to say: "We will be putting ourselves at the mercy of future blackmail by Sadat being able to threaten us to return to his original supplier—the Soviet Union—unless we supply him with more and more arms. The time to end this fatal cycle is before it begins."[118]

Even stranger was the argument used by Senator Mike Mansfield—this time in support of the C-130 sale and of further sales if required. "After all," he said, "if we can create divisions among the Arab states, I think it's in

[114] *Ibid.*
[115] *New York Times*, 29 September 1976.
[116] *Congressional Record* (Senate), 4 June 1976, p. S8547.
[117] *Congressional Record* (House), 5 April 1976, p. H2880.
[118] *Ibid.*

our interest, and I think it is in the interest of Israel as well."[119] In the end Egypt obtained the planes. The tactic of the Administration was to present the sale not so much in terms of its intrinsic value, but rather as a symbol of US intentions to reward Egypt in the wake of Sinai II and the erosion of Soviet influence.

Committee on Foreign Relations Hearings

During May, June, and July, the Committee on Foreign Relations of the Senate conducted extensive hearings on the subject of "Prospects for Peace in the Middle East," with special sessions devoted to the Palestine question, the civil war in Lebanon and its international implications, the oil factor, and the conditions of a general peace settlement. The number of participants in these sessions was high and included many Near East experts from institutions of higher learning and government. Their statements covered a wide spectrum of opinion from pro-Israeli to "evenhanded" to pro-Arab.

Generally, there was some criticism expressed for the step-by-step diplomacy inaugurated by Dr. Henry Kissinger, with many witnesses actually attributing the civil war in Lebanon and the deterioration of the situation in the Near East to it. For instance, Senator Adlai Stevenson's opening statement stressed this fact: "For many years American policy in the Middle East has consisted of little more than a series of efforts to buy time; the passage of time without movement toward peace has moved the situation toward war."[120] He went on to add that "the most charitable thing that can be said about step-by-step diplomacy is that it has run its course."[121]

Senator Abourezk made a plea for the adoption of a US policy that would be consistent with the wide-ranging US interests in the Near East, including the all-important question of bringing a just peace to the area. "The reason why we haven't done that," he stressed, "is because we have always adopted not a United States Middle East foreign policy, but an Israeli Middle East foreign policy."[122] He also predicted that the continued Israeli practice of creating new settlements in the occupied territories would provoke more guerrilla attacks and a full outbreak of war.[123]

---

[119] *Congressional Record* (Senate), 5 April 1976, p. S4870.

[120] US Senate, Committee on Foreign Relations, *Hearings on Prospects for Peace in the Middle East*, 94th Congress (Washington: Government Printing Office, 1976), p. 4.

[121] *Ibid.*, p. 5.

[122] *Ibid.*, p. 13.

[123] *Ibid.*, p. 14.

Senator Floyd Haskell of Colorado, who had just returned from a visit to the Near East, reported that he had found the Arab states he visited much more receptive and flexible toward peace than Israel. In Israel, he said, "I found really no—how to say it—there was no receptivity of anything except the status quo and I found that depressing."[124] He urged that the United States convene all the parties to a peace conference, "with the broad outline for a settlement."[125] This included the establishment of a Palestinian state, recognition of Israel and guarantees of non-aggression, withdrawal of Israel "to borders suggested by UN Resolution 242,"[126] and significantly, the inclusion of the PLO as a participant in the conference. In the ensuing discussions, more Senators were prepared to see Yasir Arafat as a responsible Arab leader eager to make a success of the projected Palestinian state in the West Bank and Gaza.

Other speakers included Hishām Sharābī, who underlined that the political paralysis of the Israeli government with respect to the peace settlement in the Middle East stemmed from the fact that the Israelis "want peace and territory at the same time."[127] He showed the extent of the contradictions between the declared objectives of American foreign policy and their implementation. Moreover, American diplomacy was interested in dealing with peripheral issues only; the Nixon and Ford administrations lacked the will to resist Israeli leverage.

On the thorny question of the Lebanese civil war, the hearings were held in June against the backdrop of the murders of US Ambassador to Lebanon Francis Meloy and Economic Counselor Robert Waring. One of the key witnesses in this session of the hearings was Dean Brown, who had been involved as special envoy on a mission to Lebanon earlier in the year. He characterized the war in Lebanon as more than a civil war involving "right, left, Christian, Moslem, rich or poor."[128] Involved also were many non-Lebanese actors and elements. He did not think that the violence would stop easily or soon. He saw it also as a crisis in leadership. "The Lebanese leaders," he said, "feel helpless in the situation and many of them incompetent in the situation."[129] Another tragic factor was that there could not possibly be "a settlement in

---

[124] *Ibid.*, p. 15.
[125] *Ibid.*
[126] *Ibid.*
[127] *Ibid.*, p. 43.
[128] *Ibid.*, p. 125.
[129] *Ibid.*

Lebanon by the Lebanese alone."[130] He did not think that the United States could play much of a role at the present moment: "Perhaps it is up to the Arabs to provide the kind of settlement that will be needed; perhaps all the United States can offer now is sympathy."[131]

---

[130] *Ibid.*, p. 126.
[131] *Ibid.*

19

Realities and Illusions in America's Middle Eastern Policy*

UNLIKE THE OTHER POWERS, past or present, large or medium, who became attracted to the strategic importance, economic wealth, and political advantages of the Middle East, the United States developed an interest in the region relatively late: culturally, during the second half of the nineteenth century; economically, in the 1920s and principally over the question of oil concessions; and strategically, during the Second World War. This comparatively late entrance on the scene has often been put forward as an explanation—or an excuse—for the alleged inexperience of United States policy formulators and decision-makers, and their characteristic trial-and-error—mostly error—approach toward the Middle East.

This picture is, however, somewhat deceptive. The strategic importance and immutable role of the Middle East in global politics and balance of power did not escape United States notice altogether. It was, after all, an American naval strategist, Admiral Alfred Mahan, who first "invented" the term Middle East in 1902, and drew attention to its destiny as a necessary and permanent region of strategic and geopolitical confrontation between rival powers.[1]

There are, in addition, a number of overarching constants, not very difficult to detect, which make for continuity in United States policy. Yet it is often claimed that America does not have a policy toward the Middle East

---

*From the original English text translated into Arabic and published as "Al-Ḥaqā'iq wa-l-awhām fī l-siyāsa al-amīrkīya fī l-Sharq al-Awsaṭ," the Introduction to *Al-Siyāsa al-amīrkīya fī l-Sharq al-Awsaṭ: Nixon—Ford—Carter—Reagan*, edited by Laila Baroody and Marwan Buheiry (Beirut: Institute for Palestine Studies, 1984), xi–xxvi.

[1][On Mahan and the term "Middle East," see above, pp. 157–69.]

in general, and the Arab states in particular. This writer, however, believes otherwise; and the nine contributions, from widely different perspectives as they are, tend to support his contention. The problem appears less an absence of policy than an inability to maintain a regular and sustained course of action because of a complex combination of structural, functional, and perceptual factors including the nature of the Presidential and Congressional systems, the influence that special interest groups—such as the pro-Israel lobby—can exercise on specific occasions, and certain obsessions that are clarified by the contributions in the volume. The reality is that the Arabs have had to put up with, indeed have been caught between, two contradictory sets of American foreign policy behavioral modes: the Hamlet complex and the King Lear complex.

The questions that are posed and answered in the nine studies comprised in this volume center around the following: the constants and shifts in American interests and policy, the dominant schools of thought in the formulation of policy, instruments of implementation, the influence of special interest groups, the critique of US policy, and the ability of Israel, as implicit or explicit strategic ally, to preempt, derail, circumvent, or freeze American initiatives.

There are various ways of explaining decision-making in American foreign policy. One leading analyst, William Quandt, sees it in terms of "four distinctive, though often complementary, approaches:"

> 1. *The strategic or national-interest perspective*, which is probably the most commonly employed and which stresses the global view. In this respect the region is seen, almost exclusively, as a function of the world balance between the two superpower blocs.
> 2. *The domestic politics perspective*, which stresses the role of lobbies, Congress, and public opinion in formulating policies.
> 3. *The bureaucratic politics perspective*, which emphasizes the role of the executive branch and the professionals in shaping and implementating policies.
> 4. *The Presidential leadership perspective*, which emphasizes the view that it is the President and his closest advisers who make high-level policy. This perspective tends to assume that foreign policy is the product not of abstract forces but of individuals.[2]

---

[2] William Quandt, *Decade of Decisions* (Berkeley: University of California Press, 1977), pp. 3–4.

The first perspective focuses on foreign policy as the "rational adaptation of means (resources) to ends (national interests)," the use of economic and military power to attain desirable goals. In this respect the Arab world is seen in terms of a global strategy dominated by superpower rivalry. Typically, American strategic analysis will emphasize the pattern of alliances, the nuclear balance, and the control of vital resources (energy, investments, and markets) and their denial to rivals. The Arab world and the Middle East in general are viewed as part of the American and West European global defense system against the Soviet Union. The doctrine of "containment" of the Soviet Union is held sacrosanct; détente tends to remain a tactical tool, despite the rhetoric.

Strategically important as it is, in both geopolitical and oil terms, the Middle East is frequently perceived by American decision-makers as being also "strategically the most dangerous region in the world because both powers are engaged and spheres of influence are not carefully drawn; in these respects the Middle East differs from both Southeast Asia, where the danger of Soviet intervention seems slight, and Europe, where the boundaries between east and west are clearly marked and carefully respected."[3] In the light of this danger, two schools of thought have developed: one advocating a balanced and evenhanded policy, especially with Jordan and Egypt, and the second (the more frequent and influential) calling for the "maintenance of Israel's military strength at a high level as a deterrent against an Arab or Soviet attack."[4] Writing in late 1971, William Quandt predicted that President Sadat might have to resort to war in the not too distant future because Egyptian diplomacy was getting nowhere. America and Israel wanted to maintain the status quo. No new initiative appeared likely; and, "on balance, it seemed as if the United States would have less and less to offer President Sadat as time went by."[5] Egypt did go to war in 1973.

The joint contribution by Richard Barnet, David Dellinger, and Richard Falk represents the radical and oppositional American critique of US foreign policy. Its relevance is manifest. "All the major US initiatives in foreign policy, however they started out, have been developed and justified within the framework of the assumptions of the most reactionary part of the American political establishment," writes Richard Falk, adding: "This represents

---

[3] *Idem*, "The Middle East Conflict in US Strategy, 1970–1971," *Journal of Palestine Studies*, 1.1 (Autumn 1971), p. 40 [translated as "Nizāʿ al-Sharq al-Awsaṭ fī istrātījīyat al-Wilāyāt al-Muttaḥida," in *Al-Siyāsa al-amīrkīya*, p. 2].

[4] *Ibid.*, p. 41 [= *Al-Siyāsa al-amīrkīya*, p. 4].

[5] *Ibid.*, pp. 51–52 [= *Al-Siyāsa al-amīrkīya*, p. 21].

a triumph on the domestic scene in the United States for those advocating a more militaristic approach to foreign policy."[6] This oil-hungry militarism is on the increase and represents a constraint: "To understand US foreign policy, one needs to ask why, in virtually all critical policy areas, President Carter, unabashedly liberal and humane in style, has become increasingly militaristic and reactionary in practice."[7] Thus American foreign policy towards the Middle East proceeds from what he calls "an imperial orientation," and policy-makers apparently lack the "imagination to find a successful, non-military way of defending Western and American interests."[8] Moreover, Falk views the US "as a declining empire," and, as such, entailing "a dangerous transition because, during that decline, the imperial nation only has its still-formidable military power to arrest the adverse trend."[9]

Former Under-Secretary of State George Ball's analysis of America's policy shortcomings springs from an entirely different tradition than that of the radical-oppositional view already outlined briefly. In 1977, he published a controversial article—by the standards of the American political establishment to which he belongs—in *Foreign Affairs* entitled, "How to Save Israel in Spite of Herself," wherein he advocated putting official pressure on Israel to abide by UN Security Council Resolution 242.[10] A year later his views were expressed even more explicitly. Ball affirmed that the interests of Israel and the United States did not coincide:

> ...In the manner in which some of the Israeli leadership conceives its interests, there is divergence....Some Israeli leaders tend to equate territory and security. I think that is an illusion. Israel in the long term can have no real security unless it is prepared to withdraw substantially to the pre-1967 borders.[11]

[6]Richard Barnet, David Dellinger, and Richard Falk, "US Policy in the Middle East," *Journal of Palestine Studies*, 10.1 (Autumn 1980), p. 7 [translated as "Siyāsat al-Wilāyāt al-Muttaḥida al-khārijīya fī l-Sharq al Awsaṭ," in *Al-Siyāsa al-amīrkīya*, p. 99].

[7]*Ibid.*, p. 8 [= *Al-Siyāsa al-amīrkīya*, p. 100].

[8]*Ibid.*, pp. 9–10 [= *Al-Siyāsa al-amīrkīya*, p. 102].

[9]*Ibid.*, p. 11 [= *Al-Siyāsa al-amīrkīya*, p. 106].

[10][George W. Ball, "How to Save Israel in Spite of Herself," *Foreign Affairs*, 55.3 (April 1977), pp. 453–71.]

[11]George Ball, "American Policy on Trial," interview in *Journal of Palestine Studies*, 7.3 (Spring 1978), p. 21 [translated as "Al-Siyāsa al-amīrkīya ʿalā l-maḥk," in *Al-Siyāsa al-amīrkīya*, p. 28].

Giving sophisticated arms in abundance to Israel did not promote peace. On the contrary, "if the Israelis are strongly armed and there is a military imbalance, Israel's incentive to make peace would be less."[12]

* * * *

If the first perspective, that of the strategic or national-interest perspective, concentrates on the global view, the confrontation with the Soviet Union, and oil as the major constant, the second perspective tends to focus attention on the domestic realities of American politics: the activities of the lobbies, Congressional behavior, election issues, and the mood of the public. As far as the Middle East is concerned, the oil lobby, the defense lobby, and the various pro-Israel lobbies, particularly the American Israel Public Affairs Committee (AIPAC), have shaped or obstructed the formulation and implementation of policy at certain crucial moments.

Ghassan Bishara's detailed study "Israel's Power in the US Senate" is a vivid illustration of this reality. In an unprecedented step, President Carter disavowed the affirmative vote of the United States on UN Security Council Resolution 465 of 1 March 1980, which strongly deplored Israel's settlements policy and called for the dismantling of existing settlements, including those in Jerusalem.[13] The episode was officially explained as a "foul-up" in communications between the White House, the State Department, and the US delegation at the UN headquarters in New York. Far from being a "foul-up," President Carter, in the words of Bishara, "could not withstand the pressure initiated by the Jewish community in the United States and by Israel itself, and had to retreat from his administration's position of support for the resolution."[14]

Another example is to be found in Bishara Bahbah's study "The United States and Israel's Energy Security," which concludes that no country in the world, not even a NATO ally, enjoys "the privileges and security guarantees extended to Israel by the US in the fields of energy."[15] The US has persuaded non-OPEC countries to provide oil to Israel, has placed Alaskan oil reserves

---

[12] *Ibid.*, p. 30 [= *Al-Siyāsa al-amīrkīya*, p. 40].

[13] Ghassan Bishara, "Israel's Power in the US Senate," *Journal of Palestine Studies*, 10.1 (Autumn 1980), p. 58 [translated as "Qūwat Isrā'īl fī Majlis al-Shuyūkh fī l-Wilāyāt al-Muttahida," in *Al-Siyāsa al-amīrkīya*, p. 61].

[14] *Ibid.*, p. 76 [= *Al-Siyāsa al-amīrkīya*, p. 87].

[15] Bishara A. Bahbah, "The United States and Israel's Energy Security," *Journal of Palestine Studies*, 11.2 (Winter 1982), p. 130 [translated as "Al-Wilāyāt al-Muttahida wa-amn ṭāqat Isrā'īl," in *Al-Siyāsa al-amīrkīya*, p. 129].

at its disposal, and has given Israel $2.35 billion in compensation for the Sinai oil fields. However, there is some question as to whether Israel's oil dependence has increased US leverage over Israel. And the same question marks apply to other areas as well: sophisticated arms transfers, technology transfers, and the mammoth aid bill.

Marwan Buheiry's study "The Saunders Document" is yet another illustration of Israel's ability—and the constraining influence of US domestic politics—to negate real progress towards a resolution of the Arab-Israeli conflict. Saunders' initiative, described best as a trial balloon seeking to attract the attention of the PLO, was immediately deflated by the Israelis. And as soon as it drew Israeli and Congressional fire, Henry Kissinger dismissed the Saunders Document as "a somewhat academic exercise explaining in a purely theoretical manner several aspects of the Palestine problem as [Deputy Assistant Secretary of State] Saunders saw them."[16]

Other examples abound. Claudia Wright's study "Shadow on Sand" argues that President Carter's moves toward a comprehensive settlement of the Arab-Israel conflict involving a Geneva conference, PLO representation and an acknowledgement of the Palestinian rights to statehood, and the participation of the Soviet Union, were derailed by domestic pro-Israel opposition.[17]

In addition to direct and explicit opposition, there are indirect and implicit forms of pressure. The pro-Israel lobbies, because of the "law of anticipated reaction," act as powerful constrainers on policy-makers. In other words, they do not always need to mobilize support in a confrontation with the White House: their mere presence and the nuisance value of their "anticipated reaction" is often as effective in the formulation and implementation of policy.[18]

* * * *

The third perspective emphasizes the importance of the rivalries among the various bureaucracies controlling the vast field of foreign affairs: rivalries

---

[16] Marwan Buheiry, "The Saunders Document," *Journal of Palestine Studies*, 8.1 (Autumn 1978), p. 35 [translated as "Wathīqat Saunders: al-qaḍīya al-filasṭīnīya fī l-siyāsa al-amīrkīya," in *Al-Siyāsa al-amīrkīya*, p. 52. Also see above, p. 424.]

[17] Claudia Wright, "Shadow on Sand: Strategy and Deception in Reagan's Policy Towards the Arabs," *Journal of Palestine Studies*, 11.3 (Spring 1982), p. 43 [translated as "Ẓill fawqa al-raml: al-istrātījīya wa-l-khidāʿ fī siyāsat Reagan tujāha al-ʿarab," in *Al-Siyāsa al-amīrkīya*, p. 210].

[18] Quandt, *Decade of Decisions*, p. 20.

between the State Department, the Pentagon, the CIA, and the National Security Council (NSC), with the White House often making political capital out of these divergences. Classical examples of bureaucratic rivalries have been those between the State Department and the White House during, for instance, Truman's policy of recognition and support of Israel in 1948, and between the State Department and the NSC (more specially between William Rogers and Henry Kissinger) during the whole episode of the ill-fated Rogers Plan, as well as between Cyrus Vance and Zbigniew Brzezinski in the Carter years.

In this connection the crucial role of the NSC deserves careful study. During the short period that General George Marshall held the office of Secretary of State (1947–49) in the Truman administration, far-reaching changes occurred in the formulation and implementation of American foreign policy. As one analyst put it:

> Marshall himself played a major role in the development of new administrative devices to meet the challenge of the Cold War. In July 1947, the National Security Act became law, creating a new agency, the National Security Council, to coordinate military and foreign policy in the interest of national defense and security. Although that agency recognized the supremacy of the civilian authorities in the determination of foreign policy, it gave new importance to military factors. The Secretary of State was a member of the Council, but he was seemingly outflanked by the military departments, for the Secretaries of Defense, the Army, the Navy, and the Air Force were also members. Since Marshall himself was a soldier and since other soldiers held important diplomatic posts, it appeared to critics that the military had indeed captured control of foreign policy.[19]

Although the military content of the NSC eventually became less conspicuous, and despite the fact that the fortunes of the NSC have varied—with each President using it in different ways—in time it helped to displace the State Department as the fulcrum of decision-making. And while it is true that in the Johnson years the NSC lost some of its decisive attributes, yet with the Nixon-Kissinger tandem in the White House it not only regained its losses but surged forward to become the effective rival of the State Department.

---

[19] Norman Craebner, *An Uncertain Tradition: American Secretaries of State in the Twentieth Century* (New York: McGraw-Hill, 1961), p. 160.

* * * *

A major assumption is that the President plays a pivotal role in foreign policy matters, although there are sharp differences of opinion as to the definition of this role. This is of course the fourth approach: the Presidential leadership perspective. But the question of the psychology of decision-making and the personality of the President remain central. This is how Quandt sees the problem:

> It is less the personality of the President that must be understood than the way he and his advisers view the world and how they reason. Policy-making is an intellectual process embedded in a social context. It is not merely an acting out of one's deepest fears, anxieties, and aspirations. Two points can be made to clarify the ambiguous link between personality and policy-making. First, individuals with remarkably different personal backgrounds are typically found supporting similar policies. In fact, it is rare that serious arguments over policy take place at high levels in government. The tendency is toward consensus and toward reinforcement of prevailing views....Second, the same individual, with no noteworthy alteration in his personality or his psychodynamics, may very well change position on given policy issues....The question to be asked is not whether policy decisions are rational or irrational, but rather what kind of calculation goes into them....On most issues of importance, policy-makers operate in an environment in which uncertainty and complexity are the dominant realities....The result is often a cautious style of decision-making that strives merely to make incremental changes in existing policies.[20]

In short, policy-making appears here as rational calculations by Presidents and their closest advisers acting in a given social context with well-established guidelines: a reinforcement of continuity and consensus. How then can change take place? And what is the importance of Presidential leadership in this connection? The key lies in the frequency and magnitude of crisis situations, for it is in such moments that a President becomes personally involved in management. Large crises often cause surprises, bring a sense

---

[20]Quandt, *Decade of Decisions*, pp. 29–31.

of urgency into decision-making, expose the defects in older guidelines and assumptions, and can, on occasion, produce change in both perspective and policy.

Because the Middle East is the region of the world where crises occur very frequently (usually provoked by superpower interplay and Israel), one would expect to read a story of *change* rather than of *continuity* in American policies. Yet, it is the latter trend that tends to dominate the dismal story. The question is why? The answer is because as soon as the crisis is managed or resolved, the old stable *conventional wisdom* reasserts itself, the new nuances perceived in the heat of the crisis regress, and the Administration tends to slide back into the traditional modes and premises, with minor cosmetic changes here and there when necessary.

Of course, the policy-making elite in the United States is far from being a monolithic bloc; any discussion of the conjunctures that lead to continuity or change must take account of the important dichotomy between the "Cold Warriors" school and the "Regionalist" school. As outlined by Malcolm Kerr in his valuable study, *America's Middle East Policy: Kissinger, Carter and the Future*:

> The Cold Warriors' school of thought is based on the idea of the balance of power, a conception with strong roots in the European diplomatic tradition from Machiavelli to Talleyrand to Bismarck to Churchill....Since 1945 in America it has focused on the Soviet Union as a strategic rival, and on the post-colonial Third World as a soft area of "power vacuums" that one of the two superpowers must inevitably fill, before the other one does, by cultivating local clients if not by inserting its own direct control....The opposing school of thought, which we shall term the Regionalists, does not deny the importance of the American-Soviet global rivalry, but denies that local issues around the world should be primarily approached in those terms; instead, the Regionalists insist, it should always be recognized that local problems have their own substance to be dealt with in their own terms, if the US is to hope for positive relationships with the local societies and their governments. Nor are these societies inevitably the exclusive clients of any great power: their outside attachments, including their orientation to Cold War issues between the super-

The Formation and Perception of the Modern Arab World

powers, will depend significantly on who assists them in solving problems that they cannot solve alone.[21]

Leading Cold Warriors include Hans Morgenthau, Dean Acheson, John Foster Dulles, Henry Kissinger, John Connolly, Henry Jackson, Ronald Reagan, and Alexander Haig. The smaller and far less influential Regionalist school has included Dean Rusk, Adlai Stevenson, George Ball, J. William Fulbright, William Rogers, Cyrus Vance, and Jimmy Carter (at least at the outset of his administration).[22]

Some attention must also be paid to the "Arabist" presence in the State Department, which has been under constant attack by the powerful pro-Israel lobbies. "Arabists" tend to include career diplomats with long service in the Arab countries who believe that it is in the US national interest to improve relations with the Arab world by developing "even-handed" policies and correcting the persistent pro-Israel tilt. However, they are not a cohesive group, and their ability to influence policy has not always been decisive, particularly when brow-beaten by Israel and its lobbies. Arabists, for instance, were strongly divided over the proper policy toward Nasser's Egypt. The Rogers Plan represents perhaps the apogee of their influence. Moreover, because of the dynamics of crisis situations, analyzed above, the chances of having their policy recommendations adopted tend to recede.

Manifestly critical of the dominant Cold Warrior school, Malcolm Kerr also takes to task Washington for its disregard of European Community peace initiatives. He believes that Western Europe, joined by Japan, would render a service to everyone "if they will push their [Venice 1980] initiative in Washington for all it is worth as a fundamental element of future American-European cooperation." And he adds: "The Middle East conflict is no longer a safe preserve for America to practice Disneyland diplomacy, but a vital arena in which the whole world is involved, and in which America, like everyone else, should prepare to take the advice of her own allies seriously."[23]

Likewise, a major contribution to the fourth, or presidential, perspective is Claudia Wright's "Shadow on Sand." The only time that a US President can be seriously expected to make up his mind about the Middle East is his fifth year of elected office, observes Wright, adding: "But since 1945 only two

---

[21] Malcolm Kerr, *America's Middle East Policy: Kissinger, Carter and the Future* (Beirut: Institute for Palestine Studies, 1980), pp. 10–11 [translated as "Al-Siyāsa al-amīrkīya fī l-Sharq al-Awsaṭ: Kissinger, Carter wa-l-mustaqbal," in *Al-Siyāsa al-amīrkīya*, pp. 177–79].

[22] *Ibid.* [= *Al-Siyāsa al-amīrkīya*, pp. 178–79].

[23] *Ibid.*, p. 32 [= *Al-Siyāsa al-amīrkīya*, p. 206].

Presidents have lasted that long—Eisenhower and Nixon—and they took no initiative, but had to deal instead with the aftermath of the Suez War of 1956 and the Ramadan War of 1973."[24] The widely held view that the American presidency is a powerful institution is an illusion, especially in regard to policy toward the Arab-Israeli conflict. The presidency is constrained by the factionalism of its subordinate components, and it takes a great deal of effort and talent to "distinguish the multiple policy tracks being developed below the President's range of vision, in his name."[25] Wright is of the opinion that to this date only Carter was capable of reading these multiple tracks. Moreover, she suggests that Reagan's policy in 1981–82 "encouraged rather than deterred the aggression and intimidation to which the Arab states have been exposed from Israel in Lebanon, Syria, Jordan, Iraq, and Saudi Arabia." And in the case of Reagan's policy towards the Fahd Plan, "A vacillating White House attacked its most durable European ally, Britain, at the behest of the Israelis."[26]

* * * *

What about future prospects? This perennial question is addressed in Camille Mansour's study "L'Avenir des relations israélo-américaines." Analysts have often speculated on the deterioration of US-Israeli relations and the consequent loss by Israel of its privileged status—a speculation which, in Mansour's view, is particularly complex and fraught with contradictory strands of analysis. The two states are united by a tight network of special relations and a convergence of important interests in the strategic, political, military, economic, historical, and cultural fields. The divergences, on the other hand, are less pronounced and not as consequential as the convergences, with one important exception, the West Bank: "En fait, la Cisjordanie constitue le seul sujet de tension véritable entre l'Amérique et Israel puisqu'elle est perçue comme une question d'intérêt vital par les Israeliéns et les Arabes."[27] But even here Mansour suspects that future accommodation between American and Israeli positions is likely.

---

[24] Wright, "Shadow on Sand," p. 4 [= *Al-Siyāsa al-amīrkīya*, p. 208].

[25] *Ibid.*, p. 14 [= *Al-Siyāsa al-amīrkīya*, p. 224].

[26] *Ibid.*, p. 34 [= *Al-Siyāsa al-amīrkīya*, p. 257].

[27] "Camille Mansour, "L'Avenir des relations israélo-américaines après la guerre du Liban," *Revue d'études palestiniennes*, 7 (Spring 1983), p. 93 [translated as "Mustaqbal al-ʿalāqāt al-isrāʾīlī—al-amīrkīya baʿda ḥarb Lubnān," in *Al-Siyāsa al-amīrkīya*, pp. 273-74].

As to the lessons to be drawn by the Arabs from the nature and mechanism of these special relations, of their divergences and convergences, "too much attention," Mansour concludes, "has been given by Arabs to the Americans as privileged mediators; and the Arabs have not paid sufficient attention to the importance of internal development in Israel, nor have they explored the possibilities that flow from there." And instead of looking for the privileged interlocutor in Washington, who thereby doubly profits, "would it not be better to confront him, in peace or war, in Palestine itself?"[28]

* * * *

In a recent study, "America in the Middle East: A Breakdown in Foreign Policy," George Ball reflected, once again, on the feature of constant subservience of US policy to Israel, epitomized in President Reagan's handling of the Israeli invasion of Lebanon. "History has proved," he said, "that Israel almost invariably wins any test of will with the United States." The experience in Lebanon "proved for the hundredth time that, when the United States and Israel are eyeball to eyeball, we (American decision-makers) habitually blink." Ball's analysis is very much to the point and deserves lengthy quoting:

> Lacking a coherent Middle East policy of our own, we have reacted without thought or foresight to the policies, decisions, and actions of the Israeli government, whose interests and objectives in Lebanon, as it conceives them, diverge sharply from our own. Rather than pursuing our own objectives and looking out for our own interests, we have offered ourselves to the Israeli government as the uncritical, undemanding supporter of its objectives, prepared to help it achieve goals not our own and then to sweep up the breakage created by its violent pursuit of excessive ambitions.[29]

This constant feature in American political behavior (President Eisenhower is the one exception) is likely to persist for the foreseeable future. The present environment of global confrontation with the Soviet Union will probably help to foster it, despite the important change in American interests from oil to the recycling of oil revenue through the use, *inter alia*, of

---

[28] *Ibid.* [= *Al-Siyāsa al-amīrkīya*, p. 274].

[29] George Ball, "America in the Middle East: A Breakdown in Foreign Policy," *Journal of Palestine Studies*, 13.3 (Spring 1984), p. 4.

expensive arms sales. The Americans appear either happy or resigned to live with this state of affairs. The views of the Globalists and Cold Warriors are more likely to prevail than those of the Regionalist minority.

This does not mean, however, that the Arab world is powerless. It is quite capable of devising both its own policies and the strategies to fulfill them. It is quite capable, even when engaged in diversionary or peripheral issues, to serve notice that it is not prepared to take American initiatives urging a Middle East peace seriously while America continues to provide Israel with the economic and military power to negate or derail that objective. Nor must it succumb to the attraction of the Globalists.

Part III

Economic History of the Middle East

20

The Rise of the City of Beirut*

IN 1825 THERE WAS little indication that Beirut would become the first city of Lebanon. In terms of trade, population, and construction activity, the cities of Sidon and Tripoli were probably more important. Yet in the short space of one generation, Beirut overtook and surpassed her rivals to become the leading port on the Mediterranean seaboard and eventually the nation's capital. To account for this complex phenomenon in any comprehensive manner is, of course, beyond the scope of this short introduction. Instead, we have provided the testimony of three perceptive Lebanese and foreign residents of the 1850s: Thomson, Farley, and Rizkallāh.

The military campaigns of Ibrāhīm Pāshā and the intervention of the European powers had stimulated the economy and attracted an influx of money and goods. Moreover, Beirut was selected as the quarantine station, with all ships obliged to call there. It also became a military headquarters during the long years of the campaigns. Following Ibrāhām Pāshā's defeat and return to Egypt in 1841, the city's new breed of middle class entrepreneurs moved ahead very quickly to consolidate the advantages secured from such a conjuncture of events and factors.

Writing in the 1850s, W.M. Thomson, a Beirut resident and author of *The Land and The Book*, remarked:

> Thirty years ago, the population was 5000, and the shops and markets were dependent for supplies on Sidon; now there are

*From the Introduction to Marwan R. Buheiry and Leila Ghantus Buheiry, *The Splendor of Lebanon: Eighteenth and Nineteenth-Century Artists and Travellers* (Delmar, New York: Caravan Books, 1978), xvii-xix. © 1978 by Caravan Books. Reprinted courtesy of Caravan Books. A French version of this essay, "Beyrouth d'hier," was published in *Le commerce du Levant*, 50, no. 4693 (29 March 1979), pp. 36-38.

not less than 40,000 inhabitants, and Sidon is wholly dependent on Beirut. Thirty years ago there was scarcely a decent house outside the walls; now two-thirds of the population reside in the gardens, and hundreds of convenient dwellings, and not a few large and noble mansions, adorn the charming suburbs.[1]

Thomson went on to add that perhaps no other city in the whole of the Turkish empire had witnessed such rapid expansion.

J. Lewis Farley, Chief Accountant of the newly established Ottoman Bank in Beirut, writing in the late 1850s, was also struck by the intense construction activity in progress:

> Even during my own short residence—less than two years—new streets have been made, large buildings have been erected towards Ras-el-Beyrout, to which the Post-office and French consulate have been removed, and several new cafés have been established, provided, as I understand, with good billiard-tables. A group of old houses, not far from the Hotel de Belle Vue, have been pulled down, and in their place are now to be seen several handsome suites of offices, two of which are occupied by English merchants. Outside the town building has also been carried on to a considerable extent. The head of the wealthy house of Bustros and Nephew has erected a princely mansion, and Mr. Muchaka has built a magnificent house....[2]

In 1858 a French enterprise began the construction of a good carriage road between Beirut and Damascus, a profitable investment which introduced stagecoach travel in the area as well as rapid communications with the hinterland. In the same year, Khalīl al-Khūrī printed the first newspaper in Beirut, *Ḥadīqat al-akhbār.* Twenty years later there were a dozen newspapers in circulation in the city, including *Lisān al-ḥāl,* founded by Khalīl Sarkīs in 1877. An equal number of journals, pillars of the cultural renaissance in the Near East, were also in circulation by then, including *Al-Majma' al-vatikānī,* founded by the Jesuits in 1870, Buṭrus al-Bustānī's *Al-Jinān,* founded in the same year, and *Al-Muqtaṭaf,* founded by Ya'qūb Sarrūf and Fāris Nimr in 1876. There was even a medical journal in circulation, *Al-Ṭabīb,* founded by Dr. George Post of the Syrian Protestant

---

[1] W.M. Thomson, *The Land and the Book; or, Biblical Illustrations Drawn from the Manners and Customs, the Scenes and Scenery of the Holy Land* (London: Nelson, 1863), p. 37.

[2] J. Lewis Farley *Two Years in Syria* (London: Saunders and Otley, 1858), p. 28.

College (presently called the American University of Beirut). The city was well on its way to becoming the intellectual and informational center of the country. In contrast, Tripoli's first newspaper, Muḥammad Kāmil Buḥayrī's *Ṭarābulus*, appeared in 1893. As to Sidon, it was only in 1911 that Aḥmad 'Ārif al-Zayn's *Jabal 'Āmil* was printed.

The third witness to the growth of Beirut in mid-century is Ḥabīb Rizkallāh of Shwayfāt. His vivid description of Beirut is quoted at length:

> Beyrout has rapidly risen into considerable importance; and it may be considered now the chief entrepôt of Syrian commerce. At that period (1840) there were barely three or four European families established; and an English vessel only occasionally touched at the port; now (1853), merchants, artizans, and shopkeepers, from all parts of Europe have flocked into the town; and scarcely a week passes by without three or more vessels arriving in the roads from different ports of Europe. The roadstead presents a gay appearance on Sunday, when all the different vessels display the ensigns of their respective nations, and corresponding flags are hoisted from the tops of the consulates on shore. English, French, Sardinian, Austrian, American, Portugese, Spanish, Dutch, Danish, Norwegian, and Swedish ships are daily arriving at, or sailing out of the port, bringing manufactures from Manchester, colonial produce from London, sugar from Hamburg, assorted cargoes from France and Italy, and numberless requisites and necessaries from other parts of the world; whilst they export from Beyrout, silk reeled in the many factories situated in the immediate neighbourhood and on Lebanon, grain from the interior, raw silk, of which some portion is contributed from my native village, and lately an enterprising American has carried off ship-loads of our Beyrout and Syrian olive oil, timber, nuts, and specimens of dried and preserved fruits. The population is rapidly increasing, the wealth augmenting, new firms are being established, fresh channels of commerce discovered, houses being built, gardens enclosed, grounds purchased and planted, till the once quiet, secluded, and almost desolate-looking Beyrout, many of whose decayed and dilapidated ruins crumbled into dust under the severe shocks of the great earthquake of 1821, has been rapidly metamorphosed into a pleasant and flourishing town, replete with handsome buildings and luxuriant gardens, presenting,

as viewed from the sea, one of the handsomest marine pictures possible for the pencil of the painter to depict, or the lay of the poet to celebrate. Please God, I hope yet to see the day when much loved Beyrout shall rival and surpass in every sense Smyrna, and even Stamboul.[3]

What was life like in Beirut a hundred and ten years ago? Let us assume that in 1888 a Beiruti merchant wanted to meet a European counterpart arriving on one of twelve steamship company boats which called regularly every week. He would probably find him at Hotel Bassoul or Hotel Bellevue (10 to 15 francs for full board) in Zaytūneh unless the visitor was in search of local color, in which case he might locate him either in Hotel Kawkab al-Sharq on the Place des Canons where Salīm Shāmī, the owner, charged two francs for the night, or else at Madame Pascall's Furnished Rooms in Zaytūneh where the charge was equally modest. In actual fact, Amīn Khūrī's guide to Beirut in 1889, Al-Jāmi'a, lists seventeen hotels. Having found him, and if the visitor expressed interest in a Turkish bath, they would proceed to one of the following hammāms: Al-Kabīr near Bāb al-Derkeh, Al-Zuhūr on the Damascus Road, Al-Barghūth near the Ottoman army central barracks, Al-Shafā, and Al-Bashūra. A swim could even be proposed in one of three newly installed bathing establishments in the Zaytūneh and Mudawwar districts.

Refreshed, the visitor could next embark on an industrial tour beginning with the newly installed match factory (1881) owned by 'Adwān Khūrī, the Sultānī Soap Factory owned by Jurjī Ṣābūnjī, and the brand new marble factory of Ibrāhīm Shāmī and Ṭannūs Sha'yā near the telegraph office. A comprehensive tour of silk factories would normally include Constantine Najjār's (formerly owned by Daḥdāḥ), the Pedroni factory in the Ḥursh area, Naṣr's on the Damascus Road, and the establishments of Salīm Jubaylī and Antoine Wardī in the Nahr area. The roof-tile factory, after an auspicious start, had closed. But if the paper business interested him he could visit the establishment of Aḥmad 'Ītānī or the carton factory attached to the Jesuit Printing Press.

The great topic of the day was the 99-year port concession granted to Joseph Muṭrān and the formation of the Société ottomane du port des quais et entrepôts de Beyrout (1888) with the participation of the Imperial Ottoman Bank, the Comptoir d'escompte de Paris, and the Compagnie des

---

[3]Habeeb Risk Allah, *The Thistle and the Cedar of Lebanon*, 2nd edition (London: James Madden, 1854), pp. 52–53.

messageries maritimes. In March of 1888 the city was lit by gaslight through a concession obtained by a French company. The municipality had contracted for a network of 656 posts, but the people of Beirut preferred their petroleum lamps to this newcomer; the gas company therefore diversified its operations by providing the city with ice.

Banking services were in great demand. The merchant and his friend would probably choose one of the following establishments: the Imperial Ottoman Bank in Khān Anṭūn Bey, Bank Jabbūr Ṭabīb and Co. in Khān Fakhrī Bey, Bank Sursuq in Sūq Sursuq, or the Firʿawn and Shīḥā Bank near Wikālat al-Shikāl. There was also a large number of small exchange and credit houses.

The characteristic jewelry of the Levant would be obtained in Sūq Raʿd wa-Hānī from Ilyās Nicholas Ḥomṣī, Bāsil Ṭūqatlī, Ḥabīb Dhiyāb, or Salīm Fīʿānī. Western influences were permeating the entire fabric of society and European-style taylors were very much in demand: Jurjī ʿAramān near Khān Fakhrī Bey, Jurjī Khadīj in Sūq Ayyās, and Yūsuf Shāwūl in Sūq al-Ḥarīr. Mr. Bianchi was certain to provide one with the latest male fashions. As to Oriental-style taylors, Ḥannā Flayfil, in Sūq Bāzārkhān, Sulaymān Abū Shākir, and Muḥammad Balṭajī would guarantee entire satisfaction.

Traditionally, the Lebanese mountain had played the role of a refuge. But during the troubled twenty years of intercommunal strife in Mount Lebanon (1840–61), Beirut took over as the new sanctuary, attracting an influx of refugees. With this increase of the population there was a corresponding expansion of medical services. Among the many doctors practicing their art in 1888 were Ibrāhīm Ṣāfī, Ilyās Shukrallāh, Shākir Khūrī, Ibrāhīm Maṭar, Adīb Qaddūra, and the doctors of the American and Jesuit universities. Dr. H. Ṣabra, a woman, received women patients. For dental care the choice was more limited and included Ilyās and Nicolas Yuwākīm, Christo Anastāsī and Asʿad ʿAbduh Charles, but pharmacies were abundant and numbered at least fifteen. Among the leading pharmacists were Masʿūd Ḥaymarī (established in 1850), Elie ʿArab, Elie Thābit, Iskandar Ḥelū, Murād Bārūdī, Yamīn and Ṣūrātī, and the Maṭar brothers.

The city continued to grow, attracting more educational establishments, more ships, and more competition between international firms. In fact, it became the market for the imports and exports of the Syrian hinterland. At the turn of the century, bilingualism and trilingualism were common among the upper middle class, giving Beirut a cosmopolitan style of its own: a meeting place of the world, an entrepôt of material goods, and a crucible for ideas and politics.

21

British Official Sources and the Economic History of Lebanon: 1835–1914*

THIS SURVEY WILL EXAMINE a selection of British official source material that is available for the still-neglected study of the economic history of Lebanon in the period 1835 to 1914. These include: 1) two comprehensive printed reports that were specially commissioned; 2) the *Annual Series of Consular Reports on the Trade and Commerce of Beirut* in printed form;[1] and 3) the voluminous unpublished commercial correspondence in the Foreign Office archives (FO), which may be consulted under the code references FO 78, FO 195, FO 371, FO 368, and FO 226. The first two categories are conveniently located in the Official Publications Library (OPL) in the British Museum, London. The third category is stored in the Public Record Office (PRO), Kew, Surrey—an hour by train from the center of London. The ordering procedure for this last category is computerized.

The date 1835 was chosen as a convenient starting point because it marks the revival of British interest in Lebanon and the Middle East, which was partly caused by the challenge of Muḥammad ʿAlī's territorial expansion and his economic policies combining monopoly practices and industrialization. Yet, at the same time, Britain was also very conscious of the enormous growth of Beirut as a trading and transit center, which it attributed to perhaps an exaggerated extent to the Egyptian occupation. Consul Moore's

---

*From *Dirāsāt: Lettres et sciences humaines*, 11 (1984), pp. 9–16. ©1984 by the Université Libanaise. Reprinted courtesy of the Faculté de Pédagogie, Université Libanaise.

[1][More specifically, the reports described here may be consulted in the OPL in the *Accounts and Papers* series of the Sessional Papers of the House of Commons. Consular reports for a given year are arranged alphabetically by country and published in the papers of the following year.]

economic report of 16 November 1835 (FO 78/264) is very eloquent on this point, describing as it does the transformation of Beirut into "a flourishing city" as well as into the port for Damascus and the hinterland. Equally, it served as the "market for the sale of large quantities of English manufactures and colonial produce" in the context of Britain's industrial revolution and the expansion of steam navigation.[2] At about this time, John Bowring, a distinguished economist of the free-trade school, prepared the first British comprehensive and modern statistical and economic study of Lebanon, Syria, and Palestine for Lord Palmerston, Britain's Minister for Foreign Affairs.[3]

Similarly, at the other end of the spectrum, the cut-off date of 1914 was an appropriate choice because it marked the end of an epoch, but also because at about this time, an even more comprehensive survey than Bowring's was prepared by Ernest Weakley for the Board of Trade, Commercial Intelligence Committee.[4] These two valuable sources for the economic history of Lebanon and Syria serve as a convenient time-frame for this survey.

Briefly stated, this period, 1835–1914, prepared the ground for the transition from a traditional feudal society to that of modern Lebanon. Beginning with Muḥammad ʿAlī's campaigns and the Ottoman Tanẓīmāt, there was better enforcement of law and order, as well as the consecration of private property through the Land Law of 1858. It is also a period of mounting Western educational presence, economic penetration, and technological application, particularly in the silk industry and the utilization of machinery in printing and in the flour mills. Equally important are the various infrastructural investments in ports, banking, railways, and other concessions. The sharp rise in trade, urban construction, and the professions stimulated the development of a Lebanese middle class oriented towards consumer behavior.

The Reports of Bowring and Weakley

John Bowring's *Report on the Commercial Statistics of Syria* was addressed to Palmerston and presented to both Houses of Parliament in a printed account of 144 pages, containing a useful index. It was compiled by one of Britain's most experienced statisticians and political economists from detailed questionnaires addressed to Britain's consuls in Beirut, Damascus,

---

[2][On the rise of Beirut, see above, pp. 483–87.]

[3][John Bowring, *Report on the Commercial Statistics of Syria* (London: H.M. Stationery Office, 1840).]

[4][Ernest Weakley, *Report Upon the Conditions and Prospects of British Trade in Syria* (London: H.M. Stationery Office, 1911).]

and Aleppo, as well as from other sources. Beirut and to a lesser extent Mount Lebanon figure prominently in the report. The rapid increase of silk and agricultural produce is noted with care, as are the local manufactures of textiles. The problem of fluctuating currency, the general expansion of trade and of house construction, and the special share of Britain in the market are treated. Some attention is also given to population statistics, the still primitive communications network, the taxation system, wages and the price of food, the mode of sales and payments, and even the state of education. Bowring often provides explanations for new developments and fluctuations. The report is impressive by any standards and reflects: 1) the urgent search for markets forced by the frenetic pace of industrial production in England and the expansion of steam navigation; 2) the geopolitical interest of Britain in the eastern Mediterranean; and 3) the improvement of statistical and economic modes of analysis.

A very useful table deals with the export of silk from the port of Beirut: 582 bales in 1833, 1464 bales in 1834, 1035 bales in 1835, 1760 bales in 1836, with a total value of about 8.5 million francs for the four years.[5] The principal countries of destination were France, Egypt, and Tuscany. The report estimates the number of textile looms in operation in Mount Lebanon as 1200, divided as follows: 300 for silk and cotton fabrics, 300 for woolen abas, and 600 for coarse cotton used in shirt making.

Approximately 75 years later, Ernest Weakley prepared his valuable study entitled *Report Upon the Condition and Prospects of British Trade in Syria* for the Commercial Intelligence Committee of the Board of Trade. It was printed as a parliamentary paper in the *Accounts and Papers* series, vol. 87 (1911), and was therefore accessible to the general public of the time. Again the rising share of England in the imports of the Beirut market is measured, and great attention is also devoted to areas of competition with the other exporting nations. But there is also much information on investment opportunities and on the performance of existing concessions such as the Beirut customs house, the Port Company, the Water Company, which was a British investment, the Beirut Gas Company, the Electric Tramway Company, the various post offices, and the railways. Some attention is also given to Tripoli and Sidon. The present state as well as the potential growth of local manufactures are carefully monitored, as is the import and utilization of machinery. And there are several sectoral studies made on the principal articles of exports from the Lebanese coast. The accent is of course on the

---

[5] Bowring, *Report*, p. 58. A standard bale of silk weighed approximately 100 kg.

prospects of Britain's leading position in the imports of Beirut and on the complicated game of concessions. And there is a great deal of advice given to commercial interests. The report is more than 200 printed pages long.

Weakley made a successful attempt to measure the dimension and implications of emigration, which he described as "a special feature in the economy of the country." He noted that it was a "drain of the able-bodied population," but that it was compensated by the considerable sums of money remitted by emigrants and estimated at about £1 million in 1908, of which about half was remitted through the Beirut branch of the Imperial Ottoman Bank.[6] He also provided a detailed table of emigration through Beirut and Tripoli for the year 1909:

	By Italian Steamers			*By French Messageries Steamers*		
	From Tripoli	From Beirut	Total	From Tripoli	From Beirut	Total
Jan.	38	42	80	66	45	111
Feb.	–	67	67	17	110	127
March	110	178	288	445	395	810
April	83	210	293	252	260	512
May	186	395	581	302	520	822
June	148	390	538	60	100	160
July	140	175	315	185	340	525
August	280	405	685	610	475	1085
Sept.	285	540	825	810	610	1450
Oct.	440	800	1240	765	980	1745
Nov.	97	800	897	217	445	662
Total	1807	4002	5809	3759	4280	8039

Consular Reports on the Trade and Commerce of Beirut

This Annual Series was inaugurated by the Foreign Office in 1886 and is particularly valuable in the charting of growths and declines over a period of time. The reports are quite substantial, averaging 20 printed pages each. Taking a typical report, that of 1899 for instance, the breakdown of the subject matter is as follows. The consul begins by making remarks for

---

[6] Weakley, *Report*, pp. 10–11.

the year in question: "It is beyond all question that the trade of Beirut was very satisfactory for the year 1899. Both imports and exports show a marked difference on the preceding year, especially the latter, on account of larger exports of silk thread, and the high prices realised in France for that article."[7] He then moves to a detailed discussion of shipping, exports, imports, and foreign competition; and, in the 1899 case, there is a section analyzing the Italian trade. This is followed by a short section on emigration with some statistical information and by a description of the major infrastructural projects under construction or already in operation. The report contains many appropriate statistical tables and also a brief picture of the trade of Tripoli by Vice-Consul T.S. Abela and another of the trade of Sidon by Vice-Consul S. Abela. Incidentally, there is an interesting reference to the village of Shaḥīm in the Shūf district of Mount Lebanon as a manufacturing center for textiles made of goat's hair, which was in demand as carpeting and tenting by the bedouins. Shaḥīm apparently sent 2,000 bales worth £20,000 to Gaza during 1899.[8]

As we get closer to 1905, the annual reports display a growing interest in the importation of railway equipment and its effect upon shipping. Equal attention is focused on wheat and barley shipments from the interior to the coast. The report for the year 1905 speaks of an increase in the grain trade stimulated by the Rīyāq-Ḥomṣ-Ḥamāh railway line and the ensuing "divertion of a large part of Tripoli's exports to Beirut."[9] At about this time. the orange trade from Sidon to Britain, which began in 1901, stabilized.

Below is a listing of the Foreign Office Annual Series (FOAS) of Consular Reports:

1. FOAS, no. 8: *Report on the Trade of Beyrout for the Year 1885*, by H. Eyres.

2. FOAS, no. 114: *Report for the Year 1886 on the Trade of Beyrout*, by H. Eyres.

3. FOAS, no. 290: *Report for the Year 1887 on the Trade of Beyrout*, by G. Eldridge.

---

[7][R. Drummond-Hay, *Report for the Year 1899 on the Trade and Commerce of Beirut and the Coast of Syria*, FOAS, no. 2441, p. 3.]

[8][*Ibid.*, p. 18.]

[9]R. Drummond-Hay, *Report for the Year 1905 on the Trade and Commerce of Beirut and the Coast of Syria*, FOAS, no. 3569, p. 4.

4. FOAS, no. 508: *Report for the Year 1888 on the Trade of Beyrout,* by G. Eldridge.

5. FOAS, no. 720: *Report for the Year 1889 on the Trade of Beyrout,* by H. Eyres.

6. FOAS, no. 908: *Report for the Year 1890 on the Trade of Beyrout,* by H. Trotter.

7. FOAS, no. 1279: *Report for the Year 1891-92 on the Trade of Beyrout,* by H. Trotter.

8. FOAS, no. 1418: *Report for the Year 1893 on the Trade of Beyrout,* by H. Eyres.

9. FOAS, no. 1626: *Report for the Year 1894 on the Trade of Beyrout,* by R. Drummond-Hay.

10. FOAS, no. 1790: *Report for the Year 1895 on the Trade of Beyrout,* by R. Drummond-Hay.

11. FOAS, no. 1970: *Report for the Year 1896 on the Trade of Beyrout,* by R. Drummond-Hay.

12. FOAS, no. 2116: *Report for the Year 1897 on the Trade and Commerce of Beirut and the Coast of Syria,* by R. Drummond-Hay.

13. FOAS, no. 2286: *Report for the Year 1898 on the Trade and Commerce of Beirut and the Coast of Syria,* by R. Drummond-Hay.

14. FOAS, no. 2441: *Report for the Year 1899 on the Trade and Commerce of Beirut and the Coast of Syria,* by R. Drummond-Hay.

15. FOAS, no. 2662: *Report for the Year 1900 on the Trade and Commerce of Beirut and the Coast of Syria,* by R. Drummond-Hay.

16. FOAS, no. 2836: *Report of the Year 1901 on the Trade and Commerce of Beirut and the Coast of Syria,* by R. Drummond-Hay.

17. FOAS, no. 3026: *Report for the Year 1902 on the Trade and Commerce of Beirut and the Coast of Syria,* by R. Drummond-Hay.

18. FOAS, no. 3192: *Report for the Year 1903 on the Trade and Commerce of Beirut and the Coast of Syria,* by R. Drummond-Hay.

19. FOAS, no. 3459: *Report for the Year 1904 on the Trade and Commerce of Beirut and the Coast of Syria*, by R. Drummond-Hay.

20. FOAS, no. 3569: *Report for the Year 1905 on the Trade and Commerce of Beirut and the Coast of Syria*, by R. Drummond-Hay.

Unpublished Commercial Correspondence

Very briefly, this presents many problems for the researcher, including the problem of handwritten documents, repetition, the mixture of trivial information with the important, classification, and, of course, the reference codes (FO 78, FO 195, FO 226, FO 368, and FO 371). But they are nevertheless indispensable for any thorough work on at least the British dimension and perception of economic relations with Lebanon.

The code FO 78 refers to the general correspondence of Turkey and contains the letters emanating from the consulate of Beirut. It is important to consult both the political and commercial volumes. As examples, we list the following volumes for Beirut:

1879	FO 78/2989	(political)	FO 78/3016	(commercial)
1880	FO 78/3130	”	FO 78/3136	”
1881	FO 78/3314	”	FO 78/3340	”
1882	FO 78/3417	”	FO 78/3423	”
1883	FO 78/3532	”	FO 78/3536	”
1884	FO 78/3642	”	FO 78/3648	”
1885	FO 78/3774	”	FO 78/3779	”

After 1906 the code FO 78 is replaced by FO 371 for the political correspondence and FO 368 for the commercial. The code FO 195 also refers to correspondence involving Beirut. Equally valuable, although duplicating the above, are the 310 files of the Consulate-General of Beirut under FO 226 from 1810 to 1914 and 1942 to 1945, arranged chronologically, but also topically in the sense that generally the files have specific titles. For instance, FO 226/68 of 1839 contains a listing of towns damaged by the earthquakes of 1837. File FO 226/124 of 1858 is devoted to an evaluation of the Beirut-Damascus carriage road project together with an English translation of the original *firmān*. Files FO 226/126 and 130 of 1858 and 1859 contain the grievances of British merchants residing in Beirut during the economic crisis caused by the Peasant Revolt in Kisrawān. File FO 226/158 of 1861 includes a detailed survey of the population of Mount Lebanon during the crucial discussions over the establishment of the *mutaṣarrifīya*. File FO 226/184 of 1875 is a survey of the state of affairs in Mount Lebanon with some emphasis on the scramble for offices in the administration, the impact of tobacco smuggling on the economy, and the growing indebtedness of the peasantry. File FO 226/198 of 1878 is devoted to the economic impact of the Russo-Turkish War of 1878 on Mount Lebanon, while FO 226/209 of 1887 dealt with the newly established Beirut Chamber of Commerce.[10]

Concluding Remarks

The foregoing British official sources are impressive, composed as they are by experienced staff in the service of a powerful trading nation with strategic and political interests in the Middle East. Thus, the sources contain a wealth of information on Lebanon's importation of textiles, particularly of cotton goods, and of other less important products from the point of view of British trade with the country such as petroleum, hardware goods, building materials, coffee, and sugar, to mention only a few. Somewhat less emphasis was placed on the exports picture, except insofar as it affected British shipping. But generally Britain's share of Lebanon's exports, unlike France's share, remained slight.

The sources are very useful also in charting the growing interest in concessions and investment opportunities: in railways, public utilities, banking, and the transfer of technology. However, they are less useful for the domestic picture, and they often convey a partial or distorted image of this important reality.

Not surprisingly, the attention is almost exclusively focused on Beirut and to a lesser extent on Tripoli and Sidon. The rest of the country is largely neglected. The sources are therefore of less use in the examination of internal developments, such as in land tenure, in handicrafts, and in income.

---

[10]With respect to the bibliographical literature on the subject of British trade and consular views one ought to mention two articles by Charles Issawi: "British Consular Views on Syria's Economy in the 1850's–1860's," in *American University of Beirut Festival Book*, edited by Fuad Sarruf and Suha Tamim (Beirut: American University of Beirut, 1967), pp. 103–20; and "British Trade and the Rise of Beirut, 1830–1860," *International Journal of Middle East Studies*, 8 (1977), pp. 91–101.

Finally, there is little information concerning new social formations and local entrepreneurial activity. There is an underlying current of awareness regarding the growing importance of a commercial and professional middle class produced by Western education, but, paradoxically, the implications of these important developments are to be found in the political correspondence of the same consuls who drafted the economic reports.

22

The Peasant Revolt of 1858 in Mount Lebanon: Rising Expectations, Economic Malaise, and the Incentive to Arm*

AMONG HISTORIANS of the Middle East, serious attention to agrarian studies is of relatively recent date. The peasantry—men, women, and children who till the soil and engage in cottage crafts—has had to take second place to approaches stressing great ideas, politics, diplomacy, urban culture, and the great-man syndrome.[1] This bias is in part explained by the fact that historiography has traditionally been an urban profession. One might recall, to cite an example, Marx's extraordinary claim that the bourgeoisie had "rescued a considerable part of the population from the idiocy of rural life."[2]

There are of course exceptions. But in general terms, on the rare occasions when the peasant enters into the pages of history books it is during famines, for which he is frequently blamed, or when he is in a state of rebellion, for which he is more often romanticized than understood.

In Lebanese history, the period 1820–61 was convulsed by four or perhaps even five rural uprisings. This paper concentrates on the peasant insurrection of 1858 in the *muqāṭaʿa* or district of Kisrawān in Mount Lebanon

---

*From *Land Tenure and Social Transformation in the Middle East*, edited by Tarif Khalidi (Beirut: American University of Beirut, 1984), pp. 291–301. © 1984 by the American University of Beirut. Reprinted courtesy of the American University of Beirut.

[1] *The Peasantry in the Old Regime: Conditions and Protests*, edited by Isser Woloch (New York: Holt, Rinehart, and Winston, 1970), p. 1.

[2] Karl Marx and Friedrich Engels, *The Communist Manifesto*, translated by Samuel Moore (London: Penguin, 1967), p. 84.

which was directed against the Khāzins, who were the traditional landed shaykhs, local *multazims* (tax-farmers), and *muqāṭaʿjīs*, this last being a title which the shaykhs bore proudly and which had developed a specific, "quasi-feudal" connotation in the region.[3] The origins, objectives, and consequences of this important episode in Lebanese history have received adequate attention from scholars both in the past and today. In reviewing this rich corpus of material it is possible to divide the contributions into three categories.

The first category includes the valuable testimony of local chroniclers such as Anṭūn al-ʿAqīqī and Manṣūr al-Ḥattūnī, together with those of their Western contemporaries who wrote soon after the events: Colonel Charles Churchill (a British resident widely known as Sharshar Bey), Richard Edwards, Jean Joseph Poujoulat, and Eugène Poujade.[4] To these must be added the voluminous consular reports among which only the French and the British appear to have been fully utilized so far, with far more attention being paid to the political than to the commercial correspondence. Belgian, Austrian, Russian, Italian, and Vatican archives, on the other hand, are rarely cited. For this present paper the *Recueil consulaire belge* proved to be a particularly rewarding source. The great lacuna, however, remains the absence of the story from the point of view of the Ottoman state.

---

[3]The *Imāra* of Mount Lebanon developed a form of *de facto* private landownership (usufructory in nature) which in turn stimulated the growth of a class of local landed shaykhs—a "shaykhocracy"—able to pass on their holdings as hereditary possessions. In the Maʿnī or Shihābī *imāra*, the Amīr—a principal landowner—also served as principal tax-farmer (*multazim*) who in turn farmed out the taxes to the leading shaykhs. In fact, Mount Lebanon was divided into 24 districts or *muqāṭaʿāt*—Kisrawān under the Khāzins was one of them—which are often described in the literature as feudal, giving rise to controversy.

If by feudal we mean the European institution of lord and vassal and their relationships with each other and with the peasantry, the holding of land in fee, obligations such as homage, service under arms and in court, wardship, forfeiture, and local exercise of the functions of government, and the imposition of seigneurial *corvée*—all carefully regulated by legal, contractual, and ceremonial arrangements in which religion figured prominently, then the term is not applicable to Mount Lebanon. A more appropriate characterization would be that of "quasi-feudal."

[4]Anṭūn al-ʿAqīqī, *Thawra wa-fitna fī Lubnān*, edited by Yūsuf Ibrāhīm Yazbak (Beirut: Maṭbaʿat al-ittiḥād, 1939); Manṣūr al-Ḥattūnī, *Nubdha taʾrīkhīya fī l-muqāṭaʿa al-kisrawānīya*, 2nd edition (Beirut: Y.I. Yazbak, 1956); Charles Churchill, *The Druzes and the Maronites Under the Turkish Rule from 1840 to 1860* (London: Bernard Quaritch, 1862); Richard Edwards, *La Syrie: 1845–1862* (Paris: Amyot, 1862); Eugène Poujade, *Le Liban et la Syrie 1845–1860* (Paris: Librairie Nouvelle, 1860); Baptistin Poujoulat, *La Vérité sur la Syrie et l'expédition française* (Paris: Gaume Frères et J. Duprey, 1861).

For the 1858 events the most important sources by far in this first category are the papers of the Maronite Patriarchate, the numerous and little-explored holdings of individual monasteries, and the thousands of documents held by various members of the Khāzin family and by the Archives Department of Lebanon's National Museum. This large corpus of Lebanese and foreign material contains the accounts closest in time to the 1858 revolt.

The second category of sources—books, monographs, and articles written in the past 35 years—includes the contributions of Kamal Salibi, Dominique Chevallier, Adel Ismail, Yūsuf Ibrāhīm Yazbak, Malcolm Kerr, Irena Smilianskaya, Toufic Touma, Fu'ād Qāzān, Mary-Jane Deeb, Yehoshua Porath, 'Abdallāh Ḥannā, and, more recently, Wajīh Kawtharānī, Mas'ūd Ḍāhir, Gabriel Baer, Samir Khalaf, and Axel Havemann. These authors are of course very varied in methodological approach and scope: the liberal and *Annales* schools are represented, as is the Marxist school. But the historiographical tradition of Labrousse is largely absent.[5]

---

[5] Kamal Salibi, *The Modern History of Lebanon* (London: Weidenfeld and Nicolson, 1965); Dominique Chevallier, "Aspects sociaux de la question d'Orient: aux origines des troubles agraires libanais en 1858," *Annales: économies, sociétés, civilisations*, 14 (1959), pp. 35–64; Adel Ismail, *Histoire du Liban du XVIIe siècle à nos jours, IV: Redressement et déclin du féodalisme libanais, 1840–1861* (Beirut: Adel Ismail, 1958); Yūsuf Ibrāhīm Yazbak, editor of the al-'Aqīqī manuscript and of a valuable collection of letters from the Archives of the Maronite Patriarchate; Malcolm Kerr, *Lebanon in the Last Years of Feudalism 1848–1868* (Beirut: American University of Beirut, 1959), a translation of the al-'Aqīqī manuscript and of the letters published by Yazbak—Kerr's edition has been used for this study and will be referred to hereafter as 'Aqīqī-Kerr, *Lebanon*; Irena Smilianskaya, *Al-Ḥaraka al-fallāḥīya fī Lubnān*, translated by 'Adnān Jāmūs (Beirut: Dār al-Fārābī, 1972); Toufic Touma, *Paysans et institutions féodales chez les druses et les maronites du Liban du XVIIè siècle à 1914* (Beirut: Université Libanaise, 1971), in two volumes; Fu'ād Qāzān, "Al-Thawra al-fallāḥīya al-sha'bīya fī l-qarn al-tāsi' 'ashar bi-qiyādat Ṭānyūs Shāhīn," *Al-Ṭarīq*, 29 (March 1970), pp. 75–125; Mary-Jane Deeb, "The Khazin Family: A Case Study of the Effect of Social Change on Traditional Roles" (M.A. thesis: American University in Cairo, 1972); Yehoshua Porath, "The Peasant Revolt of 1858–61 in Kisrawān," *Asian and African Studies*, 2 (1966), pp. 77–157; 'Abdallāh Ḥannā, *Al-Qaḍīya al-zirā'īya wa-l-ḥarakāt al-fallāḥīya fī Sūriyā wa-Lubnān 1820–1920* (Beirut: Dār al-Fārābī, 1975–78), in two volumes; Wajīh Kawtharānī, *Al-Ittijāhāt al-ijtimā'īya al-siyāsīya fī Jabal Lubnān wa-l-mashriq al-'arabī, 1860–1920* (Beirut: Ma'had al-inmā' al-'arabī, 1976); Mas'ūd Ḍāhir, *Al-Judhūr al-ta'rīkhīya li-l-mas'ala al-zirā'īya al-lubnānīya 1900–50* (Beirut: Ma'had al-inmā' al-'arabī, 1983); Gabriel Baer, *Fellah and Townsman in the Middle East* (London: Frank Cass, 1982); Samir Khalaf, *Persistence and Change in 19th Century Lebanon* (Beirut: American University of Beirut, 1979); Axel Havemann, *Rurale Bewegungen im Libanongebirge des 19. Jahrhunderts* (Berlin: Schwarz, 1983).

In between the contemporary sources and archives and the more modern literature, and in a sense spanning the two, is the 1908 book of Būluṣ Nujaym, a Kisrawānite, who compared the peasant movement in Mount Lebanon to that of the French peasants of 1789.[6] Similarly, Gabriel Baer has compared the list of demands of the Kisrawān peasant insurgents with the twelve *Artikel* of the German *Bauernkrieg*, or Peasant War, of 1525.[7] Indeed, Nujaym (1908) and Baer (1982) are rare examples of the comparative approach to the 1858 Kisrawān peasant revolt. Lebanese rural historiography would surely profit from a wider application of such comparative methodology.

* * * *

Located a few miles north of the expanding city of Beirut, the *muqāṭaʿa* of Kisrawān roughly encompassed the territory between the Nahr al-Kalb and Nahr Ibrāhīm. By the middle of the nineteenth century it contained about fifty villages and small towns, forty monasteries and convents, and a growing population of 35,000 inhabitants: 70 percent Maronites, 25 percent Greek Catholic Uniates, and five percent Shīʿite Muslims.[8] Rising gradually from the Mediterranean coastline to the *jurd* or heights of Mount Lebanon, this hilly and carefully terraced agricultural region specialized in the production of silk, the principal cash crop and mainstay of the economy at the time.

A gradual, yet significant, social transformation occurred in the first half of the nineteenth century. The traditional polarized picture of a landowning "shaykhocracy" and a landless peasantry had eroded and was being replaced by a more complex relationship between class origins and landownership. A few of the six hundred or so Khāzins living throughout the *muqāṭaʿa* still possessed large holdings, but a majority of the shaykhs remained only just above subsistence level, given their propensity for extravagant expenses connected with status and the struggle for political influence within an evolving amīrate

---

[6] Būluṣ Nujaym wrote, under the pseudonym Paul Jouplain, *La Question du Liban*, 2nd edition (Jounieh: Fouad Biban et Cie., 1961). See Marwan Buheiry, "Bulus Nujaym and the Grand Liban Ideal 1908–1919," in *Intellectual Life in the Arab East, 1890–1939*, edited by Marwan Buheiry (Beirut: American University of Beirut, 1981), pp. 62–83 [= pp. 573–92 below].

[7] Gabriel Baer, *Fellah and Townsman*, pp. 272, 278.

[8] Al-Ḥattūnī, *Nubdha taʾrīkhīya*, pp. 27–32.

and qā'imaqāmate system. In addition, as noted by Nujaym (Jouplain), a stratum of impoverished and turbulent Khāzin squires had emerged.[9]

The peasantry, too, presented a variegated picture of landless share-croppers, sharecroppers with small and often fractioned holdings, and more well-to-do peasant proprietors. But most significant in terms of social trans-formation was the rise of a rural bourgeoisie of landowning peasants with access to the lucrative silk-trading centers in nearby Beirut, and with po-litical ambitions to match their growing economic and social status. The chronicles of al-Ḥattūnī and al-'Aqīqī highlight the increasingly important role of this peasant elite—particularly the *shuyūkh shabāb* and the *wakīls*—who constituted a wedge in the "quasi-feudal" system of *muqāṭa'a* and *il-tizām*, providing a grassroots type of popular leadership cabable of articulat-ing grievances, formulating demands, gaining the support of the influential clergy in Kisrawān, and making representations to Ottoman administrators and European consuls.[10]

The present study, which is in the nature of a reconsideration of certain aspects of the Kisrawān peasant revolt of 1858, will stress two factors in the etiology of immediate causes (often referred to as precipitants). Only passing attention will be devoted to long-range causes. In the literature on internal conflict a distinction is generally made between long-range causes or preconditions, and the more immediate causes, which are viewed as accelera-tors and triggers. It is of course difficult to always maintain this distinction, but it does make for conceptual clarity and is useful in organizing evidence, data, and interpretative insights.

Many of the long-range causes or preconditions for the 1858 outbreak are directly related to land tenure. For while there was a transition from landless to landowning peasants, it is clear that the land tenure and con-tractual system in the Kisrawān made it very difficult for an expanding peasantry, with an eye on sericulture and mulberry trees, to acquire more land from the Khāzins. Most sources, including Dominique Chevallier's ground-breaking "Aux origines des troubles agraires libanais en 1858," note that the system imposed by the landed shaykhs on their peasant *sharīk*s or *métayers* in the Kisrawān did not involve the transfer of property. Simi-

---

[9]Nujaym, *La Question du Liban*, p. 341. From 1840 Nujaym noted an expansion of impoverished Khāzins who appeared to side with the peasantry on many occasions. Nujaym referred to this stratum as "les cadets de la noblesse maronite."

[10]Al-Ḥattūnī, *Nubdha ta'rīkhīya*, p. 269; 'Aqīqī-Kerr, *Lebanon*, pp. 45–47 and letters of the *wakīl*s to the Maronite Patriarch, Būluṣ Mas'ad, pp. 110–11; Porath, "The Peasant Revolt," pp. 84, 92–93.

larly, to reduce the impact of continuous parcelling of property over time through inheritance, the Khāzins resorted on occasion to private family *waqf*s. The peasantry, furthermore, could not acquire land held as *waqf* by the monasteries and orders. One may note, in this respect, the consolidation and expansion of property held by the convents in contrast to the fragmentation and occasional loss of property through sales by the Khāzins.[11]

Elsewhere in Mount Lebanon there was a more favorable system open to the peasant: local variants of the system of *mughārasa* (Toufic Touma refers to it also as *munāṣaba*) where the proprietor would concede a parcel of land to a peasant *sharīk* who was in turn obliged to plant it with trees and share the proceeds.[12] After a lapse of between five and ten years, however, the *sharīk* acquired a quarter or a half of the land and trees in question as his own private holding.

To the scarcity of suitable land, the absence of a *mughārasa* system, and the demographic pressure leading on occasion to emigration from the *muqāṭaʿa*, must be added another aggravating factor: the full burden of taxation that the shaykhs simply transferred to their peasant *sharīk*s.[13] Other grievances included the imposition of humiliating and increasingly anachronistic "quasi-feudal" homage and *ʿīdīya* (presents), often transcribed into the contractual arrangements with the *sharīk*. Regular as well as *ad hoc* *ʿīdīya* increasingly took the form of products that had to be purchased from urban markets, such as soap, coffee, and sugar.[14] In a sense, although the *ʿīdīya* was a drain on the peasant's monetary resources and a symbol of his servitude, it also served to maintain his contact with urban market places,

---

[11] Chevallier, "Aspects sociaux," pp. 54–55.

[12] Touma, *Paysans et institutions*, pp. 584, 588, 616–17; André Latron, *La Vie rurale en Syrie et au Liban* (Beirut: Institut Français de Damas, 1936), pp. 48–58, 65–72.

[13] Nujaym, *La Question du Liban*, p. 340. An analysis of the dynamics of population growth for nineteenth-century Mount Lebanon is not yet possible due to the absence of birth rate, death rate, and migration rate statistics. Nujaym, however, appears to attach a great deal of importance to emigration out of Mount Lebanon as early as 1850: another indicator, perhaps of the rising expectations of a peasantry seeking to improve its place in the sun.

[14] ʿAqīqī-Kerr, *Lebanon*, pp. 97, 111. The third item in the peasant petition (*ibid.*, p. 98) addressed to Patriarch Būlus Masʿad is clear on the subject of *ʿīdīya*: "The presents and marriage taxes currently paid to their excellencies the Shaikhs in certain places, or the presents to the Shaikhs attached to the sale of their goods to the people, must be discontinued and removed in their entirety." See also I.F. Harik, "The *Iqṭāʿ* System in Lebanon: A Comparative Political View," *Middle East Journal*, 19 (1965), p. 418; and Chevallier, "Aspects sociaux," p. 50.

particularly in Beirut. Paradoxically, therefore, the *'īdīya* became a contributory factor to the erosion of the "quasi-feudal" system.

On the political front, the Khāzins were involved in an expensive and deeply divisive struggle between Bashīr Aḥmad, the *qā'imaqām*, and his rival Bashīr 'Assāf, while at the same time they were losing the support of the clergy. As for the peasantry, participation in earlier rural movements had enhanced their collective consciousness, self-esteem, and powers of organization. The emergence of *shuyūkh shabāb* and *wakīls* weakened the traditional leadership of the Khāzins, and the rise of urban centers in Kisrawān such as Jounieh and Zūq Mkāyil added to this erosion, as did the growing economic ties with Beirut and the profound economic changes brought about by Western industrial and commercial penetration throughout the Levant. The introduction of new techniques by French silk manufacturers established in the Matn, in the outskirts of Beirut, and more rarely in the Kisrawān, changed the nature of the demand for silk. Traditionally, Mount Lebanon produced only hand-reeled raw silk thread. The new French factories in the area, however, were more interested in purchasing silk cocoons as raw material for their mechanical reels. There is evidence that the Khāzins did not adapt to these new market conditions and continued to think in terms of thread rather than the increasingly lucrative cocoon.[15] The peasant proprietors, on the other hand, were more responsive to change and economic opportunity.

In short, there was a situation of multiple disfunction: a social, economic, and political breakdown of the internal cohesion of the Khāzin elite compounded by intransigence on the one hand and a corresponding gain of strength and expectations among the peasant insurgents on the other. Holding the balance of power in this contest, the clergy were more inclined to sympathize with the peasant community. This, in brief, summarizes the long-range causes or preconditions of the 1858 revolt.[16]

Turning to the immediate causes or precipitants of the revolt, our examination will involve two factors that have not received adequate attention in the literature. The first of these is the sharp and unexpected economic

---

[15] Chevallier, "Aspects sociaux," p. 54.

[16] From the rich literature on the theory of internal wars and revolts the following proved particularly useful: Harry Eckstien, "On the Etiology of Internal Wars," *History and Theory*, 4 (1965), pp. 133–63; Lawrence Stone, "Theories of Revolution," *World Politics*, 18 (1965-66), pp. 159–76; Chalmers Johnson, *Revolution and the Social System* (Stanford: Hoover Institution, 1964); James C. Davies, "Toward a Theory of Revolution," *American Sociological Review*, 27 (1962), pp. 5–19.

downturn beginning in 1856, following two decades of sustained growth and
prosperity in sericulture. It is suggested that sustained economic improvement interrupted by a sudden setback, as in 1856–58, is profoundly destabilizing and a precipitant for revolt when the preconditions are right. The
social and economic conjuncture in Kisrawān would therefore appear to fit
the "J-curve" pattern outlined by James C. Davies:

> Revolutions are most likely to occur when a prolonged period of
> objective economic and social development is followed by a short
> period of sharp reversal. The all-important effect on the minds
> of people in a particular society is to produce, during the former
> period, an expectation of continued ability to satisfy needs—
> which continue to rise—and, during the latter, a mental state of
> anxiety and frustration when manifest reality breaks away from
> anticipated reality.[17]

The second factor relates to the arming of the peasantry, which acted as
both a trigger, and when the revolt gathered momentum, as a deterrent to
reaction by the "shaykhocracy." A peasantry armed, even with small-caliber
Belgian muzzleloaders, is a peasantry that has been socially transformed, and
is psychologically more secure and self-confident in the face of enemies such
as the Khāzins: it is a peasantry in a position to back its demands with
visible armed strength.

Writing in 1857, the Belgian consul in Beirut, H. De Turck, dwelt on the
disasters caused by climatic conditions. The work huts of the silkgrowers
were swept away by unseasonal and torrential rains, killing large numbers
of the maturing silkworms. In addition, disease reduced the grape crop to
about one-twentieth of normal production, and the olive harvest was a failure
as well.[18] Manṣūr al-Ḥattūnī recorded 1857 as being one of the most severe
of winters in terms of cold temperatures and abundant snowfalls.[19]

Equally gloomy was De Turck's report for the following year, which
he characterized as a year of continuing economic calamities. An intense
drought damaged the olive crop once again. Even more serious was the
plight of Beirut's silk merchants, who were badly affected by the virtual collapse of the silk industry in Lyon, Lebanon's principal export market. The
silk industry in the south of France was itself going through a severe crisis

---

[17]Davies, "Toward a Theory of Revolution," p. 6; Roland Mousnier, "Conjuncture and
Circumstance in Popular Uprisings," in *The Peasantry in the Old Regime*, pp. 52–58.

[18]Royaume de Belgique, *Recueil consulaire*, III (1857), De Turck's report, pp. 140–41.

[19]Al-Ḥattūnī, *Nubdha ta'rīkhīya*, p. 266.

at this time caused by a silkworm disease that devastated French production in the Rhône Valley and Languedoc, and paralyzed the weavers of the region.[20] Many of the leading Lebanese silk merchants were ruined and the commerce of Beirut and Mount Lebanon was gravely disturbed. "Après tant de faillités successives," De Turck wrote, "on n'ose plus croire à la solidité d'aucun négociant, d'aucune maison de commerce. Notre banque anglaise, qui prospérait à Beyrout, sous le nom de Banque Ottomane, a cessé, momentanément et par prudence, ses opérations."[21]

This picture is corroborated by British consular reports from Beirut, although British trade, containing a high proportion of goods in transit to Damascus and Baghdad, fared better than its European rivals. Consul Moore underlined the "general monetary crisis" and the sharp fall in Lebanese exports to France (consisting mainly of silk). He also estimated a 50 percent drop in local silk production. At the same time, he noted a movement from cottage industry to agricultural pursuits under the impact of English manufactures.[22] Similarly, Beirut's first newspaper, the newly established *Ḥadīqat al-akhbār*, reflected the disturbed state of the market (shortage, stagnation, and lack of credit) and a movement of grain from Beirut to Jounieh.[23] This acute and widespread economic crisis was all the more disturbing coming, as it did, after a prolonged period of sustained growth, soaring prices for silk, and heightened expectations.[24]

As to the second factor in this reconsideration of the immediate causes of the Kisrawān peasant revolt—the flow of arms and the arming of the peasantry—it is now clear that the influx of Belgian muskets and shotguns to Beirut during 1855, 1856, 1857, and 1858 was enormous. Again the evidence of Consul De Turck is illuminating, for beside his consular duties he was a trader in Belgian arms and a principal importer of this lucrative commodity. Such massive infusions of this particular product of Western industry and technology is a qualitative factor in the internal wars and conflicts of the nineteenth century Middle East—one that requires further investigation,

[20] Marcel Emerit, "La crise syrienne et l'expansion économique française en 1860," *Revue historique*, 207 (1952), pp. 224–25.
[21] Royaume de Belgique, *Recueil consulaire*, IV (1858), De Turck's report, p. 72.
[22] Great Britain, *Parliamentary Papers*, XXX (1859), report by Moore, pp. 451–52.
[23] *Ḥadīqat al-akhbār*, 1 (1858), nos. 26 to 37, July to September.
[24] Gaston Ducousso, *L'Industrie de la soie en Syrie et au Liban* (Beirut: Imprimerie catholique, 1913), p. 108. Ducousso points to the phenomenal increase in prices for silk cocoons within a decade of the establishment of French factories in Mount Lebanon: from ten to twelve piastres an *ocke*, to 25 and even 34 piastres.

particularly in view of the fact that the pattern of arms import for Beirut is repeated in other ports of the region, such as Jaffa.

De Turck's statistics for Belgian guns cleared (quite legally) through the Beirut customs are as follows:[25]

Year	Cases	No. of Guns	Av. Price Per Gun
1855	43	1075	12.50 francs
1856	573	14325	16 francs
1857	849	21225	25 francs
1858	229	5725	21 francs

The consul reported that his figures for 1855 were only partial and that for 1858 there were more shipments on the way. He also noted that other traders may have placed orders with Belgian manufacturers without his knowledge. To this, one would have to add imports from other European countries, although these would have been much dearer than the Belgian product: for instance, French guns were nearly double the price. Nor should one underestimate the number of guns smuggled into the country whenever the demand was stimulated by the prospect of conflict. It is therefore safe to say that there were enough guns in the area to arm and rearm the peasantry and the tribes of the hinterland from Aleppo to Gaza.

Who was buying this weaponry? Direct and conclusive evidence is fragmentary, but for the Kisrawān both consuls and chroniclers agree on the intensive arming of the peasantry and also on direct purchases by the peasants themselves.[26] Another British consul reported large consignments of Belgian guns arriving in 1858 in steamships:

> I have heard of one mercantile house (Maltese) in Beyrout having within two years made immense imports with profit. The articles were all sold, even before arrival. During the same period, one shop in Jerusalem has sold 30,000, imported via Jaffa, and they were distributed at that port to Gaza, Hebron, etc. At this moment more are on the passage out, but all these are inferior in number to the sales in Beyrout. Such numbers are

---

[25] Royaume de Belgique, *Recueil consulaire*, I (1855); III (1857); IV (1858). A case contained 25 guns.

[26] 'Aqīqī-Kerr, *Lebanon*, pp. 53, 100, 114, 117; al-Ḥattūnī, *Nubdha ta'rīkhīya*, pp. 272–75, 289.

scarcely conceivable to be true....The peasantry, notwithstanding the losses sustained by extortion of their own Sheikhs and of
the tax-farmers, have accumulated an unprecedented degree of
wealth....The people are therefore able to purchase arms, both
numerous and of strong quality, and many a rustic is in possession
of two or three guns of his own property, besides the never-failing
short swords called khanjars.[27]

A Belgian gun represented an average investment of 100 piasters or one gold
pound for a peasant, the price of three *ockes* of fresh silk cocoons and well
within his means.[28] Thus, al-'Aqīqī's and al-Ḥattūnī's reports of concentrations of 400, 600, or even 800 armed peasants, led by their *shuyūkh, shabāb,*
and *wakīls,* are plausible, as is the statement of the Khāzin shaykhs, in a
petition to European consuls, that the peasant insurgents "drove us away
under showers of musketry, with various kinds of insults to us jointly and
severally."[29] Similarly, in a letter to Patriarch Būluṣ Mas'ad by 'Abbās
Shaybān al-Khāzin, the shaykh complained that: "The people of 'Ajaltūn
brandished their weapons at our cousins, insulted them with unbearably
insolent words, and threatened them with destruction....In brief, the immi-
nence of bloodshed has become closer than the eyelid is to the eye."[30] Yet
there was surprisingly little bloodshed during the three years of the peasant insurrection, for only three Khāzins were killed. Indeed, there was not
much the Khāzins could do against such concentrations of armed peasants:
deterrence in this case had proved to be credible.

* * * *

One of Alexis de Tocqueville's major contributions to peasant studies is
the thesis that revolutionary protest occurs when conditions are improving:

---

[27] Great Britain, *Parliamentary Papers,* LXIX (1860), *Despatches from Her Majesty's
Consuls in the Levant Respecting Past or Apprehended Disturbances in Syria 1858–60,* p.
42, Consul Finn to the Earl of Malmesbury, 9 October 1858.

[28] It is interesting to note that one gold pound today is worth roughly 500 Lebanese
pounds on the Beirut market, which is also the price of a Kalashnikov assault rifle in
Beirut.

[29] Memorial of the Khāzin Family signed by 30 shaykhs to the European consuls, in Great
Britain, *Parliamentary Papers,* LXIX (1860), *Despatches from Her Majesty's Consuls in
the Levant Respecting Past or Apprehended Disturbances in Syria 1858–60,* pp. 87–88;
'Aqīqī-Kerr, *Lebanon,* pp. 53, 100, 114, 117.

[30] 'Aqīqī-Kerr, *Lebanon,* p. 100.

It was precisely in those parts of France where there had been most improvement that popular discontent ran highest. This may seem illogical—but history is full of such paradoxes. For it is not always when things are going from bad to worse that revolutions break out. On the contrary, it oftener happens that when a people which has put up with an oppressive rule over a long period without protest suddenly finds the government relaxing its pressure, it takes up arms against it. ...Patiently endured so long as it seemed beyond redress, a grievance comes to appear intolerable once the possibility of removing it crosses men's minds. ...At the height of its power feudalism did not inspire as much hatred as it did on the eve of its eclipse.[31]

This pattern of insurgency in the closing days of France's Ancien Régime is also applicable to the peasantry of Kisrawān under the Khāzins. A further question may be raised regarding the specificity of the Kisrawān revolt in the regional conflict which engulfed the coast and hinterland of the Levant from Aleppo in the north to Gaza in the south between 1858 and 1860. Villages in the vicinity of Aleppo were attacked by nomads. In the 'Alawite mountains there was a sharp conflict between the 'Alawites and the Dandāshlīs. In north Lebanon rival clans in Bsharrī and Zghartā clashed. In the Kisrawān, Christian peasants revolted against their Christian "shaykhocracy" in 1858. In the Shūf and Matn, Druze overlords led their peasants in a bitter civil war against Maronite overlords and their peasants in 1860. In the 'Arqūb region, there was an obscure peasant war in which, according to a British consular source, at least 200 lives were lost in one season alone. The rival leaders in this conflict were 'Uthmān Laḥḥām and his cousin Muḥammad 'Atallāh, and the war ended with the banishment of both to Cyprus.[32] In the region of Nablus there was a bitter outbreak between the 'Abd al-Hādī family and their tribal allies (the Ghazawīya and 'Adwān) on the one hand, and the Ṭūqāns and their tribal allies (the 'Abbād and Banū Ṣaqr) on the other.[33] In Damascus, there was urban violence, which degenerated into the

---

[31]The Tocqueville quote is from *The Economic Origins of the French Revolution: Poverty or Prosperity*, edited by Ralph W. Greenlaw (Boston: D.C. Heath and Co., 1958), p. 13.

[32]Great Britain, *Parliamentary Papers*, LXIX (1860), *Despatches*, pp. 44, 535 (Consul Finn, 9 October 1858 and 17 November 1859).

[33]Miriam Hoexter, "The Role of the Qays and Yaman Factions in Local Political Divisions: Jabal Nablus Compared with the Judean Hills in the First Half of the Nineteenth Century," *Asian and African Studies*, 9 (1973), p. 278.

notorious sectarian massacres of 1861. And in Gaza there were tribal wars spilling into the city.

In this general picture of conflict the case of Kisrawān is specific in a number of ways. First, it pitted Maronite shaykhs against Maronite peasants. Second, the peasant leadership drew up a program that culminated in the setting up of a popular republic functioning under the authority of a republican-type government: *bi-qūwat al-ḥukūma al-jumhurīya*, as al-'Aqīqī characterized it.[34] And third, the leadership appeared to be aware of the Ottoman *Khaṭṭ-i hümayūn*, and the "ideology" of their revolt stressed "universal equality and complete freedom...no distinctions or degradations in addressing persons."[35] In fact, Nujaym (1908) characterized the revolt as a popular democratic movement.[36] Notwithstanding the specificity of Kisrawān, the remarkable phenomenon of regional conjunction begs explanation. One is reminded of Metternich's observation that when Paris sneezed Europe caught a cold, as in 1830 and 1848. Was there a Paris in the Syrian-Lebanese-Palestinian conjunction of 1858? And if so, where was it? These are questions that still await investigation.

---

[34] 'Aqīqī-Kerr, *Lebanon*, p. 53.

[35] *Ibid.*, p. 98.

[36] Nujaym, *La Question du Liban*, p. 347.

23

The Agricultural Exports of Southern Palestine, 1885-1914*

THE PRINCIPAL AIM of this study is to survey and quantify the agricultural exports of southern Palestine for the 30-year period between 1885 and 1914 in contribution to the much-neglected economic history of the Arab East, and in the hope that some light may be shed on the role of foreign trade in the economic development of Palestine in the half century before the First World War. The main stress is on agricultural and related products destined for export to Europe, Egypt, and parts of the Ottoman Empire. A second aim is to evaluate British source material, particularly the Foreign Office "Annual and Miscellaneous Series of Reports on Trade and Commerce" from the consulate of Jerusalem, which forms the main corpus of documentation used in this study. Compiled by experienced consular staff in Jerusalem, Jaffa, and later in Gaza, the reports are a mine of information and constitute valuable research sources.

Southern Palestine is here defined as the Ottoman province of Jerusalem, established as an autonomous *sanjaq* or *mutaṣarrifīya* in 1873 and encompassing one *markaz-liwā'* (*al-Quds*, i.e. Jerusalem), three *qaḍā*'s (Jaffa, Gaza, and Hebron), and two *nāhiyas* (Bethlehem and Ramla). In 1899 the *qaḍā'* of Beersheba was established in a move to better control the increasingly important border zone with Egypt. In 1906 the *qaḍā'* of Nazareth was detached from the *vilāyet* of Beirut and was added to Jerusalem for a short span of about two years.

---

*From the *Journal of Palestine Studies*, 10.4 (Summer 1981), pp. 61–81. © 1981 by the Institute for Palestine Studies. Reprinted courtesy of the Institute for Palestine Studies.

The Expansion of Europe and the Dependent Status of the Ottoman Economy

Palestine, together with other parts of Bilād al-Shām (geographical Syria), was brought into the European economic system as a dependent producer of raw materials and cereals and as a docile market for manufactured goods and investments early in the seventeenth century, and with increased vigor during the last 150 years. This was accomplished under a process that began with indirect forms of control (the Capitulations[1] granted to Europeans by the Ottoman sultanate) and that ended—for Palestine—in direct annexation and domination of the land and the expulsion of a considerable proportion of its people.

Building to some extent upon the political and economic gains of the Crusades, Europe embarked on a systematic program of global exploration. The consequences of such relentlessly pursued activity were the control and colonization of territories vastly superior to it in size and natural resources. The new acquisitions yielded three groups of interrelated dimensions connected with the rise of the West to a position of political and economic hegemony over the rest of the world. In the first place, quantities of gold and silver were extracted, which stimulated the use of money and the growth of a capitalist economy. Secondly, millions of Africans were transported as slaves to North, Central, and South America and the Caribbean islands to provide the cheapest possible manpower for the production of key agricultural commodities, such as cotton, sugar, indigo, and tobacco, as well as for labor in the gold and silver mines.[2] Thirdly, the new possessions provided European nations with opportunities to establish plantations also in Asia and lucrative markets in the four corners of the earth, thus helping to make it worthwhile for division of labor practices to develop in the budding industrial sectors of the West. At the same time, placed in a state of subservience,

---

[1]The term "Capitulations" is derived from the Latin *capitula*, i.e. chapters. In formal terms, the first Capitulations were granted by Sultan Sulaymān to France in 1528 and 1535; the practice of maintaining, indeed of enlarging the scale and scope of such privileges, was followed by the succeeding sultans. Some of the privileges included the right to act as protector of the Holy Places in Palestine, the authorization of European ships to trade in Ottoman ports, the right of having European residents in the Empire tried and disciplined by their own consular courts, not by Ottoman authorities, and all kinds of tax exemptions on residence, profit, travel, and exports. See *Le Régime des Capitulations* (Paris: Plon, 1898), pp. 55, 60, 81.

[2]Estimates for the number of slaves transported from Africa to America vary: about one million in the sixteenth century, rising to three million in the eighteenth. See Eric J. Hobsbawn, *Industry and Empire* (London: Penguin, 1969), p. 52.

these vast colonial markets acted as shock-absorbers for the numerous economic crises in Europe during the past two centuries. The industrial take-off and sustained growth of the Western economy would not have been possible without the large-scale plunder and intensive exploitation of Europe's formal and informal overseas possessions.

A distinctive feature of Ottoman policy was the granting of Capitulations to Europe: these were concessions of extraterritorial privileges that amounted in effect to a self-imposed loss of sovereignty. Surprisingly, the Capitulations were not extracted by force; they were awarded by a magnanimous sultan at the height of Ottoman power, with little foresight as to their implications for the future. Europe was invited to come in and take over, for a start, control of the Empire's international trade, an invitation gladly accepted.

In time, the Capitulations, matched by Europe's irrepressible will to power, proved fatal to the economic independence of the Ottoman Empire: they signified, in fact, that Turkey could levy only two percent tax on European imports in the sixteenth century, rising gradually to a maximum of 10–11 percent in the twentieth.[3] In 1907, it was only about eight percent. Consequently, the realm of the Sultan was saddled with a permanent handicap in the form of low tariff barriers that played havoc with the manufacturing potential of local urban and rural producers.

The stranglehold on the Ottoman Empire and on Bilād al–Shām was tightened following the Industrial Revolution. The commercial treaty with Turkey in 1838 symbolized the growing needs of European society and its ability to pressure its way into world markets: old Capitulations were confirmed and additional ones imposed. Then in 1867, the right to purchase property was granted by the Ottoman government to foreigners. The Capitulations also served as a convenient avenue through which massive investments were channelled as soon as sufficient surplus capital accumulated in the advanced industrial societies. The banks in the Empire were generally foreign: even the Ottoman Bank was an Anglo-French enterprise. By the last quarter of the nineteenth century, imports, exports, mining concessions, ports, railways, water, and technology were largely under foreign control. By then the Ottoman Empire was literally bankrupt, unable to meet even half the interest on its massive foreign debt. After 1882, the administration of the Ottoman Debt Commission, a body grouping the Big Powers, took

---

[3] Z.Y. Hershlag, *Introduction to the Modern Economic History of the Middle East* (Leiden: E.J. Brill, 1964), p. 43.

over the revenues of such lucrative monopolies as tobacco and salt, together with other sources of income. The subservience and peripheralization of the Ottoman economy had reached a high point.[4]

Thus, at the dawn of the twentieth century the Big Powers had already partitioned the Ottoman Empire into spheres of economic influence. This has been demonstrated by Rashid Khalidi in his *British Policy Towards Syria and Palestine, 1906-1914*, with special reference to the intricate Anglo-French railway negotiations, which are characterized as the "beginnings of partitions."[5] In other words, the economic partition of Bilād al-Shām was the prelude to the political partition that was planned on the eve of the First World War and put into effect with major modifications immediately after it.[6]

The Agricultural Trade of Palestine in Historical Perspective

The economic importance of Palestine has traditionally been underestimated, generally for myth-construction purposes: a dominant theme, taken for granted by the Western world, is the Zionist claim that the region was a desert which bloomed with the arrival of the first wave of Jewish colon-pioneers late in the nineteenth century.[7] In fact, Palestine has always been

---

[4] H. Islamoglu and C. Keyder, "Agenda for Ottoman History," *Review* (Summer 1977), p. 54.

[5] Rashid Khalidi, *British Policy Towards Syria and Palestine, 1906–1914* (London: Ithaca Press, 1980), p. 113.

[6] H.F. Frischwasser-Ra'anan, *The Frontiers of a Nation: A Re-examination of the Forces Which Created the Palestine Mandate and Determined Its Territorial Shape* (London: Batchworth Press, 1955), p. 27. The author argues (*ibid.*) that economic partition was accomplished between 1906 and 1914 and that it "established the bases for the secret wartime agreements on the partition of the Turkish Empire and, consequently, for the post-war division of the Middle East."

[7] The economic literature on Palestine is richer for the post-First World War period than it is for the Ottoman centuries. Nevertheless, the following works are of value: John Bowring, *Report on the Commercial Statistics of Syria* (London: H.M. Stationery Office, 1840); Ernest Weakley, *Report Upon the Conditions and Prospects of British Trade in Syria*, prepared for the Board of Trade, Commercial Intelligence Committee (London: H.M. Stationery Office, 1911); Vital Cuinet, *Syrie, Liban et Palestine* (Paris: E. Leroux, 1896); Noel Verney and George Dambmann, *Les Puissances étrangères dans le Levant et en Palestine* (Paris: Guillaumin, 1900); Alfred Bonné, *Palästina, Land und Wirtschaft* (Leipzig: Deutsche wissenschaftliche Buchhandlung, 1932); Abraham Granovsky, *Land Problems in Palestine* (London: Routledge, 1926); Ḥannā Ṣalāḥ, *Filasṭīn wa-tajdīd ḥayātihā* (New York: Palestine Anti-Zionism Society, 1919); Nabīl Badrān, "Al-Rīf al-filasṭīnī qabla l-ḥarb al-'alamīya al-ūlā," *Shu'ūn filasṭīnīya*, 7 (March 1972), pp.

an important producer of key agricultural commodities and was experiencing a significant expansion of agriculture and allied manufactures at least two generations before the arrival of the first colons from eastern Europe,[8] who were able to maintain their farms only with the help of Arab labor and the massive financial subsidies of Baron Edmund de Rothschild.[9]

As far back as the tenth century, the Palestinian geographer al-Muqaddasī had stressed the importance of Palestine's olive oil, cotton, grapes, sugar cane, and the manufacture of silk and cotton cloths and soap.[10] Likewise, Fra Francesco Suriano, a Franciscan father and long-time resident of Palestine in the sixteenth century, described the abundance of its production. In addition to sugar cane, citrus fruits, and apples, he reported:

> They have an infinite number of bushes which yield cotton [and] other bushes which produce a seed...from which they make oil called sesame, which is better than olive oil when cooked and even better than butter. And they produce such quantities of this that it supplies all Syria and Egypt.[11]

A few centuries later, more specifically in 1911, Ernest Weakley's comprehensive report on economic conditions in Syria also noted the importance of the sesame crop: "The districts of Haifa and Jaffa produce the largest quantity of sesame seed in Syria, and a normal harvest in these districts will allow of some 9,000 to 14,000 tons being exported. The quality of this seed is the best known in the Levant, and yields a good quantity of oil."[12]

Throughout the sixteenth, seventeenth, and eighteenth centuries, substantial shipments of cotton and grains were exported from various Bilād al-Shām ports, usually by European merchants residing in the area and protected by the Capitulations; the ports of Sidon and Acre played a prominent role in this trade.[13] At first used in the making of candle wicks, cotton was

---

116–29; M. Maoz, *Studies on Palestine During the Ottoman Period* (Jerusalem: Magnes Press, 1975); and especially Alexander Schölch, "The Economic Development of Palestine, 1856–1882," *Journal of Palestine Studies*, 10.3 (Spring 1981), pp. 35–58.

[8] Bowring, *Report*, p. 133.

[9] William E. Curtis, *To-day in Syria and Palestine* (Chicago: Revell, 1903), p. 327.

[10] Carl Johan Lamm, *Cotton in Mediaeval Textiles of the Near East* (Paris: Geuthner, 1937), p. 232.

[11] Fra Francesco Suriano, *Treatise on the Holy Land, 1516* (Jerusalem: Franciscan Press, 1949), p. 233.

[12] Weakley, *Report*, p. 198.

[13] Lamm, *Cotton in Mediaeval Textiles*, p. 234; Paul Masson, *Histoire du commerce français dans le Levant au 17e siècle* (Paris: Hachette, 1896), p. 390; Ralph Davis,

later much sought after as raw material for the European textile industry. The demand for cotton remained important during the seventeenth century and most of the eighteenth, and was further stimulated in the final decades of the eighteenth; in fact, it became a leading factor in the genesis of the Industrial Revolution.[14]

It is significant to note that the steady demand for this valuable commodity in the West was reflected in the expansion of cotton cultivation in Palestine throughout the eighteenth century, reaching new heights in the 1790s, the acknowledged take-off period for the Industrial Revolution, and that this increase also provided the economic bases for the rise of the Zaydānī family, culminating in the dramatic career of Dāhir al-ʿUmar and the development of Acre.[15] Similarly, it would help explain the Aḥmad al-Jazzār phenomenon. Largely based on the expansion of agriculture and commerce, with cotton, silk, and grains constituting key factors, Acre rose to even greater prominence under this ruler, becoming the principal seat of power for the southern and western regions of Bilād al-Shām.[16]

Palestinian cotton was always a more important item of trade to France—especially to southern France—than it was to England. It was considered of superior quality to that of northern Syria and southern Turkey and was valued at 30 to 50 percent higher. In the 1830s the annual production, according to John Bowring's report, averaged an estimated 2,200 tons, of which three-quarters was exported.[17] But thereafter it suffered a severe decline with only a brief revival during the American Civil War, when the demand for non-American cotton was greatly stimulated.[18] In the opening years of the twentieth century, there was renewed interest in cotton, as reflected in the annual reports, with Consul Dickson providing a competent summary of the history and prospects of its cultivation in Palestine. Experiments were being

---

"British Imports From the Middle East 1580–1780," in *Studies in the Economic History of the Middle East*, edited by M.A. Cook (London: Oxford University Press, 1970), pp. 200, 204.

[14] Marwan and Leila Buheiry, *The Splendor of The Holy Land* (New York: Caravan Books, 1978), xiii–xiv.

[15] *Ibid.*

[16] A.L. Tibawi, *A Modern History of Syria* (London: Macmillan, 1969), pp. 31–32; Charles Issawi, "British Trade and the Rise of Beirut, 1830–1860," *International Journal of Middle East Studies*, 8 (1977), p. 92, explaining the economic factors in the revival of British interests in Bilād al-Shām.

[17] Bowring, *Report*, pp. 13–14, 58.

[18] "Cotton Growing in Palestine," *Levant Trade Review*, 2.3 (December 1912), pp. 363–64.

carried out which yielded fair results, and even steam ploughs and tractors were in use as early as 1910.[19] It is quite clear that by 1906 British business interests and Zionist colonization were aware of the cotton-producing potential of Palestine and that this resource may have been an added incentive in the economic partition of the area, which, as has already been suggested, was the prelude to the political partition of the post-1914 era.[20]

Of greater—because of more lasting—importance than cotton in the export trade of Palestine were wheat, barley, citrus fruit, olive oil, soap, and sesame. The latter was in demand particularly by the oil and soap industry of Marseilles, which imported substantial shipments in the late nineteenth century. In the best years (1889–97), exports from Jaffa would climb to between £50,000 and £110,000 a year, roughly equivalent to orange exports. But thereafter there appears to have been a steep decline in sesame exports (1898–1905), while orange exports rose to ever higher levels (see Table 2 at the end of this study).

Wheat, of course, had once played a considerable role in commercial exchange with Europe. According to Paul Masson, the economic historian of Marseilles, wheat shipments obtained in Syrian ports, especially at Acre, helped to save southern France from famine on numerous occasions in the seventeenth and eighteenth centuries: he quotes a French traveller, Fermanel, who witnessed 32 ships in Acre in 1630, all waiting at the same time to load the wheat.[21]

Despite much fluctuation and a massive drop in its export from Jaffa (particularly after 1890), wheat remained important for the Italian trade, and its "hard" quality was much esteemed for the macaroni industry: in fact, Italian demand for this hard wheat remained high in spite of the lower market price of Russian wheat shipped from the Black Sea port of Odessa.[22]

---

[19] Foreign Office Annual Series (cited hereafter as FOAS), no. 3223, *Trade and Commerce of Palestine*, 1904, pp. 6–7.

[20] Ernest Weakley in his *Report* to the Commercial Intelligence Committee of the British Board of Trade in 1911 (pp. 56–57, 130) described the soil of Jordan as particularly suited to cotton growing. Also, the *Levant Trade Review* article on "Cotton Growing in Palestine" (pp. 363–64) described British attempts to grow cotton in various parts of Palestine, including the Jaffa area, and stressed that land prices were about 15 percent less than in Egypt. It added that the adoption of newly invented American cotton-picking machinery would be the answer to the problem of labor costs.

[21] Masson, *Histoire du commerce français dans le Levant au 17è siècle*, p. 390, n. 13; also his *Histoire du commerce français ... au 18è siècle*, pp. 441, 458, 463.

[22] Masson, *Histoire du commerce français ... au 18è siècle*, p. 513; Verney and Dambmann, *Les Puissances étrangères*, p. 637.

In good years, exports of Palestinian wheat from the various ports reached substantial figures. According to A. Ruppin, the Zionist Organization's principal land colonization expert, the Jewish colonies during the period 1901–1907 turned to wheat cultivation, each colonist being given large plots averaging 250 dunums, "under the direction of the Jewish Colonization Association."[23] Yet the results did not seem encouraging. Describing the dismal and despairing conditions of 25 agricultural settlements cultivating 350,000 dunums of land in 1908, Ruppin recalled:

> There are few things sadder to imagine than [their] state of mind...round about the year 1908. The older generation was grown weary and sullen with the labour and toil of a quarter century, without the faintest hope for the future or the slightest enjoyment of the present, the younger generation wished but one thing, namely to leave agriculture..., and to find a "better" occupation in the outside world.[24]

Barley was another valuable export crop, associated principally with the Gaza region. Because of its superb quality, it was in great demand by the breweries of England, Scotland, and Germany: annual production for ex-

---

[23] Arthur Ruppin, *The Agricultural Colonization of the Zionist Organization in Palestine* (London: Martin Hopkinson, 1926), p. 4. Ruppin divides Zionist colonization into four periods: 1) the period 1880 to 1900, characterized by the Rothschild administration and the dependence on wine; 2) the period 1901–1907, with the focus on wheat cultivation under the direction of the Jewish Colonization Association; 3) the period 1908–20, with attention on mixed farming; 4) the period after 1921, when large-scale means were employed and attention devoted to the acquisition of connecting land areas. Furthermore, N. Weinstock, in his *Le Sionisme contre Israël* (Paris: Maspero, 1969), p. 77, points out the massive subsidies accorded to Jewish colons by the "patriarchal" administration of the Rothschilds: 360 families had been subsidized at a cost of 40 million francs by 1900. Yet by 1908, and in spite of this enormous investment, Arthur Ruppin could paint such a dismal picture of the total effort.

[24] Ruppin, *Agricultural Colonization*, p. 6. The myth of the Zionist colon's "genius" for agriculture (set off against a background of Arab incompetence) and the myth of "the land that was desolate" have been carefully nurtured over generations and are therefore hard to dispel. Yet it is sufficient to recall the observations made in 1918 by S. Tolkowsky, a foremost agricultural engineer of the Zionist Organization, concerning Jewish colons in Palestine: "They had come to cultivate again the soil...but, as has already been mentioned, they were ignorant of the most elementary rules of agriculture. Still, far from being discouraged, they started by copying the primitive methods of their Arab neighbours; little by little they became acquainted with the nature of the land, and the requirements of the crops...." See S. Tolkowsky, *The Jewish Colonization in Palestine* (London: The Zionist Organization, 1918), p. 6.

port regularly exceeded 40,000 tons for the period 1890-1900 in Gaza alone, representing three-quarters of Palestine's total export of this cereal.[25]

A consular report for the year 1898 estimates exports to Great Britain from Gaza to be 30,000 tons of barley, 4,000 tons of wheat, and 600 tons of dura shipped on board 15 British steamers.[26] A note also adds:

> It is to be hoped that the harvest of Gaza and its neighbourhood will be of the best, especially as the districts belonging to the Bedouins of Gaza are very fertile, and more highly thought of than any other district throughout the whole of Palestine, because of their productive qualities.[27]

In fact, what is often forgotten is that the average value of Gaza's barley exports to England (35,000 tons worth £180,000) was nearly twice the average value of Jaffa's exports of oranges (£97,000 yearly average for 1901–1905) to all countries.[28] Barley was therefore the leading export item.

After 1905, there was more interest shown in the Gaza region in political as well as economic matters. Beersheba appeared more frequently in the reports "as the seat of government of the 70,000 Bedawin who inhabit the district."[29] The governor was credited with doing his best to encourage public works: mosque construction, public gardens, and a pump placed over a water well.[30]

According to Consul Blech's report for the year 1907, barley was laid out on the beach in the form of large piles and served as a peculiar landmark for captains of steamers. Exports of this valuable grain had risen to between £200,000 and £250,000 a year by 1907.[31] The chief import from England in the Gaza district was unbleached calico cloth, the standard item of popular clothing, which was dyed blue locally using German anilines.

---

[25] Verney and Dambmann, *Les Puissances étrangères*, pp. 350, 645; Weakley, *Report*, p. 197.

[26] FOAS, no. 2217, *Trade and Commerce of the Consular District of Jerusalem*, 1899, p. 7.

[27] *Ibid.*

[28] FOAS, no. 3561, *Trade and Commerce of Palestine*, 1906, p. 10.

[29] *Ibid.*, p. 9.

[30] FOAS, no. 3771, *Trade and Commerce of Palestine*, 1907. B. Abu Manneh in "The Rise of the *Sanjak* of Jerusalem in the Late 19th Century," *The Palestinians and the Middle East Conflict* (Ramat Gan: Turtledove Publishing, 1978), pp. 24–25, documents the creation of the Beersheba qaḍāʾ, but neglects to mention the addition of the qaḍāʾ of Nazareth to the *sanjaq*.

[31] FOAS, no. 3974, *Trade of Palestine*, 1908.

With regard to the orange and olive on which much of the agricultural fame of Palestine rested, they represented valuable cash crops for the *sanjaq* of Jerusalem, as they did for the *sanjaq*s of Acre and Balqā' (Nablus).[32] In this respect, it is interesting to note that according to Weakley's competent estimates contained in his *Report upon the Conditions and Prospects of British Trade in Syria* (1911), Palestine as a whole produced over 40 percent more olive oil than the total production of the *mutaṣarrifīya* of Mount Lebanon, the *sanjaq* of Beirut, and the *sanjaq* of Tripoli.[33]

The annual reports on the trade of Jaffa reveal the fluctuating nature of olive oil exports. For instance, in 1892 the value of this export was only £1,358 as against £20,700 in 1891; this is accounted for by the fact that the olive crop is plentiful every alternate year.[34] In bad years, olive oil would be imported from Greece: in 1901, from Mitylene [Mitilini].[35] Table 2 would indicate a huge drop in olive oil exports from Jaffa after 1891 but a corresponding near-tripling in the export of soap (£33,600 for 1889 against £124,000 for 1891 and £114,000 for 1894). There was obviously more oil being converted to soap for export (mostly to Egypt, but also to the Ḥijāz and Yemen), and this is further corroborated by Consul Dickson's report for the year 1899. However, despite the importance of olive oil and soap, the annual reports devote, on the whole, very little attention to this subject. For the 21-year period between 1885 and 1905, the total value of oil and soap exported from Jaffa slightly exceeded the total value of orange exports.

Of course, the port of Jaffa, the gateway to Palestine, was the center of orange exports. According to a French source of 1900, nine-tenths of total exports went to Britain between 1885 and 1900, due to three factors: increased demand for this fruit in England, more British shipping serving Palestinian ports, and the substantial loans and advances made to Palestinian producers by British firms.[36] Ten years later, a British source claimed that 50 percent of Jaffa's orange exports went to England and that the British market preferred smaller oranges packed 144 to a case, whereas the Austrians and Russians preferred the larger fruit packed 96 to a case of similar size: the

---

[32] Vital Cuinet, *Syrie, Liban et Palestine* (Paris: E. Leroux, 1986), pp. 25–26, 34, 95, 99; Verney and Dambmann, *Les Puissances étrangères*, pp. 641–45; Weakley, *Report*, pp. 59, 193, 194.

[33] Weakley, *Report*, p. 59.

[34] FOAS, no. 1186, *Trade of Palestine*, 1893, p. 2.

[35] FOAS, no. 2822, *Trade and Commerce of Palestine*, 1902, p. 6.

[36] Verney and Dambmann, *Les Puissances étrangères*, p. 645.

cost per case was five shillings (FOB) and the number of cases was as follows: 1905–456,000; 1906–548,000; 1907–631,000; 1908–676,000; 1909–709,000.[37]

This, then, is a brief survey of Palestinian agricultural production exports, with the principal emphasis placed on shipments to Europe, as reflected in the annual reports. If to this is added the significantly large exports to Egypt and Turkey, it is clear that Palestine, far from being the "land that was desolate" as characterized by Zionist and some Western literature, in fact yielded a substantial surplus for export, and helped to finance the crushing Ottoman Public Debt, before any significant contributions were made by the Jewish colonies and the agricultural colonization schemes of the Zionist Organization.

But Palestine was not only an exporting land; it also provided a docile market for the consumer goods relentlessly ground out by Western industry. Already by 1830, the region was exporting raw cotton and importing even greater quantities of cheap cotton manufactures.[38] The steady destruction of the Syrian and Palestinian cottage industries, which had provided local needs and employment opportunities, persisted throughout the nineteenth century. As late as 1906, Reverend C.T. Wilson reported: "In a village I know, where a few years ago forty looms were in full work, only six are now to be found."[39] In the same year, Consul Freeman (Jaffa) emphasized the dramatic increase of cotton goods imports, which had doubled in quantity and quadrupled in value in seven years. He cited two causes: a) "native looms have mostly fallen into disuse;" and b) "cotton flannelette in colours have replaced woollen stuffs."[40]

The British Annual Reports and the Agricultural Exports of Southern Palestine: An Assessment

According to one British consul and "old Turkish hand," Robert Stuart, the Ottoman Empire required the special skills of experienced staff: "The Consul is always regarded as a political and representative officer, and as a repository of the views of his government on questions of state policy."[41] On

---

[37] Weakley, *Report*, p. 194.

[38] Bowring, *Report*, pp. 36–37.

[39] Rev. C.T. Wilson, *Peasant Life in the Holy Land* (London: John Murray, 1906), p. 5.

[40] FOAS, no. 3771, *Commerce of Palestine*, 1903.

[41] Gordon L. Iseminger, "The Old Turkish Hands: The British Levantine Consuls, 1856–1876," *Middle East Journal*, 22 (1968), p. 306, quoting Great Britain, *Accounts and Papers*, LX (1872), pt. 3, pp. 10–11.

the thorny question of qualifications Stuart was equally emphatic. A consul had to see things "through the English medium" because:

> If his notions and sympathies are local, they influence his judge-
> ment, his mode of reasoning, and habit of thought. They colour
> his despatches, so that, writing according to his own apprecia-
> tions, he might, in all good faith, represent a state of things very
> different to what it would appear to English eyes. Now, it is the
> English, not the Eastern, view of things that is required by our
> Government....Our Government as well as our capitalists and
> merchants, are directly interested in knowing the real state of
> things in Turkey. And for such knowledge they are almost, if not
> altogether dependent on Consular Reports.[42]

With this observation in mind, how useful are the data and the description of agricultural conditions, including trade, contained in the annual
reports? To begin with, one must stress that two areas, orange growing
and wine production, are given the bulk of attention while other products
of the land—cereals, olive, sesame, colocynth, and watermelon—are dealt
with mainly to the extent of their constituting export items, particularly to
England and Europe (in that order).

There is usually a brief paragraph on the general condition of crops in
every annual report. For instance, for 1886 Consular Agent Amzalak wrote
from Jaffa:

> The severe sirocco winds, which blew during the month of April
> last year, caused great damage to the principal productions of
> the country: such as wheat, barley, beans, lupins, etc....I regret
> also to add that the blossoms of the most important production
> of Palestine, the olive tree, were nearly all destroyed by those
> sirocco winds.[43]

However, for the next three years, information is particularly scarce. The
only references to agriculture in Amzalak's report for 1887 concern the expansion and high quality of wine production in the German colonies and the
somewhat puzzling note, in answer to Foreign Office circulars, that "agriculture is carried on in Palestine in too primitive a mode for information in

[42] *Ibid.*
[43] FOAS, no. 164, *Trade of Jaffa*, 1887, p. 1.

regard to it to be of any interest or utility to British farmers."[44] But he may have had second thoughts with respect to the value of agricultural information from Palestine. In 1893 he reported: "Attention has been drawn to the superior qualities of the [orange] fruit, both at the Cape and in Australia, and these colonies may find it advantageous to promote the planting and cultivation of young trees procured from Jaffa."[45] In this regard the American consul in Jerusalem, Henry Gillman, is much more emphatic about the usefulness of Palestinian lessons in agriculture. In a remarkable report dated 1886, he outlined the reasons why orange growers in Florida would find it advantageous to adopt Palestinian techniques of grafting directly onto lemon trees.[46]

The single reference in the 1888 British consular report is that Rishon Le Zion has planted about 2,000,000 vines, and that "all the colonists are good labourers."[47] There was hardly a word on agriculture in the 1889 report by Amzalak.[48] Therefore, for the years 1886 to 1889, the information is of little value except as an indication of the particular bias of the consular agent in question. His superior in Jerusalem, Consul Noel Temple Moore, merely transmitted the reports without useful comments of his own.

Thereafter, and for the next fifteen years (1890–1905), the informational picture improved, with Consul John Dickson in Jerusalem exercising what appears to be a closer supervision of Consular Agent Amzalak in Jaffa, in addition to providing his own assessment and data on a variety of agricultural subjects. In this respect, the report for 1891 would serve as a good example:

> Agriculture in 1891 was not in such a flourishing condition as in 1890, the crops having failed in several districts. The price of wheat and barley was consequently high. The outbreak of cholera, moreover, in the neighbourhood of Damascus during the summer caused the establishment of sanitary cordons at various places on the borders of this province. All communication with the infected districts was prevented and internal traffic and the transport of produce from one part of the country to another was suspended. Cereals consequently rose in price, and farmers of the tithes who had made their contracts with the Government,

---

[44]FOAS, no. 363, *Trade of Jerusalem and Jaffa*, 1888, pp. 1–2.

[45]FOAS, no. 1350, *Trade of the Consular District of Jerusalem*, 1894, p. 2.

[46]United States, *Documents of the Jerusalem Consulate*, Henry Gillman to J.D. Porter, "Report For the Year Ending September 30, 1886" (dated 16 December 1886).

[47]FOAS, no. 529, *Trade of Jaffa*, 1889, p. 3.

[48]FOAS, no. 773, *Trade of Jaffa*, 1890.

before the appearance of the epidemic were enabled, by the sale of this produce, to reap very considerable profits. Grain is exported almost entirely from Gaza, but statistics as to the amount that is annually shipped are not procurable. As far, however, as can be ascertained, over 1,000,000 bushels of wheat and barley are each year sent out of the country.[49]

The report for 1892 mentioned that "a considerable quantity of colocynth is anually exported from Gaza, as well as from Jaffa, to Europe for use as a drug, and the trade in this article is increasing."[50] This fruit (*Citrullus colocynthis*), a drastic purgative, was widely used in the pharmaceutical and veterinary fields. Dickson also mentioned the planting of half a million young American vines in the colony of Petah Tikva alone. As one might guess, the consular reports emphasized information on agricultural pursuits in the Jewish colonies, and showed a particular bent for wine production. And for succeeding years, the volume of news of commercial and agricultural activities in these colonies increased, as they also did with respect to the German colonies in southern Palestine. The report for 1894 has a subtitle "colonization" and a semiecstatic note—repeated year after year—on the quality of the wines of Rishon Le Zion.[51] The section on agriculture in the report for the year 1895 is entirely devoted to the Jewish colonies, with references to the fact that they are not "altogether self-supporting," and that they use European farming methods in sowing and reaping.[52] There is a great deal of detail concerning the quantity of wine and cognac exported to Europe in barrels and bottles in the report for 1897.[53] Consular Agent Amzalak in his report for the year 1898 writes that "the settlers in the colony of Petah Tikva have begun to plant a large part of their grounds with orange trees," and that the planting of mulberry trees for the rearing of silkworms was being expanded.[54]

For 1901, the Jaffa Consulate reported: "Several families from the Jewish agricultural colonies in Palestine are emigrating to Australia and America in search of work, which is attributed to the recent changes adopted under

[49]FOAS, no. 1023, *Trade of Palestine*, 1892, p. 4.

[50]FOAS, no. 1186, *Trade of Palestine*, 1893, p. 3.

[51]FOAS, no. 1540, *Trade of Jaffa*, 1895, p. 2.

[52]FOAS, no. 1698, *Trade of the Consular District of Jerusalem*, 1896, pp. 4–5.

[53]FOAS, no. 2050, *Trade and Commerce of Jerusalem and District*, 1898, p. 10.

[54]FOAS, no. 2217, *Trade and Commerce of the Consular District of Jerusalem*, 1899, p. 8.

the new rules by which the colonies are administered."[55] A later report explains the details of the transfer of the Rothschild colonies to the Jewish Colonization Association, whereby the settlements were "thrown into a state of ferment, and not merely single individuals but entire families left for the United States, Canada, Australia, and South Africa." The report also mentioned that "numerous Arab peasants who had been employed in the colonies received their dismissal."[56]

For the period up to 1905, the most detailed account of the Jewish and German colonies in the *muṭaṣarrifīya* of Jerusalem are to be found in Consul Dickson's 1904 report.[57] The Germans consisted mainly of Wurtembergers who founded Sarona and Wilhelma and two other similar settlements in Jaffa itself and near Jerusalem. The Jewish colonies in the district included Petah Tikva (Mulebbis), Richon Le Zion, Ekron, Katra, Kustineh, Rehobot, Wady-Hanein, Artuf, and Mozah (the spelling of the annual report).[58]

As noted earlier, the Jewish and German colonies were given considerable prominence and exaggerated importance in the reports. Whatever the reasons for this inclination on the part of the Consuls—political, cultural, ease of access to information—it could not have been on rational economic grounds. The agricultural contribution of the German and Jewish colonies was limited, if not marginal, and was restricted in the main to the export of wines and cognac. To set this contribution in proper perspective, it was roughly equivalent to Jaffa's watermelon export (see Table 2 for the years 1897 to 1905).

This brings us to the last observation: the assessment of the Jaffa orange industry as reflected in the consular reports. To begin with, attention is drawn to a valuable study which was translated by the consular authorities and printed in the Foreign Office Miscellaneous Series (No. 300, 1893) as "Report on Irrigation and Orange Growing at Jaffa," drawn up by G. Franghia (perhaps Franjīya), "the local Government Engineer" as he is described by Consul Dickson. A concession for irrigating the gardens of Jaffa by using the water of the River Auja had been granted in Constantinople to Philip Malhameh; Franghia's work was in the nature of a feasibility study. What was of interest, apart from the detailed breakdown of the costs of laying-out, planting, irrigating, and maintaining an average garden, was the observation that "orange growing in Syria is conducted exclusively by na-

---

[55] FOAS, no. 2822, *Trade and Commerce of Palestine*, 1902, p. 7.

[56] FOAS, no. 3410, *Trade and Commerce of Palestine*, 1905, p. 11.

[57] *Ibid.*, pp. 7–11.

[58] *Ibid.*

tives" and that due to the trade in this citrus fruit "Jaffa now ranks next after Beyrouth in importance among Syrian coast towns."[59]

As to the annual reports themselves, they contain a mass of details concerning market conditions, current prices, prospects for the year, current packing and freight charges, the competition from other countries and shipping, and trans-shipment. And it is perhaps in this regard that they remain most significant for research in the agricultural trade of southern Palestine. The reports, of course, were meant to serve the requirements of British policy, trade, and shipping.

In 1891, Consul Dickson provided data on participants in this growing trade: "The firm of Messrs. Houghton and Co., of London, annually send out an agent to Jaffa, who collects carefully and ships the choicest crop of the season for the London market."[60] And in the following year, there was more of the same:

> The export of oranges to the United Kingdom has of late been on the increase, and last autumn a line of British steamers was established with the object of shipping oranges direct to Liverpool. The firm of Messrs. Goodyear and Co., sent on an average a steamer every 10 days from the commencement of the orange crop, each vessel loading from 15,000 to 20,000 boxes at a time. . . a profitable business for the steamship companies.[61]

In a later report, the reader is informed that "a well-known firm in Glasgow has opened an agency in this port [Jaffa] for obtaining consignments of oranges to Glasgow and shippers seem to have been satisfied with this new market."[62]

In the view of the consuls, the quick rise of Great Britain to a dominant position in the Jaffa orange trade was due to such factors as direct and regular shipping service from Jaffa to Liverpool and money advances made by British merchants to Palestinian growers and speculators.

In his report for the year 1907, Consul Blech charted the growing importance of orange production and provided a detailed breakdown of the costs of establishing an orange grove of 100 dunums (25 acres). "In 1897," he wrote,

---

[59] Foreign Office, Miscellaneous Series, no. 300, *Report on Irrigation and Orange Growing at Jaffa*, 1893, pp. 1–10. For a competent treatment of orange exports in the post-Crimean War period, see Schölch, "The Economic Development of Palestine, 1856–1882," p. 49.

[60] FOAS, no. 1023, *Trade of Palestine*, 1892, pp. 1–2.

[61] FOAS, no. 1186, *Trade of Palestine*, 1893, p. 3.

[62] FOAS, no. 1698, *Trade of the Consular District of Jerusalem*, 1896, p. 7.

"only 290,000 cases were exported; the total has now risen to 630,000 cases, and it is confidently expected that within a very few years the output will reach 1,000,000 cases."[63] These cases contained 120 to 150 oranges weighing approximately 80 pounds and were admitted duty free in English ports: the price on the British market was eight to ten shillings per case. As to the methods of business transactions, Blech described them as follows:

> It is usual for the owners of orange gardens to sell the produce long before it is ripe to speculators, who thus take off their hands all further trouble and responsibility. The price obtained by the grower is about 3 francs (2 shillings 4 1/2 d.) per case; the cost of packing is about 1 1/2 fr. (1 s. 2 d.); the freight is 1s. 3d. per case. Anything obtained over 4s. 9 1/2 d. per case at Liverpool represents the speculators' profit.[64]

Establishing an orange grove of 100 dunums (25 acres) with 6,000 cuttings required a considerable investment in 1907. Blech's estimates included £800 for the land (at £8 per dunum); £950 for sinking an 18-meter well, purchasing a motor pump, constructing a reservoir and irrigation channels; £500 for the orange cuttings, hedges, labor, fertilizer, etc., making a total outlay of £2,250 for the first year. To this must be added maintenance costs and interest until the actual production stage was attained in the sixth year after planting, so that the total outlay on one grove in fact rose to £4,500. In the seventh year, the grove would normally produce one case of oranges per tree, thereafter one and a half cases.[65]

Consul Blech's projection of the million cases target was soon to materialize. In 1911, Jaffa's orange export figure reached 869,800 cases valued at £217,000; in 1912, it climbed to 1,418,000 cases valued at £283,000; and in 1913, according to Consul McGregor's figures, a high point of 1,608,570 cases valued at £297,700 was reached, shipped to the following ports and countries:

By way of contrast, in the same year Jaffa's exports of soap were valued at £200,000.[66]

---

[63] FOAS, no. 3974, *Trade of Palestine*, 1908.

[64] *Ibid.*

[65] *Ibid.*

[66] FOAS, no. 5339, *Trade of the Consular District of Jerusalem*, 1914.

Liverpool	825,455	cases
Manchester	10,632	cases
London	14,348	cases
Other British ports	10,737	cases
Marseilles	3,568	cases
Hamburg	13,317	cases
Trieste	52,594	cases
Odessa	152,942	cases
Egypt	233,291	cases
Turkey	291,024	cases
Romania	5,087	cases

Concluding Remarks

1. The annual reports consulted reveal a wealth of material on the transfer and application of technology, the importation of textiles, hardware, building materials, petroleum, rice, flour, coffee, and tobacco. They are equally useful for charting the growing interest in investment opportunities, railway construction, public utilities, banks, and shipping.[67] However, as sources for the agriculture of southern Palestine, they tend to convey only a partial and sometimes distorted image of reality. Nonetheless, the statistical information contained in the reports allows for cumulative analysis and therefore can help to correct the picture.

2. With respect to the significant growth of soap exports, Table 2 indicates a drop in olive oil exports from Jaffa after 1891, but a corresponding near-tripling in soap exports (£33,600 for 1889 against £124,000 for 1891, and £114,000 for 1894). Clearly, more oil was being converted to soap in response to increased demand in Egypt, the Ḥijāz, and Yemen. However, despite the importance of the soap-olive oil dimension, the annual reports devoted only passing attention to it. And yet, for the 21-year period between 1885 and 1905, the total value of oil and soap exports from Jaffa was not less than the total value of orange exports.

3. Recalling Consul Stuart's emphatic advice to view things "through the English medium" and not succumb to "Eastern" modes, it is clear that this

---

[67]Foreign Office, Miscellaneous Series, no. 288, *Report on the Jaffa-Jerusalem Railway*, 1893.

dictum was closely adhered to, particularly in the reporting on agriculture and investments. The attention of the consuls was focused on 1) foreign agricultural intrusion (e.g., the German and Jewish colonies and their wine production); and 2) orange production and its British connections: capital investments and shipping. But although the reports reveal the Arab nature of this valuable agricultural enterprise, they provide no sociological information on the new "class" of Arab entrepreneurs, its origin, and impact on the socio-political scene. It is implied that this "class" is dependent on Europe for its rise and growing wealth, yet the crucial fact that it is also forging increased ties with markets nearer home in the Ottoman Empire and Egypt is ignored. The regional network of economic relations acquires additional importance: a phenomenon worthy of careful study.

4. Little attention is devoted to other centers of southern Palestine such as Hebron, Ramla, Ramallah, and even Bethlehem. The reports are, therefore, not particularly useful to students of the internal domestic scene: land tenure, income, taxation, markets, handicrafts, and economic geography.

5. A great deal of interest is shown in the cotton question, its past history in Palestine, the various experiments conducted from time to time, and its future prospects.

	WHEAT Quarters	MAIZE Quarters	OLIVE OIL Lbs.	SESAME Tons	SOAP Tons	WOOL Lbs.	ORANGES Boxes	COLOCYNTH Lbs.	HIDES Lbs.	WINES & SPIRITS Kilos	HANDICRAFTS
1885	2.25	7.05	2021.25	2.40	0.43	165.-	106.-	27.50	44.-	–	–
1886	1.90	9.-	–	3.10	0.28	209.-	98.-	60.50	36.-	–	–
1887	12.50	24.-	605.-	2.12	1.20	247.50	180.-	27.50	24.-	–	–
1888	6.25	21.20	1512.50	1.87	1.50	160.-	221.-	60.-	18.-	–	–
1889	14.13	22.75	2052.60	4.32	1.05	264.-	20.50	48.40	–	–	–
1890	20.80	17.47	5817.25	7.26	1.41	221.75	200.-	49.50	564.50	–	–
1891	2.70	18.32	1529.-	1.89	4.25	422.40	270.-	93.40	462.-	–	–
1892	–	0.69	11.-	5.-	1.80	380.-	248.-	88.70	372.-	–	–
1893	–	3.24	1159.20	4.-	3.90	239.20	278.-	42.-	248.-	–	–
1894	–	2.35	643.05	4.12	4.-	33.-	280.-	16.50	90.-	–	–
1895	4.97	4.72	286.-	3.69	4.44	240.77	260.-	18.66	280.-	–	–
1896	1.09	20.85	414.44	4.60	4.91	324.-	242.-	33.33	488.89	–	–
1897	–	8.75	250.-	3.12	3.15	275.-	290.-	44.-	308.-	–	–
1898	10.-	3.-	330.-	2.-	2.75	264.-	330.-	42.50	254.-	–	–
1899	–	3.-	81.25	1.50	5.25	68.75	310.-	38.55	555.50	366.-	–
1900	–	3.75	598.-	2.30	1.63	83.-	251.07	45.50	120.-	1365.-	–
1901	–	0.12	96.-	1.71	2.21	188.-	361.45	34.70	279.-	2443.-	–
1902	–	1.30	–	6.40	0.74	130.-	304.09	24.40	125.58	1202.79	2.20
1903	–	–	414.50	2.16	2.81	320.50	447.67	71.16	128.60	2805.79	0.58
1904	–	–	80.90	1.67	2.64	349.-	467.50	57.-	267.50	3512.58	0.65
1905	7.66	–	–	0.98	2.27	275.75	456.15	52.50	506.60	3708.40	0.98
Total	84.25	171.56	17901.94	66.21	52.62	4860.62	5621.43	976.30	5172.17	15403.56	4.41

TABLE I

Principal Exports of Jaffa, 1885–1905

Source: Foreign Office Annual Series for the respective years
(quantities expressed in thousands)

	WHEAT £	MAIZE £	OLIVE OIL £	SESAME £	SOAP £	WOOL £	ORANGES £	COLOCYNTH £	HIDES £	WINES & SPIRITS £	WATERMELONS £	HANDICRAFTS £	OTHER ARTICLES £
1885	3.60	7.87	25.26	32.–	13.72	2.40	26.50	0.80	0.64	–	–	–	19.77
1886	3.32	9.–	–	45.53	8.96	3.70	29.40	2.15	0.56	–	–	–	18.93
1887	15.–	21.–	7.55	42.50	38.40	3.60	36.–	1.60	1.–	–	–	–	19.72
1888	7.80	16.96	20.62	28.12	45.–	2.–	55.–	2.–	0.75	–	–	–	26.06
1889	16.95	18.20	26.43	62.66	33.60	2.30	51.20	1.80	–	–	–	–	30.40
1890	19.92	11.24	75.08	109.32	44.70	4.56	83.12	2.20	7.24	–	–	–	89.62
1891	3.30	17.30	20.70	30.80	124.–	4.30	108.40	3.80	8.60	–	–	–	79.33
1892	–	0.42	1.35	69.35	46.80	5.55	62.–	2.58	7.10	–	–	–	63.30
1893	–	2.58	13.84	54.94	112.–	2.40	69.50	0.95	4.07	–	–	–	73.34
1894	–	2.–	9.05	42.15	114.–	0.4	51.–	0.80	1.20	–	–	–	65.–
1895	3.56	3.20	2.60	42.75	93.24	2.07	65.–	1.40	3.08	–	–	–	65.37
1896	1.92	14.17	6.05	59.80	113.11	5.32	72.60	2.50	14.27	–	–	–	83.69
1897	–	8.45	3.50	40.–	81.90	4.–	75.80	1.–	9.80	–	26.–	–	58.93
1898	14.–	3.–	4.50	28.–	62.–	3.36	82.50	1.40	8.10	–	24.85	–	75.07
1899	–	1.22	1.35	21.–	125.75	1.75	77.–	1.30	10.25	2.90	26.10	–	47.52
1900	–	2.95	9.11	30.56	44.55	1.36	74.21	1.88	1.61	21.84	24.50	–	52.37
1901	–	0.12	1.50	25.20	57.–	2.15	86.52	2.19	3.45	35.35	21.75	–	42.40
1902	–	1.45	–	29.26	18.76	1.32	86.50	1.45	2.98	18.40	17.65	4.85	20.77
1903	–	–	5.33	30.04	77.65	4.50	93.43	3.70	4.–	30.35	19.–	7.10	47.23
1904	–	–	0.95	23.35	62.–	7.93	103.95	3.65	6.–	37.86	11.–	9.–	29.61
1905	11.–	–	–	13.82	56.91	4.54	114.65	3.37	8.11	47.02	18.80	12.58	77.01
Total	100.37	141.13	234.77	861.15	1374.05	70.51	1504.28	42.52	102.81	193.72	189.65	33.53	1085.44

TABLE II

Total Value of Exports from Jaffa, 1885–1905

Sources: Foreign Office Annual Series for the respective years

(values expressed in thousands)

	GREAT BRITAIN £	TURKEY £	FRANCE £	ITALY £	EGYPT £	RUSSIA £	AMERICA £	GERMANY £	AUSTRIA £	OTHER COUNTRIES £	TOTAL £
1885	23,799	18,075	29,353	17,055	30,142	6,785	600	—	6,770	—	132,579
1886	25,890	15,110	30,200	13,505	24,022	5,308	—	—	5,520	—	119,555
1887	42,200	25,100	32,350	18,255	36,300	7,800	5,000	6,500	—	12,866	186,371
1888	50,300	35,830	36,200	15,205	30,200	10,180	3,700	7,200	—	15,500	204,315
1889	64,200	42,300	46,000	21,000	35,600	12,200	3,500	8,600	—	11,161	244,561
1890	102,630	88,600	109,404	12,976	96,000	13,600	2,200	9,060	—	2,540	447,010
1891	99,800	80,000	101,000	11,900	49,000	11,700	2,000	17,000	—	38,130	410,530
1892	71,610	31,356	53,000	8,000	52,000	9,000	1,000	5,600	—	26,900	258,466
1893	69,968	51,200	49,736	3,664	125,240	2,160	1,540	6,000	—	23,120	332,628
1894	52,600	45,000	43,100	2,700	115,200	1,800	1,200	4,080	—	19,924	285,604
1895	40,600	49,600	39,750	3,500	108,600	2,700	1,820	5,200	—	31,136	282,906
1896	55,800	68,700	59,320	7,680	125,300	4,100	1,650	7,400	—	43,497	373,447
1897	59,500	62,500	52,100	6,800	84,300	3,700	1,100	6,200	—	33,189	309,389
1898	61,800	60,500	59,280	7,500	81,900	4,300	1,300	7,200	—	23,000	306,780
1899	65,965	54,800	61,200	8,750	87,750	8,900	2,100	11,150	—	15,543	316,158
1900	77,000	31,500	50,300	7,200	61,400	10,000	2,000	13,400	—	12,150	264,950
1901	74,500	25,700	41,000	10,000	55,000	8,000	3,500	17,500	12,000	30,435	277,635
1902	70,000	22,000	28,000	8,000	32,000	6,000	4,000	15,000	10,000	8,390	203,390
1903	95,000	25,000	30,000	13,000	65,000	12,000	7,000	30,000	20,000	25,335	322,335
1904	98,000	20,000	24,000	7,000	75,000	8,000	8,000	32,000	12,000	11,300	295,300
1905	122,000	31,000	27,000	10,000	86,000	9,500	9,000	35,000	17,000	21,320	367,820
Total	1,423,162	883,871	1,002,293	213,690	1,455,954	157,733	62,210	254,090	83,290	405,436	5,941,729

TABLE III

Total Value of Exports From Jaffa Per Country, 1885–1905
Source: Foreign Office Annual Series for the respective years

	1906		1907		1908	
	£	£	£	£	£	£
	Imports From	Exports To	Imports From	Exports To	Imports From	Exports To
Britain	65,000	145,000	74,000	160,000	80,000	164,000
Brit. Colonies	40,000	12,000	43,000	15,000	44,000	16,000
Turkey	210,000	50,000	257,000	51,000	260,000	59,000
Austria	100,000	24,000	129,000	20,000	85,000	14,000
Russia	40,000	12,000	51,000	9,000	69,000	11,000
Germany	39,000	47,000	54,000	50,000	56,000	46,000
France	43,000	40,000	50,000	30,000	54,000	32,000
Egypt	50,000	116,000	42,000	100,000	49,000	165,000
Belgium	25,000	11,000	33,000	10,000	42,000	11,000
Italy	20,000	12,000	26,000	13,000	31,000	15,000
United States	10,000	12,000	16,000	15,000	12,000	13,000
Others	18,000	19,000	34,000	12,000	22,000	11,000
Total	660,000	500,000	809,000	485,000	804,000	557,000

TABLE IV

The Trade of Jaffa

Source: Ernest Weakley, *Report Upon the Conditions
and Prospect of British Trade in Syria*
(London: H. M. Stationary Office, 1911), p. 16.

24

Beirut's Role in the Political Economy of the French Mandate: 1919–39*

THE PRIMARY OBJECTIVE of this paper is to examine the development of Beirut as a regional trade and cultural center under the French mandate and some of the conflicting perceptions of the city's economic prospects in the wake of dramatic transformations in the map of the Levant brought about by the Franco-British partition of the Ottoman Empire's Arab provinces. It comprises six sections: first, a brief survey of Beirut's meteoric rise to preeminence among the ports of the eastern Mediterranean between the years 1840 and 1914; second, the important transitional year of 1919, when Lebanese Francophiles analyzed the future economic prospects of Greater Lebanon; third, the French mandate's contribution to the modernization of Beirut through programs of urban planning and infrastructural investments designed to encourage the services sector and to promote the city as a show-piece of the Mandate; fourth, the challenge posed by the growth of Haifa; fifth, the political and economic fears of the *ahl al-sāḥil* (the people of the Coast), who represented the opposition to the Mandate, and their attitude toward the *ahl al-jabal* (the people of the Mountain), the long-standing allies of France; sixth, in conclusion, a few remarks on the Mandate's performance and legacy.

The principal sources consulted include the French Haut Commissariat's statistical bulletins; Jadʿūn's series of *Al-Dalīl al-sūrī*; the Beirut press; the bulletins of the two associations of French interests: L'Union économique de

*From the English typescript of the paper presented at the conference "The Middle East in the Inter-War Period," held at the Institut für europaische Geschichte, Bad Hamburg, August 1984. While this volume was in press, a further version of this study was published by the Centre for Lebanese Studies in its *Papers on Lebanon* series, no. 4 (Oxford, 1988).

Syrie (UES) and L'Association des commerçants et industriels français du Levant (ACIFL); the bulletins of the Banque de Syrie et du Grand Liban; and various pamphlets by Lebanese economic interests. Some interviewing (incomplete to date) of businessmen familiar with the Mandate period was also conducted.

The Rise of Beirut: 1840–1914

Even as late as 1825 there was little indication that Beirut would become the first city of Lebanon. In terms of population size, construction activity, artisanal production, and trade, the cities of Sidon and Tripoli were probably more important. Yet in the short span of one generation Beirut surpassed her rivals to become the leading port of the eastern Mediterranean seaboard.[1] Then in 1888 the city became the administrative capital of a new Ottoman *vilāyet* bearing its name which encompassed, in addition to the Lebanese coastal regions, the northern half of Palestine, including the ports of Acre and Haifa, and a considerable stretch of Syria's coastline and hinterland, including the port of Latakia. Finally, in the first decade of the French mandate Beirut became the capital of the Lebanese Republic.

To account for this remarkable growth properly is beyond the scope of this paper. Briefly, the military campaigns of Ibrāhīm Pāshā in geographical Syria and the intervention of several European powers to check this Egyptian expansion in the late 1830s had stimulated the economy and attracted an influx of money, goods, and consumers. Beirut served as a quarantine station, a military headquarters, and a garrison during the decade of Egyptian occupation. Following Ibrāhīm Pāshā's defeat and return to Egypt in 1841, the city's growing stratum of traders and entrepreneurs took full advantage of a favorable conjuncture of events and factors. These included the Industrial Revolution and Manchester cotton, the expansion of steamship navigation, increased security along the coast, the stimulation to sericulture given by the introduction of new French techniques and investors, and the intense competition for influence between Protestant Anglophone and Catholic Francophone missionaries.[2]

---

[1] [On the rise of Beirut in the nineteenth century, see pp. 483–87 above.]

[2] Charles Issawi, "British Trade and the Rise of Beirut, 1830–1860," *International Journal of Middle East Studies*, 8 (1977), pp. 92–93; Dominique Chevallier, *La Société du Mont Liban à l'époque de la révolution industrielle en Europe* (Paris: Paul Geuthner, 1971), pp. 182–84; Roger Owen, *The Middle East in the World Economy, 1800–1914* (London: Methuen, 1981), pp. 165–67.

Most accounts of Beirut's surge in the nineteenth century stress external—generally Western—inputs, while at the same time neglecting the importance of military garrisons and expenditures as stimulants of growth (which this writer would like to stress as a recurring dimension in the palmy but also stormy affluence of the city in both the nineteenth and twentieth centuries). Recently, however, Leila Tarazi Fawaz has provided a more accurate analysis of Beirut's rise to prominence by demonstrating the significance of the relationship between migration and urbanization, and by giving equal attention to local and regional determinants.[3]

A branch of the Ottoman Bank was established in Beirut in the 1850s, and the Beirut-Damascus carriage road was constructed by a French company in 1858, introducing rapid communications with the hinterland. In the same year, the first newspaper of the city, *Ḥadīqat al-akhbār*, was published, and within 20 years there were a dozen newspapers in circulation, together with an equal number of journals—the pillars of the *nahḍa*, or cultural renaissance. The city had become the intellectual and informational center of the country, the port of the hinterland, and the principal entrepôt of goods and political currents.[4]

During the last quarter of the nineteenth century, Beirut witnessed the occidentalization of life-style and manners among its privileged classes, a social process of transformation recently analyzed by Nada Sehnaoui in "L'Occidentalisation de la vie quotidienne à Beyrouth 1860–1914."[5] Christian and Muslim merchant notables from such families as the Sursuq, Busṭrus, Ṭrād, Bayhum, and Dā'ūq gradually moved to newly created suburbs and lived, in Kamal Salibi's words, "in large Italianate mansions furnished and decorated mostly in European style,"[6] providing the principal impetus to the creation of a distinctive Beiruti Baroque atmosphere and sensibility.[7]

At this time also the city experienced a marked expansion of banking, money-lending, and allied services to take care of emigrants' remittances, sericulture, the import and growing transit trade, speculation in

---

[3]Leila Tarazi Fawaz, *Merchants and Migrants in Nineteenth-Century Beirut* (Cambridge, Mass.: Harvard University Press, 1983), pp. 2–4.

[4]The *nahḍa* or cultural renaissance finds detailed treatment in Albert Hourani, *Arabic Thought in the Liberal Age 1798–1939* (London: Oxford University Press, 1962).

[5]Nada Sehnaoui, "L'Occidentalisation de la vie quotidienne à Beyrouth 1860–1914," MA Thesis, University of Paris, 1981.

[6]Kamal Salibi, *The Modern History of Lebanon* (London: Weidenfeld and Nicolson, 1965), p. 142.

[7]Marwan Buheiry, "Beirut Baroque, 1850–1914," a lecture given in the "Frontiers of Learning" series at the American University of Beirut, November 1983, mimeographed.

international stocks and shares, and ventures in real estate and agricultural land. Likewise, a scramble for concessions developed between local and foreign entrepreneurs—with French investors leading the hunt—in railways, tramways, waterworks, port construction, and communications.

To sum up, with a newly constructed port, a railway line (DHP) serving the Syrian interior, an ever-expanding marketplace, and a sophisticated network of economic, cultural, and political relations with Europe and America, Beirut on the eve of the First World War was indeed the proud capital of a prospering *vilāyet* that administered its Palestinian, Lebanese, and Syrian maritime rivals: Haifa, Acre, Tyre, Sidon, Tripoli, and Latakia. French influence in the economic sphere, particularly in infrastructural investments and in the link between Lyon and local silk producers, as well as in the spheres of education, language, and political patronage, was paramount. To an influential portion of its occidentalized merchant notables and professional middle classes, Beirut was by then Ottoman only in the sense that the Ottoman Bank was Ottoman.

1919: Transition and Examination of Future Prospects

In that crucial year of 1919, when the fate of the Arab provinces of the Ottoman Empire was being decided at Versailles and the transition made from Ottoman to French rule for Lebanon and Syria, some Lebanese Christian intellectuals wrote about their future prospects from the standpoint of political economy. Lebanese Francophiles, including Būlus Nujaym, Albert Naqqāsh, Charles Corm (editor of *La Revue phénicienne*), Michel Shīḥā, Emile 'Arab, Jacques and Ibrāhīm Thābit, Jean de Frayj, and Fu'ād al-Khūrī, argued that their economic future depended largely on the creation of an expanded Lebanon in its "natural frontiers"—the Grand Liban (a term that they were probably the first to introduce in 1919), and in what may be broadly described as a service-oriented economy with trade, transit, banking, and tourism as its main features. The example of Switzerland was evoked and appears to have served as inspiration.[8]

Albert Naqqāsh remarked that "the all-important economic question has been relegated to an inferior position, and yet it should form the basis of Lebanese demands," adding: "Lebanon's economic future is intimately linked to the political economy in store for it."[9] In normal times the "eco-

---

[8] *Revue phénicienne*, edited by Charles Corm, July to December 1919.

[9] Albert Naqqāsh, "Notre avenir économique," *Revue phénicienne*, July 1919, p. 2.

nomic equilibrium" of Mutaṣarrifate Lebanon presented the following picture as established by Naqqāsh:

Income	Million Piastres	Expenditures	Million Piastres
Gold transfers by emigrants	100	Wheat imports	40
Silk production	50	Other cereals	40
Textile manufactures	20	Cattle imports	10
Income from tourism	20	Building materials	10
Agricultural industry	20	Foodstuffs	10
Agricultural products	20	Skins	5
		Textile thread	5
		Clothing	70
		Others	10
Total	230		200

Thus the "economic equilibrium" depended on three principal factors, all external: 1) the unimpeded transfer of gold from the Americas; 2) the freedom to import silkworm eggs from France and Italy and to export, in return, silk in various forms; and 3) the unrestricted import of wheat and other cereals from the Syrian interior.[10] A serious blow to any one of the three factors would be fatal to the economy of "Smaller Lebanon," Mutaṣarrifate Lebanon, and lead, as in the First World War, to famine. A Lebanon expanded to its natural borders, "Grand Liban," could on the other hand constitute a more viable economic and national unit. The country was evolving in the direction of light industry despite the blockages of the Turkish regime. Hydraulic power was available and Grand Liban could emulate Switzerland and Piedmont.[11] In the same month and journal, Amīn Mushahwar contributed a study entitled "Nos resources agricoles, industrielles, commerciales et minières" in which he drew attention to the fact that "for some time, our country has been attracting the attention of the West."[12] He estimated that 90 percent of Beirut's merchants were importers: "Ce sont des commisionnaires, representants de fabriques, agents transitaires, grossistes,

---

[10] *Ibid.*, p. 4.

[11] *Ibid.*, p. 6.

[12] Amīn Mushahwar, "Nos resources agricoles, industrielles, commerciales et minières," *Revue phénicienne*, July 1919, p. 21.

pour leur compte propre, ou traitant les marchandises en consignation."[13] Exporters, on the other hand, were only a handful. But Beirut remained the general entrepôt for Syria for imports serving the cities and regions in the following proportion:

For Aleppo and its interior	20 percent
For Palestine	15 percent
For Damascus, Ḥomṣ, and Ḥamāh	35 percent
For Beirut and Mount Lebanon	30 percent

There was, he felt, little danger of competition from the ports of the eastern Mediterranean seaboard, with one exception—Haifa:

> L'on se demande si après la conclusion de la paix et la délimitation de la frontière syrienne, le port de Beyrouth gardera sa prépondérance antérieure ou bien, concurrencé par Haifa, il ne sera plus le grand port de la Syrie, mais uniquement celui du Liban et de la Bekah. L'avenir peut nous réserver des surprises désagréables.[14]

The Swiss example is also clearly revealed in Fu'ād al-Khūrī's article on "L'Industrie hôtelière au Liban." Nature and climate, he affirmed, were the true riches of the country. Lebanon's future rested on the development of summer resorts and transit facilities for the city dwellers of Syria, Palestine, Anatolia, Egypt, and even Europe. He did not deny the possibility of progress in commercial, industrial, and agricultural enterprise, but believed the process to be slow, painful, and requiring enormous capital investments from Europe and America which he doubted would be forthcoming.[15] The answer was to emulate the Swiss and to become the "Switzerland of the Orient:"

> Le peuple suisse a donc trouvé dans ses montagnes même la source de profits abondants, et l'argent que laissent chaque année les troupes d'étrangers qui visitent la Suisse ou y séjournent, n'a pas peu contribué à la mise en valeur de leur sol si pauvre soit-il.
>   Espérons que ce rêve sera bientôt réalisé dans notre pays. Si nous n'avons pas du capital-argent, nous avons un capital-beauté

---

[13] *Ibid.*, p. 24.

[14] *Ibid.*

[15] Fu'ād al-Khūrī, "L'Industrie hôtelière au Liban," *Revue phénicienne*, July 1919, p. 37.

et un capital-climat uniques au monde. Mettons nous à l'oeuvre pour les faire valoir et fructifier, et nous verrons le Liban devenir avant longtemps la Suisse de l'Orient.[16]

This theme finds further elaboration and a more comprehensive treatment in Jacques Thābit's *Pour faire du Liban la Suisse du Levant.*[17]

Similar conclusions on the importance of tourism and summer resorts were also drawn by Albert Naqqāsh in "L'Industrie de la villégiature au Liban," in which he pointed out the attractions of various locations. Beirut merchants favored Aley because of its relative proximity and rapid communications with the city. The summer resort of Ṣofar, on the other hand, with its elegant villas and prestigious Grand Hotel-Casino, attracted a different clientele: wealthy Lebanese and Egyptian families, the rentiers of Syria, and the well-heeled amateurs of the card tables: "L'absence de bois et de verdures semble pour les habitués, avantageusement remplacés par le tapis vert où la dame de coeur et le valet de pique se prélassent amoureusement."[18] The immediate task, as he saw it, was to complete the network of roads in Mount Lebanon, to create a sense of order and public purpose in the rural municipalities, and to establish an overall plan for the development of tourism and summer resorts in the country.[19]

As to the future of Beirut, Ibrāhīm J. Thābit, in "L'Avenir de Beyrouth," invited the French authorities to enlarge its port and improve the railway network, while "maintaining the city as terminus for all interior lines" and giving up plans to develop the harbor of Tripoli. This, he felt, was all the more necessary for the French because Beirut constituted the center for French action in Syria.[20]

Among the large group of Francophone and Francophile intellectuals and members of the professional middle classes who pondered over the political and economic future of Lebanon in the pages of the *Revue phénicienne* in 1919, perhaps the most articulate defender of the Grand Liban thesis was Būluṣ Nujaym.[21] The expansion of Smaller Lebanon (Mutaṣarrifate

---

[16] *Ibid.*, p. 39.

[17] Jacques Thābit, *Pour faire du Liban la Suisse du Levant: aperçu sur les conditions politiques, économiques et touristiques des deux pays* (Paris: Imprimerie Ramlot, 1924).

[18] Albert Naqqāsh, "L'Industrie de la villégiature au Liban," *Revue phénicienne*, December 1919, p. 209.

[19] *Ibid.*, p. 213.

[20] Ibrāhīm J. Thābit, "L'Avenir de Beyrouth," *Revue phénicienne*, December 1919, p. 253.

[21] Būluṣ Nujaym, "La Question du Liban: étude de politique économique et de statistique descriptive," *Revue phénicienne*, August 1919, pp. 66–81.

Lebanon) to its natural borders, he affirmed in "La Question du Liban: étude de politique économique et de statistique descriptive," was of greater priority than the nature of the regime or the form of government placed over the country. Drawing liberally on Albert Naqqāsh's statistical data and analysis of Lebanon's economic equilibrium, Nujaym argued that Smaller Lebanon's chances of survival were in doubt. Natural LEBANON (i.e. the inclusion of the coastal cities, the Biqā' valley, the Anti-Lebanon range, and southern Lebanon) would, on the other hand, constitute a viable economic and national unit.[22] This would mean, of course, the addition of roughly 150,000 Sunnīs and 100,000 Shī'tes to the population of Mutaṣarrifate Lebanon, with the Maronites finally forming about a third of a total population of 900,000. Yet, unlike many of his coreligionists, Nujaym did not view this prospect with alarm, believing the Lebanese to be "sufficiently mature for a democratic regime" and to have formed an organic whole "united by a glorious past, common tradition, and national history, with everyone belonging to the same race."[23]

Viewed in retrospect, the general outlook of these intellectuals was substantially in harmony with the economic perceptions and policies of the French mandate as they developed. However, this general outlook, which emphasized a Grand Liban independent from Syria under French tutelage and with an orientation toward tourism and a service economy, was not shared by the equally influential Arab nationalist, Syrian nationalist, or pro-Fayṣal Muslim opinion, represented, for instance, in the Municipal Council of Beirut, and in a political alliance known as the Conference of the Coast (*Mu'tamar al-sāḥil wa-l-aqḍiya al-arba'a*), who wanted to maintain their close economic and family ties with the cities of the hinterland and the political unity of Syria.

The Modernization of Beirut

In geo-strategic and geo-economic terms, the French envisioned two main parallel axes for the Mandate territories and their neighbors: 1) in the north, the *Transarménien* (to use Duchâtel's terminology and thesis) beginning at Alexandretta and serving Aleppo, Mosul, southern Turkey (particularly Diyārbakr and the mining region of Arghāna), Armenia, northern Persia and

---

[22] Marwan Buheiry, "Bulus Nujaym and the Grand Liban Ideal: 1908–1919," in *Intellectual Life in the Arab East: 1890–1939*, edited by Marwan Buheiry (Beirut: American University of Beirut, 1981), p. 80 [= pp. 589–90 below].

[23] Nujaym, "La Question du Liban," p. 75.

Tibriz, and Adharbayjān; 2) in the south, the *Transdésertique* beginning at Beirut and serving Syria, Palestine, Iraq, southern Persia, and Arabia.[24] In addition to this regional role, Beirut was the general headquarters for the French mandate, and, having been selected as a showpiece for French accomplishment and the *mission civilisatrice*, it received a great deal of attention from the Administration.

Deeply impressed by the material and human losses caused by the First World War, the French administration wasted little time in implementing a crash program of relief and reconstruction. As soon as the Turks departed, the harbor was cleared of wartime wrecks, some dating back to the Turkish-Italian War of 1912, and dredging operations were begun with the help of heavy equipment rented from the Suez Canal Company.[25] Emergency supplies were brought in to feed a population decimated by famine by an estimated one third.[26] Health clinics were set up for the sick: Haut Commissiariat statistics indicate that 10,000 children were hospitalized in Beirut in the space of twelve months, while 138,000 adults received intensive care in emergency clinics. The number of hospitals tripled in the short space of two years following the French presence.[27] Equally important was the French contribution to the restoration of confidence in the market. In fact, a successful international fair was organized in Beirut in 1921.[28] The merit and scale of this early French effort in all the fields outlined above can scarcely be minimized. The impact on Lebanese opinion was positive, and despite political controversy and disenchantment, the Mandate began on an auspicious note.

Next, the French administration took up an item of high priority in its economic policy: the modernization of Beirut. An elegant quarter, adjacent to the harbor and bounded by three newly created principal avenues (Foch, Allenby, and Weygand), was founded as the new business center. A second quarter, in the familiar *étoile* pattern, incorporating some traditional sites and elements, was built next to it, with a parliament house occupying the central Place de l'Étoile. Administrateur Poupon in Beirut,

---

[24] Duchâtel, "Une Grande voie internationale: l'avenir d'Alexandrette," *Bulletin de l'union économique de Syrie*, 7 (1928), pp. 97–99.

[25] Haut Commissiariat de la République Française en Syrie et au Liban (HCRFSL), *La Syrie et le Liban en 1922* (Paris: Emile Larose, 1922), pp. 127–28.

[26] *Ibid.*, p. 4.

[27] *Ibid.*, p. 5.

[28] HCRFSL, *La Syrie et le Liban en 1921: la foire-exposition de Beyrouth* (Paris: Emile Larose, 1922), pp. 1–3.

who contributed so much to the embellishment and modernization of the capital, wrote two important articles entitled "La Modernisation de Beyrouth" in the *Bulletin de l'union économique de Syrie* in 1928 and 1929 in which he pointed to the widespread boom in real estate brought about by this urban planning (prices doubling or nearly tripling in five years), not to mention the greatly augmented receipts and taxes of the Beirut municipality.[29]

Likewise, considerable effort went into building public squares and gardens, widening streets, and paving old and new roads. Plans for a national museum were finalized, and to crown this urbanization activity that transformed Beirut, a comprehensive network of sewers was laid, mechanized equipment totalling over 40 items replaced the mules of the municipality, and more electric power and street lighting were made available.[30] Finally, Radio-Orient was founded as a modern communications center, with powerful transmitters at Khaldeh and receivers in Ras Beirut, linking the capital with Paris and New York, and rendering obsolete the British cable link via Egypt. In fact, the *Bulletin de l'union économique de Syrie* claimed that Beirut became the communications center for places as far away as Persia, and demand from Palestine for the services of Radio-Orient was always high. In the early years of the Mandate, the Haut Commissariat also planned to turn Beirut into a broadcasting center for the "rayonnement de la pensée française à travers tout ce Moyen Orient si fidèle à notre langue et si attentif à toutes les manifestations de notre culture."[31]

The capital of Lebanon responded very quickly to this surge of infrastructural investment and modernization, as indicated in the following three tables of growth,[32] population increase,[33] and construction activity.[34]

---

[29] Poupon, "La Modernisation de Beyrouth," *Bulletin de l'union économique de Syrie*, 9 (1930), pp. 10–11.

[30] *Ibid.*

[31] "Le Centre de T.S.F. de Beyrouth," *Bulletin de l'union économique de Syrie*, 9 (1930), pp. 10–11.

[32] Indicators for 1889 are from Amīn Khūrī, *Al-Jāmi'a, aw dalīl Bayrūt* (Beirut: Al-Maṭba'a al-adabīya, 1889), pp. 46–63; for 1923 and 1928, from Ilyās and Jurjī Jad'ūn, *Al-Dalīl al-sūrī* (Beirut: Maṭba'at Jad'ūn, 1923 and 1928).

[33] Statistics do not include foreign military personnel and foreign civilian residents or visitors. Statistics for the 1921 census as cited in Jad'ūn, *Al-Dalīl al-sūrī*, 1923, p. 184; statistics for the 1932 census as cited in *Bulletin de l'union économique de Syrie*, 11 (1932), p. 162.

[34] *Bulletin de l'union économique de Syrie*, 11 (1932), p. 238.

	(1889)	1923	1928
Hotels	(15)	35	62
Restaurants	(6)	21	32
Cafés		22	26
Travel agencies		6	10
Travel goods shops		6	11
Advertising agencies		2	7
Clearing agencies (customs)		14	24
Insurance companies		26	45
Banks		24	52
Credit and exchange houses		20	43
Lawyers	(12)	86	111
Real estate brokers		17	21
Doctors	(31)	164	239
Architect-engineers		13	57
Négociants (in manufactures)		210	324
Négociants commissionnaires		164	194
Printing presses	(13)	23	27
Cinemas		6	10

Miscellaneous Indicators of the Growth of Beirut, 1923–28

	1921 Census	1932 Census
Sunnī	32,884	51,906
Shī'ite	3,274	11,379
Druze	1,522	4,225
Maronite	17,763	28,995
Greek Orthodox	12,672	19,993
Greek Catholic	4,256	8,397
Protestant	544	3,684
Armenian Gregorian	-	18,604
Armenian Catholic	-	4,385
Syriac Orthodox	-	1,745
Syriac Catholic	-	2,169
Jews and others	4,907	6,000
	77,820	161,382

Population of Beirut

Thus, the population of Beirut doubled in the eleven years between the censuses of 1921 and 1932, with the Sunnī, Maronite, and Greek Orthodox population growing by just over 50 percent, while the Shī'tes more than tripled and the Druze nearly tripled. There were also an additional 28,000 newcomers composed of Armenians (Gregorians, Catholics, and Protestants) and Syrians (Orthodox and Catholics).

	1-2 Rooms	3-4 Rooms	Complete house
1929	541	246	334
1930	614	768	315
1931	679	341	466

Construction permits delivered, 1929–31

Other sectors also received attention. In industry and agriculture, silk was granted special consideration and a promising revival was in progress before adverse developments in the world silk market, competition from artificial silk, and changes in taste forced a collapse of Lebanon's sericulture, which, it must be recalled, was a Christian (and Mount Lebanon) dominated activity. Official policy aimed, with mixed success, at encouraging the formation of a class of small and medium property owners, potentially loyal to the Mandate, through such measures as the cadastre and the extension of agricultural credit. Under the capable direction of C. Duraffourd, the cadastre surveyed, delimitated plots, settled disputes of ownership, and made proper registration possible.[35] But this widely praised initiative worked better in areas close to the capital than in remote regions such as the 'Akkār in northern Lebanon. Michael Gilsenan has recently argued that such reforms paradoxically served to reinforce *iqṭā'īya* or feudality in the 'Akkār:

> When the French instituted a cadastral survey in order to rationalise land ownership (in their view), regulate private property in land, and aid in the creation of an independent landholding peasantry as the motor of agricultural change and progress it was actually the lords who benefitted. Collective holdings and rights were indeed fragmented, and often acquired by the beys, but the *latifundia*, to use the term employed by French officials, were expanded and strengthened rather than also broken up into smaller units as had been intended.[36]

Finally, in the tourism sector, the Société des grands hotels du Levant affiliated to the Banque de Syrie et du Grand Liban provided Beirut in 1932 with the prestigious Hotel Saint Georges, a shining symbol of the French mandate's interest in infrastructural promotion.

The Challenge of Haifa

By the end of the Mandate's first decade, the Beirut-transdesertic axis was under pressure and the city's future as the *Porte de l'Orient* was jeopardized by developments in Palestine, specifically by the double threat posed by Haifa as a modern port offering better facilities and as the terminal for the Iraq Petroleum Company pipeline from the Kirkuk and Mosul oilfields.

---

[35] C. Duraffourd, "Cadastre et amélioration foncière des états du Levant sous mandat français," *Bulletin de l'union économique de Syrie*, 7 (1928), pp. 103–108; S.H. Longrigg, *Syria and Lebanon Under the French Mandate* (London: Oxford University Press, 1958), p. 280.

[36] Michael Gilsenan, "A Modern Feudality? Land and Labour in North Lebanon, 1858–1950," in *Land Tenure and Social Transformation in the Middle East*, edited by Tarif Khalidi (Beirut: American University of Beirut, 1984), p. 459.

In addition, Palestine's industrial development was proceeding at a much faster rate than Lebanon's. Opinion in Beirut felt that a momentous struggle was in progress between two competing economic zones, Syria-Lebanon and Palestine-Transjordan-Iraq, controlled by the rival mandatory powers. "The beautiful dream," as one writer put it, "of Beirut—as the only important port of the whole region—becoming in no time the port of transit of Mesopotamia, Persia, Afghanistan, and even India, was close to being shattered."[37] Nearly twice the size of Beirut's harbor, and with the prospect of better communications with Iraq through a projected railway, Haifa was widely perceived in Beirut as a formidable threat. One writer suggested that the struggle between the two mandatory powers had shifted from politics to economics, and that the British had embarked on a vigorous press campaign in Iraq aimed at undermining Beirut's preeminent position by allegations that the transdesertic axis through Damascus was insecure.[38]

An editorial by Karam Milḥim Karam in *Al-ʿĀṣifa* (1934) entitled *"Bayrūt tamūt!"* ("Beirut is Dying") placed the blame squarely on the Sykes-Picot Agreement because it had segmented an integrated region in which Beirut held a privileged position of trade and commerce. The British mandate, in his view, appeared more cognizant and decisive in economic matters than its French counterpart. And one of the consequences of the disastrous Sykes-Picot Agreement was that "Britain constructed a modern port in Haifa to combat Beirut while France merely looked on."[39] Britain's policy was to promote and defend its long-term interests, while France was content to focus attention on the immediate and the temporary.[40]

Amīn Abū ʿIzz al-Dīn expressed substantially similar views about Haifa, less stridently and more comprehensively, in a series of three articles in the weekly *Al-Maʿraḍ al-usbūʿī* (early 1935) entitled "Trade Routes and Communications in the Near East." Again the economic war between the two mandatory powers was stressed, as was the strategic importance of the oil port and the projected railway to Iraq for the British Empire—a second route to India, as he saw it. Abū ʿIzz al-Dīn estimated that Beirut was still holding its own in the lucrative Iraq and Iran transit, but that it would have to face increasing pressure in the future, not only from Haifa, but also from

---

[37]X.X., "La Lutte économique dans le Proche-Orient," *Correspondance d'Orient*, 1929, pp. 9–10.

[38]*Ibid.*, pp. 10–11.

[39]Karam Milḥim Karam, "Bayrūt tamūt!," *Al-ʿĀṣifa*, III, 15 April 1934, p. 1.

[40]*Ibid.*

the port of Mersin, the projected expansion of which appeared to be an item of high priority in Turkish planning in response to Haifa's ascendancy.[41]

As he had done earlier in connection with the Iraqi pipeline, 'Umar Dā'ūq, president of the Beirut Chamber of Commerce, campaigned vigorously for the protection of the city's trading link with the interior, the transdesertic axis, and for the expansion and modernization of harbor facilities in response to Haifa's growing challenge. In early 1933 he petitioned the Haut Commissariat to take effective action:

> Beirut is threatened by the large modern port of Haifa. The construction of a railway linking Haifa to Baghdad has also been decided. Turkey, for her part, is bent on gaining the commercial traffic with Persia. The Lebanese economy is on the decline, the re-exportation trade is inhibited by newly imposed customs duties, agricultural output is falling, and the transit trade is seriously jeopardized. Such palliatives as the construction of additional warehouses and the signing of commercial agreements are without effect. Iraq and Persia are both looking for an outlet on the Mediterranean, and transdesertic traffic is increasing.[42]

In conclusion, 'Umar Dā'ūq urged the immediate establishment of Beirut as a free port or at least the creation of a free zone, measures that French economic interests led by the Beirut Port Company supported. Other proposals included the construction of a railway linking Tripoli with the Palestinian border at al-Nāqūra and the reduction of customs duties. The Mandate authorities responded positively by establishing a comprehensive free zone, which included the possibility of certain forms of industrial production within its precinct.

On the basis of a preliminary survey, it would appear that the double threat posed by Haifa as a modern port and pipeline terminus (and the reaction in Alexandria and Mersin) were recurring themes in the Beirut press. On these issues there was a broad consensus, which was echoed by both French and Lebanese economic interests as well as by the Haut Commissariat: compare, for instance, the views of 'Umar Dā'ūq, the *Bulletin de l'union économique de Syrie*, Karam Milḥim Karam, and Amīn Abū 'Izz al-Dīn. From about 1929 onward, Haut Commissaires, particularly Henri

---

[41] Amīn Abū 'Izz al-Dīn, "Al-Ṭuruq al-barrīya li-l-naql al-tijārī wa-l-muwāṣalāt fī l-Sharq al-Adnā," *Al-Ma'raḍ al-usbū'ī*, 6 February 1935, pp. 25–26.

[42] As quoted in Raoul Colonna de Lega, *La Zone franche du port de Beyrouth* (Beirut: Faculté de droit de Beyrouth, 1957), pp. 23–24.

Ponsot and Count Damien de Martel, found it useful to concentrate on economic matters, not only because of the deepening world depression, but also as an antidote to politics. Ponsot had declared in 1929 that he wanted above all to be an economic high commissioner.[43] President Bishāra al-Khūrī, in his memoirs, also credited de Martel for the energetic pursuit of infrastructural development, including the construction of the harbor's "second basin" and the Beirut airport.[44] It is perhaps interesting to note that the challenge of Haifa served as a catalyst for the convergence of French and Lebanese economic interests, not least those of the Muslim merchant community of Beirut, during a troubled period of political divergence and disenchantment.

Ahl al-sāḥil Opposition and Other Areas of Friction

It has been suggested above that Francophile Christian interests and their intellectuals found early expression in the 1919 debates in the *Revue phénicienne* on the future political economy of Grand Liban, and that their equally influential Muslim Francophobe and Arab nationalist (or pro-Fayṣal) counterparts did not share their vision of an economy emphasizing services and tourism modelled on the Swiss. About twelve months later, in January 1921, the Parti progressiste (*Ḥizb al-taraqqī*), having as its motto "Pour le Liban, avec la France," was created with a 15-member directing committee composed, according to the *Correspondance d'Orient*, of the following Christian personalities:

> Marquis Jean de Frayj, *propriétaire* (President)
> Na"ūm Bākhūs, attorney (Vice President)
> Emile Eddeh, attorney (Secretary)
> Emile Khāshū, Director of the Banque de Syrie (Treasurer)
> Emile 'Arab, physician
> Salīm Aṣfar, *propriétaire*
> Michel Shīḥā, banker
> Shukrī Qardāḥī, attorney
> Bishāra al-Khūrī, attorney
> Albert Naqqāsh, attorney
> Alphonse Zaynīya, attorney

[43] X.X., "Lettre de Beyrouth: politique économique," *Correspondance d'Orient*, 1929, p. 250.
[44] Bishāra al-Khūrī, *Ḥaqā'iq lubnānīya* (Dar'ūn-Ḥarīṣā: Bāsīl lkhwān, 1960–61), I, 184.

To the above list, President Bishāra al-Khūrī has added in his memoirs the name of Yūsuf al-Jumayyil.[45] Two points of the party's three-point program underlined "the maintenance of the political independence of Grand Liban under the French mandate" and "the defense of national traditions and religious liberties." But the third point was altogether more controversial. For it proposed "electoral representation under a system to be determined later, and an organized structure which would take into account only the factors of competence and merit."[46] In the environment of a Mandate struggling to consolidate its hold, the third point would give the French-educated Christian communities a considerable early advantage in the political organization of the country. The implications were clear: the opposition to the Mandate, centered for the most part in the Muslim urban community, could presumably be denied access on grounds of merit.

Muslims were grouped around institutions dating from the period of the *vilāyet* of Beirut, such as the Maqāṣid Association, the Beirut Chamber of Commerce, the Beirut Municipal Council, and the Beirut Reform Committee (a platform for the extension of Arab rights in the Ottoman state), but also around new political formations such as the Syrian Congress, the Conference of the Coast, the Association of Muslim Youth, and the National Muslim Congress. The leadership was largely provided by Muslim Sunnī families of urban notables: Bayhum, Dā'ūq, Salām, and Yāfi' (for Beirut); Karāmī, Aḥdab, and Jisr (for Tripoli); Ṣulḥ and Bizrī (for Sidon). But equally important for the development of Lebanese political pluralism, a significant number of influential Shī'ite and Greek Orthodox leaders had joined the Conference of the Coast from its inception.

While the politics of Sunnī Muslims have been adequately studied, much less attention has been devoted to their economic thought and experience under the Ottomans or the Mandate. Direct self-perception, as found, for instance, in the *Revue phénicienne* for the intellectual and political elites of Christian Francophiles, is rarely available, and the evidence remains fragmentary. The fact that leading Sunnī intellectuals and politicians were in active opposition to the Mandate, and therefore under constant threat of imprisonment, exile, and economic reprisal—the examples of Riyāḍ al-Ṣulḥ, Salīm 'Alī Salām, Ṣalāḥ Bayhum, Salīm Ṭayyāra, and Ḥassān al-Qāḍī come to mind—may have acted as a powerful constraint.[47] One Sunnī personal-

[45] Al-Khūrī, *Ḥaqā'iq lubnānīya*, I, 115.

[46] *Correspondance d'Orient*, 1921, pp. 126–27.

[47] Salīm 'Alī Salām, *Mudhakkirāt*, edited by Ḥassān 'Alī Ḥallāq (Beirut: Al-Dār al-jāmi'īya, 1982), p. 62.

ity interviewed on this subject suggested that the pressing problems that retained the attention of his community were political and ideological. The economic unity of Syria was not at stake, but its political and territorial dismemberment was. He also recalled that he was not as fascinated by Western socio-economic models as some of his Christian colleagues were in the thirties.

Muslim urban communities formed the largest constituency of the *ahl al-sāḥil*, the "people of the coast," in distinction to the *ahl al-jabal*, "the people of the Mountain." Both terms were in frequent use in the literature of the Mandate. As far back as the 1880s the Muslims of the *ahl al-sāḥil* had provided the political and administrative leadership of the *vilāyet* of Beirut: an experience they recalled with fondness and also with pride in having helped in the joint creation, with Christian (mostly Greek Orthodox and Greek Catholic) merchant notables, of a distinctive "ideology of the city" marked by a degree of openness to the outside world and of internal coexistence. This phenomenon has been analyzed, with great perception, in Albert Hourani's "Ideologies of the Mountain and the City."[48] An expression of this ethos is to be found in one of the sample interviews of a Sunnī engineer recorded by Claude Dubar and Salim Nasr in their groundbreaking study *Les Classes sociales au Liban*:

> ...Nous sommes des habitants de la côte; ceux-ci n'émigrent pas. Ils sont plus ouverts. Plutôt que de faire la guerre aux civilisations qui nous sont venues, nous leur avons ouvert nos ports. Ce sont ceux de la Montagne retranchés dans leurs villages et leurs châteaux forts qui sont fanatiques et émigrent. Ce que je vous dit peut vous paraître bizarre; c'est le fruit de mon expérience et de ma réflexion; je suis marié a une chrétienne de la Montagne. Il y a une très grande différence de mentalité. Et pourtant sa famille n'est qu'à 15–20 km de Beyrouth. Plus loin, c'est plus accentué encore.[49]

The allegiance of the Muslims of the coast, supported by their Christian allies, was to Arab nationalism and Fayṣal, in opposition to the French mandate. Emphasis was placed on the unity, sovereignty, independence, territorial integrity, and cultural specificity of Syria, including Lebanon, Palestine,

---

[48]Albert Hourani, "Ideologies of the Mountain and the City," in *Essays on the Crisis in Lebanon*, edited by Roger Owen (London: Ithaca Press, 1976), pp. 33–41.

[49]Claude Dubar and Salim Nasr, *Les Classes sociales au Liban* (Paris: Presses de la Fondation Nationale des Sciences Politiques, 1976), p. 125.

and Cilicia, albeit with a special status reserved for Mount Lebanon. Traditionally, they saw the Mountain as a physical and perhaps psychological obstacle, as something to cross over hastily on the way to the Biqā', Damascus, the hinterland, and the centers of Islam. However, after 1936 the stress on Syrian political unity gradually evolved into a grudging recognition of the reality of the Lebanese Republic. But the idea of economic union with Syria persisted until the 1950s.

As mentioned earlier, one of the most important expressions of Muslim political activity in Beirut was a regular forum called the Conference of the Coast and of the Four *Qaḍā's*—i.e. Ḥaṣbayya, Rāshayya, B'albak, and 'Akkār—which convened under the presidency of Salīm 'Alī Salām. The proceedings of the 1933 meeting and the list of grievances submitted to the Mandate authorities contain valuable insights into the economic perceptions of Lebanese Muslims: first, that the dismemberment of Syria and the concomittant expansion in administrative budgets and personnel had placed a heavy burden on both countries, and secondly, that "whereas the *ahl al-sāḥil* (as they were called in the memorandum) contributed 82 percent of revenue for the treasury, 80 percent of the same revenue was spent in Mount Lebanon on salaries, road construction, tourist promotion, and assistance to municipalities, schools, and hospitals."[50] In the third place, it was noted that the "sons of Old Lebanon" (i.e. the inhabitants of the Mutaṣarrifate of Mount Lebanon) occupied the senior positions in the administration in violation of the constitutional clause specifying the proportional distribution of posts among the various religious communities. Fourthly, the Mandate authorities were blamed for their failure to deal with the unending economic malaise. Finally, the memorandum stated that French control over the economy, and especially over customs tariffs, had been very detrimental to the prosperity of the country; the Mandate was invited to refrain from subsidizing foreign companies.

Similar overtones and undertones were reflected a decade later in the course of a meeting between Riyāḍ al-Ṣulḥ and Geoffrey Furlonge, a senior official of the Foreign Office. The Muslim leader requested that Furlonge transmit his views to General Edward Spears as representing the views of his community:

He (Riyāḍ al-Ṣulḥ) complained that the Moslems, who after all form nearly one-half of the total population of the Lebanon, are

---

[50] Ḥassān Ḥallāq, *Mu'tamar al-sāḥil wa-l-aqḍiya al-arba'a* (Beirut: Al-Dār al-jam'īya, 1982), pp. 176–77.

still suffering from twenty years of systematic discrimination, practiced against them by the Mandatory authorities, whose policy was to back the Christians and to regard the Moslems as potential enemies. The Christians were, moreover, very largely favoured in the educational field. The Christian communities not only had a much larger number of private schools than the Moslems, but had much freer access to the numerous French-supported schools. The standard of education and of European culture was therefore far higher amongst the Christians. As a result, a much greater proportion of Christians spoke good French and could get on social terms with foreign officials. The Christian point of view was therefore put much more prominently than the Moslem before the occupying authorities; furthermore, the number of Moslems occupying State posts was much inferior to the number of Christians. The Moslem community was thus resentful as they felt that they were being unfairly treated.[51]

This sense of structural and institutional injustice remained profoundly ingrained in Muslim consciousness. Ten years after Riyāḍ al-Ṣulḥ's message to Edward Spears, Shaykh Shafīq Yamūt read from the pulpit of the Grand 'Umarī Mosque of Beirut a critical manifesto sponsored by a dozen Muslim Sunnī and Shī'ite associations grouped under the Permanent Conference of Muslim Organizations of Lebanon. The 13 points of this 1953 manifesto called for various urgent reforms and initiatives, including a census of Lebanon's inhabitants, a statistical study of the allocation of state posts by sect, an end to the Department of Tourism campaign that sought to present Lebanon to tourists as an exclusively Christian country, and economic unity between Lebanon and Syria.[52] Concurrently with the manifesto, Dr. Mustafa Khalidi's controversial pamphlet "Muslim Lebanon Today" outlined the essential grievances of his community in a bitter attack on Maronite hegemony.[53]

Finally, as one of the interviewed Sunnī intellectuals put it, together with the sense of injustice there was a "sour grapes" element in the attitude of Muslim merchants, urban politicians, and *'ulamā'* toward the frenetic energy and sophisticated performance of Christian entrepreneurs engaged

---

[51] Great Britain, Foreign Office, FO 226/223, Furlonge to Spears, Beirut, 8 June 1942.

[52] Mustafa Khalidi, *Muslim Lebanon Today*, 2nd edition (Beirut: Beirut Arab University, 1977), pp. 46–47.

[53] *Ibid.*, pp. 38–40.

in the fiercely competitive areas of international trade, finance, the services sector, and modern education.

Concluding Remarks

To be sure, the *ahl al-sāḥil* and the *ahl al-jabal* are meant to represent trends rather than archetypal categories. Geography was preponderant, not exclusive. To cite an example, the *sāḥil* of Jounieh and of Jubayl related much more to the ideology of the Mountain than to that of the City. And again, the Shī'ites of Jabal 'Āmil were deeply involved in the politics of the Conference of the Coast, offering armed insurrection against the Mandate on many occasions. In the *ahl al-jabal* and *ahl al-sāḥil* divide, Jabal 'Āmil remains a special (and much neglected) case, deserving much more scholarly research and assessment. One recent contribution, however, does delineate some of its social and intellectual horizons and self-images, Tarif Khalidi's "Shaykh Ahmad 'Arif al-Zayn and *al-'Irfan*."[54]

Returning to more typical examples, the *ahl al-jabal* included three main constituencies based on allegiance, religious affiliation, and political economy: Grand Liban nationalists, Petit Liban nationalists, and Druze nationalists. Grand Liban nationalists, it is recalled, owed their allegiance to an enlarged Lebanon defined in terms of natural frontiers (including northern Galilee), Christian historical development with secular overtones, and a general Western political and economic orientation. They remained, with some important exceptions, the most enthusiastic supporters of the French mandate between 1919 and 1939. The Petit Liban nationalists, on the other hand, believed in a smaller territorial unit, thus ensuring Maronite demographic, political, and economic supremacy. Populist in expression and tradition, they remained suspicious of the Vatican's doctrinal influence and of the French Third Republic's policy of integrating large numbers of Sunnī and Shī'ite Muslims in an enlarged Lebanon. Their political fortunes suffered a steady decline from 1926 on. Also understudied as far as the Mandate era is concerned, the Druze nationalists are not easy to assess. Deeply loyal to their religious tradition, social organization, and lines of authority, and on the decline demographically and economically compared to other communities, they nevertheless displayed great skill and determination in retaining

[54]Tarif Khalidi, "Shaykh Ahmad 'Arif al-Zayn and *al-'Irfan*," in *Intellectual Life in the Arab East 1890–1939*, edited by Marwan Buheiry (Beirut: American University of Beirut, 1981), pp. 110–24.

the political initiative. Significantly, some of their powerful leaders sup-ported the Mandate.

By and large the French mandate has been the subject of severe, often unwarranted, criticism. Nonetheless, it did make a distinct contribution to Lebanese politics and national life by providing a controlled forum in Beirut for a rapprochement between the *ahl al-jabal* and the *ahl al-sāḥil*, provoking in some degree the Beirutization of the "Old Lebanese" and the Libanization of Beirutis (or the sāḥilization of the *jabal* and the jabalization of the *sāḥil*). In this process, which helped pave the way to the National Pact of 1943, the Maronites emerged as self-appointed spokesmen of the Christian communities and the Sunnīs as self-appointed spokesmen of the Muslim communities. Yet it is clear that the phenomenon of atavistic and reciprocal phobias of hegemony persisted. Muslims continued to look to the days of the *vilāyet* of Beirut—cradle of liberal Ottomanism and Arab nationalism—with some nostalgia. For Beirut was then the capital of a growing maritime, trading, and largely urban *vilāyet* of the *sāḥil*, which provided them with a large majority of lucrative posts in the expanding bureaucracy and municipal councils, and where their rank, self-esteem, and social status vis-à-vis other communities remained particularly high. The Mandate, on the other hand, had favored the "sons of Old Lebanon," their rivals of the Mountain, who now appeared to be lording it in the City as relative newcomers. For their part, the Maronites feared that their refuge would be swamped by Muslim populations and Arab nationalist ideologies.

Another observation concerning the Mandate's performance and legacy is in order. Despite Christian and Muslim opposition to the Mandate poli-cies on the tobacco monopoly, the regulation of the currency following re-peated falls in the value of the franc, taxation, and tariffs, and the clear bias in favor of French enterprise and personnel in Lebanon, the economic performance of the Mandate was more appealing (and met with perhaps less overall criticism) than its heavy-handed and often insensitive politics. By enhancing Beirut's role as an entrepôt and cultural center, by expanding the scope of secondary, professional, and university education, and by actively pursuing a policy of modernization, the Mandate found increased support in a wide spectrum of rising middle-class interests and traditional political notables from every community. Yet, paradoxically, this phenomenon also heightened future expectations that could only be realized under national independence: thus, it worked against the Mandate in the long run (and with the help of Britain during the Second World War).

Finally, Charles Issawi has suggested that the Middle East is "over-urbanized."[55] This is certainly true for Beirut. In favoring the urban areas, particularly, and neglecting the rural countryside and its agrarian population, the Mandate authority helped to precipitate massive migration to an unprepared city, and the concomittant social and political problems. While Beirut on the whole prospered, albeit unevenly, in the sectors of trade, real estate, communications, education, and the services generally, the rest of the country received only scant and begrudging attention. Or, in the words of Roger Owen, "by splitting off Grand Liban from its natural hinterland the French not only confirmed the financial and commercial hegemony of Beirut over the Mountain, but also strengthened a pattern of economic activity in which agriculture and industry had become more and more subordinate to banking and trade."[56]

In retrospect, the price paid in national terms for the modernization of Beirut and its promotion as a seductive showpiece for France may have been too high. Yet while some blame could be placed on the Mandate authority for helping to create a Leviathan (or a Young Frankenstein-sur-Mer), it is also a sad fact that the Lebanese in the aftermath of independence did not seem to mind nurturing it very much.

---

[55] Charles Issawi, *An Economic History of the Middle East and North Africa* (New York: Columbia University Press, 1982), p. 102.

[56] Roger Owen, "The Political Economy of Grand Liban 1920–1970," in *Essays on the Crisis in Lebanon*, p. 24.

Part IV

Intellectual and Artistic History

25

The Camera-Eye in Nineteenth-Century Lebanon*

IN HIS REVEALING BOOK of meditations on photography, *La Chambre claire* (1980), Roland Barthes recalled the sensation of seeing, for the first time, a photograph taken in 1852 of Prince Jerome, Napoleon's youngest brother. "I realised then," he wrote, "with an amazement I have not been able to lessen since: I am looking at eyes that looked at the Emperor."[1] This phenomenon is not a mere return to a lost world or a capture of nostalgic moments. Old photographs have the magical property of unblocking time and distance, inviting the viewer to participate in an act of creative reconstitution.

In this exhibition[2] we may be looking at eyes and monuments that witnessed the extraordinary as well as the mundane: eyes that saw such eminent representatives of the nineteenth-century *nahḍa* (Arab cultural renaissance) in Lebanon as Buṭrus al-Bustānī, Shaykh Ḥusayn al-Jisr, and Amīr Shakīb Arslān; or watched Védrines delicately poising his Blériot, the first airplane to land in Beirut, on 27 December 1913; or wept for the martyrs of the country's independence during the First World War; or glanced at the rapid changes in fashions and social conventions before the age of electricity. A

---

*From *Romantic Lebanon: The European View, 1700–1900* (London: The British Lebanese Association, 1986), pp. 72–77. © 1986 by the British Lebanese Association. Reprinted courtesy of the British Lebanese Association.

[1] Roland Barthes, *Camera Lucida: Reflections on Photography*, translated by Richard Howard (London: Hill and Wang, 1984), p. 3.

[2] ["Romantic Lebanon: The European View, 1700–1900," organized by the British Lebanese Association, was on view at Leighton House, London, from 10 February to 8 March 1986.]

563

few discerning eyes may have focused on the photographer's lens-eye with mixed feelings. For the portrait-photograph, in the words of Barthes, is a "closed field of forces:"

> Four image-repertoires intersect here, oppose and distort each other. In front of the lens, I am at the same time: the one I think I am, the one I want others to think I am, the one the photographer thinks I am, and the one he makes use of to exhibit his art.[3]

From the Camera Obscura to the Excursions

At the height of the Italian Renaissance, the camera obscura (dark chamber with a tiny hole and precursor to the modern camera) was no longer a mystery. Leonardo da Vinci described it on two occasions in his notebooks, while Giovanni Battista Porta provided additional data and perhaps the first written analysis of its use as a practical aid to artists and draftsmen. However, it is less generally known that the camera obscura was also familiar to Arab scholars five hundred years earlier: as far back as the tenth century, particularly to Ibn al-Haytham (al-Ḥasan ibn al-Ḥasan, or Alhazen in the West). Arthur Goldsmith described his important contribution:

> The earliest written account we have of a camera obscura is attributed to a Moslem scholar, Hassan Ibn Hassan, better known by his Latinized name of Alhazen, who lived from 965 to 1038 AD. Writing in Arabic, in a manuscript now preserved in a London archive, he described a technique for observing an eclipse of the sun without looking directly at it. You must place a small hole at an opening in the outside wall of a darkened room, he instructed, so that an image of the sun is projected on the opposite wall. Then, as the eclipse takes place, you will see a changing, crescent-shaped image. However, Alhazen warned, the hole must be quite small. Otherwise, rather than an image of the sun you will merely get an image of the hole itself, whatever shape it might be.[4]

---

[3] Barthes, *Camera Lucida*, p. 13

[4] Arthur Goldsmith, *The Camera and Its Images* (New York: Ridge Press, 1979), p. 12.

The next steps on the long road to modern photography involved advances in optics and chemistry aimed at improving and preserving the elusive image on sensitized surfaces. By 1827 the patient experiments of Joseph Niepce, one of three founding fathers of photography, yielded spectacular results: the earliest surviving picture (an exposure of eight hours in bright sunlight) was taken from the artist's attic in Le Gras.

A decade later the second founding father, L.J.M. Daguerre, was producing his magical daguerreotypes for the commercial market, aided by the light-sensitive properties of iodine in contact with silver. This was a complicated single-image process yielding one (and only one) unrepeatable photo, and represented in this exhibition by an engraving of Frederic Goupil-Fesquet's daguerreotype image of Beirut in 1839: the earliest photograph known to have been taken in Lebanon as part of N.P. Lerebours' sponsored photographic expedition, the *Excursions daguerriennes.*

At about this time also, William Henry Fox Talbot of Dorset, the third founding father of photography and one of the best scientific minds of his generation, invented the negative-positive process: paper coated first with silver nitrate, then with silver chloride, which could be printed on another paper surface. A further improvement led to the Talbotype or calotype process which he wrote about in his classic treatise on photography *The Pencil of Nature* (1844) and *Sun Pictures of Scotland* (1844). Talbot's studio in Regent Street, London, was called "The Sun Picture Rooms" and, on an anecdotal note, his wife insisted on referring to his cameras as "mousetraps." The calotype process is represented in this exhibition by several photographers: Benecke, Maxime Du Camp, Ostheim, and Wheelhouse.

It is interesting to note that many nineteenth-century Lebanese photographers proudly displayed the "trinity" of Niepce, Daguerre, and Talbot in their logotypes and colophons, and that the Arabic word for photographer was *muṣawwir shamsī*—a person who draws with the sun.

As to the more advanced wet collodion process, introduced in the late 1850s, the remaining eleven photographers in the exhibition—Bedford, Bonfils, Charlier-Bezies, Cramb, Dumas, Ferkh, Frith, Good, Khoury, Saboungi, and Sarrafian—all used it. The collodion process (glass plate coated with nitrocellulose dissolved in ether and alcohol and sensitized with potassium iodide and silver nitrate) required a dark tent, a cumbersome piece of equipment on long expeditions. But it needed shorter exposures and produced sharper definitions.

After 1900 the first Kodak cameras (created by George Eastman), with the slogan "You press the button; we do the rest," were carried by tourists in the Near East. No longer a difficult and mysterious craft, photography became the hobby for thousands of amateurs.

Lebanon in the Nineteenth Century

A number of important economic, political, and cultural developments in nineteenth-century Lebanon serve as a backdrop to the growing flood of travellers, artists, scholars, pilgrims, photographers, and other visitors to the country and region. In rough chronological order these included: 1) Napoleon's military and scientific expedition to the Near East and the revival of interest in ancient civilizations and cultures; 2) the industrial revolution, the rapid expansion of steamship navigation, and the establishment of a complex network of modern communications which stimulated the growth of a Lebanese middle class closely tied to European trade and capital, and serving the hinterland; 3) the new strategic turn-around in the Eastern Question and the profound changes in the regional balance of power provoked by the expansionist ambitions of Muḥammad ʿAlī of Egypt in the Levant, and the ensuing military intervention of European powers to check this critical development (it is at this point that Daguerre's cameras and Talbot's "mousetraps" also intervene in the general picture); 4) the arrival of Protestant missionaries and Biblical scholars and the predictable rivalry with long-established Catholic missions in education, professional training, book publishing, and the press, and the consequent attraction on the part of many Lebanese to the various and sometimes opposing spheres of political, economic, and cultural influence; 5) the Civil War of 1860 in Mount Lebanon, France's military intervention, and the creation of the Mutaṣarrifate of Mount Lebanon—a new administratively autonomous unit ruled by a non-Lebanese Ottoman Christian *mutaṣarrif* approved by the European powers (at this point, French photographers—notably Dumas and Bonfils—opened studios in Beirut, followed closely by the first generation of Lebanese photographers headed by Saboungi); 6) the development of the cultural and political *nahḍa*, which expressed the critical and reformist ideas of Lebanese intellectuals; and 7) the relentless growth of Beirut against a background of intense international rivalry for political and economic influence in the Levant as a whole (by this time the combined output of the photographers in the exhibition constitutes a rich archive for the art and social history of Lebanon).[5]

---

[5] Marwan Buheiry, "Beyrouth d'hier: page d'une histoire vieille d'un siècle," *Le Commerce du Levant*, 50, no. 4693 (29 March 1979), p. 36 [= p. 483 above].

Much has been written, and still needs to be written, about the art, spiritual sensibilities, and politics of early Western photographers in the Near East. Some, like Bedford, Frith, and Good, have been studied by Michael Bartram as exponents of "the pre-Raphaelite camera," exalting the natural and seeking to render the distinct character and details of every subject matter.[6] A few were clearly obsessed by the search for the exotic and by the Orientalist tradition or fantasy which, in the words of Edward Said, aimed at "restructuring, and having authority over the Orient."[7] Others specialized in archaeological and ethnographic subjects, or retraced with a camera the footsteps of Jesus and the Apostles, virtually ignoring the rest of the topography or the reality of everyday people in their own natural setting. Others again must have behaved like curious tourists everywhere, taking pictures without too many psychological or political constraints. Many professional photographers like Bonfils, Saboungi, and Sarrafian, were eclectic in their instruments, art, and choice of subjects. They may even be accused of catering, on occasion, to what may be called an "Orientalism for the Market."

Nonetheless, the value of their combined photographic contribution is undeniable. Together they provide a unique record of a bygone age, whatever the motivation and the mode of representation.

---

[6] Michael Bartram, *The Pre-Raphaelite Camera: Aspects of Victorian Photography* (London: Weidenfeld and Nicolson, 1985), pp. 100–102.

[7] Edward Said, *Orientalism* (New York: Vintage Books, 1978), pp. 2–3.

26

Notes on the Beginnings of the English Open-Air Theater at the SPC and Its Social Context*

THE HISTORY of English dramatics at AUB—or the Syrian Protestant College, as it was called—is indeed a long one: apparently the first major production on record was *Julius Caesar*, staged on 8 and 9 May 1903. It was followed in 1905 by *Scenes from Shakespeare*, and in the following year *Hamlet* was produced by the Senior Class in Daniel Bliss Hall.[1] Thereafter the English theater—especially in the traditional indoor staging—remained a regular feature of college life, with the Shakespearean repertoire as a clear favorite.

In contrast, the origins of the open-air theater at the SPC are traced to 1907 with the launching of Shakespeare's comedy *As You Like It*, followed three years later with Tennyson's *The Foresters*, a dramatization of the tale of Robin Hood and his bold bandits of Sherwood Forest who robbed the wealthy to help the poor. Detailed information of the first production has been difficult to locate (any assistance in this connection from readers, especially from older alumni,[2] would be gratefully received). However, there is abundant material in the pages of the first volume of *Al-Kulliyah* (1910) concerning the second production, *The Foresters*.

---

*From *Al-Kulliyah*, Spring-Summer 1974, pp. 7–9. Reprinted courtesy of the American University of Beirut.

[1] "College History in Memorabilia," *Al-Kulliyah*, 1 (1910).

[2] [*Al-Kulliyah* is the bulletin of the Alumni Association of the American University of Beirut.]

To be sure, the SPC cannot lay claim as the pioneer of theater in the Arab provinces of the Ottoman Empire. Over a quarter of a century before the College was founded, and a good fifty years before its staging of *Julius Caesar*, Mārūn al-Naqqāsh[3] had produced in Beirut his adaptation of Molière's *L'Avare* in Arabic and also what may very well be the first original contribution to the Arabic theater in modern times, his *Riwāyat Hārūn al-Rashīd*. David Urquhart, a British traveller in Lebanon (1849–50), left a valuable—albeit unsympathetic—account of the Hārūn al-Rashīd play:

> After the Megilis, we went to the Play! The piece, for the opening of the first Arab theater, was written by the son of one of the members of the Megilis:—was to be acted by the family, which was a large one, in their house in the suburbs [of Beirut]. They were Maronites and their name Maron....The subject announced was "Aroun el Raschid and Jaffer;" the piece was said to be composed in the high Arab style, and interspersed with poetry, which was to be sung....
>
> The theater was the front of the house itself; which was exactly what we seek to imitate by our scenes. There was in the centre a door, on each side of it two windows, and two above; the wings were the advanced part of the court with side doors. The stage was a raised platform in front. The audience was in the court, protected by sails spread over....As to costume there was the design at least of observing the proprieties; and, as regards the women, that is the boys dressed up as such, [they performed] with perfect success. As there were no women on the stage, so were there none in the court, and not even at the windows which opened on the stage....
>
> Between the acts we retired to the divan hané, where refreshments were served; and, though it was long, very long, no one went away, and every one seemed content and merry. Frequent applause rewarded the author and the actors; and at the close Jaffer, to act his part to the life, threw handfuls of coin amongst us, on which the stage was assailed from all sides with showers of

---

[3]Information on Mārūn al-Naqqāsh may be obtained from the following sources: "Al-Tamthīl al-'arabī," *Al-Hilāl*, May 1910, pp. 468–70; Muḥammad Yūsuf Najm, *Al-Masrahīya fī l-adab al-'arabī al-hadīth* (Beirut: Dār Bayrūt, 1956); *idem*, "Madrasat Mārūn al-Naqqāsh," *Al-Adīb*, 14.3 (March 1955), pp. 24–26; Jacob M. Landau, *Studies in the Arab Theater and Cinema* (Philadelphia: University of Pennsylvania Press, 1958).

roses....A short farce occupied the interval between the second and third acts....

The acting was awkward, the singing abominable; but the piece was evidently managed with considerable art....They are now to build a theater, and other pieces are in preparation. The author told me, that they were painting a drop-scene with the ruins of Baalbec; on expressing my astonishment at their selecting something not their own, but Greek and Roman of the bad time, he asked me to suggest something else. I asked in return if they had anything peculiarly their own, and peculiarly beautiful. He answered at once—THE CEDARS.[4]

The *Foresters* Production of 1910

In reviewing this open-air production, *Al-Kulliyah* prefaced an article "The Dramatics of 1910" as follows:

It is a far cry from the shores of the Mediterranean to the forests and glades of Merrie England, and the years are long that separate the Syrian of today from the time when Richard Lion Heart fought in this land for its shrines and its holy places....We were carried across seas and back in time eight hundred years to witness strange doings, grave and gay, and good and evil, of a different people in a different country.[5]

In the play Robin Hood is presented as a loyal defender of King Richard the Lionhearted, who is away on a Crusade. The royal scepter is in the hands of his scheming brother, Prince John. The principal female character, Maid Marian, the beautiful daughter of a Saxon nobleman, is in love with Robin Hood, who has been unjustly outlawed by Prince John and has become a sort of avenger of the people from his hideout in Sherwood Forest. Prince John, in turn, having heard of Maid Marian's accomplished charms, wants to have her for himself. The play, as is to be expected, ends on a happy note: King Richard turns up in the nick of time to put his treacherous brother to flight; Robin Hood is rewarded and marries Marian. The cause of right triumphs while the oppressors receive their just due.

---

[4] David Urquhart, *The Lebanon (Mount Souria): A History and a Diary* (London: Newby, 1860), II, 178–81.

[5] *Al-Kulliyah*, 1 (1910), p. 149.

In addition to the obvious "good guys—bad guys" dichotomy, the play also displays the cultural and political split between Normans and Saxons. Prince John and his clique represent the interests of the Norman invaders, whereas Robin Hood, as a noble bandit, champions the cause of the native Saxons, and emerges as the symbol of resistance to foreign control.

Tennyson's *Foresters*, although by no means a great play, offers attractive possibilities for an open-air production which apparently materialized in the 1910 performance. The stage was set in the pines in front of Post Hall. The old carriage drive—now asphalted and decorated with traffic bumps—served as a no-man's-land between actors and spectators. There were no elaborate scenic effects: "The pine trees themselves," as we are told by the reviewer William T. Bliss, "was all the setting that was needed and a simple battlement wall in two of the scenes sufficiently suggested the castle of Robin Hood."[6]

As in the 1849 production of al-Naqqāsh's *Riwāyat Hārūn al-Rashīd*, the female parts at SPC were played by men: Spiridon Abu Mes'ud as Maid Marian and Mikha'il Dumit as her attendant (see the complete list of players below). Likewise, singing was incorporated in the production. It would be interesting to establish who was the first actress to appear on an SPC or AUB stage in a major production, and when.

Social Protest in Disguise?

Speculating on the socio-political, as opposed to the aesthetic, impact of the play on the students of the Syrian Protestant College in the years preceding the First World War is hazardous but worthwhile.

That the play was well-received is evident and easily explained. Themes depicting the age-old clash between "good and bad guys" possess universal appeal. Likewise, the sight of a joyous gang linked together by the bonds of brotherhood served to win a congenial audience. Nevertheless, other reasons, grounded in the political climate of the time and the social composition of the student body, may have contributed significantly to the successful reception of the Robin Hood theme.

In political terms, students by 1910 were progressing beyond the proto-nationalist phase characterized by the cultural *nahḍa* to a more active—albeit covert—national risorgimento, a familiar mutation in the annals of national self-consciousness and assertion. Feelings of cultural pride were

---

[6] *Ibid.*, p. 152.

being reinforced by longings for political independence, or, at the very least, for complete regional autonomy. And the Ottoman Turk was perceived, all the more, as an unwanted intruder by the native, in much the same manner as the Saxon—whose cause was championed by Robin Hood—viewed the Norman topdog.

In social terms, the typical SPC student did not belong to the privileged classes. He was an underdog, but with two crucial differences. Firstly, through education his prospects for a higher level of status and income than his father's were particularly bright. In fact, education followed by emigration, was virtually the sole avenue to upward social mobility. Secondly, he tended to belong to highly motivated minority groups: Armenians, Greek Orthodox, and especially to the newcomers to an already intricate minorities scene, the Protestants. In brief, then, the typical SPC student had a heightened self-consciousness, an uncompromising resentment against the existing order, high expectations, and, most important of all, a somewhat protected field where this explosive mixture could be enacted in the form of covert protest activity.

Noble brigands or social bandits[7] like Robin Hood of England, Diego Corrientes of Spain, Angelo Duca (Angiolillo) of Italy, and, with many reservations, Ṭāniyūs Shāhīn of Mount Lebanon, articulate and reflect modes of protest inherent in agrarian society, particularly during periods of transition to modernity. They express the deep-seated hatred towards exploitation by feudal and semi-feudal landlords, tax collectors, money lenders, and the habitual injustice meted out by ruling elites. In the example of Robin Hood there is the added dimension of a native hero—the insider—who carries the fight against foreign intruders.

Undoubtedly, the round of enthusiastic applause that greeted the performances of *The Foresters* in 1910 conveyed a special meaning to the insiders.

The Cast of *The Foresters* (1910)

King Richard .... Taufik Jureidini
Prince John, brother of King Richard .... Nimr Salibi
Robin Hood, Earl of Huntingdon .... Henry Glockler
Sir Richard of the Lea .... Dikran Utijian

---

[7]The term is borrowed from Eric J. Hobsbawm, *Primitive Rebels: Studies in Archaic Forms of Social Movement in the 19th and 20th Centuries* (Manchester: University of Manchester Press, 1959), p. 13.

Walter Lea, son of Sir Richard .... Wadi' Abu-Nadir
The Baron of York .... Antun Zarzur
Sheriff of Nottingham .... Salim Shihadeh
Followers of Robin:
    Little John .... Garabed Batmanian
    Will Scarlet .... Alfred Deyo
    The Butcher .... Vahan Kalbian
    Much, the Miller's son .... Aziz Marmoura
A Justiciary .... William Topuskhanian
Persuivant .... Wadi' Abu-Nadir
A Sailor .... Ibrahim Dada
Maid Marian, daughter of Sir Richard .... Spiridon Abu-Mes'ud
Kate, attendant on Marian .... Mikha'il Dumit
An Old Woman .... Musa Balutin

Three Ragged Retainers

Wadi' Nasr .... Suleiman Izz-ud-Din .... George Khaiyat

Foresters

Bedros Kumkumian .... Taufic Kurban .... George Suki
Krikor Krikorian .... Isaac Lewin .... Jurji Tahhan
Khalil Jebbur

Mercenaries

Wadi' Nasr .... Kamil 'Id .... Adib Faris
Suleiman Izz-ud-Din .... Amin Saikali

Beggars

Kamil 'Id .... Izzet Sureiyeh .... Wadi' Nasr

Peddlers

Musa Balutin .... George Khaiyat .... Adib Faris

Citizen and Wife

Ibrahim Dada .... Amin Saikali

Heralds

Benjamin Nasif .... Hagop Serrikian

27

Būluṣ Nujaym and the Grand Liban Ideal, 1908–1919*

IN THE HALCYON DAYS preceding the First World War and in the portentous political atmosphere of the last decade of the Ottoman Empire, a book was published in Paris by M. Jouplain entitled *La Question du Liban: étude d'histoire diplomatique et de droit international* (1908).[1] It was a substantial work of 550 pages, bearing the signs and quality of a doctoral dissertation. Jouplain began by broadly surveying the historical development of Syria and Lebanon from early times to Muḥammad 'Alī's campaigns, taking up about 40 percent of the work. Thereafter he narrowed down the scope by focusing attention on the stormy internal affairs of Mount Lebanon from 1841 to the eve of the Young Turk revolution, with some emphasis on the interplay of the Concert of Europe in the Lebanese question.

While analyzing the checkered history of the *mutaṣarrifīya* of Mount Lebanon, the author also proposed far-reaching reforms, including increased autonomy from the Ottoman Empire, more democratic institutions, a radical solution to land held by the monastic orders, and, above all, the addition of territories on the northern, eastern, and southern borders, plus the city of Beirut: in effect more than doubling its area. The project was seen as a reconstitution of "le Liban de la grande époque," the Lebanon of Fakhr al-Dīn and the Amīr Bashīr, in its "natural frontiers" as drawn in the 1861 and 1863 staff maps of the French military expedition to Syria. Such far-reaching

---

*From *Intellectual Life in the Arab East, 1882–1939*, edited by Marwan Buheiry (Beirut: American University of Beirut, 1979), pp. 62–83. © 1979 by the American University of Beirut. Reprinted courtesy of the American University of Beirut.

[1] M. Jouplain, *La Question du Liban: étude d'histoire diplomatique et de droit international*, 2nd edition (Jounieh: Fouad Biban et Cie., 1961).

changes would be achieved under the auspices of the big European powers with a special role reserved for France. Throughout, Jouplain was at pains to accentuate the themes of autonomy and particularism in Lebanon's historical experience. The irredentist tone, supported by arguments of economic self-sufficiency, was unmistakable.

The identity of Jouplain was revealed eleven years later. In August 1919, a short-lived but important Beirut journal, *La Revue phénicienne*, published an article entitled "La Question du Liban: étude de politique économique et de statistique descriptive" in which the author, Būluṣ (or Paul) Nujaym, let it be known that Jouplain was none other than himself, that the pseudonym M. Jouplain was in fact an anagram of Paul Noujaim.[2] Again, as in 1908, the author called for the creation of "le Liban de la grande époque," but this time he also named it specifically "Le Grand Liban," a term which he used twice in the article, and always in italics. The article, bearing the dateline of Jounieh, 10 July 1919, constitutes, together with Albert Naqqāsh's "Notre avenir économique," published also in *La Revue phénicienne* (July 1919), perhaps some of the earliest written and public references to a Grand Liban.[3] For instance, the term does not appear to have been used seven months earlier by the first Lebanese delegation to Paris—at least not in its official releases. Or to cite a later example, the term was not used in the important correspondence from Clemenceau to Maronite Patriarch Ḥuwāyik dated 10 November 1919.[4]

---

[2] Paul Noujaim, "La Question du Liban: étude de politique économique et de statistique descriptive," *La Revue phénicienne*, August 1919, pp. 66–81. For the crucial year of 1919, other contributors on economic, political, and cultural subjects to this valuable if largely under-utilized journal include Charles Corm, Albert Naqqāsh, Jean Jalkh, Joseph Jumayyil, Emile 'Arab, Auguste Adīb, Shukrī Ghānim, Michel Shīḥa, 'Abdallāh Khayr, Philippe de Ṭarrāzī, Hektor Khlāṭ, Yūsuf al-Khāzin, 'Azīz Zabbāl, Ibrāhīm Thābit, and Ilyās Ḥāyik. [On these essays in *La Revue phénicienne*, see above, pp. 540–44.]. I am grateful to Dave Corm for his generous gift of rare copies of *La Revue phénicienne*, and equally to Victor Jabre, a nephew of B. Nujaym, for a copy of his uncle's principal work, *La Question du Liban*.

[3] [On Naqqāsh's study, see above, pp. 540–41.].

[4] The text of this letter is in Zeine N. Zeine, *The Struggle For Arab Independence* (Beirut: Khayat's, 1960), pp. 263–64. In her recent and valuable study, *Daoud Ammoun et la creation de l'état Libanais* (Paris: Klincksieck, 1978), p. 73, Lyne Loheac quotes excerpts from a private letter from Da'ūd 'Ammūn to his wife, dated 12 December 1918, in which this Lebanese statesman uses the term *Grand-Liban*: "Vous connaissez mon programme du Grand-Liban; je l'ai fait adopter par tout le monde ici, y compris le gouvernement français. Le Conseil Administratif l'a fait sien. Il a voté à l'unanimité, druses et musulmans compris, l'envoi d'une délégation. . . à Paris pour défendre ce projet à la Conférence de la Paix. Je fais partie de cette délégation avec le titre de Premier Délégué." It is perhaps

There is no doubt that Nujaym was formulating his ideas under pressure of momentous events in that summer of 1919, when a delegation led by the Maronite Patriarch left Jounieh on 15 July on board a French warship—first to Rome and the Vatican, then to Paris and the Versailles Peace Conference—and when an American fact-finding mission despatched by President Wilson, the King-Crane Commission, was attempting to assess the political wishes of various communities in Syria, Lebanon, and Palestine. Another cause of concern in many Maronite and Catholic Melchite circles were the aspirations of the Syrian Congress, which sought complete independence for the whole of geographic Syria, "with the Amir Faysal as king under a democratic, civil, and constitutional monarchy."[5]

In between the two works mentioned above, Nujaym also contributed chapters on the history of Lebanon in Ismāʿīl Ḥaqqī, *Lubnān: mabāḥith ʿilmīya wa-ijtimāʿīya.* He covered the period from the Arab conquest to 1914, while Father Louis Cheikho contributed the chapters for the earlier epochs. Pressured, no doubt, by the dangers and arbitrary rule of the Turkish military regime in wartime, Nujaym ended his narrative with the hope for a speedy end to the First World War and the return of prosperity to Lebanon "under the shadow of His Majesty the sultan Muḥammad Rashād."[6] In this third work Nujaym was circumspect in his treatment of the themes of autonomy and particularism, and of the national achievements of his heroes. The chapters are of lesser importance, insofar as this study is concerned, except for the fact that he appears to have retreated from the radical, progressive, and thought-provoking interpretation of the Kisrawān peasant revolts of 1858 expressed in *La Question du Liban* in 1908.[7]

The principal objectives of this study are to examine the intellectual contributions of this talented member of the rising professional middle class, and

significant, however, that the four-point program, voted by the Conseil Administratif of Mount Lebanon on 9 December 1918 does not use the term *Grand-Liban.*

[5] Harry N. Howard, *The King-Crane Commission* (Beirut: Khayat's, 1963), p. 120.

[6] *Lubnān: mabāḥith ʿilmīya wa-ijtimāʿīya*, edited by Ismāʿīl Ḥaqqī, 2nd edition (Beirut: Lebanese University, 1961), I, 364.

[7] One of Nujaym's distinctive contributions to the historiography of conflict in Lebanon is his perceptive interpretation of the civil strife in Mount Lebanon, 1858–60, which he saw in terms of social revolution and class struggle. He criticized the representatives of the European powers in Istanbul and in Syria for their portrayal of the origins of conflict as being almost exclusively religious, whereas in fact, "la cause première... a été un conflit social entre les seigneurs et les paysans. Il n'y a pas eu lutte entre deux communautés religieuses hostiles l'une à l'autre. La religion n'a été mêlée à ce conflit qu'assez tard." See *La Question du Liban*, pp. 282, 288, 543. [Buheiry developed this point in a later study. See above, pp. 499–511.].

his understanding of important features of Lebanese history as determinants of his national political vision and program. These include the historical origins of Syria and Lebanon, the role of Fakhr al-Dīn and the Amīr Bashīr in the formation of what Nujaym saw as a distinctive Lebanese polity which cut across communal lines, the dashed hopes and rising expectations of the *mutaṣarrifīya,* and the urgency and nature of reforms in the political, economic, and territorial spheres. Finally, to compare his Grand Liban concept with other formulations by Maronites and Catholic Melchites in the period under consideration, 1908 to 1919.

* * * *

Būluṣ Nujaym was born in 1880 in Jounieh, Kisrawān, into a family that had produced many a bishop to the Maronite church.[8] He studied at the prestigious 'Anṭūra College. His father, Fāris Nujaym, cited in one pre-1914 source as the dean of Mount Lebanon's doctors, was a prominent member of the medical profession, widely respected for his art and human qualities.[9] Fāris belonged to one of the early groups of Lebanese students to have studied in the Cairo School of Medicine (ca. 1860), which included many Maronites, as did the group entering in 1868. According to Dr. Shākir Khūrī, himself a graduate of the Cairo school, the Khedive had regularly earmarked ten scholarships in medicine for students from Syria and Lebanon.[10] To date these early graduates from Lebanon have not been the subject of comprehensive study. They, of course, predate the first generation of doctors formed in Lebanon by the Syrian Protestant College (forerunner of the American University of Beirut), and the Jesuit Université St. Joseph.

---

[8]Manṣūr al-Ḥattūnī, *Nubdha ta'rīkhīya fī l-muqāṭa'a al-kisrawānīya,* 2nd edition (Beirut: Y.I. Yazbak, 1956), pp. 28, 146. Al-Ḥattūnī cites, for instance, Yūsuf and Urmīya Nujaym.

[9]*Le Réveil,* 691 (21 October 1913).

[10]Shākir Khūrī, *Kitāb tuhfat al-rāghib* (Beirut 1879), pp. 3–4. The first group of doctors to have studied in Egypt, beginning in 1837, included Ibrāhīm Najjār of Dayr al-Qamar, Ghālib Khūrī of Ba'aqlīn, Yūsuf Jalkh, and Yūsuf Mirhij Lṭayf. Dr. Ibrāhīm Najjār is widely recognized as the first trained Lebanese surgeon, and has given his name to the old Quarantine Hospital in Beirut. See *Al-Ḥayāt,* 11 August 1971, and *Le Jour,* 15 November 1970. Some of the specific perceptions of this new middle class are worthy of note. Būluṣ Nujaym, for instance, sees a conflict of economic and electoral interest in Mount Lebanon between the *gros bourg,* growing in importance and infrastructural development, and the humble *hameau.* Another distinction is that the *gros bourg* tended to be located either virtually on, or else within easy reach of, the seacoast, whereas the *hameau* was perched high in the mountains and was hostile to social and economic changes and political reforms. See *La Question du Liban,* p. 480.

By the third quarter of the nineteenth century the professional middle class had become quite visible, in the coastal cities as well as in the more prosperous towns of Mount Lebanon; likewise, some of the behavioral traits of this class were predictable: of Dr. Fāris Nujaym's two sons, Saʿīd followed in his father's footsteps by studying medicine—in France—and setting up his clinic in Jounieh, while Būluṣ took a doctorate in law and a doctorate in political science from the Faculté de Droit, Paris, and turned to politics. For the generation of the sons, the French dimension was also predictable.

The French dimension, while predominant in the sphere of economic concessions, education, language, and life-styles of the elite and upper middle class, also permeated the politics of the *vilāyet* of Beirut and the *mutaṣarri-fīya* of Mount Lebanon. This is particularly true of the last decades before the First World War. Take, for instance, the year 1913. In the opening months, the Beirut press discussed the implications of Poincaré's assertion that France had extracted from Britain a recognition of her own special sphere of interest in Syria and Lebanon. At the same time, the Lebanese committee in Paris continued its agitation for reforms and territorial expansion under French auspices. In mid-year the Beirut Reform Committee, one of the more prestigious political associations, and in many ways the most sophisticated in Lebanon, participated in the Arab Congress which was held in Paris (not in Istanbul, Rome, Berlin, Geneva, or London). Then toward the end of the year a well-publicized visit by the French fleet occupied the headlines and provided an occasion for some local *zajal* poets to compose ringing verses in honor of the French navy. Furthermore, at this time the Lebanese were caught by the aviation fever, a French fever. The much-publicized "raid" by Daucourt and Roux in a Oiseau Bleu never made it to Beirut. The plane crashed north of Aleppo. However, a few weeks later (on 27 December 1913) Védrines landed his Blériot, with its ten-meter wing span, in a specially prepared field near the Quarantine, in East Beirut.[11] Three days later (on 30 December) another French pilot, Bonnier, landed his plane, this time in the sands of Bīr Ḥasan, in West Beirut. In the meantime, a French theater group, the Troupe de Madame Jeanne Rolly and Gaston Bubosc, arrived in Beirut and opened its program with Maurice Donnay's *La Bascule*; while at the Cinema Gaumont, which normally specialized in French movies, the program alternated between "The Sinking of the Titanic," "The

---

[11]ʿAnbara Salām al-Khālidī, *Jawla fī l-dhikrāyāt bayna Lubnān wa-Filasṭīn* (Beirut: Dār al-nahār, 1978), p. 48. See also Laḥd Khaṭīr, *ʿAhd al-mutaṣarrifīn fī Lubnān, 1861–1918* (Beirut: Lebanese University, 1967), p. 196.

Manoeuvres of the Ottoman Army," and perhaps aptly, "Quo Vadis?" The other cinema in town, Le Grand Cirque Ribera, specialized inevitably in the Vitagraph and American movies.

Moreover, in the economic sphere, the end of the year 1913 witnessed a determined campaign by the Quai d'Orsay to break the British monopoly of oil explorations in Syria, held by Boxall's company. On 22 December 1913 Sir Edward Grey assured the French government that Britain was seeking only one oil concession in Syria and that "there was no question of any attempt to obtain a monopoly of such enterprise."[12] From the crude gravity of the petroleum question to the flighty thrills of aviation, French influence tended to reign unchallenged in the Syria-Lebanon of 1913. In fact, in purely economic terms, the Mandates of Syria, Lebanon, and Palestine could be said to have been already in place by 1912.

After his return from France (ca. 1908), Būluṣ Nujaym participated in the political life of the Kisrawān province during the last days of the *mutaṣarrif-īya*. An important source for the history of the period, Yūsuf al-Ḥakīm, related that the struggle for influence in the Kisrawān was "between the party of the Khāzin shaykhs and the people's party *(al-jabha al-shaʿbīya)* led by Ḥabīb al-Bīṭār, George Zuwayn, Būluṣ Nujaym, and Naʿūm Bākhūs."[13] The issues were often parochial; but they also involved, on the higher level, an intense competition for the lucrative positions in the administration under a *mutaṣarrif* who retained absolute power in appointing or revoking civil servants, including the seven *qāʾimaqām*s and 47 *mudīr*s. Significantly, Nujaym publicly opposed the official Ottoman policy of restrictions on steamship

[12]William Shorrock, *French Imperialism in the Middle East* (Madison: University of Wisconsin Press, 1976), pp. 134–35. For a perceptive analysis of the strategic and economic importance of the Anglo-French railway agreements (1910) over Syria as factors in the partition of influence, see Rashid Khalidi, *British Policy Towards Syria and Palestine* (London: Ithaca Press, 1980), p. 113. Nujaym deplored the decline of French economic influence and the growth of German influence in the region. Nonetheless, he believed that France's earlier position of prominence could be swiftly restored: "Le prestige moral de la France est encore énorme dans le Liban et dans toute la Syrie. C'est la langue française qu'apprennent les jeunes Libanais; ce sont dans des écoles françaises qu'ils vont s'instruire. C'est à l'Université française de Beyrouth qu'ils étudient la médecine. C'est en France qu'ils viennent pour achever leurs études. Ils veulent être et ils sont toujours les 'Français du Levant.' A la France de les soutenir, de déployer une plus grande activité économique en Syrie. Grâce aux sympathies ardentes des Syriens et des Libanais en particulier, elle y reprendra vite le premier rang parmi les puissances commerciales." See *La Question du Liban*, p. 501.

[13]Yūsuf al-Ḥakīm, *Bayrūt wa-Lubnān fī ʿahd āl ʿUthmān* (Beirut: Catholic Press, 1964), pp. 44, 52. See also Khaṭīr, *ʿAhd al-mutaṣarrifīn fī Lubnān*, pp. 181–84.

navigation in such Mount Lebanon ports as Jounieh. In November 1909, he joined Bishāra 'Azzī and Sejean 'Arayj in signing a widely distributed protest pamphlet entitled *Le Liban et ses ports*.[14]

There were other economic incentives as well for the rising Lebanese middle class. New opportunities were created by the scramble for concessions, including railways, port facilities, irrigation, and hydroelectric schemes, which brought together French financial interests and local entrepreneurs around the turn of the century. A good example of this trend was the Beirut-M'āmaltayn railway, with the options of extensions both northward and southward, sponsored jointly by the Khaḍra brothers of Ṣarba (Kisrawān) and a consortium of French banks and companies. The speculative element in much of this activity, the expansion of credit, the promise of substantial returns, and new jobs, provided ideal ground for the interplay of political patronage.

Early in 1913 the newly appointed *mutaṣarrif*, Ohannes Kuyumjian, proceeded with a thorough revision of the administration, appointing among others Būluṣ Nujaym as director of the foreign affairs bureau *(ra'īs al-qalam al-ajnabī)*, a measure which was generally well-received. A pro-French newspaper of Beirut commented at the time that "Nujaym's appointment was greeted with satisfaction in Lebanon as a sign that the government intended henceforth to select young talent capable of providing a new and progressive impulse to a fatigued administration."[15]

During the First World War he was exiled by Jamāl Pāshā. Under the French mandate he became *procureur général* of the Appeals Court. He died in France in 1931.

In what sense was Būluṣ Nujaym a representative of the rising intelligentsia? It has been suggested by Herbert Passin that societies entering "the cycle of modernization must at some point break through in three fields: political and social reform, language, and journalism." The breakthroughs may occur simultaneously, as they did in China during the 4 May movement of 1919 when, in the words of Passin, there was "a simultaneous climax of literary, philosophical and political ideas seeking to burst free of the restraints

---

[14] Wajīh Kawtharānī, *Al-Ittijāhāt al-ijtimā'īya al-siyāsīya fī Jabal Lubnān* (Beirut: Ma'had al-inmā' al-'arabī, 1978), p. 229. This book by Kawtharānī, together with his *Bilād al-Shām* (Beirut: Ma'had al-inmā' al-'arabī, 1980), constitute valuable sources for the study of French political and economic influence in Lebanon and Syria during the period 1860 to 1920, as does John Spagnola's *France and Ottoman Lebanon 1861–1914* (Oxford: Ithaca Press, 1977).

[15] *Le Réveil*, 591 (25 February 1913).

of the half-emancipation of the 1911 revolution."[16] Something similar did happen in the Arab provinces of the Ottoman Empire in the aftermath of the Young Turk revolution of 1908, although the breakthroughs in language and journalism preceded the breakthrough in political and social reform by perhaps a decade. Indeed, new channels of communications such as books, newspapers, and periodicals played crucial roles as solvents of the traditional order in the Arab East, roles that deserve more study.

Describing the intellectual scene in the decade before the First World War, K.T. Khairallah senses this ferment:

> Beyrout, où afflue la jeunesse lettrée du Liban, est la capitale intellectuelle de la Syrie. C'est dans son sein une telle fermentation d'idées et de sentiments qu'on a peine à s'y reconnaître. On a peine à croire l'audace des théories sociales et littéraires qui s'y développent. Cette audace a stimulé du moins cette vieille société orientale et y entretient un puissant courant qui la pousse en avant.[17]

Of course the case for the new channels of communications must not be overstressed. Economic and demographic pressures, such as the ones present in Mount Lebanon in 1858, and even earlier in Beirut, Sidon, and Tripoli, were equally powerful solvents. Nonetheless, the articulation and diffusion of issues deemed vital proved useful in maintaining the tempo of erosion and bringing about change. And it is at this point that the intelligentsia found its calling, becoming in time an institution in its own right.

The French-educated Maronite intelligentsia of Mount Lebanon (or the *vilāyet* of Beirut) of which Būlus Nujaym was a member asked roughly the same basic questions, and displayed the same critical faculty, as the rising group of Muslim intelligentsia of the cities represented, for instance, by a 'Abd al-Ghanī al-'Uraysī. But if the questions were similar the answers often differed. The questions asked included: Who are we? Where is the blame? Who are our friends? What is to be done? The contrast between Nujaym's and al-'Uraysī's answers is indeed striking.[18]

---

[16] Herbert Passin, "Writer and Journalist in the Transitional Society," in *Communications and Political Development*, edited by Lucian Pye (Princeton: Princeton University Press, 1963), p. 82. See also Samir Khalaf, *Persistence and Change in 19th-Century Lebanon: A Sociological Essay* (Beirut: American University of Beirut, 1979), p. 118.

[17] K. T. Khairallah, *La Syrie* (Paris: E. Leroux, 1912), p. 112.

[18] See Rashid Khalidi, " 'Abd al-Ghani al-'Uraisi and *Al-Mufid*: The Press and Arab Nationalism Before 1914," in *Intellectual Life in the Arab East, 1890–1939*, edited by Marwan Buheiry (Beirut: American University of Beirut, 1981), pp. 38–61.

* * * *

The opening sentences of Būluṣ Nujaym's *La Question du Liban* (published in 1908) clearly reveal the broad lines of his historical vision. His avowed intention was "to retrace the history of this small Lebanese territory, of this small nation, which despite its size has played and continues to play such a large role in the Orient."[19] In ancient times he saw it as a center of advanced civilization. In the Ottoman period, although incorporated into an empire, it nevertheless succeeded in retaining a large measure of autonomy due to factors of geographic location and historical circumstance. Within Syria, the Lebanon developed "its own particular figure, in the religious as well as in the political and economic spheres."[20] In short, he viewed Lebanon's history as going beyond the Syrian framework and with wider implications. Throughout the nineteenth century it was the special concern of European diplomacy; with the end of Muḥammad 'Alī's intervention in 1840, "the Lebanese question became an international question, with the Lebanese claiming for themselves the largest autonomy possible."[21] In this respect France had a special role to play because of her long tradition of religious, linguistic, educational, political, and economic ties with the coast and the mountain.

This in a nutshell is the argument. When it came to filling in the details, Nujaym began by setting the geographic scene for Syria and Lebanon, displaying in the process a marked bias for geographic determinism. The influence of Elisée Reclus is revealed by the frequency of citations. "Two geographical facts," Nujaym writes, "have determined the history and ethnicity of Syria: firstly, its composition as a narrow territorial band hemmed in between the Mediterranean and the desert, and secondly, its mountainous nature."[22] He described the whole region as a crossroad of nations, a communications center, the only land route between Asia and Africa, the shortest route between the Mediterranean and the Indian Ocean, and the natural

---

[19] Jouplain, *La Question du Liban*, p. ix.

[20] *Ibid.*

[21] *Ibid.* p. x. It is indeed surprising that Būluṣ Nujaym has not received the attention he so rightly deserves. Two notable exceptions are A.H. Hourani, "Historians of Lebanon," in *Historians of the Middle East*, edited by Bernard Lewis and P.M. Holt (London: Oxford University Press, 1962), p. 238; and Kamal Salibi, *The Modern History of Lebanon* (London: Weidenfeld and Nicolson, 1965), pp. 118–19. At one point Nujaym used the English term "self-government" to clarify the kind of autonomy he had in mind for Mount Lebanon in 1908 (*La Question du Liban*, p. 531).

[22] Jouplain, *La Question du Liban*, p. 1.

meeting place of Orient and Occident. However, the predominantly mountainous nature of the land was also seen as a factor of division: it tended to keep the diverse elements of the population apart. All he saw by way of historical development were tiny states in perpetual internecine conflict, hence easy prey to conquest by foreign invaders. But at this point Nujaym introduced a social-Darwinian dimension in his argument. The most robust elements of the various Syrian populations would retreat into the natural fortresses of the land—particularly in Mount Lebanon, Anti-Lebanon, and Mount Hermon—where favorable geographic conditions would help them conserve and develop autonomy, particularly during periods of declining central authority.

Basically, Nujaym showed great admiration for the achievements of the Phoenicians, although he does not spend more than a couple of pages out of 550 on them. He shows what may be described as indifference to the Graeco-Roman period, dismissing it in one paragraph. He displays a marked hostility toward the Byzantines, holding them responsible for the ruin of geographical Syria. In fact, all he sees in the Byzantine epoch is administrative corruption, cruel civil servants, social and economic injustice, heavy taxation, heresies and persecutions, and religious orders with substantial economic privileges contributing little or nothing to the overall economic life of the region.[23] Consequently, Byzantium was in no position to halt the advance of the Arabs, especially as the Syrian population had not really assimilated Hellenism. They remained, in the words of Nujaym, always Semites, treating the Byzantines as strangers and the Arabs as brothers of the same race. "The majority of the Syrians," wrote Nujaym, "greeted with joy the coming of the Arabs and the defeat of the Byzantine persecutors."[24]

The author displayed, in fact, a positive attitude toward the Arab conquest. He saw it as the revenge of the Semitic principle over the nine centuries of control by Hellenism, and the return of Syria to its proper historical course: "A Semitic civilization, profoundly rooted in the geographic and ethnic features of the land and the true heir of the ancient civilization of the Orient, could henceforth develop."[25] And he concludes: "With the Arabs, Syria became once more the center of Semitism...and the cradle of Arab or Muslim civilization."[26] In fact, with the Umayyads it became the center of the civilized world: "Ce furent les Omaiyades qui firent éclore la civilisation

---

[23] *Ibid.*, pp. 4, 7.

[24] *Ibid.*, p. 7.

[25] *Ibid.*, p. 9.

[26] *Ibid.*, p. 10.

musulmane ou arabe, la plus belle du haut moyen âge. Leur empire arabo-syrien était certainement l'Etat le plus civilisé et le plus florissant des VIIè et VIIIè siècles. La Syrie était véritablement le centre du monde civilisé."[27]

In addition, the coming of the Arabs was also the starting point of the Maronite experience: "C'est dans cette époque, sans doute, qu'il faut placer l'origine historique d'une peuplade qui devait jouer dans la suite un rôle prépondérant dans le Liban et en Syrie, de la peuplade des *Maronites*...Dès le début de la conquête arabe, le Liban devait ainsi jouer un rôle particulier en Syrie, que nous montrerons dans son ensemble."[28] Likewise, Nujaym briefly discussed the origins of the Muslim Tanūkhs, the Shī'ite Qarāmiṭa, and the Druzes insofar as the history of Lebanon is concerned. The sources he utilized were varied but substantial: Diercks, al-Duwayhī, Yūsuf Dibs, Azar, al-Shidyāq, Ibn Yaḥyā, Churchill, Lammens, de Sacy, Guys, Jawdat Pāshā, de Goeje, Ibn Khaldūn, al-Ṭabarī, and al-Wāqidī, to mention but a few.

* * * *

It is not this paper's intention to examine Nujaym's assessment of historical developments under the 'Abbāsids, Fāṭimids, Seljuks, and Crusaders, except to note three of his characteristic interpretations. First, in reaction to the Seljuks, who introduced into Syria a military-feudal organization, the Maronites in turn "adopted this military organization, which was that of an armed nation (*nation armée*) with a hierarchy of feudal lords composed of chieftains, *amīrs*, and shaykhs."[29] Second, under the Crusaders Syria became the natural meeting ground of the Occident and Orient, "from which the Latin Knights" took back with them the seeds of a new civilization which saw the full light of day in the Renaissance.[30] Third, the Crusades created indissoluble links between the Franks and the Christians of Syria, particularly the Maronites. From this period on the Maronites became "the Frenchmen of the Levant (*Français du Levant*) and the champions of Christian France in Syria."[31]

---

[27] *Ibid.*, p. 20.

[28] *Ibid.*, p. 12. Nujaym inevitably enters into polemical discussions with other authors on the subject of the Maronites. He disagrees with many of R.P. Azar's assertions (p. 36), and he draws a distinction between the Mardaites and the Maronites (p. 42).

[29] *Ibid.*, p. 536.

[30] *Ibid.*, p. 537.

[31] *Ibid.*

To Fakhr al-Dīn and the Amīr Bashīr, Nujaym reserved special treatment. The cult of the Maʿnid prince that one tends to see in later historiography (for instance in Michel Shiblī or Adel Ismail) is already in forceful evidence. To Nujaym, Fakhr al-Dīn was not only the organizer of an efficient military establishment, he was above all a monarch creating a sovereign state by bringing the various communities into a harmonious unity. He saw him as an enlightened prince eager to stimulate economic growth, and as a "colbertiste avant Colbert" seeking self-sufficiency, protectionism, the regulation of the economy, and wide-scale infrastructure development with the help of the European experts and technology.[32] In short, to quote Nujaym:

> Fakhr al-Dīn fashioned a powerful and well-organized state with Lebanon as its center....It was no longer a Turkish province but a state with a life of its own, resembling more the civilized countries of Western Europe than a *vilāyet* of the Sublime Porte. Led by an enlightened despot, it experienced the splendor of an [Italian] Renaissance.[33]

Nujaym does recognize the errors of Fakhr al-Dīn; the fact that he lacked moderation and was in too great a hurry. He also notes a tendency toward economic oppression toward the end of his career. Nevertheless, Nujaym's verdict was clear:

> Ainsi mourût le prince le plus remarquable qui eut jamais gouverné la Montagne. Son génie est incontestable. Il en a laissé des monuments impérissables: c'est d'abord la prospérité économique de Beyrouth et du Liban, qui est son oeuvre, et qui aujourd'hui encore, les place au premier rang des pays du Levant; c'est ensuite la création d'une unité politique du Liban, d'un Etat libanais, capable de jouer un grand rôle en Syrie et dans tout l'Orient, un Etat prospère qui avait attiré sur lui l'attention bienveillante même de l'Europe. Sans doute, il avait échoué, mais il avait montré la voie aux Libanais, Druses et Maronites, qui était l'unité de tous pour la défense de l'autonomie; il avait cimenté cette unité par les traditions glorieuses de son gouvernement; il avait éveillé chez tous les Montagnards la conscience de leur unité nationale; il les avait placés au premier rang de tous

---

[32] *Ibid.*, p. 110.
[33] *Ibid.*, p. 111.

les peuples syriens. Désormais, il était évident que le salut, que l'indépendance de la Syrie ne pouvait venir que du Liban.[34]

As to the controversial Amīr Bashīr, Nujaym concentrated on his politics, which he characterized as one of calculated neutrality between the Turkish governors of the Syrian provinces with the aim of perpetually holding the balance of power between Damascus and Acre. Internally he worked hard to weaken the powerful shaykhs and the *iqṭāʿ* system and to strengthen his own hold over the mountain and the coast, particularly in terms of economic control and administrative centralization. To Nujaym, Bashīr had a special genius for dissimulation and could present himself in various religious garbs to suit his multi-religious communities. Nujaym does not raise the possibility of this being a myth and assumes that Lebanese Muslims, Christians, and Druzes were fooled by Bashīr's stratagem.

Yet Bashīr could not remain neutral forever. By 1831, according to Nujaym, "he was forced by circumstances to abandon [neutrality] and to choose between Turkey and Egypt."[35] It was to cause his downfall and the end of the Shihābī epoch. But to Nujaym the Bashīr experience contained many positive elements: 1) the alliance between Muḥammad ʿAlī and Bashīr reinforced the trend toward the centralization of power; 2) despite earlier tensions between Druzes and Maronites, deliberately triggered by Bashīr and Muḥammad ʿAlī, the two communities buried their differences and antagonisms and signed the Dayr al-Qamar pact of 1840; 3) the final fight against Muḥammad ʿAlī brought all the communities into a common front, thus helping to forge some sort of unity; 4) vast quantities of gold, food, weapons, and ammunition were landed by the British to sustain the revolt against the Egyptians; 5) finally, the Syrian question, particularly in its Lebanese dimension, was no longer an internal Ottoman affair. It became internationalized ("elle est entrée définitivement dans le domaine international")[36]—a development which Nujaym welcomed. Nonetheless, in supporting Muḥammad ʿAlī France had lost ground; her role of moderator between the Ottoman State and the Christian communities was taken over by the Concert of Europe led by England.

Throughout the Maʿnid and early Shihābī periods, in short, Nujaym saw religious-based politics recede before the politics of the *imāra* and revised *iqṭāʿ* system, and the creation of a class of notables whose economic interests

---

[34] *Ibid.*, p. 116.
[35] *Ibid.*, p. 168.
[36] *Ibid.*

cut across religious affiliation. Thus the political dichotomy of Lebanon was not so much a Druze-Maronite division as it was a Qaysī-Yamanī one. Besides, all communities had an interest in keeping the Ottomans out and to defend a precarious autonomy. It is in this sense that a polity was forged serving as a base for the "movement of liberation and independence from the Ottomans."[37]

Another crucial landmark in Lebanon's historical experience was the *mutaṣarrifīya*. In drawing his balance sheet Nujaym carefully analyzed its positive results and dashed hopes before embarking on his program of political and economic reform. The positive elements, he believed, were numerous. Firstly, "Mount Lebanon," as he put it, "was removed from the direct authority of the Ottoman Porte and placed squarely under the collective trusteeship (*tutelle*) of the powers, whose representatives actually participated in the nomination of the *mutaṣarrif*."[38] The autonomy of Lebanon was growing, providing a model for the other provinces of Syria. Secondly, internal peace became a reality and the 1860 events were being gradually forgotten. Thirdly, despite all kinds of difficulties, a national and political life focused—"as was the case in Western Europe"—on political and economic issues, and programs irrespective of religious affiliation did develop. In short, he claimed that there was a "continued evolution of democracy in Lebanon."[39] Fourthly, there was some progress in economic development, not so much on the level of trade as in infrastructure.

Nonetheless, the dashed hopes were also many. For a start, Nujaym argued, the Mountain in territorial terms was mutilated by the Règlement of 1861. The territorial rearrangement which broke up the land artificially was all the more incongruous to Nujaym because it was done by the same European powers who helped to fashion Italian and German unity.[40] Moreover, the policy of granting absolute powers to a *mutaṣarrif* was a retrograde step. In any case this dignitary ought to be selected from the indigenous population. Then, also, confessionalism had received official consecration.[41]

---

[37] *Ibid.*, p. 167.

[38] *Ibid.*, p. 544. For a different reading of the Ottoman experience and of the potential for progress, see Sulaymān al-Bustānī, *'Ibra wa-dhikra aw al-dawla al-'uthmānīya qabla l-dustūr wa ba'dahu*, new edition (Beirut: Dār al-ṭalī'a, 1978), pp. 214–29.

[39] Jouplain, *La Question du Liban*, p. 544.

[40] *Ibid.*, p. 531.

[41] *Ibid.*, p. 477. Nujaym's hostility to the mustaṣarrifate, particularly to Da'ūd Pāshā Yeramian, is intense. Asad Rustum has noted this feature in Nujaym's writings and has criticized him for it in *Lubnān fī 'ahd al-mutaṣarrifīya* (Beirut: Dār al-nahār, 1973), p. 85.

Finally, the Mountain became depopulated at the rate of about a third of its inhabitants in the 30-year period between 1870 and 1900, and to the gain of North and South America and Egypt.

Where was the blame and what was to be done? For a start he saw the Lebanese as the most active and industrious portion of the Syrian population, with a vanguard role to play in bringing national unity and progress to Syria: "Ils sont seuls aptes à jouer dans ces régions autrefois si glorieuses le rôle que le Piémont a joué en Italie. [Les Libanais] sont les Piémontais de la Syrie. Que les puissances leur permettent au moins de remplir le rôle des Piémontais."[42] Clearly then, in 1908 Nujaym envisioned a Lebanon within a Syrian national framework, and in a vanguard role. As to his analogy with Piedmont, it was noteworthy and original in terms of topography, religion, and the importance of the silk factor. To accomplish this required the reconstitution of natural Lebanon, the restitution of, as he put it, Tripoli and the 'Akkār, the Biqā', Marj 'Uyūn, the Ḥūlah region of Galilee, Sidon, and of course, Beirut.

Equally crucial was the need to stem the flood of emigration to the Americas. At this point Nujaym proposed a radical and highly controversial measure, the only one, he insisted, that could solve the problem of emigration: the suppression of mortmain property, (*mainmorte*)—the suppression, that is, of lands held impersonally and inalienably by the ecclesiastical orders and convents.[43] He did not want it to appear, he says, "as a measure of anti-clerical fanaticism."[44] Rather, he wanted it to be seen in terms of the public interest. The priestly establishment, he insisted, had a disastrous effect on the economy because its policy was merely to acquire more and more mortmain property, which would then be left unproductive and inaccessible to the land-hungry peasantry. How best to proceed? A radical solution was necessary: the confiscation of the major holdings of the ecclesiastical orders, with compensation, "and a law passed to inhibit their right to acquire more land."[45] In addition, he proposed that the powerful priestly establishment fall under the same tax laws as everyone else in the country. One must recall that Nujaym was writing in France with the anti-clerical legislation of the Third Republic as backdrop, and it is clear that he was profoundly influenced by this current.

[42] Jouplain, *La Question du Liban*, p. 531.
[43] *Ibid.*, p. 530.
[44] *Ibid.*, p. 526.
[45] *Ibid.*, p. 527.

So much for the question as seen in 1908. If there appears to be some ambiguity or even confusion regarding the terms Syria or Lebanon, this is natural. One would notice the same ambiguity in Muṭrān Yūsuf Dibs' multi-volume *Ta'rīkh Sūriya*, representing the best of Maronite historiography, as well as in K.T. Khairallah's *La Syrie* published in 1912, representing the secular trend.[46] At this juncture, and despite the obvious emphasis on the themes of particularism and special relationship with France, Nujaym nevertheless viewed the Lebanese as the vanguard of a Syrian nation of the future: the Piedmont formula, to use a European analogy which he used. In other words, at this stage, he would probably not have differed too much with the Syrian Committee in Paris led by George Samna and Shukrī Ghānim.

* * * *

The importance of the year 1919 is hard to exaggerate. The allies at Versailles were getting nowhere in their attempt to reach an agreement on Syria. An American source, Wickham Steed, in describing the intense atmosphere of the March 1919 negotiations wrote: "The meetings discussed the question of Syria and the Franco-British agreements in regard to it, as well as the Secret Treaties in general, with the result that confusion became more confounded. President Wilson came out of the meeting cursing everybody and everything, saying that he had done nothing but talk for forty-eight hours and was getting disgusted with the whole business."[47] Soon afterwards, in April, Clemenceau and the Amīr Fayṣal met and tried to narrow down their different viewpoints. France's draft proposal, which was in fact withdrawn when Fayṣal's draft reply was rejected by the French government, significantly agreed "to recognize the right of Syria to independence in the form of a federation of local autonomies reflecting the traditions and wishes of the populations."[48] Some of this information may have leaked to Lebanese pressure groups in Paris as well as to pro-French circles in Beirut. In any case, according to Gontaut-Biron, who made a detailed study of the year 1918-19 in his book *Comment la France s'est installée en Syrie,* Maronites and Catholic Melchites were disturbed by a January 1919 speech of Georges Picot in Damascus implying close relations between France and Fayṣal.[49]

---

[46] Khairallah, *La Syrie*, pp. 139–40.

[47] Zeine, *The Struggle for Arab Independence*, p. 79.

[48] *Ibid.*, p. 81.

[49] R. de Gontaut-Biron, *Comment la France s'est installée en Syrie 1918–1919* (Paris: Plon, 1922), p. 233.

With Fayṣal's arrival in Beirut from France on board a French warship in April, the anxiety of those who preferred to see an independent Lebanon under French control rose even higher. And when it was revealed that an American commission would visit the Near East to ascertain the wishes of the people on the spot, the supporters of France mobilized effectively to insure that their voice was heard.

How did Nujaym see "La Question du Liban" in July 1919? He begins his article by arguing that "La Nation Libanaise [spelled in capital letters], jealously guarding its independence"[50] and concerned about its national sovereignty, is claiming for itself a free and independent political existence, suited to its own geographic situation and historical past. To Nujaym, this meant in effect the reconstitution of the "Liban de la grande époque: *Le Grand Liban.*"[51]

The addition of the territories already outlined, he urged, was of greater priority than the nature of the regime or the form of government placed over the country. This may sound surprising at first sight. But the reasons were clear: a small Lebanon, the constricted Lebanon of the Mutaṣarrifate, was economically vulnerable and could hardly survive on the two months' supply of wheat that it produced. Drawing heavily on Albert Naqqāsh's perceptive analysis of Lebanon's economic future, Nujaym explained that in normal times the economic equilibrium of the country depended on three principal factors, all of which were external. The first was unimpeded transfer of gold from the Americas by Lebanese emigrants, representing in net terms 100 million piastres per annum. The second was the freedom to import silkworm eggs from France and Italy and to export, in return, silk in various forms. The third was the unimpeded import of wheat and other cereals from the interior, at an average rate of 80 million piastres per annum.[52] Any serious perturbation would bring the whole economy of "smaller Lebanon" to a standstill and lead, as in the First World War, to famine. A greater Lebanon, drawn along the lines of the French General Staff maps of 1861 and 1863 would, on the other hand, constitute a viable economic and national unit. According to the statistical charts he provided, this signified the addition of roughly 150,000 Sunnīs and 90,000 Shī'ites to the population of *mutaṣarrifīya* Lebanon. In short, the Maronites would end up forming 275,000 out of a population of 850,000. Nujaym did not appear to view this prospect with

---

[50] Jouplain, *La Question du Liban,* p. 66.

[51] *Ibid.*

[52] *Ibid.,* p. 75.

any alarm. He believed the Lebanese to be "ready for a democratic regime, free from all external affinities (mûrs pour un régime démocratique, libre de toute affinité extérieure)."[53] Besides, he believed the Lebanese formed an organic whole, a national entity, "united by a glorious past, common tradition, national history, with everyone belonging to the same race."[54]

There is one puzzling note in this 1919 article: Nujaym, living under the shadow of a French military administration, did not call for a French Mandate, as so many other figures of the Francophile intelligentsia were doing in the pages of the same journal and elsewhere. How is one to interpret this? Did Nujaym have a premonition that his country would be trading one *mutaṣarrif* for another: a Muẓaffar Pāshā for a Georges Picot? Did his student days in Paris reveal to him the true nature of a French colonial administration? Was he a shrewd enough politician to realize that many things could emerge out of the flux of 1919 and that it would be wise to keep as many options open? Nor is this surprising when it is recalled that the first Lebanese delegation to Versailles in January 1919 accepted as one option an "internal autonomy within a Greater Syria under French influence."[55] Whatever the answers, one thing is nevertheless clear: Nujaym rejected the idea of a small enclave for his community; instead he envisioned a democratic Lebanon, economically viable, and multi-confessional. The principal difference between the 1908 and 1919 writings is that the Syria dimension appears to have receded and the Piedmont model is no longer there.

* * * *

What is the place of Nujaym's ideas in the wide spectrum of Maronite and Catholic Melchite intelligentsia thought regarding the future of Lebanon? At one end of the spectrum, the Pan-Arab end, he has little in common with the trend represented by Negib Azoury's program of the "Ligue de la patrie arabe," except for the Francophile element and the stress on Lebanon's autonomy. Azoury had asserted that: "From the Tigris to the Isthmus of Suez and from the Mediterrranean to the Sea of Oman, there is only one nation, the Arab nation, speaking the same language, possessing the same historical traditions, studying the same literature, and with each individual of this ethnic mass proud of being a citizen of the Arab fatherland."[56]

[53] *Ibid.*, p. 77.
[54] *Ibid.*, p. 75.
[55] George Samna, *La Syrie* (Paris: Bossards, 1920), pp. 231–32 n.
[56] Negib Azoury, *Le Réveil de la nation arabe* (Paris: Plon, 1905), p. 164.

Nor at the other end of the spectrum, which may be termed the "Frankish Lebanon" end, did Nujaym share the views of a Ferdinand Tyan, who in 1917 saw Lebanon in terms of a "protectorat modelé sur le protectorat franc des Croisés" with a hereditary Maronite *amīr* in control of local affairs, leaving external affairs in the hands of a French Governor General residing in Damascus.[57] To complicate matters further, this French governor would, in Beirut, also serve as the "Résident Général de France auprès de l'Emir du Liban." And at this point Tyan adds: "C'est dire que la Syrie pourrait être colonisée à l'instar de l'Algérie, mais à la condition de n'établir qu'une sorte de protectorat sur la Montagne du Liban."[58] The official language of the Amīrate would be French and the senior posts of the local administration would be shared "on a fraternal basis" with Frenchmen.

Nor were his views compatible, particularly after 1919, with the views expressed by a Syrian integralist like Nadra Muṭrān, or those expressed by Shukrī Ghānim and George Samna who advocated Lebanon's membership in a large Syrian confederation or federation, with France assuming the role of a guide under the mandate system, and with Fayṣal out.

Nadra Muṭrān read his history very differently from Būluṣ Nujaym. In 1916 he wrote: "Lebanon is an integral part of Syria; from the viewpoints of history, ethnic composition, and trade, there is nothing to distinguish it from Syria."[59] He was critical of the prevalent "political psychology" which sought to spin myths and legends about the Lebanese question. "For a start," he said, "Lebanon was never independent."[60] The autonomy enjoyed before 1860 "was only illusory and no different from the autonomy enjoyed by nearly all the Syrian provinces."[61]

As to George Samna, he argued in 1919 and 1920 that "Lebanon could easily incorporate into a Syrian confederation, without the loss of its rights and privileges."[62] And he warned: "Lebanese autonomy is meaningless without a Greater Syria framework; even with Beirut and the Biqā', the Mountain isolated from the Syrian body... would be reduced to a mediocre and uncertain life, a life without future."[63]

---

[57] Ferdinand Tyan, *France et Liban: défense des intérêts français en Syrie* (Paris: Perrin et Cie., 1917), p. 78.

[58] *Ibid.*, p. 77.

[59] Nadra Muṭrān, *La Syrie de demain* (Paris: Plon, 1917), p. 97.

[60] *Ibid.*, p. 98.

[61] *Ibid.*

[62] Samna, *La Syrie*, p. 232.

[63] *Ibid.*

Finally, Nujaym had little sympathy for the pro-Fayṣal trend represented by an Iskandar ʿAmmūn or Saʿdallāh Ḥuwāyik. His ideal from 1908 to 1919 remained the "Liban de la grande époque," evolving into a "Grand Liban." His originality was the careful use of geopolitics and economics to bolster the vision and program of a liberal nationalist, sensitive both to the pluralist composition of Lebanese society and to the leadership role of his own community.

28

Vignettes from the Marwan R. Buheiry Photograph Collection

One of Marwan Buheiry's keenest interests was photography and photographic history, a field in which he was decisively influenced by his grandfather, Abraham Sarrafian. The Sarrafian brothers, Abraham, Boghos, and Samuel, were pioneering photographers in late Ottoman Lebanon. Abraham learned his trade from Protestant missionaries in central Turkey and in Berlin in the early 1890s, and established the family business in Beirut and Jerusalem shortly thereafter. The brothers not only did the usual portrait work and posed "oriental" scenes, but also travelled widely to record series of photographic studies of what they realized was a rapidly changing Arab world. Most of this work was done between the 1890s and 1920s, and in terms of both professional technique and cultural interest the Sarrafian series were of a very high standard. The brothers were appointed photographers to the Syrian Protestant College (SPC, later the American University of Beirut), and in 1905 they won the first prize in photography at the Ottoman Exhibition in Shweir, Mount Lebanon.

As a youth in the early 1950s, Buheiry was fascinated by his grandfather's work. During his summer holidays he worked at the family business in Bab Edriss, and it was Abraham Sarrafian who gave him his first camera. With his developing interest in history, Buheiry appreciated the importance of the Sarrafian photographs and began to collect and save as many of them as possible. He inherited a large collection from his family, and also began to purchase photographs, not only by the Sarrafians, but also by others who had worked in the Arab world and elsewhere. This ultimately resulted in

595

a large collection covering Europe and most of the Middle East, including much rare and unpublished material.

Buheiry deemed his photograph collection an integral part of his work as a historian, and in his teaching, lecturing, and research he used it extensively as an aid to the understanding and assessment of modern Arab history. Of particular importance was an illustrated lecture entitled "Beirut Baroque," delivered at the American University of Beirut in 1983, and his active participation in the exhibition "Romantic Lebanon," on display in February and March 1986 at Leighton House in London.

The inclusion here of a selection from the Buheiry collection seemed not only appropriate, but also an excellent opportunity to illustrate topics discussed in the studies above. The 49 items reproduced in the following plates fall into several distinct groups: a series of scenes in Beirut and elsewhere in Lebanon by Dumas, Moore, and the Sarrafians, a group of Sarrafian photographs (with one by Moore) taken at the SPC, a selection of prints from Syria and Palestine, mostly by the Maison Bonfils, a Sarrafian series from Turkey, mainly Diyarbakir, and a final Sarrafian series taken in the Yemen on the eve of the First World War. These represent only a small sample from that part of the collection presently accessible in London, and as is often the case with old photographs, most can be only approximately dated.

Photographic material has in recent years come to be acknowledged as a resource of great importance to the study of Middle East history. Buheiry certainly recognized it as such, for vignettes like these capture precious moments in the process to which he devoted his academic career, the formation and perception of the modern Arab world.

List of Plates

1. **Beirut: Place des Canons, View from the South**
   Tancrède Dumas, *c.* 1880

2. **Beirut: The Hotel Angleterre at the Place des Canons**
   Dumas, *c.* 1880

3. **Beirut: Place des Canons, View from the Southeast**
   Sarrafian, *c.* 1920

4. **Beirut: An American Warship at Anchor in the Port**
   Sarrafian, *c.* 1905

5. **Beirut: The Landing of Védrine's Blériot at Ḥorsh**
   Sarrafian, 27 December 1913. Note the large number of
   European-style umbrellas.

6. **Beirut: A Group of Freemasons and Their Insignia**
   Sarrafian, c. 1900

7. **Beirut: Fishing Boats at Ain Mreisse**
   Sarrafian, c. 1905

8. **Beirut: Rue Jeanne d'Arc, Looking Toward the SPC Campus**
   Franklin T. Moore, c. 1900

9. **Beirut: View Eastward from the Tower of College Hall, SPC**
   Moore, c. 1900. Note the open fields to the right, later
   developed into the city's main shopping district.

10. **Beirut: Staff and Students of the SPC**
    Sarrafian, c. 1900. Note the veiled woman at the left end
    of the second row.

11. **Beirut: Library of the SPC (College Hall)**
    Sarrafian, c. 1904. Note the closed-stack system and the
    combination of gas and electric lighting.

12. **Beirut: Class in Pharmacy at the SPC**
    Sarrafian, c. 1904

13. **Beirut: An Anatomy Lesson (SPC?)**
    Moore, c. 1910

14. **Beirut: The Boy Scout Troop of the SPC**
    Sarrafian, c. 1908

15. **Beirut: Red Cross Field Hospital on the SPC Campus**
    Sarrafian, c. 1917. The site is now AUB's "Green Oval".

16. **Beirut: Red Cross Field Hospital on the SPC Campus**
    Sarrafian, c. 1917

17. **Beirut: The Medical Gate and Medical School, SPC**
    Sarrafian, c. 1904

18. **Tripoli (Lebanon): The Citadel and the Qadīsha River**
    Sarrafian, c. 1900

19. **Lebanon: A Mountain Scene**
    Sarrafian, *c.* 1900

20. **Sidon: The Sea Castle and Fishing Harbor**
    Sarrafian, *c.* 1905

21. **Jerusalem: The Pool of Hezekiah**
    Maison Bonfils, *c.* 1880

22. **Jerusalem: The Armenian Patriarch**
    Maison Bonfils, *c.* 1880

23. **Jerusalem: The Church of Mary Magdalene and the Old City**
    Maison Bonfils, *c.* 1885

24. **Jerusalem: Gethsemane and the Church of Mary Magdalene**
    Zangaki, *c.* 1885

25. **Bethlehem: Pilgrims on Christmas Day**
    Maison Bonfils, *c.* 1880

26. **Jaffa: View from the Sea**
    Maison Bonfils, *c.* 1880

27. **Gaza: A General View**
    Maison Bonfils, *c.* 1880

28. **Boaz (Palestine): A Scene at Harvest Time**
    Maison Bonfils, *c.* 1880

29. **Bethlehem: Two Young Girls**
    Maison Bonfils, *c.* 1880

30. **Syria: Breadmaking in a Village**
    Maison Bonfils, *c.* 1880

31. **Syria: Two Muslim Women in Town Dress**
    Maison Bonfils, *c.* 1880

32. **Palestine: An Elderly Man**
    Sarrafian, *c.* 1919

33. **Diyarbakir: A Summer View**
    Sarrafian, *c.* 1904. The beds are on the rooftops to benefit
    from the evening breeze, the mattresses and covers being
    folded over the ends of the beds during the day.

34. **Turkey: Sirri Pasha in His Study**
Sarrafian, *c.* 1904

35. **Turkey: Asto Pasha and His Son**
Sarrafian, *c.* 1904

36. **Diyarbakir: Turkish Troops on 'Īd al-Aḍḥā**
Sarrafian, *c.* 1904

37. **Diyarbakir: Laborers at a Silk Works**
Sarrafian, *c.* 1904. The workers are stacking mulberry
branches in preparation for removing the silkworm cocoons.

38. **Sanaa: House of a Notable**
Sarrafian, *c.* 1913

39. **Sanaa: The Bazaar**
Sarrafian, *c.* 1913

40. **Sanaa: Bāb al-Yaman (the South Gate)**
Sarrafian, *c.* 1913

41. **Sanaa: A Mosque Minaret**
Sarrafian, *c.* 1913

42. **Sanaa: House of Notables**
Sarrafian, *c.* 1913

43. **Sanaa: Bāb al-Salām (the Gate of Peace)**
Sarrafian, *c.* 1913

44. **Zibid: A General View**
Sarrafian, *c.* 1913

45. **Hodeida: An Arab Sayyid**
Sarrafian, *c.* 1913

46. **Yemen: A Fortified Village**
Sarrafian, *c.* 1913

47. **Yemen: Farm Laborers**
Sarrafian, *c.* 1913

48. **Yemen: Gem Dealers**
Sarrafian, *c.* 1913

49. **Yemen: A Field Guard**
Sarrafian, *c.* 1913

Ed.

Plate 1

Plate 2

Plate 3

Plate 4

Plate 5

Plate 6

Plate 7

Plate 8

Plate 9

Plate 10

Plate 11

Plate 12

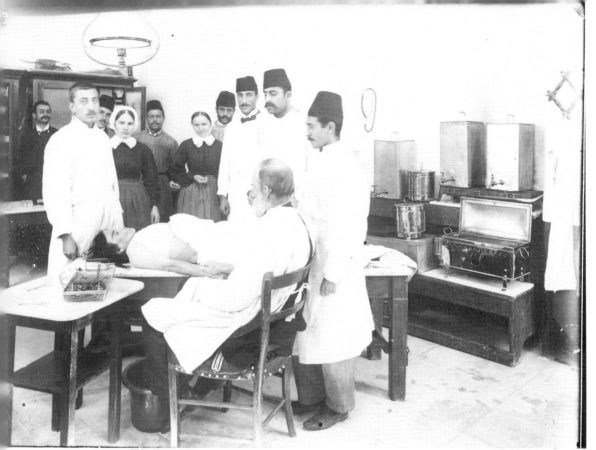

Plate 13

Plate 14

Plate 15

Plate 16

Plate 17

Plate 18

Plate 19

Plate 20

Plate 21

Plate 22

Plate 23

Plate 24

Plate 25

Plate 26

Plate 27

Plate 28

Plate 29

Plate 30

Plate 31

Plate 32

Plate 33

Plate 34

Plate 35

HAMIDIA SOLDIERS IN TURKISH UNIFORM

Plate 36

Plate 37

Plate 38

Plate 39

Plate 40

Plate 41   Plate 42

Plate 43

Plate 44

Plate 45

Plate 46

Plate 47

Plate 48

Plate 49

INDEX